THE CRIMINAL PROCESS

PROCESS

Fifth Edition

LIZ CAMPBELL
ANDREW ASHWORTH
MIKE REDMAYNE

OXFORD
UNIVERSITY PRESS

OXFORD
UNIVERSITY PRESS

Great Clarendon Street, Oxford, OX2 6DP,
United Kingdom

Oxford University Press is a department of the University of Oxford.
It furthers the University's objective of excellence in research, scholarship,
and education by publishing worldwide. Oxford is a registered trade mark of
Oxford University Press in the UK and in certain other countries

Second edition 1998
Third edition 2005
Fourth edition 2010

Impression: 1

Published in the United States of America by Oxford University Press
198 Madison Avenue, New York, NY 10016, United States of America

British Library Cataloguing in Publication Data
Data available

Library of Congress Control Number: 2019940147

ISBN 978–0–19–881840–3

Printed in Great Britain by
Bell & Bain Ltd., Glasgow

THE CRIMINAL PROCESS

PREFACE

The fourth edition of *The Criminal Process* was published in 2010. The plan was that Mike Redmayne would take charge of the fifth edition, either alone or with a new co-author. Tragically, Mike died in 2015 after a brave battle with cancer. The loss of such an outstanding scholar—see his monograph on *Character in the Criminal Trial*, published in 2015 just before his death—has been widely felt. But the book should live on, and I am delighted that Professor Liz Campbell accepted the invitation to prepare the fifth edition. She brings to the task a wide range of expertise and understanding, and I am confident that this edition will be welcomed by scholars and students alike.

Andrew Ashworth
December 2018

It was a bittersweet privilege to be asked by Andrew Ashworth to take over the fifth edition of *The Criminal Process*. I have tried to honour Mike Redmayne's legacy and memory in my approach, as well as seeking to complement the remarkable contribution that Andrew has made and continues to make to criminal law scholarship. I can only hope that I do them both justice.

In the eight years since the fourth edition, the pace of change in the criminal process has continued to be rapid, both in a legislative and policy sense. The Criminal Procedure Rules play a central and ever-strengthening role; issues relating to disclosure of evidence have led to talks of crises in criminal justice, while legal aid cuts continue to bite. In addition, the prospect of the UK's departure from the EU and the lack of clarity as to the parameters and meanings of 'Brexit' have resulted in a great degree of political and legal uncertainty, neither of which look likely to be resolved soon. Moreover, despite political rhetoric and commitments to the contrary, human rights still play a significant role in the criminal process, and throughout the book we continue to place considerable emphasis on European human rights law. As well as developments relating to the confrontation and protection of witnesses, since the last edition legislative change has been prompted by a significant decision from Strasbourg relating to the retention of DNA profiles, for instance.

The aim of the book remains that of providing a reflective, contextualized consideration of doctrinal, practical, and normative issues in criminal processes and procedures, drawing on arguments from the law, research, policy, and principle. It focuses on England and Wales, with occasional comparative references. Rather than being an exhaustive account of the criminal process, it subjects a range of key issues to deeper examination than would be possible were the book to aim for wider coverage. Its primary focus is on the impact of the criminal process on the individual, although some consideration is also given to the corporate suspect.

The structure remains broadly similar to that of previous editions. The book opens with a chapter setting out the context for recent changes to the English criminal process. A theoretical framework is advanced in Chapter 2. This chapter centres on the European Convention on Human Rights, and seeks to develop a human rights approach to resolving issues in the criminal process. Chapter 3 focuses on the occupational cultures of criminal justice professionals and on questions of legal ethics that arise at various stages. The book then goes on to deal with ten key issues in the criminal process, integrating and commenting upon developments in law and practice. The order of Chapters 4 and 5 has been reversed, so as to consider evidence collection more broadly before police questioning. Chapter 4 analyses the powers and practices in relation to the investigation of crime and the gathering of evidence. This is followed in Chapter 5 with an examination of the questioning stage of the criminal process, looking at the role and powers of the police. Chapter 6 focuses on the decision as to whether a suspect should be prosecuted or diverted from the formal criminal process, and looks at the range of out–of-court disposals and the implications of deploying these. Then Chapter 7 looks at cases that are charged and subjected to prosecutorial review, and includes detailed consideration of the functions and performance of the Crown Prosecution Service. In Chapter 8, remand decisions are analysed, scrutinizing the justifications for removing liberty before trial. Chapter 9 reviews a number of pre-trial rights and duties, including particularly contentious issues such as the disclosure of evidence. In Chapter 10, the laws and practice on plea negotiation are explored. Chapter 11 turns to the criminal trial itself, raising questions about the roles of judge and jury. Chapter 12 examines the appeals system and the possibility of post-conviction review of cases, and Chapter 13 scrutinizes the development and subsequent amendment of civil preventive orders.

The writing of the text was completed in late November 2018, and I hope to have taken into account major legal and policy changes up to then.

Liz Campbell
Melbourne, December 2018

CONTENTS

TABLE OF CASES

For R v Defendant see under name of Defendant. Judicial Review cases are found under R

TABLE OF STATUTES

INTERNATIONAL LEGISLATION
AND CONVENTIONS

TABLE OF SECONDARY LEGISLATION; CODES OF CONDUCT; CODES OF PRACTICE; PRACTICE DIRECTIONS

PRACTICE DIRECTIONS

1

INTRODUCTION TO THE ENGLISH CRIMINAL PROCESS

Issues of criminal process are rarely out of the news. As our work on the fifth edition of this book was drawing to a close, media reports focused on stop and search powers as a way of dealing with knife crime; the use of facial recognition technology by police to scan crowds at public events; the disclosure of evidence by prosecutors; and the treatment of victims during the criminal trial, to name just a few. As well as this intense and continuous media focus, it is a time of remarkable change for the criminal process, driven by swingeing cuts, technological advances, as well as changing public expectations. By 2020, there will have been a 40 per cent reduction in the Ministry of Justice budget,[1] criminal barristers have been on numerous strikes over legal aid cuts,[2] and many court buildings have been closed.[3] Though ostensibly underpinned by efficiency savings, there are ideological reasons for the retrenchment of state provision of legal aid, and the alterations to the infrastructure of the court process, to take just two key examples.

Each of this wide set of issues is relevant to the criminal process. This book explores these topics and more, and assesses critically the relevant laws and practice, as well as the context around them. The present chapter sketches briefly the key stages and decisions of the criminal process and their significance, and classifies them according to their nature and consequence. It differentiates between the criminal process and the system. Finally, it orients the reader by outlining significant reforms that have shaped the criminal process in the past decades.

1.1 KEY STAGES AND DECISIONS IN THE CRIMINAL PROCESS

The criminal process is part of the state response to crime, part of the mechanisms by which the state applies substantive criminal law to its citizens and legal persons. At its

---

[1] Ministry of Justice: Public Expenditure: Written question—112641; answered 16 November 2017.

[2] 'Barristers step back from escalating legal aid strikes', *Financial Times*, 24 May 2018; 'Barristers and solicitors walk out over cuts to legal aid fees', *The Guardian*, 5 January 2014. http://www.bbc.co.uk/news/uk-43594546; https://www.theyworkforyou.com/debates/?id=2018–05–08b.627.0.

[3] N. Padfield, 'Even More Court Closures' [2018] *Crim LR* 351; https://www.nao.org.uk/report/early-progress-in-transforming-courts-and-tribunals/.

most expansive, it covers a range of procedures and decisions from the investigation and questioning of possible suspects through to appeals against conviction and other means of challenging convictions or acquittals. The criminal process forms part of the wider criminal justice system, which includes all the agencies and institutions (police, prosecutors, public defenders, judges, probation officers, prison officers, and so on) as well as the criminal law itself and the sentencing system. In this book, we focus on the criminal process, but it is not easy to define exactly what this is, and, indeed, views on its parameters and dimensions may differ. That said, our chief concern lies with the processes and procedures whereby the criminal justice system deals with potential suspects, suspects, and defendants.[4]

Before drawing attention to its key stages, it is important to put the criminal process in perspective by reflecting on its use in practice. The criminal process is presented sometimes as if it were a vital tool of crime control, but the majority of crime never comes to the attention of the police or other enforcement agencies, and even when offences are brought to official attention they do not always elicit a formal response. It is estimated that less than half of crimes are reported to the police and, of those, between four-fifths and two-thirds are recorded; and these figures vary depending on the offence type.[5] An increased focus on improving recording practices has led to a greater proportion of reported crimes being recorded by the police,[6] but this means that an increase in the number of crimes recorded by the police does not necessarily mean the level of crime has worsened. Offences of interpersonal and sexual violence are still significantly under-recorded by the police. Moreover, even when crime is reported to and recorded by the police, the police will not be able to identify a suspect in the vast majority of cases. In the year ending March 2018, police forces closed almost half (48 per cent) of offences with no suspect identified, a similar proportion to the previous year.[7]

Although it is not easy to define exactly what the criminal process is, we take it as starting with the identification of one or more suspects by the police—our attention thus is partial, in term of crimes committed. Nonetheless, it is at this stage that fundamental issues of criminal procedure arise. If the police identify someone who they suspect has committed a crime, often they will wish to take steps towards initiating

---

[4] The term 'suspect' describes a person who is not yet the subject of formal criminal proceedings but who has experienced some police intervention or state suspicion; 'defendant' means a person who has been charged or summonsed; and 'offender' denotes a person who has admitted guilt, or who has been found guilty in court (see CPS, *The Code for Crown Prosecutors* (2018), 1.4).

[5] HM Inspectorate of Constabulary (HMIC) found that the police are failing to record a large proportion of the crimes reported to them. Over 800,000 crimes reported to the police have gone unrecorded each year, which is an under-recording of 19 per cent. The rates for violence against the person and sexual offences are 33 per cent and 26 per cent respectively. HMIC, *Crime-recording: making the victim count. The final report of an inspection of crime data integrity in police forces in England and Wales* (2014), 7.1.

[6] Office for National Statistics, *Crime Survey for England and Wales, Crime in England and Wales: year ending March 2018* (2019), CSEW, https://www.ons.gov.uk/peoplepopulationandcommunity/crimeandjustice/bulletins/crimeinenglandandwales/yearendingmarch2018#whats-happened-to-the-volume-of-crime-recorded-by-the-police.

[7] Home Office, *Crime outcomes in England and Wales: year ending March 2018*, Statistical Bulletin HOSB 10/18 (2018).

a prosecution. In minor cases, the police are likely to proceed by issuing a summons against the suspect, which will require him[8] to attend court. In more serious cases, the police are likely to arrest the suspect and take him to a police station,[9] though interview on the street is becoming more common. The regime in the police station is intended to offer the suspect certain protections—for example, against unnecessary detention or unduly aggressive questioning. In all police stations where suspects may be detained, a police officer is given the role of 'custody officer'. This person plays an important role in ensuring that the protective regime operates properly. When the suspect is brought to the police station, the custody officer has to decide whether he should be released without charge, charged, or detained for questioning, if it is thought necessary to do so to obtain further evidence.[10] Detention must be reviewed after six hours, and there are procedures for renewal and varying limits.[11] The custody officer must record these decisions on a custody sheet, and the suspect must be informed of the right to free and confidential legal advice. The Codes of Practice issued under the Police and Criminal Evidence Act 1984 (PACE) set out standards for the conduct of police investigations. For example, they impose restrictions on the manner in which the police may question a suspect,[12] and on the handling of identification procedures. These procedures will be examined in Chapter 5, where actual practice as well as legal doctrine will be discussed. In addition, the police will seek to question the victim at an early stage, and should inform victims of violent offences of the existence of the Criminal Injuries Compensation Authority. The police may also put the victim in touch with Victim Support or other similar agencies. Inquiries in a case may be completed quickly or may spread over a considerable time, in which case the police have a duty to keep the victim informed of the progress of the case. Beyond such police procedures, other investigating agencies, such as the HM Revenue and Customs, are subject to the Codes of Practice also, although there are fewer controls over investigations by the many regulatory agencies such as Health and Safety Executive (HSE) and the Environment Agency (EA).

The general principle throughout, however, is that a person may only be questioned before charge and not afterwards. Once there is sufficient evidence, the suspect should be charged. However, charging is not the only way of commencing a prosecution; the alternative method is for a police officer to lay an 'information' stating the offence the defendant has allegedly committed before a magistrate or justices' clerk, as a result of which a summons will be issued and served on the defendant. This summons procedure is used more commonly for minor offences: the power of arrest, which places considerable discretion in the hands of the police, typically is used for more serious offences, but can also be deployed for relatively minor offences against public order.

At this stage of the criminal process, the police are trying to build a case against the suspect. Even if a suspect has been caught 'red-handed', so to speak, a conviction will not be guaranteed should the case progress to court. The case must appear strong and

---

[8] Given that the majority of suspects and defendants are male, the male pronoun is used generally throughout the book.

[9] See Ch 4.   [10] PACE, s 37.   [11] PACE, ss 40–44.

[12] Taken in conjunction with PACE, ss 76, 78, and 67(1).

convincing, first to the prosecutor who decides on the charge, and then to the court. In such a 'red-handed' case the police will want to take statements from any witnesses and write up their own reports of the incident. Of course, a confession from the suspect would also strengthen the case. In other situations, the police may want to gather further evidence, for example by holding an identification parade, taking a DNA sample from a suspect, or searching his house. These evidence-gathering activities are regulated in various ways, and have different aims and implications. For instance, the regulation of identity parades is intended largely to secure the reliability of evidence produced, whereas with DNA samples and searches of property, other interests—such as privacy and bodily integrity—are at stake.

It has been assumed so far that the progression from sufficient evidence to charge or summons is natural or inevitable, but that is far from true. An authority with the power to prosecute may decide to take no formal action, perhaps believing that the experience of detection or an informal warning is sufficient, or it may decide that a formal caution or warning is appropriate. During the latter part of the twentieth century, the police developed the practice of issuing a formal caution to certain offenders, particularly the young and those whose offences were very minor (see further Chapter 6). Many regulatory agencies also have powers to issue formal warnings to employers and companies; most prefer this approach in the hope of maximizing compliance with the law rather than pursing prosecution, in the first instance at least.

One significant trend concerns the growing circumvention of the criminal trial, through out-of-court penalties and deferrals of prosecution. Some agencies have long had powers to exact financial penalties from offenders without bringing a prosecution: for instance, HM Revenue and Customs will agree not to investigate criminally with a view to prosecuting someone for deliberate conduct outlined in a Contractual Disclosure Facility contract.[13] Furthermore, the police can impose Fixed Penalty Notices on road traffic offenders, and Penalty Notices for Disorder.[14] Deferred prosecution agreements are a cognate but distinct mechanism available for corporate defendants only.[15] All these measures have considerable implications both for the place and status of the criminal trial and for the significant discretion of the police and the relevant prosecutor.[16]

If the prosecution follows, and it proceeds by way of summons, the defendant will be given a date for first appearance in a magistrates' court. If it proceeds by arrest, the police officer has a power to grant bail to the suspect without going to the police station—a power known colloquially as 'street bail'.[17] However, in many cases the officer

[13] https://www.gov.uk/guidance/admitting-tax-fraud-the-contractual-disclosure-facility-cdf#what-happens-if-you-own-up-to-committing-fraud. See P. Alldridge, *Criminal Justice and Taxation* (2017), 131.

[14] Criminal Justice and Police Act 2001, ss 1–11, and the Police Reform Act 2002, Sch 4. These powers are discussed in detail in Ch 6.

[15] See Ch 6.

[16] A. Ashworth and L. Zedner, 'Defending the Criminal Law: Reflections on the Changing Character of Crime, Procedure and Sanctions' (2008) 2 *Crim Law & Phil* 21.

[17] Criminal Justice Act 2003, Part 2; see A. Hucklesby, 'Not Necessarily a Trip to the Police Station: The Introduction of Street Bail' [2004] *Crim LR* 803.

will take the suspect to the police station and, if it is decided that the suspect is to be charged, the officer must then decide whether the suspect is to be bailed or remanded in police custody after charge. There is a duty to ensure that a defendant is brought before a court as soon as practicable, which is often the morning after arrest (or on Monday morning if the arrest takes place on a Saturday). The defendant may be bailed to appear in court or, if there are reasonable grounds for believing that detention is necessary, the police may keep the defendant in custody until the first court appearance.[18] At first appearance, the magistrates' court must either dispose of the case or, if not (and particularly in serious cases which will be committed to the Crown Court for trial), the court must decide whether to release the defendant on bail or to make a custodial remand. The Bail Act 1976 proclaims a presumption in favour of bail, but also sets out potential reasons for the refusal of bail: see Chapter 8.

Despite considerable budgetary cuts,[19] legal assistance is available at several stages in the process.[20] There is a right to free legal advice at the police station, with duty so-licitor schemes to facilitate this and to advise on representation in court. The Criminal Defence Service (CDS) was established in 2001 within the Legal Services Commission. The Commission was replaced by the Legal Aid Agency in 2013, and the CDS and a Public Defender Service remain,[21] though its financial basis remains a question of controversy. Moreover, far fewer solicitors' firms now accept criminal work,[22] and the Ministry of Justice wishes to reduce the number of providers still further.[23] Low salaries are a significant barrier to working in the legal aid sector. Moreover, the number of Crown Prosecution Service (CPS) lawyers has fallen by 27 per cent since March 2010, and the CPS struggles to find counsel to prosecute cases.[24] Indeed, overall the landscape of criminal advocacy is changing with an ageing workforce, less work that is less well paid, and some concerns about the quality of advocacy.[25]

The Legal Aid Act 1988 once required magistrates' courts to grant legal aid to de-fendants who were to be tried in the Crown Court, and there was a discretion to do so for summary trials.[26] Now the rules about who qualifies for legal aid are set out in the Legal Aid, Sentencing and Punishment of Offenders Act 2012 and the Criminal Legal Aid (General) Regulations 2013. To be eligible, an individual's gross annual income must not exceed £12,475; or if it does but is less than £22,325, his annual disposable

---

[18] PACE, s 38.

[19] See Ministry of Justice, *Transforming Legal Aid: Delivering a more credible and efficient system* (2013) and *Transforming Legal Aid: Next Steps* (2013).

[20] See generally E. Cape, 'The Rise (and Fall) of a Criminal Defence Profession' [2004] *Crim LR* 401.

[21] See https://www.gov.uk/topic/legal-aid-for-providers/crime; https://publicdefenderservice.org.uk.

[22] In 2001/2, the number of firms offering criminal defence services declined from 3,500 to 2,909 firms in a year; by 2006/7 it was 2,510 and in 2012/13 1,599: Legal Services Commission, *Annual Report and Accounts 2012–13* (2013), 23.

[23] Ministry of Justice, *Transforming Legal Aid: Delivering a more credible and efficient system* (2013), 2.7.

[24] House of Commons Committee of Public Accounts, *The Criminal Justice System*, Fifty-Ninth Report of Session 2013–14, HC 1115, 6.

[25] Sir Bill Jeffrey, *Independent Criminal Advocacy in England and Wales* (2014), 2.1–2.9, 4.1 and 4.2.

[26] See R. Young and A. Wilcox, 'The Merits of Legal Aid in the Magistrates' Courts Revisited' [2007] *Crim LR* 109.

income must not exceed £3,398.[27] This means test threshold entails that thousands are ineligible for legal aid but unable to afford legal advice, with no choice but to represent themselves.[28] As we discuss in Chapters 11 and 12, this poses particular problems for the trial and appeals stages of the process. These cuts, which are animated by concerns with performance and cost-effectiveness, principally affect marginalized defendants, but also impact on well-off defendants prosecuted and tried in serious fraud cases.[29]

As for legal representation, expenditure on legal aid fell 33 per cent in real terms between 2011–12 and 2017–18.[30] Criminal defence advocates receive legal aid payments under the Advocates' Graduate Fee Scheme, under which rates have not increased since 2007 and have been subject to some reductions.[31] The Litigators' Graduated Fee Scheme, which applies to those representing clients in Crown Court cases, includes a cap on the number of pages of prosecution evidence (PPE) for which the defence solicitor receives payment under the graduated fee. This stood at 10,000 pages until 2017, but was lowered to 6,000, until a successful judicial review in August 2018.[32]

While formerly the police took the decision whether or not to charge the defendant, now the CPS determines the charge in most cases, though the power to charge is moving back to the police in some instances.[33] The CPS has the power to discontinue prosecutions in magistrates' courts,[34] and may drop a case when it is brought to trial in the Crown Court, but statutory charging has had the effect of reducing the use of these powers. If it is a Crown Court case, the indictment must be drafted.[35] If the defendant has been remanded in custody, time limits apply to the period between first appearance in the magistrates' court and committal (70 days), and between committal to the Crown Court and trial (112 days).[36] The prosecution may apply for an extension, but if there are insufficient grounds the accused must be released on bail until the trial.

The choice of charge determines the mode of trial. Most minor offences are triable summarily only, in the magistrates' courts. Most serious offences are triable only on indictment, in the Crown Court. The intermediate category of offences triable either way may be tried in a magistrates' court or at the Crown Court. In these cases, a defendant is asked by the magistrates whether he intends to plead guilty or otherwise. If he indicates his intention to plead guilty, the magistrates' court becomes seized of the case (under the 'plea before venue' procedure) and may proceed to pass sentence or, if it believes its sentencing powers are inadequate, may commit the case to the Crown

---

[27] Reg 18.

[28] See V. Kemp, *Transforming Legal Aid: Access to Criminal Defence Services* (2010), available at http://eprints.nottingham.ac.uk/27833/1/Kemp%20Transforming%20CD%202010.pdf.

[29] A. Jordanoska, 'Case Management in Complex Fraud Trials: Actors and Strategies in Achieving Procedural Efficiency' (2017) *Int J Law in Context* 336.

[30] House of Commons Justice Committee, *Criminal Legal Aid*, Twelfth Report of Session 2017–19, HC 1069 (2018), [79].

[31] Ibid, [3].   [32] *R (The Law Society) v The Lord Chancellor* [2018] EWHC 2094 (Admin).

[33] See Ch 6.   [34] Prosecution of Offences Act 1985, s 23.

[35] For details, see J. Sprack, *A Practical Approach to Criminal Procedure* (15th edn, 2016), ch 15.

[36] Prosecution of Offences Act 1985, s 22; for analysis of the regulations and cases, see *Blackstone's Criminal Practice* (2019), D10.4.

Court for sentence. If, on the other hand, the defendant indicates an intention to plead not guilty, the magistrates have to decide, having heard representations, whether to commit the case to the Crown Court for trial. Even if they decide not to do so, taking the view that the case is suitable for summary trial, the defendant has an unfettered right to elect Crown Court trial.

In terms of criminal procedure, the Criminal Procedure Rules (CPR) are regarded as having brought about a 'fundamental change'[37] and 'effected a sea change to the way cases are to be conducted'.[38] The CPR, which set out the duties of the parties and the courts in relation to the conduct of criminal proceedings, were introduced in 2005 and have been amended a number of times since.[39] Rule 1.1 sets out the 'overriding objective', which is 'that criminal cases be dealt with justly'.

(2) Dealing with a criminal case justly includes—

    (a) acquitting the innocent and convicting the guilty;

    (b) dealing with the prosecution and the defence fairly;

    (c) recognising the rights of a defendant, particularly those under Article 6 of the European Convention on Human Rights;

    (d) respecting the interests of witnesses, victims and jurors and keeping them informed of the progress of the case;

    (e) dealing with the case efficiently and expeditiously;

    (f) ensuring that appropriate information is available to the court when bail and sentence are considered; and

    (g) dealing with the case in ways that take into account—

        (i) the gravity of the offence alleged,

        (ii) the complexity of what is in issue,

        (iii) the severity of the consequences for the defendant and others affected, and

        (iv) the needs of other cases.[40]

Rule 1.2 places a duty on the parties to 'prepare and conduct the case in accordance with the overriding objective', and rule 1.3 requires the courts to further the objective when dealing with cases. Rule 3.2 further specifies the duty of the courts:

(1) The court must further the overriding objective by actively managing the case.

(2) Active case management includes—

    (a) the early identification of the real issues;

    (b) the early identification of the needs of witnesses;

---

[37] *Lawson v Stafford Magistrates' Court* [2007] EWHC 2490 (Admin), [30].

[38] *CPS v Cipriani*, Westminster Magistrates' Court, 24 June 2016, 6f.

[39] The CPR are made by the Criminal Procedure Rule Committee, including the DPP and chaired by the Lord Chief Justice.

[40] CPR 2018, r 1.1(2).

(c) achieving certainty as to what must be done, by whom, and when, in particular by the early setting of a timetable for the progress of the case;

(d) monitoring the progress of the case and compliance with directions;

(e) ensuring that evidence, whether disputed or not, is presented in the shortest and clearest way;

(f) discouraging delay, dealing with as many aspects of the case as possible on the same occasion, and avoiding unnecessary hearings;

(g) encouraging the participants to co-operate in the progression of the case; and

(h) making use of technology.

(3) The court must actively manage the case by giving any direction appropriate to the needs of that case as early as possible.

Rule 3.3 obliges the parties to assist the court in its pursuit of the overriding objective. It imposes an explicit duty on the parties to every case to communicate with each other, to find out whether the defendant is likely to plead guilty or not guilty; what is agreed and what is likely to be disputed; what information, or other material, is required by one party of another, and why; and what is to be done, by whom, and when.

After these general pronouncements, the rules move to the level of procedural detail, setting out how the stages of litigation should proceed. We refer to the CPR throughout the chapters that follow.

The CPR are significant in that they indicate that the defence's concern should not just be to win its own case, but to ensure that the case is dealt with justly, where justice includes the conviction of the guilty. While Darbyshire sees the CPR as continuing case management practices that predated them,[41] McConville and Marsh are less sanguine.[42] For them, the CPR do more than merely consolidate and simplify rules of procedure, in that they increase the role of the defence in the prosecution enterprise and shift the role of judges in formalizing a duty to further that overriding objective by 'actively' managing cases. They speak of the tension faced by trial judges under the CPR when 'managing' defence counsel who seek to assert their 'right' to adversarial protections.[43]

Lord Justice Irwin extolled the virtues of 'firm case management' stating that, 'whether the court is constituted by a professional District Judge or by lay magistrates . . . [it] must consider the Criminal Procedure Rules, which are there to be employed actively so as to preclude game playing and ensure that the courts only have to address real issues with some substance'.[44] That said, there appears to be a gap between doctrine and practice here, between what Sir Brian Leveson called 'the excellent work of the Criminal Procedure Rules Committee and the daily diet of the Crown Court'.[45]

---

[41] P. Darbyshire, 'Judicial Case Management in Ten Crown Courts' [2014] *Crim LR* 30, 48.

[42] M. McConville and L. Marsh, 'Adversarialism goes West: Case Management in Criminal Courts' (2015) 19 *IJEP* 172, 176.

[43] Ibid, 173.

[44] *R (on the application of Hassani) v West London Magistrates' Court* [2017] EWHC 1270 (Admin).

[45] The Rt Hon. Sir Brian Leveson President of the Queen's Bench Division, *Review of Efficiency in Criminal Proceedings* (2015), [192].

There is evidence that a considerable proportion of the Bar and the Bench are not familiar with and do not cite the CPR.[46]

If a defendant indicates an intention to plead not guilty, there will be various exchanges between prosecution and defence before the date set for trial. In the magistrates' courts there may be a pre-trial review, and in the Crown Court there will be a Plea and Trial Preparation Hearing (PTPH). In more complex cases a Further Case Management Hearing (FCMH) may be needed. In many cases, there will be discussion between prosecuting counsel and defence counsel on the day before, or the very day of, the Crown Court trial. In some cases, there may be a preliminary discussion with the judge. Defence counsel may then discuss the case with the defendant, and a change of plea to guilty may take place. This part of the process, sometimes described as 'plea-bargaining', is unregulated by statute and little regulated by the Court of Appeal. The many issues arising are discussed in Chapter 10.

A defendant who pleads guilty will be sentenced by the magistrates or by the Crown Court judge, after hearing a statement of facts from the prosecution and a plea in mitigation from the defence, and in non-minor cases after receiving a pre-sentence report. A defendant who pleads not guilty will be tried in the appropriate court. Magistrates' courts tend to be less formal, with less strict adherence to the law of evidence but also with a greater sense of briskness.[47] In the Crown Court, the trial will be before judge and jury, and matters are unfolded in greater detail.

A defendant convicted by a magistrates' court may appeal against conviction or sentence to the Crown Court, where the appeal takes the form of a rehearing. If either the defence or the prosecution wish to appeal on a point of law, the magistrates may be asked to state a case to the Divisional Court. A defendant convicted in the Crown Court may appeal against conviction and/or sentence to the Court of Appeal (Criminal Division). After the appeal process has been exhausted, there is provision for a case to be referred to or taken up by the Criminal Cases Review Commission and, if the Commission so decides, to be referred back to the Court of Appeal. This arrangement is intended to remedy the defects that led to the long delays in dealing with what became the notorious cases of miscarriage of justice uncovered in the late 1980s and early 1990s. These issues are further examined in Chapter 12.

The numerous stages outlined above comprise the general format of the process, although as noted there are some differences between the powers and practices of the police and of the regulatory agencies. Moreover, there are important differences in respect of cases involving certain types of suspect or defendant, and certain types of alleged offence. Where the suspect or defendant is a young person, aged between 10 and 18, special procedures and safeguards are in place. There are also special provisions for suspects and defendants with mental disorders, and for persons requiring interpreters

---

[46] Darbyshire, n 41; The Rt Hon. The Lord Thomas of Cwmgiedd, 'The Criminal Procedure Rules: 10 Years On' [2015] *Crim LR* 395, 397.

[47] P. Darbyshire, *Sitting in Judgment: The Working Lives of Judges* (2011), 171; cf L. Welsh, 'Are magistrates' courts really a 'law free zone'? Participant observation and specialist use of language' (2013) 13 *Papers from the British Criminology Conference* 3–16.

or other assistance. Certain procedures apply to corporate defendants only. As for types of offence, there are different legal regimes for motoring offences, as well as for persons suspected of terrorist offences or of serious fraud. Many motoring offences may be dealt with by a fixed penalty without a court appearance or through the online 'Make A Plea' scheme,[48] and some of those that have to be brought to court do not require the appearance of the defendant. The police are given considerably greater powers in the investigation of suspected terrorist offences, under a series of statutes. In terms of fraud, the Criminal Justice Act 1987 (as amended) gives enhanced powers to the Serious Fraud Office when investigating persons suspected of involvement in large-scale frauds, including a special procedure for bringing such cases to trial.

These different stages and decisions are part of a larger context. They are not discrete, individual acts in isolated conditions, but rather entail decisions taken either by individuals or by agencies, working within a given professional setting. The individual police officer or prosecutor is likely to be affected, for example, not only by the working practices and expectations of colleagues, but also by decisions taken by others beforehand and decisions likely to be taken at subsequent stages. The factual basis for the decision may well have been constructed by others, in a way that depends on selection and interpretation. This point is developed throughout the book: it is crucial to emphasize the context and nature of human decisions, which are situated in particular places and structures.

1.2 DISTINGUISHING TYPES OF DECISION

The legal procedures and methods described in section 1.1 combine to affect the ways particular suspects and defendants are processed by officials. Formal procedures do not necessarily determine that treatment, since suspects and defendants experience the working practices of officials, which may be more or less faithful to the rules. Indeed, in some instances the law may leave discretion rather than imposing strict rules.

It is noticeable, however, that the decisions outlined above are not all of the same kind. Most of them might be described as 'processual', in that they are decisions about the processing of the case from initial charge through to trial and appeal. But there are certain decisions that may be described more accurately as 'dispositive', in that they are concerned with the disposal of the case. Two key examples of this are the decisions whether to 'prosecute or divert', and whether to impose an out-of-court penalty. The 'prosecute or divert' decision is whether to give a police caution, conditional caution, or warning, or to take no formal action, rather than to prosecute. This decision, whether taken by the police, the CPS, or a regulatory agency, may be regarded as analogous to sentencing. It disposes of the case (which goes no further), and it may carry a form of censure, though unlike sentencing no court is involved. Diversion is premised

---

[48] See https://www.gov.uk/make-a-plea.

on the belief that the case does not warrant full processing and a court appearance. The second example, whether to impose an out-of-court penalty, leaves considerable discretion in the hands of the police or other law enforcement agency, and on many occasions the possibility of refusing the penalty and opting for a court appearance may be more theoretical than real. While there are other stages in the criminal process which have a dispositive element—for example, the CPS decision to discontinue a case, the decision on mode of trial and, more especially, the decision to accept a guilty plea to a lesser offence or to fewer charges than originally preferred—the 'prosecution or divert' decision and the question of imposing out-of-court penalties raise particular issues of principle about the proper role of the criminal courts and the amount and type of discretion that law enforcement agencies should be allowed to wield.[49]

Distinguishing between processual and dispositive decisions is important, as different considerations will apply in their taking—this is clear from the analogy between dispositive decisions and sentencing, which has no application to the processing of cases. Nonetheless, the distinction may be less sharp in practice than in theory. Moreover, there is at least one type of decision that is neither processual nor dispositive: whether to grant bail or to remand in custody. The remand decision has no direct bearing on whether the prosecution will be continued or discontinued, nor on mode of trial or plea, nor is it a way of removing a case from the system and dealing with it otherwise. It is *sui generis*, and is best described as a temporizing decision, in that it arises solely if and when a case cannot be dealt with at the first court appearance. The adjective 'temporizing' refers only to why this decision is necessary rather than to the nature of the issues it raises; these are discussed further in Chapter 8.

1.3 PROCESS AND SYSTEM

This book focuses on and refers to the criminal process rather than 'the criminal justice system'. This is because it is not a 'system' in the sense of a coherent or closed set of coordinated decision-making bodies. Many entities working within criminal justice are relatively autonomous and enjoy considerable discretion in their decisions and determinations. Nonetheless, the inaccuracy and inappropriateness of the term 'system' should not obscure the practical interdependence of the agencies. Many rely on other entities for their caseloads or information, and decisions taken by one body can impinge on those taken by others. The CPS depends largely on the police for the information on which it bases its decisions, and those CPS decisions in turn affect the caseload of the courts, and may constrain the powers of magistrates' courts and of defendants to determine the mode of trial. Many other examples of interdependence and influence can be found throughout the book, and decisions should be viewed within this setting rather than as discrete and objectively based determinations.

[49] See further Ch 6.

Referring to systems and interdependence runs the risk of overlooking the human dimensions and impact of the criminal process. Of course, the process impinges directly on victims, suspects, and defendants, in the form of multiple contacts and decisions. A defendant who has been questioned by the police, charged, kept in police custody, remanded by the court, perhaps offered a plea bargain, and then tried in court is likely to feel 'punished', irrespective of whether a guilty verdict and sentence follow. Indeed, a person who is acquitted after such a sequence of events may well feel 'punished' by the process to which he has been subjected, even if relieved at the ultimate outcome. Though this is a misuse of the legal term punishment, which should be confined strictly speaking to sentences imposed by courts after findings of guilt, it accords with the research findings of American criminologist Malcolm Feeley, encapsulated in the title of his book *The Process is the Punishment*.[50] Suspects and defendants often feel that the way in which they are treated is equivalent to punishment, in the sense that it inflicts on them deprivations (of liberty, of reputation) akin to those resulting from a sentence. This is particularly true for defendants who have been remanded in custody, but also may flow from a single decision such as to prosecute. It may also be a consequence, not so much of decisions taken in their case, but rather of what they regard as disrespect for their rights by the relevant officials. For present purposes, it is sufficient to note that the criminal process is a process to which defendants are subjected by officials who have considerable de facto power as well as the power of law behind them. It amounts to and involves an exercise of state power, and so we consider the proper standards, fair procedures, accountability, and other issues relevant to such dealings between the state and individual citizens.

Clearly, it is not just defendants but also victims and witnesses whose interests should be protected. Long overlooked in respect of police practice as well as adversarial court proceedings, victims who report crimes often experience 'secondary victimization' at the hands of police, prosecutors, and courts.[51] While some steps have been taken to reduce these effects by improving techniques of police questioning, granting anonymity to victims of certain offences, and using video links in court, many victims suffer psychologically and socially from their involvement in the criminal process, beyond experiencing the crime itself. Although efforts are made to ameliorate such secondary victimization, the criminal process can be said to be a process to which victims of crime, too, are subjected by officials.

1.4 REFORMS OF THE CRIMINAL PROCESS

Criminal procedure reform often occurs in response to a miscarriage of justice of some sort, or a critical event, perceived or otherwise. While certain crises can prompt or expedite much-needed action, this is not always the ideal climate in which to contemplate

---

[50] M. Feeley, *The Process is the Punishment* (1979).

[51] See C. Hoyle and L. Zedner, 'Victims, Victimization and Criminal Justice' in M. Maguire, R. Morgan, and R. Reiner (eds), *The Oxford Handbook of Criminology* (4th edn, 2007), esp 468–70.

reform and then legislate reactively. Moreover, '[o]ur conduct of criminal trials was designed in the 19th century with many changes and reforms bolted on, especially over the last 30 years'.[52] What is evident is that much reform has been incremental and cumulative, rather than being introduced on a blank slate, as it were.

PACE was introduced to address the findings of the Philips Royal Commission,[53] which examined police powers and prosecutions after the extension of an inquiry into the *Confait* case where three young men were convicted of murder on the basis of confessions later shown to be false.[54] *Confait* had highlighted the lack of regulation in the police station as well as the significance of false confessions; the initial inquiry indicated that there were systemic problems that could not be examined within the confines of the review of a single case. So, the Philips Commission covered police powers and prosecutions more broadly, and ultimately formed the basis of PACE, which remains central. PACE extended police powers of arrest, and stop and search, and formalized the regime for detention in the police station, imposing time limits on detention and introducing the role of the custody officer. For the first time, legislation clearly provided suspects with a right of access to legal advice while in police custody. PACE is accompanied by a series of Codes of Practice which elaborate on the legislative provisions, explaining how certain powers and procedures are to be given effect: for example, Code C on the detention and questioning of suspects and Code D on identification procedures. The other major piece of legislation to result from the Philips Commission was the Prosecution of Offences Act 1985, which took responsibility for the prosecution of offences away from the police and gave it to the newly established CPS.

A series of miscarriage of justice cases, recognized as such in the late 1980s and early 1990s, highlighted more problems with the criminal justice process.[55] The Birmingham Six, the Guildford Four, the Maguire family, and Judith Ward all had been convicted of offences arising out of the bombing campaign conducted by Irish nationalists during the 1970s. Some of the defendants had confessed falsely, allegedly because of considerable pressure and violence on the part of the police. Several of the cases involved forensic science evidence, thereby doubting the independence and neutrality of forensic scientists. There had also been failures to disclose evidence to the defence and, in some cases, failure by the police to disclose evidence to the prosecutor. Another disturbing feature was that in several cases the allegations of false conviction had been long-running. The Birmingham Six, for example, had had their case heard twice by the Court of Appeal before the convictions were quashed in 1991.[56] Questions about how the criminal process deals with appeals and allegations of miscarriage of justice were

---

[52] Courts and Tribunals Judiciary, 'Sir Brian Leveson's Review of Efficiency in Criminal Proceedings published', Media Release, 23 January 2015.

[53] Royal Commission on Criminal Procedure, *Report* (1981).

[54] *Report of an Inquiry by the Hon. Sir Henry Fisher into the circumstances leading to the trial of three persons on charges arising out of the death of Maxwell Confait and the fire at 27 Doggett Road, London SE6* (1977).

[55] J. Rozenberg, 'Miscarriages of Justice' in E. Stockdale and S. Casale (eds), *Criminal Justice under Stress* (1993).

[56] *McIlkenny et al* (1991) 93 Cr App R 287.

brought to the fore, as well as about the operation of the early stages of the criminal process.

The official response was to set up another Royal Commission to consider the implications of these cases and to suggest reforms. The Runciman Commission reported in 1993,[57] but its proposals were nowhere near as far-reaching as those of Philips. Many of the cases involved convictions secured before the PACE protections were introduced.[58] While the Runciman Commission recommended new procedures for appeals against conviction and for post-appeal review of alleged miscarriages of justice, many of its proposals involved fine-tuning rather than radical reform. Other proposals were unconnected to miscarriages of justice, such as on the way cases are allocated between the Crown Court and magistrates' court and on plea-bargaining, both of which were controversial.

The killing of Stephen Lawrence, a young black man, in a racist attack in 1993 brought to the fore concerns about endemic racism in the police, and about a miscarriage of justice of a different kind. While police inquiries ensued, and five young white men were interviewed, no prosecution was brought at the time.[59] The Lawrence family launched a private prosecution against those five individuals but the case was stopped when the judge ruled the evidence against them insufficient. The government set up an inquiry chaired by High Court judge Sir William Macpherson. The report in 1999 concluded that the investigation into the murder was 'marred by a combination of professional incompetence, institutional racism and a failure of leadership by senior officers'.[60] Much of the report was concerned with police investigative procedures and criticisms of what took place in that particular case, but two other points are of particular importance here. First, the report identified 'institutional racism' in the police: though the definition of institutional racism is controversial (in that it can elide racist behaviour and attitudes with practices that unintentionally have the effect of disadvantaging members of minority ethnic groups[61]), the report succeeded in drawing attention to deep-seated problems of discrimination in criminal justice. Secondly, the report argued in favour of a re-examination of the double jeopardy rule that prevented the prosecution of a person already acquitted. That issue was referred to the Law Commission, which favoured relaxing the rule,[62] and Part 10 of the Criminal Justice Act 2003, as examined in Chapter 12, broadly implemented that recommendation. The Macpherson report therefore showed how concern about unpursued prosecutions, unmerited acquittals, racial discrimination, and the treatment of victims and

---

[57] Royal Commission on Criminal Justice, *Report* (1993).

[58] There were exceptions, such as a number of cases involving the West Midlands Serious Crime Squad. See T. Kaye, *'Unsafe and Unsatisfactory'? Report of the Independent Inquiry into the Working Practices of the West Midlands Serious Crime Squad* (1991).

[59] Two of the men involved were tried and convicted of his murder in 2012.

[60] *The Stephen Lawrence Inquiry: Report of an Inquiry by Sir William Macpherson of Cluny* (1999): quotation at 46.1.

[61] See e.g. the critique by M. Tonry, *Punishment and Politics* (2004), ch 4.

[62] Law Commission, *Double Jeopardy and Prosecution Appeals*, Law Com No 267 (2001).

their families can motivate reform of the criminal process, just as concern about false convictions.

It is important to note the changing political climate surrounding criminal justice reform. For much of the twentieth century, criminal justice was not politically controversial,[63] and there was a broad consensus between the main political parties as to how policy should develop. That changed at the 1979 general election, which the Conservative Party fought partly on 'Law and Order' issues. In the 1980s, the police made clear their support for a Conservative rather than Labour administration, a move which helped to confirm the former as the party of law and order. This marked the end of the bipartisan consensus: criminal justice had become a political and therefore an electoral issue. The first major piece of criminal justice legislation after the Runciman Commission was the Criminal Justice and Public Order Act 1994. This contained provisions—advocated by the government but not supported by the Commission's report—allowing juries to draw inferences against defendants who are silent at trial or during police questioning. The following years saw Runciman's proposals translated into legislation: the Criminal Appeal Act 1995 contained reforms of the appeals and post-appeals process and the Criminal Procedure and Investigations Act 1996 made significant changes to the disclosure regime.

Two other aspects of the political climate surrounding criminal justice reform are worth highlighting: namely, the politicization of criminal justice policy, and the associated drive for efficiency with its focus on managerialism. Now the politicization of criminal justice policy is embedded. After its electoral defeat in 1992, the Labour Party began to rethink its policies, including criminal justice: 'Tough on crime, tough on the causes of crime' was the new Labour slogan. Labour was now prepared to embrace criminal process reforms which it would once have vehemently opposed. When in government, Labour criminal justice policy was presented as toughening the criminal justice system and promoting the interests of victims rather than those of defendants.[64] Since the Conservatives regained office in 2010, governing in coalition with the Liberal Democrats until 2015, there has been some moderating of views in terms of civil liberties and consideration of the causes of crime, and even apparent swapping of positions with Labour.[65] Criminal justice policy might be 'volatile and contradictory',[66] but it has considerable traction and remains a prominent issue in political manifestos.

The Runciman report in 1993 was concerned with increasing the efficiency of the criminal justice system, such as in its recommendations on the mode of trial and plea-bargaining. This reflects a wider shift in emphasis in criminal justice policy during

---

[63] See I. Loader, 'Fall of the Platonic Guardians: Liberalism, Criminology and Responses to Crime in England and Wales' (2006) 46 *Brit J Criminol* 561.

[64] See e.g. Home Office, *Rebalancing the Criminal Justice System in Favour of the Law-Abiding Majority: a consultation paper* (2006).

[65] See R. Reiner, 'Conservatives and the Constabulary in Great Britain: Cross-Dressing Conundrums' in M. Deflem (ed), *The Politics of Policing: Between Force and Legitimacy, Sociology of Crime, Law and Deviance* (2016), 79.

[66] P. O'Malley, 'Volatile and Contradictory Punishment' (1999) 3 *Theoretical Criminology* 175.

the 1990s, to prioritizing managerial concerns and efficiency over the accused's rights. Such themes were to the fore in the Auld Review's terms of reference,[67] and the drive for efficiency has even more salience in the context of the Conservative government's preference for privatization as well as its austerity agenda. Case management, for instance, is much more significant in these straitened times, and while it purports to improve efficiency, is underlined by distinct ideological reasons.

In 2014, Sir Brian Leveson was asked to conduct a review into the efficiency of criminal proceedings 'to demonstrate ways in which, consistent with the interests of justice, it might be possible to streamline the disposal of criminal cases thereby reducing the cost of criminal proceedings for all public bodies'.[68] The terms of reference of the review were:

(1) While taking into account—

(a) current initiatives to improve the efficiency and speed of the criminal justice system (in particular recent changes relating to the early guilty plea scheme);

the need for robust case management;

recommendations made in previous reviews of the criminal justice system, including those not implemented at the time; and

Government reforms to the criminal justice system;

(2) Review current practice and procedures from charge to conviction or acquittal, with a particular focus on pre-trial hearings and recommend ways in which such procedures could be:

(a) further reduced or streamlined;

improved with the use of technology both to minimise the number of such hearings or, alternatively, conducted (whether by telephone, or internet based video solutions) without requiring the attendance of advocates.

(3) Review the Criminal Procedure Rules to ensure that:

(a) maximum efficiency is required from every participant within the system; and

any changes proposed are fully supported by the Rules.

(4) Report to the Lord Chief Justice within 9 months.

The overarching principles or themes of the review are:

- Getting it Right First Time
- Case Ownership
- Duty of Direct Engagement
- Consistent judicial case management.[69]

[67] The Rt Hon. Lord Justice Auld, *Review of the Criminal Courts of England and Wales: Report* (2001), [1.5]. For an earlier example, see M. Narey, *Review of Delay in the Criminal Justice System* (1997).
[68] *Review of Efficiency in Criminal Proceedings* (2015), 1.1.   [69] Ibid, ch 2.

This review was wide-ranging and was conducted in a remarkably short time frame. The final report, published in January 2015, recommended, inter alia: a greater use of video and other conferencing technology; more flexible opening hours in magistrates' courts; tighter judicial case management by judges; mechanism to incentivize early guilty pleas. Reference to the report, and its influence, is made through the book. Overall, we endorse the view of Luke Marsh that this is the latest effort 'under the guise of "efficiency" measures, to scale back protections traditionally afforded to criminal defendants and has dramatic implications for the maintenance of accurate case outcomes' and that it adopts a narrow approach to 'efficiency' which takes no account of the interest in the accuracy of verdicts.[70] The review will have no bearing upon the real inefficiencies of the process, namely wrong verdicts; collapse of prosecutions in respect of cracked trials and ineffective trials; and ordered and directed acquittals.[71]

Linked to the Leveson review are a number of schemes that are referred to throughout this book. Better Case Management (BCM) is a judicially-led initiative, which forms part of the implementation of the review, and seeks to improve the way cases are processed through the system. BCM introduced two major case management initiatives: a uniform national Early Guilty Plea scheme (EGP) and Crown Court Disclosure in document-heavy cases. Transforming Summary Justice (TSJ), a scheme to improve the efficiency and effectiveness of the magistrates' courts, was introduced in 2015 in an effort to reduce delays in the magistrates' courts, hold fewer hearings per case, and increase the number of trials that go ahead the first time that they are listed. TSJ was supported and endorsed by Sir Brian Leveson.[72] The TSJ programme contains ten characteristics including anticipated plea hearings; early receipt of initial details of the prosecution case; streamlined disclosure; clear expectations of effectiveness; and connectivity (wi-fi) for each agency at court.

The National Audit Office echoed Sir Brian Leveson's concerns, stating that reducing inefficiency in the justice system is essential if the increasing demand and reduced funding are not to lead to slower, less accessible justice.[73] Notwithstanding various efforts and schemes, the House of Commons Committee of Public Accounts did not pull any punches in its report on efficiency in the criminal justice system.[74] It described the criminal justice system as overstretched and close to breaking point, with delays, inefficiencies, lack of shared accountability, insufficient focus on victims, and significant regional variations in performance.[75] Crucially, the Committee considered that the Ministry of Justice has exhausted the scope to make more cuts without further

---

[70] L. Marsh, 'Leveson's Narrow Pursuit of Justice: Efficiency and Outcomes in the Criminal Process' (2016) 45(1) *Common Law World Review* 51.

[71] Ibid, 60.

[72] The Rt Hon. Sir Brian Leveson President of the Queen's Bench Division, *Review of Efficiency in Criminal Proceedings* (2015), 5.1.1.

[73] National Audit Office, *Efficiency in the Criminal Justice System*, Session 2015–16, HC 852 (2016), 17.

[74] House of Commons. Committee of Public Accounts. *Efficiency in the criminal justice system*, First Report of Session 2016–17, HC 72 (2016).

[75] Ibid, 3.

detriment to performance. Another House of Commons Committee has described matters raised before it as symptomatic of a criminal justice system under significant strain.[76] Whether these points are absorbed and understood by the government remains to be seen.

Central to the efficiency discourse and drive, managerialism in the criminal process is pronounced and embedded in England and Wales. Both the language and practices of management and of audit are now commonplace, with efficiency, key performance indicators (KPIs), etc to the fore in government rhetoric and policy. While an increased focus on management may have some positive implications in terms of consistency and accountability, it is more likely that it results in centralized control with efficiency and economy savers as the drivers behind legal and policy developments. Moreover, one major worry is that institutionally derived managerial goals become paramount, rather than those originating from normative or social goals.

Jenny McEwan observes that the emergence of a managerialist system of criminal justice has not been accompanied by a consideration of the values that underpinned traditional structures in England and Wales, but rather has evolved through a series of independent ad hoc measures that fundamentally change pre-trial processes and trial procedures.[77] She suggests that the absence of any normative underpinning of these developments poses problems, in overlooking adversarialism's commitment to allowing the parties, rather than the state, to direct proceedings, in that managerialism is indifferent to the fair trial rights protected by both traditional models in their different ways, and in its compromising of crime control goals.

In addition, scientific advances prompt some review and reform of the criminal process. Technological developments, wider availability of and cheaper devices for investigators and prosecutors, combined with perceived efficiencies have led to even greater drives for digitalization. In 2011, the CJS Efficiency Programme was established,[78] followed in 2012 by the Ministry of Justice Digital Strategy which aimed to have a 'digital by default approach to all services by 2013'[79]. Despite these initiatives, progress in improving IT systems is slow, with many disparate systems which fail to operate together.[80] A joint inspection of digital case preparation and presentation in the criminal justice system in 2016 found that training provided to staff across criminal justice partners was variable,[81] that inefficiencies in the digital process remain, with police spending time converting paper information into digital format,[82] and limited

[76] House of Commons Justice Committee, *Disclosure of evidence in criminal cases*, Eleventh Report of Session 2017–19, HC 859 (2018), [50].

[77] J. McEwan, 'From Adversarialism to Managerialism: Criminal Justice in Transition' (2011) 31 *Legal Studies* 519, 524.

[78] Ministry of Justice, *Modernising the Criminal Justice System: The CJS Efficiency Programme* (2011).

[79] Ministry of Justice, *Digital Strategy* (2012).

[80] Committee of Public Accounts, *The Criminal Justice System* (2014), 6.

[81] HM Crown Prosecution Service Inspectorate (HMCPSI) and HMIC, *Delivering Justice in a Digital Age: Joint inspection of digital case preparation and presentation in the criminal justice system* (2016), 1.27; also National Audit Office, n 73, 4.8.

[82] HMCPSI and HMIC ibid, 1.32.   [83] Ibid, 1.39.

positive impact on victims and witnesses resulting from the digitization.[83] Crucially, there is scant regard for the defendant in any of these reviews, and on the fact that the use of technology may marginalize the accused.[84] Again, while ostensibly the drive is to improve technology, there is an ideological dimension to this. The HM Courts and Tribunals Service 'transformation' programme seeks to upgrade technology and building, but also to '[revisit] our fundamental assumptions about how justice can best be served to the people that need it, in a modern era'.[85]

The treatment and experiences of victims and witnesses in the criminal process were focused on in *Speaking Up for Justice*, the report of a Home Office Working Party in 1998.[86] It raised concerns about the way in which the process of giving evidence in court may be unduly stressful for such witnesses. Many of its proposals found their way into the Youth Justice and Criminal Evidence Act 1999, subsequently developed in Part 8 of the Criminal Justice Act 2003.[87] Since then, the interests and rights of victims have been strengthened through the Right to Review Scheme, and by the EU Directive on Victims Rights.[88]

Not all change to the criminal process is accepted, and there has been some pushback against government reform, both at consultation stage as well as after enactment. For instance, in 2015 the government introduced the Criminal Courts Charge, in an effort to recover some of the costs of the criminal courts from offenders, thereby reducing the burden on taxpayers.[89] This mandatory charge was to be imposed after conviction, and ranged from £150 to £1,200, depending on 'factors that drive cost' such as the offence type, whether it was dealt with in the magistrates' or the Crown Court, and whether or not the offender pleaded guilty. The Criminal Courts Charge was met with much opposition,[90] including the resignation of 30 magistrates in protest in August 2015. A highly critical report from the House of Commons Justice Committee highlighted how it could incentivize guilty pleas; that the levels of the charge were grossly disproportionate to the means of many offenders and the gravity of the offences; the lack of discretion enjoyed by sentencers on whether to impose the charge and if so at what level; the creation of perverse incentives affecting defendant and sentencer behaviour; and the detrimental impact on victims and the CPS from sentencers reducing awards of compensation and prosecution costs.[91] The Criminal Courts Charge was abolished in December 2015.

[84] Marsh, n 70, 55.

[85] https://insidehmcts.blog.gov.uk/2017/03/31/hmcts-improving-the-justice-system/.

[86] Home Office, *Speaking Up for Justice* (1998).

[87] For a detailed account of the background to the 1999 Act and related legislation, see P. Rock, *Constructing Victims' Rights: the Home Office, New Labour and Victims* (2004).

[88] See ch 7.

[89] Criminal Justice and Courts Act 2015, s 54; see https://www.gov.uk/government/uploads/system/uploads/attachment_data/file/336085/fact-sheet-criminal-courts-charge.pdf.

[90] See E. Johnston, 'The Innocent Cannot Afford to Plead Guilty: The Impact of the Criminal Court Charge' (2015) 179 *Criminal Law and Justice Weekly* 670–1.

[91] House of Commons Justice Committee, *Criminal courts charge*, Second Report of Session 2015–16, HC 586 (2015).

As we noted in the previous edition, the most significant legislative reform of the 1990s did not relate to criminal justice specifically, but rather was the Human Rights Act 1998 which gave effect to the European Convention on Human Rights in English law. Despite some calls for the UK's withdrawal, this has not (yet) materialized: the Act remains of great importance for many areas of the criminal process: detention and questioning in the police station, the right to silence and the privilege against self-incrimination, remand decision making, disclosure, and the rules of evidence. Assessing the actual and potential impact of the Convention on the criminal process is a major concern of this book.

The final change on the horizon concerns the withdrawal of the UK from the EU. The EU has only recently and to a limited extent concerned itself with matters of criminal justice. Currently, the UK enjoys a 'special status' in relation to EU cooperation on matters of Justice and Home Affairs, insofar as it has negotiated the right to 'opt in' to provisions rather than being automatically bound, and so can be regarded as having a 'varied'[92] participation in some areas of EU criminal law. At the expiry in 2014 of the transitional protocols after the Lisbon Treaty, the UK opted out of all pre-Lisbon instruments, then opted back into 35 of those measures. When the UK leaves the EU in 2019, it will also leave these 35 measures.

1.5 CONCLUSION

This preliminary overview of criminal process reform has two goals. One is to familiarize readers with some of the major reports and pieces of legislation which will be discussed in later chapters. The other is to give some sense of the forces shaping criminal justice policy. The reform process is often event-driven, with proposals responding to particular problems in the criminal process which have gained publicity. At times, this can make the reform process seem somewhat haphazard: if the initial failed prosecution of the suspects in the Stephen Lawrence case had not received the media attention that it did, it seems unlikely that the double jeopardy rule would have been the subject of provisions in the Criminal Justice Act 2003. It would be wrong, however, to suggest that there is some simple causal process whereby a failing in the system leads to reform. The account has drawn attention to the politically charged climate in which reforms of the criminal process take place. The major political parties seek to sell their criminal justice policies to the electorate; there is an important populist element in the way in which criminal justice policy is framed.[93] The shared assumption of the parties seems to be that being seen to be tough on crime, and claiming to promote the interests of victims rather than defendants, will bring electoral success. This assumption plays an

---

[92] See V. Mitsilegas, 'The Uneasy Relationship between the UK and European Criminal Law: From Opt-Outs to Brexit?' [2016] *Crim LR* 517, 522.

[93] See further J. Pratt, *Penal Populism* (2007).

important part in moulding the criminal process as it undergoes a seemingly continual round of reforms.

It is evident that many elements of the criminal process call for clear and careful justification. We now move, in Chapter 2, towards an exploration of the sources of justification and of critique of the English criminal process. The examination of principles continues in Chapter 3, where we look particularly at ethical issues in relation to the working practices of criminal justice professionals. Those general chapters are then followed by chapters on particular stages of the criminal process—questioning; gathering evidence; diversion; charging and prosecutorial review; remands; pre-trial rights and duties; plea changing; trial procedures; and appeals.

2

TOWARDS A FRAMEWORK FOR EVALUATING THE CRIMINAL PROCESS

What should the (or a) criminal process do? What aims should underpin it, and what values should be respected? In answering these questions, we must be mindful of the links between the different parts and rules of the criminal justice system overall. The purpose and scope of the substantive criminal law have a bearing on pre-trial matters such as powers of arrest and plea negotiation. The rules of evidence at trial may limit the investigative powers of the police and other enforcement agencies. And the principles of sentencing are critical to the criteria for diversion from the criminal process and to plea negotiation. This chapter will keep those wider relationships in view while focusing on developing a framework for evaluating the criminal process.

2.1 A THEORY OF CRIMINAL PROCESS

Chapter 1 provided an outline of the criminal process in England and Wales, depicting a sequential process with suspects first identified by the police or other agency, and cases then progressing to and through further stages. At different points suspects may be removed from or drop out of the process, perhaps because the evidence is thought not to be strong enough, or it is decided that the case is suitable for diversion. Potentially, suspects can continue to trial, which may result in conviction or acquittal; then after trial, appeal may be possible. Next, we explore what this process is about and what values should animate it.

Here we aim to develop a normative framework which can be used to understand and evaluate the criminal process; this complements the description in Chapter 1. Account must be taken of the complexity of the criminal process and its embodiment of different aims and values, as well as jurisdictional variations. Perhaps it would be possible to develop a single normative model that is sufficiently detailed to ascertain whether certain actual criminal processes (perhaps all adversarial ones) are in some way deficient. This would be an ambitious enterprise, and arguably unattainable—not least because some aspects of the criminal process (such as the type of fact-finder used) may reflect values which have relatively little to do with the criminal process itself. Institutions such as the jury may exist for historical and political reasons which make them more appropriate for some jurisdictions than for others.

One way of proceeding would therefore be to draw a distinction between internal and external values in the criminal process. Internal values are taken to be the core values of criminal process, ones which all criminal processes should embody. One would expect such a theory to be relatively thin and lacking in detail. Something could then be said about the external values which, in a particular jurisdiction such as England and Wales, might fill in the details. There is some merit in this approach, but there are also problems. One is that it may prove difficult to distinguish between internal and external values. The criminal process is part of a wider criminal justice system, and there are many theories of criminal justice. A given theory of criminal justice may be related to some wider political theory, at which stage there are further choices of approach to be made. The situation is rather like a set of Russian dolls, where the core values of the political theory at the centre play a role in shaping the outer layers such as the criminal process. It may therefore be difficult to find agreement on internal values of criminal process that may be claimed to apply across all jurisdictions.

Because of this problem, we should say a little more about the basic values we believe should play a role in shaping the criminal process. The thin, internal account we start with reflects the values of a liberal state, where state power is limited, and citizens are bearers of rights. In terms of criminal justice—and this will become important as we add detail to the thin theory—we subscribe to a retributive, or desert-based, rationale for punishment. On this view, the institution of punishment is justified by the moral appropriateness of visiting censure on citizens for crimes as wrongs, and the need to reinforce that with sanctions in order that the censure be taken seriously. It is appropriate that the state should maintain a system for enforcement and adjudication, so as to ensure a public, authoritative, and consistent approach to the imposition of censure. But a proper relationship between the coercive state and its citizens as rational and rights-bearing subjects means that a punishment should always be proportionate to the seriousness of the crime, and not disproportionate so as to fail to respect the offender.[1] Those principles of proportionality and respect for the suspect/defendant/offender as a rational rights-bearing subject should also underpin the criminal process, though of course this is complicated somewhat in the context of corporate defendants. A criminal process based on deterrence, or on principles of restorative justice, might differ significantly from one based on desert.[2]

What, then, are the purposes of the criminal process, and what values should it reflect? One simple point can be made at the outset. The laws, regulations, and institutions that make up the criminal process provide a set of rules, standards, and areas of discretion for decision making. These rules or procedures have an immediate value, no matter what their content. Rules are intended to guide decision makers and to control

---

[1] For elaboration, see A. von Hirsch and A. Ashworth, *Proportionate Sentencing* (2005), ch 2.
[2] See section 2.5.

their discretion. Procedure has a coordinating function, crucial given the complexity of the criminal process, which involves many different actors. It allows different decision makers to work together by giving them some knowledge of what other actors will have done or at least a framework of what they could do. Set procedures also allow for transparency: they allow rules to be made accessible to the public as well as to the actors in the process. Thus, procedure should serve the rule of law, by making decisions more consistent, more predictable, and less arbitrary. These simple points do not say anything about the contents of the rules and standards; they merely suggest the basic value of having some set of procedures. As we shall see, this emphasis on proper procedures rather than arbitrariness lies at the core of the European Convention on Human Rights (ECHR).

Moving beyond this, it is obvious that the criminal process is part of the state response to crime. There are, however, many ways in which the state responds to crime which do not invoke criminal procedure. Much of the state's strategy against crime is preventive: it includes things as diverse as education, street lighting, and the maintenance of a visible police presence. The criminal process (as understood for the purposes of this book) is narrower than this. It is the mechanism that authorizes the state to apply the criminal law to its citizens. It is invoked only when it is suspected that a crime has been committed. Again, though, the state can respond to suspected crime in many ways. Minor offences may be ignored or met with a warning. Some offences, such as driving offences, are dealt with by way of fixed penalty notices. The point is even more obvious regarding agencies other than the police: for example, the Health and Safety Executive often responds to breaches of the criminal law through processes designed to ensure future compliance; prosecution is used as a last resort.[3] We will say more about these responses to crime in Chapter 6; the discussion of 'dispositive values' in section 2.6 of this chapter is also relevant. Many such responses are said to involve 'diversion' from the criminal process, indicating that the criminal process is involved in a minimal sense only. Nevertheless, the principles underlying diversion are important, in part because of the light they shed on those cases which do enter the criminal process more fully. The 'full' criminal process is involved where a relatively formal response to crime is taken: where, in the conventional situation, the police respond to a suspected offence with a view to prosecution. The possible end result of the process is adjudicative: a trial. Whether a trial is held will depend on many other factors. As has been emphasized, many suspects drop out of the process for a variety of reasons. But what matters is the potential, not the probability.

This characterization of criminal procedure enables something to be said about its purposes. The function of criminal procedure is to regulate and facilitate the preparation of cases for trial; this suggests that the purposes of criminal trials will determine in a little more detail the functions of criminal procedure. The criminal trial seeks to determine whether or not a person has committed a particular criminal offence and to do so fairly, according to certain rules and values. This suggests that one important

---

[3] K. Hawkins, *Law as Last Resort* (2003).

focus of criminal procedure is, broadly speaking, investigation. Criminal procedure should provide mechanisms to regulate the gathering of evidence so as to allow adjudicative decisions to be made accurately and fairly.

An investigation into a suspected criminal offence is unlikely to progress far unless the police are given certain coercive powers over suspects. Justifications may therefore be found for giving the police powers enabling them, for example, to detain suspects and to take fingerprints and DNA samples. Moreover, trials, as inquiries into a defendant's guilt or innocence, are likely to be most effective if the defendant is present. This provides the basis for other coercive powers, such as the power to remand in custody, to ensure that the defendant is present at trial, and to summon witnesses to attend trial.

An obvious, but important, point should be made at this stage. Although criminal procedure exists to ensure a particular end result—an effective criminal trial—it is not a mechanized process, but rather a way of dealing with people, who should be treated with dignity, and their rights respected. Here we are drawing on the wider principles of justice within which our account of the criminal process is embedded. Given that effective criminal procedure requires that prosecuting agencies be given coercive powers, a key facet of criminal procedure is to limit those powers to ensure that the human interests connected to the respect for dignity are not infringed unnecessarily. This is the central dilemma of criminal procedure: how to reconcile a process which will bring cases to effective trial with the protection of human rights, including the requirement of a fair trial.

Recognizing the human impact of the criminal process has several implications in terms of filtering out cases which do not merit prosecution. Waiting for trial imposes considerable stress on people, especially those remanded in custody, and so cases should not be pursued, maintained, or prolonged without good reason. The criminal process deals with people suspected of crimes of varying seriousness. In the least serious cases, the principle of proportionality suggests that the pressures and effects of a trial may not be justified. This underlines the importance of diversion in an account of the criminal process. However, the need to filter cases is not just to limit the application of coercive procedures, or to minimize the considerable stress suffered by people awaiting trial. It is also important because trials are fallible and somewhat unpredictable. The danger that a mistake will be made at trial provides further reason for filtering cases during the pre-trial stage, to remove cases where there is limited evidence. Moreover, efficiency, the costs of procedure, and trials, provide further reasons for filtering: indeed, the system, such as it is, would not be sustainable were all cases to be pursued to trial and contested.

In addition, any convincing normative theory of the criminal process needs to be connected to empirical facts about actual criminal processes and the practices of the relevant agencies. Thus, reference to the stress of waiting for trial was made in order to explain the importance of filtering cases which are in the system. There are other facts about the system which it is important to take into account. In Chapter 1, reference was made to miscarriages of justice which have played a role in shaping the system. Sometimes the police are over-eager to secure a conviction, and so often they will focus on an initial suspect at the expense of considering alternative lines of inquiry.[4] Police officers have been prepared to put considerable pressure on suspects in order to extract confessions—at one time, the use of violence was not uncommon. Suspects sometimes confess falsely,[5] and other sources of evidence too are fallible, such as eye-witness evidence.[6] Nonetheless, the frailty of such evidence can be difficult to detect at trial. So, a primary function of criminal procedure is to provide rules to ensure that reliable evidence is produced which can form the basis of an effective and legitimate trial. Criminal procedure should therefore provide safeguards against unreliable forms of evidence. Concern for human dignity is another reason for this: aggressive or violent questioning infringes fundamental human interests.

Notwithstanding the relative infrequency of contested trials, our theory of criminal procedure is trial-centred; it assumes that preparation of cases for possible trial is the principal objective of the investigative and pre-trial stages. It was suggested earlier that the objectives of the criminal trial are to determine accurately and fairly whether or not a person has committed a particular criminal offence. But this may be too simple; saying a little more about trials generates a slightly richer theory of criminal process. Accurate decision making is an important function of criminal trials, but complete accuracy is unattainable: trials are fallible. Of the two sorts of 'concluding' errors in a criminal trial—acquitting a guilty person or convicting an innocent person—the latter is more serious, since it involves a grievous wrong against a specific individual whereas the former does not, although it reflects badly on the system, may disappoint or hurt the victim or witnesses, and may reduce community confidence. To protect against convicting the innocent, the prosecution must prove its case beyond reasonable doubt. The implication of this heavy burden of proof is that of the errors made by criminal courts, more will involve acquitting the guilty than convicting the innocent. Criminal trials thus incorporate an 'error preference'; this is a cardinal value of the criminal process. Though it is arguable that this error preference should influence the pre-trial process just as it moulds the trial,[7] we suggest otherwise: one should actually be wary of seeing criminal procedure as an obstacle course which seeks to stymie the securing of convictions.[8] While features of English criminal procedure appear to apply this error preference at the pre-trial stage (see the rules protecting defendants against false confession or mistaken eyewitness identification, for example), in fact they help to ensure an effective trial by safeguarding the reliability of evidence. Moreover, filtering of cases can also be explained without reference to error preference. While it is true that the CPS decision whether or not to continue a prosecution is informed by the

---

[4] See K. Findley and M. Scott, 'The Multiple Dimensions of Tunnel Vision in Criminal Cases' (2006) *Wisconsin L Rev* 291; K. Rossmo (ed), *Criminal Investigative Failures* (2008).

[5] Royal Commission on Criminal Justice, *Report* (1993), 57, and see Chs 4 and 5 in this book.

[6] See Ch 4.4.

[7] See L. Campbell, 'Criminal Labels, the European Convention on Human Rights and the Presumption of Innocence' (2013) 76 *MLR* 681–707.

[8] This obstacle-course depiction of the pre-trial process is one problem with Packer's Due Process model, discussed further later in the chapter.

high standard of proof at trial, this is due to the predictive nature of the prosecutors' decision at this stage.[9]

The trial is not just about accurate fact-finding: principles of fairness lie at the heart of the trial in particular, as well as the criminal process in general. Thus, the trial is not just a diagnostic procedure, of which the sole purpose is to establish as accurately as possible (subject to the standard of proof) what happened. Trial verdicts must be legitimate, and this has consequences for the use of tactics such as entrapment.[10] Moreover, Antony Duff and co-authors argue that the trial should also be seen as a communicative process, whereby the state tries to let the convicted defendant know, in terms which he can understand, why he is to be subjected to the censure of the criminal sanction. In doing so, the state must also establish the legitimacy of its own claim to hold the defendant to account, notably by observing 'norms that require defendants to be treated as citizens of a liberal polity'.[11]

One obvious objection to a trial-centred theory of criminal process is that in reality the criminal process in England and Wales hinges on trial-avoidance.[12] Guilty pleas, as discussed in detail in Chapter 10, are the normal method of disposing of criminal cases. That said, such pleas do not avoid trial and judicial involvement completely: bearing in mind the retributive background to our account of criminal process, sentencing is an important function of the trial, and the court plays a role as a sentencing venue here. Further, reliance on guilty pleas does not undermine the importance of the criminal process as an investigative mechanism. A desert-based theory of sentencing emphasizes that sentences should be proportional to wrongdoing, which makes accurate investigation important, even if there will be no contested trial. In fact, one of the problems of the system of guilty pleas in England and Wales is that it may allow sentencing to be carried out without accurate knowledge of the facts of the offence: the gravity of the offending may be downplayed as part of a charge-bargain, or a defendant may plead guilty when factually innocent in order to take advantage of a sentence discount. But the emphasis on trials, and accurate fact-finding, allows us to criticize the systematic encouragement of guilty pleas for these very reasons. That is one of the themes of Chapter 10.

2.2 INTERNAL AND EXTERNAL VALUES

We have argued that the purposes of the criminal process are accurate determinations and fair procedures, and have suggested that the criminal trial should be regarded as the focus of the process, even though the majority of cases do not go to trial. Our theory is partly instrumental, giving an account of the sorts of things the criminal process

---

[9] See Ch 7.   [10] I. Dennis, *The Law of Evidence* (6th edn, 2017), ch 8.

[11] A. Duff, L. Farmer, S. Marshall, and V. Tadros, *The Trial on Trial, Vol 3: Towards a Normative Theory of the Criminal Trial* (2007), 288. For discussion, see M. Redmayne, 'Theorizing the Criminal Trial' (2009) 12 *New Crim LR* 287.

[12] M. Langer, 'From Legal Transplants to Legal Translations: the Globalization of Plea-Bargaining and the Americanization Thesis in Criminal Procedure' (2004) *Harvard Int LJ* 1.

will need to do and the sorts of powers (to arrest and detain suspects, to filter cases) needed to achieve those ends. But just as important are the values—respecting human rights—that should mould the way in which these ends are achieved. The theory is thin and relatively generic—an 'internal' theory in the sense outlined earlier. We now turn to consider external values, and how they inform a theory of criminal process.

Some external values are jurisdictionally specific. One example, mentioned earlier, relates to the use of lay fact-finders in the English criminal process (lay magistrates and juries).[13] Many other systems of criminal procedure make some use of lay fact-finders, whereas some do not use them at all. Much has been written about the value that lay justice—particularly trial by jury—brings to the criminal process. The point of identifying lay justice as an external value is to suggest that those systems which rely on it do so partly for particular historical and political reasons, and that there is not necessarily anything deficient or preferable, as systems of criminal procedure, in those systems which do not.[14]

Another example of an external value is adversarialism. Although the classification of systems of criminal process is complex and contested, the basic point is that adversarial systems, such as those operating in England and Wales and the United States, give a far greater role to the parties in developing the case and conducting the trial than do 'inquisitorial' systems, such as those operating in continental Europe. In some ways, these different systems reflect competing political philosophies. In French criminal procedure, for example, the role of the state in protecting its citizens' interests is emphasized. Giving too great a role to defence lawyers is seen as disruptive and potentially inegalitarian, and also as something for which there is little need because the state can be trusted to look out for the accused.[15] This is anathema in Anglo-American criminal procedure. Damaška has also suggested that Anglo-American criminal procedure differs from continental criminal procedure in the extent to which it is 'policy-implementing'. An example is that in England and the United States, criminal procedure is prepared to forego effective fact-finding at trial, either to uphold the integrity of the system or in the hope of exerting some influence over the way in which the police gather evidence. Unfairly or illegally obtained evidence may thus be ruled inadmissible at trial. Continental systems, historically at least, have tended to see control over the police as being better exercised in other ways.[16]

Our account of criminal process emphasizes the importance of rights. The fact that the criminal process should respect rights is an internal value, but the content of those

[13] See S. Doran and R. Glenn, *Lay Involvement in Adjudication* (2000).

[14] See T Hörnle, 'Democratic Accountability and Lay Participation in Criminal Trials' in A. Duff et al (eds), *The Trial on Trial, Vol 2: Judgment and Calling to Account* (2006).

[15] See J. Hodgson, 'Human Rights and French Criminal Justice: Opening the Door to Pre-Trial Defence Rights' in S. Halliday and P. Schmidt (eds), *Human Rights Brought Home: Socio-Economic Perspectives on Human Rights in the National Context* (2004); J. L. Sauron, 'Les Vertus de l'inquisitoire, ou l'Etat au service des droits' (1990) 55 *Pouvoirs* 53.

[16] See R. Frase, 'France' in C. Bradley (ed), *Criminal Procedure: A Worldwide Study* (1999), 161–2; C. Bradley, 'The Emerging International Consensus as to Criminal Procedure Rules' (1993) 14 *Michigan J Int Law* 171.

rights is best seen as being set externally to the process. A theory of criminal process cannot tell us very much about what rights people have. While some rights are specific to the criminal process (such as the presumption of innocence) many rights which place important constraints on criminal process (such as the rights to bodily integrity and to respect for private life), have wider significance and application. But saying that such rights are determined externally to the criminal process is not the same as saying that the rights are jurisdictionally specific. While there may be some things which we refer to as rights which have a particular significance in certain jurisdictions (the right to legal advice in the police station, for example[17]), there are many rights which any criminal process should respect. This is reflected in the fact that many international human rights documents include rights which have immense significance to the criminal process. Examining these documents and rights adds more detail and texture to our (so far) rather thin account of the criminal process. In the next section, the discussion will be more descriptive, focusing on the ECHR. The material remains relevant to a normative account of criminal process, however, for it identifies the most important of the rights which should shape the criminal process. The discussion also starts to analyse the way in which we should think about rights by showing some of the problems in the claim that rights can be 'balanced' against other values.

2.3 FUNDAMENTAL RIGHTS AND THE ECHR

(A) INTERNATIONAL HUMAN RIGHTS OBLIGATIONS

The UK is subject to several international declarations of human rights, of which three will be mentioned before the ECHR is considered in detail. One is the International Covenant on Civil and Political Rights (ICCPR), drawn up by the United Nations and monitored by the ICCPR Human Rights Committee. The extent and formulation of rights in the ICCPR differ in some respects from those in the ECHR. The ICCPR remains a document of some importance,[18] not least because reference has been made to it (in view of its wider international status) when interpreting the ECHR.[19]

A second instrument of importance is the United Nations Convention on the Rights of the Child. Though this does not refer to criminal proceedings primarily, it does declare a number of rights of children who are either defendants in criminal cases or sentenced following a finding of guilt.[20] As with the ICCPR, the Convention on the

---

[17] The European Court of Human Rights has held that the right of access to legal advice takes on particular importance when inferences may be drawn from silence at police interview: *Murray v UK* (1996) 22 EHRR 29. On the different attitude to legal advice in France, see n 15.

[18] See the essays in D. J. Harris and S. Joseph (eds), *The International Covenant on Civil and Political Rights and United Kingdom Law* (1995).

[19] See e.g. *John Murray v UK* (1996) 22 EHRR 29.

[20] G. van Bueren, *Commentary on the UN Convention on the Rights of the Child* (2005); L. Lundy, U. Kilkelly, B. Byrne, and J. Kang, *The UN Convention on the Rights of the Child: a study of legal implementation in 12 countries* (UNICEF, 2012).

Rights of the Child has been used by the European Court of Human Rights (ECtHR) as a source of rights applicable to children and young people.[21]

A third instrument is the Charter of Fundamental Rights approved by the EU in 2000, brought into force in 2003, and forming part of the Treaty establishing a Constitution for Europe signed in Rome in 2004. This contains several Articles devoted to safeguards in the criminal justice system, some of which go further than those currently recognized under the Convention.[22] The imminent departure of the UK from the EU in 2019 will result in the exclusion of the Charter, through the European Union (Withdrawal) Bill.

Those three instruments should be kept in mind as we turn to the ECHR, now the foremost authoritative source of rights in this country both generally and for the criminal process. The Convention was signed in 1950, ratified by the UK in 1951, and came into force in 1953. It has been ratified by all Member States of the Council of Europe. Since 1966, the UK has allowed individual petition to the ECtHR. Thus, any individual may make an application to the ECtHR, provided that domestic avenues of challenge have been exhausted. The Court will adjudicate on whether or not the complaint is admissible. Admissible cases are then heard by a section of the Court. If the Court rules against the Member State, the state will usually alter the law so as to comply with the judgment, but there is no absolute obligation to do so. The Committee of Ministers monitors state responses to findings of the Court.

(B) THE HUMAN RIGHTS ACT 1998

The UK was the subject of many adverse judgments in Strasbourg in the 1980s and 1990s, due in part to the fact that courts across the UK were unable to apply the ECHR when hearing domestic cases. When the Labour government was elected in 1997, it adopted the view that it was frustrating and unnecessary that individuals had to go outside the UK to secure the enforcement of rights to which the British government committed itself long ago. The Human Rights Act was passed in 1998, and came into force in 2000. For present purposes, there are four principal provisions. The first is s 6, which requires all courts and public authorities (such as the police and the CPS) to conform with the Convention in their decisions and policies. Section 3 imposes a strong interpretive duty, requiring courts to interpret statutes so far as possible in a way that gives effect to Convention rights. Sections 3 and 6 should be read together with s 2, which requires courts to take account of the decisions of the ECtHR. This does not require courts always to follow decisions of the Court in interpreting the Convention, although good reasons should be given for not doing so.[23] Unlike some constitutions such as that of the United States, the Convention does not (under the Human Rights

---

[21] See e.g. *V and T v UK* (2000) 30 EHRR 121.

[22] See S. Peers, T. Hervey, J. Kenner, and A. Ward, *The EU Charter of Fundamental Rights: A Commentary* (2014).

[23] As stated by the senior Law Lord, Lord Bingham, in *Anderson v Home Secretary* [2002] 4 All ER 1089, [18].

Act) have priority over legislation. If a higher court finds that a UK statute cannot be interpreted so as to be compatible with the Convention, the court may make a 'declaration of incompatibility' under s 4; there is then provision for the government, if it wishes, to initiate a fast-track procedure for parliamentary amendment of legislation which falls foul of the Convention. We will note, at appropriate points in the following chapters, how the courts have adapted to the duties and powers given to them by the Human Rights Act.

(C) CONVENTION RIGHTS AND THE CRIMINAL PROCESS

For present purposes, a general overview of those Convention rights relevant to the criminal process will be given. Each of the relevant Articles will be set out, and a few illustrative comments added.

Article 2

1. Everyone's right to life shall be protected by law. No one shall be deprived of his life intentionally save in the execution of a sentence of a court following his conviction of a crime for which this penalty is provided by law.

2. Deprivation of life shall not be regarded as inflicted in contravention of this Article when it results from the use of force which is no more than absolutely necessary:

   (a) in defence of any person from unlawful violence;

   (b) in order to effect a lawful arrest or to prevent the escape of a person lawfully detained;

   (c) in action lawfully taken for the purpose of quelling a riot or insurrection.

This Article's relevance here lies in para 2(b) and its impact on the use of force in arrest or the prevention of escape. The leading ECtHR case is *McCann v UK*.[24] An undercover team of specially trained soldiers were surveilling three IRA members in Gibraltar, in the belief that the latter were about to carry out a bombing. When they thought that the three were about to detonate the bomb, they shot and killed them. In fact, there was no detonator and no bomb. The ECtHR found that the planning of the operation was so defective that it made the killings foreseeable, although avoidable, and that this breached the victims' right to life under Art 2(1). Controversially, the majority of the Court held that the shooting did not fall within the 'absolute necessity' exception in Art 2(2), and therefore held the UK in violation of the Article. Some years earlier in *Kelly v UK*,[25] the European Commission had held that the action of a soldier in shooting at a car that had failed to stop at a checkpoint in Northern Ireland, killing one of the occupants, was 'absolutely necessary . . . in order to effect an arrest'. Article 2 is not well drafted in this respect: it contains no reference

---

[24] (1996) 21 EHRR 97.
[25] (1993) 74 DR 139, on which see the critical discussion by Sir John Smith at (1994) *New LJ* 354.

to the purpose of the arrest, and fails to confront the obvious point that one cannot arrest a person who has just been killed.

Article 3

No one shall be subjected to torture or to inhuman or degrading treatment or punishment.

A critical and controversial case on this Article is *Ireland v UK*,[26] in which the Court ruled that the notorious 'five techniques'[27] used in the interrogation of suspected terrorists by the authorities in Northern Ireland did not amount to 'torture', but rather 'inhuman and degrading treatment'. This judgment was affirmed in 2018, when the ECtHR rejected the Irish government's application to revise the original judgment on the basis that the UK had withheld evidence from the Court in 1978, which could have shown that the treatment constituted torture.[28]

In *Jalloh v Germany*, the Court ruled on whether the forced administration of an emetic to a suspected offender amounted to a breach of Art 3:[29] in finding a breach, the Court suggested that the 'inhuman and degrading' part of Art 3 should be treated as less powerful than the prohibition on torture. This problematic hierarchy seems to have been tempered in *Gäfgen v Germany*, a case involving threats of violence to a man suspected of involvement in the disappearance of a child.[30] The Court stressed that: 'The philosophical basis underpinning the absolute nature of the right under Article 3 does not allow for any exceptions or justifying factors or balancing of interests, irrespective of the conduct of the person concerned and the nature of the offence at issue.'[31]

In other judgments, the Court has been developing the positive duties that flow from Art 3, holding the UK to account for failing to provide proper facilities for disabled prisoners[32] and for failing to provide proper medical care for prisoners who present a known risk of suicide.[33] One difficulty is that many of those in detention are unable to pursue claims in order to draw attention to the conditions, and so the European Committee on the Prevention of Torture and Inhuman and Degrading Treatment has been established, with authority to inspect the prisons and police stations of all Member States. It has inspected prisons across the UK, and has made a number of critical reports.[34]

Article 5

1. Everyone has the right to liberty and security of person. No one shall be deprived of his liberty save in the following cases and in accordance with a procedure prescribed by law . . . c) the lawful arrest or detention of a person effected for the purpose of bringing him before the competent legal authority on reasonable suspicion

---

[26] (1978) 2 EHRR 25.
[27] Wall standing, hooding, subjection to noise, deprivation of sleep, and deprivation of food and drink.
[28] *Ireland v UK* (2018) 67 EHRR SE1.   [29] *Jalloh v Germany* (2007) 44 EHRR 667.
[30] (2010) 52 EHRR 1, [2010] ECHR 759   [31] [107].   [32] *Price v UK* (2001) 34 EHRR 53.
[33] *Keenan v UK* (2001) 33 EHRR 38.
[34] Available at https://www.coe.int/en/web/cpt/united-kingdom.

of having committed an offence, or when it is reasonably considered necessary to prevent his committing an offence or fleeing after having done so . . .

2. Everyone who is arrested shall be informed promptly, in a language which he understands, of the reasons for his arrest and of any charge against him.

3. Everyone arrested or detained in accordance with the provisions of paragraph 1(c) of this Article shall be brought promptly before a judge or other officer authorised by law to exercise judicial power and shall be entitled to trial within a reasonable time or to release pending trial. Release may be conditioned by guarantee to appear for trial.

4. Everyone who is deprived of his liberty by arrest or detention shall be entitled to take proceedings by which the lawfulness of his detention shall be decided speedily by a court and his release ordered if the detention is not lawful.

5. Everyone who has been the victim of arrest or detention in contravention of the provisions of this Article shall have an enforceable right to compensation.

This Article covers a great deal of ground, and has been developed considerably by the Court. Since one of its purposes is to guarantee the right to liberty, it is vital to those stages of the pre-trial process at which liberty is curtailed—that is, arrest, remand by the police and by a court, and trial within a reasonable time. Although Art 5 does provide (circumscribed) exceptions to deal with detention for those purposes, it makes no allowance for detention without charge or trial. For this reason, the government had to derogate from Art 5 when Parliament enacted the Anti-Terrorism, Crime and Security Act 2001, ss 21–3 of which provide for the indefinite detention of persons certified to be 'suspected international terrorists'. The House of Lords held this provision and the derogation from Art 5 to be incompatible with the Convention,[35] and so in the Prevention of Terrorism Act 2005 the 'control order' was created. The particular use of this power by the government was held to amount to a 'deprivation of liberty' contrary to Art 5,[36] and the terms of the orders were altered so as to reduce the number of hours of home detention. As is examined in Chapter 13, control orders themselves have been replaced by Terrorism Prevention and Investigation Measures.

Article 5 does allow for the detention of a person on reasonable suspicion of having committed an offence. In the leading case of *Fox, Campbell and Hartley v UK*,[37] the ECtHR held that:

the exigencies of dealing with terrorist crime cannot justify stretching the notion of reasonableness to the point where the essence of the safeguard secured by Article 5(1)(c) is impaired.

In that case, the UK was held to have violated Art 5, because the only grounds for arrest were that two of the three had previous convictions for terrorist offences.

[35] *A v Secretary of State for Home Affairs* [2004] UKHL 56.
[36] *Secretary of State for the Home Department v JJ* [2007] UKHL 45. Other House of Lords decisions have held that the control order regime fails to satisfy the fair trial requirements of Art 6: *Secretary of State for the Home Department v AF* [2009] UKHL 28.
[37] (1990) 13 EHRR 157.

However, in *O'Hara v UK*,[38] the Court held that the requirement of reasonable suspicion was fulfilled when the police arrested the applicant on information received,
even though that information was not revealed to the Court. Article 5 requires an
arrestee to be brought promptly before a court, and in *Brogan v UK*[39] the Court held
that detention for longer than four days violated this provision. In order to determine whether it is justifiable to detain a defendant before trial, under Art 5(3), the
Court has developed an extensive jurisprudence which emphasizes the presumption
of liberty and the presumption of innocence, and which requires courts to avoid
stereotypical reasoning (e.g. that someone with previous convictions will therefore
commit offences if granted bail) and to assess each case on its facts.[40] The Court has
also sought to place limits on the length of time for which a person may be detained
before trial (in conjunction with the right to trial within a reasonable time under Art
6, below),[41] and has insisted on the importance of regular review of the continued
justification for detention.[42]

Article 6

1. In the determination of his civil rights and obligations or of any criminal charge
    against him, everyone is entitled to a fair and public hearing within a reasonable
    time by an independent and impartial tribunal established by law . . .

2. Everyone charged with a criminal offence shall be presumed innocent until proved
    guilty according to law.

3. Everyone charged with a criminal offence has the following minimum rights:

    (a) to be informed promptly, in a language which he understands and in detail, of
        the nature and cause of the accusation against him;

    (b) to have adequate time and facilities for the preparation of his defence;

    (c) to defend himself in person or through legal assistance of his own choosing or,
        if he has not sufficient means to pay for legal assistance, to be given it free when
        the interests of justice so require;

    (d) to examine or have examined witnesses against him and to obtain the attendance and examination of witnesses on his behalf under the same conditions as
        witnesses against him;

    (e) to have the free assistance of an interpreter if he cannot understand or speak the
        language used in court.

This Article has many different implications, but its central aim is to guarantee the
right to a fair trial. Thus, the opening words of the Article, which apply also to civil
proceedings, guarantee three free-standing rights: to a fair and public hearing; to trial
within a reasonable time; and to an independent and impartial tribunal. The remaining

---

[38] [2002] *Crim LR* 493.
[39] (1989) 11 EHRR 117; a breach of this provision was also found in *O'Hara v UK* (n 38).
[40] Discussed further in Ch 8; see generally the decision in *Nikolova v Bulgaria* (2000) 31 EHRR 64.
[41] See Ch 9 on delay.
[42] E.g. *Jablonski v Poland* (2003) 36 EHRR 455; cf also Art 5(4) on review of detention.

rights in Art 6 apply only to criminal proceedings, but this in itself has become a matter of controversy. The ECtHR has insisted that the phrase 'charged with a criminal offence' has an autonomous meaning, thereby preventing Member States from subverting the special protections in Art 6 by framing proceedings as civil.[43]

Article 6(2) declares the presumption of innocence. While this provision might be thought to restrict the placing of burdens of proof on defendants, it has been the subject of loose and unconvincing judgments.[44] The minimum rights in Art 6(3) can be seen as non-exhaustive elaborations of the basic right to a fair trial; many of these specific rights are discussed in later chapters. The boundaries of the right to free legal aid (Art 6(3)(c)) have not yet been fully established, but it should certainly be provided when a person is in danger of being committed to prison.[45] Moreover, Art 6(3)(d) has a bearing on the use of anonymous witnesses and of statements from witnesses unable to attend court.

No less significant have been the rights the ECtHR has implied into Art 6 as concomitants of the general right to a fair trial. Probably the foremost example of this is the principle of equality of arms, which has crystallized as the right of a defendant to have disclosure of 'all material evidence for or against the accused',[46] subject to circumscribed exceptions.[47] The Court has also implied into Art 6 the right of silence and the privilege against self-incrimination, describing them as 'generally recognised international standards which lie at the heart of the notion of fair procedure under Article 6'.[48] In *Teixeira de Castro v Portugal*,[49] the Court confirmed that the right to a fair trial extends to the right to fair pre-trial procedures, and found a violation when a court had received and acted upon evidence obtained by entrapment. However, both express and implied rights may occasionally have to give way to countervailing rights of others involved in criminal proceedings: thus in *Doorson v Netherlands*,[50] the Court held that a defendant's right of confrontation under Art 6(3)(d) may have to be somewhat curtailed in cases where witnesses have been threatened with violence and therefore ought to be questioned by the judge in the presence of counsel (but not the accused). The rights of the witnesses under Art 5 (security of person) and Art 8 (respect for private life) were rightly protected in those circumstances.

We do not consider Art 7 in detail, which declares the right not to be convicted or punished as a result of a law coming into force after the relevant act or omission. Suffice it to say, that it has important implications for the substantive criminal law, and

[43] Compare the leading cases of *Engel v Netherlands* (1979) 1 EHRR 647 and *Benham v UK* (1966) 22 EHRR 293 with the decision of the House of Lords in *Clingham v Kensington and Chelsea LBC; R (McCann) v Manchester Crown Court* [2003] 1 AC 787, and see the discussion in Ch 13.

[44] *Salabiaku v France* (1989) 13 EHRR 379; cf the stricter interpretation of Art 6(2) by the English courts in *Attorney General's Reference (No 4 of 2002); Sheldrake v DPP* [2004] UKHL 43.

[45] See *Benham v UK*, n 43.   [46] *Edwards v UK* (1993) 15 EHRR 417.

[47] Cf *Edwards and Lewis v UK* (2005) 40 EHRR 593 with *A and others v UK* (2009) 49 EHRR 625.

[48] *John Murray v UK* (1996) 22 EHRR 29, [45].   [49] (1998) 28 EHRR 101, discussed in Ch 9.5.

[50] (1996) 22 EHRR 330.

that it is an aspect of the general requirement that criminal offences be defined with sufficient certainty.[51]

Article 8

1. Everyone has the right to respect for his private and family life, his home and his correspondence.

2. There shall be no interference by a public authority with the exercise of this right except such as is in accordance with the law and is necessary in a democratic society in the interests of national security, public safety or the economic well-being of the country, for the prevention of disorder or crime, for the protection of health or morals, or for the protection of the rights and freedoms of others.

This Article sets out the right to privacy. Once the right is engaged, it is still possible for the state to justify interfering with it, so long as the requirements of Art 8(2) are fulfilled. Innocuous as the first requirement of Art 8(2) ('in accordance with the law') may appear, the fact is that the UK lost many cases before the ECtHR because of the absence—at least until the Regulation of Investigatory Powers Act 2000—of a proper statutory framework for electronic and other forms of surveillance.[52] Even if the 2000 Act removed objections of 'arbitrariness' from the previous approach, any interference with the right to privacy must also be 'necessary in a democratic society' and required for one of the reasons set out in Art 8(2). The Court has developed various general principles for interpreting the exceptions to declared rights. Not only must the exception be prescribed by law, but account must also be taken of the principles of proportionality (significant intrusions into privacy only for serious offences), subsidiarity (intrusive techniques must be the last resort), accountability (prior independent authorization for intrusions on the declared right, supported by record-keeping and monitoring), and finality (information obtained by exceptional means should be used only for the purpose for which it was obtained).

These principles lend greater detail and weight to the exceptions to the declared rights, not only to Art 8 but also to the right of freedom of thought and religion (Art 9), the right to freedom of expression (Art 10), and the right to freedom of assembly and association (Art 11). Articles 9–11 all include a second paragraph along the same lines as Art 8(2), and all have been subject to interpretation by the Court.[53]

Article 14

The enjoyment of the rights and freedoms set forth in this Convention shall be secured without discrimination on any ground such as sex, race, colour, language, religion, political or other opinion, national or social origin, association with a national minority, property, birth or other status.

---

[51] See further B. Emmerson, A. Ashworth, and A. Macdonald, *Human Rights and Criminal Justice* (3rd edn, 2012), ch 17.

[52] E.g. *Khan v UK* (2000) 31 EHRR 1016; *PG and JH v UK* [2002] *Crim LR* 308.

[53] For a full discussion, see D. Harris, M. O'Boyle, E. Bates, and C. Buckley, *Harris, O'Boyle, and Warbrick's Law of the European Convention on Human Rights* (3rd edn, 2014), chs 11–15.

This does not amount to a general right not to be discriminated against: its terms are restricted to discrimination in relation to Convention rights, and therefore it can only be used in a situation where a violation of one of the other Convention rights is found.

This brief introduction to the key Convention rights gives an outline of the interaction between the ECHR and the rules of the criminal process. Detailed consideration of that interaction will be found in the relevant chapters: what is evident from their inclusion in the Convention and from the enactment of the Human Rights Act is that they should have a special place in English law generally and in the criminal process specifically—they are deemed more fundamental than other rights not so recognized, and have what might be termed a 'constitutional' dimension of added weight. In this context, there are two other particular aspects of the Convention which are crucial to the arguments of this chapter, and to a theory of the criminal process. The first concerns the prioritization or ranking of rights under the Convention, in terms of their differing strengths. The second, to which we will return later, concerns the patterns of reasoning when applying Convention rights.

(D) PRIORITY AMONG CONVENTION RIGHTS

One problem with rights-based accounts of the criminal process such as ours is that rights may conflict with each other or with other social values. Some rights may seem to be more important, or weightier, than others, giving the impression that rights can be traded off against one another and against other values. This, in turn, might lead one to conclude that because rights do not have an absolute value, they have no special value at all, and that a rights-based approach is in fact no different from a consequentialist approach (discussed further later). This line of reasoning is mistaken. While it is correct insofar as rights can conflict and can be ranked roughly in terms of importance, it is wrong in concluding that rights can be traded off against other values, or that rights-based approaches are not distinctive. We suggest that insight on some of these questions can be gained by looking at how they are dealt with within the ECHR framework.

It may already have become apparent that some of the Convention rights have different strengths, or more flexible exceptions, but the key to the ranking of Convention rights is to be found in Art 15:

Article 15

1. In time of war or other public emergency threatening the life of the nation any High Contracting Party may take measures derogating from its obligations under this Convention to the extent strictly required by the exigencies of the situation, provided that such measures are not inconsistent with its other obligations under international law.

2. No derogation from Article 2, except in relation to deaths resulting from lawful acts of war, or from Article 3, 4 (paragraph 1) and 7 shall be made under this provision ...

So, it is permissible for states to derogate from various Convention rights if the conditions for doing so are satisfied, but no derogation at all is allowed from four particular rights. This establishes an order of priority. The non-derogable rights are:

- the right to life (Art 2);
- the right not to be subjected to torture or inhuman or degrading treatment (Art 3);
- the right not to be subjected to forced labour (Art 4(1)); and
- the right not to be subjected to retrospective criminal laws or penalties (Art 7).

The fact that they are non-derogable indicates that they are the most basic of the fundamental rights in the Convention. Of course, their meaning and reach are subject to interpretation, and in that sense they are not *absolute* rights—or, at least, not until the scope of their application has been determined. But it is plain that they are not intended to give way to 'public interest' considerations: the metaphor of 'balancing' should not be applied here.

Another category of Convention rights might be termed qualified or prima facie rights—the right is declared, but it is also declared that interference is permissible on certain grounds, to the minimum extent possible. We have already noted examples of this in respect of Arts 8–11. All these qualified rights are subject to interference, if it can be established that this is 'necessary in a democratic society' on one of the stated grounds. As outlined earlier,[54] the ECtHR has interpreted the second paragraphs of these Articles in such a way as to impose meaningful limitations on state interference with the rights.

Situated between non-derogable rights and qualified rights is an intermediate category, which is less easy to label and less easy to assess. This category includes the right to liberty and security of the person (Art 5) and the right to a fair trial (Art 6). Unlike Arts 8–11, the rights in Arts 5 and 6 are not at all qualified on the face of the Convention. In the internal logic of the Convention, this may prove to be quite a significant distinction. What it suggests is that, although these rights are less fundamental than the non-derogable rights, any arguments for curtailment must at least be more powerful than the kind of 'necessary in a democratic society' argument that is needed to establish the acceptability of interference with a qualified right.

More will be said in section 2.4 about rights-based reasoning. The important point here is that it would not be accurate to state that human rights can be 'balanced' against public interest considerations. In the jurisprudence of the ECtHR, the vague notion of balancing does not dominate the interpretation of the Convention. Unfortunately, as we will see, the same is not always true of the English courts, where some judges have seized on the notion of balancing and a distorted version of the proportionality requirement to make significant inroads into the protection of rights.

Although we have concentrated on rights in this section, there are many values which are not to be found in documents such as the ECHR but which play an important role

---

[54] See n 53.

in shaping the criminal process. These include the values associated with the involvement of lay people in criminal justice decision making, the values associated with adversarialism, and the value of respect for victims of crime, for example. There are also the values reflected in treating defendants as an integral part of the process—as being called to account, in the terminology of Duff et al,[55] rather than as simple objects of the process, about whom judgements can be made without their being involved in the process in any significant way. Complex, late-modern societies may recognize a wide range of other values, and these should be reflected in an institution such as the criminal process.

2.4 EVALUATING THE CRIMINAL PROCESS

Thus far in this chapter we have sought to develop and to justify a theory that accords twin purposes to the criminal process—accurate determinations and fair procedures. The trial has been treated as the focus of the criminal process, and in that respect we have argued for the importance of regulating preparation for an effective criminal trial and of ensuring respect for rights and other important values. We have added a certain amount of detail to the theory by situating it in an analysis of the rights to be found in the ECHR. We now go on to show how and why our approach differs from certain other accounts of the criminal process.

(A) DUE PROCESS AND CRIME CONTROL: HERBERT PACKER'S MODELS

One well-known framework for evaluating the criminal process was developed by Herbert Packer in the 1960s.[56] While it has been the subject of considerable criticism and modification since, and is not adopted as a starting point here, it provides a useful frame for interpreting trends in criminal procedure: indeed, Packer did not propose his scheme as a normative theory but rather advanced two models as aids to interpretation.

Packer suggested that mechanisms and developments in criminal justice could be evaluated by reference to two models, the Crime Control model and the Due Process model. 'The value system that underlies the Crime Control model is based on the proposition that the repression of criminal conduct is by far the most important function to be performed by the criminal process.'[57] This calls for 'a high rate of apprehension and conviction', placing a 'premium on speed and finality', and therefore preferring informal to formal procedures, with minimal opportunity for challenge. To work efficiently, weak cases should be discarded at the earliest opportunity and strong cases

---

[55] A. Duff, L. Farmer, S. Marshall, and V. Tadros, *The Trial on Trial, Vol 3: Towards a Normative Theory of the Criminal Trial* (2007).

[56] H. Packer, *The Limits of the Criminal Sanction* (1968).   [57] Ibid, 158.

taken forward to conviction and sentence as expeditiously as possible. The police are in the best position to judge guilt, and, if they form the view after investigation that a person is guilty, the subsequent stages of the process should be as truncated as possible. In contrast, the Due Process model takes cognizance of the stigma and loss of liberty that results from the criminal process, and so insists on various protections for the suspect or defendant. Thus, the emphasis should be on formal and open adjudication of the facts in court, with the possibility of appeal.

These models are, of course, artificial constructs which list the features of a 'pure' or extreme form of a particular approach. They are designed as interpretive tools, to enable us to tell, say, how far in a particular direction a given criminal justice system tends, and they do not of themselves suggest that one approach is preferable to the other. Stuart Macdonald argues that what Packer intended to produce was not models but Weberian ideal-types.[58] However, the terminology of models has been adopted widely, and various objections have been raised against Packer's approach:

- Most fundamentally, it is curious to suggest that Crime Control and Due Process should be recognized as the two main objectives of the system. Due process cannot be an objective—rather it provides the safeguards in attaining the aim of Crime Control. In terms of their relationship Packer failed to give a clear explanation: while he recognized that 'the polarity of the two models is not absolute',[59] and stated that the ideology of Due Process 'is not the converse of that underlying the Crime Control model', since 'it does not rest on the idea that it is not socially desirable to repress crime',[60] it is not clear if Due Process and Crime Control are opposite ends of a continuum or two sides of the same coin. His models could be reconstructed so as to indicate that Crime Control is the underlying purpose of the system, and that pursuit of this purpose should be qualified out of respect to Due Process.

- Moreover, Packer's use of the term Crime *Control* presupposes that pre-trial justice is capable of affecting the crime rate, which is questionable. It is true that Packer included powers of arrest and detection rates in his discussion, but evidence is needed of a significant relationship between the extent of police powers and the crime rate.[61] Variations in crime rates are influenced more greatly by social and economic factors. The notion that different methods of processing defendants before trial might affect crime rates is not only unproven but also question-begging: Packer's models could be more persuasive if he cited conviction of the guilty as the primary state interest in pre-trial processes rather than controlling crime.

- Related to this, Packer underestimated the importance of resource management as an element in the criminal process. As noted in Chapter 1, this has assumed

---

[58] S. Macdonald, 'Constructing a Framework for Criminal Justice Research: Learning from Packer's Mistakes' (2008) 11 *New Crim LR* 257.

[59] See n 56, 154.   [60] Ibid, 163.

[61] For a review of the evidence up to the mid-1990s, see D. Dixon, *Law in Policing* (1997), 81–8.

greater significance in the years since Packer wrote, as governments have come under much greater financial pressure, and have brought this pressure to bear on criminal justice agencies.[62] Efficiency and managerialism are now to the fore. Any contemporary model of criminal justice ought to take account of the influence of targets, performance indicators, and other bureaucratic goals on the workings of the main agencies (e.g. police, prosecutors).[63]

- Packer's models make no allowance for victim-related matters. Again, this may be because there was far less consciousness of victims' interests and rights in the 1960s, but it is a significant omission and compromises the value of Packer's models today. Indeed, the existing scheme could probably not be adapted to accommodate this perspective: a new model or dimension would need to be added.

- Furthermore, it is possible to mount various internal critiques of the two models. One example is the premium on speed, which Packer describes as an element in the Crime Control model. However, delays are a source of considerable anxiety and inconvenience, and occasionally prolonged loss of liberty, to defendants. A more developed notion of Due Process would insist that there be no unreasonable delay.[64]

Consideration of Packer's models demonstrates the complexity of the criminal process and the problems of devising a satisfactory theoretical framework. The models may help us to identify elements of two important strands, but they neglect other, conflicting tendencies. One could try to remedy the defects by constructing further possible models. A wider and more differentiated scheme was presented by Michael King: beyond the models of due process and crime control, he outlined the medical model, in which the courts have a pastoral and rehabilitative role; the bureaucratic model, whereby courts seek to process individuals quickly and cheaply; the 'status passage' model which centres on the public denouncement of the individual and the criminal acts, and the associated affirmation of community values; and the 'power model' whereby the process reinforces class values and divisions.[65] More recently, Kent Roach has developed two models incorporating victims' rights, the construction of which amply demonstrates the politicization of victims' rights rather than the rational pursuit of victim-centred objectives.[66] Macdonald has proposed a reconfiguration of the due process model as an ideal-type based on a defensive criminal law designed to protect individuals against abuses of state power; he also warns against any simplistic balancing, and instead emphasizes the importance of taking account of 'the competing demands of many values', including those of efficiency and reliability.

---

[62] However, A. E. Bottoms and J. D. McClean took up this point only eight years after Packer had written: *Defendants in the Criminal Process* (1976), ch 9.

[63] See A. Ludlow, 'Marketizing Criminal Justice' in A. Liebling, S. Maruna, and L. McAra (eds), *The Oxford Handbook of Criminology* (6th edn, 2017).

[64] See the discussion in Ch 9.4.   [65] M. King, *The Framework of Criminal Justice* (1981).

[66] K. Roach, *Due Process and Victims' Rights: The New Law and Politics of Criminal Justice* (1999); for a survey of proposed readjustments and additions to Packer's framework, see Macdonald, n 58, 263–71.

(B) THE METAPHOR OF BALANCING

Much discussion of criminal justice by governments, courts, and official bodies gives
a central role to the notion of balance. Clear examples are to be found in the report
of the Royal Commission on Criminal Justice in 1993, in some of the leading judgments under the Human Rights Act and the ECHR, and in government claims about
the rights of victims of crime. In our view, the metaphor of balancing is a rhetorical
device of which one must be extremely wary. At worst, it is a substitute for principled
argument: 'achieving a balance' is put forward as if it were self-evidently a worthy and
respectable goal, rather like 'achieving justice'. Who, after all, would argue in favour
of injustice or an unbalanced system? Of course, it is important to recognize that the
criminal process is the scene of considerable conflict and tension between diverse aims
and interests. Regrettably, many of those who employ this terminology fail to stipu-
late exactly what is being balanced, what factors and interests are to be included or
excluded, what weight is being assigned to particular values and interests, and so on.

One example comes from a number of decisions of the British courts applying the
Convention under the Human Rights Act 1998. By far the most significant was the
first judgment handed down by the Privy Council after the 1998 Act came into force.
In *Brown v Stott*,[67] an appeal from Scotland raised the question whether the privilege
against self-incrimination, recognized as an implied right under Art 6,[68] protects the
owner of a car from criminal conviction for failing to declare who was driving it at a
given time and place. Of greater interest than the Privy Council's conclusion that the
privilege should not apply in this situation was the reasoning of Lord Bingham. Having
explained that motoring laws are socially important because of the risk of death and
injury from bad driving, he went on:

> If one asks whether section 172 [requiring owners to declare who was driving] represents
> a disproportionate response to the problem of maintaining road safety, whether the bal-
> ance between the interests of the community at large and the interests of the individual is
> struck in a manner unduly prejudicial to the individual, whether (in short) the leading of
> this evidence would infringe a basic human right of the respondent, I would feel bound to
> give negative answers.[69]

This is a crucial passage, setting the tone for many of the subsequent decisions under
the Human Rights Act. Yet it is flawed. The plausibility of the reasoning derives from
the reliance on two key concepts, 'balance' and 'proportionality', which seem to be understood in terms of some kind of trade-off between a conception of the public interest
(in which human rights apparently have no part) and the rights of the individual. Even
if those concepts can be constructed in a defensible way, the point is that they do not
belong here. As argued earlier, the right to a fair trial in Art 6 is a strong right under
the Convention, and its constituent rights cannot simply be traded off by reference to
the public interest. However, it must be said that ECHR jurisprudence is now equivocal as to the proper place of that mode of reasoning in Art 6 cases: within a week of

---

[67] [2003] 1 AC 681.   [68] See n 48 and accompanying text.   [69] [2003] 1 AC 681.

Brown v Stott, the ECtHR held that the privilege against self-incrimination could not be outweighed by the social importance of anti-terrorist laws[70] and, on facts similar to those in *Brown v Stott*, the ECtHR quoted the above passage from Lord Bingham with approval.[71] Furthermore, there is a role for the concept of proportionality in Convention cases, but that is chiefly in respect of Arts 8–11, as part of a specified mode of reasoning under the second paragraph of those Articles. It is relevant in considering whether the interference with the individual's right can be justified as 'necessary in a democratic society' for one of the listed reasons, and in its proper rigour should require a four-stage analysis.

(1) Is the purpose of any rights restriction a legitimate democratic purpose?

(2) Is the measure suitable for attaining that purpose?

(3) Is it the least restrictive measure for attaining that purpose?

(4) Is the measure proportionate in the strict sense, striking the proper balance between the purpose and the relevant individual rights?[72]

Lord Bingham's use of the concept in relation to Art 6 was far less disciplined and more opaque, whereas (because the Art 6 right is stronger than Arts 8–11) it should have been at least as rigorous as that four-stage analysis. We will return to this point later.

A second example involves the rights of victims. These will be discussed in more detail in later chapters, but at this point the debate about victims is a useful illustration of how the balancing metaphor is sometimes misleading. For instance, the Home Office recently claimed that 'Reforms to pre-charge bail balance carefully the interests of victims and witnesses, those on bail and the police.'[73] The metaphor can imply that the lot of suspects or defendants has to be made worse in order to improve that of victims.[74] But many victim-centred reforms—better courtroom facilities, better support, and keeping victims properly informed of the progress of their cases—do not affect suspects or defendants in any way. Other measures do affect defendants, for example restrictions on how vulnerable witnesses can be cross-examined.[75] Here the rebalancing metaphor is more appropriate, though it may still mislead. It might be taken to suggest that there is an inevitable clash between the rights of defendants and those of witnesses when in fact there is not. Vulnerable witnesses protections are generally intended to allow such people to give their 'best evidence'; but of course no defendant has a legitimate interest in a witness giving unreliable evidence, or in their feeling intimidated. If there *is* a balancing going on here, it does not involve balancing two rights. A further reason why the (re-)balancing metaphor may mislead is that it tends to suggest that victims have an interest in increased conviction rates, no matter how

---

[70] *Heaney and McGuinness v Ireland* (2000) 33 EHRR 12.

[71] *O'Halloran and Francis v UK* (2008) 46 EHRR 407.

[72] This four-stage analysis is taken from the report by B. Goold, L. Lazarus, and G. Swiney, *Public Protection, Proportionality and the Search for Balance* (Ministry of Justice, 2007).

[73] https://homeofficemedia.blog.gov.uk/2018/03/30/statement-on-pre-charge-bail/.

[74] Home Office, *Rebalancing the Criminal Justice System in Favour of the Law Abiding Majority* (2006).

[75] See Ch 11.

that increase is produced. Defendants share many of the interests of victims: interests in fair and dignified treatment, and in accurate fact-finding. This is something that the rebalancing metaphor only serves to obscure.

Our criticisms here are aimed at the vague and unprincipled use of the concept of 'balancing', a seductive notion that exudes fairness to the point of incontrovertibility. Yet talk of 'balancing' often assumes a kind of hydraulic relationship between human rights safeguards and the promotion of public safety, an assumption that cannot be made. Another problem with the 'balancing' metaphor is that it may lead to restrictions on a minority in the hope of enhancing the security of the majority.[76] A further difficulty is that too frequently no account is taken of the increase in state power that accompanies curtailments of individual rights, whereas one of the fundamental purposes of human rights is to protect individuals against arbitrary exercises of state power. Moreover, even for rights in respect of which balancing is proper, the exercise should be conducted in a particular way. That is, the concept of 'balance' should be reserved for the conclusion of a lengthy and careful process, whereby rights and interests are identified; arguments for including some and excluding others are set out; appropriate weights or priorities are assigned to particular rights and interests, either generally or in specific contexts; and so forth. Above all, this must be a reasoned, principled, and empirically grounded course of argument, not simply the pronouncement of a conclusion. We will pursue this claim further later. Prior to that, it will be helpful to illustrate some of the problems of balancing with reference to consequentialist theories of criminal process, which tend to rely heavily on this device.

(C) CONSEQUENTIALISM IN THE CRIMINAL PROCESS

Jeremy Bentham and John Stuart Mill are known for their espousal of utilitarianism: though the theory may take more or less sophisticated forms, in essence it provides that social policies both generally and in respect of criminal justice should be determined by calculating what approach would conduce to the greatest happiness of the greatest number of people.[77] A 'felicific calculus', measuring pain and pleasure, is used to determine the approach that would produce least pain overall. An obvious criticism of such a consequentialist approach is that its chief concern is with aggregate benefits, and that it may therefore jeopardize particular individuals or minorities in order to benefit the majority. Torture is the most provocative example: human rights instruments prohibit it absolutely, whereas utilitarians might accept it when it seems likely to yield a benefit for the majority. More prosaically, human rights instruments often proclaim the presumption of innocence in criminal proceedings, whereas on a

---

[76] For further critique of 'balancing', see J. Waldron, 'Security and Liberty: The Image of Balance' (2003) 11 J Political Philosophy 191; L. Zedner, 'Seeking Security by Eroding Rights: The Side-stepping of Due Process' and A. Ashworth, 'Security, Terrorism and the Value of Human Rights', both in B. Goold and L. Lazarus (eds), Security and Human Rights (2007).

[77] A good account of consequentialism is in W. Kymlicka, Contemporary Political Philosophy: An Introduction (2nd edn, 2002), ch 2.

utilitarian calculus it may often benefit the community more if defendants were required to prove, for example, any defence that they wished to raise.

Rights theories, on the other hand, are anti-consequentialist: the whole point of recognizing a right is to uphold the claim of an individual to protection from treatment of certain kinds, even though such treatment may accord with the wishes of the majority or be for the overall benefit of the community. This does not mean that consequentialist reasoning is always inappropriate, but it does imply that in certain spheres of activity consequentialism must give way to recognized rights. There has been a recent revival of consequentialist theories in criminal justice; two are mentioned here. John Braithwaite and Phillip Pettit argue that the ultimate determinant should be the republican ideal of liberty: clashes between individual rights and public interests should be resolved by calculating which approach advances 'dominion' on a greater scale, where dominion means non-interference by others.[78] One difficulty with this form of theory is that it appears not to recognize anything other than vague outer limits on state intervention in individual lives. Thus, its authors refer to the need to provide reassurance to the community and to espouse incapacitative penal strategies: 'crucial to the promotion of community reassurance' is the power to 'escalate responses' as 'an offender displays more and more intransigence about offending against others'.[79] Although primarily directed at sentencing rather than at pre-trial processes, this approach provides no principled restraints on state intervention, and it is unclear whether and to what extent it would recognize individual rights. Whatever the merits of the republican ideal, the absence of principled limits means that the theory leaves individuals too much at the mercy of the state.

Andrew Sanders, Richard Young, and Mandy Burton adopt a distinct form of consequentialism, though one that has marked similarities to Braithwaite and Pettit's. For Sanders, Young, and Burton, the value to be maximized is 'freedom', rather than dominion. They argue that when human rights and other interests are being compared, the approach that is likely to enhance freedom the most should be chosen, since the various conflicting considerations (human rights, protecting the innocent, convicting the guilty, protecting victims, maintaining public order, etc) should be seen as means to achieving the overriding goal of freedom. Thus 'all we have to do is to prioritise the goal that is likely to enhance freedom the most'.[80] Two difficulties with this approach concern the definition of freedom and the approach to balancing that it requires. The meaning of freedom is highly contestable—as the classic essay by Isaiah Berlin on negative liberty and positive liberty shows[81]—and these concerns are compounded when the authors state that they include the freedom 'of the community at large'.[82] Their fundamental

---

[78] J. Braithwaite and P. Pettit, *Not Just Deserts: A Republican Theory of Criminal Justice* (1990).

[79] For brief contributions to the debate, see P. Pettit with J. Braithwaite, 'Republicanism in Sentencing: Recognition, Recompense and Reassurance', and A. Ashworth and A. von Hirsch, 'Desert and the Three Rs', both in A. von Hirsch and A. Ashworth (eds), *Principled Sentencing: Readings on Theory and Policy* (2nd edn, 1998).

[80] A. Sanders, R. Young, and M. Burton *Criminal Justice* (4th edn, 2010), 48.

[81] I. Berlin, 'Two Concepts of Liberty' in A. Quinton (ed), *Political Philosophy* (1967).

[82] Cf Sanders, Young, and Burton, n 80, 49, for a defence of their use of the idea of the 'freedom of the community at large'.

concept seems to us to be under-determined, and it is not clear how they would deal with the weighting of 'competing goals, interests and rights' that is necessary.[83] They certainly recognize the need to assign weights to them, but their confidence in 'the language of freedom' to smooth the path by providing a 'common currency' may be overstated. However, we support their recognition of the sheer range of relevant interests to be considered, and their recognition that assigning weight to each of them in particular contexts is an essential precondition of any kind of 'balancing' operation.

In summary, the principal problem with consequentialist theories is that they allow rights to be overridden in pursuit of other values. Even the sophisticated theories of Braithwaite and Pettit and Sanders, Young, and Burton appear to allow violations of human rights if to do so would ultimately promote dominion or freedom: Sanders, Young, and Burton say not, but that suggests some kind of special protection for human rights in their freedom-based calculations, the implications of which are not articulated. When one considers the sheer number of different values relevant to criminal justice in a complex society, many of which conflict, it is difficult to believe that they can be reduced to a single core value. To take some examples mentioned earlier: the choice between an adversarial or inquisitorial system, or between lay or professional fact-finders, cannot be made in terms of which promotes dominion or freedom better. Moreover, the value of confrontation between defendant and witness, which features in the ECHR,[84] cannot be conceptualized or assessed easily in those terms either. One should be suspicious of theories that attempt, as consequentialist theories do, to reduce all human values to a single metric.

(D) DEVELOPING THE RIGHTS PERSPECTIVE

Our approach to criminal process differs from those just described in that it is rights-based. This is not to say that the purpose of the criminal process is to implement human rights, but that in the pursuit of retributive justice respect for rights is essential. Respect for rights should be seen as a concomitant aim of criminal process—not merely a side-constraint on the pursuit of accuracy or 'rectitude' in convicting the guilty and acquitting the innocent, but an objective to be attained while pursuing that aim. Thus, the ECHR is taken to be part of the normative framework for the criminal process, as indeed it is in terms of both UK law (following the Human Rights Act) and the country's international obligations. But the Convention is not the full extent of our normative arguments. It has limitations, in respect of discrimination, victims and witnesses, and young suspects and defendants, for example. Furthermore, as we have noted, values beyond those contained in human rights documents play a legitimate role in shaping the criminal process.

The particular contribution of the human rights perspective is in its subtle weighting of different rights, and its structuring of arguments for making exceptions to rights. As noted, certain rights allow for interference and for a balancing process to determine

---

[83] Ibid, 62.   [84] Art 6(3)(d), the right to examine witnesses; see *Al-Khawaja v UK* (2012) 54 EHRR 23.

whether the interference is justified. But the kind of balancing that is permitted under the Convention is a far cry from the vague and undisciplined concept criticized earlier.[85]

Our starting point is the hierarchy of Convention rights (sketched in section 2.3(D) earlier) which distinguishes between non-derogable rights, strong rights, and qualified rights. Non-derogable rights permit no balancing in the public interest. For example, arguments that torturing certain people would be in the public interest cannot be entertained, as the ECtHR held in *Chahal*[86]. On the other hand, qualified rights self-evidently are open to balancing. But this is not some vague exercise of trying to measure the individual's right against the wider public interest, but rather a structured process of reasoning indicated by the wording of the second paragraph of those rights and developed in the jurisprudence of the Court. Of course, courts can reach different conclusions about whether an interference is 'necessary in a democratic society'. The argument is that the structure of reasoning required in order to justify interference with a qualified right provides a guide to the weighting of the right and the circumstances in which it can be outweighed.

More difficult are the two strong rights declared by Arts 5 and 6. It must be said that the ECtHR has not been entirely consistent in its judgments. There are some decisions on Arts 5 and 6 where it has stated either that a particular right is not absolute, or that it may be necessary to balance a right against some other interest. This proposition must be treated with care, and not as a licence for vague and undisciplined 'balancing'. The ECtHR has said that both the right of silence and the privilege against self-incrimination are not absolute,[87] yet, emphatically, that does not mean that they can be 'balanced' freely against public interest considerations. What it means in respect of the right of silence is that there may be 'situations calling for an explanation from' the accused, in which adverse inferences may justifiably be drawn from the accused's silence: this is a significant qualification, but it refers only to the evidential situation in the case. The fact that a power is believed to be essential in the fight against terrorism has been held insufficient to justify an exception to the privilege against self-incrimination, but it remains to be seen whether the Court will continue to hold this line.[88]

As for balancing an Art 6 right against another Convention right, the principal example of this is *Doorson v Netherlands*,[89] where the Court held that the defendant's right to examine witnesses against him has to be balanced against the rights of the witnesses themselves, notably where a witness has reason to fear violent reprisals if her or his identity is revealed. But, again, this decision does not license some vague kind of 'balancing'. In the first place, the interests 'balanced' were both rights of individuals, not any public interests. Moreover, the process of 'balancing' was quite rigidly

---

[85] See section 2.4(B).   [86] (1996) 23 EHRR 413.

[87] E.g. in *John Murray v UK* (1996) 22 EHRR 29 and in *Saunders v UK* (1997) 23 EHRR 313.

[88] Compare *Heaney and McGuinness v Ireland* (2000) 33 EHRR 12 (fight against terrorism insufficient to justify exception) with *Jalloh v Germany* (2007) 44 EHRR 667 (seriousness of offence a relevant consideration). For principled discussion, see e.g. A. Ashworth, *Human Rights, Serious Crime and Criminal Procedure* (2002), 108–18.

[89] (1996) 22 EHRR 330.

structured: the Court insisted that, although it was proper to protect the identity of the witness, defence rights must be curtailed as little as possible. Thus, the 'handicaps under which the defence laboured [must be] sufficiently counterbalanced by the procedures followed by the judicial authorities', such as appropriate directions from the judge; and any conviction should not be based 'solely or mainly' on the evidence of the witnesses who were thus allowed to give their evidence anonymously.[90] All these requirements, indeterminate as they may be in their application, constitute an advance on general notions of 'balancing', by showing how a right can continue to exert influence even where its application is curtailed.

Another example of a structured approach may be found in the Court's judgments on the prosecution's duty to disclose documents to the defence, and the claim of 'public interest immunity' from having to disclose certain evidence. In the leading decision of *Rowe and Davis v UK*,[91] the Court held that the principle of equality of arms is a requirement of fairness under Art 6, but that:

> the entitlement to disclosure of relevant evidence is not an absolute right. In any criminal proceedings there may be competing interests, such as national security or the need to protect witnesses at risk of reprisals or keep secret police methods of investigating crime. In some cases it may be necessary to withhold certain evidence from the defence so as to preserve the fundamental rights of another individual or to safeguard an important public interest. However, only such measures restricting the rights of the defence which are strictly necessary are permissible under Article 6(1). Moreover, in order to ensure that the accused receives a fair trial, any difficulties caused to the defence by a limitation on its rights must be sufficiently counterbalanced by the procedures followed by the judicial authorities.[92]

Subsequent judgments re-examined the 'counterbalancing' procedures in cases of public interest immunity, finding that the combination of non-disclosure with the special counsel system may be insufficient to comply with the requirements of a fair trial.[93]

These examples demonstrate that, on the rare occasions when the ECtHR has recognized that a degree of balancing may enter into the determination of certain rights under Arts 5 and 6, it has insisted on structured reasoning. It has not allowed a right simply to be 'balanced away',[94] but has concentrated on preserving the essence of the defendant's right while giving some weight to pressing public interest considerations. As argued earlier, even the justifications for interfering with the qualified rights under Arts 8–11 must be reasoned according to a particular structure of requirements: this renders all the more cogent the argument that rigorous and structured reasoning

---

[90] Ibid, [72]; cf *Van Mechelen v Netherlands* (1997) 25 EHRR 547.

[91] (2000) 30 EHRR 1.

[92] Ibid, [61].

[93] See e.g. *A v UK* (2009) 49 EHRR 625, *Secretary of State for the Home Department v AF* [2009] UKHL 28.

[94] Even in *O'Halloran and Francis v UK* (2008) 46 EHRR 407, where the Court quoted with approval Lord Bingham's passage about balancing rights against the public interest, the Court took account of other factors in coming to its decision.

should be used when there is a question of 'balancing' certain (not all) rights under the stronger Arts 5 and 6 against some public interests.

That said, structured reasoning only takes one so far: it offers a procedure, but no ultimate criterion for making choices. Human rights standards are open-textured in places, perhaps more than some rules of domestic law. Because human rights are as much political as legal, their reach inevitably will generate controversy. But we have argued that the structure of the Convention sets certain markers and establishes an order of priority, which may be used as a basis for reasoned argument. In respect of Arts 5 and 6, which are the rights primarily relevant to the criminal process, it should be recognized that they essentially 'trump' considerations of public interest. There may be limited circumstances in which certain rights may be 'over-trumped' by extreme and urgent considerations of public interest. But, even then, the ECtHR has shown that policies relating to the fight against terrorism or drugs cannot be taken as sufficient for these purposes.[95] Consequentialist approaches might well lead to other conclusions in these scenarios: that marks a significant difference in our emphasis.

2.5 DEVELOPING THE RIGHTS PERSPECTIVE: THE STATE AND VICTIMS

Our theory of the criminal process—one that has the twin goals of regulating the processes for bringing suspected offenders to trial so as to produce accurate determinations, and of ensuring that fundamental rights are protected in those processes—still needs to be supplemented and adapted in several ways. Of course, it is important to reflect on the suspect who is at the heart of the criminal process, given the critical and sometimes intersecting characteristics of sex, gender, race, age, class, and so on. While many texts, doctrines, and protections are conceived of with the individual adult in mind, the suspect or accused may also be a child or a legal person. Differences of approach may be necessary when dealing with young suspects, for example. It is necessary to look to the United Nations Convention on the Rights of the Child (1990), whose wide-ranging list of rights includes those in Art 40 on 'the administration of juvenile justice'. A further question is whether all the rights in the Convention ought to apply to corporate bodies as well as to individuals: how ought the right to liberty and security of the person (Art 5) or the right to a fair trial (Art 6) apply to companies?[96]

It is also necessary to assess the relevance of what are claimed to be victims' rights. Until the end of the last century, victims' needs for support, respect, and compensation were neglected. Now there is increasing recognition that the victims of crime have

---

[95] E.g. *Heaney and McGuinness*, n 87; *Brogan v UK*, n 39; and, on drugs, *Teixeira de Castro v Portugal* (1999) 28 EHRR 101.

[96] See D. Spielmann, 'Companies in the Strasbourg Courtroom' (2016) 5 *Cambridge J Int and Comp L* 404; P. Van Kempen, 'The Recognition of Legal Persons in International Human Rights Instruments: Protection Against and Through Criminal Justice?' in M. Pieth and R. Ivory (eds), *Corporate Criminal Liability: Emergence, Convergence, and Risk* (2011), 355–389.

rights to respectful and sympathetic treatment from law enforcement agents; to support and help in the aftermath of the offence; to proper information about the progress of their case; to facilities at courtrooms that separate them from other members of the public; and to compensation for the crime, either from the offender or (if that is not possible) from the state, at least for crimes of violence. These rights to particular treatment and services should be regarded as an important element in social provision for those harmed or disadvantaged by crime, and those working in the criminal justice system should ensure that they are recognized and fulfilled. But completely different justifications are needed if it is claimed that victims have procedural rights in the criminal process. Should victims have the right to be consulted on decisions whether or not to prosecute, on bail/custody decisions, on the acceptance of a plea to a lesser offence or to fewer offences, or on sentence? Though some victims and victims' families want this kind of involvement,[97] the question here is whether there are good arguments for recognizing such wishes or claims as rights.

An essential first step is to consider what the role of the state should be in the criminal process. One familiar argument is that the state's leading role is a social necessity: if it were left to victims, their families, and their supporters to deal with people who break the rules, this would open the way to revenge, retaliation, vigilantism, and serious injustice, if not anarchy. This consequentialist argument does not establish, however, why it should be the state—as opposed to local communities, for example—that should have the overall responsibility and power. For this, one needs a conception of the state's proper functions. The state has as one of its major functions the prevention or reduction of harm, and this includes responding to wrongs done by censuring those who commit them. The state can and should do this in a way that shows respect for the (alleged) offender as a rational citizen (e.g. by conforming to human rights), and which adopts a fair and consistent approach to the task.[98] These last specifications have particular resonance for the criminal process, in the investigatory, pre-trial, and trial stages: a major role of the state is as guarantor of the rights of all those involved, as well as providing official agencies (such as the police, public prosecutors, and courts) to carry out the essential functions of law enforcement.

This may be regarded as a general argument of principle. It may have to cede, to some extent, if the reality is that a certain state is failing to perform its proper role—where, for example, there is widespread mistrust among the people because of long-running social divisions; or even where it is evident that there is a vitiating gulf between provision for wealthier citizens (who can afford extra security measures) and provision for the poor, a social problem that may be no less manifest in law enforcement than in health or education.[99] But the argument of principle—the starting point, informed by the commitment to retributive justice—is that the primary interests in the application of the criminal sanction through the processes of the criminal justice system are

[97] See Victim Support, *The Rights of Victims of Crime* (1995).
[98] See further A. von Hirsch and A. Ashworth, *Proportionality in Sentencing* (2005), ch 2.
[99] See A. Ashworth, 'Responsibilities, Rights and Restorative Justice' (2002) 42 *BJ Crim* 578, 580–1.

those of the state and the suspect/defendant/offender. Then, in respect of sentencing, the court should take a decision according to the law, and the victim's personal view should be no more relevant to this than that of any other individual. The rule of law, embodied in the ECHR and other human rights documents, requires decisions to be taken by an independent and impartial tribunal according to settled rules announced beforehand. A particular victim may be vindictive or forgiving, demanding or afraid of the offender, and it would be an abdication of the state's responsibility to allow such individual feelings to influence the sentence. The same reasoning applies to the key stages of the criminal process, such as the decision to investigate, the decision to prosecute, and the acceptance of a plea to a different charge: the rule of law requires these decisions to be taken impartially and independently, and not influenced by the wishes of a particular individual. In practice, the willingness of a victim or complainant to become involved, by making a statement or alternatively by declining to give evidence in court, can often determine whether an inquiry or prosecution is taken forward. But those facts do not alter the legal rules and appraisal; indeed, in some types of case (such as domestic violence) prosecutions may be brought without the victim's cooperation.[100]

The implication of this reasoning is that there are no convincing arguments for accepting that victims or their families have a right to influence any of the key decisions in the criminal process. Whether there is still good reason to say that the police or prosecutors should 'take account of' victims' wishes before taking decisions is a moot point: this could be criticized as a sham if at the same time we maintain that the decisions should not be *influenced* by the victim's wishes, because victims might feel they are being misled and might feel disappointed if their wishes are not followed.[101] However, this is the position in respect of Victim Personal Statements (VPSs), which are submitted by victims to the court: as the Criminal Practice Directions 2015 state, 'The opinions of the victim or the victim's close relatives as to what the sentence should be are therefore not relevant, unlike the consequences of the offence on them.'[102] Information contained in the VPS may be relevant when assessing the consequences of the offence for the victim, and at remand proceedings—there are cases where it would be important to know about the alleged victim's apprehensions about (further) violence or harassment. This shows the distinction between information from the victim (which may be relevant) and the opinions of the victim (which should not be relevant).

An independent review in 2015 revealed that many victims of crime regarded their experience of engaging with the criminal justice system as being 'almost worse than the actual journey of being a victim'.[103] With that in mind, it is imperative that victims are treated with dignity, though we argue that they should not be granted procedural rights that enable them to influence decisions in the criminal process. This leaves

---

[100] See the discussion in Ch 7.

[101] See the research into the pilot project on submitting victim statements to prosecutors, discussed by A. Sanders, C. Hoyle, R. Morgan, and E. Cape, 'Victim Impact Statements: Can't Work, Won't Work' [2001] *Crim LR* 447.

[102] Criminal Practice Directions 2015, Division VII Sentencing, F.3.

[103] Victims' Commissioner, *A Review of Complaints and Resolution For Victims of Crime* (2015), 25.

untouched the need to review and improve rules relating to investigations, procedure, and evidence in particular types of case—notably cases of sexual assault, where victims remain open to questioning, in and out of court, on details of their past which are of questionable relevance to the proper interests of the defendant.[104] Similarly, we endorse strongly arguments in favour of improved support, information, and compensation for victims. For many years, victims were not always kept informed about the progress of 'their' case through the system: though we question this characterization of the case, it is not appropriate that victims are informed of developments like a plea of guilty to a lesser offence only at a much later stage in process, or by happenstance. The publication of a Code of Practice for Victims of Crime under the Domestic Violence, Crime and Victims Act 2004 was a welcome step, but the Act stopped short of establishing statutory rights to services for victims. The Code was revised in 2013 to reflect the commitments in the EU Victims' Directive (2012/29/EU) in terms of service provision and the Victims' Right to Review scheme.[105]

How do these conclusions on the role of the state and on victims' rights relate to initiatives in restorative justice? In the precise sphere of this book, the implications are limited because it is usually a precondition of a defendant entering restorative justice that he or she admits guilt. Restorative justice is not put forward as a means of resolving factual disputes or a substitute for trials, though it does replace other state reactions to admissions of guilt. Restorative justice challenges the view that the state should have exclusive responsibility for the administration of criminal justice, and employs 'restorative conferences' (composed of victims and their families, offenders and their families, and community representatives) or other means of communication to allow victims and offenders to come to terms with what happened and to determine the response to offences.[106] Although it is said to be essential that the offender consents to participate and can withdraw at any time, it is plain that the conferences take place in the shadow of the formal legal system and that any consent is therefore somewhat bounded. Victims clearly have a significant role in deciding the outcome, and this goes against the rule-of-law principles of independent and impartial judgement by making it likely that outcomes will depend to some extent on whether the victim is forgiving or otherwise.[107] Advocates of restorative justice view this as less important than whether the offender comes forth with an apology to the victim and whether the victim feels better having entered into a dialogue with the offender. To relate this back to Packer's two models of the criminal process (see section 2.4(A)), we can see that an entirely different model is needed to interpret trends and tendencies from the victim's point of view.[108]

---

[104] See C. McGlynn, 'Rape Trials and Sexual History Evidence: Reforming the Law on Third Party Evidence' (2017) 81 *J Crim L* 367–392.

[105] See Ch 7.

[106] See further G. Johnstone, *Restorative Justice: Ideas, Values, Debates* (2nd edn, 2011); and see Ch 6 of this book.

[107] See the criticisms by A. Ashworth, 'Responsibilities, Rights and Restorative Justice' (2002) 42 *BJ Crim* 578, and the reply by A. Morris, 'Critiquing the Critics: A Brief Response to Critics of Restorative Justice', ibid, 596.

[108] See K. Roach, 'Criminal Process' in P. Cane and M. Tushnet (eds), *The Oxford Handbook of Legal Studies* (2003), 780–1.

Insofar as restorative justice is invoked to deal with cases at the lower end of the scale of seriousness, there may be advantages in experimenting with it to see whether it yields the benefits (in terms of community reintegration and crime prevention) that tend to be claimed for it. But as the seriousness of the offences increases, so the importance of maintaining rule-of-law standards and respecting the rights of defendants in the face of sanctions imposed upon them increases.[109] This issue is pursued further below.

2.6 DISPOSITIVE VALUES

The discussion thus far has focused on values in the context of a theory of the criminal process. Now we return to the 'dispositive' values which underpin pre-trial decisions. These include the prevention of crime; consent; the compensation of victims; and proportionality of imposition. Our focus here is on police cautions, conditional cautions, final warnings, Fixed Penalty Notices, Penalty Notices for Disorder (PNDs), restorative justice conferences, and other forms of diversion from the formal trial process.[110] To a large extent, the values relevant here reflect the purposes at the stage of sentencing, which is the best-known and most widely publicized dispositive decision, but it is important also to retain a philosophical connection with the principles discussed earlier in relation to process values. In particular, the right of an innocent person not to be punished is relevant to both types of decision.

(A) PREVENTION OF CRIME

The prevention of crime is among the reasons for having a criminal justice system, including police, courts, and sentences. Indeed, in section 2.5 we argued that this should be a primary function of the state. It is also an underlying reason for diversion, but this is not to say that it should be determinative in individual cases. It is one thing to argue that the system of diversion should operate so as to contribute to the overall prevention of crime, at least by dealing with offenders in ways that do not increase the chances of further law-breaking by them or others. It is another thing to maintain that the prospect of a particular person not reoffending should be a necessary or sufficient reason for diverting that offender from the formal criminal process: that might conflict with the principle of proportionality (see section 2.6(D)). The point here is that, since dispositive decisions without trial may be regarded as part of or analogous to the sentencing system, they should not be invoked in a way that increases the probability of people committing offences.

---

[109] See C. McGlynn, N. Westmarland, and N. Godden, "'I Just Wanted Him to Hear Me": Sexual Violence and the Possibilities of Restorative Justice' (2012) 39 *J L and Soc* 213–40.

[110] These were introduced in Ch 1, and will be discussed in detail in Ch 6.

(B) CONSENT AND FAIRNESS

The system should ensure that, as far as possible, a person's decision whether or not to accept diversion is a free and informed one, and that there is a right of access to a court if guilt is disputed.[111] This principle has a direct connection with process values. The idea of a completely free decision in this context may be regarded as illusory, in the sense that the alternative of going to court will often be perceived as more stressful, but there are ways of maximizing consent. For example, legal advice should be available so as to help a suspect with this decision, not least because cautions, final warnings, and PNDs are recorded and may be cited in subsequent proceedings, and also because restorative justice conferences are sometimes less benign than they might seem.[112] PNDs, unlike other out-of-court disposals, do not require an admission of guilt by the ticketed person; they do not rank as convictions, yet they are recorded on the Police National Computer and may be used against a person in various circumstances. This underlines the need to ensure that methods of diversion do not become methods of subverting fairness and the protection of the innocent.

(C) VICTIM COMPENSATION

Any arrangement for diversion should ensure that the victim does not thereby lose a right to compensation. This does not mean that offenders should be required to pay full compensation to their victims in order to be eligible for diversion: as in formal sentencing proceedings, compensation should reflect the offender's means, too. Again, the statutory requirements for conditional cautions appear to deal properly with this question, but for informal processes such as restorative conferences there is no legal framework.

(D) PROPORTIONALITY OF IMPOSITION

There should be a sense of proportion between the seriousness of the offence and that to which the offender is asked to agree as part of the diversion. This is not merely to ensure that consent is as voluntary as possible, but is also a basic element of desert in sentencing: a person who has committed an offence deserves to be punished only to an extent that is appropriate to the seriousness of the offence committed, in terms of harm and culpability. Thus, the impositions on those who are 'diverted' must be proportionate to one another, in the sense that more serious cases should involve more onerous requirements and vice versa. The impositions should also be of modest severity overall, so as to be ranked below court-imposed penalties appropriately.

In terms of the human rights discussed in section 2.3(C), why is proportionality of sentencing so important? Apart from the strong arguments of principle for ensuring

---

[111] As required under Art 6: *Ozturk v Germany* (1984) 6 EHRR 409.

[112] This is not to imply that legal advice necessarily leads to the best outcome for an accused person: see Ch 3 on the ethics of defence lawyers, and Ch 10 on lawyers' advice on plea.

that punishment is proportionate so as to deal fairly with individuals,[113] the ECtHR has insisted that punishments must not be so disproportionate as to constitute 'inhuman and degrading' punishment under Art 3;[114] the Charter of Fundamental Rights of the European Union, in force since 2003, declares in Art 49(3) that 'the severity of penalties should not be disproportionate to the criminal offence'; and there are other examples of human rights documents insisting on this limitation of state punishment.[115] In terms of human rights law, therefore, the right not to be punished disproportionately to the seriousness of the offence committed seems well established. That said, one emergent difficulty, as suggested earlier, is that some processes which are intended to be beneficial to the offender will in fact be more onerous, in terms of the requirements they impose, than is justified by reference to the seriousness of the offence. This may be a problem with the outcomes of some restorative conferences, and there is therefore an argument in favour of taking steps to limit the impositions that may be made or 'agreed', or to require court approval of the outcome. The same difficulty may arise with some rehabilitative programmes offered as part of diversion: there is a developing range of programmes to tackle alcohol or substance abuse, to manage anger, etc, and the degree of commitment required may be considerable. Proponents of these programmes often claim that it is no use if offenders participate in them for less than the full course; but if this means months of attendance, and therefore considerable impositions by comparison with the seriousness of the offence, there are questions of disproportionality to be addressed.

2.7 CONCLUSION: THE CRIMINAL PROCESS AND THE LIMITATIONS OF HUMAN RIGHTS

In this chapter we sketched a rights-based theory of the criminal process, suggesting that the process should have the coexisting goals of regulating the procedures for bringing suspected offenders to trial so as to produce accurate determinations, and of ensuring that fundamental rights are protected in those processes. We have offered arguments for our belief that this approach should be adopted in England and Wales— both on principle and because it is implicit in international documents such as the ECHR that now play a fundamental role in English law. However, we have also recognized the need to supplement the Convention rights and to develop a fuller statement of rights that would include (for example) the rights of young people and the rights of victims. We have also proposed separate objectives for dispositive decisions, notably the decision to divert a person from the criminal process without trial. We have not overlooked the many conflicts that inevitably occur in the criminal process and the

[113] For elaboration, see A. von Hirsch and A. Ashworth, *Proportionate Sentencing* (2005), chs 1 and 2.

[114] *Weeks v UK* (1988) 10 EHRR 293, and other authorities discussed in Emmerson, Ashworth, and Macdonald, n 51, ch 20.

[115] See D. van Zyl Smit and A. Ashworth, 'Disproportionate Sentences as Human Rights Violations' (2004) 67 *MLR* 541.

many difficult decisions those require: the human rights framework has been offered as a way of dealing with those conflicts that has a firmer moral and political foundation than consequentialist theories and has greater integrity and transparency than approaches that simply refer to 'balancing'. However, two limitations of rights theories must be kept firmly in view—the gap between the law in action and the law in the books, and the political volatility of criminal justice systems.

(A) RIGHTS, RHETORIC, AND REALITY

Theories of rights are normative: they indicate what should or should not be done, what should be protected, and when. To recognize a right is important, but to ensure its respect in practice is different. Our human rights approach does not purport to be a description of the present system in operation. Thus we do not overlook the variable gap, sometimes small and sometimes large, between passing a law that recognizes and protects a right and ensuring that the right-holders are in a position to exercise that right as intended. Wherever relevant in this book, we refer to empirical evidence that sheds light on whether certain rights or procedures are properly implemented in practice. We will argue that due protection is not always given to established rights in decisions by police, Crown prosecutors, magistrates at remand proceedings and on the acceptance of pleas of guilty (to take some examples).

Generally speaking, what is required to ensure that declared rights are respected in actuality is not only an ethical commitment on behalf of the relevant agency to respecting those rights (see Chapter 3), but also proper information to suspects/defendants about their rights and ready access to legal advice relating to their situation. The same applies to information about victims' rights, and access to support or information about support and service. Though improvements have been attempted, it is a longstanding complaint that neither suspects nor victims and witnesses have all the information they are entitled to expect about their rights and how to exercise them. If they do not, it is likely that there will be a significant gap between the law as declared and the law in practice.

(B) THE POLITICAL VOLATILITY OF THE CRIMINAL PROCESS

The criminal justice system is a forum for political posturing.[116] It is not so much that the leading political parties have conflicting approaches, but rather that they often try to outdo one another in the 'toughness' of their rhetoric. In the mid-1990s, the Conservatives bolstered their political cause through the words and policies of the then Home Secretary, Michael Howard, who proclaimed that 'prison works'. As the re-shaping of 'New Labour' began around that time, 'weak' policies on law and order were identified as a potential threat to its other policies and to electoral success. Since the election of the Conservatives in 2010, there has been an emphasis

---

[116] See M. Tonry, *Punishment and Politics* (2004).

on efficiency, cost-cutting, and pragmatism. This was tempered somewhat by the presence of the Liberal Democrats in coalition from 2010 to 2015. Overall, criminal justice policy is inconsistent and often unprincipled, and changes to the criminal process are not predicated on any firm research base from the Home Office or other state entities.

Moreover, the government's pronouncements are often antagonistic as to human rights, certainly those deriving from the ECHR. Although the Labour government introduced the Human Rights Act, its criminal policy statements paid limited attention to the issue, and often seem to make a virtue out of avoiding or minimizing human rights protections. A succession of reports from the Joint Committee on Human Rights have forced the government to be explicit about the relationship between legislative proposals and relevant human rights. There has been some degree of improvement: now the government provides an ECHR Memorandum which, though often unduly optimistic, is relied on by the Joint Committee on Human Rights in its scrutiny of Bills' compatibility with the ECHR.

Rarely do the media or the government talk about criminal policy in general or in a holistic sense. More commonly, they identify particular types of crime and criminal. More stringent or tougher measures are needed (we are told) for the fight against terrorism, to combat organized crime, and so forth. This might sound convincing if it were not placed in the context of a society that aspires to the rule of law and which has long proclaimed its adherence to various international treaties on human rights. It is, as we argued earlier, a complete misconception to argue that human rights become less important whenever the detection and prosecution of serious crime is the objective. On the contrary, at a theoretical level human rights are safeguards against arbitrary action by governments, for example by failing to observe proper procedural protections when dealing with suspects and defendants. And in terms of the jurisprudence of the ECtHR, there are many pronouncements showing that governments cannot simply remove safeguards under Arts 5 and 6 in the name of the fight against terrorism or other serious crimes.[117] Few government statements on the criminal process discuss these issues in relation to new policies. The rhetoric is all about taking tough measures and protecting victims, within the confines of an under-resourced and under-efficient system. There is little about upholding human rights (which is also in the public interest), and the rhetoric of protecting victims would not be sustainable on a proper analysis of the ways of protecting people that are likely to be most effective on the available evidence. Our rights approach indicates a framework for dealing with apparent conflicts between individual rights and 'the public interest'—one that urges greater transparency about the weighting of rights, and closer attention to claims about the need to diminish rights and the outcome of doing so, but no meta-principle that purports to resolve all difficult cases.[118]

---

[117] See the cases cited in nn 87 and 88.

[118] See also Waldron, n 76.

FURTHER READING

DUFF A., FARMER, L., MARSHALL, S., and TADROS, V., *The Trial on Trial, Vol 3: Towards a Normative Theory of the Criminal Trial*, Oxford: Hart Publishing, 2007.

REDMAYNE, M., 'Theorizing the Criminal Trial' (2009) 12 *New Crim LR* 287.

ROACH, K., 'Criminal Process' in P. Cane and M. Tushnet (eds), *The Oxford Handbook of Legal Studies*, Oxford: Oxford University Press, 2003.

QUESTIONS FOR DISCUSSION

1. Do Packer's models still have a valuable role to play in analysing developments in the criminal process?

2. What is the purpose, or what are the purposes, of the criminal trial?

3. What should be the role of victims in decision making in the criminal process?

4. How should one decide which theory of the criminal process is the most satisfactory?

3

ETHICS, CONFLICTS, AND CONDUCT

Chapter 2 sketched a normative model of the criminal process in which the pursuit of a particular end—retributive justice—was constituted and constrained by respect for rights and other values. This chapter examines one way in which the demands of this rather abstract model can be put into practice: through the consideration of ethics. Ethics are important for a number of interconnected reasons: first, as we have just noted, ethical principles can help to close the gap between our aspirations and our day-to-day actions. This is reflected in the fact that ethical codes exist to guide the conduct of numerous actors in the criminal process. Secondly, while the criminal process is structured by a framework of rules, discretionary decision making plays a crucial role. Rules always leave room for interpretation, and often preserve discretion deliberately. Such discretion should be exercised in an ethical way. A third reason why ethics are important is that the question of what conduct is ethically right is often not easy to answer. It is not much use responding to someone who asks how to exercise their discretion by telling them to do so in a way that both pursues retributive justice and respects rights. This is in part because different actors in the criminal process play different roles, and we expect these roles to mould the way in which they act. Thus, to take the most obvious example, we expect the defence lawyer advising her client to act differently to the police officers who are questioning him. The consideration of ethics involves considering how such roles should guide conduct, and there is room for debate about the correct principles.[1] Finally, ethics are important because actors in the criminal process may be tempted to subvert the rules and principles intended to govern their conduct, even when the rules leave little room for interpretation. The criminal process deals with people who have done, or—the qualification is significant—are alleged to have done, all manner of unattractive things, and judgements of 'moral character' may lure officials into bending the rules in order to ensure that such people are convicted, or treated harshly.[2] This is perhaps the greatest challenge to the pursuit of

---

[1] Cf the classic articles by W. H. Simon, 'The Ethics of Criminal Defense' (1993) 91 *Mich LR* 1703 and D. Luban, 'Are Criminal Defenders Different?' (1993) 91 *Mich LR* 1729.

[2] On judgements of moral character, see e.g. K. Hawkins, *Law as Last Resort* (2003), at 183, 243, and 334–5 on Health and Safety inspectors, and H. Parker, M. Sumner, and G. Jarvis, *Unmasking the Magistrates* (1989) on the magistracy.

justice in the criminal process. It is not only police officers who could subvert the rules or act inappropriately; as we will see, defence lawyers, prosecutors, and judges all face comparable temptations. A strong commitment to ethics, and a clear understanding of the ethical implications of one's role in the system, are therefore cornerstones of the criminal process.

The chapter opens with a brief discussion of the idea of ethical conduct. Next it outlines some *un*ethical practices, and then attempts to examine and reconstruct some possible justifications for such practices. Consideration is then given to the problems of displacing the occupational cultures and other influences which may lead to resistance against change. Formal accountability systems are also discussed, and the chapter concludes with a consideration of the prospects for bringing about changes in the conduct of practitioners within the system.

3.1 RULES, ROLES, AND ETHICS

Is there any need to discuss ethics when there are so many legal rules, codes, and guidelines impinging on the work of law enforcement agents? Is there really any room for moral disputation when we have such documents as the Police and Criminal Evidence Act 1984 (PACE) and its Codes of Practice, the Code for Crown Prosecutors, the Code of Practice for Victims of Crime, and countless statutes on criminal justice? Three good reasons may be offered for our stressing the significance of ethics.

First, ethical principles apply to those who lay down rules and guidelines as well as to those who are subject to them. The decisions of members of the legislature, the Home Secretary, the Director of Public Prosecutions (DPP), and the Lord Chief Justice should be equally subject to appraisal on ethical grounds as the acts and decisions of prosecutors, criminal defence lawyers, and police officers on the street. The function of ethical principles is to supply strong reasons for adopting and applying a particular rule. Though the European Convention on Human Rights is a formal source of ethical principles for policymakers, as we saw in Chapter 2, it does not contain all the rights and principles that ought properly to be upheld. Thus, clear ethical principles and processes are necessary for policymakers, and the judiciary.

Secondly, the criminal justice system is not covered completely by rules and clear-cut guidance. Recent years have seen greater efforts to introduce various forms of guidance and accountability, but there are still vast tracts of discretion, some of it deliberate so as to enable flexibility, some eked out by practitioners. Wherever there is discretion, and even where there are rules, there may be choices between following ethical principles and other policies or preferences.

Thirdly, there are strong occupational cultures among the different professional groups in the criminal justice system. For example, a study of detectives for the Royal Commission on Criminal Justice spoke of faults in the traditional 'detective culture' ('macho' and 'elitist' attitudes, belief that 'rules are there to be bent', excessive secrecy and suspicion of outsiders, and so on).[3] In his *Review of Efficiency in Criminal Proceedings*, Sir Brian Leveson spoke of elements of the 'present culture' of the Crown Prosecution Service (CPS) in which failures to concentrate on the case file and defence requests until the door of the court are commonplace.[4] The significance of culture and the need for a shift in this respect was also emphasized in the 2017 joint inspection on disclosure.[5]

Research into the conduct of criminal defence lawyers has also shown how the culture of many solicitors' firms operates so as to adapt the law and the lawyer's role, in ways that differ from the formal rhetoric and procedures, and which result in less than full protection for suspect-defendants.[6] There is evidence that judges sitting in the Court of Appeal were received into an occupational culture which, for many years, resulted in a particularly restrictive approach to the exercise of the court's statutory powers.[7] Embedded norms in subsets of occupational culture lead to certain practices like plea-bargaining being more common in certain circuits.[8] In the face of such well-entrenched cultures, what are the prospects for rules, let alone guidelines or unfettered discretion? In practical terms, these cultures seem to be direct competitors with ethical principles, partly because they often put sectional interests first, but partly also because they sometimes challenge the values of those who argue for the recognition of rights. Exploration of these occupational cultures will be one of the principal tasks in this chapter.

What kind of principle may be described as ethical? It should be a principle that is impartial as between persons, and for which one can give reasons which show a respect for the rights and interests that have a good claim to be protected. Impartiality in this context requires that no preference should be shown towards persons (whether suspects, victims, defendants, or whatever) on extraneous grounds such as sex, race, wealth, social connections, and so forth. It also forbids conduct based on the self-interest of the official or criminal justice practitioner, who ought to act out the ethical commitments attached to the assigned role (e.g. investigating officer, defence lawyer) and set aside personal convenience, profit, or other extraneous motivation. As for rights and interests, this refers not merely to the interests discussed in Chapter 2, but also to the fundamental orientation of the criminal process towards either an inquisitorial or an adversarial approach. Although several of the procedures in English criminal justice blur the line between the two, and this convergence is more apparent with the strengthening role of the Criminal Procedure Rules (CPR), the fundamental orientation is towards an adversarial model. This, in

---

[3] M. Maguire and C. Norris, *The Conduct and Supervision of Criminal Investigations* (1992).

[4] The Rt Hon. Sir Brian Leveson President of the Queen's Bench Division, *Review of Efficiency in Criminal Proceedings* (2015), [141].

[5] HMCPSI and HMIC, *Making It Fair: A Joint Inspection of the Disclosure of Unused Material in Volume Crown Court Cases* (2017), [1.4].

[6] M. McConville, J. Hodgson, L. Bridges, and A. Pavlovic, *Standing Accused* (1994); M. Travers, *The Reality of Law* (1997); D. Newman, *Legal Aid Lawyers and the Quest for Justice* (2013).

[7] R. Nobles and D. Schiff, *Understanding Miscarriages of Justice* (2000), ch 3.

[8] P. Darbyshire, *Sitting in Judgment: The Working Lives of Judges* (2011) chs 8 and 9.

turn, invests actors with certain role responsibilities. Thus, the duty of the lawyer is to 'promote fearlessly and by all proper and lawful means the *client's* best interests',[9] though as McConville and Marsh note, this duty is out of alignment with the 'judicial overreach into the conduct of the defence case' that is entailed by the CPR.[10] It is also tempered by the countervailing duty of the lawyer to the court, particularly the duty not to mislead the court.[11]

Whereas the defence lawyer's role is essentially partisan, that of the prosecuting lawyer should be impartial, not seeking convictions as such but taking on the role of a 'minister of justice'.[12] The prosecutor's goal should be to conduct the case dispassionately, seeking justice according to the law (not relying, for example, on inadmissible evidence) and disclosing to the defence all evidence that should be disclosed. As noted in Chapter 9, the ongoing failure of prosecuting lawyers to disclose evidence to the defence lies at the root of some of the notorious cases of miscarriage of justice.

3.2 IDENTIFYING 'UNETHICAL' PRACTICES

In order to provide a factual basis for the discussion in the rest of the chapter, it is now proposed to sketch some presumptively unethical practices. Many of them are discussed in greater detail later in the book, but it is important at this early stage to illustrate the context in which ethical arguments take place. Whether the practices can properly be termed 'unethical' will not be determined until we have discussed the explanations for them, but they are discussed here because they appear to be so. There is no suggestion that all the practices are widespread, but they do occur occasionally.

(A) 'HELPING THE POLICE WITH THEIR INQUIRIES'

One of the purposes of introducing rules on detention in police stations under PACE was to ensure that persons brought to police stations under arrest were detained only if it was necessary to do so, and if there was sufficient evidence for a charge.[13] Early research showed that custody officers routinely authorized detention without an examination of the sufficiency of evidence,[14] and a subsequent Home Office study found the same situation: 'it was exceptional for detention not to be authorised', namely in

---

[9] Bar Standards Board, *The Bar Standards Board Handbook* (3rd edn, 2017), r C15: https://www.barstandardsboard.org.uk/media/1901336/bsb_handbook_version_3.1_november_2017.pdf.

[10] M. McConville and L. Marsh, 'Adversarialism Goes West: Case Management in Criminal Courts' (2015) 19 *IJEP* 172, 173.

[11] BSB, r C3, n 9.

[12] Crompton J in *Puddick* (1865) 1 F & F 497. While this phrase was mentioned in the General Council of the Bar, *Code of Conduct*, Annex H, para 11 such terminology is not in the new *Bar Standards Board Handbook*; R. J. Buxton, 'The Prosecutor as Minister of Justice' [2009] *Crim LR* 427.

[13] PACE, s 37.

[14] I. McKenzie, R. Morgan, and R. Reiner, 'Helping the Police with their Inquiries: the Necessity Principle and Voluntary Attendance at the Police Station' [1990] *Crim LR* 22.

only one of some 4,000 cases.[15] Dehaghani's study had similar findings.[16] This practice is unethical because it deprives suspects of protection against being detained unless it is absolutely necessary, a protection that Parliament intended to give them.[17]

(B) DEPARTURE FROM PACE AND ITS CODES OF PRACTICE

PACE and its Codes of Practice were also designed to lay down standards of fair treatment and to restate the courts' discretion to exclude evidence obtained in contravention of the standards. The reason behind these protections is to spare defendants intimidation, and to enhance the reliability of any evidence that is obtained. Yet since then there has been a stream of cases in which police officers have been found to have departed from the Codes of Practice on Questioning and on Identification.[18]

Another purpose of the 1984 Act was to require the police to inform each suspect/defendant of certain rights—the right to make a telephone call from the police station, the right to have someone informed of one's detention, and the right to have legal advice that is free, independent, and given in a private consultation. After implementation in 1986, it was found that not all suspects were being informed of these rights.[19] The relevant Code of Practice was altered in 1991, and further research showed that the rate of informing suspects had increased but was still less than complete.[20] It would be unethical for police officers to give the statement in an unclear or overly rapid fashion, or to emphasize unduly the possible problems (such as delay) in summoning legal advice. However, research indicates that there has been a positive change in police culture, and that normally suspects are informed of their right of access to a lawyer in neutral terms.[21]

(C) FAILURE TO DISCLOSE RELEVANT EVIDENCE

Similar motivation may underlie some failures by the police to disclose to the prosecution or the defence certain evidence in favour of the defence, which was a reason for quashing the convictions in the cases of the Maguire Seven, the Birmingham Six, and Judith Ward.[22] The Attorney General's Guidelines on disclosure were not in force at

[15] C. Phillips and D. Brown, *Entry into the Criminal Justice System* (1998), 49.

[16] R. Dehaghani, 'Automatic Authorisation: An Exploration of the Decision to Detain in Police Custody' [2017] *Crim LR* 187.

[17] E. Cape, *Defending Suspects at Police Stations* (7th edn, 2017), 2–76, citing the statement of the Home Office minister in 1984 that the detention must be necessary, 'not desirable, convenient or a good idea but necessary'.

[18] See generally Cape, ibid, ch 8; among the examples are *Forbes* [2001] 1 AC 473 and *Harris* [2003] EWCA Crim 174.

[19] A. Sanders and L. Bridges, 'Access to Legal Advice and Police Malpractice' [1990] *Crim LR* 494.

[20] D. Brown, T. Ellis, and K. Larcombe, *Changing the Code: Police Detention under the Revised PACE Codes of Practice* (1993).

[21] E. Cape and J. Hodgson, 'The Right of Access to a Lawyer at Police Stations: Making the European Union Directive Work in Practice' (2014) 5 *New J European Crim L* 450, 458.

[22] See J. Rozenberg, 'Miscarriages of Justice' in E. Stockdale and S. Casale (eds), *Criminal Justice under Stress* (1993).

the time of the original trials in these cases, but the principle of disclosure did exist. Similarly, in the case of the Maguire Seven, the outcome of certain tests carried out by the Forensic Science Service, with results favourable to the defendants, was not notified to the defence. Non-disclosure of forensic evidence also occurred in the cases of the Birmingham Six and Judith Ward. These omissions can be regarded as unethical. Breaches of the disclosure rules were not confined to the 1970s, as subsequent appellate decisions[23] and the collapse of cases again Liam Allan and other suspects illustrate.[24] Failure to follow statutory requirements conscientiously is unethical, whether by the police, the prosecution, or the defence.

(D) FAILURE TO PROTECT A CLIENT AT INTERVIEW

One of the reasons for the right to consult a lawyer at a police station is to ensure that the conduct of the police towards the suspect is scrupulously fair. However, in some cases legal advisers are reluctant to intervene to protect their client, allowing hostile and hectoring modes of questioning to pass without comment.[25] In clear cases, this is unethical conduct by the legal adviser, particularly where the lawyer's motivation for failing to intervene is not related to advancing the interests of that client.

(E) FAILURE TO DISCONTINUE A WEAK CASE

A primary reason for creating the CPS was to bring a professional prosecutorial review into the system, to prevent weak or inappropriate cases from going to court.[26] The CPS was given a power of discontinuance,[27] and subsequently given the power to charge suspects ('statutory charging', discussed in Chapter 7). Were the CPS to pursue a case where there is insufficient evidence, perhaps to retain good relations with the police,[28] this would be unethical.

(F) AVOIDANCE OF 'PRESUMPTIVE' MODE OF TRIAL

Under the existing system for determining mode of trial, cases have arisen in which the prosecution has preferred an either way charge, the defendant has elected Crown Court trial, and the prosecution has thereupon dropped the either way charge and brought a charge that is triable summarily only, in a magistrates' court. Defendants have challenged these tactics by means of judicial review, and the Divisional Court has held that in general the choice of charge lies within the discretion of the prosecutor so long as the substituted charge is not inappropriate and there is no bad faith,

---

[23] E.g. *Fergus* (1994) 98 Cr App R 313.   [24] For discussion, see Ch 9.

[25] See e.g. D. Roberts, 'Questioning the Suspect: The Solicitor's Role' [1993] *Crim LR* 368, and Newman, n 6.

[26] Royal Commission on Criminal Procedure, *Report* (1981), para 7.6.

[27] Prosecution of Offences Act 1985, s 23, discussed in Ch 7.

[28] J. Baldwin, 'Understanding Judge Ordered and Directed Acquittals in the Crown Court' [1997] *Crim LR* 536, esp at 550–2; see further Ch 7.

oppression, or prejudice.[29] The CPS Code now instructs prosecutors not to prefer a higher charge in this situation, save in exceptional circumstances:

> Prosecutors should not change the charge simply because of the decision made by the court or the defendant about where the case will be heard.[30]

It remains possible to alter the charges before the mode of trial proceedings have begun, which also raises ethical issues.[31]

It is one thing to lower the charge to ensure that the case is heard quickly (avoiding the waiting time for the Crown Court) if there are good reasons for this, perhaps connected with victims or other witnesses; it is quite another thing to do this in the hope of taking advantage of the higher conviction rate in magistrates' courts.

> Speed must never be the only reason for asking for a case to stay in the magistrates' court. But prosecutors should consider the effect of any likely delay if a case is sent to the Crown Court, including the possible effect on any victim or witness.[32]

Admittedly, the ethical argument here is complex, but the temptations for prosecutors require careful assessment.

3.3 UNDERSTANDING 'UNETHICAL' BEHAVIOUR

The preceding section has set out some examples of behaviour that might be described as 'unethical', in the sense that it fails to show proper respect for citizens and often removes, circumvents, or weakens certain rights that should be accorded to the suspect or defendant. There may be other sources of miscarriages of justice, but the focus here is on conduct that may be said to involve some conscious circumvention of the rules. Suspending final judgement on whether these practices are to be termed unethical, we must first inquire into the reasons for them.

There is often a tendency to regard practices of this kind as the product of individuals, exercising a discretion unconstrained by structure, context, or colleagues. This is the 'rotten apple' theory, assuming that a small number of 'rogue' individuals decide to defy the rules. This ignores the fact that these individuals work in a professional context in which organizational rules and occupational pressures operate, sometimes fuelled by the unrealistic expectations of the public and others,[33] and exacerbated by the demands and limitations resulting from budget cuts. Thus, research into the police

---

[29] *R v Liverpool Stipendiary Magistrate, ex p Ellison* [1989] *Crim LR* 369; cf the similar legal and ethical problems raised by preferring a new charge and thereby obtaining an extension of time limits, *R v Leeds Crown Court, ex p Wardle* [2001] UKHL 12 and *R v J* [2005] 1 AC 562.

[30] Crown Prosecution Service, *Code for Crown Prosecutors* (2018), 6.4.

[31] Ibid, 6.5: 'Prosecutors must take account of any relevant change in circumstances as the case progresses after charge.'

[32] Ibid, 8.2.

[33] K. Hawkins, 'The Use of Legal Discretion: Perspectives from Law and Social Science' in K. Hawkins (ed), *The Uses of Discretion* (1992), 22.

has often concluded that much police behaviour is influenced by a particular 'cop culture'. Four elements seem to be at the core of such a dominant and problematic culture:

(1) support for colleagues' decisions and rejection of close supervision;

(2) machismo, which includes heavy drinking and physical presence, and may extend to sexist and racist attitudes;

(3) the sense of mission in police work; and

(4) the idea that rules are there to be used creatively and 'bent' if necessary to achieve 'justice'.[34]

The suggestion is that these and similar attitudes are widespread and embedded, not that they are universal. There may be differences from division to division, particularly between rural and urban areas, and many individuals or groups, particularly women and some younger police officers, might accept few or no aspects of the prevailing norms in a given occupational context. That there are negative elements in police cultures has been observed so frequently that their existence (even dominance)[35] in some quarters cannot be doubted, but the cultures are diverse and complex and certainly not monolithic.[36]

In attempting to unravel the reasons which underlie the problematic culture, we first consider (1) support for colleagues' decisions and the inappropriateness of close supervision. Two research studies for the Royal Commission on Criminal Justice in the 1990s found that supervision of junior officers in the conduct of inquiries and in questioning was not the norm and was often regarded as a breach of trust.[37] This was linked to the idea of police solidarity and the duty to support a fellow officer, although it may have a darker side, as the Royal Commission recognized in its reference to officers and civilian staff being 'deterred by the prevailing culture from complaining openly about malpractice'.[38] To some extent the isolated position of the police in society may breed a form of solidarity and defensiveness and the culture may reflect the differing perspectives of police officers 'at the sharp end' and those officers who are managers, with the lower ranks covering for one another and trying to shield from senior officers various deviations from the rules.[39]

There is well-established evidence of the existence in the British police of (2) machismo, manifest in the physical dangers of the job, 'the alcoholic and sexual indulgences' of male police officers, and the struggle of women police officers to gain acceptance.[40] There are, however, important points to be made about this aspect of

---

[34] For detailed discussion, see e.g. J. Skolnick, *Justice without Trial* (1966); J. Chan, 'Changing Police Culture' (1996) 36 *BJ Crim* 109; D. Dixon, *Law in Policing: Legal Regulation and Police Practices* (1997); S. Choongh, 'Policing the Dross: A Social Disciplinary Model of Policing' (1998) 38 *BJ Crim* 623.

[35] B. Loftus, 'Dominant Culture Interrupted' (2008) 48 *BJ Crim* 756, and B. Loftus, *Police Culture in a Changing World* (2009).

[36] See L. Westmarland, 'Police Cultures' in T. Newburn (ed), *Handbook of Policing* (2008).

[37] J. Baldwin, *Supervision of Police Investigations in Serious Criminal Cases* (1992); Maguire and Norris, n 3.

[38] Royal Commission on Criminal Justice, *Report*, para 2.65.

[39] R. Reiner, *The Politics of the Police* (4th edn, 2010), 122.   [40] Ibid, 128.

'cop culture'. First, it does not follow that there is a precise correlation between the way the police talk and behave when off-duty, and their conduct of their duties.[41] The demanding nature of police work may be said to make it necessary to 'let off steam' when off-duty or in the canteen, and it does not necessarily mean that this translates into conduct at work.[42] Secondly, on the allegation that racism forms part of the police culture, Robert Reiner suggests that some interpretations fail to take proper account of the nature of police work in a society that places ethnic minorities at a disadvantage in many respects.[43] Indeed, Reiner argues more generally that, just as it is unrealistic to regard police malpractices as stemming from isolated individuals without reference to the wider police culture, it is equally unrealistic to focus on the culture without reference to the social structures that contribute to and sustain it.[44] Account must be taken of the role assigned to the police in society—as a form of social service that has to deal with the least advantaged people, as well as meeting targets that often imply a degree of control over social events that they simply cannot exert.

In a sense, these typical elements of 'cop culture' may appear to be odd bedfellows of (3), the sense of mission in police work. This is a serious-minded, socially conservative cluster of attitudes which celebrate the position of the police as a 'thin blue line' standing between order and chaos. Of course, it is not claimed that the mission, any more than the culture, is monolithic. Indeed, the conflict in police ideologies between advocates of 'zero tolerance' and advocates of the 'problem-solving' approach demonstrates one clear difference. The research evidence regards the mission as strengthened by seeing the police as being on the side of the right, serving society and ranged against offenders and other miscreants who are in the wrong. Reiner describes the subtle interplay of three themes: 'of mission, hedonistic love of action, and pessimistic cynicism' that constitute the core of the police outlook.[45] Many officers join the police with a sense of mission, in terms of defending society and its institutions against attack and disorder, and then develop a kind of cynicism about social trends that seem to threaten existing ways of doing things.

To be sceptical about the moral quality of this police mission would be easy: it certainly contains its contradictions, in that it emphasizes established moral values while some officers do not adhere to such standards, and it adopts a puritanical attitude towards drug-users when police alcoholism is a long-standing problem.[46] Yet, these contradictions apart, the police perform an essential and central social function, about which there is a justifiable sense of mission, such as that of doctors and nurses in the health system, say. But while the vital nature of this social function of policing cannot be disputed, some interpretations of its mission can be—not

[41] C. Hoyle, *Negotiating Domestic Violence* (1998), ch 4, for a sustained discussion of both empirical evidence and theoretical interpretations.
[42] P. A. J. Waddington, 'Police (Canteen) Culture: an Appreciation' (1999) 39 *BJ Crim* 286.
[43] Reiner, above n 39, 129; cf J. Foster, 'Police Cultures' in T. Newburn (ed), *Handbook of Policing* (2003), 215–18.
[44] R. Reiner, 'Is Police Culture Cultural?' (2017) 11 *Policing: A Journal of Policy and Practice* 236, 240.
[45] Reiner, n 39, 121.   [46] Ibid, 128.

least when this leads to forms of so-called 'noble cause corruption', with officers succumbing to the temptation to seek justice summarily, and to regard outcomes as more important than processes.[47] Similar conflicts may arise in the context of 'consumer demand' for certain services from the police, which leads to government targets and to dilemmas for officers.[48]

This leads us directly to (4): the idea that rules are there to be used creatively and bent. The sense of mission may be so powerful that it displaces respect for the laws. There are two strands to this. The first emphasizes the use of the criminal law as a resource for legitimating or reinforcing police handling of a situation: the police officer has available a range of offences with which to support his or her authority, and may decide whether or not to invoke one of them as a reason for arrest and charge.[49] Of course, this is hardly applicable to crimes such as murder, rape, and armed robbery, but it can be applied to the range of public order offences, obstruction, and assault on police officers, for instance. The primary objective of the police may be to keep the peace and to manage situations; in this they use and exert authority; anyone who resists that authority may be arrested and even charged. The second strand concerns the various procedural rules about questioning, notably the Codes of Practice under PACE. One reason these rules are broken from time to time may be that they are seen as impediments to proper police work, standing in the way of vigorous questioning which will get at the truth or will produce the results which senior police officers or the media seem to want. On the one hand, there is pressure arising from the high expectations of others; on the other, there is a belief that those expectations cannot be met when lawmakers fail to understand the realities of police work.

Reiner reminds us that police culture is not the primary cause of police practice, but rather they are interdependent, and both shaped by structural pressures.[50] Numerous studies have revealed polarities in police culture including determinism/autonomy; social/individual; macro/micro factors, all of which mean that aspects of police culture and practice, like discrimination, can only be alleviated somewhat by reform policies.[51] Indeed, classic and more recent studies indicate the resilience of questionable perspectives, despite decades of reform initiatives.[52]

Such reforms include the College of Policing's Code of Ethics and the National Decision Model (NDM).[53] Following a Home Affairs Committee report on *Leadership and*

---

[47] See P. Neyroud, 'Policing and Ethics' in T. Newburn (ed), *Handbook of Policing* (2008).

[48] See P. Neyroud, 'Ethics in Policing: Performance and the Personalization of Accountability in British Policing and Criminal Justice' (2006) 9 *Legal Ethics* 16.

[49] For a classic study on this, see E. Bittner, 'The Police on Skid Row: A Study in Peacekeeping' (1967) 32 *Am Soc Rev* 699.

[50] Reiner, n 44, 236–241.   [51] Ibid, 240.

[52] Ibid. B. Loftus, 'Police Occupational Culture: Classic Themes, Altered Times' (2010) 20 *Policing and Society* 1.

[53] The College of Policing was established in 2012 as a statutory body that sets standards for policing in England and Wales. HM Inspectorate of Constabulary (HMIC) inspects forces against the standards set by the College.

standards in the police,[54] the College of Policing issued a Code of Ethics,[55] centering on nine policing principles: accountability; integrity; openness; fairness; leadership; respect; honesty; objectivity; and selflessness. The Code of Ethics is closely linked to the NDM, which is the primary decision model for the police service.[56] The NDM puts the Code of Ethics at the heart of all police decision making, and both seek to embed ethical reasoning in accordance with policing principles and expected standards of behaviour.[57]

Despite the intention that these ethical principles would underpin and strengthen existing procedures for ensuring standards of professional police behaviour, HM Inspectorate of Constabulary has found that the use of the Code of Ethics varies across forces, with some forces using their own set of values instead, or confusing the priority between the Code and their own values.[58] The House of Commons Home Affairs Committee reiterated these concerns, stressing that the Code of Ethics must be 'fully embraced by Chief Constables and serving officers so that it becomes rooted in police culture, throughout the ranks'.[59] In 2015, the Independent Police Complaints Commission raised concerns about discrimination cases not being referred appropriately,[60] and this was echoed, with disappointment, by HM Inspectorate of Constabulary and Fire & Rescue Services (HMICFRS) in 2017.[61] More positively, the third annual report of HMICFRS in 2017 on the legitimacy of police forces[62] suggested that forces are good at ensuring that their workforces behave ethically and lawfully, though we suggest this is a rather generous interpretation of the rather uneven findings.[63] Again, the gaps between aspiration, policy, and working practices are pronounced. HMICFRS emphasized that the best way to prevent police wrongdoing is to promote an ethical working environment or culture,[64] through effective vetting procedures, encouraging and

---

[54] Home Affairs Committee, *Leadership and standards in the police*, Third Report, Session 2013–14, HC 67-I (2014).

[55] College of Policing, *A Code of Practice for the Principles and Standards of Professional Behaviour for the Policing Profession of England and Wales* (2014): http://www.college.police.uk/What-we-do/Ethics/Documents/Code_of_Ethics.pdf.

[56] College of Policing, *National Decision Model* https://www.app.college.police.uk/app-content/national-decision-model/the-national-decision-model/, [4.1.1].

[57] Ibid, 4.1.6.

[58] HMIC, *State of Policing: The Annual Assessment of Policing in England and Wales 2015* (2016), 50.

[59] House of Commons Home Affairs Committee, *College of Policing: three years on*, Fourth Report of Session 2016–17, HC 23 (2016).

[60] Independent Police Complaints Commission, *Referring complaints, conduct matters and death or serious injury matters to the IPCC—a review of current police force practice* (2015), available at: https://www.policeconduct.gov.uk/sites/default/files/.../IPCC_referrals_review.pdf.

[61] HMICFRS, *PEEL: Police legitimacy 2017: A national overview* (2017).

[62] A legitimate force is one in which those working in it are seen by the public consistently to behave fairly, ethically and within the law.

[63] HMICFRS, *PEEL 2017*, n 61, 6. HMICFRS assessed 34 forces as good and eight as requiring improvement for this inspection question. None was graded as either outstanding or inadequate. These grades are better than 2016, when 16 forces were graded as requiring improvement.

[64] Citing College of Policing, *Promoting Ethical Behaviour and Preventing Wrongdoing in Organisations* (2015), available at: http://whatworks.college.police.uk/Research/Documents/150317_Integrity_REA_FINAL_REPORT.pdf and College of Policing, *The Role of Leadership in Promoting Ethical Police Behaviour* (2015), available at: http://whatworks.college.police.uk/Research/Documents/150317_Ethical_leadership_FINAL_REPORT.pdf.

displaying strong ethical leadership at all levels, reinforcing high ethical standards in line with the Code of Ethics, and empowering the workforce to apply these standards in practice.[65] Certainly, active consideration of ethics is becoming more widespread across policing, such as in the creation of Ethics Committees.[66] Increasingly, forces are putting structures in place to support ethical decision making, although the extent to which these are embedded and established enough to be effective diverges considerably across England and Wales.

Compared with the police, rather less is known about the occupational cultures of other groups within the criminal justice system, which, of course, have working cultures which sometimes can pull against the ethical discharge of their role responsibilities. A detailed study in the mid-1990s of a number of criminal defence practices in England and Wales by McConville, Hodgson, Bridges, and Pavlovic discovered several unethical practices at different stages. Once again, the researchers did not claim that all criminal defence practices operated in this way: indeed, they pointed out that some practices were well run and properly orientated. But they drew attention to some defence lawyers' failure to protect clients in police stations from improper questioning,[67] encouraging or even engineering a plea of guilty in spite of the client's inclinations,[68] 'selling out' clients in court by using a particular phraseology that made it clear to magistrates that the lawyer believed that the client's instructions were unworthy of belief.[69] More recent ethnographic research by Daniel Newman focused on the lawyer–client relationship under legal aid.[70] He found two contradictory messages; in interviews with him, lawyers claimed to have a positive relationship with their clients, whereas under participant observation they treated their clients with disrespect, and pushed them to plead guilty, despite protestations to the contrary. Newman describes this as elevating crime control over due process, and as placing clients' access to justice in jeopardy.[71] Overall, he saw little purpose in the lawyers being present with their clients, except to facilitate efficient and swift processing of cases. Some of these unethical practices are driven by financial considerations, whereby business decisions trump justice and social welfare concerns.[72] This arises from the structure of the legal aid system, a situation which can only be exacerbated by more recent cuts.

Some defence lawyers subscribe to the theory that particular clients (or clients of a particular kind, or from a certain family or housing estate) are guilty anyway, are always committing crimes, and therefore it is pointless to go through the motions of a 'full and fearless defence'.[73] This approach may be underpinned by a desire to keep 'on the right side' of the police and the courts where possible, rather than losing credibility by mounting a vigorous defence of a presumptively guilty villain. As Ed Cape and Jenny McEwan have argued, various reforms have tended to undermine the

---

[65] HMICFRS, *PEEL 2017*, n 61, 32.   [66] Ibid, 36.
[67] McConville et al, n 6, 61–2, 112–15, and 124.   [68] Ibid, 70 and 194ff; also Travers, n 6, chs 5 and 6.
[69] Ibid, 180–1; see also A. Hucklesby, 'Remand Decision Makers' [1997] *Crim LR* 269, 278–9.
[70] Newman, n 6.   [71] Ch 6.   [72] Newman, n 6, 19.
[73] A. Mulcahy, 'The Justifications of "Justice"' (1994) 34 *BJ Crim* 411.

proper adversarial elements in criminal justice, therefore requiring more from the defence lawyer in order to protect the defendant's rights.[74] Indeed, defence lawyers may have difficulty reconciling their ethical obligations to the client with their considerably enhanced duties to the court.[75] The integration of non-adversarial elements with professional obligations predicated on adversarial processes warrants a fundamental revision of ethical codes.[76] Moreover, ethical constraints do not pull in a single direction: thus, some defence lawyers may use cross-examination to attack witnesses in a way or to a degree that strains the boundaries of ethics, sometimes to create a good impression with the client rather than because there really is a material inconsistency in a witness's story.[77]

The Bar Council now provides a confidential Ethical Enquiries Service for the benefit and assistance of barristers and staff to assist them to identify, interpret, and comply with their professional obligations under the Bar Standards Board (BSB) Handbook. There is an Ethical Enquiries Service website as well as a confidential phone and email service. The Bar Council Ethics Committee outlines a range of ethical dilemmas and possible ways to approach these issues, such as drawing barristers' attention to their obligations in relation to changes of plea, where documents are disclosed to counsel by mistake, and their duties to the court to make inquiries as to the factual basis for grounds of appeal.[78]

Similarly, the Solicitors Regulatory Authority (SRA) also provides guidance on questions of ethics, following the introduction of the SRA Handbook in 2011, which sets out the standards and requirements for solicitors. Again, sample ethical dilemmas are included, such as regarding very high-cost cases, and the answers refer to the Principles in the SRA Handbook.[79] While these initiatives are laudable, the extent to which they affect behaviour positively remains to be seen, not least given the resource pressures that may underpin some questionable practices.

What about unethical behaviour by prosecutors? In this sphere there is less research to draw upon, but there is some evidence that prosecutors sometimes resolve the conflicting pressures upon them by indulging in unethical conduct. One example already given is that prosecutors may pursue a weak case, even though aware of the weakness, for reasons which can only be described as unethical—for example, a desire to keep 'on the right side' of the police, or even agreement with the police view that the defendant deserves to be put through a trial.[80] Another closely related example is the failure to disclose unused material

---

[74] E. Cape, 'Adversarialism "lite": developments in criminal procedure and evidence under New Labour' (2010) 79 *Criminal Justice Matters* 25–7; J. McEwan, 'From Adversarialism to Managerialism: Criminal Justice in Transition' (2011) 31 *Legal Studies* 519.

[75] F. Garland and J. McEwan, 'Embracing the Overriding Objective: Difficulties and Dilemmas in the New Criminal Climate' (2012) 16 *E&P* 233.

[76] Ibid.

[77] McConville et al, n 6, 219; also P. Rock, *The Social World of an English Crown Court* (1993), ch 2.

[78] http://www.barcouncilethics.co.uk/subject/criminal/.

[79] http://www.sra.org.uk/solicitors/code-of-conduct/guidance/question-of-ethics.page.

[80] Baldwin, n 28; see also J. Jackson, 'Ethical Implications of the Enhanced Role of the Crown Prosecutor' (2006) 9 *Legal Ethics* 35.

that could assist the defence case,[81] which may sometimes be for unethical reasons. In assessing Transforming Summary Justice, HMCPSI found that CPS lawyers fail to engage effectively with the defence prior to the first hearing.[82] Though this may not always or even often be related to matters of ethics, a clear message is needed from CPS managers to staff about what is expected with regard to defence engagement.[83] Underpinning this with ethical considerations is likely to give added weight and impetus.

3.4 JUSTIFYING 'UNETHICAL' BEHAVIOUR BY CHALLENGING THE ETHICAL NORMS

In the foregoing section we discussed the occupational cultures of various criminal justice agencies and the reasons for conduct which appears unethical. One element running through these explorations is that some of those who act in the ways described may argue that their behaviour is ultimately ethical. In other words, they may argue that the notions of ethics being relied upon here are flawed, limited, and inappropriate, and so that the rules can be circumvented legitimately, or that the understanding of ethics should be reformulated.

(A) ARGUMENTS FOR CIRCUMVENTING RULES

In order to establish the context for any such redefining of the ethical, we might consider three standpoints that appear practical and sensible, especially among those who work in particular parts of the criminal justice system. The first, already mentioned, is the argument that certain rules should be circumvented because rule makers do not understand practical problems. The second is that it is wrong to expect police, prosecutors, etc to operate with 'their hands tied behind their backs'. And the third is that when the CPS drops a case or when a court gives a lenient sentence, or even when the Court of Appeal quashes a conviction, this is bad for morale in the criminal justice system. All these standpoints are connected, but deserve brief discussion individually.

Is it right to circumvent rules on the ground that the rule makers do not understand the day-to-day, on-the-ground problems of the criminal process? The claim is heard among some police officers in relation to PACE and its Codes of Practice: these are restrictions imposed by people who expect 'results' and yet do not understand the difficulties the police have to encounter. A similar claim might be heard among barristers who resent the procedural imperatives and preparation times associated with plea and case management hearings and other pre-trial assessments.[84] There are three

---

[81] While ethics are mentioned in the House of Commons Justice Committee's recent report on Disclosure, this is in relation to the police (at [107]): *Disclosure of evidence in criminal cases*, Eleventh Report of Session 2017–19, HC 859 (2018).

[82] HMCPSI, *TSJ: An early perspective of the CPS contribution report* (2016), [6.13].   [83] Ibid, 6.14.

[84] Royal Commission on Criminal Justice, *Report*, para 7.36; Auld Report, *Review of the Criminal Courts* (2001), 490–2.

problems with claims of this kind. First, there is the constitutional argument: any official or public organization that substitutes its own judgement for one reached through the appropriate democratic channels is behaving unconstitutionally. Both police and lawyers' representatives are well able to put their points in political debate, and should therefore accept the outcome in their work. Secondly, there is the values argument: the claim assumes that crime control is the only value that is in the public interest. It gives no weight to the protection of the rights of suspects, particularly in terms of the importance of procedures rather than merely outcomes. And, thirdly, there is the evidential argument: is it really true that 'the job' cannot be done if the restrictions are observed? In fact, this is less likely to be a matter of evidence than a question of values again, since the claim that the job cannot be done suppresses the unarticulated clause, 'within the prevailing culture'. If a different culture prevailed, perhaps the job could be done. One can only plausibly assert that it cannot be done if one assumes no change in the culture. These three arguments expose the weaknesses of the claim that it may be justifiable to circumvent rules made by out-of-touch rule makers.

The second claim is similar in some respects. It is that society expects the police to combat crime and prosecutors to obtain convictions with their hands tied behind their backs. The precise formulation varies, but the focus is always the 'restrictions' imposed by the legislature and the higher judiciary. The claim could be countered by means of the three arguments deployed above—the constitutional point, the values argument, and the question of evidence. However, another argument is worth raising here: the assumption that respecting the rights of suspects significantly diminishes the number of convictions and therefore the protection of the public and of victims. This is a complicated argument, requiring considerable space to develop and to rebut. Suffice it to say here that no clear evidence has been found, for instance, that the adverse inferences from silence permitted since the Criminal Justice and Public Order Act 1994 have produced a significant increase in convictions. They have produced changes in working practices within the criminal process, as Home Office research demonstrated,[85] but the failure to meet the objective of increasing the number of convictions—and critics argued that this might mean an increase in wrongful convictions—suggests that the legal distinctions that have grown up around the 1994 Act are not worthwhile and that the adverse inference provisions should be abolished.[86] Thus, giving protection to suspects does not necessarily mean fewer convictions: it is not a zero-sum game.

The third claim is that it is bad for police morale when the CPS decides against pursuing a particular case, contrary to the wishes of the police. Comparable claims are sometimes heard when a court gives a low sentence on conviction, and there is also a suggestion that station sergeants tend not to refuse charges from officers who bring in arrestees as it might affect morale. Now, as an empirical proposition these claims may well be correct. Such events may reduce police morale, as may new restrictions on their

---

[85] T. Bucke, R. Street, and D. Brown, *The Right of Silence: The Impact of the Criminal Justice and Public Order Act 1994* (2000).

[86] D. Birch, 'Suffering in Silence: A Cost-Benefit Analysis of section 34 of the Criminal Justice and Public Order Act 1994' [1999] *Crim LR* 769.

questioning of suspects, changes in their pay and conditions, and several other matters. The problem here is whether one should defer to the conservatism that underlies the morale of many professions, including the police, a conservatism no doubt linked with a sturdy defence of the police mission. The police mission is therefore a crucial element in any attempt to redefine the ethical approach. What kind of ethics, it might be asked, could call into question the vigorous pursuit of the fundamental social functions of crime prevention and conviction of the guilty?

(B) REASSESSING THE ETHICAL APPROACH

To answer this question, we might begin by constructing a model version of the mission. Some of the main elements have been described earlier, but there is a need for a rounded version that could fit the words and opinions of police officers. The key element is crime control: this is surely a primary objective of the criminal justice system. It means that law observance should be maximized. In this, the police are inevitably in the front line, having peacekeeping functions that (in terms of time spent) outstrip the processing of suspected offenders. A second element is that, where the interests of the defendant conflict with those of the victim or society, priority should be given to the latter. A third and connected element, following from the first two, is that the police should pursue this society-centred approach so far as is possible, exploiting any discretion left by the criminal justice system to further the conviction of those whom they believe to be guilty. Taken together, these elements of crime control and the protection of society may be treated as establishing a powerful case in favour of the police mission.

Assuming that there is some truth in this account, is it defensible? Almost every step suffers from confusion which, when examined, mixes overstatement with understatement and neglects important features of social life. It would be easy to claim that this is because this version of the police mission has been formulated in a way favourable to the thesis being advanced: but the counter-arguments below can be ranged against any other version of the police mission that keeps faith with what has been found by on-the-ground research.[87] The counter-arguments are these.

The first element refers to crime control as if it were to be pursued without regard to any other values. Is it plausible to advance such an uncomplicated notion? To take an extreme but telling example, does it suggest that the police should be free to use repressive measures wherever they regard them as appropriate, or that torture should be available for use on those suspected of serious crimes? If the answers are negative, as they should be, then we need to adopt a more sophisticated and sensitive notion than 'crime control'. Many people might accept at first blush that crime control is the ultimate aim of the criminal justice system, but on reflection they would surely recognize that it ought not to be pursued without qualification.

The second element is that priority should be given to the victim or society over the interests of the suspect/defendant. In essence, the interests of the 'innocent and

[87] E.g. the findings of Maguire and Norris, n 3.

good' should be preferred over those of the suspect or defendant. As one constable stated some years ago, 'Speaking from a policeman's [sic] point of view it doesn't give a damn if we oppress law-breakers, because they're oppressors in their own right.'[88] This seems to suggest that accused persons should have no rights, or few rights, or at least rights that can be overridden when that is necessary in the public interest (as interpreted by the police). This is to turn the idea of rights on its head. The whole idea of rights is that they safeguard the individual's autonomy and ensure that the individual is protected from certain kinds of inappropriate behaviour and is furnished with certain assistance when he or she is in the hands of public officials. As we saw in Chapter 2, rights are essentially anti-utilitarian claims, in the sense that they represent claims that the individual not be treated in particular ways even if that might handicap the pursuit of some collective good. However, the idea of priority for 'the interests of society' seems to accord the individual suspect or defendant no particular rights, and to deny the whole legitimacy of human rights such as those incorporated in the European Convention and discussed at Chapter 2.3(C).[89] Moreover, it does so at a stage before the suspect or defendant has been convicted, thereby affirming a strong presumption of guilt arising from the investigating officer's belief. We cannot place so much emphasis on the judgement of one or more police officers, especially if one element in police culture is a mutual support and respect for the skills of others which frowns on routine supervision.

These arguments also show the weakness of the third element, always seeking to promote the interests of society against those of the suspect. This is flawed for various reasons. Most fundamentally, suspects are members of society. Few would agree that suspects should lose all rights, and that it should be for the police to decide which suspects should be accorded rights and which not. The notorious cases of miscarriage of justice make us well aware that police officers' judgements or suspicions of someone's guilt or innocence should not be determinative. Surely the ethical approach for the police is to ensure that evidence is collected fairly and then presented to the court for its adjudication. Upholding the right to a fair trial requires procedural fairness in the gathering of evidence and in the construction of the case.

The conclusion is therefore irresistible that the 'police mission' described earlier cannot claim the moral high ground: it is not a 'noble cause', and does not justify officers in seeking to do justice summarily. It overstates the notion of crime control by assuming that this should be pursued either without qualification or with only such qualifications as the police deem appropriate. It assumes that respect for the rights of suspects is bound to detract from crime control, and does so for insufficient reason. In this, it understates the importance of respect for human rights, in terms of fair procedures for those suspected of crime. And, like the 'balancing' approaches criticized in Chapter 2, it shows no appreciation of the subtlety and structures of arguments about the reach

[88] Quoted by Reiner, n 39, 119.
[89] This is not to overlook the importance of victims' rights, which may on occasion conflict with those of suspects and defendants. But, again, there is a difference between victims' interests and the public interest: for further discussion, see Ch 2.5.

of human rights, and rather tends to assume that human rights should be overridden whenever it can be said to be in the public interest to do so.

Any challenge by prosecutors to the ethical approach might take a similar form: the essence would be that certain rules and procedures stand in the way of what is right in terms of crime control. For example, John Baldwin found that some Crown prosecutors would run a relatively weak case where the charge was a serious one: he quotes one as saying that 'the more serious the case and the more finely balanced it is, the more you stretch the point'. He concludes that 'some CPS lawyers share a common value system with the police, a core element of which is that serious cases ought to be prosecuted, almost irrespective of considerations as to evidential strength'.[90] The supporting argument would be, therefore, that this is necessary to ensure that wrongdoers are brought to book, and that the 'stretching' of the rules is justified by that end. The counter-arguments are: (1) that this is not the prosecutor's function, since the prosecutor must act in accordance with the 'overriding objective' 'that criminal cases be dealt with justly', which includes acquitting the innocent and convicting the guilty; and (2) that the purported justification that 'there is a lot more at stake in letting a potential rapist, murderer or child abuser off the hook'[91] overlooks what is at stake for the individual defendant. No doubt the CPS would regard Baldwin's findings as outdated, but, beyond the HMCPSI reports to which we allude throughout the book, there has been no independent research into prosecutors' working practices since then.

3.5 DISCRETION AND ACCOUNTABILITY

It will be evident from the foregoing paragraphs that many of the decisions to be taken by criminal justice agencies are characterized by discretion rather than by binding rules. As Keith Hawkins puts it:

> Discretion arising from a number of sources suffuses the processes of law enforcement and regulation. Discretion is plastic, shaped and given form to some extent by the institutions of law and legal arrangements and more substantially by decision-makers' framing behaviour. Systems of formal rules, for all their appearance of precision and specificity, work in only imprecise ways. Indeed, precision and consistent practice are not necessarily assisted by the drafting of ever more elaborate schemes of rules. The legal system is not neatly carved up by smoothly functioning institutional arrangements, but in reality, as a loosely coupled set of subsystems, is more messy, with internal inefficiencies and conflicts. Those enforcing rules may seek to attain the broad aim of a legal mandate in general terms, but the specific question of whether and how a particular rule applies in a particular circumstance will inevitably be reserved for, or assumed within, the discretion of the legal actor concerned.[92]

Thus, as we have seen in this chapter, whether there are rules or areas of discretion, occupational cultures and working practices may exert an influence on how people with

---

[90] Baldwin, n 28, 551.   [91] A senior Crown prosecutor, quoted by Baldwin, ibid.
[92] K. Hawkins, *Law as Last Resort* (2003), 424–5.

power of different levels and forms in the criminal process actually behave and operate. One way of trying to combat this is through codes of ethics, but their prospects of success are variable. One institutional approach to ensuring that the various authorities fulfil their functions and exercise their powers as they ought to is through systems of accountability. We have already seen how values such as the protection of declared rights (of victims and suspects or offenders) and the prevention of abuse of power by officials might be threatened if the policies or the practices of a law enforcement agency diverge from the purposes of the system. Methods of accountability should include proper scrutiny of general policies, rules, and/or guidelines for decision making, active supervision of practice, avenues for challenging decisions, and openness rather than secrecy at key stages.

In a democratic form of society, issues of public policy should be decided by the legislature. However, in matters of law enforcement the tendency has been for Parliament to avoid such issues and to leave them to each agency itself, usually without any check other than the formal requirement to submit annual reports to the House of Commons. Thus, agencies such as HM Revenue and Customs, the Environment Agency, and the Health and Safety Executive are relatively free to determine their own policies: although some of their procedures are authorized by statute, there is no overall body that reviews their policies and practices, despite their significance for the reach of the criminal process. On the other hand, the tendency has been to draw the police increasingly under a system of central control, although there remains a considerable degree of local accountability.

The Police Reform and Social Responsibility Act 2011 introduced directly elected Police and Crime Commissioners (PCCs) to replace police authorities, other than in London where the Mayor retains responsibility.[93] The PCC must secure 'the maintenance of the police force for that area' and ensure that 'the police force is efficient and effective'.[94] While turnout for their elections is remarkably low, PCCs wield power: they are the recipient of all funding for policing in their area and have responsibility for appointing, and dismissing, the chief constable.[95] So, some degree of police accountability is sought to be ensured by means of the connection between the electorate and PCCs. Chief constables and PCCs are required to have regard to the College of Policing standards in order to ensure consistency across the 43 forces in England and Wales, and HM Inspectorate of Constabulary (HMIC) inspects forces against the standards set by the College.

The Independent Office for Police Conduct (IOPC), formerly the Independent Police Complaints Commission, oversees the police complaints system in England and Wales.[96] The IOPC investigate the most serious matters, including deaths following

---

[93] Following the recommendations in Home Office, *Policing in the 21st Century: Reconnecting Police and the People* (2010).

[94] s 1.

[95] S. Lister; 'The New Politics of the Police: Police and Crime Commissioners and the 'Operational Independence' of the Police' (2013) 7 *Policing: A Journal of Policy and Practice* 239–47.

[96] Policing and Crime Act 2017, Part 2. S. Savage, 'Thinking Independence: Calling the Police to Account through the Independent Investigation of Police Complaints' (2013) 53 *BJ Crim* 94–111.

police contact, and set the standards by which the police should handle complaints. Moreover, individual officers can be held to account for their actions and decisions, through the courts refusing to accept unlawfully obtained evidence, or by internal disciplinary measures, though scepticism remains about the potency of the latter.

More generally, law enforcement bodies are subject to scrutiny from government and parliamentary sources. The Select Committee procedure applies, and thus the Justice Committee examines the performance of such organizations as the police, the CPS, and the Prison Service. Within government, the National Audit Office assesses the performance of agencies. The existence of these bodies adds to accountability, even though their direct powers are limited. Perhaps of greater operational impact are the inspectorates in the criminal justice system. The National Probation Service, the Prison Service, and the CPS (as well as the police) are overseen by Her Majesty's Inspectors, who issue annual and thematic reports that receive considerable publicity. However, other major law enforcement agencies stand outside any such system of independent inspection: neither HM Revenue and Customs, nor the Environment Agency, Health and Safety Executive, or any of the other so-called regulatory agencies is subject to inspection, and there is no such body to oversee the work of defence lawyers who receive criminal legal aid money, let alone the work of the judiciary. Indeed, HM Inspectorate of Court Administration closed in 2010 and was abolished in 2012.[97]

Are law enforcement agencies accountable to the courts? There are a number of public law doctrines available, but the tendency has been to confine judicial review to the outer limits of unreasonableness (by applying the *Wednesbury* principle).[98] There have been some cases of successful judicial review of certain policies for and against prosecution,[99] but the prevailing attitude remains one of reluctance.

Accountability of entities and individual actors in a criminal justice system is crucial. Indeed, to some extent, more oversight, or at least public visibility, is enabled through social media and mainstream media coverage.[100] Accountability encourages and is enabled by transparency, it may enhance the protection of the rights of individuals, and it helps to ensure that the power entrusted to law enforcement authorities is not abused. However, it is wrong to rely on *post hoc* accountability methods to secure these desirable goals. Transparency and accountability are increased by the involvement of members of the public in the criminal process, whether as lay visitors in police stations or through jury service. But the key objective is to ensure that rules and guidelines are applied faithfully, and not limited in their practical effect because their purpose and spirit are not accepted by those who are supposed to apply them. Thus, there is a key role for training and for ethical orientation.

---

[97] The Public Bodies (Abolition of Her Majesty's Inspectorate of Courts Administration and the Public Guardian Board) Order 2012.

[98] See P. Craig, 'Grounds for Judicial Review: Substantive Control over Discretion' in D. J. Feldman (ed), *English Public Law* (2nd edn, 2009).

[99] See Chs 6 and 7.

[100] H. Campeau, '"Police Culture" At Work: Making Sense Of Police Oversight' (2015) 55 *BJ Crim* 669.

3.6 CRIMINAL JUSTICE REFORM THROUGH ETHICS

Law enforcement agencies and the administration of criminal justice are governed by masses of legislative rules, and yet it is well established that: (1) even rules can be adapted, (2) there are wide areas of discretion; and (3) there must continue to be some areas of discretion. One step, to promote respect for 'rule of law' ideals and to avoid the kind of arbitrariness against which Arts 5 and 6 of the Convention are intended as safeguards, is to attempt to structure discretion by the use of guidance and guidelines. Other common features of reform proposals are better training of criminal justice personnel and better lines of accountability. Measures of this kind are now recognized to be far more promising than mere changes in legal rules.

The reason for this is the strength of occupational cultures within such key agencies as the police, the CPS, regulatory inspectorates, defence solicitors, the criminal Bar, and so on. More has been said here about the occupational culture(s) of the police, to some extent justifiably since they form the principal filter into the criminal justice system, but we have also reviewed evidence on occupational cultures within the CPS, among defence lawyers, and even among appellate judges. What is noticeable about at least some of the occupational cultures in criminal justice is that their concern is not simply to preserve established working practices or to defend traditional territories of influence, but also to see that 'justice' is done. This is the sense of mission. Everything turns, of course, on what one takes to be 'justice' in this context. We must refuse to accept references to 'the interests of justice', 'the public interest', and even (more emotively) 'the interests of victims'—unless it is carefully spelt out how exactly these rather sweeping claims have been arrived at. We need to identify the values that underlie such statements, and then consider what values should be recognized in criminal justice. But this essential part of the ethical approach cannot be treated in isolation: one cannot expect changes in the culture of lawyers, let alone in the culture of the police, so long as politicians and other key figures fail to show respect for the value of human rights and other ethical precepts.[101]

The development of codes of ethics, and other initiatives, is to be welcomed. To expect rules alone to change behaviour may be naïve, but without some rules or guidance it is unlikely that behaviour will be changed at all. That said, codes of ethics should not only set out the proper spirit and orientation of those performing certain functions, but like the Bar Council and SRA, also give examples of points at which an ethical approach might differ from an unethical approach.

Reflection on the proper roles of the various groups and agencies within the criminal justice system would be needed. Obtaining convictions should not be regarded as the sole or dominant aim of the prosecutor, and the concept of justice also should include recognition of certain rights of defendants and of victims. The CPS should articulate guidance on ethical approaches to situations where, for example, the prosecutor

---

[101] See the powerful argument of J. Chan, 'Changing Police Culture' (1996) 36 *BJ Crim* 109 on the link between police culture and prevailing socio-political attitudes.

realizes that the court has made an error in favour of the prosecution, or realizes that certain evidence may have been obtained unfairly, or enters into plea negotiations despite doubts that the charge(s) can be sustained in court, or is tempted to make representations at remand proceedings even though it is unclear that the statutory requirements for a custodial remand are fulfilled.[102]

In respect of defence lawyers, the reasons for spelling out the ethical approach are no less pressing. It is insufficient to state, in a broad way, that the lawyer should seek to protect the client while not misleading the court. There must be a sharper statement of the defence lawyer's guiding function, in the light of the 'overriding objective' of the CPR to deal with criminal cases justly. Among those would be the problems of defending a person believed to be guilty, particularly where the lawyer believes that perjury has been or will be committed; where the defence lawyer knows of an error of law, or alternatively an error of fact, in the proceedings which favours the defence; where advice has to be offered to a client who wishes to plead not guilty; where the client wishes the lawyer to make an application for bail against the lawyer's professional judgement; when the lawyer believes that the client is innocent, despite indicating an intention to plead guilty; and so on.[103]

The reason for emphasizing the importance of giving examples is to try to give the ethical principles the greatest chance of practical success. While one might dismiss this approach on the basis that 'each case depends on its own facts', this is not true. Some situations and ethical dilemmas are common, and for those an orientation can be given; for unusual and controversial situations, only general ethical principles may be offered. However, ethical guidance that is as detailed as possible would help to confront those elements of occupational culture that are known to give priority to unethical motivations such as financial reward, preserving contacts, and distaste for particular suspects/defendants. Defining the role responsibility of a defence lawyer, prosecutor, or police officer is the first step. But no less essential is the further step of putting together examples of situations where there may be a divergence between the ethical and other approaches.

Once this has been done, the next step would be to inculcate the principles through training and other means, in a way that engages with the contemporary policing agenda (including human rights) and is mindful of the pressures under which staff operate in straitened economic circumstances.[104] The main task would be to convey the reasons why these principles are worth adhering to, whether by abstract instruction or by

---

[102] See further M. Blake and A. Ashworth, 'Some Ethical Issues in Prosecuting and Defending Criminal Cases' [1998] *Crim LR* 16; M. Blake and A. Ashworth, 'Ethics and the Criminal Defence Lawyer' (2004) 7 *Legal Ethics* 167; and R. Young and A. Sanders, 'The Ethics of Prosecution Lawyers' (2004) 7 *Legal Ethics* 190.

[103] L. Bridges, 'Ethics of Representation on Guilty Pleas' (2006) 9 *Legal Ethics* 80; cf D. Nicolson and J. Webb, *Professional Legal Ethics* (1999), ch 7, and Legal Services Commission, *Code for the Criminal Defence Service* (2005). Section 29 of the Legal Aid, Sentencing and Punishment of Offenders (LASPO) Act 2012 provides for a code of conduct which is to be followed by Public Defender Service staff providing legal services to individuals. The code must include duties to protect the interests of clients and applies in addition to any professional code of conduct.

[104] See Neyroud, n 47.

means of role-play exercises, debates, etc. This approach must be integrated into a programme for retraining personnel at all levels, from senior management down to new
recruits. The struggle towards consistency in areas of discretionary decision making
should involve training, supervision, and review: as Field concluded from his study of
diversionary decisions in youth justice, 'reshaping the professional culture of decision-
making may be as important protection for young people as the procedural values of
due process'.[105] Even if the training is well done, a statement of ethical principles would
be a poor match for a well-entrenched occupational culture.[106] The key questions must
be addressed convincingly: why must I show respect towards someone who admits to
a dreadful crime? If I feel that I can solve a difficult case only by deviating from the
rules, is it not in the interests of society that I should do so? Both the democratic argument and ethical principles should be elaborated in reply. And, of course, these broad
prescriptions should be no less applicable to other groups such as judges, court clerks,
regulatory agencies, and so on.

3.7 CONCLUSION

No doubt some will be sceptical of the claims of the ethical approach, particularly
when pitted against entrenched occupational cultures in certain spheres. Certainly it
is not argued here that, even if successfully defined and then inculcated, it would solve
the problems of the criminal process. Rather, the argument is that it ought to be recognized as a worthwhile part of altering the orientation of the system towards the ideals
and values set out in Chapter 2 earlier. Simply declaring those principles, or other legal
rules, is unlikely to work, for reasons that have been explained. The gap between the
law in the books and the law in practice will become ever more visible in the chapters
that follow, and it is the value-systems of those people who dominate practice that
emerge as the key element.

FURTHER READING

BRIDGES, L., 'Ethics of Representation on Guilty Pleas' (2006) 9 *Legal Ethics* 80.

CAPE, E., 'Rebalancing the Criminal Justice Process: Ethical Challenges for Criminal Defence
Lawyers' (2006) 9 *Legal Ethics* 56.

GARLAND, F. and McEWAN, J., 'Embracing the Overriding Objective: Difficulties and Dilemmas
in the New Criminal Climate' (2012) 16 *E&P* 233.

LOFTUS, B., 'Police Occupational Culture: Classic Themes, Altered Times' (2010) 20 *Policing and
Society* 1.

---

[105] S. Field, 'Early Intervention and the "New" Youth Justice: a Study of Initial Decision-Making' [2008]
Crim LR 177, 189.
[106] See Loftus, n 35.

QUESTIONS FOR DISCUSSION

1. To what extent are the findings of research on 'cop culture' generalizable to other decision makers in the criminal process?

2. Are ethical conflicts inherent in the role of criminal defence lawyer in the English system?

3. Should every criminal justice agency have a code of ethics? What good would this do?

4

INVESTIGATING CRIME AND GATHERING EVIDENCE

The criminal process is, to a large extent, an investigative one, existing to prepare cases for effective trial. To this end, authorities are given powers enabling them to gather evidence. But these powers can infringe numerous interests, some relating to the workings of the process itself, in addition to external ones, such as liberty, privacy, freedom from humiliation, and bodily integrity. This chapter examines how the gathering of evidence is and should be affected by these concerns.

4.1 THE INITIATION OF CRIMINAL INVESTIGATIONS

A criminal investigation can be described as '[a]n investigation conducted by police officers with a view to it being ascertained whether a person should be charged with an offence, or whether a person charged with an offence is guilty of it'.[1] As we have seen, some prosecuting entities like the Serious Fraud Office have investigative capacities also, as do regulatory bodies like the Environment Agency, though the exercise of these powers will not always lead to criminal proceedings. Investigations can be either reactive or proactive, insofar as the authority may initiate an investigation in response to the commission of a crime witnessed by officers, or one reported to them; or it may entail the surveillance of a person or premises to ascertain whether or not a crime has been or is likely to be committed. Moreover, under Art 3 of the European Convention on Human Rights (ECHR) the state is obliged to conduct an effective investigation into crimes which involve serious violence against the person, regardless of whether that has been carried out by state agents or individual actors.[2]

The gathering of evidence is a critical part of the investigative process, though as will be seen, more speculative gathering of material also occurs, where the link to a suspected crime is more tenuous and, rather, the material is collected and retained for

---

[1] Ministry of Justice, *Criminal Procedure and Investigations Act 1996 (section 23(1)) Code of Practice* (2015), 2.1.

[2] *Commissioner of Police of the Metropolis v DSD and another* [2018] UKSC 1, per Lord Kerr at [48].

possible use or cross-checking in future. The gathering of evidence may be from a crime scene, a suspect, or a complainant, and may be for inculpatory or exculpatory purposes. Whether through stop and search, surveillance, or sample collection on arrest, evidence collection impacts on the interests and civil liberties of the individual. Simultaneously, the efforts of the police to gather evidence may be confounded by offenders who may try to prevent helpful evidence or material from being gathered, such as through the wearing of face coverings, or the subsequent burning of stolen vehicles, say.

4.2 STOP AND SEARCH

The primary purpose of stop and search is to allow police officers to eliminate or confirm suspicions about individuals without using their power of arrest.[3] Despite this value, it remains one of the most controversial police powers, given its interventionist nature, and its particular impact on minority ethnic communities,[4] as well as young people and certain socio-economic groups. As the Stephen Lawrence Inquiry observed: 'If there was one area of complaint which was universal it was the issue of "stop and search".'[5] Similarly, the Independent Police Complaints Commission regarded stop and search as 'probably the leading cause of tension between young people and the police ... [with] a significant impact on the potential for young people to engage positively in the policing of their communities'.[6]

While the Lawrence Inquiry in 1999 highlighted the racial sensitivity of stop and search and gave impetus to efforts to improve the use of the power, subsequent change has been incremental, uneven, and limited. The disproportionate use of stop and search against certain populations has not diminished and the power remains a sensitive issue.[7] In addition, a proportion of stops and searches are still carried out on dubious grounds, and it is a questionable method of investigating or disrupting crime.

Almost all searches in England and Wales are carried out under s 1 of the Police and Criminal Evidence Act 1984 (PACE), which provides a police officer with a power to stop and search persons and vehicles if he suspects reasonably that he will find stolen or prohibited articles, namely weapons or items which can be used to commit offences of dishonesty or criminal damage.[8] A number of other statutes provide

---

[3] PACE Code A (2015), 1.4.

[4] See e.g. B. Bowling and C. Phillips, *Racism, Crime and Justice* (2002), ch 5.

[5] *The Stephen Lawrence Inquiry* (1999), para 45.8.

[6] Independent Police Complaints Commission (IPCC), *Consultation Response to Police and Crime Committee, London Assembly* (2013), available at https://www.london.gov.uk/sites/default/files/gla_migrate_files_destination/14–02–06-Stop-and-search-background-information.pdf.

[7] Home Affairs Committee, *The Macpherson Report—Ten Years On* (2009), 4–5; N. Rollock/Runnymede Trust, *The Stephen Lawrence Inquiry 10 Years On: An Analysis of the Literature* (2009), 56–60. See also J. Foster, T. Newburn, and A. Souhami, *Assessing the Impact of the Stephen Lawrence Inquiry* (2005).

[8] Criminal damage was added by the Criminal Justice Act 2003, s 1. Section 1 accounted for 99.8 per cent of all stops and searches in England and Wales in the year ending 31 March 2017: Home Office, *Police powers and procedures, England and Wales, year ending 31 March 2017*, Statistical Bulletin 20/17 (2017), 4.2.

similar powers for other offences, most notably the Misuse of Drugs Act 1971, which permits searches for controlled drugs.[9] There are also significant stop and search powers under s 60 of the Criminal Justice and Public Order Act 1994 (CJPOA), and the Terrorism Act 2000 (as amended by the Protection of Freedoms Act 2012). Section 43 of the Terrorism Act 2000 allows a constable to stop and search a person whom he or she reasonably suspects to be involved in terrorist activity. Under s 60 of the Criminal Justice and Public Order Act 1994, an area may be designated as one within which a general power of stop and search for offensive weapons will exist for 24 hours. When this occurs, a police officer may stop and search persons and vehicles for weapons 'whether or not he has any grounds for suspecting that the person or vehicle is carrying weapons'.[10] The power can be used only where a senior officer believes reasonably that serious violence will take place within the area. A comparable power exists to designate an area and carry out searches for items connected with terrorism, as long as a senior police officer: (1) reasonably suspects that an act of terrorism will take place; and (2) reasonably considers that:

(i)   the authorisation is necessary to prevent such an act;

(ii) the specified area or place is no greater than is necessary to prevent such an act; and

(iii) the duration of the authorisation is no longer than is necessary to prevent such an act.[11]

Stop and search potentially impacts on Art 5 and Art 8 of the ECHR, guaranteeing the right to liberty and security of person and the right to private life, respectively. Article 5 lists a series of circumstances in which 'detention' will be permitted, but reasonable suspicion is required in the context of investigating crime. In *Gillan*, however, the House of Lords held that stop and search did not involve 'detention', so Art 5 did not apply and thus suspicionless searches under the CJPOA were prima facie Human Rights Act compliant.[12] The majority also considered that Art 8 was not engaged, though Lord Brown did consider that in certain circumstances a search would be sufficiently intrusive to raise Art 8 issues.[13] More recently, the Supreme Court found s 60 to be compatible with the right to privacy under Art 8.[14] In contrast, the European Court of Human Rights (ECtHR) held that the original suspicionless stop and search powers in the Terrorism Act 2000 violated Art 8.[15] The breadth of discretion given to the police, reflected in the number of stops, meant that the powers were 'neither sufficiently circumscribed nor subject to adequate legal safeguards against abuse' and therefore not 'in accordance with the law'.[16] As a result, the Protection of Freedoms Act 2012 repealed the stop and search powers in ss 44–47 of the Terrorism Act 2000, and

---

[9] s 23.   [10] CJPOA 1994, s 60(5).

[11] s 47A, as inserted by the Protection of Freedoms Act 2012.

[12] *R (Gillan) v Commissioner of Police of the Metropolis* [2006] UKHL 12.   [13] Ibid, [74].

[14] *R (Roberts) v Commissioner of Police of the Metropolis* [2015] UKSC 79.

[15] *Gillan and Quinton v UK* (2010) 50 EHRR 45.   [16] Ibid, [87].

inserted the aforementioned s 47A (designating an area and carrying out searches for items connected with terrorism), and s 43A (search of vehicles), inter alia.

A Code of Practice issued under PACE governs the use of stop and search powers,[17] though there is evidence that some police forces still do not comply with the Code.[18] Code A provides that stop and search involves detaining a suspect in a public place for a short period in order to search his or her outer clothing.[19] The suspect can be made to remove a jacket and gloves, but any more intrusive search should be carried out by an officer of the same sex as the suspect and in private—for example, in a police van.[20] The most intrusive searches should only be carried out at a police station or other private location.[21] The distinction between the stop and the search is significant: the officer may question the suspect before carrying out the search: questioning may be used to dispel suspicion (as when the suspect gives an explanation for his suspicious behaviour), but it should not be used to generate reasonable suspicion where none already exists.[22] Many people will be stopped but not searched; a stop which does not result in a search is less intrusive and humiliating than one that does.

One of the key concerns about stop and search is that it is deployed on the basis of stereotypes,[23] and it has been used by the police to assert authority over particular sections of the community, to break up groups of youths, and to gather intelligence.[24] So, over the years, the definition of reasonable suspicion in Code A has been expanded: there must be an 'objective basis' for the suspicion 'based on facts, information, and/ or intelligence,'[25] and reasonable suspicion 'can never be supported on the basis of personal factors', like race, age, appearance, or previous convictions.[26] But a generalization based on the suspect's behaviour, as when the suspect appears to be hiding something, is permissible.[27] The latest version of the Code (2015) advises that reasonable suspicion 'should normally be linked to accurate and current intelligence', and that searches are most effective when targeted 'in a particular area at specified crime problems'.[28] The sensitivity of the issues involved in stop and search is clear from the Code and its different iterations.

The police are required to make a record of the search—including the basis for reasonable suspicion—and to provide the suspect with a copy.[29] There has been a marked

---

[17] PACE Code A 2015: Code of practice for statutory powers of stop and search and requirements to record public encounters by police officers and staff. Also see Code of Practice—Stop and Search under the Terrorism Act 2000 (2012).

[18] Home Affairs Committee, *College of Policing: three years on*, Fourth Report of Session 2016–17, HC 23 (2016), [20]. See M. Zander, 'If the PACE Codes are Not Law, Why Do They Have to be Followed?' (2012) 176 *Criminal Law and Justice Weekly* 713.

[19] Code A, 1.2, 3.3, 3.5.   [20] Code A, 3.6; PACE, s 2(9)(a).   [21] Code A, 3.7.

[22] Code A, 2.11.

[23] P. Quinton, N. Bland, and J. Miller, *Police Stops, Decision-Making and Practice* (2000); P. Quinton, 'The formation of suspicions: police stop and search practices in England and Wales' (2011) 21 *Policing and Society* 357.

[24] M. Fitzgerald, *Final Report into Stop and Search* (1999).   [25] Code A, 2.2.   [26] Code A, 2.2B.

[27] Code A, 2.6B.   [28] Code A, 2.4A.   [29] Code A, 4.2.

improvement in how police forces record the grounds for stops and searches, but practice remains variable in quality and detail.[30] Indeed, in 2013 HM Inspectorate of Constabulary found that 27 per cent of the stop and search records it examined did not satisfy the 'reasonable grounds for suspicion' requirement, potentially calling into question the legality of a large proportion of the one million searches conducted during the previous year.[31] Moreover, though at one stage officers resorted to 'voluntary' or 'consensual' searches to avoid the Code requirements, including that of recording,[32] this is sought to be prevented by Code A which now provides that '[a]n officer must not search a person, even with his or her consent, where no power to search is applicable'.[33] A record should be made of consensual searches. The police will, however, often ask a person to account for themselves, asking what they are doing in a particular street, or why they are carrying a particular object. Just as anyone can ask a question of a person on the street, no legal power is needed to enable the police to ask such questions. While citizens are under no legal duty to answer, the fact that police officers are figures of authority makes such encounters of dubious consensuality. A recommendation of the Lawrence Inquiry was therefore that instances of 'stop and account' should be recorded, with a copy of the record given to the person questioned, though this has not been enacted.[34]

The Home Office compiles statistics on the use of stop and search powers, including information on the race of those stopped, though ascertaining the true extent of stop and search rates remains problematic due to issues with police recording.[35] Moreover, there is little focus in these data on children specifically, or a breakdown of the figures by age.[36] Despite these issues, the data do tell us something about trends and about the racial disparities in the application of the power, and indeed some positive changes are evident.

In the year ending March 2017, police conducted 303,845 stops and searches in England and Wales, 21 per cent fewer than the previous year, and the lowest number since current data collection began in 2002.[37] In contrast, 1,035,438 stops were recorded in 2007/8, for instance.[38] Some of this decrease can be ascribed to initiatives

---

[30] HM Inspectorate of Constabulary and Fire & Rescue Services (HMICFRS), *PEEL: Police Legitimacy* (2017), 22.

[31] HM Inspectorate of Constabulary, *Stop and search powers: Are the police using them effectively and fairly?* (2013), 6.

[32] See D. Dixon, *Law in Policing: Legal Regulation and Police Practices* (1997), 93–104.

[33] Code A, 1.5.   [34] See Code A, 4.12.

[35] Equality and Human Rights Commission, *Briefing paper: Race disproportionality in stops and searches under Section 60 of the Criminal Justice and Public Order Act 1994* (2012), 5; also HMICFRS, *PEEL 2017*, n 30, 28, 29.

[36] All Party Parliamentary Group for Children, '*It's all about trust': Building good relationships between children and the police Report of the inquiry held by the All Party Parliamentary Group for Children 2013–2014* (2014), 2.3; S. Flacks, 'The Stop and Search of Minors: A "Vital Police Tool"?' (2017) 18 *Criminol & Crim Justice* 364.

[37] Home Office, *Police powers and procedures, England and Wales, year ending 31 March 2017*, Statistical Bulletin 20/17 (2017), 2.2.

[38] Ministry of Justice, *Statistics on Race and the Criminal Justice System 2007/8* (2009), 27.

like the 'Best Use of Stop and Search' (BUSS) scheme, which the Home Office and College of Policing launched in an effort to improve transparency, encourage community involvement in the use of stop and search powers, and to support a more intelligence-led approach.[39] Stop and searches have fallen across all ethnic groups but at different rates:[40] stops of white individuals have fallen by the most (28 per cent), while stops of non-white individuals have fallen 11 per cent. Individuals from Black, Asian, and Minority ethnic (BAME) groups are just under four times as likely to be stopped and searched compared with those who are white, and in particular, individuals who are black (or Black British) are over eight times more likely to be stopped than those who are white. In both cases, the figures from 2016/17 are higher than the previous year, which is concerning. In 2016/17, compared with the White ethnic group, stops and searches proportionate to population size were more likely to be carried out on the Black (eight times as likely), Mixed (between two and three times as likely), Asian (just over two times as likely), and Chinese or Other (one and a half as likely) ethnic groups.[41] As Lammy noted, '[G]rievances over policing tactics, particularly the disproportionate use of Stop and Search, drain trust in the CJS in BAME communities'.[42] Ironically, if these decisions undermine the legitimacy of the police, they are likely to weaken the public's willingness to comply with the law.[43] Moreover, drawing more BAME into the criminal justice system in this way helps to lead to their pronounced over-representation on the DNA database.[44]

In terms of s 60 specifically, there has been a drastic decline in its use, from a peak of around 150,000 searches in the year ending March 2009, to 617 in the year ending March 2017.[45] This itself is a fall of 36 per cent from 970 in 2016. In contrast to the situation regarding s 1, the number of stop and searches conducted on white suspects under s 60 has increased by 14 percentage points over the same time period, from 45 per cent to 59 per cent, whilst the percentage of s 60 stop and searches on black and Asian suspects over the past five years has decreased by 6 percentage points from 38 per cent to 32 per cent for black suspects and 11 per cent to 5 per cent for Asian suspects. That said, s 60 stop and searches form less than 1 per cent of all stop and searches.[46]

In the year ending 31 March 2018, 768 persons were stopped and searched under s 43 of the Terrorism Act 2000. This represents an increase of 70 per cent on the previous year's total of 453 and is the highest number of searches in a year since the year ending

[39] Best Use of Stop and Search (BUSS) scheme: see https://www.justiceinspectorates.gov.uk/hmicfrs/wp-content/uploads/best-use-of-stop-and-search-scheme.pdf.

[40] Home Office, *Police powers and procedures* (2017), 2.2.

[41] Ministry of Justice, *Statistics on Race and the Criminal Justice System 2016* (2017), 8; HMICFRS, *PEEL 2017*, n 30, 20.

[42] *The Lammy Review: An Independent Review into the Treatment of, and outcomes for, Black, Asian and Minority Ethnic Individuals in the Criminal Justice System* (2017), 17.

[43] Equality & Human Rights Commission, *Stop and think* (2010), 5. See T. Tyler, *Why People Obey the Law* (1990).

[44] See section 4.6.   [45] Home Office, *Police powers and procedures* (2017), 4.3.

[46] Ministry of Justice, *Statistics on Race and the Criminal Justice System 2016* (2017), 25–6.

31 March 2012 (819).[47] In the latest year, there were 64 arrests resulting from a s 43 stop and search, the second highest number in a financial year since the data collection began, after the 67 arrested in the year ending March 2016.

Section 47A of the Terrorism Act 2000 was not used until 2017,[48] in contrast to its precursor provision which was relied on widely, with the whole of the Metropolitan Police area designated for 'suspicionless' stops for terrorist items since 2003 until 2012.[49] Following the attack on Parsons Green in September 2017, the authorization of the power of stop and search under s 47A was used for the first time, and it has been authorized by four forces.[50]

Code A explains that 'the primary purpose of stop and search powers is to allow officers to allay or confirm suspicions about individuals without using their power of arrest'.[51] More often than not, suspicions turn out to be unfounded. In its 2017 *Report on Legitimacy*, HM Inspectorate of Constabulary and Fire & Rescue Services (HMICFRS) assessed that of the 8,574 records it reviewed, 12 per cent were likely to have resulted in an arrest had the stop and search power not been available.[52] This was framed as an effective use of the powers, as the persons were instead eliminated from suspicion. That said, HMICFRS expressed concern that 61 per cent of the sample were searches for drugs, of which 70 per cent involved a suspicion of possession only as opposed to a supply-type offence, suggesting that in many instances stop and search is still not deployed against more serious priority crimes.[53]

In terms of 'find rates', that is, searches that confirm suspicion, the item searched for was found in 24 per cent of the 8,574 records in the HMICFRS 2017 Report, though there was a wide range between forces.[54] The general find rates for stop and searches across different ethnicities were broadly similar,[55] though in terms of the subset of drugs searches, those involving black people were less likely to result in drugs being found compared with those involving white people or other ethnic groups.[56] The disparity in find rates is troubling; it suggests that black people are stopped and searched on weaker grounds for suspicion.

Overall, arrest rates following stop and search are continuing to rise: in the year ending March 2017, 17 per cent of stop and searches led to an arrest, up 1 per cent from

---

[47] Home Office, *Operation of police powers under the Terrorism Act 2000 and subsequent legislation: Arrests, outcomes, and stop and search, Great Britain, financial year ending March 2018*, Statistical Bulletin 09/18 (2018), 6.2.

[48] See G. Lennon, 'Stop and Search Powers in UK Terrorism Investigations: A Limited Judicial Oversight?' (2016) 20 *Int J HR* 634–48; B. Bowling and E. Marks, 'The Rise and Fall of Suspicionless Searches' (2017) 28 *King's LJ* 62–88.

[49] See *R (Gillan) v Commissioner of Police of the Metropolis* [2006] UKHL 12.

[50] Home Office, *Operation of police powers under the Terrorism Act 2000 and subsequent legislation: Arrests, outcomes, and stop and search, Great Britain, quarterly update to September 2017*, Statistical Bulletin 24/17 (2017), 19–20.

[51] Code A, 1.4.   [52] HMICFRS, *PEEL 2017*, n 30, 24.   [53] Ibid, 26.   [54] Ibid, 24.

[55] Ibid, 29.

[56] Ibid, 29–30. This was consistently the case with the find rate for: drug searches overall (33 per cent white and 26 per cent black); those where the suspicion was possession (36 per cent white and 30 per cent black); and those where the recorded grounds involved only the smell of cannabis (37 per cent white and 29 per cent black).

2016 and the highest since data collection began.[57] In 21 per cent of stops and searches, the outcome of the search was linked to the initial reason for the search; that is, the officer found what they were searching for.[58]

Being a target of stop and search has been found to be correlated with having less confidence in the police.[59] By alienating young people, stop and search is counterproductive.[60] Moreover, stop and search makes a limited contribution to crime control, as there is no strong connection between crime rates and stop rates.[61] No doubt, a visible police presence on the streets deters some crime, but beyond this stop and search probably adds little in terms of deterrence. Home Office research from 2016 on the use of weapons searches in ten London boroughs found no indication that substantial, targeted increases in stop and search reduced crime.[62] The study could not assess whether stop and search in itself works, though stated that a base level of stop and search could possibly be effective at reducing crime, or might work in highly focused locations. Similarly, a College of Policing report assessed the relationship between stop and search and crime at a borough level in the Metropolitan Police over a ten-year period.[63] Overall, it suggests that higher rates of stop and search (under any power) were associated with very slightly lower than expected rates of crime in the following week or month. The inconsistent nature and weakness of these associations provided only limited evidence of stop and search having acted as a deterrent at a borough level. As for detecting crime, stop and search does play a role: as noted earlier, around 17 per cent result in arrests. Support for the powers remains, especially in terms of responding to knife crime, however.[64]

Despite some improvement and purported, if minor, benefits, concerns about stop and search persist, yet it is notably resistant to abolition.[65] If the power to stop and search were taken away from the police there would probably be minimal impact on the prevention and detection of crime, but there might be other negative effects. Arrest can be justified on very similar grounds to stop and search—both powers hinge on reasonable suspicion.[66] The arrest power allows the police to take a suspect to a police station and to detain him for a considerable length of time. The greatest negative

---

[57] Home Office, *Police powers and procedures* (2017), 2.2 and 4.2.

[58] Ministry of Justice, *Statistics on Race and the Criminal Justice System 2016* (2017), 31.

[59] J. Miller, N. Bland, and P. Quinton, *The Impact of Stops and Searches on Crime and the Community* (2000), 51–2.

[60] See M. Fitzgerald, *Final Report into Stop and Search* (1999).

[61] Miller et al, n 59, ch 3, B. Bradford 'Unintended Consequences' and R. Delsol, 'Effectiveness' in R. Delsol and M. Shiner (eds), *Stop and Search: The Anatomy of a Police Power* (2015).

[62] R. McCandless, A. Feist, J. Allan, and N. Morgan, *Do initiatives involving substantial increases in stop and search reduce crime? Assessing the impact of Operation BLUNT 2*, (2016).

[63] P. Quinton, M. Tiratelli, and B. Bradford, *Does More Stop and Search Mean Less Crime? Analysis of Metropolitan Police Service Panel Data, 2004–14* (2017).

[64] See e.g. 'Stop and search harms fight against knife crime, Met officer says', *The Guardian*, 13 March 2018; 'David Lammy criticises Sadiq Khan over vow to increase stop and search', *The Guardian*, 14 January 2018.

[65] K. Murray, 'The Modern Making of Stop and Search: The Rise of Preventative in Post-War Britain' (2018) 58 *BJC* 588, 589; V. Stone and N. Pettigrew, *The Views of the Public on Stops and Searches* (2000), 41.

[66] See Ch 5.

impact of removing stop and search powers, then, would probably be an increase in the number of low-suspicion arrests.

4.3 SURVEILLANCE

The use of surveillance techniques by law enforcement agencies has grown exponentially and is likely to increase further with technological advances. Many offences are committed or planned by electronic means, whether through encrypted messaging, social media, or the dark net, and there is a range of techniques and devices for the surveillance of citizens; so it is understandable why law enforcement agencies wish to take advantage of any technology which improves the detection of crimes. Surveillance techniques that involve (for example) electronic eavesdropping or imaging may promise a high degree of reliability. However, they also raise a number of human rights concerns, and it is these concerns that have led to various changes in English law.

The general approach of the common law to the interception of communications is that this is permissible unless specifically made unlawful. Thus, until the 1980s, telephone-tapping was authorized by the Home Secretary, without a relevant legal framework. When this was challenged in *Malone v UK*,[67] it was found to be in breach of Art 8 of the ECHR, which safeguards an individual's right to respect for private life, home, and correspondence. Article 8(2) permits interference with the right on certain grounds that make it 'necessary in a democratic society', but the interference must be 'in accordance with the law', to ensure that it is not arbitrary but has procedural safeguards. Soon after the decision, the Interception of Communications Act 1985 was passed. This introduced a statutory authorization scheme for telephone-tapping, but failed to deal with surveillance generally. Other methods remained unregulated, save for Home Office guidelines.

Among the subsequent challenges was that in *Khan v UK*,[68] where police officers had placed a listening device on the wall of a private house and recorded incriminating conversations. The police officers had followed the procedure of obtaining the chief constable's authority, but there was no legislative framework in England and so the interference with the targeted person's right to respect for private life was not 'in accordance with the law'. The government anticipated this ruling by promoting the provisions that became Part III of the Police Act 1997, which provides an authorization procedure for surveillance involving entry on to property. However, this piecemeal approach to legislation still failed to provide a general framework for all forms of intrusive surveillance, and adverse decisions from Strasbourg continued.[69]

---

[67] (1985) 7 EHRR 14.   [68] (2000) 31 EHRR 1016.
[69] E.g. *Govell v UK* [1999] EHRLR 121; *Halford v UK* (1997) 24 EHRR 523; and, also relating to an investigation in the 1990s, *PG and JH v UK* [2002] *Crim LR* 308.

Many of the points of principle about safeguarding human rights in the process of using surveillance were accepted in a White Paper,[70] resulting in the Regulation of Investigatory Powers Act 2000 (RIPA). Although much more general than previous legislation, it failed to integrate or incorporate the provisions in Part III of the Police Act 1997, which remain in force. In outline,[71] the first part of the 2000 Act replaced the Interception of Communications Act 1985 with a new framework that extends to communications on public and private networks. It provided a procedure whereby the Home Secretary may issue a warrant, and ss 5(2) and 5(3) reflect the language of Art 8(2) in referring to proportionality and the various reasons for which interference may be held necessary in a democratic society. The second part of the 2000 Act, in outline, introduces a regulatory framework for three forms of surveillance. *Directed surveillance* is covert surveillance that is not intrusive in its method but is likely to reveal matters within the protection of Art 8(1). *Intrusive surveillance* is covert surveillance that does involve intrusion into private premises or a vehicle. *Covert human intelligence sources* are persons who maintain a close relationship with a target suspect and thereby obtain information falling within the ambit of Art 8(1). The Act required authorization by a senior police officer, on the statutory grounds, before directed surveillance or covert human intelligence sources were deployed; and required authorization of intrusive surveillance at the level of chief constable or, if the matter was urgent, by a senior police officer. The Act established a Commissioner to review warrants issued and a tribunal to deal with complaints; the most intrusive forms of surveillance require prior authorization by a Commissioner. Commissioners also carry out regular inspections in order to audit compliance. This was more or less a continuation of the previous system, and it is doubtful whether it was Convention-compliant. The ECtHR has held more than once that a procedure for interference with Art 8 rights must require judicial authorization,[72] and it must be highly doubtful whether the procedures for authorization by middle-ranking police officers (in respect of directed surveillance, covert human sources, and, in some circumstances, intrusive surveillance) satisfy this requirement. Moreover, there is room for argument about the vagueness of some key terms in the Act—such as 'serious crime'—now that the ECtHR is taking a more stringent approach to cases of state interference with Art 8 rights.[73]

One flaw in the RIPA scheme was that the hierarchy of levels of surveillance was drafted in rather simple terms. 'Intrusive surveillance', which generally requires prior

---

[70] Home Office, *Interception of Communications in the United Kingdom* (Cm 4368, 1999), prompted by JUSTICE, *Under Surveillance* (1998).

[71] For discussion of the 2000 Act, see S. Bailey and N. Taylor, *Civil Liberties: Cases, Materials and Commentary* (6th edn, 2009), 578–600.

[72] E.g. most clearly in *Kopp v Switzerland* (1999) 27 EHRR 91, [74].

[73] The government relied on two decisions of the Commission, *Hewitt and Harman v UK*, App No 20317/92 and *Christie v UK* (1994) 78A DR 119, as confirming that the phrases 'in the interests of national security' and 'the economic well-being of the country' are sufficiently certain; but in recent years the Court itself has signalled a greater emphasis on certainty in decisions such as *Valenzuela v Spain* (1998) 28 EHRR 483 and *Amann v Switzerland* (2000) 30 EHRR 843.

approval by a Commissioner, involves surveillance of residential premises or a private vehicle,[74] but people may engage in highly sensitive communications, with expectations of privacy, outside such areas. In *McE v Prison Service of Northern Ireland*, the House of Lords considered appeals by detainees who complained about the possibility that their discussions with legal advisers and doctors might be subject to surveillance.[75] The House of Lords held that while such surveillance was permissible under the Act—and that the Act's provision of authority to carry out covert surveillance overrode a suspect's right to consult a solicitor in private guaranteed in s 58 of PACE[76]—to comply with Art 8 it needed to be authorized at the higher level required for intrusive surveillance, rather than at the internal police level deemed appropriate for directed surveillance.

The annual reports by the Surveillance Commissioner[77] suggested that requests for authorization by the Commissioner were seldom refused: appeals against refusals are extremely rare, there being one or none each year. And while there are over 2,000 authorizations for property interferences granted by the police each year, very few (usually six or less) are quashed by the Commissioner, suggesting a permissive regime. While the Commissioner's monitoring reveals various unauthorized instances of surveillance, those examples that come to his attention usually seem to involve surveillance equipment being left in a premises after an operation has ended. The case law reveals occasional more serious abuses of surveillance powers.[78] One notable trend has been a decline over the years in the number of 'Covert Human Intelligence Sources' (CHIS)—informers—registered by the police. Whether this is because of a drift away from this sort of operation—puzzling, as the Commissioner notes, given the modern emphasis on 'intelligence led' policing[79]—or because some informers are redesignated as 'tasked witnesses' in order to evade the regulatory scheme,[80] is hard to say. This has continued: at the end of March 2017, 2,299 CHIS remained authorized, which is about half the number from a decade ago.[81]

There has been a series of judgments and subsequent lawmaking, both domestically and transnationally, which seeks to grapple with the tension between the pursuit of crime and the protection of privacy and civil liberties. Mass surveillance through the retention of communications data was facilitated across Europe by Directive 2006/24/EC (the Data Retention Directive). After this was deemed to be invalid in 2014 by the Grand Chamber of the European Court of Justice (ECJ) on the ground that EU legislators had exceeded the limits of proportionality, the UK government introduced the Data Retention and Investigatory Powers Act 2014

---

[74] Regulation of Investigatory Powers Act 2000, s 26(3).   [75] [2009] UKHL 15.

[76] Lord Phillips dissented on this point: see at [24]–[25].

[77] Available at www.surveillancecommissioners.gov.uk/about_annual.html.

[78] *R v Grant* [2005] 2 Cr App R 28.   [79] See n 77, 2005–6 Report, 7.4.

[80] Ibid, 2006–7 Report, 2.3.

[81] *Annual Report of the Chief Surveillance Commissioner to the Prime Minister and to the Scottish Ministers for 2016–2017*, HC 299 SG/2017/222 (2017), [11.11].

(DRIPA). That same year, the UK government asked David Anderson, the Independent Reviewer of Terrorism Legislation, to review the operation and regulation of investigatory powers, in particular the interception of communications and communications data. His report was published in June 2015,[82] and recommended a new law to clarify these powers. On 21 December 2016, the ECJ ruled that DRIPA was unlawful.[83] DRIPA was repealed on 31 December 2016 and replaced by the Investigatory Powers Act 2016.

The Investigatory Powers Act 2016 (IPA) repealed Part I, Chapters 1 and 2 of RIPA 2000, and provided a framework for the lawful use of investigatory powers to obtain and retain communications and communications data, through interception and other interference. It set out the statutory tests that must be met before a power may be used and the authorization regime for each investigative tool, including a new requirement for Judicial Commissioners to approve the issuing of warrants for the most sensitive and intrusive powers. The Act also created an Investigatory Powers Commissioner to oversee the use of these powers.

The Act was not fully implemented immediately, and on November 2017 the Home Office published proposals to amend the Act in order to comply with a decision of the Court of Justice of the European Union in which DRIPA had been challenged successfully.[84] Moreover, in a claim for judicial review by Liberty the High Court ruled that Part 4 of the 2016 Act was incompatible with fundamental rights in EU law in that access to the retained data was not limited to the purpose of combating 'serious crime', and was not subject to prior review by a court or an independent administrative body.[85] The court concluded that the legislation must be amended by 1 November 2018, and this was done by means of the Data Retention and Acquisition Regulations 2018. However, the definition of 'serious crime' in the Regulations, of offences that attract a 12-month custodial sentence or more, is problematic in its breadth in respect of bulk surveillance.

In conclusion, RIPA and the IPA represented a significant step towards protecting human rights in the process of gathering evidence through surveillance methods. While it is unfortunate that the government adopted such a minimalist view of the requirements of Art 8 on such questions as judicial authorization, defining the grounds for interference, and informing individuals that they have been subject to surveillance, surveillance by law enforcement officers is now more fully regulated than it was two decades ago, though the scheme remains permissive. There is a pronounced interplay between courts and legislature at both the domestic and EU levels, whereby the courts have reined in the expansionist tendencies of the Executive, which continues to prioritize crime control.

---

[82] https://www.gov.uk/government/publications/a-question-of-trust-report-of-the-investigatory-powers-review.

[83] Cases C-203/15 and C-698/15 *Tele2 Sverige AB v Postoch telestyrelsen* and *Secretary of State for the Home Department v Tom Watson and others* (2016).

[84] Ibid.   [85] *Liberty v Secretary of State for the Home Department* [2018] EWHC 975 (Admin), [186].

4.4 EYEWITNESS IDENTIFICATION EVIDENCE

(A) BACKGROUND ISSUES

Eyewitness identification evidence has long played a significant role in criminal investigations and the criminal process overall.[86] Yet it is not always robust evidence, and has been of significance in a number of miscarriages of justice. Writing in 1972, the Criminal Law Revision Committee suggested that mistaken eyewitness identifications were 'by far the greatest cause of actual or possible wrong convictions'.[87] More recently, the Innocence Project, which uses DNA evidence to identify and overturn wrongful convictions, suggests that eyewitness identification played an important role in more than 70 per cent of these cases in the United States.[88]

The primary concern of the criminal process regarding eyewitness identification evidence is to ensure it is reliable. There are a number of factors that may affect this. Some of these relate to the witness, such as eyesight, memory, the conditions in which the offence was observed: distance from the offender, duration of the incident, quality of light, etc.[89] The criminal process has relatively little control over these 'estimator variables', though at trial the court should draw these to the fact-finder's attention. The criminal process has much more control over 'system variables', such as how identification is carried out, whether through a 'parade' or whether the witness is asked to identify the suspect as the offender at trial, standing in the dock. There are more subtle factors, too, over which the process has some influence, such as the time between the crime and the identification procedure, and whether the witness might have seen media images of the suspect before being asked to make an identification.

As Seale-Carlisle reminds us, 'Line-up procedures . . . were not developed by scientists and then implemented in the field, but were instead developed by law enforcement agencies who have no objective basis for preferring one procedure to another.'[90] Because of the importance of eyewitness identification evidence, and the recognition of its potential frailty, there is a considerable body of psychological research examining what affects its quality.[91] It is worth highlighting some factors that have been shown to influence eyewitness identification. In the typical situation, a person has observed a crime being committed, and later is shown a suspect by the police and asked whether

---

[86] M. Zander and P. Henderson, *Crown Court Study* (1993), para 3.3.1; G. Pike, N. Brace, and S. Kynan, *The Visual Identification of Suspects: Procedures and Practice*, Home Office Briefing Note 2/02.

[87] Criminal Law Revision Committee, *Eleventh Report: Evidence (General)* (Cmnd 4991, 1972), para 196.

[88] See www.innocenceproject.org/understand/Eyewitness-Misidentification.php; also B. Garrett, *Convicting the Innocent: Where Criminal Prosecutions Go Wrong* (2011).

[89] A useful overview of the literature is G. Wells, A. Memon, and S. Penrod, 'Eyewitness Evidence: Improving its Probative Value' (2006) 7 *Psychological Science in the Public Interest* 45.

[90] T. M. Seale-Carlisle and L. Mickes, 'US line-ups outperform UK line-ups' (2016) 3 *Royal Society Open Science* doi:10.1098/rsos.160300.

[91] See e.g. Wells et al, n 89; G. Wells and E. Olson, 'Eyewitness Identification' (2003) 54 *Annual Rev of Psychology* 277; T. Horry et al, 'Archival analyses of eyewitness identification test outcomes: what can they tell us about eyewitness memory?' (2014) 38 *Law & Human Behavior* 94.

this is the person seen earlier. Memory plays a crucial role here: the witness is being asked to compare a remembered image with the person shown to her. Memories fade over time, so in general the sooner the procedure is held, the better. Memories, and therefore the identification process, are also open to suggestion. The significance of this point cannot be overemphasized. As detailed in Chapter 5, sometimes suggestion can lead to false confessions, so it is no surprise that suggestion can affect visual memories comparably. Indeed, a good example of the power of suggestion is that experiments have shown that fingerprint examiners, who make visual comparisons between prints without having to rely on memory, can be manipulated by suggestion into being more or less likely to declare a match between prints.[92]

The standard process for identification in England and Wales is a video identification procedure (VIP),[93] and it likely that more that 80,000 take place per year.[94] Here the witness is shown images of the suspect along with various other people (known as 'fillers' or 'foils'). It is important to avoid suggestion with this process. If the person conducting the VIP holds their breath, say, when the image of the suspect appears, there is a risk of suggestion; therefore the best procedures will, like medical trials, be double-blind, so that the administrator is either unaware of who the suspect is or cannot tell when the witness is looking at the suspect's image.[95]

'Street identification' also occurs relatively frequently, in an informal procedure whereby witnesses attempt to identify an offender, usually close in time and space to the commission of a crime. If the police arrive at the scene of a street robbery shortly after the incident occurred, they may know that the perpetrator will still be in the vicinity, but not know whom to suspect among the numerous people in the area. In this situation, it will be tempting to involve the complainant in picking out the perpetrator on the street. This may be by means of a 'drive by' or in a 'confrontation conducted in the street'.[96] If the complainant does identify someone, the police will then have a suspect to arrest. Indeed, street identification should occur only where there are insufficient grounds for suspicion to warrant an arrest,[97] which is the test under PACE Code D for imposing a requirement, where appropriate, to conduct a VIP. As is detailed later, unlike video identification, street ID does not attract PACE safeguards. If the suspect's

---

[92] I. Dror and R. Rosenthal, 'Meta-Analytically Quantifying the Reliability and Biasability of Forensic Experts' (2008) 53 *J Forensic Sciences* 900; I. Dror and P. Fraser-Mackenzie, 'Cognitive Biases in Human Perception, Judgement, and Decision Making: Bridging Theory and the Real World' in D. Rossmo (ed), *Criminal Investigative Failures* (2009).

[93] This is often referred to as *VIPER*, standing for Video Identification Parade by Electronic Recording.

[94] T. Valentine, C. Hughes, and R. Munro, 'Recent Developments in Eyewitness Identification Procedures in the United Kingdom' in R. Bull, T. Valentine, and T. Williamson (eds), *Handbook of Psychology of Investigative Interviewing: Current Developments and Future Directions* (2009), 231.

[95] M. Phillips et al, 'Double-Blind Photoarray Administration as a Safeguard Against Investigator Bias' (1999) 84 *J Applied Psychology* 940; R. Horry, A. Memon, R. Milne, D. Wright, and G. Dalton, 'Video Identification of Suspects: A Discussion of Current Practice and Policy in the United Kingdom' (2013) 7 *Policing: A Journal of Policy and Practice* 307.

[96] A. Roberts, J. Davis, T. Valentine, and A. Memon, 'Should We Be Concerned about Street Identifications?' [2014] *Crim LR* 633, 635.

[97] See Ch 5.

identity is known to the police and he is 'available', a street identification should not
be carried out, but instead the procedure should be video identification, identification
parade, or group identification.[98] The research of Roberts et al found that street identification procedures were used far more frequently than formal procedures, and that
the number of street identifications conducted annually in England and Wales likely
runs into the thousands, possibly tens of thousands.[99]

The first data of street identifications in England were provided in a study by Davis
et al.[100] They found that 'street identification *attempts* are common (22 per cent of
robbery cases), although less than one in five (17 per cent) result in a suspect identification'. Crucially, a street identification has a very strong influence: '61 per cent of
identified robbery suspects . . . and 66.7 per cent from all crime types . . . were charged
or cautioned'. This underlines how an innocent suspect's interests may not be served by
participation in a second identification procedure, though refusing to cooperate with
the police may not assist the case in court.[101]

While the foregoing suggests that some identification procedures pose greater risks
to innocent suspects than do others, it is very difficult to generalize about what level
of risk actual procedures pose. Research in England and Wales suggests that in actual
cases witnesses picked fillers about 20 per cent of the time.[102] If identification procedures involve eight fillers in addition to the suspect,[103] then an innocent suspect would
bear a risk of being identified of just over 2 per cent. However, this assumes that an
innocent suspect is no more likely to be picked than any of the fillers. It is plausible that
an innocent suspect will often have been arrested because of his resemblance to the
perpetrator, and it may be difficult to find fillers who look like the perpetrator to a similar degree, so that if innocent suspects often look more like the perpetrator than does
anyone else in the array he may bear a considerably higher risk of false incrimination.

(B) REGULATING IDENTIFICATION PROCEDURES

Formal identification procedures are governed by PACE Code D. An identification
procedure should be held in situations where a witness may be able to identify the perpetrator of a crime.[104] Responsibility for organizing identification procedures is given
to an identification officer, who must be of at least the rank of inspector and must not
be involved with the relevant investigation.[105] Since its introduction in the early 2000s,

[98] Code D Revised, Code of Practice for the identification of persons by Police Officers (2017), 3.4.
[99] Roberts et al, n 96, 646–7. See also T. Valentine, J. Davis, A. Memon, and A. Roberts 'Live Showups and
Their Influence on a Subsequent Video Line-Up' (2012) 26 *Applied Cognitive Psychology* 1–23.
[100] J. Davis, T. Valentine, A. Memon, and A. Roberts, 'Identification on the Street: A field comparison of
police street identifications and video lineups in England' (2015) 21 *Pyschology, Crime & Law* 9, 22.
[101] Ibid, 23.
[102] See T. Valentine, 'Forensic Facial Identification' in A. Heaton-Armstrong et al (eds), *Witness Testimony:
Psychological, Investigative and Evidential Perspectives* (2006), 290–1. Note that this research involved live identification parades, rather than the currently used video identification.
[103] This is the minimum number required by Code D, Annex A, 2.   [104] Code D, 3.12.
[105] Code D, 3.11.

video identification has become the standard procedure. Here, the witness is shown images of the suspect and several other—usually eight—fillers, selected from a large database.[106] The video images show each person looking at the camera and turning their head in each direction to present side views. Video identifications have a number of advantages over live parades;[107] they can be arranged far more quickly and easily, and they proceed sequentially. Use of a database makes it easier to find fillers who resemble the suspect, and research has found that VIPs are fairer in this respect than live parades: observers provided with the witness's description of the suspect could guess who the suspect was 15 per cent of the time when viewing video arrays, as opposed to 25 per cent of the time with live parades (one would expect 11 per cent of guesses to be correct by chance alone).[108]

While the Code includes important safeguards, such as recording the witness's description of the perpetrator before any identification procedure is conducted, and warning the witness that the person they saw may not be present in the set of images, there is no requirement that video identifications be double-blind, so it is possible for the identification officer, consciously or not, to alert the witness to the identity of the suspect. Relatively simple arrangements could solve this problem (the witness could view the images on a screen out of the identification officer's sight, and with the suspect's position among the video clips selected at random); a double-blind requirement would therefore be a sensible addition to Code D.[109] Another potential problem is that, while video identification is a sequential process, Code D contains provisions which undermine some of the advantages sequential procedures are thought to offer in promoting absolute over relative judgements. In a strict sequential procedure, the witness would only see each image once and would have to make a 'yes' or 'no' decision, without knowing how many images they would see. A positive response would bring the procedure to an end, and revisiting images would not be possible. Code D, however, provides that the witness 'should be asked not to make any decision as to whether the person they saw is on the set of images until they have seen the whole set at least twice'.[110] The witness can also ask to view particular images repeatedly; these provisions obviously make it easier for the witness to rely on a judgement of relative likeness. In an interesting study, however, Valentine et al compared the Code D provisions to a strict sequential procedure and found that, contrary to expectations, a strict procedure offered no advantages.[111] While, in line with previous research, strict procedures led to fewer correct identifications, unlike in previous research they offered no benefits in terms of a reduced risk of false identification.

Code D and the identification procedures apply where the police have a suspect whom they can involve in an identification procedure and are intended to give suspects

---

[106] See Valentine, n 102.

[107] See T. Valentine, S. Darling, and A. Memon, 'Do Strict Rules and Moving Images Increase the Reliability of Sequential Identification Procedures?' (2006) 21 *Applied Cognitive Psychology* 933, 934.

[108] T. Valentine and P. Heaton, 'An Evaluation of the Fairness of Police Lineups and Video Identifications' (1999) 13 *Applied Cognitive Psychology* 59.

[109] See Valentine, n 102. Horry et al, n 95, 311.   [110] Code D, Annex A.11.   [111] See n 107.

some protection from biased and suggestive practices. It will be very difficult to avoid bias and suggestion where identification takes place on the street. Code D does contain provisions on this situation, referring to 'cases where the suspect's identity is not known'.[112] Here:

> an eye-witness may be taken to a particular neighbourhood, or place to see whether they can identify the person they saw . . . the principles applicable to the formal procedures . . . should be followed as far as practicable. For example: . . . Care must be taken not provide the eye-witness with any information concerning the description of the suspect (if such information is available) and not to direct the eye-witness' [sic] attention to any individual unless, taking into account all the circumstances, this cannot be avoided. However, this does not prevent an eye-witness being asked to look carefully at the people around at the time or to look towards a group or in a particular direction.[113]

The police should keep a record of what takes place and, as in all cases, the witness should be asked to provide a description of the perpetrator before any identification is attempted.

Given the increased risk of false identification in this situation, the question of the distinction between cases where the suspect's identity is known and where it is not is an important one. It seems that once the police have sufficient evidence to arrest a particular suspect, the suspect's identity will be known and a formal identification procedure should take place if he disputes the identification. Arrest requires reasonable suspicion, a criterion sufficiently vague that the known/not known distinction is imprecise, and there is room for argument about just where the distinction should lie. Although there is normally good reason to minimize the use of arrest, because of the interference with the right to liberty,[114] in cases where identity is potentially an issue arrest might be in the suspect's interest, by engaging the requirement of formal identification procedures. Indeed, it has been suggested that wider use of arrest powers could be used to more or less eliminate the need for street identifications.[115] This is probably unrealistic, as there will often be more than one potential suspect in the vicinity of the crime.

Case law is unclear as to when arrest should take place. According to the House of Lords in *Forbes*, there needs to be 'some apparently reliable evidence implicating' the person arrested.[116] In *K v DPP*,[117] the police arrived at the scene of a street robbery shortly after it had been committed. A sniffer dog was used to follow the trail of the perpetrators; D was found nearby, and was brought towards the police car where he was identified by V. The Court of Appeal was concerned by the use of this extremely suggestive procedure. It found that here there was sufficient evidence to arrest D and that this would have been the proper course. In *Toth*,[118] however, customs officers observed a car being used for a drug deal. One of the officers who had witnessed the

---

[112] Code D, 3.2.   [113] Ibid.   [114] Code G, 1.2.

[115] D. Wolchover and A. Heaton-Armstrong, 'Ending the Farce of Staged Street Identifications' (2004) 3 *Arch News* 5. See also 'Improving Visual Identification Procedures Under PACE Code D' in *Witness Testimony*, n 102.

[116] *R v Forbes* [2001] 1 AC 473, 482.   [117] [2003] EWHC 351 (Admin).

[118] [2005] EWCA Crim 754.

transaction then went to the address of the vehicle's registered keeper. The keeper was identified by the officer and then arrested. The Court of Appeal thought that this was appropriate, and that there was not sufficient evidence to arrest the vehicle's registered keeper without an identification of him as having been present at the scene. While the facts of the cases are very different, it is not obvious that *Toth* can be reconciled with the less permissive approach in *K*, where all that was known seems to have been that D was standing on the street somewhere in the direction that the perpetrators had run.

The concern about street identifications is that there is a greater risk of mistaken identification because they lack the safeguards of formal procedures. And, of course, mistaken identifications in a street identification can only be of the police suspect.[119] The empirical research carried out by Roberts et al suggests such procedures may be no less reliable than video identification, in terms of the risk of mistaken identification of innocent suspects.[120] That said, mistaken identification of an innocent suspect in a street identification entails a very high likelihood that a formal procedure involving the same suspect and witness will result in the suspect being identified again.[121] Their findings are consistent with previous research that found that a witness is much more likely to identify a suspect in a VIP where she has seen the suspect in a prior identification procedure.[122]

Once a suspect is identified through street identification, then the suspect is 'known' and the PACE safeguards will apply. As we have seen, this means that if the suspect disputes the identification, then an identification procedure, usually video identification, should be held. However, the Code contains a significant caveat to this requirement: '(i) it is not practicable to hold any such procedure; or (ii) any such procedure would serve no useful purpose in proving or disproving whether the suspect was involved in committing the offence, for example where the suspect admits being at the scene of the crime and gives an account of what took place and the eye-witness does not see anything which contradicts that; or when it is not disputed that the suspect is already known to the eye-witness who claims to have recognised them when seeing them commit the crime.'[123] This 'no useful purpose' qualification was added to the Code after the House of Lords' decision in *Forbes*,[124] which held that the previous language of the Code made identification procedures mandatory so long as the suspect disputed identity. In *Forbes*, the suspect had become known to the police through a street identification, and it appeared rather odd that a formal identification procedure was required in this situation, because once a witness has picked out someone on the street an identification procedure does not seem to offer very much in terms of testing their recollection of who they saw committing the offence (as opposed to their memory of whom they later picked out). The 'no useful purpose' language was doubtless intended to give the police more discretion in this situation, though Wolchover and Heaton-Armstrong suggest that this is a discretion 'which can only be exercised one way'.[125] It seems to

[119] Davis et al, n 100, 2.   [120] Roberts et al, n 96, 633.   [121] Ibid, 634.   [122] Ibid, 653.
[123] Code D, 3.12.   [124] See n 116.
[125] D. Wolchover and A. Heaton-Armstrong, 'Street Identification' [2014] *CJ&L* 178.

have resulted in some uncertainty as to when an identification procedure should be held,[126] but the courts have continued to hold that the requirement is a strict one, and cite *Forbes* as authority that an identification procedure is a mandatory requirement in this situation.[127] As it was put in *R v Callie*, the words 'no useful purpose' 'are strong and the Code is mandatory. They do not allow a proportionality exercise so that the Code . . . would not apply if some, but very limited, purpose would be served.'[128] As for the specific example given by the Code—where it is not disputed that the suspect is already well known to the witness—the courts have taken a fairly strict line here too, holding that someone last seen some years ago is not 'well known'.[129] As we will see, though, the courts rarely hold that breaches of the Code in these situations are grounds for excluding identification evidence, and this has doubtless contributed to there being a steady stream of cases where the Code has been breached.

Suspects have some rights in this context, relating to the information they must be told, including that they need not consent to an identification procedure.[130] Regardless, the police may attempt to hold an identification procedure without their consent, for example by using an image from CCTV or holding a group identification, where the suspect is seen as part of an informal group such as among people leaving his place of work. Refusal to consent can also be given in evidence at any subsequent trial. If the police reasonably suspect that the suspect will not cooperate, they can proceed to capture his image covertly without giving notice of rights. Once this is done, however, the suspect should be given the opportunity to cooperate in providing more suitable images for use in a VIP.[131] The suspect and his adviser can view the set of images compiled for video identification, and make objections which should be taken into account 'if practicable'.[132] Roberts et al suggest that while Code D is currently drafted in a way that establishes a presumption that a video identification procedure is to be conducted following identification of a suspect in a confrontation conducted in the street, it would be preferable for the duty to conduct a formal procedure to be triggered by a suspect's request for one, to acknowledge the autonomy of the suspect and his or her status as the holder of a procedural right to participate in a formal identification procedure.[133]

(C) EYEWITNESS EVIDENCE IN COURT

When a case involving identification evidence proceeds to court, two important issues arise: (1) what should happen if Code D has been breached; and (2) what should the jury be told about identification evidence, given its obvious weaknesses? If there has been a breach of Code D, a defendant will often argue that identification evidence

[126] See Criminal Justice Joint Inspection,*Streets Ahead: A Joint Inspection of the Street Crime Initiative* (2003), 60–1.
[127] E.g. *R v Harris* [2003] EWCA Crim 174, [26]; *R v Darren B* [2005] EWCA Crim 538, [12]; *R v Muhidiniz* [2005] EWCA Crim 2464, [14]; *R v Gojra* [2010] EWCA Crim 1939.
[128] [2009] EWCA Crim 283, [22].
[129] E.g. *Harris*, n 127; *Darren B*, n 127; *McKenna v DPP* [2005] EWHC 677 (Admin).
[130] Code D, 3.17.   [131] Code D, 3.20.   [132] Code D, Annex A.7.   [133] Roberts et al, n 96, 653.

should be excluded (if the breach involved no identification procedure being held, the argument will usually be that a prior street identification or recognition should be excluded, or, if there is no eyewitness identification, that proceedings should be stayed as an abuse of process).[134] However, exclusion is by no means automatic. The case law here is part of the wider case law on s 78 of PACE, under which evidence may be excluded if it would render the proceedings unfair. As far as Code D is concerned, the cases suggest that evidence will be excluded if there has been a 'significant and substantial' breach of its provisions. Factors taken into consideration include whether the police have acted in bad faith, and whether the defendant has been disadvantaged by the breach.[135] Even then, exclusion is by no means automatic. In *Wellington*, a 'non-technical' breach of the Code, which was held to have deprived D of one means of challenging the evidence against him, was held not to lead to exclusion.[136] One reason for this is that the courts emphasize the overall state of the evidence against D—exclusion is less likely if the identification is corroborated.[137] Thus, in *Forbes*, while the House of Lords interpreted Code D strictly, it held that the evidence obtained in breach of Code D was properly admitted in court. It endorsed the Court of Appeal's observation that:

> The evidence was compelling and untainted, and was supported by the evidence (which it was open to the jury to accept) of what the appellant had said at the scene. It did not suffer from such problems or weaknesses as sometimes attend evidence of this kind: as, for example, where the suspect is already visibly in the hands of the police at the moment he is identified to them by the complainant.[138]

The House of Lords did hold, though, that in cases where an identification procedure had not been held in breach of Code D the jury should be told that such a procedure 'enables a suspect to put the reliability of an eyewitness's evidence to the test, that the suspect has lost the benefit of that safeguard and that the jury should take account of that fact in its assessment of the whole case, giving it such weight as it thinks fair'.[139] The courts now seem to put considerable emphasis on whether or not a '*Forbes* warning' was given; often this will be seen as a sufficient remedy even where D has suffered some disadvantage through the breach.[140] This is not a convincing approach. Although often not deliberate, in these cases the actions of the police have deprived the defendant of one means of testing the evidence against him, such as by denying him a video identification or failing to record the witness's first description of the suspect, making the trial as a whole a less reliable means of establishing guilt. A *Forbes* warning appears to be a rather ineffectual response to this: how is the jury to take into account, for example, the fact that, had it been recorded, the witness's description might have been

---

[134] See generally A. Roberts, 'Pre-Trial Defence Rights and the Fair Use of Eyewitness Identification Procedures' (2008) 71 *MLR* 331.

[135] For reviews of the case law, see I. Dennis, *The Law of Evidence* (6th edn, 2017), 8-015–8-027.

[136] *R (on the application of Wellington) v DPP* [2007] EWHC 1061 (Admin).

[137] See *McKenna*, n 129, at [16]: 'when one comes to consider the fairness of the position under s 78, one looks at all the evidence'. See also *R v B* [2008] EWCA Crim 1524.

[138] See n 116, [32].   [139] Ibid, [27].

[140] See e.g. *Muhidiniz*, n 127; *Darren B*, n 127; *Harris*, n 127; *R v Lewis and Thomas* [2006] EWCA Crim 2895.

a poor fit for D? The proper response in most of these cases would be to exclude the identification evidence.[141]

Moving on from breaches of Code D, the remaining question is how the courts warn juries about the inherent frailties of eyewitness identification evidence. In the wake of the Devlin Committee's report, the Court of Appeal laid down guidelines on this issue in *R v Turnbull*.[142] *Turnbull* requires judges to warn juries about the dangers of mistaken identification. Whenever a case depends 'wholly or substantially' on identification evidence, the judge should warn the jury of the special need for caution before convicting on such evidence. The warning should go into a reasonable amount of detail, informing jurors that even convincing witnesses, or more than one witness, can be mistaken, that innocent people have been convicted on the basis of mistaken eyewitness evidence, and drawing their attention to the details of the identification in issue.[143] In cases where the quality of identification evidence is poor—for example, an identification based on a fleeting glance 'or on a longer observation made in difficult conditions'—the judge should go further. The case should be withdrawn from the jury unless there is evidence to support the identification. If there is supporting evidence, then the judge should bring it to the jury's attention; oddly, though, there is no requirement for the jury to accept the supporting evidence before convicting: thus, a jury can still, in theory, convict on poor quality identification evidence alone.[144]

Turnbull is a welcome safeguard, though it is not without its problems. The courts have considerable leeway in deciding just how *Turnbull* applies, especially when it comes to the distinction between good and poor quality evidence. According to *Turnbull*, quality is good 'for example when the identification is made after a long period of observation, or in satisfactory conditions by a relative, a neighbour, a close friend, a workmate and the like'.[145] The example of poor quality evidence that is given is 'a fleeting glance or . . . a longer observation made in difficult conditions'.[146] There is quite a gap between these examples: should a short, but not fleeting, observation in good conditions be classified as good or poor quality? It is not surprising to find in the case law some inconsistency as to when the *Turnbull* requirements on supporting evidence apply.[147] And the standard for 'good quality' can be rather low. In *Williams*, a two-second observation of a person in a moving vehicle was held not to be poor quality because it was made by a police officer.[148] Despite the Devlin Committee's observation that cross-examination is little use as a means of testing identification evidence,[149] there remains a tendency to put much trust in the jury. Thus, in *Waterfield*, the victim of a stressful sexual assault, who had been tired and had been drinking before the incident, identified D at a video

---

[141] For more detailed discussion of possible remedies, see Roberts, n 134.   [142] [1977] QB 224.

[143] On the importance of covering all of the elements in *Turnbull*, see *R v Nash* [2004] EWCA Crim 2696.

[144] This point, always apparent on a literal reading of *Turnbull*, is confirmed in *R v Ley* [2006] EWCA Crim 3063.

[145] See n 142, 229.   [146] Ibid.

[147] Cf *Oakwell* [1978] 1 All ER 1223; *Curry* [1983] *Crim LR* 737; *Bowden* [1993] *Crim LR* 379.

[148] *The Times*, 7 October 1994.

[149] P. Devlin, *Report to the Secretary of State for the Home Department of the Departmental Committee on Evidence of Identification in Criminal Cases*, HC 338 (1976), 4.25.

identification 22 days later.[150] The Court of Appeal did not think that these factors made the identification 'inherently unreliable', and considered that the jury was in the best position to consider the impact of the various factors on the identification evidence.

It has been questioned whether the courts should rely at all here on the good/poor quality distinction. The Devlin Committee had not distinguished between good and poor evidence, and had recommended directing juries in all cases that 'it is not safe to convict upon eye-witness evidence unless the circumstances of the identification are exceptional or the eye-witness evidence is supported by substantial evidence of another sort'.[151] There is something to be said for this approach. All the evidence suggests that there are limits to the strength of eyewitness evidence: the figures, reviewed earlier, on the likelihood of an innocent suspect being picked out on an identification procedure are a graphic illustration of this. Most defendants plead guilty, and if it is likely that few innocents plead guilty, the proportion of cases involving mistaken identification at trial will be much higher than the proportion of mistaken identifications occurring at identification procedures.[152] The basic fact is that some types of evidence are simply not powerful enough to justify conviction unless there is supporting evidence. Of course, even the Devlin Committee recognized that a rule with too bright a line might be problematic: exceptional circumstances would justify conviction on an eyewitness identification alone. The sorts of situations described in *Turnbull* as constituting good quality evidence might be thought to justify a conviction when standing alone. But in all other cases, the Devlin Committee's approach seems appropriate.

In conclusion, the system for regulating the production of eyewitness evidence in England and Wales is relatively robust. The use of video identification, and the detailed rules in Code D, offer significant safeguards to suspects, notwithstanding some points of criticism, such as the absence of a requirement for procedures to be double-blind.[153] While the courts may have done well to emphasize the importance of identification procedures in the face of the ambiguous language of Code D ('no useful purpose'), they have done less well in giving clear guidance on the admittedly difficult question of when street identifications are appropriate. There is also room for concern that, despite the difficulties that juries must face in gauging the accuracy of eyewitness identifications, the courts continue to put too much faith in juries, both when it comes to responding to breaches of Code D—over-reliance on *Forbes* warnings—and in letting juries convict on eyewitness evidence alone in too wide a range of cases.

4.5 VOICE IDENTIFICATION

In some instances, a witness may not have seen the offender's face, but has heard his voice; so voice identification may be crucial. It raises many of the same concerns as visual identification, with psychological research suggesting that it is even less reliable.[154]

[150] [2009] EWCA Crim 1815.   [151] See n 149, para 8.4.
[152] This is the 'pleading effect', discussed in Wells et al, n 89, 51–2.
[153] For other suggestions, see Valentine, n 102.
[154] See D. Ormerod, 'Sounds Familiar?—Voice Identification Evidence' [2001] *Crim LR* 595.

Voice identification procedures exist but are not used consistently by police forces, with some forces having decided as a matter of policy not to use them.[155] Perhaps for this reason, Code D says almost nothing about voice identification, simply noting that '[w]hile this code concentrates on visual identification procedures, it does not prevent the police making use of aural identification procedures such as a "voice identification parade", where they judge that appropriate'.[156] In the previous edition of this book, we expressed disappointment at the brevity of the statement in the 2008 version of the Code, and there has been no elaboration in the 2011 or 2017 revisions. That said, the Home Office did issue a Circular in 2003, endorsing guidance first developed by the Metropolitan Police for use in a particular case,[157] but there is no other standardization in this context. The Home Office Circular lacks the mandatory force of Code D, and makes no requirement that an identification procedure be held in a particular case. It outlines how to set up a voice identification parade, avoiding potential pitfalls such as having participants read a set text (which can apparently lead to unnatural inflection), by using interview recordings, and suggests the use of experts in selecting appropriate excerpts. The selection of recordings should be played to a number of mock witnesses, who know nothing more than what can be gleaned from a description of the crime, to see if the suspect's voice stands out.

The courts are reasonably alert to the dangers posed by voice identification. In contrast to disputed eyewitness identification, there is no duty to conduct a voice 'parade'.[158] When used, a suitably modified *Turnbull* direction is recommended—though one might wonder if a stronger warning is appropriate—and the Court of Appeal is critical where this is not given.[159] The majority of cases seem to involve voice recognition, that is, witnesses who claim to recognize the perpetrator's voice. While this may well be more reliable than the identification of a voice only heard during the crime, it is worth noting that in visual identification cases involving recognition, the courts often hold that an identification procedure is required.[160] This might well be appropriate in cases of voice recognition, even ones involving recent familiarity (as the Court of Appeal has noted, in experiments people can fail to recognize the voices of intimates speaking over a telephone[161]), so it is disappointing that neither the courts, nor the Home Office through Code D, have taken the initiative here. The courts have done better where the police have purported to recognize recorded voices, being very critical of this move.[162] In summary, while there is awareness of the difficulties involved in voice identification and voice recognition, more needs to be done to hold the police to best practice in this area.

---

[155] J. Robson, 'A Fair Hearing? The Use of Voice Identification Parades in Criminal Investigations in England and Wales' [2017] *Crim LR* 36.

[156] Code D, 1.2. See also 1.8.   [157] Home Office Circular 057/2003.

[158] *Gummerson* [1999] Crim LR 680, CA. See Robson, n 155, 37.

[159] *R v Hersey* [1988] *Crim LR* 281; *R v Phillips* [2007] EWCA Crim 1042.   [160] See n 127.

[161] *R v Flynn* [2008] 2 Cr App R 20, [16].

[162] Ibid. For similar concerns about police visual identification from CCTV, see *R v Smith* [2009] 1 Cr App R 36.

4.6 THE COLLECTION AND RETENTION OF FORENSIC AND BIOMETRIC SAMPLES

The collection and analysis of forensic samples (such as tissue, blood, and other bodily fluids) from victims, suspects, and crime scenes, is an increasingly important part of investigating and prosecuting crime. Moreover, biometric technology enables the automated recognition of individuals based on their biological and behavioural characteristics, such as through fingerprints, DNA, retina, gait, and facial features.[163] It is vital that such forensic and biometric samples are collected and preserved in a manner that impacts to the lowest possible extent on individuals' bodily integrity and other rights, yet in such a way as to prevent or minimize degradation or contamination of valuable material that can be highly relevant and probative.

Fingerprints may be taken from an arrested person without consent,[164] and his photograph taken.[165] Intimate samples, such as a dental impression or sample of blood, semen, or any other tissue fluid, urine, or pubic hair, or a swab taken from any part of a person's genitals, may be taken from a person in police detention if a police officer of at least the rank of inspector authorizes it to be taken; and the person consents.[166] A non-intimate sample, such as saliva, a sample of hair, or a sample taken from or under a nail, may be taken from an arrestee in police detention, and reasonable force may be used, if necessary.[167] These samples may be checked against other retained samples.[168]

Since the development of DNA 'profiling' in 1984,[169] DNA evidence has become an important part of the criminal justice landscape in England and Wales. No one can doubt the utility of DNA evidence in identifying offenders and building a powerful case against them. What has been more controversial has been the creation and growth of a large DNA database against which samples of DNA found at crime scenes can be checked. At one stage, because of regular expansion of police powers to take DNA samples from suspects,[170] the database held the DNA profiles of more than 4.2 million people, or some 7 per cent of the population.[171] This has been checked somewhat latterly.

---

[163] Automated facial recognition (AFR), for instance, involves the identification of an individual based on an analysis of the geometric features of his or her face, and a comparison between the algorithm created from the captured image and one already stored, such as from a custody image or social media photographs. See J. Purshouse and L. Campbell, 'Privacy, Crime Control and Police use of Automated Facial Recognition Technology' [2019] *Crim LR* 188.

[164] PACE, s 61. See Ch 5 on re-arrest and detention.   [165] PACE, s 64A.   [166] PACE, s 62.
[167] PACE, s 63.   [168] PACE, s 63A.
[169] P. Gill, A. Jeffreys, and D. Werrett, 'Forensic application of DNA "fingerprints"' (1985) 318 *Nature* 577. A DNA profile may be from a sample: it is a set of identifying characteristics from regions of DNA that are not known to provide for any physical characteristics or medical conditions of the person. It consists of a list of numbers based on specific areas of DNA known as short tandem repeats, and is only able to be read by trained professionals using computer programs. Parliamentary Office of Science and Technology, 'The National DNA Database', *Postnote* (February 2006) at Box 1.
[170] For the history of the expansion of the relevant powers, see C. McCartney, *Forensic Identification and Criminal Justice: Forensic Science, Justice and Risk* (2006), ch 1.
[171] Hansard, 10 November 2008, col 799W (Alan Campbell MP, written answer).

Originally, under PACE, samples could be obtained from those suspected of involvement in serious arrestable offences only, and when the DNA database was first established in 1995 profiles could not be retained unless a person was convicted. But after changes introduced by the Criminal Justice Act 2003, DNA samples could be taken, without consent, from anyone *arrested* for a recordable offence, irrespective of whether they were convicted or even prosecuted, and whether or not the sample would be useful in investigating the offence for which they had been arrested.[172] The sample, as well as a DNA profile obtained from it and entered on the database, could be retained indefinitely. These wide powers of retention led to the UK being held in breach of Art 8 by the ECtHR in *Marper v UK*.[173] As a result, restrictions on the power to retain DNA profiles on the database were included in the Crime and Security Act 2010, and the Protection of Freedoms Act 2012.

DNA contains a range of sensitive personal information, such as information about our ancestry and susceptibility to disease. DNA profiles, however, contain information taken from very small portions of the genome. The relevant portions are 'non-coding', in other words they do not play a role in determining the features or development (the 'phenotype') of the person concerned. That said, because even non-coding DNA is inherited, DNA profiles contain some information about who is related to whom. It is also possible to make limited inferences about a person's ethnicity on the basis of a DNA profile.[174]

When the House of Lords had considered *Marper*, a majority held that retention of DNA profiles raised no privacy issues.[175] The ECtHR, however, came to the opposite conclusion, finding that the ability to explore genetic relationships and make inferences about ethnicity meant that DNA profiles enable 'the authorities to go well beyond neutral identification'.[176] One might quibble with some of this. Inferences about ethnicity would not be drawn from the profiles in issue in *Marper*, because these are taken from known people and details about the person's ethnic appearance will be recorded along with other relevant information such as name and date of birth. Inferences about ethnicity will only be made where a DNA sample is found at a crime scene, and in the absence of a match to the database the police want information about the offender's possible ethnic appearance. This practice was simply not in issue in *Marper*. The point about genetic relationships is a sounder one, but it is still important to understand just what occurs. If a crime scene sample is checked against the database but no match is reported, a search may be conducted for near matches, on the assumption that these may involve the offender's relatives. The police might then approach the source of a close match, and ask this person to name close relatives, who might then come under suspicion. So while the database provides a lead, information about

---

[172] PACE, s 63.

[173] *S and Marper v UK* (2009) 48 EHRR 50. See L. Campbell, 'A Rights-Based Analysis of DNA Retention: "Non-Conviction" Databases and the Liberal State' [2010] *Crim LR* 889.

[174] See Nuffield Council on Bioethics, *The Forensic Use of Bioinformation: Ethical Issues* (2007), 2.15–2.21.

[175] [2004] UKHL 39. Baroness Hale dissented on this point: see at [67]–[79].

[176] *S and Marper*, n 173, [75].

relatedness will come, if at all, from the person approached by the police, who is under no legal obligation to comply. Nevertheless, as a report issued by the Nuffield Council on Bioethics noted, familial searching needs to be carried out with great sensitivity.[177] Even had there been no concerns about sensitive information, the ECtHR would still have held that DNA profiles raise issues under Art 8, for in the same judgment it also considered the retention of fingerprints, finding that 'fingerprints objectively contain unique information about the individual concerned allowing his or her identification with precision in a wide range of circumstances. They are thus capable of affecting his or her private life.'[178]

This led the Court to a consideration of whether retention of DNA profiles and fingerprints was justified under Art 8(2). Though all European jurisdictions allow the retention of such material in some circumstances, *Marper* highlighted the exceptionally wide powers available in England and Wales—neither applicant had been convicted, and yet their profiles would be retained indefinitely. The Court found that the 'blanket and indiscriminate nature' of the powers 'fails to strike a fair balance between the competing public and private interests'.[179] While the government had provided some evidence that retention of DNA from those arrested but not convicted contributed to identifying offenders, the Court thought that insufficient detail was given to make the government's case for wide retention.

The ECtHR cited with approval the 'Scottish model', which was endorsed by the Nuffield Council on Bioethics also.[180] Under this approach, profiles are only retained from those arrested for violent and sexual offences, and for a limited period of three years, though the police can apply for a two-year extension.[181] It is not clear what the argument for this position is, especially as it might be said to stigmatize a certain group of arrestees. More serious offences tend to have lower recidivism rates than less serious ones, so in terms of risk of reoffending the Scottish policy might even be said to target the wrong people. Obviously, it is more important to convict people of serious offences, but this does not provide a straightforward case for singling out those who have been arrested for sexual and violent offences. Versatility in offending—some offenders who commit serious crimes commit less serious ones as well—means that there may be a case for retaining profiles of those arrested for minor crimes in order later to gain convictions for more serious ones.[182]

The applicants claimed that retention cast suspicion on unconvicted persons implying that they were not 'wholly innocent'.[183] Although the Court of Appeal noted that a constable could destroy DNA evidence if the person were free from 'any taint of suspicion',[184] the ECtHR expressed concern that unconvicted persons, who 'are entitled

[177] See n 174, 6.11.   [178] *S and Marper*, n 173, [84].   [179] Ibid, [35].
[180] See n 174, xv.
[181] L. Campbell, 'DNA Databases and Innocent Persons: Lessons From Scotland?' [2010] *The Juridical Review* 285–97.
[182] See M. Gottfredson and T. Hirschi, *A General Theory of Crime* (1990); Home Office, *Keeping the Right People on the DNA Database: Science and Public Protection* (2009), 34–5.
[183] *S and Marper*, n 173, [89].   [184] Ibid [14].

to the presumption of innocence, are treated in the same way as convicted persons'.[185] That said, this factor underpinned its final judgment on Art 8 regarding privacy, rather than constituting a separate line of argument under Art 6.[186]

The government responded to *Marper* with a rather rushed consultation paper,[187] leading to the publishing of the Crime and Security Bill in November 2009. Though enacted in April 2010, its provisions on the retention of DNA were not brought into force following the election. Instead the Coalition government introduced a new Protection of Freedoms Bill with much stricter rules on the retention of innocent people's DNA records and fingerprints. The Protection of Freedoms Act 2012 imposes a differentiated scheme of DNA collection and retention. The Act requires all DNA samples to be destroyed within six months of being taken, which allows sufficient time for the sample to be analysed and a DNA profile to be produced for use on the database. When an individual is suspected of an offence, his DNA may be collected, speculatively searched, but not retained past the conclusion of the investigation or proceedings.[188] The profile of someone arrested for or charged with a minor offence is not retained, unless he is convicted, or has previously been convicted of a serious recordable offence, in which case the material may be retained indefinitely.[189] For a minor offence resulting in a Penalty Notice for Disorder, the profile is retained for two years.[190] If an individual is arrested for or charged with a qualifying offence (i.e. a serious violent or sexual offence, terrorism offence, or burglary offence) but is not convicted, retention is for three years (or indefinitely if he has a previous conviction for a recordable offence) plus a possible two-year extension on application to the magistrates' court.[191]

Arguments about who should be included on the DNA database and for how long are complex.[192] Unfortunately, beyond various anecdotes we have little reliable information about how important the DNA database is in securing convictions against people in various groups: the convicted and the unconvicted, and those arrested for more and less serious crimes. The annual report of the National DNA Database (NDNAD) Strategy Board claims that the increase in the number of matches between crime scene profiles and a subject profile on the NDNAD demonstrates the continued effectiveness of the NDNAD.[193] While matches demonstrate the database's value in the investigation of crime, its effectiveness in terms of impacting on conviction rates, or on deterring crime, is less evident.

We also have limited information about the attitudes of the general public to inclusion on the database;[194] of course, popular support would not necessarily warrant a wider or universal database. The most contentious issue is whether DNA profiles and

---

[185] Ibid [122].

[186] L. Campbell, 'Criminal Labels, the European Convention on Human Rights and the Presumption of Innocence' (2013) 76 *MLR* 681–707.

[187] Home Office, n 182.   [188] PACE, s 63E.   [189] PACE, s 63H.   [190] PACE, s 63L.

[191] PACE, s 63F.

[192] See generally D. Lazer (ed), *DNA and the Criminal Justice System: The Technology of Justice* (2004).

[193] The National DNA Database Strategy Board, *Annual Report 2016/17* (2018), i.

[194] The Human Genetics Commission, *Nothing to Hide, Nothing to Fear? Balancing Individual Rights and the Public Interest in the Governance and Use of the National DNA Database* (2009).

fingerprints should be retained from those who have not been convicted of an offence, but the question of how long the profiles of the convicted should be retained is significant too. It might be argued that if the convicted remain at a higher risk of offending, then they are likely to be rearrested at some point, in which case a new profile can be taken.[195] When it comes to the unconvicted, in the response to the consultation it seems that a majority were opposed to retention.[196] This stance is initially attractive, but it does have its problems. Police forces often keep records about those they arrest, detailing names, reason for arrest, and the like, and it might be questioned why there is such concern about DNA profiles but not about these other forms of recorded information. What about DNA makes its retention particularly sensitive and problematic? Further, if it is conceded that the profiles of the convicted should be retained for at least some period, and if this concession is based on risk of reoffending, then we must consider whether those arrested but not convicted have a higher risk of offending than the general population.[197]

Ethnic disproportion on the database is marked: at one stage, one in three young black males had a profile on the database, compared to one in eight young white males. This results from the ability of the police to take profiles on arrest, and as we will see further in Chapter 5, there is evidence that BAME people are arrested on a lower evidence base than white people. The equality issue was highlighted as a cause for concern in the Nuffield report,[198] but was not mentioned in the consultation paper. Evidently, the database is not a direct cause of inequality but rather a manifestation of police decision making. But to argue that the database simply reflects problems elsewhere in the criminal process is to ignore the fact that white people have significantly less chance of being arrested as a result of a database match to a crime scene profile than do black people. In this way, by putting black people at a greater risk of conviction, the database amplifies over-representation in the criminal justice system. This is sometimes used as an argument for having a truly universal database, with people included at birth.[199] Indeed, the Human Genetics Commission found considerable public support for this idea, but was not itself convinced that equality provided good reasons for a universal database.[200] While a universal database would, by definition, mitigate any biases in selective DNA collection and retention, it would be a disproportionate incursion on the right to privacy, and one likely to entail considerable costs in its creation, maintenance, searching, and safeguarding.

In 2017, NDNAD held 6,024,032 subject profile records and 555,362 crime scene profile records, and of which 269,489 and 40,829 respectively had been loaded in the

---

[195] See K. Soothill, 'Keeping the DNA Link' (2009) 159 *NLJ* 1021.
[196] Home Office, *Keeping the Right People on the DNA Database: Science and Public Protection, Summary of Responses, Public Consultation 7 May–7 August 2009* (2009), 2.1.
[197] See Home Office, *DNA Retention Policy: Re-Arrest Hazard Rate Analysis* (2009).
[198] See n 174, 4.63–4.66.
[199] See D. Kaye and M. Smith, 'DNA Databases for Law Enforcement: The Coverage Question and the Case for a Population-Wide Database' in Lazer, n 192.
[200] Human Genetics Commission, n 194, paras 3.40–3.45.

preceding year.[201] Now 7.5 per cent of the subject profile records on the NDNAD are from black individuals, as determined by the sampling officer, 5.2 per cent from Asian individuals, 75 per cent from white, and 8 per cent unknown.[202]

In summary, there is no obvious place to draw the line when it comes to deciding whose DNA profiles and other samples should be retained on databases. But once the debate moves on to degrees of risk, as it now seems to have done, questions are raised about whether there is a strong case for retaining the profiles of the convicted for an indefinite period when those of the unconvicted are not.

4.7 THE PRIVILEGE AGAINST SELF-INCRIMINATION

A key constraint on the ability of the state to gather and use evidence against suspects is the privilege against self-incrimination. While recognized in international human rights documents,[203] and implied into the ECHR, its scope and underlying justification are difficult to determine, and our understanding of the privilege has shifted over time.[204] While acknowledging those points, we begin by noting that certain aspects of the privilege appear to have universal support. In English law, its most fundamental application is at trial, in the form of the rule that the defendant is not a compellable witness at his own trial. The significance of this is that the defendant can refuse to testify, and cannot be held in contempt of court for this refusal. In the discussion to follow, we will try to show some of the values that underpin the privilege against self-incrimination, concentrating on the way the privilege has been developed under the ECHR,[205] and linking it to the gathering of evidence specifically.

(A) WHEN DOES THE PRIVILEGE APPLY?

In 1993, in *Funke v France*,[206] the ECtHR recognized the privilege as being part of the fair trial guarantee in Art 6. The applicant was suspected of tax evasion. The authorities demanded that he provide them with details of his bank accounts; when Funke did not do so the French court fined him 50 francs a day. The Court found that: 'The special features of customs law . . . cannot justify such an infringement of the right of anyone "charged with a criminal offence" . . . to remain silent and not to contribute to incriminating himself.'[207] Some years later, in *Saunders v UK*, it expanded on these rather cryptic comments.[208] Saunders had been investigated under the Companies Act

---

[201] The National DNA Database Strategy Board, *Annual Report 2016/17* (2018), 1.2.1.   [202] Ibid, 14.
[203] International Covenant on Civil and Political Rights, Art 14; Inter-American Convention on Human Rights, Art 8.
[204] See R. Helmholz et al, *The Privilege Against Self Incrimination: Its Origins and Development* (1997); M. MacNair, 'The Early Development of the Privilege Against Self-Incrimination' (1990) 10 *OJLS* 66.
[205] For a more detailed review of the ECHR case law, see A. Ashworth, 'Self-Incrimination in European Human Rights Law—A Pregnant Pragmatism?' (2008) 30 *Cardozo L Rev* 751.
[206] (1993) 16 EHRR 297.   [207] Ibid, [44].   [208] (1997) 23 EHRR 313.

1985 after he had been suspected of illegally boosting the price of shares in his company. Under the Act, inspectors had the power to require that he produce documents and answer questions put to him. Refusal could be punished as contempt of court and any information gained through this process could be used against Saunders at trial. The ECtHR found the latter point significant: its 'sole concern', it explained, was 'with the use made of the relevant statements made at the applicant's criminal trial'.[209] The fact that his statements had been used against him at trial put those proceedings in breach of Art 6. This time the Court said something more about the justification for the privilege against self-incrimination:

> [The] rationale lies, *inter alia*, in the protection of the accused against improper compulsion by the authorities thereby contributing to the avoidance of miscarriages of justice and to the fulfilment of the aims of Art 6. The right not to incriminate oneself, in particular, presupposes that the prosecution in a criminal case seek to prove their case against the accused without resort to evidence obtained through methods of coercion or oppression in defiance of the will of the accused. In this sense the right is closely linked to the presumption of innocence. . . . The right not to incriminate oneself is primarily concerned, however, with respecting the will of an accused person to remain silent. As commonly understood in the legal systems of the Contracting Parties to the Convention and elsewhere, it does not extend to the use in criminal proceedings of material which may be obtained from the accused through the use of compulsory powers but which has an existence independent of the will of the suspect such as, *inter alia*, documents acquired pursuant to a warrant, breath, blood and urine samples and bodily tissue for the purposes of DNA testing.[210]

This passage has been repeated, with minor variations, in several other cases.[211]

The effect of *Saunders* in English law was that a number of statutes giving similar 'inquisitorial' powers to investigators were modified by the introduction of 'use immunity'.[212] Use immunity means that, although a suspect can be subjected to sanctions—such as a fine, or being held in contempt of court[213]—for refusing to answer questions or provide information, the information so obtained cannot then be used in court. (This position, whereby investigators can gain information but not use it to gain a conviction, has been described as 'the worst of all possible worlds' by one commentator.[214]) Use immunity has received some emphasis in later ECtHR decisions. In *Heaney and McGuiness v Ireland*, the defendants had been found close to the scene of a terrorist bombing.[215] Under Irish law, they could be asked to provide an account of their movements in the preceding 24 hours; refusal to do so was a criminal offence. The Court again found a breach of the ECHR, noting that the situation as to whether or not the applicants' answers to such questions could be used at a trial for the offence under investigation was unclear. And in *Marttinnen*,[216] the defendant faced criminal liability for refusing to disclose details of his assets in debt enforcement proceedings;

---

[209] Ibid, 67.   [210] Ibid, 68–9.   [211] E.g. *JB v Switzerland* [2001] *Crim LR* 748.
[212] Youth Justice and Criminal Evidence Act 1999, s 59.
[213] *IJL and others v UK*, App No 29522/95, 19 September 2000.
[214] S. Sedley, 'Wringing Out the Fault: Self-Incrimination in the 21st Century' (2001) 52 *NILQ* 107, 120.
[215] (2000) 33 EHRR 12.   [216] *Marttinnen v Finland*, ECtHR, 21 April 2009.

this was held to breach Art 6 because again there was no guarantee that information disclosed could not be used against him in proceedings for debt fraud, an investigation of which was under way.

That use immunity should play a role in the case law is perhaps not surprising. The privilege protects against self-incrimination. If information provided carries no risk of self-incrimination, the privilege does not apply. This means that some requests by the state for information are perfectly legitimate so far as the privilege is concerned. Thus, in *King v UK*,[217] King was held to have been properly fined for failing to provide information about his tax liability, because he was not being prosecuted for a tax offence beyond the one involving his refusal to provide information. Similarly, in *Weh v Austria*, the applicant was asked to provide details of who was driving his car on a particular date when it was seen to break the speed limit; when he gave vague details he was fined for providing inaccurate information.[218] As criminal proceedings had not been commenced against Weh in respect of the speeding offence (the authorities had charged 'unknown offenders'), he was held not to benefit from the privilege against self-incrimination. This is a rather fine distinction, and is in tension with some of the reasoning in *Marttinnen*.[219]

The scope of the privilege against self-incrimination is limited in another way: in the view of the ECtHR in *Saunders* it does not apply to material which has an existence 'independent of the will' of the subject 'such as, *inter alia*, documents acquired pursuant to a warrant, breath, blood and urine samples and bodily tissue for the purposes of DNA testing'. This pronouncement has caused much bemusement. After all, many of the cases where the Court has held that the privilege does apply involve material which appears to have an existence independent of the will: *Funke* and *Marttinnen* involved financial details. In *Jalloh*,[220] the German police took a suspected drug dealer to hospital, where he was administered an emetic which made him regurgitate drugs. The drugs surely had an existence independent of the will, yet the ECtHR held that the privilege applied. The not very satisfactory reasoning used to distinguish 'breath blood and urine samples' from the swallowed drugs was that the situation in *Jalloh* involved real evidence, as opposed to material which would be examined for the presence of alcohol or drugs, and that the degree of force used in *Jalloh* was greater than in the case of a simple blood, etc test.[221] The former point received a little elucidation in *Gäfgen v Germany*, where the real evidence in *Jalloh* was said to have been elicited as a direct result of a breach of Art 3, and was contrasted with real evidence discovered as the indirect effect of a threat of violence.[222]

An interesting English case has probed the question of to which material the privilege applies. *R v S and A* involved investigation into suspected terrorism.[223] The police wanted to access encrypted files on the defendants' computer, but were unable to do so without an encryption key. Under s 49 of RIPA, the defendants were asked to provide

---

[217] (2004) STC 911.   [218] (2005) 40 EHRR 37.   [219] See n 216, esp at [64].
[220] *Jalloh v Germany* (2007) 44 EHRR 32.   [221] Ibid, [113]–[114].
[222] (2009) 48 EHRR 13, [104].   [223] [2008] EWCA Crim 2177.

the key either orally or in writing. Failure to do so was a criminal offence, punishable by a term of imprisonment. The Court of Appeal held that the key had an existence independent of the will:

> Once created, the key to the data, remains independent of the appellant's 'will' even when it is retained only in his memory. . . . In this sense the key to the computer equipment is no different to the key to a locked drawer. The contents of the drawer exist independently of the suspect: so does the key to it. The contents may or may not be incriminating: the key is neutral.[224]

The point about the neutrality of the material received further emphasis:

> The actual answers, that is to say the product of the defendants' minds, could not be incriminating. The keys themselves simply opened the locked drawer, revealing its contents. In much the same way that a blood or urine sample provided by a car driver is a fact independent of the driver, which may or may not reveal that his alcohol level exceeds the permitted maximum, whether the defendants' computers contain incriminating material or not, the keys to them are and remain an independent fact.[225]

So far we have seen that, under the ECtHR's jurisprudence, the privilege against self-incrimination applies to information which may incriminate the defendant in criminal proceedings, and which does not exist independently of his will. A further question about the privilege is whether it is absolute, or whether its breach might be justified in some situations. Here, the ECtHR's jurisprudence is not entirely satisfactory.[226] In cases such as *Saunders* and *Heaney*, the Court denied that the need to investigate complex financial transactions or serious crime—a terrorist bombing—could justify a breach of the privilege. While *Heaney* did allow that the privilege was not absolute, it suggested that any abrogation of the privilege must not destroy its 'very essence'.[227] In *Jalloh*, however, the Court slipped into the language of balancing, suggesting that 'the weight of public interest in the investigation and punishment of the offence at issue' was a relevant consideration in determining whether Art 6 had been breached.[228] But because the case involved only a minor drug-dealing offence, with the applicant receiving a suspended sentence, the breach was not justified. The real test case for breaches of the privilege has been the regulation of road traffic offences. As we have seen, in *Weh* the applicant was asked to identify who had been driving his car, and his unhelpful response gained him a criminal conviction. Powers such as this are a common way of dealing with car ownership, and have received extended discussion in the UK in *Brown v Stott*[229] and in Strasbourg in *O'Halloran and Francis v UK*.[230] In the latter case, the applicants' cars had been filmed breaking the speed limit. Section 172 of the Road Traffic Act 1988 required them to provide details of who was driving the car at the relevant

---

[224] Ibid, [20].   [225] Ibid, [21].
[226] See J. Jackson, 'Re-Conceptualizing the Right of Silence as an Effective Fair Trial Standard' (2009) 58 *ICLQ* 1.
[227] See n 215, 55.   [228] See n 220, [117].   [229] [2001] 2 WLR 817.   [230] (2008) 46 EHRR 21.

time. They alleged that this breached their privilege against self-incrimination. The ECtHR found no breach; it seemed to accept that the privilege against self-incrimination is not absolute,[231] and offered several reasons why, on the facts, 'the very essence' of the right was not negated. It noted that the compulsion involved—'a moderate and non-custodial penalty'[232]—was minor, and that the applicants had only been asked to provide a limited amount of information.[233] Both of these points are problematic.[234] As noted earlier, in *Jalloh* the level of penalty was used as evidence that the offence was not a very serious one and thus that coercive measures were not appropriate; if the penalty level can be used to argue in either direction, it is hardly a principle that can restrain breach of the privilege. As for the complexity of the information sought, what is surely more significant is that the answer to the question is capable of incriminating the subject.

The Court in *O'Halloran* was on firmer ground when, quoting from the Privy Council's decision in *Brown v Stott*, it noted that:

'All who own or drive motor cars know that by doing so they subject themselves to a regulatory regime. This regime is imposed not because owning or driving cars is a privilege or indulgence granted by the State but because the possession and use of cars (like, for example, shotguns . . .) are recognised to have the potential to cause grave injury'. Those who choose to keep and drive motor cars can be taken to have accepted certain responsibilities and obligations as part of the regulatory regime relating to motor vehicles, and in the legal framework of the United Kingdom, these responsibilities include the obligation, in the event of suspected commission of road traffic offences, to inform the authorities of the identity of the driver on that occasion.[235]

In other words, this is not so much a case of the privilege being outbalanced by the need to regulate vehicle ownership, as that there is here a clear regulatory regime, involving licensing, registration, number plates, and the like, which vehicle owners voluntary enter into. While this reasoning is perhaps not entirely satisfactory (in rural areas, vehicle ownership may be something of a necessity), it has some pedigree in the criminal law where it is an argument that sometimes features in the justification of strict liability offences.[236] It is certainly preferable to a plain balancing argument; accepting that the harm caused by cars outbalanced the applicants' rights would have obvious repercussions for cases like *Heaney*, where the privilege would easily be outbalanced by arguments about the need to respond to terrorism.[237]

---

[231] Ibid. There is some ambiguity in the judgment, e.g. at [53] it is not clear whether the Court accepts that the privilege is non-absolute as opposed to that some forms of compulsion may not breach the right in the first place.

[232] Ibid, [58], quoting from *Brown v Stott* [2001] 2 WLR 817.   [233] Ibid, [58].

[234] See Ashworth, n 205, 762–5.   [235] See n 230, [57].

[236] See R. Duff, 'Strict Liability, Legal Presumptions and the Presumption of Innocence' in A. Simester (ed), *Appraising Strict Liability* (2005), 138–41.

[237] It might, though, be argued that the privilege has more value in serious cases, and thus that the weights on either side of the balance are greater in a case like *Heaney*. That is an interesting possibility, but the argument remains to be made.

(B) SCOPE OF THE PRIVILEGE

By describing the case law, with an emphasis on ECtHR decisions, we have given some idea of what the privilege against self-incrimination involves. It should be emphasized, however, that the privilege is a controversial principle, with a number of writers questioning whether it is possible to justify it.[238] One way of approaching these more normative issues is to return to one of the questions that surfaces in the case law: to what sort of information does the privilege apply? The ECtHR has tried to delimit the privilege by arguing that it does not apply to material which has an existence independent of the subject's will, but it has been criticized for applying this criterion inconsistently by finding breaches of the privilege in cases involving the production of documents and drugs.[239] It is possible to argue that there is more consistency in the case law than might at first appear. The critical passage in *Saunders* refers to 'documents acquired pursuant to a warrant' as being outside the scope of the privilege, and in the earliest case, *Funke*, there was criticism that the authorities, 'Being unable or unwilling to procure [the documents] by some other means, . . . attempted to compel the applicant himself to provide the evidence of offences he had allegedly committed.'[240] It may be that there would have been no criticism had the authorities used their powers to find the relevant information themselves, such as by executing a search warrant. On this view, what was objectionable was that Funke and other applicants in cases involving documents were placed under a legal obligation to cooperate with the authorities by handing over incriminating information. The privilege, it could be said, is means- and not material-based, prohibiting a particular means of acquiring information rather than protecting a particular type of material.[241] This way of viewing the privilege would avoid some rather odd distinctions that have been drawn in the case law. For example, in *S and A*, the case involving the encryption key, the Court of Appeal suggested that the key existed independently of the appellants' will, equating it to a physical key or a blood or urine sample. There is a sense in which this is true, but the distinction is probably not conducive to a principled case law. Any information stored in the memory, such as Heaney's memory of what he had been doing in the preceding 24 hours, might similarly be said to have an independent existence. This would be even more obvious if Heaney kept a diary which the police asked him to hand over to them; it would seem perverse to differentiate between obliging Heaney to hand over the diary and obliging him to give a verbal account of his movements.[242] To be fair, the Court of Appeal

---

[238] See e.g. D. Dolinko, 'Is there a Rationale for the Privilege Against Self-Incrimination?' (1986) 33 *UCLA L Rev* 1063; R. Allen, 'Theorizing About Self-Incrimination' (2008) 30 *Cardozo L Rev* 751.

[239] See e.g. T. Ward and P. Gardner, 'The Privilege Against Self-Incrimination: In Search of Legal Certainty (2003) *EHRLR* 387; Dennis, n 135, 161–5.

[240] See n 206, [44].

[241] See M. Redmayne, 'Rethinking the Privilege Against Self-Incrimination' (2007) 27 *OJLS* 209; H. Stewart, 'The Privilege Against Self-Incrimination: Reconsidering Redmayne's Rethinking' (2016) *E&P* 95.

[242] But for a theory that would draw a distinction here, on the grounds that Heaney is able to lie when responding verbally but not when handing over the diary, see D. Seidmann and A. Stein, 'The Right to Silence Helps the Innocent' (2000) 114 *Harvard L Rev* 430.

in *S and A* did not overemphasize the argument that the key existed independently of the will, putting rather more weight on the argument that knowledge of the key was not in itself incriminating (and allowing that in some circumstances it might be, as where knowing the key could be used to prove the defendant's knowledge of the contents of a computer file). The court used this distinction to explain why blood and urine samples are not protected by the privilege, an argument we also find in *Jalloh*, where a distinction between directly and indirectly incriminating material appears to be drawn. Again, though, these distinctions are unappealing. There is very little difference between the drugs in *Jalloh* and a blood sample, and little too between asking the appellants in *S and A* to disclose the encryption key and to disclose the contents of the file. It is better to say that in all these situations the privilege is breached, at least prima facie, because the subject has been placed under a legal obligation to cooperate with the prosecution.

If the scope of the privilege against self-incrimination is defined in terms of whether the subject is placed under an obligation to cooperate, things such as blood and DNA samples will fall outside the protection of the privilege when they are taken by force, because this involves no cooperation. In this situation, they will be taken independently of the will just like documents found during a search of the suspect's house. This is not, of course, to say that there is nothing problematic in taking blood by force; this would be an act of violence and a significant breach of the right to bodily integrity. It may well be better to breach the privilege against self-incrimination than the right to bodily integrity, and in fact in English law it is an offence under the Road Traffic Act to refuse to supply a breath or blood sample[243] (a breach of the privilege, in terms of the account developed here), but the police have no power to take blood without consent.[244] A further implication of the argument is that in *Jalloh* there was no breach of the privilege against self-incrimination; not because the case involved real evidence, but because Jalloh was not placed under an obligation to cooperate; in fact, he refused to cooperate and was held down while the emetic was administered by force. The ECtHR, though, was quite right to find a breach of Art 3 on these facts.

Another question about the scope of the privilege concerns its connection with the right to silence, which will be discussed in the following chapter. Terminology is one problem here. To this point, we have described the privilege against self-incrimination as a principle under which the state should not place a suspect under a duty to cooperate with a prosecution which is being brought against him. For the purposes of the discussion here, we would distinguish the right to silence as being the rule that inferences should not be drawn from a suspect's failure to mention facts at police interview or failure to testify at trial. The European Court has held that this rule is not required as part of a fair trial; in other words, inferences can be drawn from silence, as under the Criminal Justice and Public Order Act 1994, without conflict with Art 6 (see Chapter 5). The Court has, however, emphasized the need to draw such inferences with care, and to offer legal advice to those held in the police station in a regime where

---

[243] Road Traffic Act 1988, ss 6, 7.   [244] PACE, s 62(1)(b).

their failure to mention facts can be used against them at trial.[245] As a matter of theory, this approach is fruitful: there is a good argument that there is no strong relationship between the right to silence, as just defined, and the privilege against self-incrimination. Drawing inferences from silence does not place a suspect under an obligation to speak; indeed, the words of the new caution begin: 'You do not have to say anything'. The Criminal Justice and Public Order Act may put a certain amount of pressure on suspects to speak, but this is not the same as obliging them to. However, as the ECtHR notes, it is important that the regime of inferences from silence is handled carefully. To the extent that silence is suspicious, it is appropriate to draw inferences from silence. But if inferences are drawn too readily, or given too much weight, the scheme of drawing inferences from silence will change from being one where suspects face the natural consequences of their suspicious behaviour, to one where the only rational explanation for inferences is that they are being used to encourage suspects to speak by penalizing non-cooperation. Once the inferences from silence regime operates in this manner, it does appear to be in tension with the privilege against self-incrimination.[246] We will also see in Chapter 5 that there is evidence that the current caution is difficult to understand. If it is interpreted by suspects as meaning that they are required to speak, then in practice there would again be a conflict with the privilege against self-incrimination.

(C) A FUNDAMENTAL RIGHT?

Until this point, we have outlined the ECtHR jurisprudence on the privilege against self-incrimination and suggested how it might be reinterpreted. In the process, something has been said about the scope of the privilege. But the hardest question remains: why should the criminal process respect a principle which places limits on its ability to obtain evidence from suspects? There is no agreed theory of the privilege's value; indeed, as noted earlier, one influential position is that no coherent normative theory of the privilege can be developed.[247] On the account developed here, the privilege protects people from being placed under an obligation to cooperate with the prosecution. At a fairly general level, then, the privilege says something about the proper relationship between citizens and the state. Criminal prosecution involves the state in one of its most powerful guises. The privilege allows citizens to keep some distance between themselves and the state, and avoids them having to make what will often be a significant personal sacrifice. Placing people under an obligation to cooperate would usually involve criminal sanctions, and this would often be an excessive response to a suspect's non-cooperation.[248]

The passage from *Saunders*, quoted earlier, mentions various values that justify the privilege, including that the privilege is connected to the presumption of innocence. This point is worth brief discussion, in part to disambiguate some of the points often made in

---

[245] *Murray v UK* (1996) 22 EHRR 29; *Condron v UK* (2001) 31 EHRR 1.
[246] See M. Redmayne, 'English Warnings' (2008) 30 *Cardozo L Rev* 1047, 1082–3.
[247] See n 238 above.
[248] For an elaboration of this account, see Redmayne, n 241.

this context. In Chapter 5, we will draw attention to Greenawalt's argument that, as a matter of basic morality, one should not be expected to respond to accusations unless they are backed up with evidence.[249] This means that it is wrong to draw inferences from silence where there is not a reasonable basis for suspecting the person involved of wrongdoing. This principle might be said to reflect the presumption of innocence, where the presumption is understood not, as evidence lawyers tend to understand it, as a rule about the standard of proof in criminal cases, but as a rule about how the state should treat citizens. The state should not treat its citizens as suspects unless it can provide reasons for doing so; it should treat people with civility.[250] This principle might be seen as connected to the privilege against self-incrimination, in that at a deeper level both principles are about the relationship between citizen and state. But for many purposes it is useful to separate the principles. The privilege is more fundamental in that even when it is appropriate to draw an inference from silence—when there is sufficient evidence against the suspect to justify doing so—the privilege holds that it is still inappropriate to require cooperation. For example, at trial an inference may be drawn from the fact that the accused does not testify after the prosecution has made out a prima facie case, but it would still be wrong to hold the accused in contempt of court for not testifying. The principles, however, overlap to this extent: if there is a situation where breach of the privilege might be justified—for example, in the situation at issue in *O'Halloran*—cooperation should not be required unless the person involved is reasonably suspected of wrongdoing.

The account of the privilege against self-incrimination developed here is broad in two respects. First, it applies to real evidence such as blood and documents as much as to answers to questions, so long as they are obtained by placing the suspect under a duty to cooperate. While this creates a prima facie conflict between the privilege and the provisions of the Road Traffic Act, requiring the owners of vehicles to provide samples and to answer questions, we have suggested how one strand of the reasoning in *O'Halloran* might be used to create an exception to the privilege in this situation without engaging in an unruly balancing of rights against social interests. A second way in which the account here is broad is that the values underpinning it seem to apply to duties to incriminate other people as much as to duties to incriminate oneself, because both involve the state imposing itself on a very personal realm.[251] To some extent the law recognizes this parallel, for there are provisions relating to spousal immunity which mean that in many cases a person cannot be compelled to testify against their spouse,[252] just as they cannot be required to testify against themselves. But consider s 38B of the Terrorism Act 2000. Under this provision, it is a criminal offence, punishable by up to five years' imprisonment, to fail to inform the authorities that another person is engaged in terrorist activity, when that other person is known or reasonably suspected to be engaged in such activity. That other person might, of course, be a spouse or sibling. If we regard it as important to maintain some distance between

---

[249] K. Greenawalt, 'Silence as a Moral and Constitutional Right' (1981) 23 *William & Mary L Rev* 15.
[250] See D. Nance, 'Civility and the Burden of Proof' (1994) 17 *Harvard J Law & Public Policy* 647.
[251] See further Redmayne, n 241.   [252] See n 135.

ourselves and the state, so that the state's ends cannot be made to become our ends, then this wide-ranging provision is as objectionable as many of those discussed earlier.

4.8 CONCLUSION

Investigating crime and gathering evidence brings the tensions between crime control and due process into sharp focus. While the sections of this chapter may seem quite freestanding, from this set of topics there emerges a picture of the complexity of criminal process, showing the varied interests and constraints that affect it. The police have extensive powers to stop and search, to monitor and record individuals, and on arrest to collect and retain forensic samples, and the exercise of these powers can be fraught, given racial and other biases. Moreover, the development and deployment of new technologies, be that DNA profile comparison, or facial recognition technology, is often in a legal vacuum, or at least in uncharted territory. There is a marked interplay between the legislature, domestic and European courts, whereby policymakers seek to enable the exploiting of new technology to the greatest extent possible. There is an apparently ineluctable drive towards the use of such technologies in investigating crime and gathering evidence, even if the benefits are unclear, and the impact on civil liberties great.

FURTHER READING

BOWLING, B. and MARKS, E., 'The Rise and Fall of Suspicionless Searches' (2017) 28 *King's LJ* 62.

CAMPBELL, L., 'Criminal Labels, the European Convention on Human Rights and the Presumption of Innocence' (2013) 76 *MLR* 681.

QUINTON, P., 'The Formation of Suspicions: Police Stop and Search Practices in England and Wales' (2011) 21 *Policing and Society* 357.

ROBSON, J., 'A Fair Hearing? The Use of Voice Identification Parades in Criminal Investigations in England and Wales' [2017] *Crim LR* 36.

QUESTIONS FOR DISCUSSION

1. Should: (a) powers to stop and search without reasonable suspicion and (b) powers to stop and search with reasonable suspicion, be abolished?

2. How well are defendants protected against the risk of false eyewitness identification by (a) Code D and (b) the courts? Could defendants be given increased protection without unduly obstructing the conviction of the guilty?

3. In what circumstances should DNA profiles and fingerprints be taken and retained from those suspected of crime?

4. What is the value, if any, of the privilege against self-incrimination?

5

QUESTIONING

Police questioning, of suspects and witnesses, is a key pressure point in criminal procedure due to its centrality to police investigative practices.[1] Over the years, police powers of arrest have been extended, allowing detention for questioning to be used in more cases. During questioning, it is perhaps not surprising that the aim of the police will be to produce a confession. The majority of suspects make some form of confession, and confessions are powerful evidence, likely to secure a conviction at trial.[2] Suspects who are not forthcoming about their guilt may be seen as obstructing the investigation, which might prompt the police to put more pressure on them, by detaining and questioning them for longer and by adopting a harsher tone.[3] A further possibility is the false attribution of incriminating statements. These are dangers against which criminal procedure must provide safeguards.

While the regulation of police detention through the Police and Criminal Evidence Act 1984 (PACE) could be viewed as remedying concerns, serious abuses and false confessions still occur.[4] Since then, considerable effort has been put into training police in less aggressive interviewing practices,[5] and there is an increased recognition of vulnerability of suspects and witnesses in interviews. Moreover, though police investigative practices are increasingly proactive, using intelligence and sting operations, many of these practices have problems of their own (see the discussion of surveillance in Chapter 4 and entrapment in Chapter 9).[6] Even if there has been a move away from aggressive interviewing, changes to the right to silence under the Criminal Justice and Public Order Act 1994 (CJPOA) have contributed to making the police interview room a more pressurized environment.

---

[1] https://www.app.college.police.uk/app-content/investigations/investigative-interviewing/.

[2] M. McConville, *Corroboration and Confessions: The Impact of a Rule Requiring that No Conviction Can Be Sustained on the Basis of Confession Evidence Alone* (1993), 32–3; C. Clarke and R. Milne, *National Evaluation of the PEACE Investigative Interviewing Course* (2001), 33.

[3] See S. Kassin et al, 'Behavioral Confirmation in the Interrogation Room: On the Dangers of Presuming Guilt' (2003) 27 *Law & Human Behavior* 187.

[4] See the cases of Miller and George Heron, discussed in G. Gudjonsson, *The Psychology of Interrogations and Confessions: A Handbook* (2003), 96–106.

[5] See G. Gudjonsson, 'Investigative Interviewing' in T. Newburn, T. Williamson, and A. Wright (eds), *Handbook of Criminal Investigation* (2007).

[6] B. Loftus and B. Goold, 'Covert surveillance and the invisibilities of policing' (2012) 12 *Criminol & Crim Justice* 275.

5.1 QUESTIONING AND CONFESSIONS:
PSYCHOLOGICAL RESEARCH

One of the most important advances in the understanding of the process by which the police elicit confessions has been the development of a sophisticated body of psychological research on questioning. Such research is important in the practice of the courts, with psychologists and psychiatrists often called to give expert evidence about the reliability of confession evidence in individual cases.[7] Psychological research also offers more general lessons to the legal system as to how it should deal with the questioning process and the evidence that results from it.

Research on police questioning tells us something about the circumstances in which suspects confess to crime. A significant finding is that the questioning process itself often does little to elicit confessions. Most suspects who confess do so at the outset of the interview, rather than in response to being challenged by the police.[8] As to why some suspects but not others decide to confess, the most significant factor appears to be the strength of evidence against them.[9] And as to whether some types of defendant are more likely to confess than others, it does not appear that intellectual ability makes them more likely to confess to the police.[10] The only individual factor which was identified as a good predictor was whether that person had taken illegal drugs in the 24 hours before arrest, as 'suspects who are dependent on illicit drugs are motivated by factors that they perceive as expediting their release from custody'.[11]

The factors described above do not distinguish between true and false confessions. It is obviously very difficult to conduct research into why people confess falsely, because the veracity or otherwise of a confession is often impossible to establish. Coercive interrogation practices were the major cause.[12] False confessions tended to occur in serious cases, where the stakes were high and where often there was little other evidence against a suspect.[13] In such circumstances, the police may put a large amount of pressure on a suspect who—the lack of evidence suggests—could well be innocent. Gudjonsson has explored the explanations given by prisoners who claim to have confessed falsely. His findings again identify police pressure as a significant factor, though prisoners also claimed to have confessed falsely out of fear of custody, and to protect other people.[14] Finally, psychological factors may contribute to false confession. Some people will confess to crime without external pressure, perhaps as a form of attention

---

[7] See e.g. *R v Antar* [2004] EWCA Crim 2708; *R v Nolan* [2006] EWCA Crim 2983; I. Blandón-Gitlin, K. Sperry, and R. Leo, 'Jurors believe interrogation tactics are not likely to elicit false confessions: will expert testimony inform them otherwise?' (2011) 17 *Psychology, Crime & Law* 239.

[8] Gudjonsson, n 5, 70, 133. But cf S. Soukara et al, 'What Really Happens in Police Interviews of Suspects? Tactics and Confessions' (2009) 15 *Psychology, Crime & Law* 493, 500–1.

[9] Gudjonsson, n 5, 153.   [10] Ibid, 73.   [11] Ibid, 71.

[12] S. Kassin, 'False Confessions: Causes, Consequences, and Implications for Reform' (2014) 1 *Policy Insights from the Behavioral and Brain Sciences* 112–21.

[13] R. Ofshe and R. Leo, 'The Decision to Confess Falsely: Rational Choice and Irrational Action' (1997) 74 *Denver U L Rev* 979.

[14] Gudjonsson, n 5, 176.

seeking.[15] Young people and those with mental disorders are over-represented in false confession cases.[16] But Gudjonsson stresses that 'false confessions are not confined to the mentally ill and those with learning disability. . . . The view that apparently normal individuals would not seriously incriminate themselves when interrogated by the police is wrong.'[17]

5.2 THE CONTEXT OF QUESTIONING

(A) ARREST AND DETENTION

In order to gain a full understanding of police questioning, we need to know something about the context in which it takes place. One reason for this should already be apparent: as has been noted, research suggests that it is in serious cases where there is little evidence against suspects that the danger of false confession is greatest. Ensuring that the police can question only those suspects against whom there is reasonable evidence of guilt will reduce the risk of false confession. On the other hand, if it is made too difficult for the police to question suspects, they may be impeded unduly in the investigation of crime. We therefore begin by considering the circumstances in which suspects can be arrested and detained in police custody. Of course, there are other issues at stake here than the reliability of evidence gained through questioning: arrest and detention is an intrusion on the liberty of suspects and there is therefore potential for breach of Art 5 of the European Convention on Human Rights (ECHR). There are good reasons to minimize arrest and detention apart from the risks they pose in terms of false confessions.

The usual process is that a suspect will be arrested and then taken to the police station where questioning is likely to ensue, though, as is explained later, the granting of 'street bail' is also a possibility. PACE gave the police fairly wide arrest powers, and these were expanded by the Serious Organised Crime and Police Act 2005.[18] Under the previous law, a distinction was drawn between 'arrestable offences' and other, less serious, 'non-arrestable offences'. The distinction embodied a basic idea of proportionality, the idea being that arrest would not normally be appropriate where the least serious offences were concerned. Here, the police could usually proceed by way of summons, requiring the person concerned to attend court at some later date.[19] But now this distinction has gone, and the police are able to arrest for any offence, no matter how trivial, so long as they reasonably believe that one of the reasons in s 24(5) of PACE applies, including enabling the person's name or address to be ascertained; preventing

---

[15] See *R v Flanagan* [2005] EWCA Crim 2286; *R v Lawless* [2009] EWCA Crim 1308.

[16] L. Malloy, E. Shulman, and E. Cauffman, 'Interrogations, confessions, and guilty pleas among serious adolescent offenders' (2014) 38 *Law and Human Behavior* 181; B. Feld, *Kids, Cops and Confessions* (2013); H. Cleary 'Police Interviewing and Interrogation of Juvenile Suspects' (2014) 38 *Law & Human Behavior* 271.

[17] See n 5, 626.   [18] See R. C. Austin, 'The New Powers of Arrest' [2007] *Crim LR* 459.

[19] PACE, s 25 did allow the police to arrest for non-arrestable offences where the issue of a summons was not practicable, e.g. if they could not be sure of the person's name and address.

loss, damage, or injury; preventing the person from disappearing, and 'to allow the prompt and effective investigation of the offence or of the conduct of the person in question'. Arrest remains discretionary, and the police may still proceed by way of summons in any case, but the criterion of allowing 'prompt and effective investigation' is sufficiently vague that it is little more than a rubber stamp which could justify arrest in any situation where the police wish to question a suspect.

A Code of Practice, Code G, has been issued under PACE, and was amended most recently and considerably in 2012. The Code provides that 'The use of the power [of arrest] must be fully justified and officers exercising the power should consider if the necessary objectives can be met by other, less intrusive means'.[20] Before deciding to arrest, the officer should take account of available facts and information, including claims of innocence.[21]

It is difficult to say how widely or justifiably arrest powers are used. Research on police decision making 'on the street' emphasizes the flexibility of police powers, which allow coercive measures such as arrest to be used for a variety of purposes, some with little connection to crime investigation.[22] Some commentators suggest that PACE led to arrests being carried out on a firmer evidential basis than was previously the case, but others doubt this.[23] After a peak in the year ending March 2008 when police made 1,475,266 arrests, there has been a downward trend: in the year ending March 2017 there were 779,660 arrests, a fall of 12 per cent from the previous year.[24] This may be due to the increased use of voluntary attendance, where an individual attends voluntarily at a police station without having been arrested for the purpose of assisting with an investigation. It is thought that the use of this practice has grown due to a more stringent application of the necessity test, where, for an arrest to be lawful, there must be reasonable grounds for believing that the arrest is necessary.[25] Moreover, there is considerable variation between forces in terms of how they use arrest powers. Notably, and worryingly, the number of arrests in domestic abuse crimes has fallen in about half the forces, and the rate at which domestic abuse perpetrators are being arrested has fallen by 15 per cent across England and Wales.[26]

Although empirical analysis suggests Black and Minority ethnic groups are less likely to commit crime, arrest rates are generally higher across these groups in comparison to the white population.[27] As in previous years, in the year ending March 2017 persons from all Black and Minority ethnic groups were proportionately over one and a half times more likely to be arrested than those who were white, and black individuals were

---

[20] PACE Code G (2012), 1.3.   [21] Ibid, 2.3A and note 2 (new in 2012 Code).

[22] See A. Sanders and R. Young, 'From Suspect to Trial' in M. Maguire, R. Morgan, and R. Reiner (eds), *The Oxford Handbook of Criminology* (4th edn, 2007).

[23] D. Brown, *PACE Ten Years On: A Review of the Research* (1997), 51–5.

[24] Home Office, *Police powers and procedures, England and Wales, year ending 31 March 2017*, Statistical Bulletin 20/17 (2017), 3.2.

[25] HMIC, *PEEL: Police effectiveness 2016: A national overview* (2017), 66, referring to PACE Code G.

[26] Ibid, 18.

[27] Ministry of Justice, *Black, Asian and Minority Ethnic disproportionality in the Criminal Justice System in England and Wales* (2016), 5.1.

over three times more likely to be arrested than those who identified as white.[28] Both black and mixed ethnic women were more than twice as likely to be arrested than white women.[29] Moreover, in 2016 Black, Asian, and Minority ethnic (BAME) children accounted for 26 per cent of all child arrests in England and Wales, and for 60 per cent of all child arrests by the Metropolitan Police Service.[30] Although BAME young males and adults were more likely than white people to be arrested, BAME young females and adults were less likely to be charged by the Crown Prosecution Service (CPS).[31]

On being arrested, a suspect should be told that he is under arrest, and the grounds for the arrest.[32] He must be told 'in simple, non-technical language that he can under-stand, the essential legal and factual grounds for his arrest', although the nature and extent of the information required depends upon the circumstances.[33] He should also be cautioned.[34] Once taken to the police station, there is a designated custody officer who is a police officer of at least sergeant rank[35] who assumes responsibility for the suspect's rights and welfare whilst he is in police custody. At the police station deten-tion is not, in theory, automatic: it must be authorized by the custody officer. PACE provides that a suspect can be detained where the custody officer reasonably believes that detention is necessary 'to secure or preserve evidence . . . or to obtain evidence by questioning him'.[36] Though the 'necessity' criterion might be thought to be relatively demanding, and while the College of Policing states that detention is the 'last resort',[37] research shows that it is very rare for custody officers to refuse to permit detention.[38] Zander describes s 37, on 'Duties of custody officer before charge', as one of the most important sections of PACE,[39] but recent empirical research carried out by Roxanna Dehaghani indicates that s 37 still has little to no impact on custody practices, in that custody officers still fail to act as a 'check' on police powers and routinely authorize detention.[40] Vicky Kemp found that pressure to prioritize police performance targets encouraged senior officers to intervene in custody decisions, so that a consequence of performance management is the potential to undermine the legal protections of those held in police custody.[41]

[28] Home Office, *Police powers and procedures*, 15; Ministry of Justice, *Statistics on Race and the Criminal Justice System 2016* (2017), 24.

[29] Ministry of Justice, n 27.

[30] Howard League, 'Howard League publishes ethnicity analysis of child arrests following the Lammy Re-view', 27 November 2017, https://howardleague.org/news/howard-league-publishes-ethnicity-analysis-of-child-arrests-following-the-lammy-review/.

[31] Ministry of Justice, n 27.   [32] PACE, s 28, Code C, 10.3 and note 10B.

[33] *Fox v UK* (1990) 13 EHRR 157, [40]; *Taylor v Chief Constable of Thames Valley Police* [2004] EWCA Civ 858.

[34] PACE, s 30; Code C, 10.4.   [35] PACE, s 36(3).

[36] PACE, s 37(2). See *Richardson v CC of West Midlands* [2011] EWHC 773 (QB) and *Hayes v CC of Mer-seyside Police* [2011] EWCA Civ 911; *Lord Hanningfield of Chelmsford v Chief Constable of Essex Police* [2013] EWHC 243 (QB).

[37] https://www.app.college.police.uk/app-content/detention-and-custody-2/response-arrest-and-detention/.

[38] Brown, n 23, 57–62.

[39] M. Zander, *Zander on PACE: The Police and Criminal Evidence Act 1984* (7th edn, 2015), 4–10.

[40] R. Dehaghani, 'Automatic Authorisation: An Exploration of the Decision to Detain in Police Custody' [2017] *Crim LR* 187.

[41] V. Kemp, 'PACE, Performance Targets and Legal Protections' [2014] *Crim LR* 278, 282.

Once arrested and taken to a police station, suspects can be detained for a considerable period before being charged. Pre-charge detention can only be authorized where there is insufficient evidence to charge a person and 'the custody officer has reasonable grounds for believing that his detention without being charged is necessary to secure or preserve evidence relating to an offence for which he is under arrest or to obtain such evidence by questioning him'.[42] As with arrest, changes to PACE have expanded powers of detention.[43] All arrestees can be detained for an initial period of 24 hours.[44] After this, a police officer of at least the rank of superintendent can authorize detention for a further 12 hours, taking the total to 36, so long as the person concerned is under arrest for an indictable offence. This may now be done by means of live video link.[45] 'Indictable' is a broad category, comprising all offences other than those which can only be tried in the magistrates' court; it includes offences such as minor theft. During this period, detention should be reviewed periodically by a senior officer: after an initial period of six hours, and then at nine-hour intervals.[46] The evidence suggests that, especially during the initial 24 hours, the process of review is routinized and is not a very effective means of limiting detention to what is necessary.[47] After 36 hours, further detention can only be authorized by the magistrates' court. The magistrates can authorize further detention, 36 hours at a time, up to a maximum of 96 hours.[48] This also may now be done by means of live link.[49] There are wider powers of detention for terrorist offences:[50] if the suspect is being held under the Terrorism Act 2000, he can be detained for up to a total of 14 days.[51]

In practice, detention is usually for a relatively short period: the average is around seven hours,[52] though Kemp found between seven and 12 hours,[53] and figures from the Metropolitan Police in 2016 indicate an average detention time with no solicitor of almost 13 hours, and with a solicitor 16 hours.[54] Kemp, Balmer, and Pleasence found a rise in the average length of detention over recent years, with a difference of around two and a half hours depending on whether legal advice was requested or not.[55] The need for an interpreter was related to large and significant increases in the length of detention.[56] This indicates that, overall, PACE has not restricted the length of detention.

If the suspect dies while in custody, in certain instances the relevant officers may be prosecuted. Section 1(2)(c) of the Corporate Manslaughter and Corporate

---

[42] PACE, s 37(2).   [43] See E. Cape, 'Modernising Police Powers—Again?' [2007] *Crim LR* 934.

[44] PACE, s 41.   [45] PACE, s 45ZA as inserted by the Policing and Crime Act (PCA) 2017.

[46] PACE, s 40.

[47] D. Dixon et al, 'Safeguarding the Rights of Suspects in Police Custody' (1990) 1 *Policing and Society* 115.

[48] PACE, ss 43, 44.   [49] PACE, s 45ZB as inserted by PCA 2017.

[50] Terrorism Act 2000, Sch 8.

[51] The Protection of Freedoms Act 2012 reduced the maximum period from 28 to 14 days.

[52] C. Phillips and D. Brown, *Entry into the Criminal Justice System* (1998), 109.

[53] V. Kemp, N. Balmer, and P. Pleasence, 'Whose Time is it Anyway? Factors Associated with Duration in Police Custody' [2012] *Crim LR* 736, 751.

[54] https://www.met.police.uk/SysSiteAssets/foi-media/metropolitan-police/disclosure_2017/february_2017/information-rights-unit---average-detention-time-for-detainees-who-used-their-right-to-legal-advice-in-the-last-12-months.

[55] Kemp, Balmer, and Pleasence, n 53, 751.   [56] Ibid, 742.

Homicide Act 2007 specifies that the Act's provisions apply to police forces. The 2017 Report of the Independent Review of Deaths and Serious Incidents in Police Custody noted that of eight prosecutions of police officers in connection with a death in custody in the last 15 years, all have ended with acquittals despite unlawful killing verdicts in Coroner's Inquests.[57] 'There are also concerns about the inadequacies of some custody detention officers employed by private companies. This includes the way in which civilian Custody Detention Officers (CDO) perform their duties, as well as training provisions and management lines between CDOs and police officers, particularly custody sergeants.'[58]

It is possible for suspects to be questioned at the police station even if they have not been formally arrested, as some people attend the police station 'voluntarily'. This process, which seems to be increasingly common,[59] avoids some of the regulations imposed by PACE, such as the detention time limits, though there are some protections in s 29 and Code C.[60]

A suspect maybe arrested and then bailed, a condition of bail being to report to the police station at a later time where they may be questioned.[61] At one stage, it seemed that about one-third of arrestees were bailed by police.[62] While bail and remand are considered more fully in Chapter 8, it is worth outlining the contours of 'street bail' and police bail here, as they relate to the investigative stage of the criminal process.

Street bail was introduced in 2003,[63] following a recommendation in the Joint Home Office/Cabinet Office Review of PACE.[64] Code G states: 'Having determined that the necessity criteria have been met and having made the arrest, the officer can then consider the use of street bail on the basis of the effective and efficient progress of the investigation of the offence in question. It gives the officer discretion to compel the person to attend a police station at a date/time that best suits the overall needs of the particular investigation. Its use is not confined to dealing with child care issues or allowing officers to attend to more urgent operational duties and granting street bail does not retrospectively negate the need to arrest.'[65]

While ostensibly this seems to enhance liberty by not entailing immediate detention of the individual, it granted extensive powers to the police to impose bail conditions. This resulted in the control of individuals, often for protracted periods of time.[66] Cape and Edwards suggested that there were strong arguments for the abolition of street

[57] Rt Hon. Dame Elish Angiolini DBE QC, *Report of the Independent Review of Deaths and Serious Incidents in Police Custody* (2017), https://www.gov.uk/government/uploads/system/uploads/attachment_data/file/655401/Report_of_Angiolini_Review_ISBN_Accessible.pdf, [20].

[58] Ibid, [76].   [59] HMIC, *PEEL 2017*, n 25, 66.   [60] Code C, 3.21–3.22.

[61] A. Hucklesby, 'Not Necessarily a Trip to the Police Station: The Introduction of Street Bail' [2004] *Crim LR* 803.

[62] House of Commons Home Affairs Committee, *Police bail*, Seventeenth Report of Session 2014–15, HC 962 (2015).

[63] PACE, ss 30A, 30B, 30C, and 30D as inserted by the Criminal Justice Act 2003, and ss 30CA and 30CB as inserted by the Police and Justice Act 2006.

[64] *Joint Home Office/Cabinet Office Review of PACE* (2002), 23.   [65] Note 2J.

[66] See e.g. *The Times*, 'Police leave businessman on bail for six years', 10 February 2016.

bail, predominantly drawing on Art 5 of the ECHR.[67] Indeed, the Northern Ireland Law Commission recommended its repeal there, citing the lack of a clear legal framework, the lack of transparency, and the potential for net-widening through its use.[68]

Pre-charge police bail concerns persons who have been arrested and taken to a police station, but who are released without having been charged. Such bail may be imposed where there is as yet insufficient evidence to charge a suspect and he is released pending further investigation,[69] or where the police consider that there is sufficient evidence to charge, but the matter must be referred to the CPS for a charging decision.[70]

Street and police bail involved no statutory time limits,[71] no cap on the number of re-bails, and no judicial oversight other than by way of judicial review.[72] Prolonged release on pre-charge bail was challenged unsuccessfully in *R (C) v Chief Constable of A and A*.[73] In addition, there were major concerns about the use of pre-charge bail by reference to ethnicity and other demographic factors, despite a marked lack of statistical data.[74] Moreover, record keeping about re-bail pending charge was found to be poor: while bail management in pre-charge cases is now better regulated, some aspects need to be improved further, such as communication of information about who was due to answer bail and how to determine how often a suspect was re-bailed pending the charging decision.[75]

After some egregiously expansive use of these powers, significant amendments were made by the Policing and Crime Act 2017, though as will be seen these have not mitigated the negative impact on suspects. Section 62 imposes an initial 28-day limit on street bail under s 30A.[76] Further extension is possible only up to three months with the authorization of a senior police officer, and to six months with magistrates' court approval. Section 52 of the 2017 Act now imposes a presumption that where an officer decides that it is appropriate to release an arrested person rather than take him to a police station, release will be without bail, unless bail is necessary and proportionate in all the circumstances and is authorized by a police officer of the rank of inspector or above. Similarly, s 54 amends ss 34 and 37 of PACE to establish a presumption that release of a person whilst an investigation continues should be without bail unless bail preconditions are satisfied. This has resulted in the unfortunate situation whereby the police seem to be releasing many suspects under investigation without bail, leaving them without any indication of whether the investigation is continuing, how long it may take, and whether they will have to return to the police station.[77]

---

[67] E. Cape and R. Edwards, 'Police Bail Without Charge: The Human Rights Implications' (2010) 69 *Cambridge LJ* 529, 560.

[68] Northern Ireland Law Commission, *Report: Bail in Criminal Proceedings*, NILC 14 (2012), paras 2.36–2.37.

[69] PACE, ss 37(2), 34(2), and 34(5).   [70] PACE, s 37(7)(a).

[71] A Home Office Circular on street bail suggested a normal maximum of six weeks: HO Circular 61/2003, Criminal Justice Act 2003: Changes Affecting PACE Section 4 Bail elsewhere than at a Police Station.

[72] E. Cape, 'The Police Bail Provisions of the Policing and Crime Act 2017' [2017] *Crim LR* 587, 589.

[73] [2006] EWHC 2352 (Admin).   [74] Cape, n 72.

[75] HMCPSI and HMIC, *Joint Inspection of the Provision of Charging Decisions* (2015), para 5.26.

[76] See n 71.   [77] Cape, n 72, 597.

Section 63 imposes a regime of time limits and extensions for pre-charge bail. A senior police officer or prosecutor may extend pre-charge bail to three months, and magistrates' court authorization is needed beyond this to six months. There must be reasonable grounds: to suspect that the person on bail is guilty of the offence for which they were arrested and are on bail, to believe either that further time is needed for the police to make a charging decision or that further investigation is necessary, to believe that the charging decision or investigation is being conducted diligently and expeditiously, and releasing the person on bail must continue to be both necessary and proportionate in all the circumstances.[78] While this purports to improve matters for suspects, initial evidence is to the contrary.[79] Research is needed on police practice following these significant legal changes.

(B) LEGAL ADVICE

The Royal Commission on Criminal Procedure in 1981 saw access to legal advice as going some way to 'minimising the effects of arrest and custody on the suspect'.[80] So, the right to legal advice is guaranteed by s 58 of PACE, which provides that 'A person arrested and held in custody in a police station or other premises shall be entitled, if he so requests, to consult a solicitor privately at any time.' Clearly, this right would be of little value if few suspects could afford legal advice, or if they did not know whom to contact, so when PACE was introduced a system of duty solicitors was put in place, providing free legal advice on a 24-hour basis—though suspects could also contact a nominated solicitor, as many did.

On arrival at the police station, an arrestee will be booked in and at this point should be offered access to legal advice. The right is absolute, in that it cannot legally be denied, though in strictly defined circumstances s 58 allows the police to delay access to legal advice. The courts have enforced a strict reading of s 58,[81] and it now seems to be rare for the police to delay access. Before PACE, around 10 per cent of suspects asked for legal advice,[82] whereas research in the 1990s found that around 40 per cent of suspects asked for legal advice,[83] and a more recent figure was 60 per cent, though this was based on research at just two police stations.[84] A larger scale study of 30,921 electronic custody records relating to 25,005 persons, across 44 police stations in four police force areas in 2009, indicated that 45.3 per cent of detainees (counting each detention period separately) requested advice, with 77.5 per cent of requests resulting in

---

[78] PACE, s 47ZC.   [79] Cape, n 72, 597.

[80] Royal Commission on Criminal Procedure, *The Investigation and Prosecution of Criminal Offences in England and Wales: The Law and Procedure* (1981), para 4.77.

[81] *R v Samuel* [1988] 1 QB 615.

[82] The figures in the literature vary considerably: see D. Brown, *PACE Ten Years On: A Review of the Research* (1997), 95.

[83] T. Bucke, R. Street, and D. Brown, *The Right of Silence: The Impact of the CJPOA 1994* (2000), 21.

[84] L. Skinns, 'I'm a Detainee; Get me Out of Here: Predictors of Access to Custodial Legal Advice in Public and Privatized Police Custody Areas in England and Wales (2009) 49 *BJ Crim* 399, 407. There was noticeable variation between the two research sites, with more requests for advice at the privately managed police station.

solicitor consultations (35.1 per cent overall).[85] The figures for suspects were 44.9 per cent and 81.3 per cent, respectively (36.5 per cent overall), and for other detainees they were 49.8 per cent and 50.6 per cent, respectively (25.2 per cent overall).[86] This study found significant variance both between stations and between forces.

Police have some ability to manipulate suspects' requests for legal advice in the manner in which they inform them of it:[87] not all suspects are told that legal advice is free, nor informed of their rights clearly, factors that are likely to influence uptake of legal advice.[88] However, Cape and Hodgson's research indicates a welcome change in police culture: the role or presence of the lawyer at the police station has gained a degree of acceptance, and so now usually suspects are informed of their right of access to a lawyer in neutral terms.[89] Code C now provides that if the detainee declines to exercise the right the officer should point out that the right includes speaking with a solicitor on the telephone.[90]

Although requesting advice does not always mean that advice is received, there has been a slow but steady increase in this respect. In the 1990s, research found that of the nearly 38 per cent requesting advice, 34 per cent received it,[91] whereas by 2007 Skinns' study found that 60 per cent requested legal advice and 48 per cent received it.[92] In 2009, Pleasence et al found that 45.3 per cent of detainees requested advice of which 77.5 per cent of requests resulted in solicitor consultations (35.1 per cent overall),[93] for figures for suspects were 44.9 per cent and 81.3 per cent, respectively (36.5 per cent overall), and for other detainees they were 49.8 per cent and 50.6 per cent, respectively (25.2 per cent overall).[94]

Although suspects who have requested legal advice should not be interviewed until they have received it, some may drop their requests, and this may well happen because of concerns about the delay that waiting for contact with a solicitor entails. Skinns found that suspects were concerned about delay, and on average had to wait nearly four hours for legal advice;[95] other research has found that those arrested during the night, when delays are likely to be longest, are more likely to cancel requests.[96] Blackstock et al also ascertained that release from police custody was often a major concern of suspects, and that for some the decision whether to request access to a solicitor depended

---

[85] P. Pleasence, V. Kemp, and N. Balmer, 'The Justice Lottery? Police Station Advice 25 Years On from PACE' [2011] *Crim LR* 3, 13.

[86] Ibid; also see V. Kemp, *Transforming Legal Aid: Access to Criminal Defence Services* (2010).

[87] A. Sanders and L. Bridges, 'Access to Legal Advice and Police Malpractice' [1990] *Crim LR* 494. Skinns, n 84, also found claims that police would use conversations during transit to the police station as a means of dissuading suspects from accessing legal advice.

[88] L. Skinns, '"Let's Get it Over With": Early Findings on the Factors Affecting Detainees' Access to Custodial Legal Advice' (2009) 19 *Policing and Society* 58, 66.

[89] E. Cape and J. Hodgson, 'The Right of Access to a Lawyer at Police Stations: Making the European Union Directive Work in Practice' (2014) 5 *New J Eur Crim L* 450, 458.

[90] Code C, 6.5.

[91] T. Bucke and D. Brown, *In Police Custody: Police Powers and Suspects' Rights under the Revised PACE Codes of Practice* (1997), 23.

[92] Skinns, n 84, 407.   [93] Pleasence, Kemp, and Balmer, n 85, 13.   [94] Ibid; also see Kemp, n 86.

[95] Skinns, n 88, 58.   [96] Phillips and Brown, n 52, 64.

upon their perception of how long they would be detained.[97] Suspects are concerned about the police inferring guilt from requests for legal advice,[98] though it appears that suspects also decline legal advice both because they believed they were innocent or because they believed themselves guilty.[99]

Black suspects are more likely to request legal advice and young people less likely to do so, although for the latter this was because they are suspected of less serious matters.[100] Kemp et al found that 15- and 16-year-olds were significantly more likely to request a solicitor than other detainees, and request rates increased markedly with offence seriousness for all ages of young people.[101] Two findings of particular concern in their study are that 10- to 13-year-olds, the most vulnerable age group, are the least likely to request and receive legal advice, and that 43 per cent of young people do not request to see a solicitor despite going on to be charged.[102]

The qualitative work by Vicky Kemp raises questions about the extent to which PACE continues to provide sufficient safeguards in relation to legal representation for those held in police custody.[103] Many suspects seem to be unaware of how a solicitor could assist them in the police station,[104] and there was a common perception among suspects that having a solicitor would lead to delays. Helping to counteract such a view in one police station was the high visibility of solicitors in the custody suite, which seemed to have a positive effect on increasing requests for legal advice. On the other hand, in two police stations where solicitors had been excluded from waiting around in the custody suite, there was evidence of police ploys using the threat of delays in order to discourage suspects from having legal advice, and the arrangements for providing access to legal advice impacted on uptake.[105]

Continued pressure to reduce spending on legal aid has had a number of effects on police station legal advice.[106] Free legal advice for certain less serious offences, including driving with excess alcohol and all non-imprisonable offences, is now restricted to advice delivered over the telephone. If detainees wish to consult a solicitor in person, they will not receive legal aid for any fees incurred. Solicitors are also now paid a fixed fee for attending the police station, rather than being paid per hour, and this may obviously encourage them to offer advice over the telephone rather than in person, though the fee for providing advice by telephone is much lower.[107] Cape and Hodgson found that most lawyer/client consultations were relatively short: an average of 26 minutes

[97] J. Blackstock, E. Cape, J. Hodgson, A. Ogorodova, and T. Spronken, *Inside Police Custody: An Empirical Account of Suspects' Rights in Four Jurisdictions* (2014), 275.

[98] L. Skinns, 'The Right to Legal Advice in the Police Station: Past, Present and Future' [2011] *Crim LR* 19, 26.

[99] Ibid, 35.   [100] Ibid, 23.

[101] V. Kemp, P. Pleasence, and N. Balmer, 'Children, Young People and Requests for Police Station Legal Advice: 25 years on from PACE' (2011) 11 *Youth Justice* 28.

[102] Ibid, 37.

[103] V. Kemp, '"No Time for a Solicitor": Implications for Delays on the Take-Up of Legal Advice' [2013] *Crim LR* 184.

[104] Ibid, 194.   [105] Ibid, 201.

[106] For a critical analysis, underlining the lack of independent research on how the changes affect detainees, see L. Bridges and E. Cape, *CDS Direct: Flying in the Face of the Evidence* (2008).

[107] Cape and Hodgson, n 89, 465.

in England and Wales.[108] Indeed, Kemp suggests that the introduction of fixed fees for police station legal advice means solicitors tend to concentrate on the offence rather than on the wider issues concerning their clients' detention.[109] This means that they tend to get involved in cases at the time of the police interview, which can be many hours following a request for legal advice. Overall, lawyers are placed in the unfortunate position of having to choose between acting in clients' best interests or in the interests of their business, the courts, and the government.[110] Moreover, some solicitors are not particularly zealous in defence of their clients,[111] and many legal advisers may prioritize the cultivation and maintenance of good relationships with the police over the robust, adversarial defence of one client.[112]

Overall, the lesson to draw from the foregoing is that while legal advice is undoubtedly an important safeguard for suspects, it would be a mistake to exaggerate its impact. The majority of suspects still do not receive legal advice and do not have a legal adviser with them during police questioning.

(C) INTERPRETATION

Persons involved in the criminal process whose first language is not English are particularly vulnerable,[113] as are those with speech or hearing impediments. Code C.13 deals with the role of interpreters at the investigative stage, and incorporates the requirements set out in Directive 2010/64/EU on the right to interpretation and translation in criminal proceedings. Before the Directive came into force in 2013, there were well-established rules on interpretation and translation, with Code C requiring, inter alia, that a person must not be interviewed in the absence of an interpreter if they have difficulty understanding English, the interviewer cannot speak the suspect's language, and the person wants an interpreter present.[114] Nonetheless, compliance with the Directive required some amendments to Code C, regarding access to a qualified interpreter and written translations of essential documents.[115] Chief police officers now must ensure that appropriately qualified and independent interpreters are available for suspects or detained persons, and for providing translations of essential documents.[116] Code C provides that 'the arrangements made and the quality of interpretation and translation provided shall be sufficient to "*safeguard the fairness of the proceedings, in particular by ensuring that suspected or accused persons have knowledge of the cases against them and are able to exercise their right of defence*".[117] This means that the suspect must be able to understand their position and be able to communicate effectively with police

---

[108] Ibid, 468. This is compared with less than 15 minutes in Scotland (on the telephone), 20 minutes in France, and 21 minutes in the Netherlands.

[109] Kemp, n 103, 202.

[110] L. Welsh, 'The effects of changes to legal aid on lawyers' professional identity and behaviour in summary criminal cases: a case study' (2017) 44 *Journal of Law and Society* 559, 561.

[111] Gudjonsson, n 5, 105.   [112] H. Quirk, *The Rise and Fall of the Right of Silence* (2016), 92.

[113] Kemp, n 86, [3.4].

[114] R. Gwynedd Parry, 'The Curse of Babel and the Criminal Process' [2014] *Crim LR* 802, 805–6.

[115] Ibid.   [116] Code C, 13.1.   [117] Code C, 13.1A.

officers, interviewers, solicitors, and appropriate adults as provided for by this and any other Code in the same way as a suspect who can speak and understand English and who does not have a hearing or speech impediment and who would therefore not require an interpreter.[118] Code C also refers to the 'provision of a written translation of all documents considered essential for the person to exercise their right of defence and to "safeguard the fairness of the proceedings".[119]

In the case of a person making a statement under caution in a language other than English:

(a) the interpreter shall record the statement in the language it is made;

(b) the person shall be invited to sign it;

(c) an official English translation shall be made in due course.[120]

Parry rightly argues that there are three principal and interrelated challenges to implementation of the Directive, namely capacity, quality, and cost, and that a cultural shift is needed within the criminal justice system, whereby the translator and interpreter become more imbedded, regulated, and mainstreamed within the corps of criminal justice personnel.[121]

(D) PRE-INTERVIEW DISCLOSURE

Pre-interview disclosure refers to the police disclosing why a person is suspected of an offence before questioning them. There may be good reasons for not disclosing too much at the start of an interview. The police worry that full disclosure of the evidence—for example, of a DNA match between suspect and scene of crime—will allow the suspect to fabricate an exculpatory story.[122] One of the themes of investigative interviewing is that the suspect should give an account which should then be challenged in terms of its fit with the evidence. Here, partial disclosure may be helpful; indeed, psychological research suggests that while it is very difficult to tell whether a suspect is lying by observing his demeanour, selective disclosure of evidence may be an effective way of detecting deceit.[123]

As the Court of Appeal put it in *R v W*, 'there is simply no rule of law or practice requiring the police to disclose the full extent of their relevant evidence before questioning a suspect'.[124] Then, in June 2014, the EU adopted the Directive on the right to information in criminal proceedings which, inter alia, requires the police to disclose why a person is suspected of an offence before questioning them. Code C was revised to encompass this new pre-interview disclosure requirement:

Before a person is interviewed, they and, if they are represented, their solicitor must be given sufficient information to enable them to understand the nature of any such offence,

---

[118] Code C, 13.1A.   [119] Code C, 13.1A.   [120] Code C, 13.4.   [121] Parry, n 114, 805–6.

[122] See HMIC, *Under the Microscope Refocused: A Revisit to the Thematic Inspection Report on Scientific and Technical Support* (2002), 10–11.

[123] M. Ioannou and L. Hammond, 'The detection of deception within investigative contexts: Key challenges and core issues' (2015) 12 *J Investigative Psychology and Offender Profiling* 107–18.

[124] [2006] EWCA Crim 1292, [8].

and why they are suspected of committing it . . . in order to allow for the effective exercise of the rights of the defence. However, whilst the information must always be sufficient for the person to understand the nature of any offence . . . this does not require the disclosure of details at a time which might prejudice the criminal investigation.[125]

The Notes for Guidance specify that:

> The requirement in paragraph 11.1A for a suspect to be given sufficient information about the offence applies prior to the interview and whether or not they are legally represented. What is sufficient will depend on the circumstances of the case, but it should normally include, as a minimum, a description of the facts relating to the suspected offence that are known to the officer, including the time and place in question. This aims to avoid suspects being confused or unclear about what they are supposed to have done and to help an innocent suspect to clear the matter up more quickly.[126]

As Sukumar et al note, even with the implementation of the EU Directive, the police can withhold much of their evidence before questioning a suspect.[127] How and when the police disclose their evidence to suspects and their lawyers during the interview process is still largely unregulated in England and Wales.[128] Moreover, police forces vary in their practices of recording the police disclosure that is provided to lawyers.[129] Ed Cape reminds us that the police are well aware of the strategic advantage that power over the release of information gives to them, and this is recognized by the use of 'phased disclosure' strategies particularly during the investigation of more serious offences.[130] There is benefit in this: it has been found that when evidence was disclosed gradually (but revealed later), interviews were generally both more skilled and involved the gaining of comprehensive accounts, whereas when evidence was disclosed either early or very late, interviews were found to be both less skilled and less likely to involve this outcome.[131] Regardless, a study carried out by Sukumar found that lawyers given pre-interview disclosure provided considerably more informed legal advice compared to those who were only provided with disclosure during the hypothetical police interview. This provides further evidence that pre-interview disclosure is essential for lawyers to deliver case-specific legal advice to suspects.[132]

---

[125] Code C, 11.1A (same wording in 2014 and 2018 revisions).   [126] Code C, note 11ZA.

[127] D. Sukumar, J. Hodgson, and K. Wade, 'Behind Closed Doors: Live Observations of Current Police Station Disclosure Practices and Lawyer–Client Consultations' [2016] *Crim LR* 900, 903.

[128] Ibid, 901: also J. Clough and A. Jackson, 'The Game is Up: Proposals on Incorporating Effective Disclosure Requirements into Criminal Investigations' [2012] *The Criminal Lawyer* 3, 4.

[129] Sukumar et al, n 127, 905.

[130] E. Cape, 'Transposing the EU Directive on the Right to Information: A Firecracker or a Damp Squib?' [2015] *Crim LR* 48, 57; D. Walsh, B. Milne, and R. Bull, 'One way or another? Criminal investigators' beliefs regarding the disclosure of evidence in interviews with suspects in England and Wales' (2016) 31 *J Police and Crim Psychology* 127.

[131] D. Walsh and R. Bull, 'Interviewing suspects: Examining the association between skills, questioning, evidence disclosure, and interview outcomes' (2015) 21 *Psychology, Crime & Law* 661.

[132] D. Sukumar, J. Hodgson, and K. Wade, 'How the timing of police evidence disclosure impacts custodial legal advice' [2016] *Int J Evidence & Proof* 200.

5.3 QUESTIONING AND INTERVIEWING SUSPECTS

(A) THE RULES

The legal regime governing the questioning and interviewing of suspects is to be found in PACE Code C,[133] and to a lesser extent in case law. Interviews after arrest should take place in the police station, as to permit otherwise would allow evasion of the police station regime protections, like access to legal advice and the recording of interviews, though there are exceptions if gaining information from a suspect is urgent.[134] Of course, the rule against interviewing outside the police station depends on the definition of 'interview': it is 'the questioning of a person regarding their involvement or suspected involvement in a criminal offence or offences which, under paragraph 10.1, must be carried out under caution'.[135] Sometimes the police will question a person regarding an incident and have their suspicions raised through the response to their questions. If questioning continues, at some point a dividing line will be crossed and the questioning will become an interview. As noted, Code C defines an interview in terms of whether the questions asked are about involvement in an offence.[136] Nevertheless, the police might claim that a suspect made admissions freely before arriving at the police station. In these circumstances, anything said should be put to the suspect at the beginning of the formal interview, giving him an opportunity to confirm or deny it.[137]

It is unclear how often suspects are interviewed outside the police station. While in some instances the courts enforce the Code C definition of interview relatively strictly,[138] no caution is needed for those questioned as non-suspects,[139] and statements made outside the police station may be admitted.[140] Given the concerns here, and the fact that an admission denied by the defendant will have little evidential value, this seems to be an area where a strict rule of inadmissibility—unless the statement is either recorded or later confirmed by the suspect—would be appropriate.[141] Any decision to admit such evidence would create incentives for the police to try to gain admissions outside the police station regime, or to 'verbal' suspects in ascribing a statement to them falsely.

In the past decade, concerns had been raised about the trend of conducting interviews at the suspect's home.[142] While ostensibly this might seem attractive to someone anxious about attending a police station, it enabled officers to exploit a gap in the

---

[133] Updated most recently in 2018.   [134] Code C, 11.1.   [135] Code C, 11.1A.

[136] Code C, 11.1A and 10.1.   [137] Code C, 11.4.

[138] E.g. *Okafor* [1994] 3 All ER 741; cf *R v Senior and Senior* [2004] Cr App R 215; *R v Bhambra* [2008] EWCA Crim 2317.

[139] *R v Shillibier* [2006] EWCA Crim 793.

[140] Statements might also be made inside the police station, before the formal interviewing process has begun: *R v Van Gelderen* [2008] EWCA Crim 422.

[141] Cf *Van Gelderen*, ibid. A statement attributed to the suspect by various police officers was held admissible, despite the fact that the statement was quickly denied when put to him at interview.

[142] R. Murray, 'Police interviewing loophole must be tackled urgently', *Law Society Gazette*, 26 April 2012.

PACE Codes which did not require them to inform the person of his right to consult a lawyer. The 2018 revision of Code C now provides that '[t]he rights, entitlements and safeguards that apply to the conduct and recording of interviews with suspects are not diminished simply because the interview is arranged on a voluntary basis'.[143] An officer interviewing a suspect on a voluntary basis must carry out many of the duties of the custody officer—inform the suspect of their right to a lawyer (and contact the Defence Solicitor Call Centre if a lawyer is requested), check whether an appropriate adult or interpreter is required, provide written notification of rights, and record the action taken.[144]

Particular issues arise in the content of questioning and interviewing young and vulnerable suspects, as they may be more suggestible and susceptible to harm. Code C provides that 'juveniles'[145] and the vulnerable[146] must not be interviewed without an appropriate adult.[147] The appropriate adult may be a relative or guardian, or a responsible adult who is independent from the police inquiry, that is, they must not be a police officer nor someone employed for, or engaged in, police work.[148] They are required to facilitate communication, advise the suspect, as well as ensure that the police are acting properly and fairly.[149] In addition to their presence at interview, an appropriate adult should also be present at other stages of the process such as charging, when cautions are given, and when warnings in relation to adverse inferences are given. The custody officer is responsible for implementing the appropriate adult safeguard, which entails that she identify that the suspect requires an appropriate adult.[150] As Roxanna Dehaghani reminds us, neither PACE nor Code C provide custody officers with information on how vulnerability should, or can, be identified.[151]

Now a person in police detention may be interviewed using a live link.[152] The custody officer must be satisfied that the live link to be used provides for accurate and secure communication with the suspect.[153] Each decision must take account of the age,

---

[143] Code C, 3.21.   [144] Code C, 3.21A and 3.21B.

[145] Code C, 1.5: 'Anyone who appears to be under 18, shall, in the absence of clear evidence that they are older, be treated as a juvenile.'

[146] According to Code C, 1.13 (d), 'vulnerable' applies to any person who, because of a mental health condition or mental disorder: (i) may have difficulty understanding or communicating effectively about the full implications for them of any procedures and processes connected with their arrest/detention/voluntary attendance at a police station and the exercise of their rights and entitlements; (ii) does not appear to understand the significance of what they are told, questions asked, or of their replies; or (iii) appears to be particularly prone to becoming confused and unclear about their position; or providing unreliable, misleading or incriminating information without knowing or wishing to do so; accepting or acting on suggestions from others without consciously knowing or wishing to do so; or readily agreeing to suggestions or proposals without any protest or question.

[147] Code C, 11.15. This is a statutory duty for young people (Crime and Disorder Act 1998, s 38(4)(a)) but not for vulnerable adults: see R. Dehaghani, 'Custody Officers, Code C and Constructing Vulnerability: Implications for Policy and Practice' (2016) 11 *Policing* 74.

[148] Code C, 1.7; note 1F.

[149] Code C, 11.17; *Home Office Guide for Appropriate Adults* (2011), https://www.gov.uk/government/uploads/system/uploads/attachment_data/file/117682/appropriate-adults-guide.pdf.

[150] Code C, 3.5.   [151] Dehaghani, n 147, 75.   [152] PACE, s 39, as amended by PCA 2017, s 75.

[153] Code C, 12.9A.

gender, and vulnerability of the suspect, the nature and circumstances of the offence and the investigation, and the impact on the suspect of carrying out the interview by means of a live link. For this reason, the custody officer must consider whether the ability of the particular suspect to communicate confidently and effectively for the purpose of the interview is likely to be adversely affected or otherwise undermined or limited if the interviewing officer is not physically present and a live link is used. While this may seem to be convenient and efficient, the impact on individuals and on the proceedings overall is underexplored. There is evidence that video hearings reduce defendants' understanding of, and respect for, the process,[154] and that defendants are less likely to take up legal advice when proceedings are virtual.[155] It remains to be seen whether interviews are affected comparably.

The suspect must be cautioned at the start of the interview.[156] After the changes to the right to silence were introduced, the caution has been in the form: 'You do not have to say anything. But it may harm your defence if you do not mention when questioned something which you later rely on in Court. Anything you do say may be given in evidence.'[157] The caution is relatively complex and, given the level of intellectual disadvantage among police suspects, there are considerable doubts about how well it is understood.[158]

The issue of the caution was complicated further by the decision of the European Court of Human Rights (ECtHR) in *Murray v UK*.[159] Here it was held that a suspect's Art 6 right to a fair trial was breached when he was denied access to legal advice in a situation where adverse inferences could be drawn from his failure to mention facts at interview.[160] As is explored in section 5.3(B), the relevant provisions have therefore been amended to prevent the drawing of adverse inferences from suspects who have not had access to legal advice, but this means that the standard caution will sometimes be misleading. Thus, if the suspect is to be interviewed outside the police station, or before consulting with a legal adviser who he has requested, or after he has been charged, the 'old' caution must be given: 'You do not have to say anything, but anything you do

---

[154] Transform Justice, *Defendants on video—conveyor belt justice or a revolution in access?* (2017), http://www.transformjustice.org.uk/wp-content/uploads/2017/10/Disconnected-Thumbnail-2.pdf.

[155] M. Terry, S. Johnson, and P. Thompson, *Virtual Court pilot: Outcome evaluation*, Ministry of Justice Research Series 21/10 (2010).

[156] Code C, 10.1. This is distinct from a police caution as a form of disposal—considered in Ch 6.

[157] Code C, 10.5.

[158] See M. Hughes, S. Bain, E. Gilchrist, and J. Boyle, 'Does providing a written version of the police caution improve comprehension in the general population?' (2013) 19 *Psychology, Crime & Law* 549–64.

[159] (1996) 22 EHRR 29.

[160] Cf *R v Ibrahim* [2008] EWCA Crim 880, holding that confessions made during an interview where legal advice has been denied, as well as inferences from lies, are admissible. In *Ibrahim v UK* (2015) 61 EHRR 9, the ECtHR held that the Terrorism Act 2000 struck an appropriate balance between the suspect's right to legal advice and the need in exceptional cases to enable the police to obtain information necessary to protect the public. Whether statements made by a suspect made during a police interview in the absence of a lawyer should be admitted at trial depended on whether doing so would cause him undue prejudice, taking into account the fairness of the proceedings as a whole. In the case of individuals suspected of having detonated bombs in central London, delaying access to legal advice had been a justified interference with Art 6(3)(c) and had not prejudiced their right to a fair trial.

say may be given in evidence.' Some suspects, at different points in time, will be given first one caution and then the other. Code C contains a form of words to explain the change,[161] but there must again be doubts about comprehensibility.

An accurate record should be made of all interviews, regardless of where they take place.[162] This should be an important safeguard, though a Criminal Justice Joint Inspectorate report in 2015 found that police summaries of interviews for the case file were inadequate in 25 per cent of the cases reviewed. The style, quality, and detail of the interview summaries varied considerably: some were too long and others did not contain any details of the questions that were put to the defendant in a 'no comment' interview.[163] The revised Code E requires all interviews of suspects conducted under caution, whether under arrest or as a volunteer, to be recorded using an 'authorised recording device', as long as such a device is available in working order and the location of the interview is suitable for such a device to be used.[164] The explanation in the Code of an 'authorised recording device' extends the range of devices that may be used to record suspect interviews: it does not specifically refer to body-worn video but such devices may be used if they comply with the revised operating specifications and the interview is conducted in accordance with the Code.[165] As Ed Cape notes, a major concern for many defence lawyers is whether this will encourage police officers to conduct interviews away from police stations.[166] Johnston and Smith characterize this as part of 'a wholesale move away from engaging the "formal" mechanisms of the PACE regulatory structure in favour of investigation based on informal, voluntary, and consensual interaction with suspects'.[167]

Despite its benefits in terms of police behaviour, audiovisual recording may bring other dangers. In an Australian study, Dixon found that judges were keen to play the tapes in court, and that judges and prosecutors believed that much could be read into the suspect's demeanour.[168] But demeanour is a poor guide to veracity at the best of times,[169] and will be even more so when the subject is seen under the stressful conditions of police questioning. Moreover, producing a transcript or summary may

---

[161] Code C, Annex C.   [162] Code C, 11.7.

[163] HMIC, *Witness for the prosecution: Identifying victim and witness vulnerability in criminal case files* (2015), 6.

[164] See generally Police and Criminal Evidence Act 1984 (PACE)—Code E Revised Code of Practice on Audio Recording Interviews with Suspects (2018), 2.1; also see Police and Criminal Evidence Act 1984 (PACE)—Code F Revised Code of Practice on Visual Recording with Sound of Interviews with Suspects (2018).

[165] Home Office, *Police and Criminal Evidence Act 1984 ('PACE') Codes of Practice Consultation Response to Home Office consultation on PACE Codes C (Detention), E (Audio recording of interviews with suspects), F (Visual recording of interviews with suspects) and H (Detention—terrorism)* (2018).

[166] E. Cape, 'Recording interviews with body-worn cameras: the latest PACE codes consultation', *The Justice Gap*, 5 November 2017. Also see 'Special Issue: Looking beyond the Lens: The Socio-Technical Implications of Body-Worn Cameras' (2018) 12 *Policing* Issue 1.

[167] E. Johnston and T. Smith, 'The digital revolution: Body worn cameras and street interviews' (2017) 181 *Criminal Law and Justice Weekly* 769.

[168] D. Dixon with G. Travers, *Interrogating Images: Audio-Visually Recorded Police Questioning of Suspects* (2007), 233–6.

[169] I. Coyle and D. Thomson, 'Opening up a can of worms: how do decision-makers decide when witnesses are telling the truth?' (2014) 21 *Psychiatry, Psychology & Law* 475.

introduce inaccuracies,[170] though modern technology has reduced costs and error somewhat. The Criminal Practice Directions provide that if the record is agreed there is usually no need for the audio or video recording to be played in court.[171]

Another limitation to the recording of interviews is that in some cases the police may rehearse what is to be said on tape, or exert pressure on suspects, before the formal interview begins. This is a further reason for concern about what is said outside the police station. Inside the station, cell visits by officers are meant to be recorded, but it is difficult to ensure against rule-breaking completely.[172] Most custody suites are now covered by CCTV, but coverage is unlikely to be absolute.[173] For instance, Skinns found evidence that 'off the record' conversations still took place, both during the journey to the police station and within it, for example when suspects were taken out to the exercise yard for a cigarette.[174]

Lengthy interviewing of suspects is problematic. In a difficult or complex case it may be justified, but in some cases prolonging the interview process may wear down and confuse the suspect. Code C contains rules on breaks between interviews for refreshments and requires suspects to have at least eight hours rest in 24, free from questioning,[175] but there is no cap on the cumulative length of questioning, other than the time limits on detention. These are not inconsiderable, as was seen earlier. Even with rules on the police station environment, the potential effects of custody on suspects should not be underestimated. Suspects are likely to be nervous and uncertain. They have little control over the environment in which they find themselves. Many complain of lack of sleep—something which has been found to impair the ability to cope with questioning.[176]

Code C does provide that questioning should end when the police have gathered a certain amount of information. The interview process should cease when the officer in charge of the investigation:

> is satisfied all the questions they consider relevant to obtaining accurate and reliable information about the offence have been put to the suspect, this includes allowing the suspect an opportunity to give an innocent explanation and asking questions to test if the explanation is accurate and reliable, e.g. to clear up ambiguities or clarify what the suspect said;
> . . . has taken account of any other available evidence; and
> . . . reasonably believes there is sufficient evidence to provide a realistic prospect of conviction for that offence. . . .[177]

PACE and its Codes regulate the environment in which interviewing takes place, but say little, however, about how interviews should be conducted. Code C lays down some

---

[170] See Royal Commission on Criminal Justice, *Report* (1993), ch 4, paras 73–80; Gudjonsson, n 5, 85.
[171] CPD, V Evidence 16C4.
[172] M. McConville, 'Videotaping Interrogations: Police Behaviour On and Off Camera' [1992] *Crim LR* 532.
[173] Another safeguard lies with custody visitors, who are volunteers who make random, unannounced visits to police custody to check on the welfare of detainees though their effectiveness is debatable: see J. Kendall, *Regulating Police Detention: Voices from Behind Closed Doors* (2018).
[174] Skinns, n 84, 409 and n 88, 66–7.   [175] Code C, 12.2.   [176] Gudjonsson, n 5, 31.
[177] Code C, 11.6.

basic rules: questioning should not be oppressive, and the police should not offer inducements such as release on bail in return for a confession.[178] However, the situation
as regards the sentence discount for a plea of guilty is unclear. As we will see in Chapter
10, those who plead guilty can obtain a sentence discount: the maximum reduction
'should only be given when a guilty plea has been indicated at the first stage of the
proceedings'.[179] If the police bring the sentence discount to the suspect's attention, does
this constitute an inducement that would breach Code C, and potentially render any
confession inadmissible? While it is not obvious why a statement that the full discount
will only be forthcoming if the suspect confesses should be different to an offer to
release on bail, a court that reached this conclusion would be faced with difficult questions about the voluntary nature of *any* guilty plea tendered in the hope of a discount,
and about the current policy of making the discount as widely known as possible.
What we do know is that some police forces have brought the sentence discount to the
attention of suspects at interview. In *Attorney General's References (Nos 14 and 15 of
2006)*, the Court of Appeal observed:

> There is a further reason why it would not be just to reduce Webster's discount in order to
> reflect the strength of the case against him. When being interviewed by the Hertfordshire
> constabulary, according to the practice then prevailing in that district, he was shown a
> notice that stated that if he admitted guilt at that interview, which was the first reasonable
> opportunity, he would receive a maximum reduction of sentence of one third. He con-
> firmed in answer to questions that he understood this to be the position and then went on
> to admit his participation in the offences.[180]

Hertfordshire Police had presumably concluded that their policy complied with Code
C, and the Court of Appeal offered no criticism—though in this case the defendant
did not challenge his confession. However inconsistent this seems, it may be that the
sentence discount constitutes a legal inducement. In this context, it is worth noting
that similar questions arise under s 73 of the Serious Organised Crime and Police Act
2005, which recognizes that defendants may be offered a reduced sentence in return
for assisting the prosecution. This was brought to the suspect's attention during police
questioning in *Ibrahim*,[181] but the admissibility of any resulting confession has not yet
been raised in court.

A few further guidelines on the interview process may be found in the case law.
As under Code C, oppression is outlawed, but the definition is narrow: confronting
the suspect with disturbing information is not regarded as oppressive.[182] In addition, a confession may be excluded if it was obtained in conditions likely to lead to
its being unreliable, or if admitting it is likely to make the trial unfair.[183] These requirements—discussed in more detail later—offer limited guidance to questioners.

---

[178] Code C, 11.5.
[179] Sentencing Council, *Reduction in Sentence for a Guilty Plea Definitive Guideline* (2017), 8.
[180] [2006] EWCA Crim 1335, [54].
[181] See n 160, [66]. This was in the context of a 'safety interview' with a terrorist suspect.
[182] PACE, s 76, interpreted in *Fulling* [1987] 2 All ER 75; see also *Foster* [2003] EWCA Crim 178.
[183] PACE, ss 76, 78.

To gain more idea of how interviews are actually conducted, it is necessary to turn to the empirical research.

After the miscarriages of justice of the 1980s and early 1990s, much effort was put into training officers to use less aggressive, 'investigative' interviewing styles.[184] The current model, which was introduced in 1992 and is informed by psychological research, goes under the mnemonic PEACE: *Planning and preparation; Engage and explain; Account, clarification and challenge; Closure; Evaluate.*[185] In essence, the idea is not simply to seek the suspect's assent to the police version of events, but to obtain an account from the suspect which is then challenged on the basis of any evidence the police have. Compliance has been uneven, and its impact questionable.[186] Clarke et al, drawing on 174 interviews with suspects from six police forces in England and Wales, concluded that although PEACE-trained officers conducted longer interviews, there were no other statistical differences in performance or skills.[187]

(B) THE RIGHT TO SILENCE

It was noted earlier that, despite the recommendations of the Royal Commission on Criminal Justice, major changes to the right to silence were introduced by the Criminal Justice and Public Order Act 1994. This legislation does not require suspects to answer questions, either during interview or at trial: in that sense, a right to silence remains. What the legislation does do is allow a court or jury to draw adverse inferences from silence in four situations. One of them—where a defendant does not testify at trial—will not be discussed here. Two of the other situations are relatively well defined. Under s 36, where a suspect fails to account for objects, substances, or marks on him or in his possession, an adverse inference can be drawn against him at trial. Under s 37, the failure to account for his presence at a particular place is treated the same way. With these sections, an inference can only be drawn if a specific question about the object/mark/ presence is put to the suspect. In contrast, s 34 is much more open-ended. Adverse inferences can be drawn where a defendant relies on a fact in his defence at trial which he failed to mention during police questioning. The fact must be one which he could reasonably have been expected to have mentioned during questioning. The discussion here will concentrate on s 34, although many of the points are also applicable to ss 36 and 37.

There are a number of arguments for and against allowing adverse inferences.[188] To start with some of the reasons why these provisions were introduced, it is often said

[184] See College of Policing, https://www.app.college.police.uk/app-content/investigations/investigative-interviewing/.

[185] See https://www.app.college.police.uk/app-content/investigations/investigative-interviewing/#peace-framework; E. Shepherd and A. Griffiths, *Investigative Interviewing: The Conversation Management Approach* (2nd edn, 2013).

[186] C. Clarke and R. Milne, *National Evaluation of the PEACE Investigative Interviewing Course* (2001), 102; Soukara et al, n 8.

[187] C. Clarke, R. Milne, and R. Bull, 'Interviewing suspects of crime: The impact of PEACE training, supervision, and the presence of a legal advisor' (2011) 8 *J Investigative Psychology and Offender Profiling* 149.

[188] See Quirk, n 112, ch 3.

that silence, of the sort targeted by s 34, is suspicious, and that it is only right to draw it to the attention of the fact-finder. There can, of course, be innocent reasons for not mentioning facts during police interview, which include feeling ill or intimidated, not trusting the police, and wanting to protect someone else.[189] But, so long as these possibilities can be effectively brought to the attention of the jury, and weighted in the evaluation of the evidence, there does not seem anything inherently wrong in asking it to consider drawing an inference from silence. Another reason given for reform was that defendants might be acquitted by producing an 'ambush' defence—one that the prosecution had no inkling of, and would not be able to rebut at trial—though there was little evidence that this was a significant problem,[190] and in any case disclosure requirements address this appropriately.[191] All the same, these are hardly an argument for the status quo, unless some positive reasons for retaining the traditional scope of the right to silence could be mustered.

What reasons are there, then, for *not* permitting inferences from silence? Strong reasons of principle are sometimes mentioned, such as that adverse inferences conflict with the privilege against self-incrimination. That claim raises a number of complex issues which were considered in Chapter 4. One problem with adverse inferences is that they put pressure on suspects to talk. This was something of concern to the Royal Commission on Criminal Justice, which worried that the pressure might lead to innocent suspects making incriminating statements. Here it quoted from the Report of the Royal Commission on Criminal Procedure, which had argued that adverse inferences 'might put strong (and additional) psychological pressure upon some suspects to answer questions without knowing precisely what was the substance of any evidence for the accusations against them. . . . This in our view might well increase the risk of innocent people, particularly those under suspicion for the first time, making damaging statements.'[192] Two comments can be made about this. First, the passage notes that any pressure brought to bear by the possibility of inferences will be additional to the existing pressures of police interview. There is little doubt that many suspects find detention and questioning an intimidating process. However, it is sometimes noted that those who are especially vulnerable to making false confessions are likely to do so anyway, even with the full protection of the right to silence. While there is some truth in this, the traditional right to silence allows legal advisers to counsel vulnerable suspects to remain silent without worrying that this may jeopardize the case in court. Allowing adverse inferences gives an additional tool to the police, who might use inferences as a particular threat in some cases. There seems to be some merit, then, to the argument about the dangers of pressurizing suspects. A second point to make about the passage just quoted is that it gestures towards another reason for the traditional right to silence: it highlights the fact that at police interview, the suspect may not know the details of

---

[189] Ibid, 18.   [190] Ibid, ch 2.

[191] The provisions are to be found in the Criminal Procedure and Investigations Act 1996, discussed further in Ch 9.

[192] Quoted in Royal Commission on Criminal Justice, n 170, ch 2, para 23.

the evidence against him. At trial, most people would think it unfair to ask a defendant to defend himself without full knowledge of the prosecution case. It is arguable that similar concerns apply at interview, and that here suspects should not be asked to engage in discussion of the case against them unless they know its details.[193] The principle here might be linked to a more theoretical defence of aspects of the right to silence made by Kent Greenawalt. According to Greenawalt, it is a basic moral principle that one should not be expected to respond to accusations in the absence of reasonable suspicion.[194]

The ECtHR cautiously accepted that these provisions are compatible with the Convention. In *Murray*,[195] a decision on similar provisions in Northern Ireland, the Court found that the right to silence is not absolute, and so found it permissible that the accused's silence, 'in situations which clearly call for an explanation from him, be taken into account in assessing the evidence adduced by the prosecution'.[196] It did, however, observe that in that case the question of what inferences to draw had been left to a professional judge, and that a number of other safeguards restricted the use of silence as evidence of guilt. It also held that the fact that Murray had been denied access to legal advice before police questioning led to a breach of Art 6: legal advice was seen as taking on particular importance in cases where inferences could be drawn from silence. This, as noted earlier, led to changes in English law and to a new caution which has to be given where a suspect is questioned without access to legal advice. The Court considered the English provisions in more detail in *Condron v UK*.[197] Again, the provisions were found to pass muster so long as they were handled carefully. In particular, it was held to be crucial to instruct the jury in some detail on the nature of inferences that can be drawn from silence. The Court endorsed the model direction on inferences from silence given by the Court of Appeal, and found that the fact that part of it had not been given by the trial judge in *Condron* led to a breach of Art 6.

A jury in an inferences from silence case must be given a number of directions.[198] It should be told that the defendant cannot be convicted solely or mainly on the basis of an inference from silence, and that an inference can only be drawn if it is satisfied that: when interviewed, the defendant could reasonably have been expected to mention the fact in question; that the only sensible explanation for his failure to do so is that he had no answer at the time or none that would stand up to scrutiny; and that without the inference from silence, the prosecution's case is so strong that it clearly calls for an answer by the defendant. The usual inference to be drawn is that the fact in question is false.

In *R v McKnight*, the Court of Appeal held that the judge had been wrong to direct the jury that they could draw an adverse inference where the defendant had made a no comment interview but had provided the police with a written defence statement.[199]

---

[193] P. Roberts and A. Zuckerman, *Criminal Evidence* (2nd edn, 2010).
[194] K. Greenawalt, 'Silence as a Moral and Constitutional Right' (1981) 23 *William & Mary L Rev* 15.
[195] See n 159.   [196] Ibid, [47].   [197] (2001) 31 EHRR 1.
[198] See *R v Argent* [1997] 2 Cr App R 27; *Crown Court Compendium* (2016), Part I, Jury and Trial Management and Summing Up, ch 17-5–17-6.
[199] *R v McKnight* [2013] EWCA Crim 937; *R v Faisal Khan-Mohammad* [2009] EWCA Crim 1871.

At his trial, D had relied upon facts that he mentioned in his written statement and, as such, no adverse inference could be drawn from his having failed to answer police questions. If the accused is cross-examined about discrepancies between his evidence and his defence statement, or if adverse comment is made, the judge must give appropriate guidance to the jury.[200] This may occur only when the trial offence does not differ from the interview offence.[201]

The issue of the drawing of inferences after an accused declines to answer police questions on legal advice has been considered in a number of cases, and the case law has been less than satisfactory. Of course, legal advice to remain silent does not insulate the accused from the possibility of inference being drawn, as this would render s 34 'wholly nugatory'.[202] Initially, it seemed that in a case where a suspect had remained silent on legal advice, the jury would have to consider whether the reasons for the advice were good ones.[203] The Court of Appeal rethought its position in *Betts and Hall*, where it noted that what really mattered was whether the defendant had remained silent because of legal advice, not whether his decision was wise or whether the advice was good.[204] For inferences not to be drawn, the explanation that the reason for not mentioning facts was that the person acted on the advice of his solicitor must be plausible, and not because he had no, or no satisfactory, answer to give.[205] But later decisions doubted this. In *Howell*, the defendant claimed that he would have been only too happy to explain himself to the police, but his legal adviser had counselled silence, and he had decided to follow this advice.[206] The Court of Appeal there held that an adverse inference could be drawn even if the defendant genuinely relied on his solicitor's advice, and what was important, instead, was whether the suspect was behaving reasonably: 'There must always be soundly based objective reasons for silence, sufficiently cogent and telling to weigh in the balance against the clear public interest in an account being given by the suspect to the police. Solicitors bearing the important responsibility of giving advice to suspects at police stations must always have that in mind.'[207] This was followed by *Hoare*, where some attempt was made to reconcile the judgments, but with the bottom line being that a jury can still draw an inference where a suspect has been advised to stay silent by his solicitor.[208] Both *Howell* and *Hoare* are marred by some very poor reasoning.[209]

In *Beckles v UK*, the ECtHR held, unanimously, that there had been a violation of Art 6(1) since the trial judge had left the jury with the option of drawing an adverse

---

[200] *R v Hanyes* [2011] EWCA Crim 3281.

[201] *R v M* [2011] EWCA Crim 86; see P. Bogan, 'Adverse Inference: When Interview and Trial Offence Differ' [2013] *Arch Rev* 4.

[202] *Condron and Condron* [1997] 1 Cr App R 185, 191.

[203] For discussion, see I. Dennis, *The Law of Evidence* (2017).

[204] [2001] EWCA Crim 224; see also *Chenia* [2003] 2 Cr App R 6.

[205] *Betts and Hall*, n 204, [53]–[54].

[206] [2003] *Crim LR* 405, confirmed in *Knight* [2004] 1 Cr App R 9. See A. Choo and A. Jennings, 'Silence on legal advice revisited: *R v Howell*' (2003) 7 *Int J Evidence and Proof* 185.

[207] *Howell*, n 206, 24.   [208] [2005] 1 Cr App R 22.

[209] See M. Redmayne, 'English Warnings' (2008) 30 *Cardozo L Rev* 1047, 1066–71.

inference from B's silence during police questioning, which he stated had followed the advice of his solicitor.[210] The ECtHR found that the jury should have been 'directed that if it was satisfied that the applicant's silence at the police interview could not sensibly be attributed to his having no answer or none that would stand up to police questioning it should not draw an adverse inference'.[211] In B's subsequent appeal against conviction, the Court of Appeal stated:

> In our judgment, in a case where a solicitor's advice is relied upon by the defendant, the ultimate question for the jury remains under section 34 whether the facts relied on at the trial were facts which the defendant could reasonably have been expected to mention at interview. If they were not, that is the end of the matter. If the jury consider that the defendant genuinely relied on the advice, that is not necessarily the end of the matter. It may still not have been reasonable for him to rely on the advice, or the advice may not have been the true explanation for his silence.[212]

In *Bresa*, Waller LJ gave guidance on how the jury ought to be directed in respect of adverse inferences under s 34:

> First there needs to be the striking of a fair balance between telling the jury of a defendant's rights, and telling the jury that the defendant has a choice not to rely on those rights. Second there needs to be an accurate identification of the facts which it is alleged a defendant might reasonably have mentioned. Third there needs to be a warning that there must be a case to answer and the jury cannot convict on inference alone. Fourth there must be a direction to the effect that the key question is whether the jury can be sure that the accused remains silent not because of any advice but because he had no satisfactory explanation to give.[213]

A defendant who adduces evidence of the content of, or reasons for, legal advice, beyond the mere fact of it, does waive privilege, at least to the extent of allowing cross-examination about what the solicitor was told and whether this can be the true explanation for the suspect's silence.[214] Most recently, the Court of Appeal held in *R v Sakyi* that a judge was entitled to comment on a defendant's silence in interview, where D claimed he was following professional advice, provided the judge gave the jury the standard directions on functions and did so fairly.[215]

As the reference to the public interest in *Howell* indicates, all of these judgments are driven by policy concerns; the courts want suspects to talk to the police. But even if it is in the public interest that suspects should talk to the police, this goes no way to justify drawing an adverse inference in individual cases. That depends, in simple terms, on whether silence is suspicious. And where a legal adviser has counselled silence, it is surely difficult to conclude that silence is suspicious; that is, that the suspect's real reason for silence is that he has no good explanation for the evidence against him rather than that he is relying on his solicitor's advice that silence is in his best interests. The

---

[210] (2003) 36 EHRR 13.   [211] [64].
[212] *Beckles* [2004] EWCA Crim 2766, at [46] per Lord Woolf CJ.
[213] *Bresa* [2005] EWCA Crim 1414, at [16] per Waller LJ.
[214] *Seaton* [2010] EWCA Crim 1980, approving *Bowden*.   [215] *R v Sakyi* [2014] EWCA Crim 1784.

most depressing thing in these judgments is Auld LJ's rhetorical question in *Hoare*: 'if [an innocent] defendant is advised to remain silent, why on earth should he do so . . . ?',[216] a question which can only make one wonder why we bother going to such trouble giving suspects access to legal advice. Insofar as there is a wider lesson to learn here, it is that there is an inevitable tension between promoting legal advice to suspects and allowing juries to draw inferences from silence. But to resolve this tension by allowing juries to draw inferences where there is no rational basis for doing so is unprincipled.

A further tension in the adverse inferences scheme concerns disclosure. We noted earlier that there are questions about whether it is fair to draw an inference from silence where a suspect does not know the details of the case against him. While the police may be under a duty not to mislead a suspect actively, for example by telling him that evidence exists where it does not,[217] as noted earlier they are under no obligation to inform suspects of what evidence there is against them. There is little to indicate that lack of disclosure should block an inference from silence; it is simply one factor that might be put to the jury.[218] There is a hint that the ECtHR might see non-disclosure as more significant. In *Murray*, it noted that inferences from silence were permissible 'in situations which clearly call for an explanation from'[219] the suspect, but this point has never been expanded on. The tension, then, is between what may be a useful police tactic of withholding evidence at interview, and drawing inferences from silence. In *Kirk*, the police did not inform the suspect that the victim of a mugging had died, leading the Court of Appeal to rule that evidence of the ensuing confession should have been excluded, because Kirk had not been able to make informed decisions about whether to answer questions and whether to consult a lawyer.[220]

As for the location of questioning, Owusu-Bempah argues that silence in response to questioning outside a police station should not be subject to the possibility of adverse inferences,[221] on the basis that the compulsion to speak might sometimes be greater; the accused is unlikely to have had an adequate opportunity to consider the situation in which he has found himself or the best course of action and, so, may be particularly susceptible to pressure or coercion.

Accurate record keeping of interviews is vital in this respect. A recent *obiter* statement from the High Court in *AB v CPS* emphasized that 'it can be problematic to draw an adverse inference from silence in an interview where the questions put to the suspect are entirely unknown'.[222] Here the appellant was interviewed under caution in the presence of his mother and solicitor, and answered 'no comment' to all questions asked of him. The interview transcript, if it had been taken, was not in evidence nor any details about the questions asked in interview.

There are clear reasons for concern about the abrogation of the right to silence in the CJPOA. While the Court of Appeal and ECtHR have gone some way to erecting

---

[216] *Hoare*, n 208, [53].   [217] *R v Mason* [1988] 1 WLR 139.
[218] See *Argent*, n 198; cf *Beckles*, n 212 [51].   [219] See n 159, 47.   [220] [2000] 1 WLR 567.
[221] A. Owusu-Bempah, 'Silence in Suspicious Circumstances' [2014] *Crim LR* 126, 133–4.
[222] *AB v CPS* [2017] EWHC 2963 (Admin), [48].

safeguards to prevent the jury putting too much weight on silence, rather less has been done to ensure that the inferences from silence regime does not operate unfairly in and beyond the police station. Requirements of disclosure before interview remain minimal and, by not taking a firmer stand on the issue of legal advice, the courts have effectively diluted its authority, strengthening the hand of the police in cases where suspects are advised to stay silent. In *Murray*, the ECtHR took a strong stand on the issue of access to legal advice before interview. In giving judgment, the Court noted that:

> at the beginning of police interrogation, an accused is confronted with a fundamental dilemma relating to his defence. If he chooses to remain silent, adverse inferences may be drawn against him. . . . On the other hand, if the accused opts to break his silence during the course of interrogation, he runs the risk of prejudicing his defence without necessarily removing the possibility of inferences being drawn against him. Under such conditions the concept of fairness enshrined in Article 6 requires that the accused has the benefit of assistance of a lawyer already at the initial stages of police interrogation.[223]

Yet most suspects still face this dilemma without the benefit of legal advice; all that is required is that they be given access to advice, something which, for various reasons, the majority still do not take up. In *Howell*, the Court of Appeal also observed that s 34 changes the context of police questioning: '[n]ow, the police interview and trial are to be seen as part of a continuous process in which the suspect is engaged from the beginning'.[224] As was noted earlier, Code C permits questioning to continue so as to test the suspect's account: so non-responses may be used as evidence, and police questioning might thus be thought to have taken on some of the nature of cross-examination.[225] Given the significance of questioning, it would seem right to strengthen the suspect's due process protections in the police station.[226] This would include stronger requirements on disclosure of the police case before interview—or, if disclosure is minimal, a bar on adverse inferences—and perhaps better access to legal advice. Suspects cannot be forced to consult lawyers if they do not want to, but it is known that some refuse legal advice so as not to prolong their detention. Having legal advisers on hand in police stations has been suggested as a way to overcome this problem, though this is unlikely to be palatable ideologically or in terms of resources.[227]

The point, then, is not that a regime which involves drawing inferences from silence in the police station is inevitably unfair, though it has been characterized aptly as introducing a system of obligatory participation in which defendants are penalized for non-cooperation.[228] Rather, its fairness is conditional on the environment in which questioning takes place. In terms of the effect of s 34 in practice, there is evidence that fewer suspects refuse to answer some or all of the questions put to them by the

---

[223] See n 159, 67.   [224] See n 206, 23.   [225] Code C, 11.6.

[226] See J. Jackson, 'Re-Conceptualizing the Right of Silence as an Effective Fair Trial Standard' (2009) 58 *ICLQ* 835.

[227] See A. Sanders, 'Can Coercive Powers be Effectively Controlled or Regulated? The Case for Anchored Pluralism' in E. Cape and R. Young (eds), *Regulating Policing: The Police and Criminal Evidence Act 1984, Past, Present and Future* (2008), 71.

[228] A. Owusu-Bempah, *Defendant Participation in the Criminal Process* (2017).

police.[229] But this provisions has not led to more confessions,[230] and there has been no discernible impact on conviction rates.[231] The most profound impact of the provision is on custodial legal advice, which is now more complex, and on the nature of the lawyer–client relationship, given that legal representatives may need to testify at their clients' trials.[232] Finally, the provisions put particular pressure on the vulnerable.[233] While there may not be anything wrong in theory with drawing inferences from silence, if the scheme cannot be made to work fairly in practice, and given the impact on the lawyer–client relationship, it would be preferable to abandon it.

5.4 INTERVIEWING VICTIMS AND WITNESSES

While the primary focus of this chapter is on the questioning of suspects, it is worth noting briefly that similar concerns apply to questioning of victims and witnesses. Like suspects, victims and witnesses can be suggestible and compliant; they need to be questioned carefully and sensitively. And whereas suspects have an interest in ensuring that what they say is not distorted by the police, victims and witnesses may be less aware of or sensitized to this prospect. They may feel that the best way to help the police is by agreeing with any suggestions put to them, or by being as definite as possible about what they saw or heard. It is therefore important to avoid putting leading questions to witnesses, or to disclose to them too much of the investigator's theory of the case.

For the police, the purpose of questioning victims and witnesses generally is to produce a statement, that is a written summary of their evidence. The statement plays an important part in the processing of the case: it will form part of the case file reviewed by the CPS in deciding whether to continue the prosecution. Cases often come to court months after the event in question, when memories may have faded. So, a witness's earlier statement is often used to 'refresh' memory, raising the possibility that inaccuracies in the statement will be repeated in the witness's testimony. And witness statements themselves can be admitted as evidence under various exceptions to the hearsay rule.[234]

The Criminal Justice Joint Inspectorates found that the file quality of cases involving vulnerable victims and witnesses was poor, and worse than that for all cases generally.[235] In 23 per cent of applicable files, the officer had not recorded whether the witness was vulnerable or intimidated, and so had particular needs that would require support, should they be required to give evidence in court. Similarly, a joint inspection on child sexual abuse cases found that only 15 per cent of police interviews recorded

---

[229] T. Bucke, R. Street, and D. Brown, *The Right of Silence: The Impact of the CJPOA 1994* (2000), 31; Quirk, n 112, ch 3.

[230] Bucke et al, ibid, 34.   [231] Quirk, n 112, 120.   [232] Ibid, 89–119.

[233] Ibid, 67.

[234] See A. Heaton-Armstrong, D. Wolchover, and A. Maxwell-Scott, 'Obtaining, Recording and Admissibility of Out-of-Court Witness Statements' in A. Heaton-Armstrong et al (eds), *Witness Testimony: Psychological, Investigative and Evidential Perspectives* (2006).

[235] HMIC, *Witness for the prosecution*, n 163, 8.

any consideration of the specific needs of the child (physical, sexual, social, cognitive, or linguistic).[236]

Moreover, what is known about the questioning of victims and witnesses suggests that standards here are worse than where suspects are concerned. Studies have indicated that police officers use tactics which shape the evidence gained from witnesses.[237] As with the questioning of suspects, there is now much emphasis on training and the PEACE model is emphasized. Specialist training is given to those interviewing sensitive and vulnerable witnesses, such as children and those in sexual offence cases.[238] This is to be welcomed, given the findings in 2001 that leading questions were common, and that the 'predominant use of closed questions and the view that interviewers were "just taking a statement" indicates that interviews were clearly highly interviewer driven, with a confirmatory bias'.[239]

The Ministry of Justice guidance *Achieving Best Evidence in Criminal Proceedings* describes good practice in interviewing victims and witnesses, and in preparing them to give their best evidence in court. Now a support person who is known to the witness may be present during the interview to provide emotional support.[240] Vulnerable witnesses are eligible for special measures, including communication through intermediaries.[241] An intermediary will assess the witness's communication needs, usually prior to the witness being interviewed by the police, and advises police officers and advocates how best to communicate.[242] In relation to child witnesses, the presence and interventions of an intermediary have been found to improve perceptions of the interview, with no effect on perceptions of the witness.[243] That said, the entitlement to an intermediary is predicated on the identification of the person as vulnerable. As Shepherd and Milne point out, problems with interview practice for all witnesses would be addressed by recording, as it would be possible to check exactly what had been said and to judge whether the interviewer had used inappropriate methods. Recording would also allow effective supervision, to help realize the efforts at training; after all, recording of interviews with suspects is one factor which has contributed to improvements in this area. Interviews with vulnerable witnesses, and significant witnesses in major inquiries, are recorded,[244] and indeed, a video-recorded interview may replace the first

---

[236] HMCPSI, *Achieving best evidence in child sexual abuse cases—a joint inspection* (2014).

[237] E. Shepherd and R. Milne, 'Full and Faithful: Ensuring Quality, Practice and Integrity of Outcome in Witness Interviews' in A. Heaton-Armstrong, D. Wolchover, and E. Shepherd (eds), *Analysing Witness Testimony* (1999).

[238] P. Radcliffe, G. Gudjonsson, A. Heaton-Armstrong, and D. Wolchover, *Witness Testimony in Sexual Cases: Evidential, Investigative and Scientific Perspectives* (2016).

[239] See Clarke and Milne, n 2, 58–9.

[240] Ministry of Justice, *Achieving Best Evidence in Criminal Proceedings: Guidance on interviewing victims and witnesses, and guidance on using special measures* (2011), 2.201.

[241] Youth Justice and Criminal Evidence Act 1999, s 11. See Ch 11.

[242] P. Cooper and M. Mattison, 'Intermediaries, vulnerable people and the quality of evidence: An international comparison of three versions of the English intermediary model' (2017) 21 *Int J Evidence & Proof* 351, 354.

[243] A. Ridley, V. Van Rheede, and R. Wilcock, 'Interviews, intermediaries and interventions: Mock-jurors', police officers' and barristers' perceptions of a child witness interview' (2015) 7 *Investigative Interviewing: Research and Practice* 21.

[244] Ministry of Justice, n 240, 8–9.

stage of a vulnerable or intimidated witness's evidence in court.[245] Given that cheap portable recording devices are now available,[246] it is surely time to require recording of all interviews which lead to the production of witness statements.

5.5 CONFESSIONS IN COURT

It has been seen that there remain concerns about how suspects are interviewed by the police, especially given changes to the right to silence. In the worst case scenario, a false confession will be the result of the interviewing process. Research suggests that confessions exert a powerful influence on juries.[247] It is therefore important to have safeguards at court which will guard against a false confession leading to a conviction.

The key legal provision in this regard is s 76 of PACE. Under this section, a confession should be ruled inadmissible if it has been obtained by oppression (s 76(2)(a)), or 'in consequence of anything said or done which was likely, in the circumstances existing at the time, to render unreliable any confession which might have been made by him in consequence thereof' (s 76(2)(b)). There is a degree of overlap between this section and s 78, which applies to confessions as well as to other prosecution evidence. Section 78 allows evidence to be excluded where its admission would render the proceedings unfair. Section 77 requires a court to caution a jury about relying on confessions made by the mentally handicapped. Here, the focus will be on s 76(2)(b).[248]

The wording of this provision is convoluted. It is not a simple 'exclude if unreliable' rule, but instead requires the court to consider *hypothetical* unreliability: the confession should be excluded, 'notwithstanding that it may be true',[249] if it was obtained in circumstances conducive to unreliability. The reason for this is presumably that the provision is intended to sanction bad questioning practices, even if they produce a confession which can be proved to be reliable, for example by evidence corroborating it or even a further admission by the defendant.[250] For the most part, then, the case law is clear: 'one cannot overcome problems about the reliability of a confession by using extrinsic evidence to show that it is likely to be true'.[251] But in *Proulx*, a case where a suspect had confessed in an undercover operation that dangled financial and romantic rewards in front of him, particular stress was put on the concept 'any confession'. This was held to mean 'any such confession', and to require examination of exactly what had

---

[245] Ibid, Appendix F. See N. Westera, M. Kebbell, and R. Milne 'Interviewing witnesses: Will investigative and evidential requirements ever concord?' (2011) 13 *Brit J Forensic Practice* 103–113, discussing the challenges of making one interview meet both investigative and evidential purposes.

[246] See n 237.

[247] See I. Blandon Gitlin, K. Sperry, and R. A. Leo, 'Jurors Believe Interrogation Tactics are not Likely to Elicit False Confessions: Will Expert Witness Testimony Inform them Otherwise?' (2011) 17 *Psychology, Crime and Law* 239–60.

[248] The oppression safeguard is important, but appears to be rarely applied. The confession of Stephen Miller seems to be the only example of an appeal court finding interviewing conduct oppressive.

[249] PACE s 76(2).   [250] As in *McGovern* (1991) 92 Cr App R 228.

[251] *R v Blackburn* [2005] EWCA Crim 1349, [62].

been said by the suspect: 'the relevant confession is thus to involvement in . . . a killing about which the applicant had already volunteered knowledge'.[252] Combined with the emphasis on the original court's assessment of the applicant, this approach comes close to looking at actual rather than hypothetical unreliability.

If a reliable confession may be excluded under s 76 because of the way in which it was obtained, it may also be true that an unreliable confession may be admitted if it was not procured by wrongdoing. The wording 'anything said or done' hints that only if the police do something wrong will the confession be excluded. There is a certain amount of uncertainty in the case law here, revolving around the question of how much emphasis should be placed on these words. For example, in *Goldenberg* the defendant had requested an interview with the police but claimed that the resulting confession was potentially unreliable because he was desperate to be bailed so as to be able to obtain heroin.[253] The Court of Appeal held that this could be ignored because he had not confessed in consequence of anything said or done by the police, but on his own initiative. This rather restrictive view was supported in *Crampton*[254] and *Wahab*,[255] but in a number of other cases factors such as a low mental age have been taken into account.[256] In *Foster*, however, the suspect's vulnerability was downplayed by the Court of Appeal because while it may have been known to the police, it had not been shown that the interviewing officers were aware of it.[257] *Crampton* also highlights the causal test in the section: the words 'in consequence of' appear twice in s 76(2)(b), and this again tends to focus the test on the role of misconduct in securing confessions. The Court of Appeal in *Crampton* referred to the pre-PACE case law, quoting from *Rennie*: 'very few confessions are inspired solely by remorse. Often the motives of an accused are mixed and include a hope that an early admission may lead to an earlier release or to a lighter sentence. If it were the law that the mere presence of such a motive, even if prompted by something said or done . . ., led inexorably to the exclusion of a confession, nearly every confession would be rendered inadmissible'.[258] In this way, the background factors, which put some pressure on all suspects to confess, can be ignored. The approach of the courts seems to be that only if the police draw the prospect of bail and the like to the suspect's attention will a confession be excluded.[259] As we saw earlier, it is not clear what the status of the sentence discount is, but given the degree of promotion it gets nowadays it may be that even if the police draw it to the suspect's attention it will be treated as a background factor.

One criticism of s 76 and its case law is that the courts have retained a reasonable degree of latitude in individual cases by never settling on a definitive interpretation of the section. In *Proulx*, it is actual reliability which is highlighted. In cases such as *Goldenberg* and *Crampton*, the focus shifts away from reliability and towards wrongdoing. It was noted previously that illicit drug taking is a factor predictive of confession, the likely explanation being that drug takers are anxious to escape from custody. It does not seem right,

---

[252] *R v Bow Street Magistrates' Court, ex p Proulx* [2001] 1 All ER 57, [46].
[253] (1989) 88 Cr App R 285.   [254] (1991) 92 Cr App R 369.   [255] [2003] 1 Cr App R 15.
[256] E.g. *Everett* [1988] *Crim LR* 826; *McGovern*, n 250.   [257] [2003] EWCA Crim 178, [63].
[258] (1982) 74 Cr App R 207, 212.   [259] See *Barry* (1992) 95 Cr App R 384; Code C, 11.5.

then, that this very real factor is ignored in the reliability determination. The emphasis on wrongdoing in the s 76 case law is not necessarily a bad thing: breach of the Code C rules will often disadvantage a suspect in some way. But a better way to scrutinize confessions would surely be for s 76(2)(b) to be focused purely on reliability, leaving concerns about fairness and wrongdoing to be dealt with through the application of s 78.

It has been seen that PACE and the Codes give little detailed guidance on what is and is not appropriate questioning. It should now be apparent that the s 76 case law adds little in the way of detail. Could more detailed guidelines be given? This is something which it is probably very difficult to do. It is not easy to say what degree of pressure it is appropriate to apply to suspects in order to gain admissions; and there are so many different ways in which pressure can be applied that creating guidelines is difficult.[260] However, one possible safeguard would be a rule that confessions be corroborated by supporting evidence. This would mean that a defendant could not be convicted on the basis of a confession alone.[261] A majority of the Royal Commission on Criminal Justice rejected such a proposal, settling instead for a requirement to warn the jury about the dangers of relying on a confession alone.[262] One reason given against a corroboration rule was that it would lead to the collapse of some cases which are at present prosecuted successfully.[263] The problem with this way of putting things is that it focuses on right and wrong convictions. It is, of course, very difficult to know whether a conviction based on no more than a confession is right or wrong in the sense of true to the facts. A more principled way of resolving the debate is to ask whether unsupported confessions are, by their nature, sufficiently strong as evidence to warrant conviction. Even a factually guilty person is not 'rightly found guilty' if that finding is based on weak or dubious evidence. Despite the improvements brought in by PACE and the awareness of the problems of false confessions, confessions remain a problematic sort of evidence. Given the context of detention in the police station, police questioning is always a process which applies pressure to suspects to confess. There are also the factors highlighted in *Rennie*: confessions will often be made in the hope that they will bring some advantage. Although a confession will probably be excluded if it can be shown to have been made as the result of an explicit offer to grant bail or the like, research suggests that offers of lenient treatment can be communicated implicitly.[264] Suspects who are addicted to drugs may be particularly keen to bring their detention to an end. And the emphasis on sentence discounts for guilty pleas and other forms of cooperation make it increasingly likely that suspects will expect to gain some advantage from confessing. The court in *Rennie* is right that such factors alone should not result in the exclusion of a confession, but they do help to make the case for a corroboration rule. In sum, there are simply too many doubts about the processes which lead suspects to confess for a conviction on a confession alone ever to be justified.

[260] For various examples of pressurizing tactics, see Gudjonsson, n 5, ch 4.

[261] In Scotland, there must be two sources of evidence in respect of each 'crucial fact' in a criminal case (*Smith v Lees* 1997 JC 73).

[262] See n 80, ch 4, para 87.   [263] Ibid, ch 4, para 71.

[264] S. Kassin and K. McNall, 'Police Interrogation and Confession: Communicating Promises and Threats by Pragmatic Implication' (1991) 5 *Law & Human Behavior* 233.

5.6 CONCLUSION

Despite real and lingering concerns about coercion, mistreatment, and false confession, under the existing regime confessions are recorded, there are rules giving suspects some respite from very lengthy questioning sessions, the presentation of false evidence is probably frowned upon, and police are trained in 'investigative' interviewing techniques. While in this chapter we have been critical of various aspects of the detention and questioning process, it is important to underline how much progress has been made.[265]

Nevertheless, however well regulated the police questioning process is, confessions remain a suspect type of evidence. Police detention will always be stressful, and innocent suspects will always have some incentives for confessing. This is why there is a case to be made for the corroboration of confessions. It is also crucial that the gains made since PACE are not undermined by government initiatives to cut costs by reducing the amount and quality of legal advice available to suspects, and by facilitating, inadvertently or otherwise, the circumvention of PACE. Finally, looking beyond confessions, we have seen the importance of safeguarding witnesses as well as suspects in the context of police interviews.

FURTHER READING

CAPE, E., 'The Police Bail Provisions of the Policing and Crime Act 2017' [2017] *Crim LR* 587, 589.

DEHAGHANI, R., 'Automatic Authorisation: An Exploration of the Decision to Detain in Police Custody' [2017] *Crim LR* 187.

KEMP, K., 'PACE, Performance Targets and Legal Protections' [2014] *Crim LR* 278, 282.

QUIRK, H., *The Rise and Fall of the Right of Silence: Principle, Politics and Policy* (2016).

SUKUMAR, D., HODGSON, J. and WADE, K., 'How the Timing of Police Evidence Disclosure Impacts Custodial Legal Advice' [2016] *Int J Evidence & Proof* 200.

QUESTIONS FOR DISCUSSION

1. Should inferences be drawn at trial from a suspect's failure to mention facts at a police interview?

2. Are defendants given sufficient protection against false conviction by (a) the rules governing detention and questioning and (b) the courts?

---

[265] See also D. Dixon, 'Authorise and Regulate: A Comparative Perspective on the Rise and Fall of a Regulatory Strategy' in Cape and Young, n 227.

6

GATEKEEPING AND DIVERSION FROM PROSECUTION

This chapter focuses on those decisions that determine whether or not an alleged offence/offender enters the formal criminal justice process and, if so, the path the case will take. These decisions were described in the first chapter as dispositive, in that decisions to divert a case from prosecution (by preferring one of the alternatives discussed in this chapter) are likely to dispose of it. Some of these offenders may breach the conditions of their diversion and be brought back into the criminal process, but in the vast majority of cases diversion has a practical finality. This makes it particularly important to explore the reasons why some cases are diverted and others are not, and to question whether diversion is always the most appropriate course for the public, the defendant, and the victim.

Out of all the criminal offences committed in any one year, only a very low proportion result in formal proceedings against a suspect/defendant. This 'attrition' is gradual but substantial. Around half of offences are never reported to the police: members of the public may choose not to report an offence because they think the police unable to help, because they regard the offence as too minor to report, because the offence is regarded as a private or domestic matter, because of fear of reprisals, or for other reasons. Of these reported crimes, between 60 to 80 per cent are recorded; the figures vary depending on the offence type.[1] The police identify a suspect in about half of these recorded cases,[2] bringing the number of offences remaining in the system to 20 per cent or below. Quite a large proportion of these will result in an informal warning or no further action at all, particularly when traced to young offenders. Some cases will be diverted, such as through formal cautions, resulting in very few of these offences being prosecuted and ultimately fewer again sentenced by the courts.

This rate of attrition does not apply equally to all crimes: in particular, more serious crimes, particularly those where the victim sees the assailant, more often end in

[1] HMIC, *Crime-recording: making the victim count. The final report of an inspection of crime data integrity in police forces in England and Wales* (2014), 7.1.

[2] Home Office, *Crime outcomes in England and Wales: year ending March 2018*, Statistical Bulletin HOSB 10/18 (2018).

conviction, though as was noted, police recording practice is not always robust here, and the conviction rate for homicide is high. Conversely, the attrition rate of sexual offences has long been a source of concern, and many surveys suggest that fewer than 7 per cent of cases end with a conviction for rape.[3]

What are the implications of this attrition rate? First, it demonstrates how questionable it is to expect sentences passed by the courts to act as a significant control on crime. Those sentences apply to a small proportion of offenders and, even if the symbolic effect of those (few) sentences is greater than their proportionate application, this suggests that crime-prevention strategies should not place great emphasis on sentencing. A second implication is that decisions taken by law enforcement agents have a considerable influence on the selection of cases that go forward into the criminal process. As we shall see, a range of diversionary disposals exists. In relation to cases that proceed to prosecution, the decisions of police and prosecutors have a qualitative as well as a quantitative effect: offenders who find themselves convicted in court are not a random group of the totality of offenders, nor necessarily are they the most serious.[4] They are chosen, when others are not, for a variety of reasons that will be explored later.

The focus of this chapter will be upon the decisions taken by these 'gatekeepers' of the criminal process. In order to facilitate the analysis of general issues, the discussion of different types of gatekeeper will be less detailed than the extensive literature would permit. The role of the police will be outlined first, followed by a comparison with the approach of regulatory bodies as agencies that select for official action certain types of person or situation, a selection that may lead either to prosecution and trial or to a form of diversion. The second section considers the range of formal responses to those who are believed to be offenders, but who are diverted, and dealt with 'out of court'. We then turn to examine issues with diversion, accountability, and the values behind some of the differing policies.

6.1 REPORTING AND ENFORCING

The public, the police, and a range of prosecuting agencies all have an impact on the reporting and enforcing of the criminal law, and so on the route that particular acts and actors take through the criminal process. The public play a key role in reporting crimes and thus in policing: the vast majority of offences are brought to the attention of the police by members of the public, and so here the police operate in a reactive role. The decision to report implies that the victim or witness expects something to be done

<hr/>

[3] K. Hohl and E. Stanko, 'Complaints of Rape and the Criminal Justice System: Fresh Evidence on the Attrition Problem in England and Wales' (2015) 12(3) *Eur J Criminol* 324; V. Munro and L. Kelly 'A Vicious Cycle?: Attrition and Conviction Patterns in Contemporary Rape Cases in England and Wales' in J. Brown and M. Horvath, (eds), *Rape: Challenging Contemporary Thinking* (2009), 281–300.

[4] Although it is probably true to say that many cases are not reported because they are thought too minor, one study of the victims of violence found that the probability of an offender being brought to court and convicted was not related to the objective seriousness of the assault: C. Clarkson et al, 'Assaults: the Relationship between Seriousness, Criminalisation and Punishment' [1994] *Crim LR* 4.

about the offence, though as noted earlier, reasons for not reporting include beliefs that the crime was insufficiently serious and that the police would not be able to do anything about it. The latter reason may betray a pessimism about police effectiveness rather than a judgement that no formal response is necessary. In practice, however, many of these cases will also involve the first reason—that the formal invocation of law enforcement machinery is not really necessary or overly robust. To that extent, then, the public filters many non-serious offences out of the system, at the earliest stage.

However, the police are not simply the agents of the public, reacting whenever re-quested; the police exert a powerful and distinct influence on reporting and enforce-ment in a number of respects. First, the police do not, and need not, record as crimes all incidents that are reported to them as crimes.[5] While rules and standards governing crime-recording practice were tightened significantly a number of decades ago,[6] there is clear evidence that crimes are not recorded in line with these counting rules.[7] Such 'gaming of the stats' is a way of achieving desired targets and other key performance indicators within a performance culture that prioritizes these over other goals.[8] As noted, HM Inspectorate of Constabulary's (HMIC's) inspection in 2014 on the integ-rity of police-recorded crime data found that 19 per cent of crimes reported to the police went unrecorded, and that levels of under-recording were highest for offences involving violence against the person and sexual offences.[9] This has prompted HM Inspectorate of Constabulary and Fire & Rescue Services (HMICFRS) to undertake a rolling programme of crime data integrity inspections of each force over a number of years, to test whether crimes are being recorded by the police when they should be and categorized correctly. This longstanding state of affairs underlines how the police oper-ate as a significant and problematic filter on public reports, and even though members of the public may want official action (and, implicitly, official recording of the offence), this may not be what occurs.

Secondly, many offences are discovered by the police themselves. While a 'crack-down' on certain forms of offences, such as soliciting for sex or drug-dealing in a par-ticular locality, may be in response to complaints from the public, it may also constitute a police 'campaign' against particular forms of offending, such as drug-dealing in clubs, and drink-driving. The police are operating proactively here, to some extent because

[5] The National Crime Recording Standard provides that 'An incident will be recorded as a crime (notifiable offence) for "victim related offences" if, on the balance of probability: (a) the circumstances of the victims report amount to a crime defined by law (the police will determine this, based on their knowledge of the law and counting rules); and (b) there is no credible evidence to the contrary immediately available.' *Home Office Counting Rules For Recorded Crime* (2018), [2.2] available at https://www.gov.uk/government/uploads/system/uploads/attachment_data/file/656791/count-general-nov-2017.pdf.

[6] See J. Simmons and T. Dodd, *Crime in England and Wales 2002/2003*, Home Office Statistical Bulletin 07/03 (2003), 32.

[7] In January 2013, the UK Statistics Authority withdrew its National Statistics designation from police-recorded crime statistics in the wake of accumulating evidence that the underlying data were not reliable: see https://www.ons.gov.uk/peoplepopulationandcommunity/crimeandjustice/methodologies/methodological-notewhydothetwodatasourcesshowdifferingtrends.

[8] V. Kemp, 'PACE, Performance Targets and Legal Protections' [2014] *Crim LR* 278, 296.

[9] HMIC, n 1, [7.1].

the crimes are victimless and therefore there is no victim to make a complaint. In this context, the patterns of law enforcement largely reflect the availability of police officers and the preferences of those in operational control: the police can only mount 'proactive' campaigns if they are not overwhelmed by the 'reactive' demands of crimes reported to them, and when they do adopt a proactive strategy there is a choice regarding what type of offence to target.

Thirdly, it is important to recall the complexity of the nature of police functions. Thus far, we have referred to police work as if its focus is enforcing the law by catching criminals, whether as a result of prompting by a member of the public or as a result of a police campaign, but these kinds of activity do not dominate everyday policing. Much of what the police do is to perform a kind of service function, attending to a wide range of incidents that require something to be done about them—from road accidents and rowdy parties to stray cattle and barking dogs. Into all these situations, the police officer brings authority and the ability to draw upon coercive powers if needed. These powers become even more prominent when there is thought to be a risk of public disorder—for example, at a demonstration or march or football match. These are the occasions on which the function of the police as maintainers of order comes to the fore. Whether the police use their coercive powers depends on a number of contingencies. If there is a genuine threat to good order they may intervene to make one or more arrests. Studies of police behaviour have long maintained that a police officer is more likely to arrest and charge someone who threatens the officer's authority by means of insults or failure to comply with the officer's commands or requests.[10] This forms part of the working culture of the police, discussed in Chapter 3. Significant as that proposition is in explaining why certain types of person come to be arrested and charged, it should not be allowed to overshadow the probability that some people clearly threaten to cause public disorder and should therefore be prevented from going further.[11] In other words, the use of arrest and criminal charges or out-of-court disposals by the police in incidents thought to threaten good order is likely to be an amalgam of some clearly justifiable cases and others that turn more on the disposition, pride, or self-image of particular officers. Any description that ignores one or the other lacks realism, as does the notion that Parliament makes the laws and the police 'merely' enforce them. The police manage situations so as to maintain order, using the offences in the Public Order Act 1986 for instance as resources to draw upon, to be invoked against those who threaten the police conception of what constitutes good order and how it should be achieved. There is a considerable amount of low-level discretion, the significance of which will become clear as this chapter progresses.

As noted in Chapter 1, though formerly the police took the decision whether or not to charge the defendant, now the Crown Prosecution Service (CPS) determines the charge in most cases, albeit that this is now shifting back to the police.[12] That said,

---

[10] The classic study is by E. Bittner, 'The Police on Skid Row: a Study in Peacekeeping' (1967) 32 *Amer Soc Rev* 699; cf the more recent research reported by S. Choongh, *Policing as Social Discipline* (1997).

[11] See R. Reiner, *The Politics of the Police* (4th edn, 2010), ch 4.   [12] See Ch 1, n 38.

a large minority of prosecutions are brought by agencies other than the CPS, mostly local authorities, the Driver and Vehicle Licensing Agency, and the Department for Work and Pensions.[13] Among the many others, the Health and Safety Executive brings prosecutions for offences concerning safety at work and in transport systems; HM Revenue and Customs bring prosecutions for offences relating to the evasion or attempted evasion of tax and customs duties; the Environment Agency brings prosecutions for offences of pollution; the Serious Fraud Office (SFO) brings prosecutions for financial offences; local consumer protection officers bring prosecutions for trading offences committed by shops and businesses; and so on. One major difference is that all these agencies (unlike the CPS) have both an investigatory function and the power to prosecute. Each of them therefore has control over all the relevant decisions. Another major difference between these agencies and the CPS is that there is no accountability structure between them. Each follows its own policies and practices, with no attempt at an overall strategy among different agencies, and few attempts to harmonize their policies with those of the police and the CPS. For these agencies, prosecution is usually regarded as a last resort, after informal settlements, civil actions, and warnings.[14]

The Environment Agency may be examined by way of illustration. The functions of the Agency include the regulation of pollution, waste disposal, wildlife conservation, fisheries, and water resources. The Agency publishes an 'enforcement and sanctions policy',[15] and the difference in emphasis from the CPS is striking:

> We aim to make sure our enforcement response is proportionate and appropriate to each situation. Our first response is usually to give advice and guidance or issue a warning to bring an offender into compliance where possible.
>
> We have a range of civil sanctions available to use for many of the offences we are responsible for enforcing. . . .
>
> We will normally consider all other options before considering criminal proceedings. Generally, prosecution is our last resort.[16]

Combined with this difference in outlook is a difference in powers. Unlike the CPS, the Environment Agency has full investigative powers, and also many powers short of prosecution—such as the power to issue enforcement notices and/or prohibition notices, and the power to suspend or revoke environmental licences. The policy then goes on to list 'public interest factors' which the Agency regards as relevant to the decision to prosecute.[17] In addition, the policy spells out a 'Common Incident Classification

---

[13] G. Slapper, *Organisational Prosecutions* (2001).

[14] R. Cranston, *Regulating Business* (1979), 107 and 168; G. Richardson, A. Ogus, and P. Burrows, *Policing Pollution* (1982); K. Hawkins, *Law as Last Resort* (2003); P. Almond, *Corporate Manslaughter and Regulatory Reform* (2013); P. Alldridge, *Criminal Justice and Taxation* (2017).

[15] See Environment Agency, *Environment Agency enforcement and sanctions policy* (2018), https://www.gov.uk/government/publications/environment-agency-enforcement-and-sanctions-policy/environment-agency-enforcement-and-sanctions-policy.

[16] Ibid, 7.

[17] Ibid, 8.1. These factors are similar to those stated in the Code for Crown Prosecutors, and the Environment Agency must meet the test set out in the Code, [5.1].

Scheme', with levels of environmental effect for which there would normally be different levels of enforcement action.[18]

Similar policies and practices are to be found in relation to the Health and Safety Executive, which uses 'a wide variety of methods to encourage and support business to manage health and safety risks in a sensible and proportionate way and secure compliance with the law'.[19] The difference of emphasis from the police and CPS is soon apparent: 'We take enforcement action to prevent harm by requiring duty holders to manage and control risks effectively. This includes: ensuring action is taken immediately to deal with serious risks; promoting and maintaining sustained compliance with the law; and ensuring that those who breach the law, including individuals who fail in their responsibilities, may be held to account (this includes bringing alleged offenders before the courts in England and Wales).'[20]

Occupying an interim position is the SFO, which is a specialist prosecuting authority that pursues cases of serious or complex fraud, bribery, and corruption in England, Wales, and Northern Ireland. Unlike the CPS, it both investigates and prosecutes cases,[21] whereas it takes a more robust approach to prosecution than the Environment Agency and the Health and Safety Executive, notwithstanding that increasingly it seeks to settle cases through the use of deferred prosecution agreements.[22]

These statements show the culture of diversion in these regulatory agencies. Prosecution is regarded as a last resort: the priority is to ensure compliance with the appropriate standards of safety. So, prosecutions are relatively rare, prompting criticisms regarding unevenness and consequent unfairness in the use of the criminal law. Some argue that the infrequency of prosecutions and the predominance of warnings and other remedial measures indicates that regulatory agencies have been 'captured' by big business, or that the structure of regulation is an attempt to persuade the public that enforcement is being taken seriously when it is not.

Empirical research into the working practices of regulatory agencies goes some way to explaining why the difference in approach has evolved and is sustained. A leading study by Keith Hawkins argued that Health and Safety inspectors are motivated, in their enforcement decisions, by considerations of morality (bad cases justify prosecution) and by considerations of commensurability (non-serious deviations from the required standards call for lesser responses than prosecution),[23] as well as being affected by staffing levels, workloads, and inspectors' perceptions of public reactions. Hawkins also confirms that individual inspectors differ in their approaches, with some more willing to bring a prosecution. Though Robert Baldwin argued that there was a significant shift towards readier resort to punitive sanctions, especially in financial and

[18] Ibid, 8.1.3.
[19] Health and Safety Executive, *Enforcement Policy Statement* (2015), [1.2] http://www.hse.gov.uk/pubns/hse41.pdf.
[20] Ibid, [3.1].
[21] See N. Garoupa, A. Ogus, and A. Sanders, 'The Investigation and Prosecution of Regulatory Offences: Is There an Economic Case for Integration?' (2011) 70 *Cambridge LJ* 236.
[22] See section 6.2(G).   [23] K. Hawkins, *Law as Last Resort* (2003), 243 and 220–6.

business regulation,[24] this is not borne out by the recent work of the SFO and the expansion of negotiated justice in the form of deferred prosecution agreements. Regardless, there is a clear contrast between the police and the regulatory agencies: the latter are still predominantly orientated towards ensuring compliance through negotiation, with their inspectors dealing on a long-term basis with businesspeople, and regarding the background threat of prosecution as more effective than its frequent use. Moreover, their staffing resources would not permit them to prosecute suspected offenders to the extent that the police resort to prosecution: bringing a prosecution is a significant drain on an inspector's time.[25]

The Environment Agency and the Health and Safety Executive have been chosen as examples of the many agencies which pursue a preventive or 'compliance' approach to enforcement, as distinct from a 'deterrence' or 'sanctioning' strategy which places greater emphasis on prosecution.[26] Compared with the approach of the police and CPS, their much greater emphasis on diversion rather than prosecution raises acute questions of social justice. Companies, or wealthy/middle-class suspects and offenders are more often dealt with by regulatory agencies, and benefit from the alternative approaches whereas more disadvantaged dishonest members of society are more likely to find their conduct defined as a police matter, with prosecution for theft or fraud. Yet, the offences may be no different in terms of seriousness. This might be defended on the principles of parsimony, of minimum intervention, and of assigning greater priority to the goal of securing maximum compliance than to equality of treatment; if effectiveness is the goal, it is often argued that regulatory approaches are superior to prosecutions in this area.[27] However, the effect is unacceptable in terms of social justice—allowing middle-class or white-collar offenders to benefit from diversion and other alternatives to prosecution, while lower-class or blue-collar offenders are processed in the 'orthodox' way.

How should this inequality be tackled? To assimilate the treatment of the clients of regulatory agencies to that of the clients of the police would increase overall suffering, and some argue that it is wrong to insist on equality if it results in equality of misery.[28] However, there are surely other ways of tackling this inequality of treatment, such as through the decriminalization of minor offences and the reduction of penalties for them, and the more robust pursuit of corporate and organizational harms through the criminal law. More fundamentally, fresh thought needs to be given to the approach of the police and prosecution service to the cases and people that come to their attention. It is worth reconsidering the need for strong sanctions for non-compliance with conditional and/or preventive orders (the regulatory

---

[24] R. Baldwin, 'The New Punitive Regulation' (2004) 67 *MLR* 351.   [25] Hawkins, n 23, 46, 300, 421–2.

[26] For further discussion, see the works at nn 10–11.

[27] Cf M. Levi, *The Investigation, Prosecution and Trial of Serious Fraud* (1993), and D. J. Middleton, 'The Legal and Regulatory Response to Solicitors Involved in Serious Fraud' (2005) 45 *BJ Crim* 810, G. Slapper and S. Tombs, *Corporate Crime* (2000), ch 8.

[28] The argument of N. Morris and M. Tonry, *Between Prison and Probation* (1990) in respect of equality of treatment in sentencing, criticized by A. Ashworth, *Sentencing and Criminal Justice* (6th edn, 2015), ch 7.7.

agencies have a more open approach to repeated non-compliance), and about the treatment of offenders with whom the police interact regularly (as do regulatory inspectors in their work). There are strong objections to any system that allows different investigative and prosecution agencies to pursue such divergent policies in respect of offences of similar levels of seriousness, without any attempt to address the inherent issues of social injustice.

6.2 THE RANGE OF DIVERSIONARY RESPONSES

The criminal law provides the framework for formal responses to alleged lawbreaking, but also functions as a resource to be invoked in situations where this is thought necessary so as to enforce compliance or to maintain order or respect.[29] Discretion is a key element in what actually happens—whether a case is diverted or sent for prosecution; and, if diverted, what form of diversion is chosen.[30]

The concept of diversion means directing cases away from the criminal courts and dealing with them in other ways, through what are called 'out-of-court disposals' (OOCD).[31] There is some concern about the adequacy of this terminology, despite its usage by practitioners, on the basis that it can lead to misunderstanding about the use and purpose of the disposals, and can undermine their positive aspects.[32] The terms 'neighbourhood' and 'community' justice have been suggested as alternatives.[33]

That aside, the attractions of diversion are that it aims to be simpler, cheaper, and less bureaucratic (in cutting police paperwork); it is a more proportionate and less stigmatic response to many minor offences; and it appears to be no less effective, in terms of reconvictions, than conviction and sentence. Though formerly it was (or purported to be) non-punitive, this is no longer a necessary feature. Overall, it provides a way of mitigating the impact of prosecution and possible punishment on the individual, though its development in England has been far from principled. Indeed, one could draw a contrast with some European systems' doctrine of compulsory prosecution (sometimes called the principle of legality), which is respected because

---

[29] See also D. Brown and T. Ellis, *Policing Low-Level Disorder*, Home Office Research Study 135 (1994), 42–3.

[30] L. Gelsthorpe and N. Padfield (eds), *Exercising Discretion: Decision-Making in the Criminal Justice System and Beyond* (2003).

[31] Office for Criminal Justice Reform, *Out-of-court Disposals for Adults: a Guide to Alternatives to Prosecution* (2007); Sentencing Council, *Out-of-court-disposals* (no date), https://www.sentencingcouncil.org.uk/explanatory-material/item/out-of-court-disposals/; College of Policing, *Prosecution and case management: Possible justice outcomes following investigation* (2018), https://www.app.college.police.uk/app-content/prosecution-and-case-management/justice-outcomes/.

[32] HMIC and HM Crown Prosecution Service Inspectorate (HMCPSI), *Exercising Discretion: The Gateway to Justice, A study by Her Majesty's Inspectorate of Constabulary and Her Majesty's Crown Prosecution Service Inspectorate on cautions, penalty notices for disorder and restorative justice* (2011), 5.

[33] Ibid.

it is said to promote legality and equal treatment, to prevent political interference with the process of justice, and also to heighten general deterrence.[34] In theory, all those who commit offences are brought before the courts for an open determination of guilt and (if convicted) for sentencing, and there is no broad discretionary power to avoid prosecution, as this might lead to local variations, allegations of political motivation or discrimination, or the undermining of law by expediency.[35] There are a number of exceptions to the principle of compulsory prosecution,[36] which might indicate that systems such as the German one are little different from the English: one proclaims a principle of compulsory prosecution and derogates from it, whereas the other recognizes from the outset that prosecution policy must be a question of expediency.[37] However, there is a substantial difference: whereas the German (and other) systems recognize explicitly the principle of compulsory prosecution because of the values (the principles of legality and equal treatment) it upholds, those funda-mental values and principles have little explicit recognition, even as starting points, in the heavily pragmatic English system. Instead, the alternatives to prosecution have developed one by one, often without statutory foundations, and hardly constitute a 'system' of diversion. However, they are used in large numbers; their form and their justifications need careful scrutiny.

The context for the evolution of the English approach to diversion was set by some major changes in the role of the police. On the one hand, the police lost their traditional dominance of decisions to prosecute when the CPS was created in 1986, and more re-cently they lost their dominance of charging decisions when the statutory charging scheme transferred much power to the CPS in 2003.[38] Having said this, the situation has reverted somewhat: now the police may charge: (1) any summary only offence (including criminal damage where the value of the loss or damage is less than £5,000) irrespective of plea; (2) any offence of retail theft (shoplifting) or attempted retail theft irrespective of plea provided it is suitable for sentence in the magistrates' court; and (3) any either way offence anticipated as a guilty plea and suitable for sentence in a magistrates' court; provided that it is not: a case requiring the consent of the Director of Prosecutions (DPP) to prosecute; a case involving a death; connected with terror-ist activity or official secrets; a case of hate crime or domestic violence; an offence of violent disorder or affray; causing grievous bodily harm or wounding, or actual bodily

---

[34] See e.g. J. Herrmann, 'The Rule of Compulsory Prosecution and the Scope of Prosecutorial Discretion in Germany' (1974) 41 *U Chi LR* 468; P. J. P. Tak, *The Legal Scope of Non-Prosecution in Europe* (1986).

[35] Herrmann, n 34; J. Herrmann, 'Bargaining Justice: a Bargain for German Criminal Justice?' (1992) 53 *U Pittsburgh LR* 755. For the somewhat similar situation in Italy (principle of compulsory prosecution, with practical derogations), see S. Maffei, 'Negotiations on Evidence and Negotiations on Sentence: Adversarial Experiments in Italian Criminal Procedure' (2004) 2 *J Int Crim J* 1050.

[36] Though s 152 of the German Code of Criminal Procedure requires the public prosecutor to bring a pros-ecution in respect of all punishable conduct, to the extent that there is sufficient evidence, in practice there are various exceptions to this, including s 153a, which allows conditional termination of proceedings.

[37] Cf H. Jung, 'Criminal Justice: A European Perspective' [1993] *Crim LR* 237, 241.

[38] See I. Brownlee, 'The Statutory Charging Scheme in England and Wales: Towards a Unified Prosecution System?' [2004] *Crim LR* 896–907; HMCPSI and HMIC, *The Joint Thematic Review of the New Charging Ar-rangements* (2008).

harm; a Sexual Offences Act offence committed by or upon a person under 18; or an offence under the Licensing Act 2003.[39]

In addition, the police were encouraged in the 1980s to increase their use of police cautions to deal with less serious cases, and they did so, exercising a dispositive discretion in relation to significant numbers of defendants. There was also what Richard Young describes as 'a drift towards summary justice' in on-the-street policing,[40] with police officers acquiring and using a range of non-criminal measures and also Penalty Notices for Disorder (PNDs), which are explicitly punitive. This tendency had become more pronounced, only to decline more recently.[41] In 2009, 38 per cent of the 1.29 million offences 'solved' by the police were dealt with by a disposal outside the court system, following a five-year period from 2003 where the number of OOCDs administered each year increased by 135 per cent, from 241,000 in 2003 to 567,000 in 2008.[42] The picture now is remarkably different: OOCDs fell by 14 per cent in 2017, driven in large part by a 28 per cent reduction in PNDs and a 19 per cent reduction in cautions. In 2017, 246,000 people were issued an out-of-court disposal, compared with 670,000 in 2007.[43] This is due to some legislative changes, which are examined later, as well as a highly critical report of HMIC in 2011.[44] This found wide and inexplicable variations in practice across police force areas in the proportion and types of offences handled out of court, as well as raising particular concerns about the use of OOCDs for persistent offenders.

We now turn to examine different forms of diversion, assuming cases in which there is evidence that the person has committed an offence. As will become evident, the role for the CPS is limited, with these powers mostly lying with the police.

(A) NO FURTHER ACTION

Despite evidential sufficiency, the police may decide to take no further action in a given case. This may occur where the defendant has already been sentenced to custody, or indicates a willingness to have the offence 'taken into consideration' in sentencing for another crime; or the offender is very young; or the offence is non-serious.

(B) WARNINGS

A second alternative is a warning, given by a police officer in circumstances where a formal caution (considered in section 6.2(C)) is considered unnecessary or inappropriate.

---

[39] Director of Public Prosecutions, *Charging (The Director's Guidance) 2013* (revised arrangements) (5th edn, 2013), 15. Available at https://www.cps.gov.uk/legal-guidance/charging-directors-guidance-2013-fifth-edition-may-2013-revised-arrangements. See further Ch 7.

[40] R. Young, 'Street Policing after PACE: The Drift to Summary Justice' in E. Cape and R. Young (eds), *Regulating Policing: the Police and Criminal Evidence Act 1984: Past, Present and Future* (2008).

[41] Transforming Justice, *Less is more— the case for dealing with offences out of court* (2017).

[42] HMIC and HMCPSI, *Exercising Discretion*, n 32, 9.

[43] Ministry of Justice, *Criminal Justice Statistics quarterly, England and Wales, 2017* (2018), 9.

[44] HMIC and HMCPSI, *Exercising Discretion*, n 32, 5–6.

Such a warning might be given by an individual officer on the beat, so that the individual is not even taken to a police station. Motorists have often benefited from informal
warnings of this kind. In addition, the regulatory agencies may use informal warnings:
for example, in the Guidance issued by the Environment Agency, there is recognition
that inspectors may occasionally give a 'site warning' that is noted on the site inspection report but does not result in the sending of a warning letter.[45]

There is a specific form of police warning for low-level drug possession. A 'cannabis
warning' was introduced in 2004 after cannabis was reclassified from Class B down
to Class C. It may be used where a person is found in possession of a small amount
of cannabis, and it is a spoken warning delivered by a police officer on the street or
at a police station.[46] Though cannabis was returned to Class B in January 2009, the
cannabis warning was retained.[47] For persons under 18, the first offence of possessing
cannabis for personal use may be followed by a cannabis warning; the second offence
should be followed by a PND (see section 6.2(E)); for third or subsequent offences,
there is a presumption in favour of prosecution.[48] Such a warning was introduced in
2014 for khat also.[49] In line with the general trend for OOCDs, the trend for cannabis
and khat warnings has been declining year on year since 2008, when 108,300 were issued, to 32,000 in 2017.[50]

(C) CAUTIONS

The third family of diversionary alternatives to be considered is the caution. A con-
certed push towards the wider use of cautioning came in the 1980s, with numerous
Home Office Circulars persuading the police to increase diversion and to reduce
the proportionate use of prosecutions. These had considerable success: for adult
males the cautioning rate rose from 5 per cent in 1984 to 18 per cent in 1991, and
for adult females from 14 to 40 per cent.[51] The Circular of 1990 went so far as to
state 'that the courts should only be used as a last resort, particularly for juveniles
and young adults'.[52] However, there was a hardening of approach in the mid-1990s:
a Home Office Circular of 1994 aimed to reduce repeat cautioning and in cautioning for indictable-only offences. The result was a significant downturn in the use of
cautions for indictable offences, from almost 250,000 in 1993 to 192,000 in 1998,
reaching a low of 143,000 in 2002. Since then, the use of cautions increased to a
peak of 362,900 in 2007, but has fallen again since then. In 2017, 84,000 offenders
were given either a simple or conditional caution, down 19 per cent from 2016.[53]

---

[45] Environment Agency, n 15, para 3.2.

[46] Ministry of Justice, *Penalty notices for disorder: guidance for police officers* (2014), 3.33.

[47] In 2012, the Home Affairs Select Committee voted 4:3 to recommend reducing the classification again:
see Home Affairs Select Committee, *Drugs: Breaking the Cycle—Formal Minutes* (2012), [12].

[48] Ministry of Justice, *PND Guidance*, n 46, 3.33.

[49] Home Office, *Khat Fact Sheet*, https://www.gov.uk/government/uploads/system/uploads/attachment_
data/file/341917/Khat_leaflet_A4_v12__2_.pdf; Ministry of Justice, *PND Guidance*, n 46, 3.32–3.37.

[50] Ministry of Justice, n 43, 13.   [51] *Criminal Statistics, England and Wales* (1986 and 1991), Table 5.5.

[52] Home Office Circular 59/1990, para 7.   [53] Ministry of Justice, n 43, 11.

Fifty-one per cent of cautions issued in 2017 were for indictable offences, of which drug offences, theft, and violence against the person accounted for 80 per cent. The volume of cautions issued to offenders for indictable sexual offences decreased by 26 per cent in 2017 compared with 2016, continuing the downward trend with a 63 per cent fall from 2007. In 2017, 2 per cent of offenders cautioned for indictable offences were cautioned for sexual offences. The overall cautioning rate has decreased to 10.7 per cent in 2017, from 12.5 per cent in 2016: for young people this is a decrease from 37.3 per cent to 35.1 per cent and for adults 11.3 per cent to 9.6 per cent.[54] The cautioning rate for indictable offences also decreased to 15.9 per cent in 2017, continuing the downward trend in each year since 2007: in 2016, the rate was 17.3 per cent and in 2007 39.6 per cent. The summary offence cautioning rate also continues to decline: from a peak of 24.3 per cent in 2007 it decreased to 8.0 per cent in 2017.[55]

We now consider simple cautions; youth cautions, and conditional cautions.

i. Simple cautions

A 'simple caution' is a formal police caution, to be distinguished from informal warnings given by individual officers. The police should offer to caution an individual only when there is sufficient evidence to prosecute; where he or she admits guilt, and agrees to the caution being administered; and it is in the public interest to dispose of the offence by way of caution. Usually the simple caution is delivered by a senior officer in uniform at a police station.

Until 2015, there was no statutory basis at all for this kind of cautioning, and still it is covered only partially by legislation.[56] Ultimately reform was prompted by concerns that the police were using simple cautions to deal with serious offending behaviour,[57] and that officers were issuing cautions without being aware of the cautioning criteria.[58] A subsequent review of simple cautions recommended in 2013 that restrictions be introduced either through legislation or guidance, and that a wider review of OOCDs be conducted.[59] Following this, the Ministry of Justice published revised guidance, and the Criminal Justice and Courts Act 2015 now limits the circumstances in which simple cautions may be used.

The principles on which the police should take their gatekeeping decisions are set out in the 2015 Ministry of Justice guidance on *Simple Cautions for Adult Offenders*, which aims to structure discretion. It states that '[t]he simple caution scheme is designed to provide a means of dealing with low-level, mainly first-time, offending without

---

[54] Ibid, 12.   [55] Ibid.

[56] Home Office Circular 16/2008, *Simple Cautioning*, was replaced on 8 April 2013 by the Ministry of Justice's *Simple Caution for Adult Offender guidance*. Following a review of simple cautions, this was further amended on 14 November 2013, and the current version is from 2015.

[57] Home Affairs Select Committee, *Out-of-Court Disposals*, Fourteenth Report (2015), [22].

[58] Kemp, n 8, 287.

[59] HM Government and College of Policing, *Review of Simple Cautions* (2013), https://www.gov.uk/government/uploads/system/uploads/attachment_data/file/257010/report-of-the-simple-cautions-review.pdf.

a prosecution',[60] and suggests that officers should refer to the gravity of the offence in question.[61] The Guidance emphasizes the need for 'a clear and reliable admission of the offence':[62] while it states explicitly that the admission of guilt does not need to be made within a formal interview under the Police and Evidence Act 1984 (PACE), the method for obtaining and recording the admission must comply with PACE.[63] The admission should be recorded;[64] the offender should be allowed access to legal advice,[65] and should be made aware that a caution will be recorded and cited in court, and that it may trigger notification requirements under the Sexual Offences Act 2003 if it is given for a sexual offence. As well as the retention of the record of the simple caution, the offender's DNA profile and fingerprints, if taken, whether before or after the simple caution has been administered, may be retained by the police. As Hynes and Elkins note, the caution 'is a hybrid and complex concept, not amounting to a conviction but recordable and . . . with the potential to have a similar effect to a conviction'.[66]

A simple caution must not be offered in order to secure an admission of guilt that could then provide sufficient evidence to meet the evidential stage of the Full Code Test,[67] which is a prerequisite to prosecution.[68] Moreover, a simple caution cannot be offered where the person admits guilt but also raises a defence.[69] The views of the victim (if any) should be sought, but should not be conclusive,[70] and it should be 'in the public interest' to use a simple caution.[71]

Generally, police officers may issue a simple caution without consulting the CPS, although they may ask prosecutors for advice on the suitability of using such a disposal.[72] However, the Criminal Justice and Courts Act 2015 provided some much-needed limits on police powers in this context. Section 17(2) prohibits the police from giving a simple caution for an indictable-only offence unless the CPS agrees, following consideration by a senior police officer who believes that exceptional circumstances exist. Similarly, simple cautions should not be given for certain specified either way offences[73] unless a senior police officer believes there are exceptional circumstances. Section 17(4) restricts the use of simple cautions for repeat offending: an offender must not be given a simple caution for a summary offence or an either way offence if in the two years before the offence was committed he or she has been convicted of, or cautioned for, a similar offence, unless a police officer of at least the rank of inspector

---

[60] Ministry of Justice, *Simple Cautions for Adult Offenders* (2015), https://assets.publishing.service.gov.uk/government/uploads/system/uploads/attachment_data/file/708595/cautions-guidance-2015.pdf, [6].

[61] Ibid, [32].   [62] Ibid, [23].   [63] Ibid, [26].   [64] Ibid.   [65] Ibid, [77]–[79].

[66] P. Hynes and M. Elkins, 'Suggestions for Reform to the Police Cautioning Procedure' [2013] *Crim LR* 966, 970.

[67] Ministry of Justice, *Simple Cautions for Adult Offenders*, n 60, [24].   [68] See Ch 7.

[69] Ministry of Justice, *Simple Cautions for Adult Offenders*, n 60, [25].   [70] Ibid, [57]–[59].

[71] Ibid, [29].

[72] CPS, *Cautioning and Diversion guidance*, https://www.cps.gov.uk/legal-guidance/cautioning-and-diversion.

[73] s 17(3). Ministry of Justice, *Simple Cautions for Adult Offenders*, n 60, Annex B. The specified either-way offences include: possession of a bladed article, offensive weapon, or firearm in public; including threatening with a bladed article or offensive weapon in a public place or a school; child prostitution and pornography, cruelty to a child, indecent photographs of children; and supplying Class A drugs.

determines that there are exceptional circumstances relating to the offender, or the previous or present offence.[74] The Home Office Select Committee suggested that these reforms would go some way to restore public confidence in simple cautions,[75] and noted that the new Guidance has already reduced the number of simple cautions for indictable offences. It expressed support for the proposal that the guidance be put on a statutory footing,[76] though this has yet to occur.

What are the advantages claimed for cautioning, rather than prosecuting? The Ministry of Justice states that the aims of the simple caution scheme are:

- To offer a proportionate response to low-level offending where the offender has admitted the offence;
- To deliver swift, simple and effective justice that carries a deterrent effect;
- To record an individual's criminal conduct for possible reference in future criminal proceedings or in criminal record or other similar checks;
- To reduce the likelihood of re-offending;
- To increase the amount of time police officers spend dealing with more serious crime and reduce the amount of time officers spend completing paperwork and attending court, whilst simultaneously reducing the burden on the courts.[77]

The first purpose refers to proportionality, implying that quicker and simpler responses are more appropriate for less serious offences, although the words 'and more cheaply' are implicit in this and point 2 also. Notably, there is no explicit mention of diversion in these aims, in contrast to the preceding Home Office Circular.[78] The third aim is to support the recording system, so that where an offender has made an admission of offending this is recorded and available when security checks are done or subsequent proceedings brought. The fourth aim makes a bold claim about effectiveness. Statistics show that some 85 per cent of those cautioned in 1985 and 1988 were not convicted of a serious offence within two years of their caution.[79] This reconviction rate of 15 per cent is much lower than that for offenders convicted at court, at least for first offenders, which is 29 per cent for those without any previous convictions.[80] It could be commented that any such comparison is flawed because the court group is likely to have a higher proportion of people with previous cautions, who are more likely to be reconvicted anyway. In 2016, young offenders in general had a proven reoffending rate of 41.6 per cent, whereas the reoffending rate for those given a youth caution was 30.1 per cent.[81] This has remained broadly stable since 2013, but has increased by around 3–4 percentage points compared to 2005. Moreover, a systematic review found that restorative justice conferences produced a 'modest, but highly cost-effective reduction

[74] Ministry of Justice, *Simple Cautions for Adult Offenders*, n 60, [38].
[75] Home Affairs Select Committee, *Out-of-Court Disposals*, n 57, [25].   [76] Ibid.
[77] Ministry of Justice, *Simple Cautions for Adult Offenders*, n 60, [5].
[78] Home Office Circular 16/2008.
[79] Home Office Statistical Bulletin 8/94, *The Criminal Histories of those Cautioned in 1985, 1988 and 1991*.
[80] G. Philpotts and L. Lancucki, *Previous Convictions, Sentence and Reconviction* (1979), 16.
[81] Ministry of Justice, *Proven Reoffending Statistics Quarterly Bulletin, April 2016 to June 2016* (2018), 8.

in repeat offending'.[82] However, those who subscribe to the principle of minimum intervention do not need to establish that cautions are more effective, in terms of reconvictions. It is sufficient to argue that they have not been shown to be less effective than conviction and sentence.

ii. Youth cautions

The practice of cautioning young offenders was developed by the police in the late 1970s, supported by a number of Home Office police circulars. These police cautions were replaced by the Crime and Disorder Act 1998, through the introduction of a system of reprimands and warnings known as the Final Warning Scheme.[83] The idea that a caution standing alone was insufficient was a major force behind this scheme, which allowed no more than one reprimand and no more than one final warning (which will 'usually be followed by a community intervention programme, involving the offender and his or her family to address the causes of the offending and so reduce the risk of further crime'), and then prescribed prosecution. This three-step approach applied even where the next offence was not otherwise serious enough to warrant prosecution. Despite this more elaborate statutory framework, Stewart Field's research led him to conclude that 'pre-charge decision-making in youth justice remains a highly discretionary process rooted in personal judgement'.[84]

In turn, the Final Warning Scheme was abolished by s 135 of the Legal Aid, Sentencing and Punishment of Offenders Act 2012 (LASPO), repealing ss 65 and 66 and inserting a new s 66ZA to reintroduce the 'youth caution', and s 66ZB, setting out its effects. As Edwards notes, this is an extraordinary change that replaces the structured approach to diversion in the 1998 Act.[85] Now a youth caution may be given for any offence where the young person (aged 10 to 17) admits the offence, and there is sufficient evidence for a realistic prospect of conviction but it is not in the public interest to prosecute.[86] If a constable gives a youth caution to a person, the constable must as soon as practicable refer the person to a youth offending team, which is part of a local council rather than the police or courts service.[87]

iii. Conditional cautions

Sections 22–27 of the Criminal Justice Act 2003 introduced a new form of diversion at the time, the conditional caution. Such a caution may only be given to a person aged

---

[82] H. Strang, L. Sherman, E. Mayo-Wilson, D. Woods, and B. Ariel, *Restorative Justice Conferencing (RJC) Using Face-to-Face Meetings of Offenders and Victims: Effects on Offender Recidivism and Victim Satisfaction. A Systematic Review* (2013), 2.

[83] For discussion of their use, see S. Field, 'Early Intervention and the "New" Youth Justice' [2008] *Crim LR* 177.

[84] Ibid, 189.

[85] A. Edwards, 'Legal Aid, Sentencing and Punishment of Offenders Act 2012—The Financial Procedural and Practical Implications' [2012] *Crim LR* 584.

[86] Crime and Disorder Act 1998, s 66ZA. See Ministry of Justice, *Youth Cautions—Guidance for Police and Youth Offending Teams* (2013).

[87] Legal Aid, Sentencing and Punishment of Offenders Act 2012, s 66ZB; set up under s 39 of the Crime and Disorder Act 1998.

18 or over, against whom there is sufficient evidence of guilt, and who has admitted guilt. Five requirements must be met before a conditional caution may be given: (1) the officer has evidence that the individual had committed an offence; (2) there is sufficient evidence to charge him with the offence; (3) the offender had admitted committing the offence to the officer; (4) the effect of the conditional caution and failure to comply were explained to the offender; and (5) the offender signed the document containing details of the offence and admission that he committed the offence, his consent to a conditional caution. and any conditions attached to it.[88] The conditions are usually related to participation in a rehabilitative programme or the making of reparation. Section 25 provides for the publication of a Code of Practice governing the use of conditional cautions.

When first introduced, these were implemented by the CPS, which determined whether a conditional caution was appropriate.[89] Although conditional cautions (like simple cautions) were administered by a police officer, and although the police could pass a case to the CPS with a recommendation for conditional caution, only a prosecutor could decide that, despite sufficient evidence to charge, a conditional caution should be given. This could be seen as remedying some of the objections to simple cautions, such as their largely discretionary nature; and the conferral of considerable disciplinary power on the police.

Nonetheless, the proposal that the police should authorize and issue conditional cautions without referral to the CPS was put out for consultation in 2010.[90] Now, s 133 of LASPO enables an 'authorised person' (a police officer not below the rank of sergeant or any person specifically authorized to do so by the DPP[91]) to make a decision to offer a conditional caution without reference to the prosecutor. In determining whether to offer a conditional caution, authorized persons and prosecutors must follow the Code of Practice for Adult Conditional Cautions 2013 and comply with the Guidance of the DPP.[92] Indictable-only offences still are to be referred to prosecutors:

> As such offences will generally attract significant custodial sentences on conviction the maintenance of public confidence in the Justice System will ordinarily require such cases to be dealt with at court. Any indictable only case considered by the police as suitable for a Conditional Caution must be referred to a prosecutor.[93]

Moreover, conditional cautions are available for all offences except for domestic violence and hate crime, which generally are excluded as not suitable.[94] There is some flexibility to this policy. Indeed, empirical research carried out by McGlynn, Westmarland, and Johnson found that every police force in England, Wales, and Northern Ireland (but not Scotland)

---

[88] Criminal Justice Act 2003, s 23.

[89] Applying CPS, *The Director's Guidance on Conditional Cautioning* (5th edn, 2007).

[90] Ministry of Justice, *Breaking the Cycle: Effective Punishment, Rehabilitation and Sentencing of Offenders* (2010).

[91] Director of Public Prosecutions, *Adult Conditional Cautions (The Director's Guidance)* (7th edn, 2013).

[92] Ibid, 1.1. [93] Ibid, 6.1. [94] Ibid, 3.1.

used out-of-court resolutions to respond to domestic abuse in 2014.[95] Moreover, in *R (Robson) v CPS* the High Court allowed Robson's application for judicial review of the CPS decision to prosecute her for damage, valued at £3,406.99, caused to the property of A, Robson's former domestic partner.[96] The police had ruled out a conditional caution, given the character of the case and the value and extent of the damage, and the CPS drew on different codes and Guidances to decide that a conditional caution could not be applied as the case involved domestic violence. The High Court held that while in most cases the application of the policy that a conditional caution should not be offered in cases of domestic violence would be entirely appropriate, there might be exceptional cases where a different outcome should be considered and where the exercise of discretion might result in the offer of a conditional caution. It was a misinterpretation to regard the Guidance as possessing no flexibility and permitting no exceptions and, accordingly, the decision to prosecute Robson was quashed.

Conditional cautions were introduced for persons under the age of 18 in 2008, where the offender has not previously been convicted of an offence, and subject to the same criteria in respect of admission of guilt and sufficiency of evidence as the adult scheme.[97] LASPO extended this to provide that conditional cautions may be used for young people convicted of other more serious offences in the past.[98]

LASPO also introduced the foreign national offender conditional caution. These are available for all summary (non-motoring) offences and either way offences with a penalty of up to two years' imprisonment. They have rehabilitative and/or reparative conditions, but the primary condition must be one which requires the individual to leave the country, cooperate with the authorities, and not return to the UK for five years.[99]

A conditional caution may incorporate a restorative justice dimension. Though it eludes a neat definition, restorative justice prioritizes restoration and reparation of harm, and encompasses a philosophy that sees crime as a conflict between individuals, which has resulted in harm to victims and communities. It seeks to provide an opportunity for 'active participation by victims, offenders and their communities'.[100] In England and Wales, restorative justice is available at all stages of the criminal process, and can take the form of victim–offender mediation either through a guided direct or indirect contact between the offender and victim, sometimes with a mediator, or a large-scale community conference particularly at resolving anti-social behaviour, or referral order panels for young offenders.[101] Given the absence of a firm statutory

---

[95] C. McGlynn, N. Westmarland, and K. Johnson, 'Under the radar: the widespread use of "Out of Court resolutions" in policing domestic violence and abuse in the United Kingdom' (2017) 58 *BJ Crim* 1–16.

[96] [2016] EWHC 2191 (Admin).

[97] s 66A of the 1998 Act, as inserted by Criminal Justice and Immigration Act 2008, Sch 9, para 3.

[98] s 136, omitting para (a) from s 66A(1) of the 1998 Act. Ministry of Justice, *Code of Practice for Youth Conditional Cautions* (2013), https://www.gov.uk/government/uploads/system/uploads/attachment_data/file/243443/9780108512179.pdf.

[99] See the Criminal Justice Act 2003 (Conditional Cautions: Code of Practice) Order 2013, and *The Director's Guidance on Adult Conditional Cautions.*

[100] See H. Strang, *Repair or Revenge: Victims and Restorative Justice* (2002); H. Strang and J. Braithwaite (eds), *Restorative Justice and Civil Society* (2001).

[101] CPS, *Restorative Justice Legal Guidance* (no date), https://www.cps.gov.uk/legal-guidance/restorative-justice.

framework for its content and nature, it is unsurprising that there are inconsistencies and variations in how restorative justice is implemented across the criminal justice system.[102] Nonetheless, the Code of Practice for Victims states that victims are entitled to receive information on restorative justice from the police.[103] Indeed, the House of Commons Justice Committee recommended a legislative right for victims to access restorative justice services, once demonstrated that the system has sufficient capacity to provide such services to all victims.[104]

The Association of Chief Police Officers (ACPO, now the National Police Chiefs' Council) outlines three different 'levels' of restorative justice that officers may use when responding to a reported incident:

> Level 1: an instant or on-street disposal, where police officers or PCSOs [Police Community Support Officers] use restorative skills . . . to resolve conflict in minor crimes and incidents . . . an alternative to a formal criminal justice process.
>
> Level 2: measures such as restorative justice conferences, and may involve more participants, risk assessments and seek longer-term solutions. A Level two restorative justice response can occur either as an alternative to criminal justice proceedings, or in addition to criminal justice proceedings, as part of a formal crime disposal.
>
> Level 3: resolutions that take place in addition to criminal justice proceedings, mainly post-sentence . . . for cases that involve serious, complex or sensitive incidents, or where offenders are being monitored by an offender management team and/or are deemed at risk of continued offending. Involvement in an RJ [restorative justice] process can either be made a part of a conditional caution where both victim and offender agree to take part; or the RJ process can itself be the way in which the conditions of the cautions are arrived at.[105]

These are not statutory provisions, and application of the guidance varies considerably. Moreover, there is some internal inconsistency: participation in a restorative justice process as a condition of the caution itself undermines the claim that restorative justice participation is truly voluntary. Moreover, in terms of its application, McGlynn et al found that every police force in England, Wales, and Northern Ireland (but not Scotland) used out-of-court resolutions to respond to domestic abuse in 2014, which is far more widespread than previously imagined. OOCD were used for a broad range of serious criminal offences which, if prosecuted, would have potential sentencing tariffs of up to life imprisonment. In addition, data revealed a potential over-representation of OOCDs in cases that involved women offenders and same-sex partners. Likewise, the approaches were predominantly informal, 'on-the-street' restorative outcomes (ACPO 'Level 1') which served almost exclusively as an alternative to prosecution.

---

[102] *Facing Up To Offending: Use of restorative justice in the criminal justice system*, A joint thematic inspection by HMIC, HMI Probation, HMI Prisons and HMCPSI (2012).

[103] Ministry of Justice, *Code of Practice for Victims of Crime* (2015), ch 2, part A, section 7, para 7.

[104] House of Commons Justice Committee, *Restorative Justice*, Fourth Report of Session 2016–17 (2016), [73].

[105] *Director's Guidance on Conditional Cautioning* (2013), Annex B.

(D) FIXED PENALTY NOTICES

Since the Road Traffic Act 1988, the police have been able to use fixed penalty notices (FPN) to deal with various motoring offences, starting with the most minor and now encompassing a wide range of road traffic offences. In addition, they may now be issued for littering and other environmental offences, graffiti, and street trading without a licence. An FPN can be issued by the police, local authority officers, or the Environment Agency, to anyone over the age of 10, and may range from £50 to £500 as stipulated in the relevant statute. The ticketed person may challenge the FPN, in which case the matter goes to court, as does any instance of non-payment.[106] There were 2,391,407 FPNs issued for motoring offences by the police in England and Wales in 2016, which is comparable to the previous year.[107] Eighty-two per cent of FPNs issued in 2016 were for speed limit offences (1,970,207), up 1 per cent from 2015 (1,944,978).[108]

(E) PENALTY NOTICES FOR DISORDER

The Criminal Justice and Police Act 2001 introduced another dispositive power for the police: the penalty notice for disorder (PND). The police themselves were the prime drivers behind this innovation, lobbying for a measure that would enhance on-the-street control and cut paperwork and police time too.[109] The PND was piloted from 2002 and rolled out nationally in 2004. Public prosecutors in many other countries have had similar powers for some years,[110] such as in Scotland, where the 'fiscal fine' was established in the 1990s.[111]

A PND can be issued by a police officer or community support officer for one of a list of possible offences: at the higher tier of £90 are the more serious offences, including wasting police time, being drunk and disorderly, shop theft under £200, criminal damage less than £500, and using threatening or abusive words contrary to s 5 of the Public Order Act; at the lower tier of £60 are the less serious offences, including railway trespass and consuming alcohol in a prohibited zone. The penalty should be paid within 21 days, or alternatively the person may request to have the case brought to court. If the person does neither, the penalty is increased by 50 per cent and registered at court as an unpaid fine, to be enforced accordingly. Only around 50 per cent pay their fines in full, a proportion that remains relatively stable, and 33 per cent are fined for late payment.[112]

LASPO made a number of changes to the 2001 Act, in both extending and circumscribing PNDs. Now PNDs may no longer be given to a person aged under 18 years.[113]

---

[106] See R. Morgan, *Summary Justice: Fast—but Fair?* (2008), 13.
[107] Office for National Statistics, *Police powers and procedures, England and Wales, year ending 31 March 2017* (2017), 7.2.
[108] Ibid, 7.3.   [109] Young, 'Street Policing after PACE', n 40, 78.
[110] J. Fionda, *Public Prosecutors and Discretion: A Comparative Study* (1995); A. Selih, 'The Prosecution Process' in Council of Europe, *Crime and Criminal Justice in Europe* (2000), 103.
[111] For discussion, see P. Duff and N. Hutton (eds), *Criminal Justice in Scotland* (1999), ch 7.
[112] *Criminal Statistics England and Wales 2007*, Table 7.2; Ministry of Justice, n 43, 10.
[113] LASPO, s 132 and Sch 23, para 15.

In addition, LASPO removed the requirements that a constable must be authorized by the chief officer of police to give a PND, and that a constable must be in uniform to give a PND.[114] There is also a new form of penalty notice with an education option, known as the PND-E: a police chief officer may establish an educational course scheme and offer a person the opportunity to discharge liability to be convicted of a penalty offence by paying for and completing an educational course relating to the offence. A person can, alternatively, opt to pay the penalty amount in full or request a court hearing as with a 'standard' PND.[115] The Ministry of Justice notes that the PND-E provisions were introduced in response to requests by chief officers of police, who can adapt how the scheme operates in their local area to best meet local needs, if they so wish but it is not mandatory to set up an educational course scheme.[116] A sum equal to one and a half times the amount of the penalty will be registered as a fine for enforcement against a recipient of a PND-E where the recipient fails within a period of 21 days beginning with the date on which the notice was given either to ask to attend an educational course, or to pay the penalty, or ask to be tried for the offence to which the notice relates, or asks within that 21-day period to attend a course, but then fails to pay the course fee or pays the fee but fails to attend or complete the course.[117]

The aims of the PND scheme are fourfold:

1. To offer operational officers a quick and effective alternative disposal option for dealing with low-level, anti-social and nuisance offending.

2. To deliver a swift and simple method of deterrence.

3. To reduce the amount of time that police officers spend completing paperwork and attending court, while simultaneously reducing the burden on the courts.

4. To increase the amount of time that constables spend on the street and dealing with more serious crime.[118]

The last two aims seem to amount to the same thing. We must now ask whether these aims should be supported, and whether they are being achieved.

There are several problems with PNDs as introduced and implemented. First, it is plain that they are mislabelled. Theft from a shop and criminal damage are not necessarily forms of disorder. The truth is that they were brought within the scheme to solve practical problems for the police, largely that of dealing with shop thefts. The first aim has accordingly been worded so as not to focus on disorder (unlike the title PND), and to include 'nuisance offending'. Secondly, there are significant implications of the PND. The officer who issues the PND must be satisfied that there is sufficient evidence to prosecute for the crime, but in an on-the-street encounter there may be serious questions about this.[119] No admission from the ticketed person is required, but the PND discharges all liability to be prosecuted for that offence and it does not rank

---

[114] LASPO, Sch 23, paras 13 and 14.   [115] Ministry of Justice, *PND Guidance*, n 46, 6.2.
[116] Ibid, 6.3 and 6.4.   [117] LASPO, Sch 23, para 6.
[118] Ministry of Justice, *PND Guidance*, n 46, 1.1.
[119] C. Kraina and L. Carroll, *Penalty Notices for Disorder: Review of Practice across Police Forces* (2006), 11.

as a conviction. However, it may be recorded on the Police National Computer, which may be disclosed as part of an enhanced Disclosure and Barring Service check, it may be cited in court as evidence of bad character, and is evidence in civil proceedings.[120] It may be true that a ticketed person who wishes to dispute the evidence can request to be brought to court, but since a PND is not a conviction and requires no admission of guilt, there is an incentive to 'cut one's losses' and 'get it all over with'. It is therefore questionable to rely on it as evidence of guilt. However, the features of the PND (not an admission, no criminal record, no prosecution for that offence) have been held not to prevent a prosecution for a more serious offence arising out of the same facts, if the grounds for doing so subsequently come to light. Thus, in *Gore and Maher* (2009)[121] the defendants had punched and kicked a man in a drunken fight; the victim said he was all right, the two men were arrested and were given PNDs, one for being drunk and disorderly and the other for causing harassment, alarm, or distress. It later emerged that the victim's arm was broken, and a CCTV recording showed the force of the blows delivered, so the two defendants were prosecuted for inflicting grievous bodily harm. The Court of Appeal held that the prosecutions were not an abuse of process, because payment of a PND merely prevents prosecution for the offence for which the PND was given, there was no implied undertaking not to prosecute for a more serious offence, if appropriate facts came to light.

Thirdly, the emphasis on reducing the workload of the lower courts raises questions about the proper function of those courts. The choice here is between police law, where the police are themselves judge and jury in relation to PNDs, and resort to an independent and impartial tribunal. It is not a decisive argument to say that the ticketed person always has the option of going to court, because there may be other pressures, particularly the fear of a heavier sentence. Nor is it sufficient to argue that the PND is not a conviction, because we have shown how ambiguous its status and implications are. The simplification of criminal justice comes at a price: in most other countries, it is the quasi-judicial figure of the public prosecutor who decides on diversionary financial penalties, and it is questionable whether such power should be given to the police on the street (with little supervision, as the research shows).[122]

The extent to which the police embraced the PND initially is evident from the statistics: 64,000 were issued in the first year (2004), and the total reached some 200,000 in both 2006 and 2007. Since then, like other OOCDs, the use of PNDs has decreased year on year. In 2017, 25,900 were issued compared with 36,200 in 2016, a 28 per cent decrease, and an 88 per cent decrease since 2007. As has been the case since their introduction in 2017, the majority of PNDs were imposed for being drunk and disorderly (41 per cent), possession of cannabis (20 per cent), retail theft of goods under the value of £100 (19 per cent), and behaviour likely to cause harassment, alarm, or distress (12 per cent).[123]

[120] Ministry of Justice, *PND Guidance*, n 46, 5.5–5.7.
[121] [2009] EWCA Crim 1424; also *R (Gavigan) v Enfield* [2013] EWHC 2805 (Admin).
[122] Kraina and Carroll, n 119, 12.   [123] Ministry of Justice, n 43, 10.

(F) COMMUNITY RESOLUTIONS

A community resolution is an informal, non-statutory mechanism used to address less serious crime and anti-social behaviour where the offender accepts responsibility.[124] It may involve restorative justice practices, and the views of the victim are taken into account in reaching an informal agreement between the parties.

(G) DEFERRED PROSECUTION AGREEMENTS

In 2014, a particular form of diversion was introduced for corporate actors only, in the form of deferred prosecution agreements (DPAs). Unlike the US prototype, which can apply to individuals as well as corporates,[125] in England and Wales a DPA is an agreement reached between the prosecutor and a corporate entity[126] which could be prosecuted for an economic crime,[127] under the supervision of a judge who must be convinced that the DPA is 'in the interests of justice' and that its terms are 'fair, reasonable and proportionate'.[128] The prosecutor charges a criminal offence but proceedings are suspended automatically if the Crown Court judge approves the DPA. The DPA entails suspension of the prosecution for a certain timeframe, as long as the corporate entity meets certain specified conditions, such as paying a financial penalty or compensation and cooperating with future prosecutions of individuals suspected of involvement in criminality. Though DPAs require agreement to a statement of facts, this is not a criminal law admission, or a guilty plea.

The SFO has stated that 'DPAs enable a corporate body to make full reparation for criminal behaviour without the collateral damage of a conviction',[129] and describes them as 'a new kind of disposal of criminal risk in this jurisdiction, conceptually . . . somewhere between a guilty plea and a civil recovery'.[130] To date, four corporations have agreed DPAs with the SFO: Standard Bank; XYZ (an anonymized small-to-medium enterprise); Rolls-Royce plc, and Tesco Stores Ltd. It is entirely understandable why a company may prefer to seek a DPA—the entity has more negotiating power and capacity, and a public trial and protracted media coverage throughout the process are avoided. So the stigma involved is lessened, with less problematic labelling throughout

[124] ACPO, *Guidance on the Use of Community Resolutions (CR) Incorporating Restorative Justice (RJ)* (2012).
[125] R. Epstein, 'Deferred Prosecution Agreements on Trial: Lessons from the Law of Unconstitutional Conditions' in A. Barkow and R. Barkow (eds), *Prosecutors in the Boardroom: Using Criminal Law to Regulate Corporate Conduct* (2011), 38; B. Garrett, *Too Big to Jail; How Prosecutors Compromise with Corporations* (2014).
[126] This is a body corporate, a partnership, or an unincorporated association, but not an individual: Crime and Courts Act 2013, Sch 17: s 4.
[127] Courts Act 2013, Sch 17, Part 2. This includes theft, fraud, forgery, money laundering, bribery, and fraudulent evasion of VAT.
[128] Crime and Courts Act 2013, s 45 and Sch 17.
[129] SFO, *Guidance, policy and protocols: Deferred Prosecution Agreements*, available at https://www.sfo.gov.uk/publications/guidance-policy-and-protocols/deferred-prosecution-agreements/.
[130] SFO Speech, 'The future of Deferred Prosecution Agreements after Rolls-Royce', 8 March 2017. https://www.sfo.gov.uk/2017/03/08/the-future-of-deferred-prosecution-agreements-after-rolls-royce/.

and post-trial. Despite support for DPAs, on the grounds that they lead to comparable alteration in business practices to criminal proceedings,[131] the shift away from the use of the criminal law in the sense of prosecution is significant in relation to corporates.

6.3 ISSUES WITH DIVERSION

Diversion and OOCDs throw up some problematic issues that merit brief discussion—the danger of net-widening, pressure on defendants to admit to offences, unfairness to victims, failure to discourage repeat offenders, and local variations.

(A) NET-WIDENING

Net-widening is the process whereby a measure serves not (or not only) to encompass the target group of offenders who would otherwise have been prosecuted, but also to drag into the 'net' people who might otherwise have benefited from a lesser response or no intervention at all. This danger, which was pointed out to the police in the Home Office Circular of 1985, is highlighted by the CPS also.[132] That said, there was little evidence that the considerable increases in cautioning during the 1980s were achieved through any significant net-widening,[133] rather the figures suggest a genuine transfer of offenders away from prosecution towards cautioning. More recently, though, Kemp identified that the pressure on the police to increase the number of detections resulted in cautions being imposed in cases where the legal criteria had not been met.[134] This suggests that net-widening is occurring nowadays.

(B) PRESSURE ON DEFENDANTS

The prospect of a caution or other OOCD may put pressure on a suspect to admit to an offence when it is not clear that he committed it. If the suspect denies knowledge of a certain fact, he might wish to decline a caution and have the point adjudicated in court. Indeed, all of the OOCDs detailed earlier allow the individual the alternative of contesting guilt in court, by declining to accept the official offer and leaving the authorities to prosecute. This is in accordance with Art 6(1) of the European Convention on Human Rights (ECHR) which has been interpreted so as to require the possibility of recourse to a court for a person who contests the decision to impose a penalty.[135] Yet, the disincentives to taking that course are so great (delay, risk of not being believed, risk of conviction) that acceptance of the caution is likely. The

---

[131] J. Arlen and C. Alexander, 'Does Conviction Matter? The Reputational and Collateral Effects of Corporate Crime' in J. Arlen (ed), *Research Handbook on Corporate Crime and Financial Misdealing* (2018), 87.
[132] https://www.cps.gov.uk/legal-guidance/cautioning-and-diversion.
[133] M. McMahon, 'Net-Widening: Vagaries in the Use of a Concept' (1990) 30 *BJ Crim* 121.
[134] Kemp, n 8, 295.
[135] *Le Compte, Van Leuven and De Meyere* [1981] ECHR 3, [23]; *De Weer* [1980] ECHR 1, [23].

pressure and stress of being detained may cloud the judgement of the individual, resulting in a quick decision without the proper and necessary reflection.[136] Despite the prominence now given in the 2015 Ministry of Justice guidance to the need to obtain a 'clear and reliable admission',[137] it remains possible that the alternative prospect of prosecution may be used to obtain an 'admission' that is not genuine.[138] It would take a strong person to refuse a caution and implicitly to challenge the police to prosecute, but such cases do occasionally happen and refusals to accept a caution may be vindicated.[139] In effect, whenever a person knows or believes that there will be a choice between accepting an OOCD and risking a prosecution, there is bound to be pressure to accept the former. The disadvantages of this must be minimized by ensuring that legal advice is always available,[140] and that there is adequate supervision from senior police officers or the CPS as the case may be. As Hynes and Elkins suggest, one way of alleviating the pressure on both the police and suspect to conclude matters relating to a possible caution with undue haste is to bail for a 14-day period to seek legal advice in appropriate circumstances.[141] The issue of safeguards is particularly important now that OOCDs may be cited in court and relied upon for Disclosure and Barring Service purposes.[142]

(C) REPEAT CAUTIONING

Another argument is that multiple OOCDs (in particular, repeat cautioning) sends the wrong message to some offenders, and fails to improve offending behaviour. The restriction on the use of simple cautions for repeat offending could be seen as an increase in legality, in reducing the discretionary elements of the system.[143] Conversely, one could argue that that discretion remains abundant, notably in giving informal warnings which do not invoke the statutory system.

(D) LOCAL VARIATIONS

One manifestation of the predominance of discretion is the apparent gap between national standards and local practices, leading to so-called 'justice by geography'. Evans and Ellis concluded, on the basis of research in late 1995, that 'the [three Home Office Circulars of 1985, 1990, and 1994] have not been successful in achieving greater consistency between forces'.[144] Despite the introduction of numerous national policies and

---

[136] Hynes and Elkins, n 66, 971.

[137] Ministry of Justice, *Simple Cautions for Adult Offenders* (2015), [23].

[138] *R v Metropolitan Police Commissioner, ex p Thompson* [1997] 1 WLR 1519.

[139] In one case a doctor who had used force to defend himself refused to accept a caution for assault, was prosecuted, and was acquitted: *The Times*, 17 June 1998.

[140] See *DPP v Ara* [2002] 1 Cr App R 159, discussed in section 6.4.

[141] Hynes and Elkins, n 66, 971.

[142] See L. Campbell, 'Criminal Records and Human Rights' [2017] *Crim LR* 695.

[143] Criminal Justice and Courts Act 2015, s 17(4).

[144] Evans and Ellis, *Police Cautioning in the 1990s* (1996), 2.

codes, on the face of it there are still significant differences in cautioning rates among police areas.[145] Moreover, the PND-E is an option with some police forces only.

When criticisms of variations in criminal justice are voiced, the reply is often that police forces are responding to local conditions and issues. It is certainly true that many worthwhile initiatives in criminal justice have come about through local attempts to address local problems; but there is also the probability that some variations stem from a stubborn and insular unwillingness to absorb national policies and to change working practices. Discretion thus opens the way to various practices, overt or covert.

6.4 ACCOUNTABILITY

It is apparent from the previous discussion that discretion is the dominant characteristic of the gatekeeping practices of the police, the regulatory agencies, and the CPS. Despite the creation of different guidance documents and increased legislative structure, their enforcement and impact is questionable. To what extent, if at all, are these decision makers accountable? The question has to be answered on two different levels: accountability for general policy, and accountability for individual decisions.

The main decision makers on cautioning and diversion overall have always been the police, and there have been significant changes to their accountability. (The CPS once had a primary role in the scheme of conditional cautions, and the next chapter examines the framework of its accountability (including the HM Crown Prosecution Service Inspectorate).) The traditional concept of constabulary independence, in which local chief constables were answerable to the law and to HM Inspectorate of Constabulary, was tempered considerably by Part 1 of the Police Reform Act 2002. That Act gave statutory authority for far greater central direction in policing, although considerable discretion remained in the hands of chief constables.[146]

In 2012, a new framework for the governance of police forces across England and Wales was introduced in the form of directly elected Police and Crime Commissioners (PCCs), one for each force area, other than London.[147] Furthermore, the Home Office increased HMIC's budget to fund a new programme of force inspections under the Police Effectiveness, Efficiency and Legitimacy (PEEL) framework, which aims to provide a regular comprehensive assessment of organizational performance. Finally, the Home Secretary has retained the power to intervene in 'failing' or significantly underperforming forces, and to direct HMIC to investigate and report on any issue involving the police. As such, there is an emerging landscape of more standardized and hierarchical accountability mechanisms within the police service, at least in theory.[148]

---

[145] HMIC and HMCPSI, *Exercising Discretion*, n 32.

[146] D. Ormerod and A. Roberts, 'The Police Reform Act 2002' [2003] *Crim LR* 141.

[147] P. Murphy, P. Eckersley, and L. Ferry, 'Accountability and transparency: Police forces in England and Wales' (2016) 32 *Public Policy and Administration* 197.

[148] Ibid.

Accountability for individual decisions depends largely on the internal structure of the agency. Within the police, there may be local police traditions or cultures that lead to variations in interpretation, even if there are clear policies. Though cases for caution must still be referred to sergeant level for approval, the interaction between the arresting officer and the station sergeant remains influential in determining what happens subsequently.[149] And the effect of force policy on those interactions is likely to be variable. The extent of a police force's commitment to cautioning will be determined by the occupational culture. This is compounded by the drive for performance management, and the presence of targets. Indeed, there have been calls to improve the formal oversight of police cautioning procedures through a review process,[150] and the creation of scrutiny panels in all police force areas, so that decisions to use OOCDs are reviewed for appropriateness and consistency.[151]

To what extent can police decisions about OOCD be challenged in the courts? The answer differs according to whether the decision is to prosecute or not to prosecute. If a person is charged, despite falling within one of the categories for cautioning outlined in the relevant guidance, it seems that judicial review may be possible but that this would be judicial review of the CPS if they decide to continue the prosecution rather than discontinuing it. This, the Divisional Court held,[152] was because the police are merely the initiators of proceedings, and the 'last and decisive word' on the issue lies with the CPS. The CPS would take this decision within the framework of the Code for Crown Prosecutors (to be discussed in Chapter 7).

However, the leading case of *L*[153] was limited expressly to decisions to prosecute young people and, although there is some authority in favour of extending the principle to decisions to prosecute adults,[154] the House of Lords decided that judicial review of decisions to prosecute should be confined to cases of dishonesty, bad faith, or some other exceptional circumstance.[155] It remains possible to allege that a particular prosecution amounts to an abuse of process, and to apply for it to be stayed on that ground.[156]

What of the situation where the police decide not to prosecute but to administer a caution of one sort or another? In these circumstances, an application for judicial review may succeed if it can be shown that the appropriate principles were not followed, whether the case concerns a young person or an adult.[157] Thus, in *P*[158] judicial review

---

[149] Kemp, n 8.   [150] Ibid, 287.

[151] Home Affairs Select Committee, *Out-of-Court Disposals*, n 57, 35–6.

[152] *R v Chief Constable of Kent, ex p L* (1991) 93 Cr App R 416, per Watkins LJ at 426.

[153] *R v Chief Constable of Kent, ex p L*, ibid.

[154] *R v Inland Revenue Commissioner, ex p Mead* [1993] 1 All ER 772, per Stuart-Smith LJ at 780.

[155] *R v DPP, ex p Kebilene* [2000] 2 AC 326; see also *R (Mondelly) v Metropolitan Police Commissioner* [2006] EWHC 2390 (Admin). See Ch 7.

[156] For discussion of the doctrine of abuse of process, see Ch 9.

[157] *R v General Council of the Bar, ex p Percival* [1990] 3 All ER 137, discussed by C. Hilson, 'Discretion to Prosecute and Judicial Review' [1993] *Crim LR* 639.

[158] *R v Metropolitan Police Commissioner, ex p P* (1995) 160 JP 367, discussed by R. Evans, 'Challenging a Police Caution using Judicial Review' [1996] *Crim LR* 104.

of a caution was granted when the police had failed to explain the role of appropriate adult to the child's mother and had failed to explain the consequences of an admission. In C,[159] judicial review of a decision not to prosecute an adult was granted to the alleged victim when it was shown that the CPS failed to have regard to a material consideration. More recently, in R (SY) v DPP the Administrative Court concluded that a decision not to charge a man with the rape of a woman with learning difficulties was not irrational.[160] The prosecutor had concluded correctly that such a prosecution would constitute an abuse of process and would therefore be stayed.

The caution itself may be challenged if the procedure leading up to the decision was unfair. Thus in R v Metropolitan Police Commissioner, ex p Thompson[161] the Divisional Court granted an order of certiorari quashing a caution. Counsel for the defendant argued that, where the police appear to be offering a caution if the defendant were to admit the offence, this is an unfair inducement which, on an analogy with the exclusion of confessions, should nullify the acceptance of the caution. The Divisional Court agreed with this proposition. The ruling is significant in two ways: first, it emphasizes the need to ensure that cautions are only offered and accepted in appropriate cases; and, secondly, it is important when cautions are recorded and may be relied upon subsequently. The ruling also shows why it is desirable to have access to legal advice before accepting a caution, a point reinforced by the decision in DPP v Ara.[162] There the police decided that a defendant was suitable for a caution as a result of what he had said during an interview. The defendant took legal advice subsequently, but his solicitor was not allowed by the police to have access to the tape recording of the interview. The Divisional Court upheld the decision of the justices to stay the prosecution on grounds of abuse of process, on the basis that a person should have access to legal advice before deciding whether to accept a caution, and the refusal to disclose the interview tape rendered informed legal advice impossible.

That said, the decision in Lee v Chief Constable of Essex Police underlines that the court will intervene only where there is a clear breach of the guidelines,[163] and not necessarily even then. There officers had administered a caution to Lee, an adult offender, in ignorance of a relevant Home Office Circular of 2008, relying instead upon the previous 2005 version. This meant they had not used the correct information form nor told Lee of all the consequences of a caution. Regardless, it was found that as they had complied substantially with the new Circular by the procedure adopted, the caution would not be quashed. The court stressed that police officers responsible for applying the Circular must enjoy a wide margin of appreciation of the nature of the case and whether the preconditions for a caution are satisfied, and even if there is a clear breach of the guidelines, the court retains a discretion not to interfere.[164]

Lee was cited in W v Chief Constable of Merseyside, where W, a vulnerable person, applied for judicial review of the imposition of a simple caution on the basis that it had

[159] R v DPP, ex p C [1995] 1 Cr App R 136.   [160] R (SY) v DPP [2018] EWHC 795 (Admin).
[161] [1997] 1 WLR 1519.   [162] [2002] 1 Cr App R 159.   [163] [2012] EWHC 283 (Admin).
[164] Ibid, [15].

not been preceded by any valid or reliable admission of guilt, had been administered contrary to the current Ministry of Justice guidance and PACE Codes, and that there had been no involvement of an appropriate adult during the stages of the administration of the caution.[165] The High Court rejected this, holding that there was undisputed evidence that he had received proper legal advice beforehand, that the defence had first suggested the caution, and that he had been appropriately supported throughout the process involved. *Lee* was also applied in *R (Manser) v Commissioner of Police of the Metropolis*[166] where M had applied for judicial review of a caution for an alleged offence of assault occasioning actual bodily harm on the basis that the police had described the victim as having a broken nose, not a suspected broken nose. This challenge was refused on the ground that there had not been a clear breach of para 76 of the Ministry of Justice Guidance on Simple Cautions for Adult Offenders, which relates to the disclosure of material evidence.

Though this line of cases demonstrates the latitude accorded to the police in relation to simple cautions, the court will quash a caution if the public interest test has not been passed and so it regards that the caution was not merited. In *Caetano v Commissioner of Police for the Metropolis*, the Administrative Court quashed a caution for Caetano (described as a 'vulnerable and unwell woman of excellent character' and at the time a PhD student at UCL) who had slapped her partner twice after he had revealed that he had sex with someone else.[167] Though the court acknowledged the difficulties for police officers 'on the ground' to 'make assessments and take decisions in often pressurised and difficult circumstances',[168] it concluded that 'not only [was] a prosecution was inconceivable . . . the public interest did not require a caution'.[169] As Ellis and Biggs note, while this outcome might appeal to common sense, many cases will be less clear and the cautioned person a less sympathetic character.[170] Moreover, Leigh is critical of Caetano's legal representative in the police station, describing the advice to accept the caution as 'indefensible'.[171] And, of course, very many of those who accept a simple caution will do so without any legal representation.[172]

Similarly, a caution was quashed in *R (Stratton) v Chief Constable of Thames Valley Police*.[173] Here, S accepted that in all the circumstances there was evidence on which a prosecution could have been brought and that the public interest test would have been met; rather, her challenge was on the basis that she had not admitted the commission of an offence and that she was not warned of the adverse consequences, especially in relation to her employment as a nanny. The Administrative Court noted that the form used by the police implied that the only consequence was use in other court proceedings, and found that as she was unrepresented and the acceptance of the caution given her occupation were so serious for her, she did not give her informed consent to the caution.[174]

---

[165] [2014] EWHC 1857 (Admin).   [166] [2015] EWHC 3642 (Admin).
[167] [2013] EWHC 375 (Admin), [44].   [168] [43].   [169] [44].
[170] R. Ellis and S. Biggs, 'Simple Cautions' [2013] *Arch Rev* 6, 8–9.
[171] L. H. Leigh, 'Cautioning—whatever happened to common sense' (2013) 177 *CL & J* 269–270.
[172] Ellis and Biggs, n 170, 9.   [173] [2013] EWHC 1561 (Admin).   [174] [54].

In relation to conditional cautions specifically, the Administrative Court in *R (Guest) v DPP*[175] quashed a decision (taken by a CPS caseworker) to administer a conditional caution in a case where the Code for Crown Prosecutors had clearly been misapplied—failing to prosecute assault occasioning actual bodily harm—and the Director's Guidance on Conditional Cautions had also been misapplied.[176] It is worth recounting in full the observation of Goldring LJ, that:

> By Part 3 of the Criminal Justice Act 2003, Parliament has decided to place very considerable responsibility on the Crown Prosecution Service. By a decision to offer a conditional caution to an offender, the court is effectively bypassed. It means that someone who is guilty of committing a criminal offence is not prosecuted, does not appear before the court and is not sentenced by the court. The importance of taking such a decision conscientiously and in accordance with the law can hardly be overstated. The effect on the victim and the damage to the criminal justice system is self-evident if such a decision is taken without proper regard to the relevant guidance.[177]

The subsequent extension of this power to issue conditional cautions to the police raises further pressing questions about the circumvention of courts, and about the care taken and the expertise needed in making such complex legal decisions.

In *R (Owusu-Yianoma) v Chief Constable of Leicestershire*, O challenged the imposition of a conditional caution upon him for an offence contrary to s 4A of the Public Order Act 1986 (causing intentional harassment, alarm, or distress) on the basis that he had been arrested under s 5 of the 1986 Act (causing harassment, alarm, or distress).[178] He resisted arrest, declined to inform anyone of his arrest, and declined the offer of legal advice. Though O signed documents to confirm that he admitted the offence and understood and accepted a conditional caution including the fact that a record would be kept and could be disclosed to certain potential employers or in connection with any future criminal proceedings, this was for an offence that differed from the arresting offence. The court agreed that there had been a failure in relation to s 23(2) so the necessary preconditions for a conditional caution had not been established. The court was unable to substitute a caution for a s 5 offence for one relating to s 4A. The applications for leave and for judicial review were granted and the conditional caution was quashed.

To what extent are the regulatory agencies accountable for their very different enforcement policies? We have noted that the annual report is practically the only means of being called to account for policy. There is no inspectorate for the regulatory agencies, no steering committee for the policies of the regulatory sector, and certainly no body charged with reviewing the relationship between regulatory policies and the approach of the police to law enforcement. As for accountability for individual decisions, research suggests that there are variations in the local culture of different parts of a single agency—one familiar finding is a divergence of approach between rural areas

---

[175] [2009] EWHC 594 (Admin). See also *R (Omar) v Chief Constable of Bedfordshire* [2002] EWHC 3060 (Admin).

[176] See Ch 7.   [177] [2009] EWHC 594 (Admin), [56].   [178] [2017] EWHC 576 (Admin).

and urban areas.[179] In his study of Health and Safety inspectors, Hawkins emphasized 'the centrality of organizations', their norms, their goals, and their culture, in determining the approach taken by individual inspectors.[180] Individual inspectors may vary in their preparedness to bring a prosecution on given facts, but part of the explanation for their behaviour may be organizational pressures. Moreover, an individual decision not to prosecute is unlikely to be reviewed, within most regulatory agencies, unless it is a case of particular sensitivity to which the attention of senior officials has been drawn. Judicial review of a decision not to prosecute would be available in theory, since most of these agencies have the 'last and decisive word' within their own sphere of operation, but there are few examples of challenges being brought in this way.

6.5 VALUES AND PRINCIPLES

In this chapter we have described a significant trend towards diversion and away from prosecution–conviction–sentence, but the different forms of diversion (especially conditional cautions and PNDs) incorporate penalties and must be characterized as forms of non-judicial punishment. This makes it all the more important to ask questions about values. Is equality of treatment ensured? Are the interests of victims properly respected? Are the rights of defendants respected? Do these developments represent an extension or a sacrifice of crime control?

(A) EQUALITY OF TREATMENT

In the previous section we saw that the due execution of stated diversionary policies is not buttressed by an effective framework of legal accountability. The legal frameworks for OOCDs are piecemeal, permissive, and leave a large swathe of discretion that is narrowed marginally by the various Guidances.

The predominance of discretion might be regarded as a contradiction of the principle of equality before the law and equal treatment. In many European countries, the considerable weight given to the principle of compulsory prosecution shows awareness of the values at stake. It is true that most countries do not regard this as an absolute principle, and now allow scope to the principle of expediency whereby certain cases are diverted from the courts, usually by prosecutors. But these can be regarded as circumscribed exceptions to the principle that criminal justice should be dispensed in open court, after a full consideration of the issues, with reasons given.[181] The major difference in England and Wales is that the issues are not even discussed in terms of the principles at stake. These decisions may profoundly affect the course of a suspect/offender's life: not only may prosecution itself be highly significant for the defendant

---

[179] See e.g. B. Hutter, *The Reasonable Arm of the Law* (1988).   [180] Hawkins, n 23, 330.
[181] See e.g. H. Lensing and L. Rayar, 'Notes on Criminal Procedure in the Netherlands' [1992] *Crim LR* 623; J. Hodgson, 'Codified Criminal Procedure and Human Rights: Some Observations on the French Experience' [2003] *Crim LR* 165.

in terms of anxiety and stress, damage to reputation, and possible loss of employment, but the choice of method of diversion may have significant implications. If discretion is to be bestowed on certain authorities, it should be structured carefully so as to achieve desired policies and properly controlled through channels of accountability.

Do diversionary practices accord appropriate treatment to vulnerable groups such as those with mental disorders? The diversion of such offenders is a well-established practice, although it has been argued that their ready referral to the mental health services and hospitals may sometimes be a disproportionately severe response, or may deprive them of rights they would have if prosecuted, or both.[182] There is evidence that in some cases the incidence of mental disorder is not recognized by the police, or indeed by the police surgeon, and that therefore appropriate safeguards are not put in place.[183] Of those whose disorder is recognized, the rate of diversion and no further action is relatively high.[184] Mentally disordered people who come into contact with the police may be taken to a 'place of safety' under ss 135–136 of the Mental Health Act 1983, and the Bradley Report recommended tightening the protocols for joint working with the health service on this issue. Some progress is being made: in 2014, a new 'liaison and diversion' model was implemented in ten areas of England, in an effort to standardize and improve the schemes in police custody suites which seek to identify and assess people with vulnerabilities as they pass through the criminal justice system.[185] For those taken to court, there is a scattering of court-based assessment and diversion schemes, one purpose of which is to identify and assess mentally disordered defendants and to see whether a form of diversion (such as immediate hospital admission) is possible and desirable.[186]

A second problem of equality of treatment concerns racial discrimination. Many studies indicate that there is discrimination against black people in respect of decisions to prosecute or caution.[187] Part of the difference in prosecution rates is due to the fact that more black people decline to admit the allegations against them, which removes their eligibility for a caution,[188] though this is understandable given the degree of mistrust of the police. Notably, the decrease in cautioning has been at a slower rate for black and Asian individuals when compared to white individuals. The Black ethnic group were just under 2.5 times more likely to be given a caution, compared with the White, Asian, and Other ethnic groups relative to the population.[189] Martina Feilzer and

---

[182] D. Carson, 'Prosecuting People with Mental Handicaps' [1989] *Crim LR* 87.

[183] See C. Phillips and D. Brown, *Entry into the Criminal Justice System* (1998), 188–9; Bradley Report, *Mentally Disordered People in the Criminal Justice System* (2009), para 16.

[184] Phillips and Brown, n 183, 188–9.

[185] E. Disley, C. Taylor, K. Kruithof, E. Winpenny, M. Liddle, A. Sutherland, R. Lilford, S. Wright, L. McAteer, and V. Francis, *Evaluation of the Offender Liaison and Diversion Trial Schemes* (2016).

[186] See J. Peay, 'Mental Health, Mental Disabilities, and Crime' in A. Liebling, S. Maruna, and L. McAra (eds), *The Oxford Handbook of Criminology* (6th edn, 2017).

[187] T. Jefferson and N. Walker, 'Ethnic Minorities in the Criminal Justice System' [1992] *Crim LR* 83, 88; Commission for Racial Equality, *Juvenile Cautioning: Ethnic Monitoring in Practice* (1992).

[188] M. Fitzgerald, *Ethnic Minorities and the Criminal Justice System* (1993), 18; see also C. Phillips and B. Bowling, 'Ethnicities, Racism, Crime and Criminal Justice' in Liebling et al, n 186.

[189] Ministry of Justice, *Statistics on Race and the Criminal Justice System 2016* (2017), 24.

Roger Hood conducted a large survey for the Youth Justice Board which found that the chances of a case involving a mixed-parentage young male being prosecuted were 2.7 times greater than that of a white young male with similar case characteristics, and that the chances of a mixed-parentage young female being prosecuted were six times that of a similarly placed white female.[190] This evidence is, as the report puts it, 'consistent with discriminatory treatment'. Moreover, in terms of PNDs, in 2016, 83 per cent of the PNDs issued were to White individuals, 6 per cent to Black individuals, 7 per cent to Asian individuals, 2 per cent to Mixed individuals, and 2 per cent to Chinese or Other individuals. For most groups, these proportions have been fairly stable, however the proportion of PNDs issued to black individuals increased from 2.6 per cent in 2012 to 6.3 per cent in 2016. While this may indicate a change in PND trends by ethnic group, caution is advised given that a new database was introduced in 2012.[191]

In terms of a possible model for reform, David Lammy endorsed a West Midlands scheme called Operation Turning Point, which involved deferral of prosecutions with conditions for offenders who would otherwise have been prosecuted.[192] Crucially, this did not require an admission of guilt. In addition, he cited victim satisfaction, reoffending rates, and cost as other positive components.

There are also differential cautioning rates along gender lines. In 2015, three-quarters of cautioned offenders were male and one-quarter female, with similar proportions to those for PNDs, and this split has remained stable.[193] The cautioning rate for women was lower than for men overall, at 12 per cent compared with 16 per cent, but higher for women in respect of indictable offences, at 28 per cent and 19 per cent respectively.[194] The difference may result from the high number of women convicted for the summary offence of TV licence evasion.[195] Fraud was the only offence for which men and women had a very similar cautioning rate, at 16 and 15 per cent respectively. For criminal damage and arson, the figures were 46 and 32 per cent, drug offences 44 and 32 per cent, and violence against the person, 44 per cent and 14 per cent respectively.

Though on the face of it women seem to receive favourable treatment in respect of some indictable offences, this interpretation fails to take account of the probability that offences of different types and different levels of seriousness would be found in the different groups. Thus, Phillips and Brown found that 'females were more likely to be cautioned because they were far more likely than men to admit their offences and more likely to be arrested for less serious offences (typically shoplifting)'.[196] However, research in the early 1990s found that whereas a majority of both sexes had no previous criminal history, cautioned males were twice as likely as females to have been previously convicted[197]—suggesting that some men were being treated more

---

[190] M. Feilzer and R. Hood, *Differences or Discrimination?* (2004).

[191] Ministry of Justice, *Statistics on Race and the Criminal Justice System 2016* (2017), 36.

[192] The Lammy Review, *An independent review into the treatment of, and outcomes for, Black, Asian and Minority Ethnic individuals in the Criminal Justice System* (2017), 28.

[193] Ministry of Justice, *Statistics on Women and the Criminal Justice System 2015* (2016), 44.

[194] Ibid, 45.   [195] Ibid, 46.   [196] Phillips and Brown, n 183, 92.

[197] C. Hedderman and M. Hough, *Does the Criminal Justice System Treat Men and Women Differently?* (1994), 2.

leniently than women, perhaps benefiting from repeat cautioning when women were not. Again the picture is far from clear, but it is not the case that women are typically treated more leniently.

(B) DEFENDANTS' RIGHTS

As noted earlier, one common feature of diversion schemes is that the defendant can decline the offer made by the police or prosecution if guilt is disputed, leaving them to prosecute in court and have the matter decided there. This is one reason why access to legal advice is important before a caution or conditional caution is issued, and why there is a 21-day period after the issue of a PND in which the ticketed person can decide to opt for a court hearing. Whilst these options are sufficient to comply with the ECHR,[198] it nonetheless leaves to the defendant a choice that is not without pressure. The making of an offer of a caution before the defendant had admitted guilt of the offence constituted the unfair procedure in *Thompson*,[199] although it is true that some suspects may know or be advised of the possibility of a caution or conditional caution if they admit the offence. In principle, however, the police should first decide what action is appropriate, and only then ask the defendant whether he admits the offence and is prepared to accept a caution. In substantive terms, it appears that neither a caution nor a conditional caution amounts to a 'criminal charge' such that all the extra safeguards in Art 6(2) and (3) of the Convention apply, and the House of Lords so held in a decision on reprimands and final warnings for young defendants.[200] However, Ian Brownlee has argued that the position might be different in the case of a conditional caution with the payment of a financial penalty as the condition,[201] a point that remains to be settled.

(C) VICTIMS' RIGHTS

Are the existing arrangements for diversion effective in securing the rights of victims? In deciding whether to offer a simple caution, it is important to establish, where appropriate and possible, and to take into account: the views of any victim about the offence and the proposed method of disposal; and the nature of any harm or loss caused by the offence and its significance to the victim.[202]

Similarly, when deciding whether to give a conditional caution the Code of Practice states that the decision maker will take into account, inter alia, any views expressed by the victim,[203] though they cannot be conclusive.[204] The victim's consent must be

---

[198] See n 135.   [199] *Thompson*, n 138, 182.
[200] *R (on application of R) v Durham Constabulary* [2005] UKHL 21.
[201] I. Brownlee, 'Conditional Cautions and Fair Trial Rights: Form versus Substance in the Diversionary Agenda' [2007] *Crim LR* 129.
[202] Ministry of Justice, *Simple Cautions for Adult Offenders*, n 60, 57.
[203] Ministry of Justice, *Code of Practice for Adult Conditional Cautions* (2013), 2.7 and 2.47.
[204] Ibid, 2.48.

obtained in any case where direct reparation or restorative justice processes are being considered or where the victim is involved directly in some way. If the victim does not consent to such conditions, the decision maker may still consider giving a conditional caution with other conditions attached that do not directly involve the victim.[205] In some circumstances, the decision maker may consider that proportionality with the level of the offence requires the inclusion of conditions that may be more or less onerous than those the victim wants. Notably, this Code of Practice predates the Anti-social Behaviour, Crime and Policing Act 2014 which amended s 23 of the Criminal Justice Act 2003 to impose a duty to consult victims about what conditions to attach to a conditional caution; 'the relevant prosecutor or the authorised person must make reasonable efforts to obtain the views of the victim . . .' and in particular their views on the actions listed in the community remedy document.[206] While it is stressed that care must be taken not to raise the expectations of the victim whilst seeking their views,[207] it is questionable whether this is attainable in practice, and whether the subtleties of obtaining but not necessarily adhering to the views of victims can be conveyed or comprehended.

Similarly, the views of the victim are important but cannot be conclusive in the making of a PND.[208] The Ministry of Justice guidance also reminds constables that while giving a PND removes the possibility of the criminal court awarding a compensation order in favour of the victim, it could save the victim from having to attend court to give evidence provided that the person does not request to be tried for the offence.[209]

On that note, the form of OOCD chosen may impact on the payment of compensation to the victim. For offenders who are cautioned there is no prospect of a binding order for compensation. That said, the scheme of conditional cautions embodies an attempt to address this problem by making the payment of reparation or compensation to the victim an enforceable condition.[210] Indeed, the Ministry of Justice guidance notes that where there has been financial loss or loss of private property to an individual, the decision maker should consider whether a conditional caution with a condition to repair damage or to pay compensation is more suitable than a simple caution.[211]

(D) CRIME CONTROL

How does the expansion and subsequent contraction of diversionary and non-judicial penalties affect effective crime control? Reconviction figures for cautions have generally been more favourable than those for convictions in court, and according to government figures—cited at a time when the diversionary regime for young offenders was being formalized by the introduction of reprimands and final warnings—it is only

[205] Ibid, 2.47.   [206] Anti-social Behaviour, Crime and Policing Act 2014, s 103.
[207] Ministry of Justice, *Code of Practice for Adult Conditional Cautions* (2013), 2.48.
[208] Ministry of Justice, *PND Guidance*, n 46, 3.60–3.61.   [209] Ibid, 3.62.
[210] Victims of violent crimes, and family members, may also be able to claim compensation from the Criminal Injuries Compensation Authority.
[211] Ministry of Justice, *Simple Cautions for Adult Offenders*, n 60, [57].

after three offences that a prosecution is less likely to be followed by reconviction than a caution.[212] As between the types of OOCD, a recent pilot programme found no statistically significant differences between pilot areas imposing conditional cautions and areas with predominantly simple cautions, relating to the likelihood of reoffending, time to reoffend, and the severity of the reoffence.[213] It is important to resist the temptation to equate greater severity with greater crime control: cautions and other forms of diversion may have no less preventive efficacy, and possibly greater preventive efficacy, than the prosecution–conviction–sentence approach. Indeed, as we saw in section 6.2, it is beliefs of this kind that make many regulatory agencies confident that their compliance-oriented approach is more effective than ready resort to the criminal courts. On the other hand, one implication of this may be that diversionary and non-judicial penalties actually extend and deepen social control over certain groups: this has been argued in the context of the change from punitive to welfare-oriented approaches to tackling prostitution,[214] and Richard Young has argued more generally that the 'drift to summary justice' penalizes the poor and marginalized.[215] Moreover, the findings of McGlynn et al may exemplify the downplaying of the gravity of certain offence types like domestic violence.[216]

6.6 CONCLUSION

The diversion of non-serious offenders away from the criminal courts has long been advocated across Europe as a necessary and desirable way of simplifying criminal justice.[217] The strongest arguments in favour of diversion are that prosecution–conviction–sentence may be a disproportionate response to some less serious forms of law breaking, and that in general the prosecution approach may be a less effective response in terms of reoffending and therefore prevention. A secondary argument—though one powerful with governments—is that diversion may save time and money. The courts are not involved, and less preparatory work is required of the police and prosecutors, so that the police (in particular) have more time to pursue serious criminals. However, we have noted earlier that a drive towards cost-cutting and simplification may lead to neglect of the rights of victims and the rights of defendants, and it remains important to ensure that this does not occur in practice even when the formal rules are designed to safeguard rights. As for corporate offenders, diversion and deferral of prosecution is seen as a way of ensuring justice of some sort, rather than risking protracted and costly trials that may result in acquittal. The difference here lies in the more limited judicial oversight, and the uneasy power dynamic when compared to cases involving individuals and the state.

---

[212] Home Office, *No More Excuses* (1997), para 5.9, referring to research by the Audit Commission.
[213] Ministry of Justice, *Out of Court Disposals Pilot: Cautions Reoffending Analysis* (2018).
[214] J. Scoular and M. O'Neill, 'Regulating Prostitution' (2007) 47 *BJ Crim* 764.
[215] Young, 'Street Policing after PACE', n 40.   [216] McGlynn et al, n 95.
[217] Council of Europe, *The Simplification of Criminal Justice* (1987).

What, for these purposes, is diversion? It is a semi-formal alternative to sending a case down the prosecution–conviction–sentence track. It is, therefore, a non-judicial form of disposal: but a form of disposal it certainly is. Thus, it empowers law enforcement agents, such as the police, community support officers, and officers of the various regulatory agencies, to impose punishment. Whether a simple caution or formal warning amounts to punishment may be debated, since there are usually no obligations attached, even though the simple caution can be cited in court subsequently as evidence that the offence was committed. But FPNs and PNDs plainly involve punishment, in the form of payment of the penalty; and conditional cautions may involve punishment—even if it is thought that requiring reparation or participation in some rehabilitative scheme does not amount to punishment, payment of a financial penalty certainly does. The powers bestowed on regulatory agencies might be termed civil sanctions, but 'fixed monetary penalties' are clearly punitive, and some of the other powers may be.

One possible objection to these references to punishment is that all the forms of diversion discussed here are voluntary, in the sense that the alleged offender always has the possibility of refusing. Though one could argue that consent is inconsistent with state punishment, this view must be dismissed as naïve: it is well known that in practice there is an element of coercion, sometimes in the background and sometimes (at least so far as it appears to the defendant) in the foreground, that renders this form of consent a rather impoverished sort. The House of Lords in *Durham Constabulary* recognized that explicit pressure to 'admit it and we'll let you off with a caution' would invalidate a subsequent admission by an individual;[218] the question is whether implicit pressure of the same kind should also be recognized. The alternative is prosecution in court, which may be considered more severe. Moreover, methods of diversion (other than no further action) may have adverse consequences: although FPNs are not recorded for use, any PND, simple caution, or conditional caution can be cited in subsequent proceedings (although a PND may be treated as evidence of bad character but not as evidence of guilt), and any caution for a sex offence entails the notification requirements of the Sexual Offences Act 2003. There are rather fewer such negative implications for a corporate entity.

The use of and framework for out-of-court disposals have evolved in a piecemeal and largely uncontrolled way.[219] The move to a legislative scheme has been slow, incremental, and reactive. A legislative framework is important in terms of human rights and rule-of-law values, but it is not clear whether it, and HMIC inspections, has much effect in curbing local variations.

It is unfortunate that there is no proper hierarchy of methods of diversion, leading to uncertainty in the relationship between simple cautions, conditional cautions, and PNDs. To some extent, this is resolved by the separate spheres in which PNDs operate,

---

[218] *R (on application of R) v Durham Constabulary* [2005] UKHL 21.
[219] HMIC and HMCPSI, *Exercising Discretion*, n 32, 4.

but not entirely: many PNDs are given for public order offences, but cautions could be considered for them,[220] and certainly cautions or conditional cautions could be considered for many of the thefts from shops and criminal damage offences than now attract PNDs. The three-stage escalation procedure for cannabis is something that could be considered more widely.[221]

Reform of OOCDs is on the horizon. The Ministry of Justice has proposed a 'simplified, two-tier' system comprising a suspended prosecution for serious offences, and a community resolution.[222] A pilot programme was launched in three police forces, whereby the only available OOCDs are conditional cautions and community resolutions, as the closest extant equivalents to the proposed scheme.[223] Regardless of whether this particular reform materializes, with any streamlining of the scheme of OOCDs more attention should be given to the proper relationship between these forms of diversion, if the aspirations to proportionality and transparency that now suffuse the various codes of practice and policy statements are to be given real purchase. If it is said that the appropriateness of a particular form of diversion is always a matter for judgement, then this revives the question whether enforcement officers should have such power in these matters. The CPS is at least a quasi-judicial body, and is not directly involved in law enforcement. The CPS is therefore a much more appropriate body to be determining these extrajudicial punishments, if we are to have them.[224] But that is unlikely to be applicable to PNDs, which are often issued on the street, unless what is issued becomes merely a notice of a PND, to be ratified subsequently by the CPS after reviewing the case. That would call for some police paperwork, however, and is likely to be dismissed as undermining the imperatives behind the introduction of the PND.

The predominant justifications for diversion by out-of-court disposals are in terms of simplification, speed, cost, and effectiveness. These are worthy objectives, but each of them should be evaluated fully rather than assumed; but even if diversion does further those goals, there are six other issues to be considered. First, proportionality of response (minor penalties for minor offences) is a laudable principle, but it is important to know how the various out-of-court disposals are being employed by the police and others. This is not just a question of monitoring by the inspectorates, but rather it calls for careful empirical research. Secondly, Rod Morgan shows that there is evidence of net-widening, and asks pertinent questions about the additional people being dragged into the criminal justice net by the expansion of out-of-court disposals: are 'offenders who were previously able to offend with virtual impunity for want of police and criminal justice attention now being brought effectively to book', or 'does it involve the criminalisation of marginally criminal behaviour which in the past was dealt with . . . through the

---

[220] Indeed this is acknowledged in Ministry of Justice, *PND Guidance*, n 46, 8.   [221] Ibid, 3.33.

[222] HM Government and College of Policing, *Out of Court Disposals Consultation Response* (2014).

[223] P. Neyroud, *Out of Court Disposals Managed by the Police: A Review of the Evidence* (2018).

[224] An argument made some years ago in A. Sanders, 'The Limits of Diversion from Prosecution' (1988) 28 *BJ Crim* 513.

application of various informal community sanctions'?[225] Thirdly, as McGlynn et al discovered, some serious cases are being dealt with informally, with consequences for the victim and the accused. The magistracy has raised this question: there may be pressures felt by the person who accepts a PND or caution, and yet if that person is to gain the equivalent of a criminal record the matter should really be ventilated in open court, not in a police station or on the street.[226] Fourthly, even if one can dispel fears that the use of out-of-court disposals is target-driven or is a means of raising revenue,[227] there are genuine questions about the level at which penalties are set, and their comparability.

Those four points emerge from Rod Morgan's forthright report. But there are two further issues to be considered. One is power relations between the police (and other enforcement agents) and the public: measures such as PNDs give police considerable de facto power, and there is a need for authoritative study of its effects on the rights of citizens. The second is social justice: in principle, the criminal justice system should respond consistently and proportionately to alleged offenders in a way that reflects the amount of harm foreseeably done and their culpability, and this principle should apply across the boundaries between the many different enforcement agencies. Why should there be differences in response to someone who pollutes a river, someone who defrauds the Revenue, someone who fails to take proper precautions for the safety of employees, someone who steals property from another, someone who sells unsound meat, and so on? One reply is that it is impossible to compare the relative seriousness of these different offences, and hence each of them must be viewed in its separate context. That is an unsatisfactory reply, since it is possible to make some progress towards a ranking of the relative seriousness of offences,[228] and to identify rankings of offences that are clearly inappropriate. The difficulty of settling on comprehensive criteria of offence-seriousness should not be deployed as an excuse for avoiding the broader questions of social justice that arise when relatively poor and powerless people are subjected to PNDs or prosecuted whereas the better connected are enabled to pay their way out of trouble without the stigma of a criminal conviction.[229]

What is necessary is a thorough review of the prosecution policies of the regulatory agencies. At present, there is little accountability, and certainly no overall accountability to a single body that can oversee consistency in matters of prosecution. It is one thing to argue that the different contexts in which some agencies work make different approaches appropriate. It is quite another thing to argue that there should be no attempt at a common starting point, and no concern with broader issues of social justice and the apparent unfairness of these differing arrangements. These fundamental issues of social justice are taken further in the next chapter, on prosecutions.

[225] Morgan, n 106, 30.   [226] Ibid, 20–1.   [227] Ibid, 27–9.
[228] For discussion, see A. Ashworth, *Sentencing and Criminal Justice* (6th edn, 2015), ch 4.
[229] Cf A. Sanders, 'Class Bias in Prosecutions' (1985) 24 *Howard JCJ* 176.

FURTHER READING

HYNES, P. and ELKINS, M., 'Suggestions for Reform to the Police Cautioning Procedure' [2013]
    Crim LR 966.

LAMMY, D., *The Lammy Review: An Independent Review into the Treatment of, and Outcomes for,
    Black, Asian and Minority Ethnic Individuals in the Criminal Justice System* (2017).

McGLYNN, C., WESTMARLAND, N., and JOHNSON, K., 'Under the radar: the widespread use of
    "Out of Court resolutions" in policing domestic violence and abuse in the United Kingdom'
    (2017) 58 *BJ Crim* 1.

QUESTIONS FOR DISCUSSION

1. Are there good arguments for expanding the use of diversion from prosecution?

2. Are there sufficient safeguards against the misuse of out-of-court penalties?

3. Should there be greater oversight of the enforcement powers of the regulatory agencies?

7

PROSECUTIONS

For many years the prosecution system in England and Wales has been organized differently from most other jurisdictions. The police exerted considerable control over prosecutions until the creation of the Crown Prosecution Service (CPS) in 1986, even after which the police retained the initial decision whether or not to prosecute, with the CPS having prosecutorial review. From 2004, a system of 'statutory charging' removed decisions to prosecute from the police to the CPS for most offences (save a few less serious ones), though latterly the situation has been reversed somewhat.[1] In a structural sense, the CPS absorbed the Revenue and Customs Prosecutions Office in 2010,[2] though the Serious Fraud Office (SFO) remains as a separate entity, along with the discrete regulatory agencies discussed in Chapter 6 that have both investigative and prosecutorial functions.[3]

This chapter begins by outlining the origins and functions of the CPS. It then moves on to discuss several aspects of the prosecutorial function in the criminal process, in the belief that the decision to prosecute someone in itself is a form of imposition by the state that requires justification: not only must there be sufficient evidence to warrant putting the person to the trouble of mounting a defence, but there should also be a system for weeding out evidentially weak cases so as to protect the innocent by removing or lessening the possibility of miscarriages of justice. Moreover, there must be good policy reasons for deciding that it is in the public interest to bring the prosecution (i.e. this must be both a proportionate and an appropriate response). In the course of exploring these issues, we raise questions about the standards and the performance of the CPS and other agencies. We also ask about the ethical orientation of English prosecutors: are they committed to the appropriate standards, and how (if at all) is compliance with ethical principles monitored? How committed are prosecutors to ensuring that human rights are respected in their decision making? The principle of equality of treatment is discussed throughout the chapter, not least in relation to the differences of approach taken by different prosecuting agencies: while some offences in English criminal law are treated as the business of the police, others are treated as the

---

[1] DPP, *Charging (The Director's Guidance) 2013*, 5th edn, https://www.cps.gov.uk/legal-guidance/charging-directors-guidance-2013-fifth-edition-may-2013-revised-arrangements, para 15. See Ch 6.

[2] CPS, *The Public Prosecution Service—Setting the Standard*, 23 July 2009.

[3] See the review by the House of Commons Justice Committee, *The Crown Prosecution Service: Gatekeeper of the Criminal Justice System* (2009), ch 5.

business of regulatory agencies, as noted above. It cannot be said that the former are invariably more serious than the latter. Questions therefore arise about the justifications for different treatment, at the stage of prosecution or diversion, of offences of similar gravity that are committed in different contexts and therefore policed and prosecuted by different entities.

7.1 THE CROWN PROSECUTION SERVICE

Whose task should it be to prosecute alleged offenders? For many centuries, the victim of the alleged offence had to be the motivating force behind the decision to prosecute, largely because there was no other entity to do this. There was no organized police force and no other body appointed by central or local government to initiate or organize prosecutions. Eventually the police became more and more involved in prosecuting, and as the regular police force was formed in the early part of the nineteenth century, it became natural to expect them not only to detect and arrest suspected offenders but also to initiate their prosecution. Doubts were expressed at the time about the propriety of giving this power to the police,[4] but these were not voices in favour of the status quo. On the contrary, the task of prosecuting was a burden on victims, and even where there were prosecution associations at work the result would still be inconsistencies of practice and inefficiencies in criminal justice. There were some arguments in favour of an independent prosecuting service, for the constitutional reason that it was inappropriate to bestow this task on a group (the police) whose principal tasks were keeping order and investigating alleged crimes.[5] Those arguments did not prevail, and the police appear to have taken over prosecutions almost by default. However, there was little doubt about the propriety of ensuring that this task was borne by a public body rather than by victims, whether individually or in association with one another: as part of its role in protecting people from crime, the state should make arrangements for the prosecution of those whose (alleged) conduct is judged to warrant that response.

Until prosecution arrangements in England and Wales were altered in the mid-1980s, there were three principal prosecuting agencies. The police, as just mentioned, had brought most prosecutions since the mid-nineteenth century. By the early 1980s, many police forces had developed or begun to develop a prosecuting solicitors' department, but it was still the police who took most of the decisions. Secondly, the Director of Public Prosecutions had a small department in London, dealing with all murder prosecutions, and with a spread of other cases concerned with such matters as national security, public figures, and alleged offences by police officers. And, thirdly, there were the various agencies such as the Inland Revenue (as it then was), the Post Office, the Health and Safety Commission (including the Factory Inspectorate), the Pollution

---

[4] See G. Dingwall and C. Harding, *Diversion in the Criminal Process* (1998), ch 2, for a brief history and further references.

[5] Ibid, 32.

Inspectorate, and local authorities (including, for example, their environmental health officers), which mostly had their own prosecutors.

Arguments in favour of changing the system were aired at various times, but perhaps the most influential event was the publication in 1970 of a report by the British section of the International Commission of Jurists.[6] This report drew upon principled arguments (that it was wrong for the police, who investigated crimes, to take decisions in relation to prosecution, which require impartiality and independence) and more pragmatic points (that the police were experts at investigation, and it would be a better use of their time to focus on this rather than to undertake all these prosecutorial duties). This report was often cited in the 1970s, but it took a spectacular miscarriage of justice to provide the impetus for reform. The report on the *Confait* case, published in 1977, made criticisms of several aspects of the criminal justice system, and proposed that changes in the prosecution system should be considered.[7] The arguments for and against change were then considered by the Royal Commission on Criminal Procedure, chaired by Sir Cyril Phillips. There was much discussion of the Scottish system, in which each area has a procurator-fiscal who directs the police in the investigation of crime, who interviews suspects and witnesses, and who has several powers similar to those of a continental examining judge.[8] On the other side, there were vigorous arguments from the police that they should retain control over prosecutions, using their experience and local knowledge.

The Royal Commission reported in 1981 in favour of the establishment of an independent public prosecutor system, endorsing a division of functions between investigators and prosecutors but placing the dividing line in a different place from the Scots system, giving fewer powers to the prosecutor.[9] After debates about whether the system should be locally accountable or national,[10] the Prosecution of Offences Act 1985 created a national Crown Prosecution Service, headed by the Director of Public Prosecutions (DPP) and formally accountable to the Attorney-General.[11] The CPS has a duty to take over all prosecutions instituted by the police (except for certain minor offences), and has a power to take over other prosecutions.[12] The CPS was therefore accorded a status independent of the police, though, as will be seen, is still heavily reliant on the police. Section 10 of the Prosecution of Offences Act 1985 lays upon it the duty to publish a Code for Crown Prosecutors and to report annually to Parliament on its work and the use of its powers. Notable among these is its power to discontinue prosecutions in the magistrates' courts.[13] Unlike public prosecutors in many other jurisdictions, it was not given powers to institute proceedings itself, to direct the police

---

[6] JUSTICE, 'The Prosecution Process in England and Wales' [1970] *Crim LR* 668.

[7] *Report of an Inquiry by the Hon. Sir Henry Fisher into the circumstances leading to the trial of three persons on charges arising out of the death of Maxwell Confait and the fire at 27 Doggett Road, London SE6* (1977).

[8] Cf Royal Commission on Criminal Procedure, *Report* (1981), ch 7, with R. M. White, 'Investigators or Prosecutors or, Desperately Seeking Scotland: Re-Formulation of the "Philips Principle"' (2006) 69 *MLR* 143.

[9] White, ibid, 153–7 and *passim*.

[10] See the White Paper, *An Independent Prosecution Service for England and Wales* (1983).

[11] See A. Sanders, 'The CPS—30 Years On' [2016] *Crim LR* 82.   [12] See section 7.7(C).

[13] Prosecution of Offences Act 1985, s 23.

to investigate any matter, or to put questions to any person.[14] However, the advent of statutory charging in 2004 gave the CPS greater powers, though this is waning again.

The CPS carries out its statutory obligation to publish its Code for Crown Prosecutors: it was published first in 1986, with subsequent editions in 1992, 1994, 2000, 2004, 2010, 2013, and 2018. The revision in 1994 was intended to ensure that the Code was phrased in plain English suitable for lay persons to read, as well as making some changes of substance which will be referred to later. There has been a welcome step towards openness, with the publication on the CPS website of considerable amounts of guidance previously confidential to prosecutors,[15] including much of what formerly appeared in the Prosecution Manuals, most notably questions relevant to decisions whether or not to prosecute for specific offences. This increases transparency, and should enable greater public understanding as well as affording possible grounds for challenge where it appears that the guidance has not been followed. Integrated into this guidance are 'Charging Standards', created jointly by CPS lawyers and the police in the late 1990s with a view to assisting the police in setting the charge at the right level initially and ensuring that the CPS has a common starting point when reviewing case files. The movement towards greater transparency in matters of policy has resulted in a wide range of other guidance documents being placed on the CPS website, dealing with such matters as consents to prosecution, international cooperation, domestic abuse, the reinstitution of proceedings, evidential considerations, case preparation, witnesses, disclosure, and many others. This is much to be welcomed: reference to the guidance is made at appropriate points in this chapter. The crucial question, however, is whether the guidance is applied faithfully, and research findings on this are discussed throughout the chapter.

There have been significant changes in the organization and working of the CPS. One of the earliest initiatives of the Labour government when it came to power in 1997 was to set up a review of the CPS. The emphasis of that review turned out to be largely managerial, and there was a disappointing reluctance to discuss major issues of policy on prosecutions.[16] The significant resultant changes in working practices include the introduction of many CPS caseworkers, not legally qualified, to deal with the preparation of cases as well as the presentation of 'straightforward' guilty plea cases in magistrates' courts. The range of their potential duties was increased in April 2004 to include appearing at early administrative hearings and at hearings after a guilty plea where the court had ordered a pre-sentence report. These changes were said to form part of the 'modernization' of the CPS,[17] but they also mean that many roles that were originally intended to be fulfilled by qualified lawyers are now being carried out by (trained) laypeople.

This could be defended as part of a strategy to deploy CPS lawyers for more important tasks. In 2001, the Auld Review called for major changes in the powers and

---

[14] For the early history of the CPS, see Lord Windlesham, *Responses to Crime: Vol 4* (2001), ch 4.
[15] See the second edition of this work, at 179.
[16] Glidewell, *The Review of the Crown Prosecution Service: a Report* (1998), reviewed at [1998] *Crim LR* 517.
[17] 'Extended Role for CPS Caseworkers', Press Release, 29 April 2004.

duties of the CPS, to allow it to take a more direct and proactive role by determining the charge and preparing the case for trial. Thus, Lord Justice Auld recommended that the CPS 'should determine the charge in all but minor, routine offences or where, because of the circumstances, there is a need for a holding charge before seeking the advice of the Service'.[18] The relevant law was changed accordingly by ss 28–30 of the Criminal Justice Act 2003, in combination with Sch 2. These provisions introduced what is known as the 'statutory charging scheme', whereby the CPS took all charging decisions at the outset in respect of all indictable only and triable either way offences, whereas many lesser offences may be charged by the police (although they may seek advice from the CPS).

> The specific aims of the new charging arrangements may be summarised as follows: the elimination at the earliest opportunity of hopeless cases, the production of more robust prosecution cases, the elimination of unnecessary or unwarranted delays in the period between charge and disposal, and the reduction of the number of trials that "crack" through the offering and acceptance of guilty pleas to reduced charges at a late stage in the process.[19]

The 2003 Act also provided for the Director's Guidance on Charging, issued under s 37(A) of the Police and Criminal Evidence Act 1984 (PACE) as amended. The first Guidance was issued in February 2004, and there have been five further versions since.

One of the anticipated benefits of statutory charging was a close working relationship between police and CPS, leading to 'joint investigation' (with the CPS involved from an early stage) and 'proactive prosecuting' (i.e. thinking of trial issues from an early stage).[20] Indeed, a joint inspection by the Inspectorates of Constabulary and the CPS in 2008 of the statutory charging arrangements was generally supportive.[21] Weak cases were being discontinued earlier, and final charging decisions by prosecutors were of good quality. The review identified a number of areas for improvement, including a simplification of the varying processes adopted for statutory charging by different areas, greater consistency of approach by prosecutors, improved file preparation by the police, and improved methods for the giving of advice by the CPS to the police.[22]

The statutory charging arrangements led to the presence of a duty prosecutor in larger police stations, and a scheme called 'CPS Direct' was developed simultaneously to provide out-of-hours telephone access to CPS charging advice. A review in 2008 of CPS Direct found that this was a particularly successful part of the new arrangements, often more flexible and more responsive to police requirements, delivering good quality advice but with an appeal process where there was disagreement. Most of the recommendations for improvement related to technology and resources rather than to the service itself.[23]

---

[18] Auld LJ, *Review of the Criminal Courts of England and Wales* (2001), 412.

[19] I. Brownlee, 'The Statutory Charging Scheme in England and Wales: Towards a Unified Prosecution System?' [2004] *Crim LR* 896, 897.

[20] Y. Moreno and P. Hughes, *Effective Prosecution* (2008), ch 2.

[21] HM Crown Prosecution Service Inspectorate (HMCPSI) and HM Inspectorate of Constabulary (HMIC), *Joint Thematic Review of the New Charging Arrangements* (2008).

[22] Ibid, ch 3.   [23] HMCPSI, *Inspection of CPS Direct* (2008), ch 3.

Two changes in the joint working arrangements were announced in 2009.[24] CPS
Direct was extended to become a 24-hour service, available also during the working
day in order to provide easier access to advice for the police.[25] At the same time, a
pilot programme was run whereby the charging of all summary only offences would
become the responsibility of the police again. Though ostensibly this was to allow the
CPS to concentrate on more serious cases, essentially it represented a step back to the
pre-CPS days, and, given the seriousness of some summary only offences (e.g. common assault, assaulting a police officer, taking a vehicle without the owner's consent), it
revived arguments around fairness, impartiality, and legal knowledge against allowing
the police to be both investigators and prosecutors in the same case.

Since then, the revisions of the Director's Guidance have extended the range of case
types in which the police can charge suspects without first referring the file to the CPS,
leading to a gradual return of charging powers to the police. As noted in Chapter 6,
now the police may charge: (1) any summary only offence (including criminal damage where the value of the loss or damage is less than £5,000) irrespective of plea; (2)
(attempted) shoplifting irrespective of plea provided it is suitable for sentence in the
magistrates' court; and (3) any either way offence anticipated as a guilty plea and suitable for sentence in a magistrates' court; provided that this is not: a case requiring the
DPP's consent to prosecute; a case involving a death; connected with terrorist activity
or official secrets; hate crime or domestic violence; an offence of violent disorder or
affray; causing grievous bodily harm or wounding, or actual bodily harm; a Sexual Offences Act offence committed by or upon a person under 18; or an offence under the
Licensing Act 2003.[26]

In addition to this gradual return to the police of categories of cases which they can
charge, there are other recent changes of note: very few prosecutors still work in police
stations; only in some of the most serious cases is there a face-to-face meeting between
the prosecutor and investigator; and case papers for charging advice are now provided
digitally by the police to the CPS.[27]

One of the overarching principles of Sir Brian Leveson's *Review of Efficiency in
Criminal Proceedings* was 'getting it right first time',[28] which implies both getting the
charging decision correct and also ensuring a clear and well-reasoned approach to the
case and prosecution strategy. These aims, and the overall fairness of the process, can
be compromised if the case file is not sufficiently clear and detailed. There have been a
number of assessments of charging decisions, most of which highlight the poor quality of files received by the CPS from the police.[29] A Joint Inspection of the Provision
of Charging Decisions in 2015 examined a sample of cases where the police took the
decision to charge the defendant. In 34 of the 99 cases in the sample (34.3 per cent)

---

[24] 'CPS and ACPO announce charging developments', Press Release, 10 November 2009.
[25] https://www.cps.gov.uk/cps-areas-and-cps-direct.   [26] DG5, n 1, para 15.
[27] HMIC and HMCPSI, *Joint Inspection of the Provision of Charging Decisions* (2015), [1.4].
[28] Sir Brian Leveson, *Review of Efficiency in Criminal Proceedings* (2015), [4.1].
[29] E.g. HMIC and HMCPSI, *Joint Inspection of the Provision of Charging Decisions*, n 27; HMCPSI, *Thematic
Review of the CPS Rape and Serious Sexual Offences Units* (2016), 36.

where the decision to charge the defendant was taken by the police it should have been referred to the CPS in accordance with the Director's Guidance.[30] Conversely, in 9.6 per cent of the cases where CPS Direct directed no further action or an out-of-court disposal (OOCD), the police should have made the decision. In particular, concern was raised by both CPS and police staff that too many cases of domestic abuse were being referred to them for charging decisions which should have been halted by a police decision maker due to a lack of evidence.[31] Thus, the Joint Inspection Report recommended a CPS review of the Director's Guidance and its domestic abuse guidelines to ensure consistency between them.

Part of Transforming Summary Justice (TSJ), the initiative to improve how cases are dealt with in the magistrates' courts, is the requirement that all cases are reviewed by the CPS prior to the first hearing, irrespective of whether they were charged by the police or the CPS, and regardless of plea.[32] An early review of TSJ by HM Crown Prosecution Service Inspectorate (HMCPSI) found that although CPS charging decisions were good, there was a failure to review the prosecution file in 37.7 per cent of the cases considered.[33] Both the quality and the timeliness of the CPS reviews needed improvement, and CPS lawyers were advised to engage more with defence solicitors before court to ensure that the first hearing is as effective as possible. The review also stated that the CPS should find a more effective way of working with the police to improve the quality of the prosecution file. More positively, a follow-up inspection found a significant increase in the quality of the initial review: in 83.3 per cent of cases in the file sample a review was conducted before the first hearing and 60.6 per cent of these fully met expectations for the type of case.[34] Regardless of one's views on the purpose and merits of initiatives like TSJ, quality and oversight of case files are vital components of a fair prosecution.

7.2 EVIDENTIAL SUFFICIENCY

It is wrong for a person to be prosecuted if the evidence is insufficient. The essence of the wrongness lies in the protection of the innocent: if this principle is taken seriously, it should mean not merely that innocent people are not convicted, but also that innocent people should not be prosecuted. That is important for two reasons: first, as a method of ensuring that innocent people are not subsequently convicted, by weeding out weak cases at an early stage; and, secondly, because being prosecuted is a considerable inconvenience (as expressed in the dictum that 'the process is the punishment'[35]),

---

[30] HMIC and HMCPSI, *Joint Inspection of the Provision of Charging Decisions*, n 27, para 7.4.
[31] Ibid, para 9.13.
[32] HMCPSI, *Transforming Summary Justice: An early perspective of the CPS contribution report* (2016), [5.5].
[33] Ibid, [5.10].
[34] HMCPSI, *Business as Usual? Transforming Summary Justice Follow-up Report* (2017), [4.21].
[35] M. Feeley, *The Process is the Punishment* (1979), ch 1; particular emphasis is placed on this by J. Rogers, 'Restructuring the Exercise of Prosecutorial Discretion in England' (2006) 26 *OJLS* 775.

often a source of profound worry, and sometimes a considerable expense, and it may also lead to an element of stigma and loss of social esteem. Thus, there are sound moral reasons for not prosecuting someone against whom the evidence is insufficient. There are good economic reasons also: it is a waste of police time to compile a full file on such a case, of prosecution time to review it, and of court time to hear it. It is therefore desirable that weak cases be eliminated as early as possible: it was for this purpose that the Royal Commission on Criminal Procedure recommended the introduction of a public prosecution service to provide independent review, and that the Auld Review recommended the extension of CPS powers to the initial laying of the charge.

There are at least three major issues to be discussed before the principle of evidential sufficiency can be translated into practice. One is the test of sufficiency—what should it be? Closely intertwined with this is the second question—should the test vary according to the stage the case has reached? And, thirdly, how can prosecutors, at the stage of prosecutorial review, be expected to assess cases on the basis of a written file? In discussing these issues, it must be borne in mind that evidential sufficiency is only one of the factors relevant in prosecutions. Another is the lawfulness of the prosecution in procedural terms—have the appropriate formalities been completed? Have the time limits been observed? Has there been a previous prosecution arising out of the incident, so as to raise considerations of double jeopardy? A further factor is the policy of diversion, discussed in the previous chapter in the context of the cautioning of offenders. Thus, even if a case satisfies the test of evidential sufficiency, the 'public interest' may be in favour of dealing with the case by means other than prosecution. In practice, questions of evidential sufficiency and public interest often interact, but for clarity of exposition this section is devoted chiefly to evidential sufficiency, and the latter is considered in section 7.3.

(A) FORMULATING THE TEST OF EVIDENTIAL SUFFICIENCY

Until the early 1980s, the police applied the 'prima facie test' in deciding whether the evidence was strong enough for prosecution: is there 'evidence on the basis of which, if it were accepted, a reasonable jury or magistrates' court would be justified in convicting'?[36] This often meant that as long as there was some evidence on the main points that needed to be proved, the defendant ought to be brought to court to answer the charge.[37] The weakness of the test was that it made no explicit reference to the strength and credibility of the evidence, nor to probable lines of defence. In his submission to the 1981 Royal Commission on Criminal Procedure, the then DPP denounced this test as inadequate: it was wrong, he argued, that a person could be prosecuted when an acquittal was more likely than a conviction, and the minimum standard should require that conviction is more probable than acquittal.[38] The

---

[36] Royal Commission on Criminal Procedure, *Report*, para 8.8.
[37] Provided, of course, that the 'public interest' test was also satisfied: see section 7.3.
[38] Royal Commission on Criminal Procedure, Vol ii, *The Law and the Procedure* (1981), Appendix 25.

Director's approach was commended by the Royal Commission on the basis that a lower standard would be 'both unfair to the accused and a waste of the restricted resources of the criminal justice system'.[39] When the CPS came into existence, the first edition of the Code for Crown Prosecutors in 1986 required a 'realistic prospect of conviction', a test that remains unchanged today.[40] Moreover, the Code requires prosecutors to take account of 'what the defence case may be, and how that is likely to affect the prospects of conviction',[41] and to consider whether the evidence can be used and is reliable and credible.[42] Prosecutors should consider whether there is any question over the admissibility of certain evidence.[43]

What is the legal basis for the 'realistic prospects' test, and what are its theoretical justifications? Clearly, it is predictive in nature: it requires the prosecutor to assess whether, on the evidence likely to be given at trial, a conviction is more probable than an acquittal. This includes matters such as the admissibility of the evidence and the likely defence. Paragraph 4.7 of the Code states that 'The finding that there is a realistic prospect of conviction is based on the prosecutor's objective assessment of the evidence.' There are two different ways in which this might be interpreted. One is a straight predictive, realist approach (sometimes termed 'the bookmaker's approach'[44]): the prosecutor's task would be to predict how the court in which the case would be tried would react to the evidence. This might require the prosecutor to take account of the different conviction rates of magistrates' courts and the Crown Court, and of any local trends in willingness or unwillingness to convict in certain types of case. An alternative is the 'intrinsic merits' or merits-based approach, according to which the task of the prosecutor is to judge the strength of evidence and to apply the law to it faithfully. On this approach, prosecutors exercise the function of keeping cases away from the lay tribunal when they judge that the evidence is insufficient, even though they think that the tribunal might well convict, and correspondingly prosecutors persevere with a case when they believe that the evidence is sufficient, even though they recognize that the local court is unlikely to convict. Thus, on the predictive view the disposition of the local courts sets the standard, whereas on the merits-based view it is a legal standard applied by prosecutors to case files that determines decisions.

Those who believe in the supreme importance of lay adjudications would favour the predictive view. Magistrates and juries should be the central figures, and prosecutors should attempt to anticipate their decisions rather than to neutralize or even bypass them. On the other hand, fidelity to law would favour the merits-based approach, since one might doubt whether there could be sufficient reason why a local bench or justices' clerk, or the juries of a particular neighbourhood, should be allowed to distort or disregard the law of the country as a whole. Thus, the American Bar Association has stated that: 'In cases which involve a serious threat to the

---

[39] Royal Commission on Criminal Procedure, *Report*, para 8.9.
[40] *Code for Crown Prosecutors* (2018), para 4.6.   [41] Ibid.   [42] Ibid, para 4.8.   [43] Ibid.
[44] See *R (on the application of B) v DPP* [2009] EWHC 106 (Admin), [49].

community, the prosecutor should not be deterred from prosecution by the fact that in the jurisdiction juries have tended to acquit persons accused of the particular kind of criminal act in question.'[45] This is also consistent with para 4.7 of the Code: 'an objective, impartial and reasonable jury or bench of magistrates or judge hearing a case alone, properly directed and acting in accordance with the law, is more likely than not to convict the defendant of the charge alleged'. Of course, 'more likely than not' is of a different standard to 'realistic prospect of conviction'.[46] This inconsistency should be addressed.

The merits-based approach has been endorsed by the Divisional Court in *R (on the application of B) v DPP*.[47] B was victim of a serious assault who had identified his attacker and given an account to the police. When it emerged that B suffered from a psychosis that sometimes led to paranoid beliefs and hallucinations, a psychiatric report was commissioned, which concluded that B's condition might affect the reliability of his perceptions and recollections. The CPS therefore discontinued the case, but the Divisional Court granted judicial review of that decision. Toulson LJ held that it was premature and unsatisfactory to drop the case without further discussion with either the victim or the psychiatrist about the reliability of his evidence. The CPS decision appears to have proceeded from either a misreading of the psychiatric report or unfounded stereotyping of the victim because of his mental disorder. The court went on to find a breach of Art 3 of the European Convention on Human Rights (ECHR), holding that the dropping of the prosecution violated the state's obligation to protect citizens from serious assaults and increased the victim's sense of being outside the law's protection, and the court awarded the victim £8,000 damages for the inhuman and degrading treatment suffered. This is a welcome decision in respect of those with forms of mental disturbance,[48] and has the wide significance of endorsing a version of the 'intrinsic merits' approach that insists on close attention to the actual evidence in the particular case.[49] Such an approach places considerable weight on prosecutors' judgements, but it should be supported since it aspires to advance the purpose of the law rather than deferring to the reaction of the (local) courts.

The evidential test was challenged under Art 2 in *Da Silva v UK*, a case arising from the failure to prosecute any of police officers involved in the fatal shooting of Jean Charles de Menezes in London in 2005, who was believed mistakenly to pose a terrorist threat.[50] The evidential test for bringing prosecutions was upheld as lawful by the European Court of Human Rights, which found that it does not violate any rights of victims to have crimes affecting them prosecuted effectively.

---

[45] *Standards for Criminal Justice: Prosecution Function* (3rd edn, 1993), paras 3–3.9(e).

[46] See J. Rogers, 'A Human Rights Perspective on the Evidential Test for Bringing Prosecutions' [2017] *Crim LR* 678, 679.

[47] [2009] EWHC 106 (Admin), [2009] *Crim LR* 652.

[48] See CPS, *Supporting Victims and Witnesses with Mental Health Issues* (2009).

[49] *R (on the application of B) v DPP*, n 47, [50]–[51].

[50] *Da Silva v UK* (2016) 63 EHRR 12; see Rogers, n 46, 678.

(B) EVIDENTIAL SUFFICIENCY AND THE STAGES
OF THE CRIMINAL PROCESS

The Code for Crown Prosecutors formerly stated a single test of evidential sufficiency: whether there is a 'realistic prospect of conviction'. As argued in previous editions of this book, that test is not suitable for practical application at all stages of the criminal process.[51] For example, at the end of questioning the police may believe that they have sufficient evidence to justify remanding a defendant in custody before first appearance at court, and the CPS may take the same view at that stage, but it may not be possible to say that there is a realistic prospect of a conviction. Similarly, in many cases the prosecutor receives a file for the first time just before remand proceedings are due to begin. This may be the morning after the defendant's arrest. The prosecutor will have had no time to listen to any interview tapes, and so it is likely that the police summary will dominate. Both the police and the prosecutor may believe that they have (or will have) sufficient evidence to justify the charge, but they may still have witnesses to interview and forensic reports to receive. In strict terms, there may not yet be a realistic prospect of conviction. Can a remand in custody be justified in these circumstances? Even one week's loss of liberty—often spent in an overcrowded prison, with poor facilities, away from family, friends, and employment (if any), and without unrestricted access to legal advice—is a serious deprivation. As we shall see in Chapter 8, the Bail Act 1976 directs a magistrates' court to have regard to the strength of the evidence; but, again, usually this is taken on trust from the CPS, which in turn may take it on trust from the police.

The CPS addressed this point in the 2004 version of the Code, and the 2018 Code (like those in 2010 and 2013) distinguishes between the 'Full Code Test', applicable in normal situations, and the 'Threshold Test', applicable in cases where it would not be appropriate to release a suspect on bail after charge but the evidence to apply the Full Code Test is not yet available. This guidance is based on Art 5(1)(c) of the ECHR, which states that no one shall be deprived of their liberty except on reasonable suspicion of having committed an offence. According to the 2018 Code, 'Prosecutors must be satisfied, on an objective assessment of the evidence, that there are reasonable grounds to suspect that the person to be charged has committed the offence.'[52] The assessment must consider the impact of any defence or information that the suspect has put forward or on which they might rely.[53]

This should be done by reference to:

- the nature, extent and admissibility of any likely further evidence and the impact it will have on the case;

- the charges that all the evidence will support;

- the reasons why the evidence is not already available;

- the time required to obtain the further evidence, including whether it could be obtained within any available detention period; and

- whether the delay in applying the Full Code Test is reasonable in all the circumstances.[54]

---

[51] See the second edition of this work at 184.   [52] *Code for Crown Prosecutors* (2018), para 5.3.
[53] Ibid.   [54] Ibid, para 5.7.

Recognition of the need for this Threshold Test was a significant step, but the robust-
ness of the 'reasonable suspicion' standard may be doubted. Indeed, the Inspectorates
suggested that the test should be clearer about the prosecutorial judgement on which
it is based, namely that it will in due course be 'possible to mount a viable case against
the suspect'.[55] Moreno and Hughes emphasize that the Threshold Test is merely an
interim measure 'to be used by prosecutors in exceptional circumstances in order to
manage high risk offenders [*sic*] whilst significant outstanding evidence is obtained by
the police within a reasonable time'. Thus, the test 'is about managing substantial bail
risks where all of the evidence is not available' and should not be regarded as a shortcut
for a charging decision.[56] Although para 5.11 of the Code recognizes these concerns its
wording should be stronger:

> A decision to charge under the Threshold Test must be kept under review. The prosecutor
> should be proactive to secure from the police the identified outstanding evidence or other
> material in accordance with an agreed timetable. The evidence must be regularly assessed
> to ensure that the charge is still appropriate and that continued objection to bail is justified.
> The Full Code Test must be applied as soon as the anticipated further evidence or material
> is received and, in any event, in Crown Court cases, usually before the formal service of
> the prosecution case.

The defendant's right to liberty under Art 5 should only be withheld temporarily on
these grounds, and it would be better to see open recognition of the principle of urgency and of the importance of ensuring that a suspect should not be kept in custody
any longer than absolutely necessary under the Threshold Test. The Inspectorates' finding in 2008 that in 57 per cent of cases where the Threshold Test was used there was not
a timely review applying the Full Code Test therefore gives cause for concern.[57]

The *Joint Inspection of the Provision of Charging Decisions* in 2015 examined a sample
of cases where the decision to charge had been made by police, finding that the police
applied the correct test, be that full or threshold, in 81.8 per cent of them.[58] The CPS
decision to charge was compliant with the Code test in 91.3 per cent,[59] and prosecutors
determined correctly in almost all (97.4 per cent) cases which test should be applied.[60]
Where the prosecutor determined that the Threshold Test was applicable, this was
agreed with by the court in 75.0 per cent of the cases, and the defendant was remanded
in custody. While cases which are charged under the Threshold Test must be subject
to a Full Code Test review as soon as is reasonably practicable and in any event before
any contested hearing,[61] only 37.5 per cent of threshold test cases had the required Full
Code Test review, which represented a decline from 2008. The Joint Inspection Report
concluded that 'The CPS must improve considerably compliance with this aspect of
performance.'[62] These findings were cited critically in a National Audit Office report

---

[55] HMCPSI and HMIC, *Joint Thematic Review of the New Charging Arrangements*, n 21, para 5.21.
[56] Moreno and Hughes, n 20, 48–50.
[57] HMCPSI and HMIC, *Joint Thematic Review of the New Charging Arrangements*, n 21, para 12.9.
[58] HMIC and HMCPSI, *Joint Inspection of the Provision of Charging Decisions*, n 27, 51.   [59] Ibid, 47.
[60] Ibid, para 8.7.   [61] Ibid, para 8.8, referring to para 13 of DG5, see n 1.   [62] Ibid, para 8.8.

on *Efficiency in the criminal justice system* in 2016,[63] and indeed there was no evidence of improvement in the HMCPSI *Review of the CPS Rape and Serious Sexual Offences Units* the same year.[64] Of the 89 relevant cases studied, the Code test was not applied correctly at charge in 10.1 per cent.[65] Despite the introduction of a new National File Standard for police, as part of *Better Case Management,* which determines the minimum requirements for the content of police files submitted to the CPS,[66] undoubtedly there remains significant room for improvement in charging practices on the part of both police and prosecution.

As for concerns about racism and bias in charging decisions, an independent review in 2017 chaired by David Lammy MP was reasonably positive.[67] The Lammy Review found that, overall, charging decisions taken by the CPS are broadly proportionate, noting that the CPS caseload is determined by police arrest rates.[68] Notwithstanding biases in arrest and stop and search,[69] once arrested, suspects from different ethnic groups are charged at relatively similar rates, with the important exceptions of rape and domestic abuse.[70] In the latter cases, black defendants and 'Chinese and Other' defendants (which includes anyone who self-identifies as 'Other ethnic group') were found to have higher prosecution rates, a concern identified by the CPS itself. Lammy called for more research, and noted the practical steps that could be taken to address this issue, such as redacting all identifying information, for example name and ethnicity, from the case information that passes between police officers and prosecutors.[71] The most recent statistics indicate that relative to the population, the rates of prosecution for indictable offences for Black and Mixed ethnic groups were four and two times higher than for the White ethnic group: for every 1,000 population members, 16 Black and nine Mixed defendants were prosecuted compared to four White defendants.[72] Drawing on Lammy's insights, it appears that this is due to arrest rather than charging practices.

7.3 THE PUBLIC INTEREST

The discussion of regulatory agencies in Chapter 6 demonstrated that there are different conceptions of the public interest at work across the broad sphere of law enforcement. Most of these agencies, which have both investigative and prosecution powers,

---

[63] National Audit Office, *Efficiency in the criminal justice system* (2016), 25.

[64] HMCPSI, *Thematic Review of the CPS Rape and Serious Sexual Offences Units,* n 29, para 4.17.

[65] Ibid.

[66] HMCPSI, *Better Case Management: A Snapshot* (2016), para 4.13.

[67] *The Lammy Review: An Independent Review into the Treatment of, and outcomes for, Black, Asian and Minority Ethnic Individuals in the Criminal Justice System* (2017), https://assets.publishing.service.gov.uk/government/uploads/system/uploads/attachment_data/file/643001/lammy-review-final-report.pdf, 17.

[68] Indeed, David Lammy suggested that other criminal justice agencies and institutions should learn lessons from the CPS, including openness to external scrutiny, systems of internal oversight, and a diverse workforce.

[69] See Ch 4.   [70] *Lammy Review,* n 67, 21.   [71] Ibid, Recommendation 8.

[72] Ministry of Justice, *Statistics on Race and the Criminal Justice System 2016* (2017), 8.

regard their primary role as securing compliance with the standards laid down by law. They are often willing to take time to achieve this, and many adopt an approach that may be termed accommodative or conciliatory—using persuasion, education, and negotiation as the principal methods, and leaving the power to prosecute as a background threat which is invoked rarely. Despite claims that some regulatory agencies were becoming more punitive,[73] the prevailing orientation is still towards persuasion and negotiation, not least by the SFO.[74]

The position of the CPS has been rather less constant. The 1986 and 1992 editions of the Code for Crown Prosecutors were phrased so as to suggest that a prosecution should only be brought if 'the public interest requires' it, a formulation which suggested that there should be a presumption in favour of diversion from prosecution, and that a good reason was needed for prosecuting. It is not clear whether this emphasis was intended, or indeed whether it was thus interpreted in practice. While the 1994 Code included a distinct shift in language, reflecting the then Home Secretary's determination to reduce the frequency of cautioning,[75] and repeated in the 2000 edition,[76] the advent of conditional cautioning in 2003 led to a further change (see Chapter 6.2(C) iii). Thus, para 4.10 of the 2018 Code now states:

> It has never been the rule that a prosecution will automatically take place once the evidential stage is met. A prosecution will usually take place unless the prosecutor is satisfied that there are public interest factors tending against prosecution which outweigh those tending in favour. In some cases the prosecutor may be satisfied that the public interest can be properly served by offering the offender the opportunity to have the matter dealt with by an out-of-court disposal rather than bringing a prosecution.

Whereas the 2010 version of the Code followed its predecessors in setting out lists of common factors for and against prosecution, the 2013 and 2018 Codes instead include questions which should be considered, concerning the seriousness of the offence committed, the level of culpability of the suspect, the circumstances of and the harm caused to the victim, whether the suspect was younger than 18 at the time of the offence, the impact on the community, whether prosecution is a proportionate response, and the need for protection of sources of information.[77]

As noted in Chapter 6, s 133 of the Legal Aid, Sentencing and Punishment of Offenders Act (LASPO) 2012 means that the issue of conditional cautions is no longer confined to prosecutors but may be granted by certain police officers also. The 2018 Code states very little about the factors that should dispose a prosecutor to select an OOCD: 'An out-of-court disposal may take the place of a prosecution if it is an

---

[73] R. Baldwin, 'The New Punitive Regulation' (2004) 67 *MLR* 351.

[74] N. Lord and C. King, 'Negotiating Non-Contention: Civil Recovery and Deferred Prosecution in Response to Transnational Corporate Bribery' in L. Campbell and N. Lord (eds), *Corruption in Commercial Enterprise: Law, Theory and Practice* (2018).

[75] A. Ashworth and J. Fionda, 'The New Code for Crown Prosecutors: Prosecution, Accountability and the Public Interest' [1994] *Crim LR* 894; cf R. Daw, 'A Response' [1994] *Crim LR* 904.

[76] *Code for Crown Prosecutors* (2000), para 6.2.

[77] *Code for Crown Prosecutors* (2013), para 4.12 and *Code for Crown Prosecutors* (2018), para 4.14.

appropriate response to the offender and/or the seriousness and consequences of the offending.'[78] The 2010 Code included the prescriptive statement that 'prosecutors will offer a conditional caution where it is a proportionate response to the seriousness and the consequences of the offending and where the conditions offered meet the aims of rehabilitation, reparation or punishment within the terms of the Criminal Justice Act 2003',[79] but there was no equivalent in the 2013 Code.

Paragraph 7.2 of the 2018 Code states:

> Prosecutors must follow any relevant guidance when asked to advise on or authorise an out-of-court disposal, including any appropriate regulatory proceedings, a punitive or civil penalty, or other disposal. They should ensure that the appropriate evidential standard for the specific out-of-court disposal is met including, where required, a clear admission of guilt, and that the public interest would be properly served by such a disposal.

In that vein, more detail is to be found in the DPP's Guidance on Conditional Cautioning.[80]

In terms of proportionality, the Code states that 'The more serious the offence, the more likely it is that a prosecution is required' and '[t]he greater the suspect's level of culpability, the more likely it is that a prosecution is required'.[81] The theory of desert or proportionality,[82] combined with the established finding that the process of being prosecuted may itself involve inconvenience, anxiety, or pain,[83] supports the proposition that a line should be drawn beyond which prosecution as a response is disproportionate and heavy-handed.

The extent to which a decision to prosecute could contravene the ECHR was examined in *SXH v CPS*, where SXH challenged under Art 8 the decision to prosecute her for possessing a false identity document.[84] She was a refugee whose application for asylum was pending; she was charged and had attended a case management hearing in the Crown Court meanwhile. After being granted asylum, the CPS offered no evidence, counsel having determined that it was not in the public interest to pursue the prosecution. So SXH was found not guilty and released from custody. She then issued proceedings against the CPS for damages on various grounds including breach of her rights under Art 8. The Supreme Court held that neither the ECHR nor domestic authorities supported the contention that the institution of criminal proceedings, for a matter which is properly the subject of the criminal law and for which there is sufficient evidence, may be open to challenge on Art 8 grounds. While the criminalization of conduct may amount to an interference with Art 8 rights, if it does not do so, then neither does the decision to prosecute for that conduct.[85] The Supreme Court held that whether it is in the public interest to prosecute is not the same as whether a

---

[78] Ibid, para 7.1.   [79] *Code for Crown Prosecutors* (2010), para 7.1.   [80] See Ch 6.

[81] *Code for Crown Prosecutors* (2018), para 4.14.

[82] See A. von Hirsch and A. Ashworth (eds), *Principled Sentencing* (2nd edn, 1998), ch 4.

[83] Royal Commission on Criminal Procedure, *Report*, para 8.7; M. McConville and J. Baldwin, *Prosecution, Courts and Conviction* (1981).

[84] [2017] UKSC 30.   [85] [31]–[32].

prosecution would breach an individual's Art 8 rights.[86] Article 8 is therefore not applicable to the decision to prosecute.[87] While the court could criticize the CPS's delayed admission that she had a defence, this failure would not amount to a breach, even if Art 8 was applicable.[88] Ultimately, the decided authorities pointed to the conclusion that 'the duty of the CPS is to the public, not to the victim or to the suspect, who have separate interests'.[89] Though the decision to prosecute here may seem unpalatable and contrary to the public interest, the issue lies predominantly with the construction of the substantive law. In terms of prosecution policy, Art 8 is not the mechanism to resolve such issues.

7.4 CPS PRACTICES AND PERFORMANCE

In this section we consider some key CPS practices in the light of evidence about their implementation, and highlight concerns that have been raised. Of course, the CPS records the decisions it makes, outlining the reasons for its determinations and processes. The CPS has the capacity to downgrade charges, and to discontinue cases, and such discretion must be exercised fairly and properly. We also examine the extent to which acquittals by a judge could or should be regarded as a measure of CPS efficiency.

(A) RECORDING DECISIONS AND REASONS

All cases dealt with by the CPS are registered on and tracked through its case management system, and prosecutors are expected to record an 'endorsement', that is, a record of the court hearings and decisions made in a given case. As HMCPSI stresses:

> The provision of high quality data is critical to maintaining the smooth administration of the criminal justice system and public confidence in it, and it must be seen to deliver robust compliance monitoring and assurance, good governance and accountability.[90]

Numerous reports have found issues with the quality of endorsements on CPS files.[91] In 2004, HMCPSI found that:

> File endorsements were of inconsistent quality and in many cases inadequate. It was often difficult to ascertain the factors taken into account at various stages of the process, whether there had been compliance with the Code and the Policy, and sometimes the actual decision made.[92]

---

[86] [34].   [87] [35].   [88] [36].   [89] [38].

[90] HMCPSI, *Case Finalisations: An Inspection into the Timeliness and Accuracy of Recording Case Finalisations onto the Crown Prosecution Service Case Management System* (2017).

[91] Gus John Partnership, *Race for Justice: a review of CPS decision making for possible racial bias at each stage of the prosecution process* (2003), para 99. The report makes similar points at paras 22, 31, 92, and 115. Also see HMCPSI, *Violence at Home* (2004), para 7.18.

[92] HMCPSI, *Violence at Home* (2004), para 7.77.

While it is possible that these were failures of record keeping rather than incorrect decisions, the reports suggest otherwise. The Inspection on Discontinuance in 2007 described as disappointing that 17.5 per cent of files on discontinued cases did not contain a proper record of the reasons for the decision.[93] More recently, HMCPSI evaluated the recording of finalizations on to the CPS case management system, finding that overall this had improved significantly.[94] That said, HMCPSI could find no 'standard' against which endorsements are being measured, other than a requirement that they be accurate and proportionate.[95] While acknowledging CPS investment in the data quality and integrity of information on the case management system, HMCPSI concluded that it needs to ensure compliance in the standardizing of records to ensure that all the necessary details are recorded.[96]

(B) DOWNGRADING OF CHARGES

A perennial concern is that prosecutors will 'downgrade' charges, either by reducing the charge to a lower level or by accepting a guilty plea to a lesser offence. Though the Glidewell Review was asked to examine this issue, its examination was rather poor in that it failed to discuss existing research and simply concluded that there was a suspicion 'that charges, particularly in relation to offences of violence and associated offences, are downgraded on occasions when they should not be'.[97] Indeed, the 'ladder' of offences of violence provided by the Offences Against the Person Act 1861 gives ample opportunity for downgrading and charge bargaining.[98]

Some downgradings may relate to mode of trial. When the CPS receives a case file from the police, it may conclude that the case ought to be tried in the magistrates' court. To achieve this it may drop the higher charge and substitute a lower one, although it is not supposed to do this after a defendant has elected Crown Court trial on an either way charge. The Code for Crown Prosecutors states that speed should never be the only reason for trying to keep a case in the magistrates' court, whereas any greater delays and stress on witnesses might be an adequate reason.[99] As for the allegedly high rate of acceptance of guilty pleas by the CPS in exchange for reducing the charge(s),[100] it is difficult to find evidence on this, though the John Report identified this tendency in respect of racially aggravated offences,[101] and it is possible that analysis of other offences might yield similar results. This would hardly be surprising, since the structure of the English criminal justice system is such as to place considerable pressure on defendants to plead guilty, and the relatively high acquittal rate in the

---

[93] HMCPSI, *Discontinuance* (2007), para 4.11.   [94] HMCPSI, *Case Finalisations*, n 90, para 1.2.

[95] Ibid, para 3.20.   [96] Ibid, 8.   [97] I. Glidewell, *Review of the Crown Prosecution Service* (1998), 85.

[98] D. Moxon and C. Hedderman, 'Mode of Trial Decisions and Sentencing Differences between Courts' (1994) 33 *Howard JCJ* 97; similarly E. Genders, 'Reform of the Offences against the Person Act: Lessons from the Law in Action' [1999] *Crim LR* 689, only 19 per cent eventually dealt with under s 18; A. Cretney and G. Davis, *Punishing Violence* (1995), 137; cf also research R. Henham, 'Further Evidence on the Significance of Plea in the Crown Court' (2002) 41 *Howard JCJ* 151, revealing differences by circuit.

[99] Para 8.2.   [100] For general discussion of 'charge-bargaining', see Ch 10.4.

[101] See n 160 and accompanying text.

Crown Court may also incline prosecutors to accept a plea to a lesser offence. The 2018 Code declares that:

9.2 Prosecutors should only accept the defendant's plea if:

- the court is able to pass a sentence that matches the seriousness of the offending, particularly where there are aggravating features;

- it enables the court to make a confiscation order in appropriate cases, where a defendant has benefitted from criminal conduct; and

- it provides the court with adequate powers to impose other ancillary orders, bearing in mind that these can be made with some offences but not with others.

9.3 Particular care must be taken when considering pleas which would enable the defendant to avoid the imposition of a mandatory minimum sentence.

9.4 Prosecutors must never accept a guilty plea just because it is convenient.

David Jeremy rightly castigates a previous version of this provision (which is the same other than it refers to Crown Prosecutors) as 'opaque to the point of being unhelpful'.[102] The reference to sentencing is disingenuous, since either the defendant has the intent for s 18 or has not. The court cannot pass sentence for a lesser offence, such as s 20, on the basis of that intent; and the sentencing ranges for s 20 are considerably below those for s 18.[103] In practice, the opaqueness of the paragraph allows the known hazards of trials and the cost-effectiveness of guilty pleas combined with the significant structural pressure within the whole system (see Chapter 10) to enter into CPS decisions.[104]

Reduction of charges may be justified if the defendant has been overcharged originally: the CPS would be performing their correct review function to insist on this. But that does not always happen. The HMCPSI report on domestic violence cases found that after CPS review the vast majority of cases proceeded on the correct charge, but they concluded that 9 per cent of cases had not proceeded on the correct charge even after CPS review of the file, leading to the raising of victim's expectations unnecessarily, and noting that the later reduction can compromise the commitment of the victim to the prosecution.[105]

One of the expectations of the statutory charging arrangements was that they would reduce overcharging and downgrading by ensuring that the correct charge is laid in the first place. Though there is no direct research on this, the 2008 Inspectorates review found that 25 per cent of file quality was good, 45 per cent was adequate, and 30 per cent was poor, adding that file quality appeared to have some correlation with the success of the outcome.[106] This was hardly a ringing endorsement of statutory charging, and may be thought to lend some credence to the fears of those who have suggested

---

[102] D. Jeremy, 'The Prosecutor's Rock and Hard Place' [2008] *Crim LR* 925, at 935; see also 931.

[103] Sentencing Council, *Assault Definitive Guideline* (2011), 3–9.

[104] The priority of obtaining a conviction, above obtaining a conviction for the most appropriate offence, was also found by E. Burney and G. Rose, *Racist Offences—How is the Law Working?* (2002), 78.

[105] HMCPSI, *Violence at Home* (2004), para 7.54.

[106] HMCPSI and HMIC, *Review of the New Charging Arrangements* (2008), paras 12.11–12.16.

that closer working between police and prosecutor might increase rather than reduce the tendency to pursue a weak case if the incident is serious. As noted, concerns about file quality persist and in its 2015 Review HMCPSI found that cases involving allegations of sexual offending or those which were said to be religiously or racially aggravated were the most problematic in terms of the quality of the charging decision.[107]

(C) DISCONTINUANCE

Sections 23 and 23A of the Prosecution of Offences Act 1985 gives the CPS the power to discontinue charges brought in the magistrates' courts and Crown Court. However, ever since the CPS was founded there has been criticism that the CPS discontinues too high a proportion of cases, and the White Paper of 2002 referred to the 13 per cent discontinuance rate in the context of 'what is not working' in the system.[108]

The percentage of cases discontinued in the magistrates' courts (including bindovers)[109] stood at 16.2 per cent in 2001–2 declining to 13.8 per cent by 2003–4,[110] 9.6 per cent in 2010–11, and 9.4 per cent in 2017–18.[111] The straightforward interpretation of this substantial change is that, prior to 2004, the police laid the original charge, often without consulting the CPS, and that was why a higher proportion of them had to be discontinued on subsequent review by the CPS; and that since 2004, as statutory charging has become embedded in police and prosecutorial practices, the initial charge is more likely to be accurate and there should be fewer occasions on which it proves necessary to discontinue. Why were cases discontinued? The Inspectorate's 2007 review of discontinuance found that 43 per cent were discontinued because of insufficient evidence, 24 per cent on public interest grounds, and 26 per cent 'unable to proceed' (which usually means that a key witness refused to give evidence). The discontinuance rate for domestic violence rates is higher than for most other offences, as discussed in section 7.5(C). Many of the discontinuances were also for motoring or public order offences that were charged initially by the police, since they fell outside the statutory charging scheme. Nonetheless, the Inspectorate raises some doubts about the quality of pre-charge decisions by prosecutors, over 10 per cent of which were found not to have complied with the Full Code Test, and also about delays in decision making about discontinuance, which affected more than a quarter of the discontinued cases.[112]

The 2015 Joint Inspection Report found that in 90.8 per cent of cases the CPS decision to charge was compliant with the Code test,[113] but only in 48 per cent was there

---

[107] HMIC and HMCPSI, *Joint Inspection of the Provision of Charging Decisions*, n 27, para 8.4.

[108] Home Office, *Justice for All* (2002), 51.

[109] I.e. the figure now includes cases that were discontinued when the defendant agreed to be bound over to keep the peace for, usually, a year. This shadowy practice calls for principled examination.

[110] CPS, *Annual Report 2003–2004*, Annex A, 5; CPS, *Annual Report 2008–2009*, Annex B, 5.

[111] CPS, response to FOI Request ref: 7927, 30 July 2018, see Tables 7.1 and 7.2.

[112] HMCPSI, *Discontinuance* (2007), paras 4.7–4.16.

[113] HMIC and HMCPSI, *Joint Inspection of the Provision of Charging Decisions*, n 27, 47.

Table 7.1 Magistrates' courts prosecution data

	2010–11	2011–12	2012–13	2013–14	2014–15	2015–16	2016–17	2017–18
Discontinuances (including bind-overs)	80,942 9.6%	75,612 9.6%	68,128 9.6%	62,227 9.7%	59,146 10.5%	55,221 10.3%	47,521 9.5%	42,406 9.4%
Total prosecuted	**841,180**	**787,958**	**707,995**	**640,919**	**563,625**	**538,716**	**499,816**	**453,071**

Source: CPS, response to FOI Request ref: 7927, 30 July 2018.

Table 7.2 Crown Court prosecution data

	2010–11	2011–12	2012–13	2013–14	2014–15	2015–16	2016–17	2017–18
Judge-ordered acquittals (including bind-overs)	15,041 12.8%	12,670 11.7%	11,338 11.5%	10,916 11.4%	12,615 12.5%	12,067 12.2%	10,225 11.6%	8,778 11.0%
Judge-directed acquittals	1,111 0.9%	871 0.8%	798 0.8%	632 0.7%	654 0.6%	683 0.7%	652 0.7%	512 0.6%
Total Prosecuted	**117,654**	**108,547**	**98,463**	**95,777**	**100,865**	**99,062**	**88,205**	**80,090**

Source: CPS, response to FOI Request ref: 7927, 30 July 2018.

timely discontinuance of non-Code compliant charges.[114] HMCPSI's Thematic Review of the CPS Rape and Serious Sexual Offences Units found that while all decisions to discontinue cases were Code-compliant, the decision to discontinue was timely in only 55.6 per cent.[115] The police were consulted in a proposed discontinuance or alteration of charges in eight of the 15 cases (53.3 per cent) and the victim was consulted in a proposed discontinuance or in relation to alteration of charges in seven of the 15 (46.7 per cent). The Code was applied incorrectly post-charge in eight of the 59 relevant cases (13.6 per cent); most of these were decisions to let a case continue when it had been wrongly charged.[116]

Barclay and Mhlanga's research showed that a much higher proportion of prosecutions brought against non-white defendants were discontinued than against white defendants, and that the grounds were mostly evidential, suggesting that more charges were brought against non-white defendants when the evidence was weak:[117] it is unclear whether statutory charging and collocation resulted in more of those cases being charged correctly in the first instance. There is no direct mention of discontinuance in the Lammy Review, which, as noted earlier, was broadly positive as to the practices and oversight of CPS decisions when viewed through the lens of ethnic background.[118]

(D) ACQUITTALS BY THE JUDGE

Whereas discontinuance rates have (not always rightly) been taken as a measure of CPS performance in summary cases, so in Crown Court cases the performance of the CPS has sometimes been measured according to how frequently cases end in an acquittal by the judge. Acquittals by judge are of two different types. A judge-ordered acquittal occurs where the prosecutor informs the court that the CPS does not wish to proceed, and the judge formally orders the jury to acquit. A directed acquittal occurs during or at the end of the prosecution's case in court, if the judge decides that there is insufficient evidence on one or more elements of the offence. Research by Block, Corbett, and Peay in the early 1990s suggested that dispassionate scrutineers could identify weak cases among those that ended in acquittals by the judge: a minimum of 22 per cent of acquittals occurred in cases that were regarded as foreseeably flawed in the opinion of a trained prosecutor,[119] and the researchers' own assessments led them to state that:

> although fewer than half of ordered acquittals were considered definitely or possibly foreseeable, three quarters of directed acquittals were so classified. This supports our view, derived from the study, that directed acquittals result largely from weak cases that should

---

[114] Ibid, 48.

[115] HMCPSI, *Thematic Review of the CPS Rape and Serious Sexual Offences Units*, n 29, para 4.49.

[116] Ibid, para 4.48.   [117] G. Barclay and B. Mhlanga, *Ethnic Differences in Decisions on Young Defendants Dealt With by the Crown Prosecution Service* (2000). See further HMCPSI, *A Follow Up Review of CPS Casework with a Minority Ethnic Dimension* (2004), paras 11.13–11.23, suggesting that the overcharging of minority ethnic defendants remains an issue.

[118] *Lammy Review*, n 67, 17.

[119] B. Block, C. Corbett, and J. Peay, *Ordered and Directed Acquittals in the Crown Court* (1993).

have been discontinued, whereas ordered acquittals result largely from unforeseeable circumstances.[120]

Baldwin conducted a somewhat similar inquiry for the CPS in 1995, with a sample of
around 100 cases ending in acquittal by judge and some 70 other cases. He found that
the ordered acquittals occurred chiefly where a key witness retracted a statement or
failed to arrive at court (48 per cent), the judge took the view at the outset that the case
was too weak (16 per cent), or the case was terminated following the convictions of
other people (14 per cent). The directed acquittals occurred chiefly because a key witness
failed to come up to proof (34 per cent), or there were problems of law or admissibility
of evidence (32 per cent), or the judge ruled the evidence insufficient (12 per cent).[121]
The important question is how many of these were foreseeable and ought to have led to
earlier discontinuance. Baldwin found that around 41 per cent of all cases resulting in
acquittal had reservations of a prosecutor entered upon the file at an early stage, and a
further 35 per cent of files mentioned reservations but discounted them. His conclusions
ran along two main lines. One was the acute difficulty of judging witness credibility and
reliability, on the basis of either case files or discussions with police officers on the case.
The advent of pre-trial witness interviews might improve matters here.[122] The other was
that three characteristics of some prosecutors—inexperience, lack of self-confidence,
and the sharing of values with the police—meant that some cases were not terminated as
early as they should have been.[123] In particular, Baldwin found that:

> some prosecutors share a common value system with the police, a core element of which is
> that serious cases ought to be prosecuted, almost irrespective of considerations as to evidential
> strength. Cases have developed a considerable momentum by the time of committal, and
> expectations build up that cases will proceed to the Crown Court. In such circumstances,
> it is easy to understand why some prosecutors, particularly when lacking in experience or
> self-confidence, hesitate in making hard decisions in complex or serious cases.[124]

Too often, therefore, cases were allowed to 'run'.

Baldwin also found that, especially in serious cases, some prosecutors were reluctant to make the 'tough' decision of terminating a weak case, but would rather pass the
responsibility for the decision to the court. As one prosecutor commented, 'the proper
forum for deciding whether a person is telling the truth is the jury'.[125] Baldwin comments that this attitude 'can often be a superficial cop-out', but it is at least worth acknowledging that the jury system can make this sort of reasoning attractive. A similar
attitude surfaced in the Stephen Lawrence Inquiry.

The initial prosecution of the murder of Stephen Lawrence was discontinued,
largely owing to problems with the eyewitness evidence in the case. The prosecutor's decision was challenged during the inquiry by counsel for the Lawrence family,
who argued that in making the decision the prosecutor was taking over the role 'of

[120] Ibid, 100.   [121] J. Baldwin, 'Understanding Judge Ordered and Directed Acquittals in the Crown
Court' [1997] *Crim LR* 536, 539.
[122] P. Roberts and C. Saunders, 'Introducing Pre-Trial Witness Interviews' [2008] *Crim LR* 831.
[123] Baldwin, n 121, 551.   [124] Ibid, 551.   [125] Ibid.

the judge or the jury', but the inquiry found that the decision had been perfectly proper.[126] One might find some support for the 'leave it to the jury' approach in the law of evidence: as we will see in Chapter 11, the *Galbraith* test does depict questions of credibility as being exclusively within the domain of the jury. When this is coupled with the ambiguity of the evidential sufficiency test (as between a predictive or intrinsic merits test), it is not surprising that prosecutors should allude to the role of the jury when continuing with a borderline case. Our view is that however difficult the decision, the paramount principle is that weak cases should not go to court. Prosecutors should not dodge their responsibility by arguing that the decision is for the jury, since it is their prior decision whether the evidence is strong enough to justify putting the defendant on trial.

Returning to acquittals by judge, is it right to regard these as a measure of CPS efficiency? The CPS resists this on the ground that judge-directed acquittals may simply mean that a key witness failed to come up to proof when the prosecution believed that they would. Thus, the CPS Inspectorate found in 1999 that some 78 per cent of cases in which a magistrates' court or judge dismissed the prosecution were cases which 'failed for reasons that the CPS could not have foreseen'.[127]

Judge-directed acquittals fell from 12 per cent of contested trials in 1991–2 to 7 per cent of contested hearings in 2002–3,[128] and 6.9 per cent in 2017 (see Table 7.3).[129] Since 2007, around 55–60 per cent of defendants acquitted in trial cases in the Crown Court were discharged by the judge.[130] It is difficult to assess the current position to ascertain whether this represents an improvement in the quality of preparation of cases and assessments of whether witnesses will come up to proof. Regardless, around 70 per cent of acquittals result from weaknesses in the prosecution case.[131]

7.5 CPS POLICIES AND DISCRETION: REFINING AND DEFINING THE CRIMINAL LAW

Sections 7.2 and 7.3 concentrated on the Code for Crown Prosecutors, as the basic CPS policy document. However, some research has suggested that prosecutors, in reaching judgements on evidential sufficiency and on the public interest, do not consult the Code frequently,[132] but rather rely on the large amount of guidance relating to specific issues and forms of crime in prosecuting.[133] These sometime cover broader policy

---

[126] Sir W. Macpherson, *The Stephen Lawrence Inquiry* (1999), paras 39-30–39-32.

[127] HMCPSI, *Adverse Cases* (1999), para 2.4.

[128] CPS, *Annual Report 2002–03*, 34; *Annual Report 2003–2004*, Annex A, 8.

[129] Criminal Court statistics quarterly, Table AC7, reproduced here as Table 7.3.   [130] Ibid.

[131] L. Marsh, 'Leveson's Narrow Pursuit of Justice: Efficiency and Outcomes in the Criminal Process' (2016) 45(1) *Common L World Rev* 51

[132] A. Hoyano et al, 'A Study of the Impact of the Revised Code for Crown Prosecutors' [1997] *Crim LR* 556.

[133] https://www.cps.gov.uk/prosecution-guidance.

Table 7.3 Defendants acquitted in trial cases in the Crown Court after a not guilty plea[1], by manner of acquittal, England and Wales, 2007–2017

Year	Total	Manner of acquittal				% of acquittals by jury verdict[3]
		Discharged by judge	Acquittal directed by judge	Jury verdict	Other acquittal[2]	
2007	17,226	10,360	1,660	5,024	182	29%
2008	16,786	10,245	1,497	4,844	200	29%
2009	18,583	11,146	1,669	5,535	233	30%
2010	20,902	13,035	1,741	5,921	205	28%
2011	19,380	11,863	1,599	5,737	181	30%
2012	17,280	10,122	1,478	5,509	171	32%
2013	15,141	8,536	1,322	5,113	170	34%
2014	16,535	9,323	1,387	5,667	158	34%
2015	17,367	9,684	1,427s	6,096	160	35%
2016	16,508	9,252	1,253	5,866	137	36%
2017	14,586	8,107	1,009	5,332	138	37%

Notes:
   1) Includes cases where defendants plead not guilty to all counts and also cases where defendants plead not guilty to some counts
   2) Other acquittals include where no plea is recorded, autrefois acquit and autrefois convict
   3) The number of defendants acquitted by the jury as a proportion of all acquittals</ext>
Source: Criminal Court statistics quarterly, Table AC7.

questions that are left to the CPS as an entity. Among the detailed policy documents are those relating to domestic abuse, sexual offences, racially and religiously aggravated offences, mentally disordered offenders, youth offenders and child witnesses, and social media offences. Any new offence, such as participating in the criminal activities of an organized crime group,[134] requires a prosecution policy for the CPS to follow. The CPS creates these policies for itself, after discussion with relevant law officers, and sometimes after public consultation. They have particular importance as effectively they define the ambit of the offence, insofar as they include some factual variations and exclude others. In addition, the CPS 'Instructions for Prosecuting Advocates' cover a wide range of procedural and substantive issues.[135] In this section we examine some key CPS policies in the light of evidence about their implementation and the degree of discretion they entail.

[134] Serious Crime Act 2015, s 45.
[135] https://www.cps.gov.uk/legal-guidance/instructions-prosecuting-advocates.

(A) ASSISTED SUICIDE

Some questions of the ambit of the criminal law and its implementation are left deliberately to the CPS to decide. One high-profile example concerns the offence of aiding and abetting suicide: in *R (on the application of Purdy) v DPP*,[136] the House of Lords allowed an application that called for the DPP to set out the factors considered relevant for and against prosecuting someone who renders assistance to another person who is terminally ill or severely and incurably disabled and who intends to commit suicide.[137]

As a result, the CPS published an Interim Policy in September 2009, which was then opened for public consultation: the CPS received more than 5,000 submissions.[138] The *Policy for Prosecutors in Respect of Cases of Encouraging or Assisting Suicide* was issued by the DPP in February 2010, and updated in October 2014.[139] The policy emphasizes that it does not in any way 'decriminalise' the offence of encouraging or assisting suicide nor does it amount to an assurance of immunity from prosecution for such acts.[140] Instead, it outlines a non-exhaustive list of public interest factors tending in favour of prosecution, such as where the victim was under 18 years of age or did not have the capacity to reach an informed decision to commit suicide; where the suspect was paid, or acting in a professional capacity, or not wholly motivated by compassion, or had a history of violence or abuse against the victim; and factors tending against prosecution, such as where the victim had reached a voluntary, clear, settled, and informed decision to commit suicide; the suspect was wholly motivated by compassion, or had sought to dissuade the victim from taking the course of action which resulted in the suicide, or where the actions of the suspect may be characterized as reluctant encouragement or assistance in the face of a determined wish on the part of the victim to commit suicide, or the suspect reported the victim's suicide to the police and fully assisted them in their inquiries into the circumstances of the suicide or the attempt and his or her part in providing encouragement or assistance.[141] Regrettably, there is no prioritization of these factors, which pertain to both the victim and the accused, nor any indication of how to resolve inevitable tensions. Indeed, Andrew Sanders is rightly critical of the CPS for failing to articulate the principles underpinning the draft policy, and for the adoption of some, but not all, of the most widely held views that it received.[142]

Cases of encouraging or assisting suicide are dealt with in the Special Crime Division in CPS Headquarters, where the head of that division reports directly to the DPP.[143] From 1 April 2009 up to 31 January 2018, 138 cases referred to the CPS by the police were recorded as assisted suicide. Of these 138 cases, 91 were not proceeded with by the CPS and 28 cases were withdrawn by the police. Three cases of assisted

[136] [2009] UKHL 45.
[137] Ibid, [55] per Lord Hope. The speech of his Lordship contains a detailed examination of the history and structure of prosecutorial discretion in this country.
[138] https://www.cps.gov.uk/publication/assisted-suicide.
[139] *Policy for Prosecutors in Respect of Cases of Encouraging or Assisting Suicide* (2010, updated 2014), https://www.cps.gov.uk/legal-guidance/suicide-policy-prosecutors-respect-cases-encouraging-or-assisting-suicide.
[140] Ibid, para 6.   [141] Ibid, paras 43–8.   [142] Sanders, n 11, 95.
[143] *Policy for Prosecutors in Respect of Cases of Encouraging or Assisting Suicide*, n 139, para 49.

attempted suicide have been successfully prosecuted. One case of assisted suicide was charged and acquitted after trial in May 2015 and seven cases were referred onwards for prosecution for homicide or other serious crime.[144]

(B) SEXUAL ACTIVITY BETWEEN CHILDREN

Another situation in which the CPS is left to determine the scope of the criminal law relates to the extensive list of offences against children in the Sexual Offences Act 2003. In broad terms, the Act criminalizes all consensual sexual touching between children, so that two 15-year-olds who kiss or fondle each other commit an offence. At the time, the government's argument was that CPS guidance would prevent inappropriate prosecutions, but that a strict law was necessary to ensure that anyone who takes advantage of a child sexually can be prosecuted to conviction. The difficulty with this argument is that provisions in many other jurisdictions (such as Scotland[145]) frame the law so as to exclude many interactions between children, usually by stating that the offence is not committed where the ages of the two young people are no more than two years apart. English law leaves this question to the CPS, whose guidance contains no such clear rule but sets out various considerations that will point in the direction of non-prosecution or prosecution. The structure of this part of sexual offences law is open to criticism, and may be contrary to the ECHR;[146] the important point in the present context, however, is that a considerable amount of discretion has been left to the CPS deliberately by the legislators. Whereas it might be said that the charging standards and legal guidance issued by the CPS on most offences amounts merely to refining the law, the significance of the discretion in this area amounts to a power, for all practical purposes, to define the law.

(C) DOMESTIC ABUSE

Over the past decades, the investigation and prosecution of domestic abuse has become a major area of critique and reassessment.[147] The issue here is the high attrition rate, and the concern that a complainant's withdrawal of the original statement may be due to pressure or threats from the abuser which make it inappropriate to drop the case.[148] It is crucial that the exercise of prosecutorial discretion, in a purported effort

[144] https://www.cps.gov.uk/publication/assisted-suicide.

[145] See J. R. Spencer, 'Child and Family Offences' [2004] *Crim LR* 347, and the Sexual Offences (Scotland) Act 2009.

[146] The House of Lords held that it is compatible with the Convention, in *G* [2008] UKHL 37; cf the critical comments at [2008] *Crim LR* 819.

[147] See C. Hoyle, *Negotiating Domestic Violence* (1998); M. M. Dempsey, *Prosecuting Domestic Violence* (2009).

[148] A similar phenomenon is also to be found in reported rape cases where victim and perpetrator had previously been in an intimate relationship, and where intimidation or economic dependence appears to be the reasons for victim withdrawal: S. Lea, U. Lanvers, and S. Shaw, 'Attrition in Rape Cases' (2003) 43 *BJ Crim* 583, 596.

to respect the wishes of the victim, does not compromise the robust pursuit of domestic abuse. Indeed, the Domestic Abuse Guidelines for Prosecutors emphasize that prosecutors may go ahead with the case even if the complainant wishes the case to be stopped.[149] Prosecution is more likely if the offence was serious. Thus:

> Where the evidential stage has been met, but the complainant is not willing to support the prosecution, prosecutors should carefully consider the public interest given the domestic nature and serious impacts of such offending. It will be rare for the public interest stage not to be met.
>
> In circumstances where a complainant is not willing to support a prosecution, prosecutors will need to consider the public interest after consideration of other independent evidence which meets the evidential stage. Careful consideration should be given to public interest factors, including the interests and safety of the complainant, other family members and any children or other dependants.[150]

In 2004, the CPS Inspectorate published the report of a joint thematic inspection with the Inspectorate of Constabulary, which showed an extremely high attrition rate (463 initial reports, 13 convictions), and found that in a number of cases the CPS guidance had not been followed.[151] The subsequent thematic review of *Discontinuance* revealed similar problems: the discontinuance rate for domestic violence cases was 24 per cent, more than double the 11 per cent for all cases, and the Inspectorate suggested that prosecutors should be identifying more of the weak cases at an earlier stage.[152] Matters are improving somewhat: in 2010, 21.7 per cent of prosecutions for domestic abuse were discontinued, no evidence offered or withdrawn, and this has been dropping slowly but steadily to 17.1 per cent in 2017.[153]

The CPS *Violence against Women and Girls crime report 2016–2017* noted that out of all domestic abuse cases prosecuted, the proportion that were unsuccessful due to so-called 'victim issues' (e.g. victim retractions, non-attendance, and where the 'evidence of the victim does not support the case') remained steady at 13.1 per cent compared to 13.4 per cent in the previous year.[154] The report emphasized that support for victims through the court process is important in reducing retractions. Beyond this, it seems that an issue is police referral rather than prosecutorial decision making: since 2015, there has been a fall in police referrals of domestic abuse,[155] which is affecting the volumes of prosecutions and convictions.[156]

---

[149] https://www.cps.gov.uk/legal-guidance/domestic-abuse-guidelines-prosecutors.   [150] Ibid.

[151] HMCPSI and HMIC, *Violence at Home: A Joint Thematic Inspection of the Investigation and Prosecution of Cases Involving Domestic Violence* (2004).

[152] HMCPSI, *Discontinuance* (2007), para 3.14.

[153] Office for National Statistics, *Domestic abuse in England and Wales—Appendix tables*: Table 23, https://www.ons.gov.uk/peoplepopulationandcommunity/crimeandjustice/datasets/domesticabuseinenglandan-dwalesappendixtables.

[154] CPS, *Violence against Women and Girls crime report 2016–2017* (2017), https://www.cps.gov.uk/sites/default/files/documents/publications/cps-vawg-report-2017_1.pdf.

[155] HMIC, *Increasingly everyone's business: A progress report on the police response to domestic abuse* (2015), 90; HMICFRS, *A progress report on the police response to domestic abuse* (2017), 50.

[156] CPS, *Violence against Women and Girls*, n 154, 6.

(D) HATE CRIME

Hate crime is described by the CPS as:

> any criminal offence which is perceived by the victim or any other person, to be motivated by hostility or prejudice based on a person's race or perceived race; religion or perceived religion; sexual orientation or perceived sexual orientation; disability or perceived disability and any crime motivated by hostility or prejudice against a person who is transgender or perceived to be transgender.[157]

One way of addressing hate crime is through the ability of a prosecutor to apply for an increase in sentence. Sections 29–32 of the Crime and Disorder Act 1998 introduced a number of racially aggravated versions of existing offences, with higher maximum penalties. This was supplemented by s 145 of the Criminal Justice Act 2003, which relates to increases in sentence for racial or religious aggravation; s 146, as amended, provides for increases in sentence for aggravation related to disability, sexual orientation, or transgender identity. At the time of their introduction, concern was expressed that there would be few convictions of these offences because the CPS would accept a guilty plea to the ordinary (non-aggravated) version of the offence. The Inspectorate's thematic report on these cases in 2002 emphasized the need to flag racially aggravated offences for special scrutiny, and to train specialist prosecutors who could supervise the processing of these cases.[158]

Though the Guidance on *Racist and Religious Hate Crime* states that '[i]t is CPS policy not to accept pleas to lesser offences, or a lesser basis of plea, or omit or minimise admissible evidence of racial or religious aggravation for the sake of expediency',[159] empirical evidence shows how these ideals have been compromised in practice. Burney and Rose's study demonstrated the relatively high level of discontinuance for racially aggravated offences, over 40 per cent in 1999.[160] Similarly, the John Report, *Race for Justice* (2003), found that of 33 case studies of racially aggravated incidents 25 were either discontinued or downgraded (by acceptance of a guilty plea) to a lesser offence. The CPS Inspectorate published a follow-up report on cases with a minority ethnic dimension in 2004.[161] Although it concluded that CPS performance had improved in the preceding two years, it still found a considerable number of racially aggravated cases 'in which we considered that the charge was reduced inappropriately . . . We still disagreed with the decision in more than one-fifth of cases in which the charge was reduced.'[162] The Inspectorate also noted variations in the willingness of prosecutors to take such offences to trial, and found that some areas had not yet designated and trained specialist prosecutors for these cases.

---

[157] https://www.cps.gov.uk/hate-crime.

[158] HMCPSI, *Casework having a Minority Ethnic Dimension* (2002).

[159] CPS, *Racist and Religious Hate Crime—Prosecution Guidance*, https://www.cps.gov.uk/legal-guidance/racist-and-religious-hate-crime-prosecution-guidance (revised March 2018).

[160] E. Burney and G. Rose, *Racist Offences—How is the Law Working?* (2002), 77.

[161] HMCPSI, *A Follow Up Review of CPS Casework with a Minority Ethnic Dimension* (2004).

[162] Ibid, para 6.52.

Moreover, the Inspectorate was not convinced that there would be rapid progress at a time when the new arrangements for statutory charging were using experienced staff and considerable resources.

In its 2014 report on *Hate Crime* the Law Commission referred to quite polarized consultation responses: some respondents identified the risk of aggravated offences being dropped or downgraded to non-aggravated offences, whereas other practitioners said that in their experience of defending clients against aggravated offence charges, the CPS policy is adhered to very strictly by prosecutors.[163] Notably, a recent study noted the concern of many Crown Court judges and independent barristers that a 'pro-charge' policy has resulted in racially or religiously aggravated offences being pursued in court where there is insufficient evidence to support the aggravated element of the offence.[164] This study found that many unsuccessful outcomes in hate crime cases are due to prosecutions being dropped (e.g. discontinued, no evidence offered, or withdrawn) and most of those (especially in disability hate crime cases) are dropped because of lack of evidence.[165]

In terms of disability hate crime, the issue is not so much charge reduction or discontinuance as CPS (and police) failure to identify crimes as such.[166] The joint inspection review follow-up published in 2015 found failures by the police to identify disability hate crimes to the CPS when seeking charging advice and a lack of provision of appropriate information to the CPS by police.[167]

As we have noted in several contexts in this book, having the law or the guidance right is a necessary first step, but there are powerful reasons for believing that policies announced at the top of large organizations are not always implemented by those who deal with matters on a day-to-day basis, or indeed known and absorbed in working practice. It is naïve to assume that rules are followed to the letter in everyday practice, and thereby to discount the effect of occupational cultures, pressures from others, and a simple desire to ease one's working life.

7.6 THE ROLE OF THE VICTIM

The victim is recognized and considered in the workings of the criminal process increasingly and with more sensitivity, though not always in a coherent or principled way. Indeed, CPS documents now refer more explicitly to the 'views of victims' rather

[163] Law Commission, *Hate Crime: Should the Current Offences be Extended?*, Law Com No 348 (2014), 4.178–4.180

[164] M. Walters, S. Wiedlitzka, A. Owusu-Bemaph, and K. Goodall, *Hate Crime And The Legal Process—Final Report* (2017), 102–3.

[165] Ibid, 5.4.

[166] HMCPSI, HMIC, and HMI Probation, *Living in a different world: Joint review of disability hate crime* (2013), 3.

[167] HMCPSI, HMIC, HMI Probation, and HMCPSI, *Joint review of disability hate crime follow up* (2015).

than simply to their 'interests' as it once did. These, of course, do not always align. The Code for Crown Prosecutors states that:

> Prosecutors should take into account the views expressed by the victim about the impact that the offence has had. In appropriate cases, this may also include the views of the victim's family.

- However, the CPS does not act for victims or their families in the same way as solicitors act for their clients, and prosecutors must form an overall view of the public interest.[168]

Slightly differently, the CPS statement on 'Care and Treatment of Victims and Witnesses' refers to views as well as interests:

> The CPS acts in the public interest and not just in the interests of any one individual. The interests of the victim are nonetheless important when deciding where the public interest lies and the CPS will take into account the consequences for the victim of the decision whether or not to prosecute and will consider any views expressed by the victim or victim's family.[169]

It is not clear why the CPS should promise to consider the views of the victim or victim's family if the decision is to be taken ultimately on public interest grounds, and such a statement may create expectations among victims that the CPS should not create.[170]

This receives a particular application in domestic abuse cases in which a victim withdraws a complaint or statement, and wants the prosecution to be dropped. In her 1990s research Carolyn Hoyle found that 'the CPS rarely proceeded with a case once the victim had withdrawn'.[171] The CPS Inspectorate concluded in 1998 that in cases of victim withdrawal 'we are not satisfied that the policy is being applied correctly or, on occasions, at all'—the policy being to proceed if possible, without reference to the victim's wishes.[172] When HMCPSI conducted its further review in 2004 to monitor progress in dealing with domestic violence, it found that around 44 per cent of withdrawal cases were proceeded with, but commented that this left 'scope for improvement' and that 'appropriate consultation with the police was not commonplace'.[173] As stated earlier, the Inspectorate's 2007 report on discontinuance again raised questions about the high discontinuance rate of domestic violence cases, and argued for improved pre-charge decision making.[174] In these cases, then, it is clear that the victim's (expressed) wishes should certainly not hold sway.

The Domestic Violence, Crime and Victims Act 2004 introduced a statutory Code of Practice for Victims of Crime that imposed certain duties on the CPS in relation to

---

[168] Code for Crown Prosecutors (2018), para 4.14(c).

[169] CPS, *Care and Treatment of Victims and Witnesses*, https://www.cps.gov.uk/legal-guidance/victims-and-witnesses-care-and-treatment.

[170] See the comments of the House of Commons Justice Committee, *The Crown Prosecution Service* (2009), para 83.

[171] C. Hoyle, *Negotiating Domestic Violence* (1998), 170.

[172] HMCPSI, *Cases involving Domestic Violence* (1998), para 12.3.

[173] HMCPSI, *Violence at Home* (2004), Appendix 5, R12.

[174] HMCPSI and HMIC, *Discontinuance* (2007), paras 3.11–3.14 and 4.15. See further, in the somewhat analogous field of rape prosecutions, the comparative research of L. Ellison, 'Promoting Effective Case-Building in Rape Cases: A Comparative Perspective' [2007] *Crim LR* 691.

communication with victims and victims' families, meaning that they are consulted and informed much more. The Code provided that victims should be given reasons when the CPS considered that there was insufficient evidence to prosecute, but initially did not include any formal system for review. It was revised in 2015 to meet the requirements of Directive 2012/29/EU establishing minimum standards on the rights, support, and protection of victims of crime, including a right to a review of a decision not to prosecute. Additionally, the CPS has published 'The Prosecutor's Pledge', which includes direct promises to victims relating to their care and treatment during the prosecution process.[175]

Under the Victim Communication and Liaison (VCL) scheme, the CPS communicates directly with identified victims to ensure they obtain the right level of information about a CPS decision to discontinue, or alter, a charge or not to prosecute.[176] Despite these commitments, HMCPSI found that the quality of explanations in letters to victims was variable and often inadequate.[177] The reason for the decision was explained clearly in only 47.9 per cent of the files sampled and partially explained in 36.5 per cent of cases. Contrary to requirements and the CPS's stated obligations, in 71.1 per cent of cases there was no evidence that victims are consulted before decisions are made to discontinue a case, or substantially alter charges against a defendant.[178]

7.7 REVIEW AND OVERSIGHT OF PROSECUTION DECISIONS AND POLICIES

To whom or what authorities and to what extent are prosecutors accountable for their decisions? (How) Can their decisions, whether to prosecute or otherwise, be reviewed? The absence of clear and effective lines of accountability for many regulatory agencies was discussed in the previous chapter. The focus here will be chiefly upon the CPS, its decisions, and its policies.

(A) REVIEWING DECISIONS NOT TO PROSECUTE

As explained earlier, a two-pronged test must be satisfied for a prosecution to be pursued—but after an offence has been committed, a decision not to prosecute can be traumatic for the victim, and/or surviving family. There can be a perception of bias on the basis of ethnicity, religion, or class as well difficulties in communicating the nuances of the hurdle posed by the Full Test in the Code. For instance, deaths of black individuals that occur in custody very rarely lead to prosecution, and none has resulted in a conviction, although inquest juries have delivered verdicts of unlawful killing in at

---

[175] https://www.cps.gov.uk/prosecutors-pledge.
[176] https://www.cps.gov.uk/legal-guidance/victim-communication-and-liaison-vcl-scheme.
[177] HMCPSI, *Communicating with victims* (2016).   [178] Ibid, 13.

least 12 cases.[179] This underlines the importance of a system of review, for both fairness and legitimacy.

The courts have stated many times their willingness to review decisions not to prosecute, whether in a generic sense or in individual cases. It was established in the first *Blackburn* case[180] that the courts would be prepared judicially to review a general policy not to prosecute for certain classes of offence, for example all thefts with a value below £100. In the third *Blackburn* case,[181] Lord Denning MR suggested that the courts would also be prepared to review an individual decision not to prosecute, and this dictum has received subsequent judicial support.[182] The primary basis for judicial review would be that either the policy or the individual decision not to prosecute was unreasonable in a *Wednesbury* sense, that is, was such that no reasonable prosecuting authority would have adopted the policy or taken the decision.[183]

As noted in the last chapter, the Divisional Court has upheld such challenges to the decision not to prosecute and the decision to caution in several decisions.[184] In *Manning*,[185] the Divisional Court quashed a CPS decision not to bring a prosecution arising out of a death in custody. Lord Bingham CJ stated that the standard of review must not be set too high, on the ground that judicial review is the only means by which the citizen can seek redress against a decision not to prosecute. That is not entirely true, since it remains possible to mount a private prosecution (on which see section 7.7(C)). But such a prosecution requires considerable time and energy, and the whole purpose of a public prosecution system is to prevent citizens from having thus to exert themselves. Essentially, both judicial review and public prosecution are costly, which precludes many complainants or families from acting. The greater difficulty with *Manning* is that it was confined to cases of deaths in custody: while Lord Bingham made it clear that the CPS ought to give reasons for not bringing a prosecution in such circumstances, there remains no obligation to give specific reasons for non-prosecution. Where reasons are given, the path to judicial review (and therefore effective accountability) is much easier. Thus, in *Jones*,[186] judicial review of a decision not to bring a manslaughter charge was granted on the ground that the DPP had failed to apply the law correctly to the facts. However, in *R (on the application of Guest) v DPP*[187] the court quashed a decision to administer a conditional caution (and, with it, the decision not to prosecute) in a case where the Code for Crown Prosecutors had clearly been misapplied—failing to prosecute for a serious assault—and the Director's Guidance on Conditional Cautions

---

[179] See Institute of Race Relations, *Dying for Justice* (2015), 38.

[180] *R v Metropolitan Police Commissioner, ex p Blackburn* [1968] 2 QB 118.

[181] *R v Metropolitan Police Commissioner, ex p Blackburn (No 3)* [1973] 1 QB 241.

[182] *R v General Council of the Bar, ex p Percival* [1990] 3 All ER 137.

[183] *Associated Provincial Picture Houses v Wednesbury Corp* [1948] 1 KB 223.   [184] See Ch 6.5.

[185] *R v DPP, ex p Manning* [2001] QB 330, analysed by M. Burton, 'Reviewing Crown Prosecution Service Decisions Not to Prosecute' [2001] *Crim LR* 374; see also *R (on application of Joseph) v DPP* [2001] *Crim LR* 489.

[186] *R v DPP, ex p Jones* [2000] *Crim LR* 858.

[187] [2009] *Crim LR* 730. See also *R (on the application of Omar) v Chief Constable of Bedfordshire* [2002] EWHC 3060 (Admin).

had also been misapplied. Whether a subsequent prosecution (by the CPS or a private prosecutor) would then be quashed for abuse of process was left open.

The aforementioned case of *R (on the application of B) v DPP*,[188] where B was the victim of an assault who suffered from mental health problems, involved an application for judicial review of a CPS decision to discontinue a prosecution on the basis that B would not have been a reliable witness. The Divisional Court held that this was an irrational decision and involved a misapplication of the Code for Crown Prosecutors.

Similarly, in *L v DPP* Sir John Thomas, President of the Queen's Bench Division, emphasized that the grounds upon which a challenge for judicial review of decisions not to prosecute can be made are very narrow and are limited to the following:

1. because there has been some unlawful policy;

2. because the Director has failed to act in accordance with his own set policy; or

3. because the decision was perverse, that is to say it is a decision that no reasonable prosecutor could have reached.[189]

Such a 'highly exceptional' step was taken in *R (on the application of F) v DPP and 'A'*, which involved the 'unusual, but not unique' application for judicial review of the DPP's refusal to initiate a prosecution for rape and/or sexual assault of the claimant by her former partner.[190] The Lord Chief Justice ordered judicial review on the basis that 'The entire body of evidence, both in relation to the nature and history of the relationship between these two people, and as it applies to each of the individual, specific occasions of complaint, requires re-examination.'[191] In contrast, *B* was considered and distinguished in *NXB v CPS*, where it was held that the decision to withdraw a prosecution for sexual offences was not irrational nor founded on a misunderstanding or misapplication of prosecutorial policy.[192]

i. Victims' right to review

The most significant change to and bolstering of victims' rights in this context came with the introduction of the Victims' Right to Review (VRR) in 2013, which made it easier for victims to seek a review of a CPS decision not to bring charges or to terminate proceedings. This scheme meets the principles outlined in *Killick*[193] and in Art 11 of the EU Directive establishing minimum standards on the rights, support, and protection of victims of crime.[194] In *Killick*, the Court of Appeal concluded that victims should have a right to seek a review of a CPS decision not to prosecute and that they should not have to seek recourse to judicial review.[195] The court observed that the right to a review should be made the subject of a clearer procedure and guidance with time limits.[196] As for police forces in England and Wales, they adopted an equivalent VRR on 1 April 2015.[197]

---

[188] [2009] EWHC 106 (Admin).   [189] *L v DPP* [2013] EWHC 1752 (Admin), [4].
[190] [2013] EWHC 945 (Admin).   [191] [27].   [192] [2015] EWHC 631 (QB).
[193] *R v Killick* [2011] EWCA Crim 1608.
[194] See K. Starmer, 'Finality in Criminal Justice: When Should the CPS Reopen a Case?' [2012] *Crim LR* 526.
[195] *Killick*, n 193, [48].   [196] [57].
[197] ACPO, *National Policing Guidelines on Police Victim Right to Review* (2015).

The VRR allows a victim (that is, 'A person who has suffered harm, including physical, mental or emotional harm or economic loss which was directly caused by criminal conduct', including close relatives of a person whose death was caused by criminal conduct; parents or guardians where the victim is aged under 18; and businesses) to seek a review of CPS decisions not to charge, to discontinue or withdraw all charges, to offer no evidence in all proceedings, or to leave all charges in the proceedings to 'lie on file'. After a request for review has been received, it is reviewed locally by a prosecutor who has not been involved with the case previously. The three possible outcomes to such 'local resolution activity' are that:

(1) the decision was wrong, and if possible proceedings will be (re)commenced;

(2) the decision was right but that further information about the decision should be provided;

(3) the decision was right and that there is no further information to be provided.

Where the CPS has been unable to resolve the issue to the victim's satisfaction at local resolution, the decision will be reviewed independently, albeit by another prosecutor, comprising a reconsideration of the evidence and public interest.

As noted by Sir John Thomas, President of the Queen's Bench Division in *L v DPP*, which predated the VRR by a number of months:

> As it is of the essence of the decision to prosecute that there is a significant margin of discretion given to the prosecutor, it can be well understood why two prosecutors might differ. That, therefore, underlines the great importance and essential contribution that the Director has made by putting in place this system of review.[198]

The Divisional Court in *S v CPS* considered the proper approach to the VRR where the original decision had been not to charge but this was altered subsequently.[199] S applied for permission to apply for judicial review of the CPS's decision to prosecute him for rape, which had come about only after the complainant requested a review of the initial decision under the VRR. S submitted that it was contrary to natural justice for a suspect not to have the opportunity to make representations to the reviewing prosecutor, and that the CPS acted unreasonably and irrationally in concluding that the earlier decision not to charge him was wrong. The court refused his application, concluding that although the VRR provided that a suspect was not to be made aware of a victim's request for a review during the process, which meant that a suspect could not make representations to the reviewing prosecutor, that did not mean it was contrary to natural justice. Overall, the court affirmed the lawfulness of the VRR.[200]

It is important to note that the VRR excludes a number of case types, such as where the police exercise their independent discretion not to investigate or not to investigate a case further; those concluded by way of out-of-court disposal (OOCD); and those where charges are brought in respect of some (but not all)

---

[198] *L v DPP* [2013] EWHC 1752 (Admin).   [199] *S v CPS* [2015] EWHC 2868 (Admin).   [200] [30].

allegations made or against some (but not all) possible suspects. The decision to exclude OOCDs from the scheme's policy is hard to fathom. Conditional cautions can be issued by the CPS for relatively serious offences such as sexual offences,[201] and given that the failure to issue one could have a comparable impact on the victim the underlying rationale for review is equivalent.[202] Moreover, as the 'relevant prosecutor or the authorised person must make reasonable efforts to obtain the views of the victim . . .' about what conditions to attach to a conditional caution,[203] it is curious to exclude them from review.

The lawfulness of the CPS policy to refuse to review decisions to prosecute some, but not all, possible suspects was affirmed in R (Chaudhry) v DPP.[204] Such decisions were a matter for independent prosecutorial judgement, and the CPS guidance provided discretion for a review in exceptional circumstances.[205] Chaudhry was applied in R (Hayes) v CPS, where the intersection of the VRR and private prosecutions was examined.[206] The CPS had taken over a private prosecution commenced by H against his former wife and decided to offer no evidence against her. H wished to exercise his right to request a review of that decision but was told by the CPS that a review would be carried out only after no evidence had been offered against her and the prosecution had come to an end. He sought judicial review of this decision. The Divisional Court accepted that the VRR is, or is operated as, an inflexible policy in respect of such cases, but that this was not unlawful.[207] Nothing in either Killick or the EU Directive explicitly prohibits the CPS from operating such a policy; and Chaudhry makes clear that there is no all-embracing right to a review in all circumstances.[208] This was not failing to provide any effective right to a review,[209] and such a restriction on the operation of the VRR was regarded as both necessary and proportionate to balance the competing interests of the victim and the accused.[210] Moreover, the policy was deemed to safeguard the operational effectiveness of the VRR.[211] Despite this conclusion, the Divisional Court observed that the references to time limits in the policy may raise false expectations in the minds of victims as meaning that a timely request for a review will be processed within the stated timescale and that the proceedings will not be concluded in the meantime, and suggested that the CPS may wish to consider whether there is a clearer way in which a victim could be informed of this aspect of her rights.[212] This is an apposite remark, and appears an ineluctable issue in relation to victims' rights more broadly.

Some concerns have been raised about the operation of the VRR. The 2015 HMIC and HMCPSI Joint Inspection noted that while the police notify the victim of the right to review when they inform her of the CPS decision to take no further action,

---

[201] C. McGlynn, N. Westmarland, and K. Johnson, 'Under the radar: the widespread use of "Out of Court resolutions" in policing domestic violence and abuse in the United Kingdom' (2017) 58 BJ Crim 1–16. See Ch 6.
[202] See Ch 6.
[203] Criminal Justice Act 2003, s 23, as amended by the Anti-social Behaviour, Crime and Policing Act 2014.
[204] DPP, ex p Chaudhry [2016] EWHC 2447 (Admin).
[205] [45]–[46].   [206] R (Hayes) v CPS [2018] EWHC 327 (Admin). See section 7.7(C).
[207] [47]–[49].   [208] [50].   [209] [51].   [210] [52].   [211] [53].   [212] [60].

not all police officers demonstrated a clear understanding of how the VRR operated
and their responsibilities, calling into question how effectively the right was communicated.[213] In addition, HMCPSI found that the VRR was not mentioned in 19
per cent of letters sent out to victims in their sample of relevant cases.[214] Furthermore, research carried out by Mary Iliadis and Asher Flynn on the first two years of
the VRR raised concerns about transparency, accessibility, and accountability which
may hinder its capacity to address victims' procedural justice needs relating to information, voice, and control thereby reducing its effectiveness.[215] They raised issues
about the limited data available on the process, which compromises transparency
and accountability.[216] The limited data recorded on the types of offences that are
withdrawn or altered limit opportunities to identify any patterns that might exist in
prosecutorial decision making regarding offence types, situational factors or victims,
and whether there may be any untoward biases that influence or shape prosecutorial
decision making when not proceeding with a case.[217] Iliadis and Flynn were given
access to previously unpublished statistics on the VRR, which showed that between
1 June 2013 and 31 March 2015, the CPS made 230,506 decisions that could qualify
for a VRR. Of these decisions, a request for review was made in 2,863 cases; 1.24 per
cent of all qualifying decisions. Though the low uptake has been ascribed to the fact
that so few victims 'feel that they need to take up the scheme',[218] the interviews by
Iliadis and Flynn indicated that it is attributable to victims not knowing about their
right to review. These inconsistencies in policy and practice must be resolved for the
scheme to attain its aims.

(B) REVIEWING DECISIONS TO PROSECUTE

Challenges to decisions to prosecute, and decisions about which offence to charge,
raise different and distinct issues. In *R v Chief Constable of Kent and another, ex p L*,[219]
the Divisional Court accepted that an individual decision to prosecute a young person
could be subject to judicial review if it were clearly contrary to a settled policy of the
DPP, that is, the Code for Crown Prosecutors. Stuart-Smith LJ in the Divisional Court
in *R v Inland Revenue Commissioners, ex p Mead*,[220] accepted that judicial review of
a decision to prosecute would also be possible where the applicant was an adult; the
other member of the court, Popplewell J, disagreed with this. The House of Lords in
Kebilene[221] held that an action for judicial review of a decision to prosecute should not
be entertained unless there is evidence of dishonesty, bad faith, or other exceptional

---

[213] HMIC and HMCPSI, *Joint Inspection of the Provision of Charging Decisions*, n 27, para 8.18.
[214] HMCPSI, *Communicating with victims*, n 177, para 5.5.
[215] M. Iliadis and A. Flynn, 'Providing a Check on Prosecutorial Decision-Making: An Analysis of the Victims' Right to Review Reform' (2017) 58 *BJ Crim* 550.
[216] Ibid, 563.   [217] Ibid, 564.
[218] According to the DPP cited in D. Shaw, 'Victims' Right of Review Scheme Sees 146 Charged', BBC News,
19 July 2014, available at http://www.bbc.com/news/uk-28377445.
[219] (1991) 93 Cr App R 416.   [220] [1993] 1 All ER 772.   [221] [2000] 2 AC 326.

circumstances—an approach that accords little significance to the pains of being prosecuted.[222] Only in 'highly exceptional' circumstances would the court disturb the decisions of an independent prosecutor and investigator.[223]

This was the situation in *R (E) v DPP*.[224] Here the court allowed a claim for judicial review from sisters, aged 12, 3, and 2 years old, where the eldest E was prosecuted for engaging in sexual activities with the younger two, as discovered through a video recording posted online. Though the Code and the relevant Guidance provided a comprehensive, appropriate, and lawful framework for prosecutorial decision making, the prosecutor had not followed or properly applied these. The local authority had convened a multi-agency strategy group which prepared a report for consideration by the CPS which opposed prosecution on the grounds of welfare, but this was either ignored or rejected by the prosecutor. Accordingly, the decision to prosecute had to be quashed.

The parameters of judicial review were noted in *R (Robson) v CPS*, involving an application for judicial review of the decision of the CPS to prosecute her for criminal damage rather than to offer her a conditional caution.[225] The decision centred on the distinction between the lawfulness of a prosecutorial policy and its application to the facts: only the latter generally is prohibited from judicial review, and instead 'would be . . . an abuse argument'.[226]

The High Court emphasized in *Hughes v DPP* that the prosecution must charge the correct or obvious offence.[227] Here H had been charged and was convicted of an offence of threatening behaviour contrary to s 4 of the Public Order Act 1986, whereas he should have been charged with assault, as his victim was hit from behind and so could not have noticed what was about to happen to him before the blow was delivered. The prosecution had charged the wrong offence, and the District Judge 'understandably, but . . . mistakenly, sought to see that at least the perpetrator of this wholly uncalled for violence did suffer at least a conviction for some sort of offence'.[228]

Finally, the courts are willing to stay proceedings for abuse of process where the prosecutor is found to have manipulated the criminal process in some way.[229] The leading case is *Abu Hamza*,[230] where the Court of Appeal emphasized that it would rarely be in the public interest to stay proceedings, but that it was prepared to do so where there had been an unequivocal representation by a prosecutor, on which the defendant had acted to his detriment. It seems that the requirement of detriment may not be insisted on, where a clear decision not to prosecute has been communicated to a defendant.[231] The issue in the appeal of *Antoine v R* was whether the

---

[222] On which see Rogers, 'Restructuring the Exercise of Prosecutorial Discretion', n 35.

[223] *R (on the application of Corner House Research) v Director of the Serious Fraud Office* [2008] UKHL 60, [30].

[224] *R (E) v DPP* [2011] EWHC 1465 (Admin), [2012] 1 Cr App R 6 (DC).

[225] *R (Robson) v CPS* [2016] EWHC 2191 (Admin); see Ch 6.   [226] [35].

[227] *Hughes v DPP* [2012] EWHC 606 (Admin).   [228] [11].

[229] For detailed analysis, see A. Choo, *Abuse of Process and Judicial Stays of Criminal Proceedings* (2nd edn, 2008), ch 2.

[230] [2007] QB 659.   [231] *H v Guildford Youth Court* [2008] EWHC 506 (Admin).

prosecution should have been stayed as an abuse of the process of the court where A had already been convicted and sentenced for lesser offences arising out of the same set of facts.[232] The Court of Appeal could not understand the charging decision:[233] A was charged with and pleaded guilty to the wrong, lesser offences under the Firearms Acts and so was dealt with in the wrong court.[234] That said, the Court of Appeal had no hesitation in concluding that the judge was justified in finding that there were special circumstances here which required that the prosecution continue, and that a stay would have brought the criminal justice system into disrepute.[235] Although serious mistakes were made, there was no bad faith and the mistakes were rectified within a very short time.[236]

(C) PRIVATE PROSECUTIONS

The right to bring a private prosecution still exists on the basis that it serves as a safeguard against unjustified or unfair prosecutorial decisions, particularly inertia on the part of either the police or CPS. Although the DPP has a statutory power to take over a private prosecution (and then to discontinue it if this is thought advisable[237]), private prosecutions come before the courts each year in small but not insignificant numbers.[238]

Their Lordships were divided in *Jones v Whalley*,[239] with Lord Bingham regarding the right of private prosecution as 'of questionable value' but Lord Mance regarding it as potentially significant. There the House of Lords held that a private prosecution may not be brought when the police or CPS have decided to issue a simple caution for an offence (and that would apply *a fortiori* to a conditional caution). Some would argue that the possibility of a judicial review of decisions by the CPS and police should be sufficient (see section 7.7(A)). There is also a strong argument that the nature of a private prosecution differs from that of a public prosecution, since a private prosecutor is bringing the case in order to achieve a particular end whereas a public prosecutor should act as a minister of justice. Sir Richard Buxton has therefore argued that private prosecutions in the Crown Court should always be conducted by counsel, and not by the applicant in person; and that in deciding whether to issue a summons to a private prosecutor, magistrates should take into account whether the prosecution is to be 'managed by counsel'.[240]

Until 2009, CPS policy was not to interfere in a private prosecution as long as there was sufficient evidence to satisfy a court that there was a case to answer, a much lower threshold than the evidential sufficiency test in the Code for Crown Prosecutors. This changed in 2009 when the Director issued guidance instructing the CPS to take over and stop private prosecutions if either the evidential sufficiency stage or the public

---

[232] *Antoine v R* [2014] EWCA Crim 197.   [233] [10].   [234] [11]–[12].   [235] [33].
[236] [34].
[237] Prosecution of Offences Act 1985, s 6(2), as interpreted in *R v DPP, ex p Duckenfield* [2000] 1 WLR 55.
[238] L. H. Leigh, 'Private Prosecutions and Diversionary Justice' [2007] *Crim LR* 289, 293–5.
[239] [2006] UKHL 41.
[240] R. Buxton, 'The Private Prosecutor as Minister of Justice' [2009] *Crim LR* 427, 431.

interest stage of the Full Code Test was not met.[241] Unlike the policy on assisted suicide, for instance, there was no public consultation.[242]

The appellant in *R (on the application of Gujra) v CPS* challenged the lawfulness of this policy on the ground that it interfered unduly with a citizen's right to institute a private prosecution.[243] Gujra had brought private prosecutions against a number of persons for common assault, but these were taken over and discontinued by the DPP. The Supreme Court held 3:2 that the application of the policy to take over a private prosecution and discontinue it unless the evidence was such as to render a prosecution more likely to result in a conviction than not, did not frustrate the policy and objects underpinning the right to maintain a private prosecution in the Prosecution of Offences Act 1985, and so was lawful. As Rogers reminds us, this was prior to the establishment of the VRR, and so Gujra was left without recourse in the criminal courts, a situation likely to be shared with others.[244]

A Divisional Court in *R (Lowden) v Gateshead Magistrates' Court* held that an individual could, in principle, bring a private prosecution against someone who had been given a prior simple caution for the same incident, where that caution was still extant. However, that was only so long as there had been no assurance at the time of administering the caution that there would be no future prosecution.[245]

(D) INTERNAL AND EXTERNAL ACCOUNTABILITY

The CPS is organized hierarchically, with local branches (13 areas and CPS Direct) and a headquarters, and internal lines of accountability that end with the DPP. He is answerable to the Attorney General, who has ministerial responsibility for the general policies pursued by the CPS but not in respect of decisions taken in individual cases. There is thus no accountability to Parliament for decisions in individual cases, but it is the practice of Members of Parliament to refer to the DPP individual cases brought to their attention by constituents or others. The Director will usually reply by letter, giving some reason for the decision.

The absence of an independent complaints mechanism was the subject of a number of very critical reports[246] until the first Independent Assessor of Complaints for the CPS was appointed in 2013.[247] The Independent Assessor reviews complaints in respect of the quality of service provided by the CPS and its adherence to its published complaints procedure and the complaints aspects of the Victims' Code, but cannot review complaints that are solely about prosecution decisions, which fall within the VRR instead.

---

[241] https://www.cps.gov.uk/legal-guidance/private-prosecutions.   [242] See section 7.5(A).

[243] [2012] UKSC 52.   [244] Rogers n 46, 691.

[245] *R (on the application of Lowden) v Gateshead Magistrates' Court* [2016] EWHC 3536 (Admin).

[246] The House of Commons Justice Committee describes this as a 'serious weakness': *The Crown Prosecution Service* (2009), para 98; also reports of HMCPSI in 2009 and 2013.

[247] https://www.cps.gov.uk/sites/default/files/documents/publications/iac_annual_report_to_cps_board_2016_2017.pdf.

The CPS is open to scrutiny by the Justice Committee of the House of Commons and by the National Audit Office also.[248] As we saw earlier, the Prosecution of Offences Act 1985 imposes on the Director a statutory responsibility to issue a code, and to report annually to Parliament. The annual reports now have to record the CPS's performance in relation to government targets, but apart from that no longer include reference to the number of discontinued cases or judge-directed acquittals.

The HMCPSI is the principal source of CPS and SFO accountability. By the mid-1990s there was still no inspectorate of the CPS, unlike the established inspectorates of constabulary, probation, and then the prisons, and it is to the credit of the CPS that it set up its own internal inspectorate, which issued several critical reports.[249] In 2000, HMCPSI was established formally, and, as alluded to throughout the text, has continued to issue incisive reports on the performance of local CPS areas and on numerous general themes. These reports note plenty of good practice, but do not give the impression that everything is for the best, as the CPS annual reports tend to do.

7.8 PROSECUTORIAL ETHICS

The CPS Code spells out the objective of impartiality:

> When making decisions, prosecutors must be fair and objective. They must not let any personal views about the ethnic or national origin, gender, disability, age, religion or belief, sexual orientation or gender identity of the suspect, defendant, victim or any witness influence their decisions. Neither must they be motivated by political considerations. Prosecutors must always act in the interests of justice and not solely for the purpose of obtaining a conviction.[250]

This aspect of an ethical orientation to prosecuting concerns fairness as impartiality, in terms of non-discrimination and non-susceptibility to pressures from others.

What about the specific ethical principles of prosecuting cases that have been charged? It may be claimed that each prosecutor, as a solicitor or barrister, is governed by the ethical code of the relevant professional organization.[251] In Chapter 3 we reviewed the various formulations of the prosecutor's role, concerned with obtaining convictions without unfairness to defendants. Various international documents now deal with these broader questions about the prosecutor's role, including the United Nations Guidelines on the Role of Prosecutors (1990), the standards agreed in 1999 by

---

[248] Ibid; and National Audit Office, *Crown Prosecution Service: Effective Use of Magistrates' Courts Hearings* (2006).

[249] E.g. the report on *Cases involving Domestic Violence* (n 172 and accompanying text), and its report on *Central Casework Section* (1999).

[250] *Code for Crown Prosecutors* (2018), para 2.7.

[251] See M. Blake and A. Ashworth, 'Some Ethical Issues in Prosecuting and Defending Criminal Cases' [1998] *Crim LR* 16.

the International Association of Prosecutors, and the Council of Europe's recommendation on the role of public prosecutors (2000).[252]

The importance of these lies in their endorsement of the argument, developed in Chapter 3, that the protection of rights should be regarded as part of the law, and not as standing in opposition to the proper role of police or prosecutors. Whilst it is true that defence lawyers have the primary task of securing the defendant's rights, prosecutors should neither indulge in nor condone unlawful or unethical practices. They should show no less respect for fairness and human rights, as embodied in principles such as those set out in Chapter 2, than for the obtaining of convictions of the guilty. Paragraph 2.10 of the Code enjoins prosecutors to apply the principles of the ECHR; but we have seen, particularly in sections 7.3 and 7.4, that an organization that works closely with the police may—on some occasions at least—become 'prosecution-minded' to an extent that compromises this broader ethical position. One way of tackling this would be to draw up some practical ethical guidance directed at the kinds of situation in which conflicts of this type are likely to arise. Guidance cannot always overwhelm occupational cultures and other more subtle pressures, but it is one step in that direction.

7.9 CONCLUSION

This chapter has outlined the purpose and functions of the CPS, evaluated some of the underpinning principles, and examined empirical evidence of performance of its various tasks. We have noted that, as with other large organizations, formulating the principles and the guidance satisfactorily is not sufficient to ensure that they are implemented in practice. Frank recognition of the gap between rhetoric and reality is rare in the CPS's own documents, but the presence of the Inspectorate (and the openness to external scrutiny, as alluded to in the Lammy Review[253]) ensures that a more in-depth and realistic view of the prosecution system can be obtained.

In this concluding section we raise three general issues. First, have the variations in charging arrangements affected the independence of prosecutors' judgements? It has always been a problem for the CPS that their information comes almost entirely from the police, who may construct a case in a way designed to incline the prosecutor towards a particular outcome. Indeed, the close relationship between the CPS and the police has been described as 'unhealthy and unfortunate' in cases of controversial deaths in custody, where the police may be implicated.[254] There seem to be two key questions: first, is there a danger that prosecutors who have to deal with police officers on a day-by-day basis come to adopt an anti-defendant and pro-prosecution philosophy, of the kind that leads them to 'run' cases where, in truth, the evidence is weak? The related

---

[252] Council of Europe, Recommendation R 19 (2000), *The Role of Public Prosecution in the Criminal Justice System*. See generally International Association of Prosecutors, *Standards for Prosecutors: an Analysis of the United Kingdom National Prosecuting Agencies* (2006).
[253] *Lammy Review*, n 67, 21.   [254] See Institute of Race Relations, *Dying for Justice* (2015), 43.

question is whether, on the other hand, prosecutors are now tending to under-charge because of the pressure of targets, which count any conviction rather than a conviction for the most appropriate offence as a positive outcome. The complexity of these issues is increased by the movement of more charging decisions back to the police.

Secondly, what should the role of the CPS be in relation to out-of-court disposals? In Chapter 6 we examined the increase and subsequent decrease in diversion through OOCD, highlighting that the central role of the police and other agencies with law enforcement duties is questionable. This suggests that the Criminal Justice Act 2003 was right to limit to the CPS the power to offer conditional cautions to offenders, although this was changed again by LASPO 2012. This undermines the rationale that legal qualified prosecutors may be seen as quasi-judicial officials who can rightly be trusted to exercise these powers fairly. The problem, as identified in Chapter 6, is that there is no overall scheme or consistency, and the powers proliferated without any overall plan or control.[255] Though reform is likely, it remains to be seen which powers are reserved for the CPS.

Thirdly, there remains the need urgently to confront the fundamental issues of social fairness raised by the different enforcement and prosecution policies of the CPS and the regulatory agencies (which tend not to prosecute frequently, but to prefer forms of diversion). This mean that citizens who commit offences that are of roughly equivalent seriousness may receive a very different response according to the agency that deals with enforcement. There should be a general review of the proper policies to be pursued by the so-called regulatory agencies, as well as the CPS, and also for a new system of accountability that applies the same standards to the CPS and the other agencies.[256] If equality before the law and equal treatment are to be realistic aspirations, this glaring anomaly in English criminal justice must no longer be left unchallenged. The Justice Committee noted the disparities and commended the Attorney General for starting work on bringing together the diverse prosecuting agencies. But the Committee did not recommend that the CPS should become the single prosecuting authority for all agencies, as in Scotland,[257] and more importantly it failed to highlight the social justice implications of the current situation.

FURTHER READING

HOUSE OF COMMONS JUSTICE COMMITTEE, *The Crown Prosecution Service: Gatekeeper of the Criminal Justice System*, London: TSO, 2009.

ILIADIS, M. and FLYNN, A., 'Providing a Check on Prosecutorial Decision-Making: An Analysis of the Victims' Right to Review Reform' (2017) 58 *BJ Crim* 550.

ROGERS, J., 'A Human Rights Perspective on the Evidential Test for Bringing Prosecutions' [2017] *Crim LR* 678.

---

[255] House of Commons Justice Committee, *Crown Prosecution Service* (2009), para 59.
[256] See White, 'Investigators or Prosecutors', n 8, 159–60. The statutory remit of HMCPSI is to inspect and report on the work carried out by the CPS and SFO, though it can inspect other prosecuting agencies by invitation, such as the Service Prosecuting Authority.
[257] House of Commons Justice Committee, *Crown Prosecution Service* (2009), paras 134–6.

QUESTIONS FOR DISCUSSION

1. Are the evidential tests in the Code for Crown Prosecutors satisfactory both in principle and in their operation?

2. Is the public interest test in the Code for Crown Prosecutors satisfactory both in principle and in its operation?

3. Should the CPS be responsible for all prosecutorial decision making, including prosecutions that regulatory agencies and local authorities wish to initiate?

4. Should private prosecutions be prohibited?

8

REMANDS BEFORE TRIAL

The bail/custody decision raises some of the most acute conflicts in the whole criminal process. On the one hand, there is the individual's right to liberty, safeguarded by Art 5 of the European Convention on Human Rights (ECHR), and the interest of anyone arrested and charged with an offence in remaining at liberty until the trial has taken place. On the other hand, there is a public interest in security and in ensuring protection from crime. Some practitioners, politicians, and commentators have concluded that the way to deal with this conflict is in each case to balance the defendant's rights with the public interests. However, the vague notion of 'balancing' that is advanced in this context is manifestly inadequate. No judgement of balance can be properly reached until there is a clear appreciation of what rights defendants (and actual or potential victims) have at this stage, as well as fuller analysis of the content and legitimacy of the claimed public interests, and of the evidential foundations for predictions of risk. As will appear during the course of this chapter, there is a wide range of relevant considerations, combined with a dearth of practical information at some crucial stages. Because of the impact on the liberty of the defendant, the issues are too important to leave to wide expanses of little-regulated discretion, whether in the hands of police officers, magistrates, or judges. The focus in this chapter will be on the issues of principle raised by the law and practice.

To grant a person bail is to accept their claim to liberty in the period before the next official proceedings; bail may be unconditional or conditional. To refuse bail means that the consequence is likely to be a remand in custody, that is, in prison. Questions of remand on bail or in custody arise at various stages in the criminal process. First, there is 'street bail', that is, the power of an officer who arrests a person for an offence to release the arrestee on bail, to report to a police station at a specified time.[1] Secondly, there is the possibility of police bail, granted at the police station, pending the first court appearance. Thirdly, there is the court's decision on remand between the first and the final court appearance. Fourthly, there is the question of remand after conviction and before sentence is passed, for example to allow time for the preparation of a report on the defendant. And, fifthly, there is the question of remand pending an appeal against verdict or sentence.[2] The fourth and fifth decisions will not be discussed here,

---

[1] See the discussion in section 8.2 and in Ch 5.
[2] Criminal Practice Directions (2015), 14H.5.

and there will be limited analysis of police bail and street bail, which were elaborated upon more fully in Chapter 5. The principal focus is on the court's decision whether to remand on bail or in custody between first appearance and trial.

8.1 REMANDS, RIGHTS, AND RISK

What rights of a defendant are at stake here? Article 5(1) of the ECHR declares the general right to liberty, but allows liberty to be taken away in six distinct situations, the third of which (in Art 5(1)(c)) is the lawful arrest or detention of a person in order to bring him before a competent legal authority on reasonable suspicion of having committed an offence.[3] Article 5(3) goes on to provide that persons detained under that paragraph shall be brought promptly before a court, and shall be entitled to trial within a reasonable time.[4] In applying these provisions, the European Court of Human Rights (ECtHR) has developed several distinct requirements. Its decisions have recognized four grounds for the refusal of bail: risk of absconding before trial, risk of interfering with the course of justice, risk of committing offences, and risk to public order.[5] More importantly, the Strasbourg organs have insisted on a number of procedural guarantees during remand proceedings, and we will see later in the chapter how these have affected or might affect English law.

For the present, our starting point is provided by three principles that stand out in the ECHR jurisprudence. The first is that the basis for considering the application of Art 5 should always be a presumption of liberty and a presumption of innocence (Art 6(2)). Thus in *Caballero v UK*,[6] the Commission stated that the judge:

> having heard the accused himself, must examine all the facts arguing for and against the interest of a genuine requirement of public interest justifying, with due regard to the presumption of innocence, a departure from the rule of respect for the accused's liberty.

The same passage goes on to articulate the second major principle prominent in the case law—the need to avoid stereotypical reasoning and to assess each case individually:

> For example, the danger of an accused's absconding cannot be gauged solely on the basis of the severity of the sentence risked.[7] As far as the danger of re-offending is concerned, a reference to a person's antecedents cannot suffice to justify refusing release.[8]

There is also authority for a third principle, evident in both the remand decisions and the decisions on trial within a reasonable time—that courts should take care to impose

---

[3] On 'reasonable suspicion', see Ch 4.

[4] For discussion of the drafting of Art 5(3) and the Court's interpretation of it, see B. Emmerson, A. Ashworth, and A. Macdonald, *Human Rights and Criminal Justice* (3rd edn, 2012), ch 8B.

[5] For elaboration, see ibid, ch 8C, and E. Player, 'Remanding Women in Custody: Concerns for Human Rights' (2007) 70 *MLR* 402.

[6] (2000) 30 EHRR 643, 652, endorsed by the Court at [21]. (The Commission decision was originally referred to as *CC v UK*, see [1999] *Crim LR* 228.)

[7] Citing *Yagci and Sargin v Turkey* (1992) 20 EHRR 505, [52].

[8] Citing *Muller v France* [1997] ECHR 113, [44].

the least restrictive regime on a defendant pending trial. Before depriving a defendant
of liberty, courts must consider 'whether there [is] another way of safeguarding public
security and preventing him from committing further offences',[9] an injunction that
points in English law towards conditional bail in one of its forms. Other judgments
emphasize the need for 'special diligence' and speed where a defendant is remanded in
custody, rather than on bail.[10]

It is not difficult to understand the reasons for the rights declared in the Convention.
In principle, it is quite wrong that anyone, including agents of law enforcement, should
be able to make an arrest, bring a charge, and then, without proving that charge in court,
secure the immediate detention of the defendant.[11] Detention without trial is regarded
as a manifestation of totalitarianism, or at least an expedient to be contemplated only
in an extreme kind of national emergency.[12] It follows, therefore, that any argument for
depriving unconvicted individuals of their liberty in civil society ought to have peculiar
strength. Indeed, that point is reinforced when one considers the potential consequences
for the defendant of a loss of liberty before trial—not just the deprivation of freedom to
live a normal life, often compounded by incarceration under the worst conditions in the
prison system, but also restricted ability to prepare a defence to the charge, loss of job,
strain on family relations and friendships, and often appearance in court in a deterio-
rated or demoralized condition. The higher rates of suicide and self-injury for unconvicted rather than convicted prisoners may have much to do with these adversities.[13]

No doubt it was considerations of this kind that led the Supreme Court of the United
States to declare that:

> this traditional right to freedom before conviction permits the unhampered preparation
> of a defence and serves to prevent the infliction of punishment prior to conviction. Unless
> this right to bail before trial is preserved, the presumption of innocence, secured only after
> centuries of struggle, would lose its meaning.[14]

Thus, in the years following this statement US law and practice tended to concentrate on
the problem of securing the attendance of defendants at trial. However, surveys showed
that courts were mostly using financial bonds (sureties) as the means to this end, and
that the result was the pre-trial imprisonment of people too poor to raise the money
for such a bond.[15] Congress passed the Federal Bail Reform Act in 1966, legislating for

---

[9] *Clooth v Belgium* (1991) 14 EHRR 717, Commission at [75]; reiterated by the Court in *Jablonski v Poland* (2003) 36 EHRR 455, [84].

[10] *Punzelt v Czech Republic* (2001) 33 EHRR 1159, [73].

[11] See R. A. Duff, *Trials and Punishments* (1986), 140, arguing that in principle custodial remands before trial are utterly inconsistent with respect for individual citizens as rational agents.

[12] This, of course, is a major reason why the provisions in ss 21–29 of the Anti-Terrorism, Crime and Secu-rity Act 2001, authorizing the detention without trial of 'suspected international terrorists', were held inconsis-tent with the Convention in *A v Home Secretary* [2004] UKHL 56.

[13] Ministry of Justice, *Safety in Custody Statistics* (2018).

[14] *Stack v Boyle*, 342 US 1 (1951), per Vinson CJ at 4.

[15] See C. Foote, 'Compelling Appearance in Court: Administration of Bail in Philadelphia' (1954) 102 *U Pa LR* 1031; on the subsequent research by the Vera Institute that led to the change in federal law, see D. J. Freed and P. Wald, *Bail in the United States* (1964).

'release on recognisance' rather than financial bonds as the normal pre-trial order.[16] The second phase was marked by a growing anxiety about the commission of offences by people on bail, a concern that culminated in Congress passing the Bail Reform Act of 1984. The main thrust of this Act was to move the rationale to prediction of future danger, allowing a court to authorize pre-trial detention if there was clear and convincing evidence that 'no condition or combination of conditions of pre-trial release will reasonably assure the safety of any other person and the community'. When this was challenged in *United States v Salerno*,[17] the majority held that pre-trial detention on these grounds was essentially regulatory, since the intent of Congress was not to impose punishment on dangerous people but rather to protect 'the safety of the community';[18] thus, as pre-trial detention is intended to manage risks rather than inflict punishment, due process standards are not applicable.[19] The minority retorted that this approach 'merely redefine[s] any measure which is claimed to be punishment as "regulation" and, magically, the Constitution no longer prohibits its imposition'.[20] This kind of argument, which we will meet again in Chapter 13, raises two questions. First, what are the proper criteria for determining whether or not a measure amounts to punishment or a penalty? One element in that question is whether a measure can be classified as punishment as well as something else (e.g. prevention, regulation), or whether the categories should be regarded as mutually exclusive. Measures such as the detention of the mentally disordered, of persons subject to quarantine, and of illegal immigrants pending deportation (as set out in Art 5.1 of the ECHR) are circumstances in which the state is justified in depriving a person of liberty even though that person has not been convicted of an offence—indeed, is not even suspected of one. Secondly, if a measure is classified as something different from punishment, what principles should be applied? In other words, we know the additional safeguards that apply to criminal proceedings involving punishment; but 'is it possible to articulate a consistent and workable jurisprudence of anticipatory governmental action'[21] or are we left with a jurisprudential black hole?[22] Whatever the classification of pre-trial detention, the justification must be strong and pressing in view of the deprivation of liberty involved. This shift from securing the defendant's attendance at trial to protecting the safety of the community occurred elsewhere at the same time,[23] raising deep

---

[16] For an outline, see P. R. Jones and J. S. Goldkamp, 'Judicial Guidelines for Pre-Trial Release: Research and Policy Developments in the United States' (1991) 30 *Howard JCJ* 140.

[17] 481 US 739 (1987).

[18] Cf the reasoning of the ECtHR on the concept of punishment in *Welch v UK* (1995) 20 EHRR 247, holding that a measure can be punitive in effect even if it is preventive in intent.

[19] See the discussion by M. Feeley and J. Simon, 'Actuarial Justice: the New Emerging Criminal Law' in D. Nelken (ed), *The Futures of Criminology* (1994), 175–81.

[20] *United States v Salerno*, at 760 per Marshall and Brennan JJ; for discussion, see A. Dershowitz, *Pre-Emption* (2006), 240–50.

[21] Dershowitz, ibid, 244.

[22] A. Ashworth, 'Criminal Law, Human Rights and Preventative Justice' in B. McSherry, A. Norrie, and S. Bronitt (eds), *Regulating Deviance* (2009).

[23] For the change in Ireland in 1996, which necessitated a constitutional referendum, see C. Fennell, *The Law of Evidence in Ireland* (2nd edn, 2003), 53–9; for Canada, see N. Padfield, 'The Right to Bail: a Canadian Perspective' [1993] *Crim LR* 510.

questions about the presumption of innocence and detention without trial. In practice, however strong the presumption of liberty at the pre-trial stage, in all judicial systems there is some provision for that presumption to be rebutted. Typical grounds for refusing bail are the risk that the defendant will not appear for trial; the risk that the defendant will commit offences unless placed in detention; and the risk that the defendant might interfere with witnesses or otherwise obstruct justice. All these grounds for pre-trial detention are phrased in terms of risk: the state is using its power by authorizing the detention of certain people to reduce certain risks to other citizens and to the criminal justice system. Are these separate grounds justifiable reasons for depriving a person of liberty? If they are, do we have sufficient knowledge to be able to assess the risks accurately?

Let us consider the first of the three main grounds for refusing bail—that otherwise the defendant is unlikely to stand trial or, alternatively put, that there is a significant risk of absconding. In terms of justification, one key question concerns the relative social importance of ensuring that persons charged with offences attend their trial on the due date. Courts are rightly reluctant to hold a trial in a defendant's absence.[24] Presumably the police could be dispatched to arrest someone who failed to attend without offering a reasonable excuse, but there might be a greater anxiety over certain defendants who seem likely to flee the country or to hide themselves away. In principle, there is a greater public interest in securing the trial of those charged with more serious rather than less serious offences. As for the assessment of risk, we saw that the ECHR jurisprudence counsels against simply assuming that persons charged with serious offences will fail to appear at trial. There must be some ground for identifying a significant risk—perhaps that the defendant had on previous occasions failed to attend trial. Even then, the court must be satisfied that no other method of securing attendance at trial would be effective (deprivation of liberty must be a last resort).

A second main ground is the probability of committing offences if granted bail. In terms of justification, it is often asserted that there is a public interest in ensuring that people already charged with an offence do not commit offences during the period before their trial. The exact basis for this is unclear. Is it that the state is somehow responsible for the conduct of persons who have been charged but not yet tried, perhaps because it is the slowness of the machinery of criminal justice that creates the opportunities? Otherwise, in what way do remandees differ from, say, people with previous convictions who are walking the streets? Surely it cannot be that anyone who has been charged may be presumed guilty, and for that reason may be thought likely to commit a further offence if left at large before the formal trial: that reasoning, with its presumption of guilt, would contradict the presumption of innocence. Indeed, this was one of the grounds on which the Irish Supreme Court refused to recognize this as a legitimate ground for pre-trial detention, commenting that 'this is a form of

[24] But there may be circumstances in which this is permissible and consistent with Art 6 of the Convention: see *Jones* [2002] UKHL 5, and Emmerson, Ashworth, and Macdonald, *Human Rights and Criminal Justice*, n 4, 580–1.

preventative justice which . . . is quite alien to the true purpose of bail'.[25] Yet the trend undoubtedly is to deny this, and for governments to regard the period between arrest and trial as a time at which they must take action to control risks to citizens, and must endeavour to promote public safety by providing for some defendants to be deprived of their liberty.[26] One argument may be that the fact that a person has been charged with an offence is crucial. In some cases, the defendant may well have confessed guilt and indicated an intention to plead guilty, which may be taken to contradict the presumption of innocence; but defendants may change their intentions when the prosecution evidence becomes clear and they have received legal advice, so it would be unwise to build too much on those foundations. More generally, it could be argued that the laying of a charge ought to be attributed significance as the Crown Prosecution Service (CPS) has primary responsibility for such decisions; but that overlooks the need for the CPS frequently to take the charging decision before all the evidence is available, and the fact that police increasingly take charging decisions for lower level offences. As we saw in Chapter 7, since 2004 the Code for Crown Prosecutors has propounded a 'threshold test' for cases where 'the suspect presents as a substantial bail risk if released from custody', that test being one of reasonable grounds to suspect the defendant of having committed the offence.[27] That standard is significantly below the 'reasonable prospect of conviction' test that is normally required. The arguments here, then, are much weaker than is commonly supposed; and none of them are compatible with the fundamental presumption of innocence, since they tend in the direction of assuming guilt. The ECtHR has insisted that the existence of reasonable suspicion of the offence is a necessary precondition for any custodial remand,[28] and that there must be persuasive evidence for concluding that there is a significant risk of serious offences being committed. That does not confront the question of why liberty should be taken away before trial, but offers a procedure that gives some recognition to the presumption of liberty, if less to the presumption of innocence.

A third ground is the probability that the defendant might interfere with witnesses or otherwise obstruct the course of justice if released on bail. In some of these cases there is a distinct justification: the risk to the security of another person. Where the rights of another citizen are shown to be at risk, perhaps in a domestic abuse case or some other instance of ongoing attacks, the protection of those rights may well provide a justification for restrictions and, in some circumstances, for the deprivation of liberty. The uttering of threats by the defendant towards the victim would be one way of demonstrating the risk. In contrast to the situation in the previous paragraph, threats

---

[25] *People (Attorney-General) v Callaghan* [1966] IR 426, per Walsh J at 516. In 1996, the Irish Constitution was amended so as to provide for pre-trial detention where reasonably necessary 'to prevent the commission of a serious offence by that person'. See further U. Ní Raifeartaigh, 'Reconciling Bail Law with the Presumption of Innocence' (1997) 17 *OJLS* 1, and see n 23.

[26] The Supreme Court of Canada reached a similar conclusion in *Morales* (1993) 77 CCC (3d) 91.

[27] See Ch 7.2(B).

[28] 'The persistence of a reasonable suspicion that the person arrested has committed an offence is a condition *sine qua non* for the lawfulness of the continued detention': *Assenov v Bulgaria* (1999) 29 EHRR 652, [154].

offer evidence of a specific risk to a particular person. Therefore, if it appears to be a choice between the defendant's liberty or the victim's freedom from probable harm, detention pending trial may be easier to justify.[29] If there is thought to be a more general risk of interfering with witnesses or obstructing the course of justice, the justification for restricting the defendant's liberty is to secure the integrity of the criminal justice system. But for any such restriction, and particularly for a deprivation of liberty, there must be persuasive evidence of the risk—perhaps evidence that the defendant may have been involved in such incidents before, or evidence of threats uttered.

The fourth ground for the refusal of bail recognized by the ECtHR is where the nature of the crime and the probable public reaction to it are such that the release of the defendant might lead to public disorder. This justification may apply where it is considered right, exceptionally, to detain a defendant for his own protection.[30]

All these grounds for the refusal of bail turn on questions of predicted risk. In relation to the most frequent ground for refusal of bail—the risk of offences being committed in the period before trial—the 'risk' consists of the probability of an offence being committed if the defendant is granted bail, and the seriousness of any likely offence. A low probability of a very serious offence ought to have more weight than a high probability of a minor offence. What we have seen in this section and will continue to see throughout this chapter is that the crucial issues are conspicuously underdetermined. We have failed to identify a persuasive reason for the state to take power over defendants in the pre-trial period, to the extent of depriving them of liberty. We have argued that the well-known fallibility of predictions of dangerous conduct applies no less in the pre-trial sphere. These themes will now be developed more specifically in relation to the relevant English law.

8.2 THE LAW RELATING TO REMANDS

This section of the chapter considers the history and current form of the law relating to remands, briefly in relation to remand decisions taken by the police, and then in relation to court remands.

(A) POLICE REMANDS

The powers of the police to remand persons whom they have interviewed and may wish to interview again, and persons whom they have charged pending their first court appearance, are contained in the Police and Criminal Evidence Act 1984, as amended

---

[29] See the considerations set out in the *CPS Domestic Abuse Guidelines for Prosecutors*, https://www.cps.gov.uk/legal-guidance/domestic-abuse-guidelines-prosecutors. On the positive duty of a state to protect individuals under threat, see *Osman v UK* (1998) 29 EHRR 245, and Emmerson, Ashworth, and Macdonald, *Human Rights and Criminal Justice*, n 4, ch 19.

[30] *Letellier v France* (1992) 14 EHRR 83.

by the Criminal Justice and Public Order Act 1994.[31] The principal change in the 1994 Act was to confer on the police the power to grant bail with conditions: previously, they were only able to grant unconditional bail or to keep the suspect in custody overnight pending court appearance. One danger of granting such a power, well known to criminologists, is that it may be used in a net-widening manner. That is, a power intended to reduce the number of remands in custody can actually be used in cases where unconditional bail was previously allowed.[32]

The Criminal Justice Act 2003 introduced the concept of 'bail elsewhere than at a police station', known as street bail. These powers are discretionary, and the provisions on 'the right to bail' in the Bail Act 1976 do not apply here: police officers *may* release an arrested person on bail, and require that person to attend at a police station. No other requirement may be imposed, which means that other forms of conditional bail are not possible 'on the street'. This scheme has recently been amended by the Police and Crime Act 2017.[33]

(B) COURT REMANDS

In England and Wales, the law relating to remands has developed in two distinct phases. The first phase focused chiefly on the problem of securing the attendance of the defendant at the trial. In *Robinson* (1854), Coleridge J held that this was the sole point to which the magistrates should give attention.[34] In *Rose* (1898),[35] Lord Russell stated that 'it cannot be too strongly impressed on the magistracy that bail is not to be withheld as a punishment but that the requirements as to bail are merely to secure the attendance of the prisoner at his trial'. It was not until the 1940s and 1950s that the English courts, with Lord Goddard as Lord Chief Justice, began to establish that an alternative ground for remanding in custody is that the defendant is likely to commit an offence if granted bail.[36] The Home Office took the unusual step of circulating to all magistrates the text of Lord Goddard's remarks in *Wharton* (1955).[37] Statutory confirmation came in the provisions of the Criminal Justice Act 1967, an Act which also introduced the possibility of granting conditional bail. So, following the United States but before Ireland and Canada,[38] the emphasis in English law changed to prevention. The relevant law is contained chiefly in the Bail Act 1976,

---

[31] For the detailed procedures, see Y. Moreno and P. Hughes, *Effective Prosecution* (2008), 44–6.

[32] J. Raine and M. Willson, 'Police Bail with Conditions' (1997) 37 *BJ Crim* 593.

[33] See Ch 5.

[34] (1854) 23 LJQB 286. For summaries of the history, see A. K. Bottomley, 'The Granting of Bail: Principles and Practice' (1968) 31 *MLR* 40, and N. Corre and D. Wolchover, *Bail in Criminal Proceedings* (3rd edn, 2004), 11–19.

[35] (1898) 78 LT 119.

[36] See *Phillips* (1947) 32 Cr App R 47; *Wharton* [1955] *Crim LR* 565 ('unless the justices felt real doubt as to the result of the case, men with bad criminal records should not be granted bail'); and *Gentry* [1956] *Crim LR* 120 (same policy reiterated).

[37] See Bottomley, n 34, 52.

[38] See nn 15–23 and accompanying text.

as amended. In essence, a court has four main alternatives: release on unconditional bail, release on conditional bail, release on bail subject to a surety or security, and remand in custody.

Little needs to be said about unconditional bail. Section 3(6) provides for conditional bail, which might include reporting to a police station; a curfew or a residence requirement;[39] a prohibition on driving;[40] or electronic monitoring.[41] Persons on bail may be required to live at an Approved Premises, formerly and colloquially known as a bail hostel. The Bail Act also provides that a court may, subject to certain restrictions, require a surety to secure the defendant's attendance at court, or require a defendant to give security for surrender to custody before release on bail. In murder cases, a Crown Court must impose conditions in accordance with s 3(6A) providing for the medical examination of the defendant.[42] Where a prosecutor asks a court to impose a condition, she must specify the condition and explain what purpose it would serve.[43] Beyond that, the court has considerable discretion.

It appears that around one-quarter to one-third of defendants granted bail are placed under conditions:[44] Raine and Willson found that the most common condition is residence at a specified address (78 per cent of conditional cases), followed by not contacting named persons (46 per cent), not going to a certain address (24 per cent), curfew (21 per cent), and reporting at a police station (18 per cent).[45] More recent data about bail conditions are limited. While it was suggested that electronic monitoring now is commonplace in the remand process,[46] its use declined by 22 per cent from 2014 to 2017.[47] Approved Premises are also little used: persons on bail and bail assessment account for a mere 0.3 per cent of residents.[48] Despite this, there is support for their more extensive use for women.[49] Furthermore, sureties are not imposed widely in England and Wales.[50] Raine and Willson also found that half their interviewees believed that bail conditions would not be enforced, a perception that clearly weakens the efficacy of conditional bail.[51] This was echoed in Cape and Smith's study: judicial and practitioner confidence in conditional bail is weakened by a lack of faith that conditions are adequately enforced, or enforceable.[52]

---

[39] R (CPS) v Chorley Justices [2002] EWHC 2162 (Admin).

[40] R v Kwame (1974) 60 Cr App R 65.

[41] s 3AB, as inserted by Criminal Justice and Immigration Act 2008, s 51 and Sch 11; previously the power was available only in respect of persons under 18.

[42] Coroners and Justice Act 2009, s 115.   [43] CPR 2017, r 14.5(4).

[44] P. M. Morgan and P. Henderson, Remand Decisions and Offending on Bail (1998), ch 4.

[45] J. Raine and M. Willson, 'The Imposition of Conditions in Bail Decisions' (1996) 35 Howard JCJ 256; very similar percentages were found by Morgan and Henderson, see n 44, 42.

[46] A. Hucklesby, Bail Support Schemes for Adults (2011), 14.

[47] Transform Justice, Presumed innocent but behind bars—is remand overused in England and Wales? (2018), 29.

[48] HM Inspectorate of Probation, Probation Hostels' (Approved Premises) Contribution to Public Protection, Rehabilitation and Resettlement (2017), 6. This is due to hostels and probation now being focused more on public protection, and on catering for offenders with complex needs on release from custody (13 and 17).

[49] Prison Reform Trust, Transforming Lives reducing women's imprisonment (2014), 36.

[50] Hucklesby, n 46, 13.   [51] See n 45.

[52] E. Cape and T. Smith, The practice of pre-trial detention in England and Wales: research report (2016), ch VI.

The centrepiece of the Bail Act is s 4, which proclaims what has been described as a general right to bail or a presumption in favour of bail. Thus, s 4(1) provides that 'a person to whom this section applies shall be granted bail except as provided in Schedule 1 to this Act'.[53] Paragraphs 2–6 of Part I of that Schedule[54] list a number of 'exceptions to the right to bail', including custodial remands for the defendant's own protection[55] and (more doubtfully) custodial remands because the court does not yet have sufficient information to take a decision on bail. The main provision is para 2:

> The defendant need not be granted bail if the court is satisfied that there are substantial grounds for believing that the defendant, if released on bail (whether subject to conditions or not), would—
>
> (a) fail to surrender to custody, or
>
> (b) commit an offence while on bail, or
>
> (c) interfere with witnesses or otherwise obstruct the course of justice, whether in relation to himself or any other person.

These three grounds correspond broadly with those approved by the ECtHR in its development of Art 5(3), and have a loose affinity with those subsequently incorporated in the Bail Reform Act of 1984 in the United States.[56] The Schedule to the English Act goes on to set out considerations to which regard should be had when taking bail/custody decisions. Among those is 'the defendant's record as respects the fulfilment of his obligations under previous grants of bail in criminal proceedings', a matter plainly relevant when the court is considering exception (a) to the right to bail.

Another consideration is 'the character, antecedents, associations and community ties of the defendant'. Community ties may be relevant to the probability that a defendant will attend his trial (exception (a)), since it may be argued that a person who is homeless or in temporary accommodation is more likely to abscond than someone with a permanent address (and a family) in the locality. However, it has been urged repeatedly that homelessness should not lead to a custodial remand without thorough exploration of other alternatives,[57] and in *Sulaoja v Estonia* the ECtHR determined that a lack of fixed residence did not justify imposing pre-trial detention.[58] In fact, Cape and Smith's research found that prosecutors viewed homelessness as one factor to be taken into account rather than the determinative reason for a pre-trial detention

---

[53] Cf the amendments relating to summary offences punishable with imprisonment, in the Criminal Justice and Immigration Act 2008, s 52 and Sch 12.

[54] Part II of the Sch deals separately with non-imprisonable offences, which will not be discussed here.

[55] The Criminal Justice Act 2003, s 13 introduces the possibility of alternatively granting conditional bail in such cases.

[56] The US Act refers to a serious risk that the defendant will flee or will obstruct justice; or where the case involves a crime of violence (very broadly defined), a major drug offence, or any crime punishable by life imprisonment; or where the case involves a felony charge against someone previously convicted of two offences in the above categories.

[57] E.g. in Home Office Circular 155/1975, *Bail Procedures*.   [58] (2006) 43 EHRR 36, [64].

request, and the relationship between lack of a fixed address and the likelihood of failing to surrender was a source of concern for judges and magistrates.[59]

The 'character and antecedents' of the defendant may give grounds for a prediction
of whether he or she is likely to offend if given bail (exception (b)). One oft-quoted
statement is that of Atkinson J in the Court of Criminal Appeal in *Phillips*,[60] where he
warned courts against granting bail to defendants with a 'record of housebreaking', and
added that 'in 19 out of 20 cases it is a mistake [to] release young housebreakers on
bail'. This is a considerable exaggeration, notwithstanding the fact that in 2010 20 per
cent of burglaries were committed by someone on bail.[61] The ECtHR has signalled the
need for courts to avoid stereotypical reasoning and therefore not to make assumptions simply on the basis of a criminal record:[62] previous convictions must be recent,
relevant, and of a certain seriousness before it will be proper to contemplate rebutting
the presumption of liberty on this ground. In addition, drug use, mental health, and
nationality were mentioned by participants in Cape and Smith's study in relation to
this exception.[63] The issue of nationality was regarded as a sensitive characteristic that
entailed a flight risk, though this could be mitigated by the prosecutor seeking the surrender of the defendant's passport as a condition of bail.[64]

A further consideration listed in para 9 is 'the nature and seriousness of the offence
or default (and the probable method of dealing with the offender for it)'. The ECtHR
has warned against a general assumption that the seriousness of the charge increases
the risk of non-appearance at trial, and there must be further and specific evidence of a
risk of this defendant absconding.[65] The seriousness of the charge ought to be relevant
to custodial remands on the second ground, in recognition that it would be wrong to
remand in custody a person whose charge (if proved) would be unlikely to result in a
custodial sentence. However, on the face of the Bail Act, and the exceptions to bail that
it enumerates, the probability of further minor offences such as shoplifting could justify a custodial remand. The Act should be amended so that exception (b) refers to the
likelihood of committing a *serious* offence whilst on bail, as does the law on custodial
remands of young people, so as to make this principle clear.

The ECHR had some effect in curtailing attempts to 'toughen up' the law of bail in
the 1990s. Section 25 of the Criminal Justice and Public Order Act 1994 sought to remove a court's powers to remand on bail any person charged with murder, attempted
murder, manslaughter, rape, or attempted rape who already has a conviction for such
an offence. In *Caballero v UK*,[66] the ECtHR confirmed that this was in breach of Art
5(3), because, as the Commission had put it, 'the exclusion from the risk assessment

---

[59] Cape and Smith, n 52, 58.   [60] (1947) 32 Cr App R 47.
[61] E.g. P. M. Morgan, *Offending Whilst on Bail* (1992); Ministry of Justice, FOI Request ref: FOI/97753, 11
August 2015.
[62] See n 6 and accompanying text.   [63] Cape and Smith, n 52, 57–70.
[64] Ibid, 58, citing *Wemhoff v Germany* (1979–80) 1 EHRR 55.
[65] See n 7 and accompanying text.
[66] (2000) 30 EHRR 643 (see n 6); the government conceded after the Commission's opinion, and so the
Court did not deliver a full judgment.

of a consideration of all the particular circumstances and facts of each accused's case (other than the two facts contained in s 25) exposes, of itself, accused persons to arbitrary deprivation of liberty'. Section 25 has been amended[67] so as to provide that a court may only grant bail to such persons if 'of the opinion' that 'there are exceptional circumstances which justify it'. This may still be thought inconsistent with the presumption of liberty implicit in Art 5(3), since the reworded s 25 establishes a presumption in these cases in favour of deprivation of liberty,[68] and the ECtHR has held that the authorities, not the defendant, must bear the burden of proving the need for detention.[69] By adopting an interpretative approach that treats as an 'exceptional circumstance' the view that the defendant appears unlikely to commit a serious offence if not remanded in custody,[70] a court could find the substance of s 25 compatible, but not the burden of proof.

Section 25 was deemed to be irrelevant in *R (Charles) v Central Criminal Court*,[71] on the basis that the claimant had not committed an earlier offence. Bail had been refused to Charles after he was charged with murder on the basis that murder was to be dealt with *sui generis* and there had to be exceptional grounds for granting bail. Judicial review was granted as the judge had failed to give adequate reasons for his decision and to refer to the correct legal test, and had taken account of a consideration that was legally irrelevant. Section 25 cannot be used to support the suggestion that bail in any murder case should be granted only in exceptional circumstances.

Other recent changes to rules relating to bail include s 115 of the Coroners and Justice Act 2009, which removed the jurisdiction of a magistrates' court to grant bail where a defendant has been charged with murder. Section 114 amended Sch 1 to the Bail Act 1976, providing that bail may not be granted to someone charged with murder unless the court is satisfied that there is no significant risk that, if released on bail, that person would commit an offence that would be likely to cause physical or mental injury to another person. In coming to that decision, the court must have regard to the nature and seriousness of the offence, the suspect's character and antecedents, and his record in relation to previous grants of bail. This was amended in turn by LASPO 2012 to apply to causing physical or mental injury or fear of this to an 'associated person', namely an intimate partner, spouse, cohabitant, or person in the same household. Despite this narrowing of scope, the same concerns about ECHR compatibility can be raised here as in relation to s 25.

Following the Law Commission's 2001 report on *Bail and the Human Rights Act 1998*, two other provisions were amended in an attempt to produce Convention

---

[67] By the Crime and Disorder Act 1998, s 56 and the Legal Aid, Sentencing and Punishment of Offenders Act 2012 (LASPO), Sch 11, para 33.

[68] Cf the unsatisfactory decision in *R v Crown Court at Harrow* [2003] 1 WLR 2756, criticized by A. Ashworth and M. Strange, 'Criminal Law and Human Rights' [2004] *EHRLR* 121, 128–9.

[69] *Reid v UK* (2003) 37 EHRR 9, [70].

[70] Adapting the Court of Appeal's sentencing judgment in *Offen (No 2)* [2001] 1 WLR 253; see Law Commission, *Bail and the Human Rights Act 1998* (2001), Part VIII.

[71] [2012] EWHC 2581 (Admin).

compatibility. Thus s 26 of the Criminal Justice and Public Order Act 1994 was amended
by s 14 of the Criminal Justice Act 2003, so as to establish a presumption that a person
should not be granted bail if it appears that he has committed an offence whilst on bail
for another charge, 'unless the court is satisfied that there is no significant risk of his
committing an offence' if granted bail. Similarly, the 2003 Act provides a presumption
that a person who has failed to appear at court without reasonable cause should not be
granted bail, and similarly a person who tests positive for a Class A drug, again unless
the court is satisfied that there is no significant risk of a further failure to surrender to
bail. The 'no significant risk' formula is linked more directly to the rationale of each
provision than 'exceptional circumstances', but it still reverses the general presumption
of liberty. It also places great weight on assessments of risk, and ought to be interpreted
as calling for sound, evidence-based reasons in favour of detention whereas, by virtue
of the presumption, the defendant has to produce evidence-based reasons why there is
no significant risk in granting him bail.

The use of remand for less serious offences has long been criticized: as Lord Woolf
noted, 'to remand a defendant in custody for an offence for which he would never be
sentenced to imprisonment can be questionable'.[72] Now, LASPO 2012 provides that
bail will be granted where there is 'no real prospect' that the defendant will be sentenced to a custodial sentence, as long as he has attained the age of 18, has not been
convicted of an offence in those proceedings, and the proceedings are not to do with
extradition, or domestic abuse.[73] While this is an understandable development, it is
questionable whether this is driven by principled or economic considerations. Ultimately, the degree and frequency of legislative change, driven by the desire to reduce
the prison population yet maintain public protection, has prompted calls for a consolidating statute, for clarity's sake.[74]

The Bail Act 1976 applies to children and young people too: there is a presumption
that such defendants have a right to bail, but in making this decision the court must have
regard to their welfare also.[75] This includes a specific obligation to consider a bail application, even if the court has refused bail twice and there is no change of circumstances
nor any considerations which were not before the court when the young person was last
remanded.[76] Art 3 of the United Nations Convention on the Rights of the Child 1989
provides that the best interests of the child shall be a primary consideration in all actions
concerning them, while the principal aim of the youth justice system in England and
Wales is to prevent offending.[77] So, for a child/young person there is an additional possibility of a bail condition being imposed for his 'own welfare or in his own interests'.[78]

---

[72] *Prison Disturbances April 1990: Report of an Inquiry by Rt Hon. Lord Justice Woolf and His Honour Judge Tumin* (1991), 63.
[73] LASPO, Sch 11, para 13(c).
[74] A. Edwards, 'Legal Aid, Sentencing and Punishment of Offenders Act 2012—The Financial Procedural and Practical Implications' [2012] *Crim LR* 584, 588.
[75] Children and Young Persons Act 1933, s 44.
[76] *R (on the application of B) v Brent Youth Court* [2010] EWHC 1893 (Admin).
[77] Crime and Disorder Act 1998, s 37.   [78] Bail Act 1976, s 3(6)(ca).

In terms of communicating to the defendant, the Criminal Procedure Rules (CPR) require the court to announce the reasons for its decision about bail 'in terms the defendant can understand (with help, if necessary)'.[79] However, as Cape and Smith note, this stops short of explicitly requiring that the reasons given deal with the facts of the individual case.[80] This led them to recommend amending the CPR to make it absolutely clear that courts must explain their decisions by reference to the specific facts of the case and to the representations made by the prosecutor and the defence lawyer.[81] In addition, since 2012 bail hearings may be by live link;[82] though this minimizes the need for travel and is arguably more efficient, it may affect adversely the ability of the defendant to effectively engage in the hearings, or the ability of their lawyer to effectively represent them.[83]

8.3 THE TREATMENT OF UNCONVICTED DEFENDANTS

The vast majority of cases in magistrates' courts do not involve any remand of the defendant, whether on bail or in custody. In 2017, bail was granted to 17 per cent of defendants prosecuted at magistrates' courts, while 4 per cent were remanded in custody and the remaining 79 per cent were not remanded.[84] The proportion of defendants remanded in custody at the Crown Court is higher, given that remand in custody is more likely for more serious, indictable offences: in 2017, 35 per cent of defendants tried at the Crown Court were remanded in custody, and 47 per cent were remanded on bail.

What is the position in the prisons? Remand prisoners have always tended to be placed in the most overcrowded conditions in the system, since they are sent to local prisons.[85] As HM Inspectorate of Prisons (HMIP) observed, remand prisoners receive notably poorer provision in comparison to sentenced offenders, despite the additional entitlements that should be afforded to them due to their status.[86] Moreover, the provision of legal advice to defendants remanded in custody is difficult, which may impair their defence.[87] All of this is certainly inconsistent with the proper treatment of people who have not yet been convicted, even if it is not formally in breach of the presumption of innocence and the right to legal assistance. The number of people in prison on remand has been fairly constant for the last few decades: the total stood at 13,400 in 2007, of which 8,000 were awaiting trial and the remainder convicted and awaiting

---

[79] Criminal Procedure Rules 2017, r 14.2(5).   [80] Cape and Smith, n 52, 15.   [81] Ibid, 9.

[82] Police and Justice Act 2006 (Commencement No 15) Order 2012 (SI 2373/2012).

[83] Cape and Smith, n 52, 96–7.

[84] Ministry of Justice, *Criminal Justice Statistics quarterly, England and Wales, 2017* (2018), 20.

[85] Prison Reform Trust, *Innocent Until Proven Guilty: Tackling the Overuse of Custodial Remand* (2011), 2.

[86] HM Inspectorate of Prisons, *Thematic Report by HM Inspectorate of Prisons Remand prisoners: A thematic review* (2012), 19.

[87] See the study of young remand prisoners by F. Brookman and H. Pierpoint, 'Access to Legal Advice for Young Suspects and Remand Prisoners' (2003) 42 *Howard JCJ* 452.

sentence.[88] On any particular day in 2014 almost 12,000 people were in prison awaiting trial or sentence.[89] Similarly, 10.9 per cent of prisoners in 2016 were on remand.[90]
Fifty-five per cent of those remanded in custody are held for either violence against
the person (22 per cent of the remand population), drug offences (17 per cent), or
theft offences (16 per cent).[91] The total proportion is higher for women: on 31 March
2018, 15 per cent of women in prison were held on remand.[92] This might be due to
a lack of available appropriate accommodation, rather than because their risk profile
or offence type necessitates it, as almost nine in ten women held on remand are low
or medium risk of serious harm. While there are limited data for children and young
people, it appears that nearly twice the proportion of adults are detained pre-trial
compared to them.[93]

Overall, the figures on remand constitute a much lower proportion of the total prison
population than a couple of decades ago, but that is because the number of convicted
and sentenced offenders in prison rose steeply in the late 1990s and subsequently sta-
bilized. The remand population remains high, particularly in respect of those who have
not yet had their trial. That said, average waiting times have fallen: for those remanded
in custody in 2007 it was 55 days, some three days fewer than the previous year.[94] In
2017, the average time spent on pre-trial remand for those subsequently convicted was
32 days for indictable offences, 28 days for triable either way offences, and 23 days for
summary offences.[95] In Cape and Smith's study, in just over 40 per cent of the sample
of cases pre-trial detention lasted for no longer than one month, and in just over two-
thirds of cases, pre-trial detention lasted for no longer than three months. However, in
nearly one-fifth of cases, pre-trial detention lasted for six months or more.[96]

Some improvements in the remand system may have taken place, but in the light
of the fundamental right to liberty enshrined in Art 5 we must continue to examine
whether it is necessary to have as many as 12,000 people in prison at any one time
awaiting trial—a figure that represents some 80,000 people remanded in custody each
year.[97] One way of examining this issue is to consider the outcomes of the cases against
those remanded in custody. In 2007, of all persons remanded in custody some 15 per
cent were acquitted, 29 per cent received a non-custodial sentence, and 52 per cent
were sent to custody.[98] This has remained stable: more recent figures shows that nearly
half of people who are kept in custody at some stage before their trial or sentence
were either found not guilty, or if found guilty, were given a non-custodial sentence.[99]
Of those defendants whose cases stayed in the magistrates' court, 58 per cent did not

[88] See E. Player, J. Roberts, J. Jacobson, M. Hough, and J. Robottom, 'Remanded in Custody: Recent Trends in England and Wales' (2010) 49 *Howard JCJ* 231–51, Table 3.
[89] Cape and Smith, n 52, 7.
[90] R. Walmsley *World pre-trial/remand imprisonment list* (3rd edn, 2017).
[91] Ministry of Justice, *Offender Management Statistics Bulletin, England and Wales Annual 2017* (2018), 3.
[92] Ministry of Justice, *Female Offender Strategy* (Cm 9642, 2018), [59].
[93] Cape and Smith, n 52, 64.   [94] Player et al, n 88.
[95] PQs 144347, 144348, and 144349, asked by Richard Burgon on 15 May 2018.
[96] Cape and Smith, n 52, 36.   [97] Ibid, 7.   [98] Ibid, Table 4.
[99] Cape and Smith, n 52, ch VIII.

receive a custodial sentence. Defendants remanded in custody at the Crown Court were more likely to receive immediate custodial sentences, though in 2016 27 per cent of all such defendants did not go on to get a custodial sentence.[100] Sentence lengths for defendants remanded in custody in the Crown Court who went on to receive an immediate custodial sentence have remained broadly similar over time. In 2016, 75 per cent of these defendants received immediate custodial sentences of 12 months or more.[101]

Women are particularly unlikely, if remanded, to receive a prison sentence. In 2016, just over 20 per cent of women who were remanded in custody during magistrates' courts proceedings received a sentence of immediate custody, though a further 35 per cent of these women were sent for trial at the Crown Court of which some will have received a sentence of immediate custody. Forty-three per cent of women who were remanded prior to a Crown Court trial were not given a prison sentence.[102]

These figures raise a number of serious questions. In the cases of those remanded in custody and subsequently acquitted or not proceeded against, the loss of liberty is particularly hard on the individuals concerned. It could be argued that these are not necessarily cases of malfunction in the criminal justice system: if a conscientious judgement was made about the probability that, if not remanded in custody, they would fail to attend trial, commit offences whilst on bail, or interfere with witnesses, none of those matters bears directly on the probability of conviction. However, the importance of these decisions for defendants means that two aspects of custodial remands require special attention. First, the ECtHR has made it clear that remanding magistrates must be satisfied of the continued existence of 'reasonable suspicion' (i.e. substantial evidence) against the defendant,[103] and para 9 of Sch 1 to the Bail Act states that the strength of the evidence should be considered. To what extent are magistrates able to do this meaningfully? It is well known that decisions by magistrates tend to correspond with recommendations by the CPS, which in turn correspond with decisions by the police. The correlations are strong, but not invariable, and therefore do not necessarily lead to inferences of undue influence or failure of decision makers to examine issues independently. Thus, Morgan and Henderson found that, in respect of those held in police custody, the CPS recommended custody for only 48 per cent, and 76 per cent of those recommendations were accepted; the CPS recommended conditional bail for a further 46 per cent, and magistrates accepted 90 per cent of those recommendations.[104] Since one-fifth of those remanded in custody are acquitted or not proceeded against, this ought to prompt inquiries into the reasons why they were remanded in custody. Morgan and Henderson identify a number of characteristics that are associated strongly with decisions to remand in custody, notably the absence of a fixed address, seriousness of charge, and bail history. It is also important to know why cases were dropped, where that was the outcome, and why this could not have happened at an earlier stage. At the very least, the figures suggest that the pain of custodial remand,

---

[100] Ministry of Justice, n 84.   [101] Ibid, 21.

[102] UK Parliament, Written question—118177, asked by Richard Burgon on 7 December 2017.

[103] See n 28 and accompanying text.   [104] Morgan and Henderson, n 44, 37.

felt so acutely by those subject to it, does not always weigh so heavily with those who take decisions in respect of defendants.[105] There are no recent comparable data.

What about those who receive non-custodial sentences after being remanded in custody? This is the outcome for about one-quarter of males and nearly one-third of all females remanded in custody before trial. Does it mean that they were unnecessarily remanded in custody in the first place?

At least four lines of argument cast doubt on this. The first is the one that most sentencers hasten to offer: that a court passing sentence must recognize the fact that the offender has already spent time in custody, and that a court may properly take this into account and impose a non-custodial sentence in a case where, if there had been no custodial remand, it would probably have imposed custody. The magistrates who pass sentence will rarely be the same individuals who refused bail and ordered the custodial remand, so the sentencing decision will be taken *de novo*. There can be no objection to the court taking account of what has already happened: indeed, this may allow the court to adopt a more constructive approach than it might otherwise have felt able to do, by making a community order rather than imposing a custodial sentence. The implication of this argument is that the imposition of a non-custodial sentence does not necessarily suggest that the custodial remand was wrong, since in many cases if there had not been a custodial remand there would have been a custodial sentence. In theory, this argument seems plausible. It is difficult, however, to determine how much substance it has in practice, since no research has been carried out into the reasoning of magistrates when sentencing offenders who have been in custody on remand. No one knows what proportion of the cases resulting in a non-custodial sentence are a response to the custodial remand, and what proportion imply that there need not have been a custodial remand in the first place.

Moreover, this first argument may prove rather more than was intended. If it is true that sentencers tend to take account of the fact that an offender has spent time in custody on remand, it may be the case that some of those given custodial sentences are sentenced in that way simply so as to facilitate their immediate release. If the court learns that an offender has been in prison for two months awaiting trial, it may feel that he or she has already been punished quite sufficiently (or even too heavily) for the offence, and may therefore impose a sentence of four months' imprisonment so as to ensure immediate release.[106] Otherwise, the court might have chosen some kind of community order as a suitable sentence. It is not known how many courts would react in this way—some might grant a conditional discharge or other sentence in these circumstances. But the point is that the number of people remanded in custody who are given custodial sentences subsequently by magistrates' courts may also include some

[105] It should also be added that this country, unlike many of its European neighbours, does not have a statutory scheme for compensating those who are remanded in custody and then acquitted, although Art 5(5) of the Convention mandates 'an enforceable right to compensation'.

[106] This is said to be the approach of some courts in other European countries: see e.g. W. Heinz, 'The Problems of Imprisonment' in R. Hood (ed), *Crime and Criminal Policy in Europe: Proceedings of a European Colloquium* (1989).

cases (we know not how many) where the court would not have imposed custody if there had been no custodial remand. To take the further step and assert that the number of those given non-custodial sentences who would have received custody but for the custodial remand is far greater than the number of those given custodial sentences who would have received non-custodial sentences but for the custodial remand is to advance into the realms of speculation. The proportions are not known.

A second argument against taking the figures at face value is that the criteria for granting or withholding bail are not directly related to the probability of a custodial sentence, despite the 'no real prospect' provision in LASPO 2012.[107] The three criteria in para 2 of the Schedule to the Bail Act focus only on the period between first court appearance and trial. It is true that para 9 of that Schedule suggests that courts should also have regard to 'the nature and seriousness of the offence and the probable method of dealing with the offender for it', but it is not clear how much separate attention has been given to this provision. Where a defendant is remanded in custody because there are substantial grounds for believing that otherwise he or she may not attend the trial, or for believing that otherwise witnesses may be threatened, these reasons have nothing to do with the likely sentence in the case. The statistics are not sharp enough to determine the relative proportions of cases. Exactly how many cases depended only on one or the other reason is unclear, but some evidently bear no relationship to the probability of a custodial sentence on conviction.

A third argument points to the divergence between the bail provisions and the relevant sentencing law. Section 152(2) of the Criminal Justice Act 2003 states that a court 'must not pass a custodial sentence' unless satisfied that the offence 'was so serious that neither a fine alone nor a community sentence can be justified for the offence'.[108] No such restrictions are to be found in the Bail Act and, except with reference to remand of young people, and despite the introduction of the 'no real prospect' test in LASPO 2012, there is no clear injunction that the court should adopt the least restrictive form of remand (unconditional bail; conditional bail) unless satisfied that the defendant would receive a custodial sentence if convicted as charged.

A fourth argument raises questions about whether the remand decisions taken in court really are considered and rounded determinations. We have already noted the findings of Morgan and Henderson that, in the majority of cases, magistrates tend to adopt the same course as that recommended by the CPS.[109] The vast majority of remand hearings are uncontested: only in 9 per cent of cases was there a different view advanced by prosecution and defence.[110] In most cases the CPS did not oppose bail, and in almost half of the cases where bail was opposed the defence did not contest this. At least two processes appear to be at work here. One is the influence of the police: if they

[107] LASPO, Sch 11, para 13(c).
[108] A similar provision has been part of the law since 1991: see Criminal Justice Act 1991, s 1(2).
[109] Morgan and Henderson, n 44; for experimental evidence to the same effect, see M. Dhami, 'Conditional Bail Decision-Making in the Magistrates' Court' (2004) 43 *Howard JCJ* 27, 40.
[110] A. Hucklesby, 'Court Culture: an Explanation of Variations in the Use of Bail at Magistrates' Courts' (1997) 36 *Howard JCJ* 129; also Cape and Smith, n 52, 53.

grant bail from the police station, it is highly unlikely that a court is going to find that
a custodial remand is needed, and the CPS would have difficulty in sustaining such an
argument.[111] The other is the influence of court culture, which sustains different rates
of remand in custody in different courts over prolonged periods of years.[112] Both influences tend to suggest that in some cases the CPS does not make the recommendation it
might think appropriate, and Hucklesby's finding that generally nearly nine out of ten
CPS recommendations are accepted by the court[113] shows that the CPS makes different recommendations on similar cases because they are to be heard in different courts,
or even by differently constituted benches. Moreover, this process of anticipating the
decisions of other parties is also evident in the approach of some defence solicitors,
who admit both to adapting their representations to the particular bench (sometimes
not applying for bail if it would be 'hopeless' in view of the constitution of the bench),
and to using tactics or coded language in order to distinguish bail applications which
they believe in from those which they make purely because the client has insisted.
This is a clear example of unethical behaviour, with defence lawyers failing to do their
best to advance a defendant's case or, as Hucklesby puts it, ranking 'their credibility
and status with the court above the interests of their clients'.[114] Hucklesby found that
the CPS usually failed to give reasons for its representations: indeed, in 60 per cent of
cases where the CPS requested a custodial remand, no reasons were stated, and even in
cases where the defence contested the hearing the CPS failed to give its reason (e.g. by
referring to a reason in the Bail Act) in many cases.[115] Insofar as these practices persist,
they constitute a clear demonstration of the way in which apparently open and formal
processes mask the reality of informal decision making, anticipation of the decisions
of others, and the drive to maintain professional respect. In the present context, the
implication is that decisions result from possibly tacit or even unconscious local coali-
tions between police practice and bench traditions, with the CPS and defence solicitors
operating in a way that sees them anticipating the decisions of others in many cases
and only rarely standing up for a view that differs from that of other key participants.
Of course, a high rate of concordance in decisions does not conclusively prove undue
influence, since it remains possible that the police, the CPS, and then the courts are applying the same criteria independently and reaching mostly the same conclusions, but
the evidence of the criminal justice practitioners interviewed by Hucklesby strongly
suggests otherwise.[116]

   Consideration of the four lines of argument against a face-value interpretation of the
statistics on trial and sentence therefore demonstrates a pervasive uncertainty about
the use of bail and of remands in custody. We lack the detailed research necessary to

---

[111] J. Burrows, P. Henderson, and P. Morgan, *Improving Bail Decisions: The Bail Process Project* (1994); for
similar findings in Canada, see G. Kellough and S. Wortley, 'Remand for Plea: Bail Decisions and Plea Bargaining as Commensurate Decisions' (2002) 42 *BJ Crim* 186, 204.
[112] A. Hucklesby, 'Court Culture: an Explanation of Variations in the Use of Bail at Magistrates' Courts'
(1997) 36 *Howard JCJ* 129; A. Hucklesby, 'Remand Decision Makers' [1997] *Crim LR* 269.
[113] Ibid, 276; also Morgan and Henderson, n 44, 35–6.
[114] Hucklesby [1997] *Crim LR* 269, 279.   [115] Ibid, 280–1.   [116] Ibid, 137–40.

establish which explanations account for what percentage of cases: Mandeep Dhami's experimental research suggests that divergences of approach are at their greatest in high-risk cases,[117] and closer monitoring of actual decisions is now needed. At the same time, however, the terms of the law on remands ought to be re-examined further, and consolidated. In principle, as the ECtHR has emphasized, the strength of the case ought to be a primary factor, before one of the specific grounds for deprivation of liberty is considered. In practice, this creates difficulties in cases where the full evidence may not have arrived by the first (or even subsequent) remand hearing, especially if the results of a forensic science test are being awaited. We saw earlier that the CPS has now acknowledged this point by lowering the standard of evidence required,[118] but it remains a key issue in custodial remands. Moreover, the 'future offences' ground should be rewritten so as to state expressly that there should be no remand in custody unless there is a substantial risk of *serious* offences being committed if the defendant were left at liberty.[119] If risk is to be a criterion, there must be legislative guidance not only on the seriousness of the probable offence but on the degree of risk and the basis for inferring it. This raises the issue of the information provided to bail decision makers, a topic taken up in section 8.5 of this chapter.

8.4 THE TREATMENT OF VICTIMS AND POTENTIAL VICTIMS

This is a provocative heading, intended to raise the question whether the public in general or victims in particular receive any benefit from having larger numbers of defendants in custody at any one time, or having particular individuals detained on remand. It would be almost impossible to trace any effects on the crime rate, largely because (1) the 'crime rate' is itself an elusive phenomenon which even surveys of victims (which are more complete than official records) have difficulty in charting,[120] and (2) even if we had a reliable measure of the number of crimes committed each year, it would necessarily be a product of several interacting influences, and it would rarely be possible to attribute particular trends to particular causes. But the question can be approached from other angles. One is to inquire into the volume of offences committed by persons who have been granted bail, perhaps with a view to suggesting that either too few people or the wrong people are remanded in custody. Another is to inquire into the proportion of those remanded in custody who are subsequently given non-custodial sentences, with a view to suggesting that it was unnecessary to order their pre-trial detention to secure public protection.

---

[117] M. Dhami, 'From Discretion to Disagreement: Explaining Disparities in Judges' Pre-Trial Decisions' (2005) 23 *Behavioural Sciences and the Law* 367.

[118] See the Code for Crown Prosecutors (2004), and subsequent revisions, discussed in Ch 7.2(B).

[119] The 1996 amendment to the Irish Constitution insists on risk of a serious offence (see n 23 above), and this is also evident in the ECHR jurisprudence (see n 29).

[120] See M. Maguire and S. McVie, 'Crime Data and Criminal Statistics: A Critical Reflection' in A. Liebling, S. Maruna, and L. McAra (eds), *The Oxford Handbook of Criminology* (2017).

The most direct sense of public protection is to protect a specified person who has been threatened with violence by the defendant or who has a well-grounded fear of violence. Such issues may arise in cases of stalking, domestic abuse, or neighbourhood disputes, for instance. The *Code of Practice for Victims of Crime* sets out the entitlements of victims and witnesses, and the duties of service providers, such as the police, the CPS, and the court service. In relation to the release on bail of persons arrested or charged, for example, the Code sets out duties of the police to keep victims informed.[121] The CPS *Policy on Prosecuting Cases of Domestic Violence* states that prosecutors should consider applying for appropriate conditions for bail or for the defendant to be remanded in custody to protect complainants and witnesses from the risk of danger, threats, pressure, or repeat offences.[122] There is also a prosecution right to appeal against the grant of bail, in respect of all imprisonable offences.[123]

Victims may mention in their victim personal statement (VPS) if they have specific concerns over their safety if the defendant is granted bail. This may assist in the construction of restraining orders as part of a bail condition, for instance. That said, official documents and guidelines are not very clear on how exactly these statements will be used and their exact limits with regards to bail.[124] Moreover, a joint inspection by HM Inspectorate of Constabulary (HMIC) and HM Crown Prosecution Service Inspectorate (HMCPSI) in 2017 on the police and CPS response to harassment and stalking found that victims were often badly let down throughout the criminal justice process, for reasons including the failure to impose bail conditions on perpetrators, which sometimes left the victim at risk of further offending.[125]

Turning to public protection in a more general sense, of great public concern are those defendants remanded on bail who are found to have committed offences during the period of remand. A study by Morgan and Henderson of some 2,300 bail cases in 1993–4 found that 17 per cent of those bailed by the courts were convicted of an offence committed during the period of bail.[126] Where an offence was committed on bail, it was particularly likely to be the same type of offence as originally charged if that charge was theft or handling (54 per cent), burglary (46 per cent), or a serious motoring offence (35 per cent).[127] As the Ministry of Justice itself states, the overwhelming majority of people bailed do not reoffend.[128] Moreover, between 2010 and 2014 the number of offenders convicted of committing any offence while on bail fell 48 per cent from 69,348 to 36,053. Most notably, 20 per cent of burglaries in 2010 were committed by someone on bail, but this fell steadily to 13 per cent in 2014.[129] Murders committed by persons on bail have been stable at around 11 per cent, though this fell to 6 per cent

[121] Ministry of Justice, *Code of Practice for Victims of Crime* (2015), para 1.5, section 2, https://www.cps.gov.uk/sites/default/files/documents/legal_guidance/OD_000049.pdf.
[122] CPS, *Policy on Prosecuting Cases of Domestic Violence*, Part 7.
[123] Criminal Justice Act 2003, s 18, amending the Bail (Amendment) Act 1993.
[124] J. Roberts and M. Manikis, *Victim Personal Statements: A Review of Empirical Research* (2011), 10.
[125] HMIC and HMCPSI, *Living in fear—the police and CPS response to harassment and stalking A joint inspection by HMIC and HMCPSI* (2017), 86.
[126] Morgan and Henderson, n 44, 44.   [127] Ibid, 46.
[128] Ministry of Justice, FOI Request ref: FOI/97753, 11 August 2015.   [129] Ibid, Table 2.

in 2014. Rapes committed by persons on bail have been stable at around 5 per cent, and fell to 2 per cent in 2014.

If public protection is to be an important purpose of the bail/custody decision, then there is a need to focus on two distinct issues. The first is whether we can predict with sufficient accuracy which offenders are more likely to offend on bail than not: the Home Office is not optimistic about this,[130] and in view of the relatively low percentage of bailed defendants proved to offend on bail this is hardly surprising. Even if the general predictive tools were more accurate, the focus ought then to be on the offences committed on bail. If the majority happen to be offences of theft or car crime, this prompts the question whether custodial remands are appropriate in these cases. It has been argued earlier that other means of restricting those whose offending behaviour is not conspicuously serious should be tried. It is important not to move directly from regarding 'offending on bail' as a problem, which it is, to regarding the use of custody as an appropriate or (in more than the short term) effective remedy. Indeed, it seems that the easiest offences to predict are likely to be lower on the scale of seriousness, raising doubts about the justification for remands in custody to prevent them.

This makes the connection between the failures of remands on bail and the failures of remands in custody. Is the public best protected by the extensive use of custodial remands? It is true that custodial remand represents a guarantee that the defendant will not commit offences against most members of the public (except, of course, those who are in prison either on conviction or on remand themselves). But deprivation of liberty remains, in principle, an incursion into a person's rights and that requires strong justification. Protecting a person against threats of violence may (in the absence of conditions that would be effective) be a sufficient reason for custodial remand. But we should ask whether protecting the public against theft or car crime is sufficient to outweigh this fundamental right. Moreover, we should recall the discussion in section 8.3 of this chapter, where it was shown that one-quarter of those remanded in custody are not convicted, and that around one-quarter receive non-custodial sentences. For the reasons there discussed, this raises serious questions about the need, from the point of view of public safety, to remand so many people in custody before trial.

8.5 PROCEDURAL JUSTICE AND REMAND DECISIONS

We now move on to consider four aspects of procedure relevant to the fairness of remand decisions—access to legal advice; bail information schemes; the speed of court hearings; and appeals.

---

[130] Morgan and Henderson, n 44, 60; Morgan and Henderson's study reports on an initiative to reduce offending on bail which had only mixed results.

(A) ACCESS TO LEGAL ADVICE AND ASSISTANCE

The ECtHR has insisted that a person should have a right to legal assistance before being deprived of liberty, especially before trial.[131] English law contains various provisions to ensure access to legal advice, both on arrest and detention and then during any custodial remand. That said, there is no provision for mandatory representation, even for young people.[132] Moreover, in practice the path towards provision of this access is not always smooth. Young remand prisoners have practical difficulties contacting their lawyers, and lawyers have practical difficulties in arranging visits to prisons, particularly within the constraints of their other obligations.[133] The geographical dispersal of women's prisons creates difficulties in meeting solicitors.[134] In view of the importance of such contacts to the preparation of a defence, and thus to respecting the right declared in Art 6(3)(b), this may amount to a significant handicap to those remanded in custody. The provision of legal advice at the police station is generally better, but the conditions for giving and receiving legal advice are not always sufficient to satisfy the Convention (e.g. by telephone within earshot of police officers).[135] Strasbourg decisions on the Convention have helped to produce a recognition that there is a duty on the prosecution to make some disclosure to the defence before bail hearings, in order to satisfy the principle of equality of arms that is established as an element of the right to a fair trial.[136] The Attorney General's Guidelines on Disclosure state that 'disclosure ought to be made of significant information that might affect a bail decision',[137] although the extent of compliance with this guidance is not known.

(B) BAIL INFORMATION SCHEMES

The problem for remand courts of obtaining relevant and verified information has been recognized for some time. If remand decision makers have insufficient information on the defendant's personal and social situation, the possibility of advancing cogent grounds for conditional or unconditional bail is diminished. The Vera Institute of Justice began programmes in the United States in the early 1960s, aimed at supplying courts with some objective data on which they could base their decisions, in particular data about the defendant's 'community ties'.[138] The idea was taken up in England and

---

[131] Emmerson, Ashworth, and Macdonald, *Human Rights and Criminal Justice*, n 4, 8–104.

[132] Cape and Smith, n 52, 3.2.

[133] See the research summarized in F. Brookman and H. Pierpoint, 'Access to Legal Advice for Young Suspects and Remand Prisoners' (2003) 42 *Howard JCJ* 452, 460–3.

[134] Player, 'Remanding Women in Custody', n 5, 423–5.

[135] Compare the strong statement of principle and its application in *Brennan v UK* (2002) 34 EHRR 18, with the unsatisfactory domestic decision in *M and La Rose v Metropolitan Police Commissioner* [2002] *Crim LR* 215.

[136] E.g. *Nikolova v Bulgaria* (1999) 31 EHRR 64; *R v DPP, ex p Lee* [1999] 2 All ER 237.

[137] *Attorney General's Guidelines on Disclosure* (2013), [14]; see CPS, *Disclosure Manual* (2018) 8; also Law Com 269, *Bail and the Human Rights Act 1998*.

[138] See Jones and Goldkamp, n 16, 1404.

Wales by the London office of the Vera Institute of Justice.[139] Since then, bail information schemes (BIS) have spread slowly to become part of the system, in both prisons
and courts. Not surprisingly, however, the quality of provision is variable.[140]

BIS aim to enable the court to make better informed bail decisions, with the possibility of reducing the number of defendants held in custody awaiting trial.[141] These
schemes exist to provide factual information about the bail decision such as specific
concerns expressed in opposition to bail, as well as drawing attention to the defendant's
character, antecedents, and community ties.[142] Lord Woolf heralded the use of BIS as a
great success in reducing the number of remand prisoners,[143] though it is more likely
that they have a limited bearing on remand decisions. The reason behind the majority
of decisions to remand in custody is the second statutory ground, the likelihood that
the defendant would commit an offence whilst on bail; BIS are not concerned principally with this ground or this group of defendants, although they may sometimes yield
information that enables a case to be made for conditional bail. Given the many other
elements in bail decisions, it may be that BIS have limited added value, but increase the
confidence of courts in their chosen outcomes.[144] Moreover, a HMIP review in 2012
of 33 local prisons found that few remand prisoners knew about the Bail Information
Officer at their establishment, and nearly half reported difficulties with obtaining bail
information.[145] Bail services varied considerably between prisons and in many cases
were not visible or active enough to ensure all who needed the support received it.[146]

(C) SPEED AND DELAY

The police are the first agency to deal with those who are arrested, and, as we have
seen, they take an initial decision whether to detain the defendant in custody pending
the court appearance or to grant police bail. The CPS is responsible for making representations to the court about bail, but in many cases the prosecutor is likely to receive
a large pile of case files on arrival at work in the morning (consisting of 'overnight
arrests' by the police) and will have to present these cases to the court that very morning. The prosecutor is therefore reliant on form MG7 prepared by the police, which
makes it particularly important that the police record details of the grounds for any
objection to bail that is proposed.[147] Indeed, Cape and Smith recommend improved
training for the police so that the summaries that they provide to the prosecution are
fair and objective.[148]

---

[139] C. Stone, *Bail Information for the Crown Prosecution Service* (1988).

[140] See the discussion of schemes in women's prisons by Player, 'Remanding Women in Custody', n 5, 424.

[141] HM Prison Service Order, *Bail Information Scheme*, Order Number 6101 (2013), 3.2.1.

[142] Ibid, 3.1.1.   [143] Lord Woolf, n 72.

[144] See the experimental research by M. Dhami, 'Do Bail Information Schemes Really Affect Bail Decisions?' (2002) 41 *Howard JCJ* 245.

[145] HMIP, n 86, 8.   [146] Ibid.   [147] Moreno and Hughes, n 31, 233–9.

[148] Cape and Smith, n 52, 116.

Prior to the remand hearing there is unlikely to be much time for a detached review of the evidence in the case. However, there is evidence that the CPS do not merely follow police decision making: research by Morgan and Henderson in 1993–4 shows that, in respect of some 1,500 defendants refused police bail and held in custody overnight, the CPS recommended a custodial remand in only 48 per cent of cases, conditional bail in a further 46 per cent of cases, and unconditional bail in 6 per cent.[149] This suggests that, despite the speed at which decisions have to be taken, a degree of independent judgement is brought to bear.

The brevity of the hearings themselves has long given cause for concern, in view of the momentous consequence of loss of liberty in some cases. It seems that many magistrates make bail decisions in a few minutes,[150] and training of magistrates in this respect still needs to be improved.[151]

No less important is the time taken to complete cases: ECHR jurisprudence requires 'particular expedition' where a person is being held in custody.[152] Figures from 2002 showed 450 prisoners on remand for more than 12 months, and a further 900 on remand for 6–12 months.[153] Comparable figures appear not to be given in the more recent statistics;[154] but insofar as some remand prisoners are held for such periods, this may involve breaches of Art 5(3).

(D) APPEALS AND REAPPLICATIONS

When a court refuses bail or attaches conditions to it, there is an obligation to state the ground(s) on which the court relies and to give reasons for bringing the case within that ground.[155] A defendant who is refused bail by a magistrates' court may make a reapplication to a judge in chambers. Correspondingly, the Bail (Amendment) Act 1993 introduced a prosecution power to appeal to a judge against the grant of bail by a magistrates' court in the face of representations by the prosecution, and the Criminal Justice Act 2003 extended that power to all imprisonable offences. The case for a defence right of reapplication is unanswerable in view of the enormity of the consequences of a decision to remand in custody. The case for a prosecution power of appeal is strong in cases where there is thought to be a clear danger to individuals if the defendant is granted liberty. Unless the power is shown to be used oppressively, it surely has a proper place in criminal procedure.

---

[149] Morgan and Henderson, n 44, 37.

[150] M. Dhami, 'Conditional Bail Decision-Making in the Magistrates' Court' (2004) 43 *Howard JCJ* 27, 28; Cape and Smith, n 52, 53.

[151] Cape and Smith, n 52, 9. The House of Commons Justice Committee spoke of serious problems with magistracy training, though there was no consideration of bail specifically in this report: House of Commons Justice Committee, *The role of the magistracy*, Sixth Report of Session 2016–17 (2016), [126].

[152] E.g. *Reid v UK* (2003) 37 EHRR 9, [78].   [153] *Prison Statistics 2002*, Table 2.5.

[154] Ministry of Justice, *Offender Management Caseload Statistics 2007* (2008).

[155] Bail Act 1976, s 5(3); for low rates of compliance in the early 1990s, see A. Hucklesby, 'Bail or Jail? The Practical Operation of the Bail Act 1976' (1996) 23 *JLS* 213—reasons only given for custodial remands in 47 per cent of cases.

8.6 EQUAL TREATMENT IN REMAND DECISIONS

To what extent do remand decisions appear to discriminate against certain sections of the population? To what extent do they fail to recognize the special needs of certain groups? These questions warrant considerable discussion in their own right, and it is possible only to give some general indications here.

The findings of research into the impact of race on remand decisions prompt questions about discrimination. In his study of over 3,000 cases, Roger Hood found that a higher proportion of defendants from an Afro-Caribbean background (26 per cent) than Whites (20 per cent) were remanded in custody pending trial and that, even after taking account of variations in the key facts of individual cases, some apparent discrimination remained.[156] The John Report found that the CPS opposed bail more frequently for African-Caribbeans than for other groups of defendants, especially on the ground of the risk of obstructing justice. File endorsements did not disclose the evidential foundations for many of the recommendations, suggesting that information from the police may have been passed on orally. The report concludes that it is probable that racial stereotyping was influencing some of these decisions.[157] In relation to young arrestees, Feilzer and Hood found higher rates of remand into secure conditions among black (10 per cent) and mixed parentage (13 per cent) young males than among those who were white (8 per cent) or from Asian or other ethnic groups (6 per cent). Moreover, 'as many as a third of cases where a black male had been remanded in custody failed to result in conviction, compared with one in five cases involving white males'.[158] A related issue was that the proportion of foreign nationals is significantly higher among remand prisoners (19 per cent) than sentenced prisoners (11 per cent).[159]

There is limited evidence of improvement. In 2016, Black and Mixed defendants were 23 per cent and 18 per cent more likely than White defendants to be remanded in custody in Crown Court for indictable offences,[160] a situation that warrants further analysis.[161] Thirty-five per cent of White defendants at the Crown Court were remanded in custody, compared with 43 per cent and 41 per cent of Black and Mixed defendants respectively.[162] A study from the Youth Justice Board in 2014–15 identified that Black, Asian, and Minority ethnic (BAME), and specifically black children, were more likely to be remanded to youth detention than their white counterparts.[163]

---

[156] R. Hood, *Race and Sentencing* (1992), 146–50; see also M. Fitzgerald, *Ethnic Minorities and the Criminal Justice System* (1993), 19–21.

[157] The Gus John Partnership, *Race for Justice: A review of CPS decision making for possible racial bias at each stage of the prosecution process* (2003), paras 16 and 28; for similar suggestions in Canada, see G. Kellough and S. Wortley, n 111, 196.

[158] M. Feilzer and R. Hood, *Differences or Discrimination?* (Youth Justice Board, 2004).

[159] Player et al, n 88.

[160] Ministry of Justice, *Statistics on Race and the Criminal Justice System 2016* (2017), 8.

[161] Ministry of Justice, *Black, Asian and Minority Ethnic disproportionality in the Criminal Justice System in England and Wales* (2016), 19.

[162] Ministry of Justice, *Statistics on Race and the Criminal Justice System 2016*, n 160, 49.   [163] Ibid, 60.

Overall, Lammy described remand decisions as a 'blindspot', recommending that the Ministry of Justice take steps to address key data gaps as part of a more detailed examination of magistrates' verdicts, with a particular focus on those affecting BAME women.[164]

Whereas the number of males on remand has remained relatively steady, by 2010 the number of women held on remand had increased by some 80 per cent,[165] though both rates are now decreasing comparably.[166] A higher proportion of the female prison population is on remand than the male prison population (15 compared with 11 per cent). Can these figures be justified by reference to the relative seriousness of the offences? Apparently not: some 20 per cent of women remandees were charged with offences of sex or violence, compared with 33 per cent for men. The largest single category for remanded women was drugs offences, and a smaller proportion of remanded women are sentenced to custody.[167] It is a serious cause for concern that fewer than half of women remanded in custody are thought to require a custodial sentence. The 'culture of neglect' to which Elaine Player has referred needs to be addressed with urgency.[168]

Special arrangements for the remand of mentally disordered defendants were introduced by the Mental Health Act 1983.[169] '[R]emands in custody [are] not only an inhumane, but an ineffective way of securing help and care for disturbed people',[170] and remand may exacerbate or cause mental health problems. Remand prisoners are at an increased risk of suicide and self-harm: nearly one-quarter of remand prisoners in HMIP's survey said they had felt depressed or suicidal when they arrived at prison, over three-quarters reported a welfare problem on arrival, and one-third or more said they had a drug or mental health problem.[171] Untried remand prisoners account for a disproportionate number of self-inflicted deaths and self-harm in prison custody: in 1999, 44 of the 91 self-inflicted deaths in prison custody were untried remand prisoners, in 2016 the figures were 24 of 122, and 2017 10 of 70.[172] By far, the vast majority of these deaths are men. In terms of self harm, in 2017 2,987 incidents were untried remand prisoners from a total of 44,651; 2,225 were men, and 762 women.[173]

Mental problems connected with substance abuse are a major concern.[174] Research by Plugge, Douglas, and Fitzpatrick found high levels of drug misuse among female remand prisoners, with half of them using heroin daily prior to their remand to prison.[175] They also found that the health of addicts improved during their stay

---

[164] The Lammy Review, *An independent review into the treatment of, and outcomes for, Black, Asian and Minority Ethnic individuals in the Criminal Justice System* (2017), 33.

[165] Player et al, n 88.   [166] Ministry of Justice, *Offender Management Statistics Bulletin 2017* (2018), 3.

[167] Ibid.   [168] Player, 'Remanding Women in Custody', n 5, 403, 425.

[169] See Ministry of Justice, *Mental Health Act 2007: Guidance for courts on remand and sentencing powers for mentally disordered offenders* (2008).

[170] G. Robertson, S. Dell, A. Grounds, and K. James, 'Mentally Disordered Remand Prisoners' (1992) 32 Home Office Research Bulletin 1.

[171] HMIP, n 86, 7.   [172] Ministry of Justice, *Self harm in prison custody* (2017), Table 1.11.

[173] Ibid, Table 2.6.

[174] HMIP, n 86, 43. D. Brooke, C. Taylor, J. Gunn, and A. Maden, 'Substance Misuse as a Marker of Vulnerability Among Male Prisoners on Remand' (2000) 177 *BJ Psychiatry* 248.

[175] E. Plugge, N. Douglas, and R. Fitzpatrick, *The Health of Women in Prison* (2006).

in prison, raising the possibility that courts were remanding some of these women in custody not by applying the statutory criteria but in order to give them access to healthcare which was unavailable or less effective in the community. This is deeply troubling and problematic.[176]

8.7 CONCLUSION

The starting point for discussion of remands should be Art 5 of the ECHR, which declares the right to liberty, and Art 6(2), which declares the presumption of innocence.[177] Detention without trial is objectionable in principle, because it negatives these rights. There are two ways of constructing a justification for depriving a defendant of these rights. The first is to argue that there is a distinct risk to the rights of another person: this may arise if the defendant has been charged with assaulting someone and there is evidence to suggest a risk of further violence (as is sometimes the case in domestic or other interpersonal abuse). Alternatively, it may arise where there is reason to believe that the defendant will threaten someone, especially a victim-complainant or witness. Previous threats could provide sufficient evidence. What emerges clearly is that such decisions should involve both principled reasoning and an assessment of risk. Although in practice much attention is often focused on risk, on the basis of submissions made by the prosecution or police, the issue of principle is no less critical. If the right to liberty is to be taken seriously, courts that do find a significant risk must still strive to preserve the defendant's liberty by seeking non-custodial means of responding to the risk through conditional bail.

A second strand of justification refers to overwhelming reasons of public interest. We have questioned the origins, nature, and strength of this public interest in the possible pre-trial conduct of persons who are presumed innocent,[178] but it seems to be a feature of many legal systems that the presumption of innocence weakens once a person has been charged by a public prosecutor. One element is the public interest in ensuring that defendants who have been charged attend their trials. Although it would be difficult to deny some such interest, it is questionable whether it is strong enough to justify taking away a person's liberty, particularly when the offence charged is not of the highest seriousness and absconding is not a certainty but a greater or lesser probability. This is, par excellence, a sphere in which non-custodial methods of securing attendance like electronic tagging are valuable.[179]

Another element of public interest may be that of minimizing the number of offences committed by persons on bail. The foundations of this interest were discussed critically in section 8.1, and the re-enactment of a provision requiring courts to treat offending on bail as an aggravating factor in sentencing demonstrates the political force of this concern.[180] However, the Bail Act's reference simply to the probability of committing

[176] As argued by Player et al, n 88.   [177] See Player, 'Remanding Women in Custody', n 5.
[178] See section 8.1.   [179] See n 41.   [180] Criminal Justice Act 2003, s 143(3).

'an offence' whilst on bail is much too weak. At the very least, the law should insist that the prosecution has satisfied the court that there is sufficient evidence against the defendant on the charge laid, and that the person is granted conditional bail only if there are good reasons against unconditional bail.

Once again, however, interacting with these issues of principle is the practical problem of risk assessment. In order to determine whether it is more likely than not that this defendant will commit an offence likely to result in imprisonment if granted bail, algorithms for the prediction of offending have been developed, such as the Harm Assessment Risk Tool being tested by Durham Constabulary.[181] In addition, research in the United States by Goldkamp and Gottfredson contains some useful pointers—for example, that reoffending and non-appearance at trial are highly correlated so that to predict one is usually to predict the other; and that bailees are more likely to offend the longer the period awaiting trial[182]—but it remains true that the number of false positives would be high. The scattered research in England suggests the same, as we saw earlier: it is easy to say that people charged with taking cars are the group most likely to offend on bail, but most of them are not in fact detected in law-breaking whilst on bail. Similarly, it is easy to claim that courts should have greater regard to objections to bail advanced by the police, but the vast majority of those to whom the court grants bail in the face of police objections are not detected in law-breaking whilst on bail.[183]

None of these observations breaks new ground, and yet their significance for bail has been accorded little attention. Thousands of people are being deprived of their liberty every year on the basis of predictions which have insecure statistical foundations. All the criminological evidence in analogous fields points to the likelihood of considerable over-prediction. If, as argued here, the primary concern is to prevent the commission of *serious* crimes in the period between arrest and trial, that makes the problem of protection harder, not easier. Serious crimes are rarer and therefore more difficult to predict than law-breaking in general, and the rate of false positives may well be very high.[184]

At a time when remand policies are inconsistent in terms of principle, and animated mostly by concerns about prison population rather than the treatment and dignity of the unconvicted, it is essential to reassert fundamental principles: the courts should operate with a strong presumption in favour of liberty and innocence; this ought not to be displaced unless the court is satisfied that there is sufficient evidence to continue with the charge, a test which should become stricter as time progresses and should require careful judgements by the CPS. The court's decision on the form of remand

---

[181] See https://www.bbc.co.uk/news/technology-39857645; http://data.parliament.uk/writtenevidence/committeeevidence.svc/evidencedocument/science-and-technology-committee/algorithms-in-decisionmaking/written/69063.html.

[182] J. Goldkamp and M. R. Gottfredson, *Policy Guidelines for Bail: An Exercise in Court Reform* (1985), based on research in Philadelphia courts.

[183] See n 126 and accompanying text.

[184] For a brief summary of the research on identifying dangerous offenders, see A. Ashworth, *Sentencing and Criminal Justice* (5th edn, 2010), ch 6.8.

should be governed by a statutory framework or by guidelines similar to those for sentencing.[185] In principle, there should be progressive levels of justification, and preferred disposals with reasons required for departing from them.[186] The preferred disposal should be unconditional bail. There should be evidence-based reasons for moving to the next level, conditional bail. The next step up, to remand in custody, should only be taken where the court is satisfied that the charge, if proved at the trial, would be likely to result in the imposition of a custodial sentence and where the evidence for the chosen ground for refusing bail is clear and convincing. Even then, the court should first consider whether conditional bail with a requirement of electronic monitoring would be adequate. If a court decides that a custodial remand is unavoidable, it should be for as short a period as possible. English law does have mechanisms to ensure this, including time limits for cases where the defendant is remanded in custody,[187] but some defendants still spend more than six months (and a few more than 12 months) awaiting their trials in custody.[188] Although waiting times are longer in most other European countries, this does not excuse long delays when they occur.

In conclusion, we make five points about remand decisions. First, they rely to a large extent on predictions, and the evidential foundations are rarely strong. That ought to counsel great caution: although it is common these days to refer to risk, public protection, and public safety, this should not be allowed to conceal the fragility of many of these predictions. Secondly, the Convention framework as developed by the ECtHR ought to be used instead of the more common references to 'balancing' the defendant's right to liberty against the need for public protection. In principle, the right to liberty should be respected, and only if there is strong evidence should one of the recognized exceptions be allowed to prevail. Moreover, the ECtHR has emphasized the evidential basis for and the seriousness of the charge. Thirdly, there must be greater willingness among decision makers to question the decisions taken previously in each case, and to reappraise the evidence and the approach to be taken. In particular, the CPS must be prepared to conduct a meaningful review of the police conclusion, and the court should likewise conduct a meaningful review of the CPS recommendation. Such changes will require alterations to the system as well as more resources, since decision makers cannot be expected to reach different decisions without (1) a little more time and (2) fresh information. Fourthly, the question of police remands must be revisited. It seems to be assumed that the only practical approach to deciding bail/custody decisions prior to a court appearance is to leave these to the police. However, that gives them considerable (bargaining) power over suspects, and a decision to refuse bail has strong correlations with subsequent decisions about loss of liberty. The question of conferring this power on a senior member of the CPS should be revisited urgently. And fifthly, courts must

---

[185] For similar proposals, see Dhami (n 117) and Player (n 5).

[186] Cf P. Robinson, 'Punishing Dangerousness: Cloaking Preventive Detention as Criminal Justice' (2001) 114 *Harvard LR* 1429, 1447.

[187] Corre and Wolchover, n 34, ch 12.

[188] See n 144 and accompanying text.

(continue to) adopt a more legalistic and rights-responsive approach to remand decisions. The right to liberty and the presumption of innocence should become part of the everyday currency of the courts, to make it clear how exceptional a remand in custody should be.[189] This has little to do with overcrowding in the prisons: even if there were many available places in the prisons, the argument for remanding an accused person in custody ought to be a strong one. The remand issue is not a prisons problem, so much as a justice problem. At the same time, and for the same reason, efforts to develop non-custodial facilities for holding defendants in the community must be redoubled.

FURTHER READING

CAPE, E. and SMITH, T., *The practice of pre-trial detention in England and Wales: research report*, Bristol: University of the West of England, 2016.

HUCKLESBY, A., *Bail Support Schemes for Adults*, Bristol: Polity Press, 2011.

PLAYER, E., 'Remanding Women in Custody: Concerns for Human Rights' (2007) 70 *MLR* 402.

QUESTIONS FOR DISCUSSION

1. Are there grounds for concern about the number of people remanded in custody who are subsequently acquitted or convicted and given a non-custodial sentence?

2. Does the English system respect the rights of defendants who have been charged but not convicted?

3. Should bail be refused in cases where a custodial sentence on conviction would be unlikely?

---

[189] A. Ashworth and L. Zedner, *Preventive Justice* (2014), 73.

9

PRE-TRIAL ISSUES: DISCLOSURE AND ABUSE OF PROCESS

As a case proceeds to court, certain measures need to be in place to ensure an effective trial. Much of this will be the prerogative and decision of the parties, who will prepare their trial strategies, ensure that witnesses are called, and so on. But not everything can be left to the parties: procedural mechanisms seek to ensure that the eventual trial runs efficiently and fairly. In this chapter, we consider some of these rules. In terms of facilitating the smooth running of the trial, we concentrate on ways of screening cases and clarifying some of the issues prior to trial. The disclosure of evidence is a fraught matter in this regard, with an impact on fairness as well as efficiency. In terms of ensuring that the defendant is not subjected to an unfair trial, we examine some questions that arise under the broad heading of abuse of process, concentrating on delay and entrapment.

9.1 FILTERING CASES PRIOR TO TRIAL

In preceding chapters it has been stressed that individuals should not face trial without good justification. This is partly because of the financial cost; partly because of the distress and inconvenience for defendants; and partly to protect the innocent from mistaken conviction. Thus, at different stages of the criminal process, there are evidential barriers to filter out weak cases. There must be 'sufficient evidence' before a defendant is charged,[1] the prosecuting body must determine that there is a reasonable prospect of conviction before taking a case to court, and prosecution must be in the public interest.[2] Even when the trial has commenced, there are evidential barriers to ensure that the defendant is not put in jeopardy of conviction without good reason. In the Crown Court, the judge should not let the case go to the jury unless there is sufficient evidence to enable a jury to find the crime charged to be proved beyond reasonable doubt;[3] there is a similar test in summary trial.

---

[1] See Ch 5 and E. Cape, 'Sufficient Evidence to Charge?' [1999] *Crim LR* 874.   [2] See Ch 7.
[3] *R v Galbraith* [1981] 1 WLR 1039, discussed in Ch 11.

Criminal cases start in the magistrates' court, where issues such as bail can be given a speedy initial determination (see Chapter 8), though the more serious criminal cases will be tried in the Crown Court. Historically, 'committal' proceedings were used to allow defendants to claim that there was insufficient evidence to justify bringing their case to trial.[4] Committal was abolished eventually for cases triable only on indictment in 2001,[5] and for either way offences by the Criminal Justice Act (CJA) 2003,[6] though it was more than a decade before these provisions were brought into force.[7] Now, if the magistrates' court decides that it would not have the power to try a cases it is transferred to the jurisdiction of the Crown Court by a relatively simple allocative mechanism, and defendants are likely to wait for the trial proper before arguing that the prosecution case is weak.

The current procedures for transferring cases to the Crown Court are, in outline, as follows. There is an initial hearing in the magistrates' court to decide the question of bail. In either way offences, there will also be a mode of trial hearing, and then, if the case is to be tried on indictment, it is transferred to the Crown Court. The defendant can apply to the Crown Court to have the case against him dismissed.[8] The judge has discretion whether or not to hear oral evidence on the application. He should dismiss the case against the accused if he considers the prosecution does not have enough evidence to enable a reasonable jury to convict.[9]

We turn now to consider the disclosure of evidence, and then the concept of abuse of process.

9.2 PRE-TRIAL DISCLOSURE

Disclosure of evidence before trial is a matter of great importance, and one of enduring controversy. From the point of view of efficiency, trials run most smoothly when each side has notice of the evidence and arguments that the opposing side will present at trial. But there are serious issues of justice at stake here also. Non-disclosure of prosecution evidence was a common factor in many of the miscarriage of justice cases of the late 1980s and early 1990s, and comparable concerns remain, not least given the increase in communications and digital data, the tightening of resources for criminal justice agencies, and the variable standards in police training and practice. Failures in prosecution disclosure continue to be a frequent ground of appeal to the Court

---

[4] The mechanism for doing so used to be the institution of the grand jury, until its abolition in 1930, so for much of the last century defendants used 'committal proceedings' before magistrates to argue against the case proceeding to jury trial.

[5] Crime and Disorder Act 1998, s 51.   [6] s 41 and Sch 3.

[7] Criminal Justice Act 2003 (Commencement No 28 and Saving Provisions) Order 2012 (SI 2012/1320).

[8] Crime and Disorder Act 1988, Sch 3; Crime and Disorder Act 1998 (Dismissal of Charges Sent) Rules 1998 (SI 1998/3048).

[9] For more detail, see *Blackstone's Criminal Practice 2018*, D10.

of Appeal, which has noted that it hears 'countless' cases on the issue.[10] Many cases referred to the court by the Criminal Cases Review Commission involve disclosure issues,[11] a point it emphasizes repeatedly.[12]

Failures of disclosure were at the core of *R v Mouncher and Others*, the case of 'The Cardiff Five' where three men were convicted wrongly of the murder in 1988 of Lynette White. The Court of Appeal quashed the convictions in 1992 on the basis that an in-criminating confession had been obtained by bullying, hostility, and intimidation. A review by HM Crown Prosecution Service Inspectorate (HMCPSI) in 2013 concluded that the prosecution had taken too narrow an approach to the disclosure test, and over-analysed the potential defence cases, which delayed disclosure of some material that could have assisted.[13] There was a failure of case management, particularly a lack of supervision of inexperienced disclosure counsel, as well as a failure to comply with the Disclosure Manual of the Crown Prosecution Service (CPS). A subsequent review, which had a broader remit in investigating the conduct of police officers assigned to the *Mouncher* inquiry, concluded that there should be national minimum standards for accrediting disclosure officers and a national training regime to eliminate regional differences.[14] The abiding principle must be: 'if in doubt disclose'.[15] The report stressed that 'the experience of Mouncher shows that disclosure failings, and in particular the most damaging failings, need not be complex'.[16]

Concerns about disclosure have not been resolved or, some would say, even addressed. A joint report by HMCPSI and HM Inspectorate of Constabulary (HMIC) in 2017 identified 'widespread failures' in this respect,[17] and later that year a number of high-profile media reports focused on the collapse of criminal cases due to failings in disclosure. This prompted a House of Commons Justice Committee inquiry,[18] and a number of separate reviews both on individual cases and sexual offences more widely.[19] The Justice Committee expressed disappointment at how long these problems

---

[10] *R v Pomfrett* [2009] EWCA Crim 1471, [4]. See further *R v Giles* [2009] EWCA Crim 1388; *R v Zengeya* [2009] EWCA Crim 1369; *Tucker v CPS* [2008] EWCA Crim 1368.

[11] See L. Elks, *Righting Miscarriages of Justice? Ten Years of the Criminal Cases Review Commission* (2008), 309–11.

[12] E.g. Criminal Cases Review Commission, *Annual Report and Accounts 2017/18* (2018), 7; *Annual Report and Accounts 2016/17* (2017), 3 and 34; also 'Text of letter sent 5 July 2016 from CCRC Chair Richard Foster to DPP, Attorney General and others': https://ccrc.gov.uk/text-of-letter-sent-5-july-2016-from-ccrc-chair-richard-foster-to-dpp-attorney-general-and-others/.

[13] HMCPSI, *Review into the Disclosure handling in the case of R v Mouncher and Others* (2013).

[14] R. Horwell, *Mouncher Investigation Report* (2017), para 24.11.   [15] Ibid.   [16] Ibid, 24.12.

[17] HMCPSI and HMIC, *Making It Fair: A Joint Inspection of the Disclosure of Unused Material in Volume Crown Court Cases* (2017), https://www.justiceinspectorates.gov.uk/cjji/inspections/making-it-fair-the-disclosure-of-unused-material-in-volume-crown-court-cases/.

[18] House of Commons Justice Committee, *Disclosure of evidence in criminal cases*, Eleventh Report of Session 2017–19, HC 859 (2018).

[19] CPS and Metropolitan Police Service, *The joint review of the disclosure process in the case of R v Allan* (2018), https://www.cps.gov.uk/sites/default/files/documents/publications/joint-review-disclosure-Allan.pdf; https://www.cps.gov.uk/cps/news/cps-publishes-outcome-sexual-offences-review; see T. Smith, 'The "Near Miss" of Liam Allan: Critical Problems in Police Disclosure, Investigation Culture and the Resourcing of Criminal Justice' [2018] *Crim LR* 711.

have endured, worsening under the former Attorney General's watch and that of the Director of Public Prosecutions (DPP).[20] Though resource was not the only issue, the Committee felt that additional resourcing must be considered.[21] Overall, the matters raised in the inquiry were seen as symptomatic of a criminal justice system under significant strain.[22] The Committee was particularly concerned that defence practitioners are not remunerated for reviewing unused material, and about the impact of reduced payment for reviewing prosecution evidence.[23] The Committee viewed the problems with disclosure as impacting on confidence in the justice system to such an extent that it is now an issue of national importance for the police.[24]

In addition to prosecution and police disclosure, which suffers from deep-seated issues, some degree of disclosure by the defence may be required to preclude or offset so-called 'ambush' defences which could not be rebutted. Imposing such a duty also entails imposing a degree of participation and cooperation that is at odds with traditional adversarial principles.

(A) PROSECUTION DISCLOSURE

There is a basic requirement that the prosecution disclose its case prior to trial. Rule 8.2 of the Criminal Procedure Rules (CPR) requires the prosecutor to provide initial details of the prosecution case as soon as practicable and no later than the beginning of the day of the first hearing in the magistrates' court, regardless of where the offence will be tried. The required content of the initial details, as outlined in r 8.3, is not extensive: prosecutors must disclose details of circumstances of the offence and the criminal record of the defendant if he is brought to court in custody, and otherwise a summary of the circumstances of the offence, any account given by the defendant in interview, any material and available written witness statement or exhibit, the defendant's criminal record, if any, and any available statement of the effect of the offence on a victim, a victim's family, or others. If the prosecutor wants to introduce information contained in a document listed in r 8.3 without making it available to the defendant, the court must allow the defendant sufficient time to consider it.[25] Now nearly all magistrates' courts are able to receive digitally from the CPS the initial details of the prosecution case,[26] though serious questions remain about the reliability of these IT systems.[27] Moreover, the advent of digital service poses problems in terms of providing unrepresented defendants with their papers.[28]

The foregoing deals with advance notice of the evidence the prosecution intends to call at trial. What of evidence that it does not intend to call? If, for example, a witness interviewed by the police fails to support the prosecution's version of events, it is

---

[20] House of Commons Justice Committee, n 18, 26.   [21] Ibid, 48.   [22] Ibid, 50.   [23] Ibid, 50.
[24] Ibid, 110.   [25] CPR, r 8.4.
[26] HMCPSI and HMIC, *Delivering Justice in a Digital Age: A Joint Inspection of Digital Case Preparation and Presentation in the Criminal Justice System* (2016), para 1.18.
[27] Ibid, 1.27.
[28] HMCPSI, *Business as Usual? Transforming Summary Justice Follow-up Report* (2017), 1.22.

unlikely that the prosecution would choose to call that person at trial. Yet knowledge of what the witness said might be of considerable importance to the defence. Rules requiring disclosure of such unused material were developed gradually by the courts,[29] and in 1996 were put on a statutory footing. The Criminal Procedure and Investigations Act 1996 (CPIA), along with the Code of Practice issued under it, laid out in some detail how prosecution disclosure should be managed and what tests should be applied to determine whether material should be disclosed. Aspects of the regime were modified by the CJA 2003,[30] and have been supplemented since by the CPR, the Judicial Protocol, and separate pieces of guidance from the CPS, the Attorney General, and the Ministry of Justice.

The principles that should apply to prosecution disclosure are reasonably straightforward. The defence has a right to disclosure of all relevant evidence; so, the prosecution should be seen as the trustee, rather than the owner, of any information gathered during the police investigation.[31] The European Commission of Human Rights expressed a similar idea in terms of equality of arms: the state's superior resources mean that the defence should have access to all relevant evidence that has been or could be gathered by the prosecution.[32] The CPIA attempts to put these principles into effect by placing an obligation on the police to list and describe unused material in a 'schedule'.[33] This schedule is crucial, as it forms the basis for prosecution decisions as to what material should be disclosed to the defence; the schedule itself is disclosed to the defence, and thus represents the primary means by which the defence can make a claim that relevant material has not been disclosed. Any material which 'might reasonably be considered capable of undermining the case for the prosecution against the accused or of assisting the case for the accused'[34] should be disclosed to the defence, and this determination should be kept under review.[35] Thus, as the facts change, and as more is learned about the defence case, further material may fall within the scope of s 3 and thereby require disclosure. As the CPS Disclosure Manual states, 'It is essential that [disclosure] is dealt with competently and fairly, ensuring a thinking approach throughout.'[36] While the statutory duty of disclosure is limited to the trial period, the common law duty of disclosure is a general duty to disclose any evidence reasonably thought capable of assisting a defendant, based on fairness.[37]

In terms of duties, the Crown, whether as investigator or prosecutor, must take reasonable steps to obtain relevant material, whether overseas or otherwise.[38] The

---

[29] For an overview of the history, see R. Leng, 'The Exchange of Information and Disclosure' in M. McConville and G. Wilson (eds), *The Handbook of the Criminal Justice Process* (2002).

[30] See generally M. Redmayne, 'Disclosure and its Discontents' [2004] *Crim LR* 441.

[31] P. O'Connor, 'Prosecution Disclosure: Principle, Practice and Justice' [1992] *Crim LR* 464.

[32] *Jespers v Belgium* (1981) 27 DR 61.

[33] CPIA, s 24.   [34] CPIA, s 3(1)(a).   [35] CPIA, s 7A.

[36] CPS, *Disclosure Manual* (2018), 3. Also *Attorney General's Guidelines on Disclosure* (2013).

[37] *R (Nunn) v Chief Constable of Suffolk* [2014] UKSC 37.

[38] *R v Flook* [2010] 1 Cr App R 30, and *R v Harris* [2017] EWCA Crim 1849, [74].

prosecutor must identify the issues in the case and guide the disclosure officer as to what is likely to be most relevant and important,[39] and disclosure officers must receive proper training.[40]

There is no category or class of material which is disclosed automatically, and the disclosure test must be applied on a case-by-case basis.[41] That said, there are exceptions to disclosure for sensitive material (material which carries a 'real risk of serious prejudice to an important public interest'[42]). Some material is prohibited from being disclosed, such as under s 17 of the Regulation of Investigatory Powers Act 2000.[43] This is recorded on a separate schedule, which is not disclosed to the defence. The framework for disclosing sensitive information is considered further later in the chapter.

Prosecution disclosure of unused material has long been controversial, and remains so. This is partly because, as noted earlier, failures in prosecution disclosure are a common element in many miscarriages of justice; it is hardly surprising that the prosecution might be reluctant to disclose to the defence material which may undermine its case. It is also because the CPIA was introduced as a result of claims by the police that the common law disclosure regime imposed too heavy a burden on them; thus, the reforms were perceived as having restricted the defence's ability to access important information. Now, the growing use of mobile phone and other communication technology mean that prosecutions involve much more data than before, and sifting through such material, which might comprise thousands of pages of electronic material, is against a backdrop of limited resources and increased demands for efficiency. Neither the Litigators' Graduated Fee Scheme nor the Advocates' Graduated Fee Scheme pay for the defence to review unused material, so it depends on the commitment of the legal representative involved to do this unpaid, a situation described by the House of Commons Justice Committee as 'fundamentally unfair, . . . likely to become unsustainable, and increasingly prejudicial to the defendant'.[44] This exemplifies the implications of legal aid cuts on the rights of the defendant and justice more broadly.

While historically disclosure was viewed as a matter to be resolved between the parties, the current regime empowers and requires judges actively to manage disclosure.[45] Part 15 of the CPR 2015 covers disclosure, and outlines the relevant law and procedures. Moreover, r 14.5(2) imposes a continuing duty upon the prosecutor to 'provide the court with all the information in the prosecutor's possession which is material to

---

[39] *Olu* [2011] 1 Cr App R 404, [33].   [40] *Malook* [2011] EWCA Crim 254.

[41] *R v Olu and 2 others* [2010] EWCA Crim 2975.

[42] *R v H & C* [2004] UKHL 3, [36].   [43] See Ch 4.

[44] House of Commons Justice Committee, *Criminal Legal Aid*, Twelfth Report of Session 2017–19, HC 1069 (2018), [99].

[45] Judiciary of England and Wales, *Judicial Protocol on the Disclosure of Unused Material in Criminal Cases* (2013), para 56: https://www.judiciary.gov.uk/wp-content/uploads/JCO/Documents/Protocols/Disclosure+Protocol.pdf.

what the court must decide' and r 24.13 provides that 'any party who introduces a document in evidence, or who otherwise uses a document in presenting that party's case, must provide a copy for each other party'.

As noted in Chapter 1, a programme called Transforming Summary Justice (TSJ) was adopted by all criminal justice agencies from June 2015. Its aim is to reform the way that criminal cases are handled in the magistrates' courts, and to create a swifter system with reduced delay and fewer hearings, through early receipt of initial details of the prosecution case and streamlined disclosure, amongst other initiatives.[46] Under TSJ, a Streamlined Disclosure Certificate should be used in all cases in which a not guilty plea is anticipated and which is expected to be tried summarily.[47] All cases should be reviewed by a CPS lawyer before the first hearing takes place, any work needed to improve the case should take place before that hearing, and unused material should be disclosed to the defence as soon as a not guilty plea is entered. HMCPSI carried out an early inspection in 2016 to assess CPS effectiveness in TSJ.[48] Eighty-one per cent of first hearings were found to be 'effective', with the right people present and the prosecutors well prepared, robust, and able to make decisions. That said, in preparing for the first hearing, the CPS's ability to manage and progress cases effectively was still seen to be hampered by the quality of the police file, often due to failure to comply with disclosure obligations.

There has been a series of reviews and reports on disclosure since the last edition of this book, the first of which was Lord Justice Gross's *Review of Disclosure in Criminal Proceedings,* published in September 2011.[49] The review was a comprehensive examination of how the CPIA regime operated in practice, with particular focus on cases in the Crown Court generating a substantial amount of paper and electronic documentation. Lord Justice Gross did not call for legislative change but rather advocated a significant improvement in the application of the existing system, led by the prosecution and supported by robust judicial case management.[50] This review considered 'the explosion in electronic communications', which was not and could not have been anticipated when the CPIA was enacted, but emphasized that the burden of disclosure 'should not render the prosecution of economic crime impractical'.[51] Though Lord Justice Gross spoke of the temptation to narrow the relevancy test by the insertion of a proportionality qualification, he was not persuaded, on the basis that a settled period of improved confidence in the prosecution's performance of its disclosure obligations was required first.[52]

---

[46] HMCPSI, *Transforming Summary Justice: An early perspective of the CPS contribution* (2016), https://www.justiceinspectorates.gov.uk/hmcpsi/inspections/transforming-summary-justice/.

[47] National Police Chiefs' Council and CPS, *The National Disclosure Standards* (2018), 2.2.2, https://www.cps.gov.uk/sites/default/files/documents/legal_guidance/National-Disclosure-Standards-2018.pdf.

[48] HMCPSI, *Transforming Summary Justice*, n 46.

[49] The Rt Hon. Lord Justice Gross, *Review of Disclosure in Criminal Proceedings* (2011), https://www.judiciary.gov.uk/wp-content/uploads/JCO/Documents/Reports/disclosure-review-september-2011.pdf.

[50] Ibid, para 115.   [51] Ibid, para 114.   [52] Ibid, para 119.

Subsequently, the Judicial Protocol was introduced.[53] Amongst its points of note are that:

> A constructive approach to disclosure is a necessary part of professional best practice, for the defence and prosecution. This does not undermine the defendant's legitimate interests, it accords with his or her obligations under the Rules and it ensures that all the relevant material is provided.[54]

Next a review of magistrates' court disclosure was carried out and its report published in May 2014.[55] This review claimed that disclosure, in terms of substance rather than process, rarely has any bearing on the outcome of cases tried summarily.[56] While, like Gross LJ, the review did not call for legislative change, it noted that there may be a longer term case for considering whether a simpler regime in magistrates' courts would be more efficient.[57] One proposition was whether one could provide the defence with all unused material in summary cases,[58] or more radically whether only Crown Court cases should remain within the CPIA regime, with a 'pragmatic and proportionate new approach' in the magistrates' court.[59] It remains to be seen whether either of this suggestions is taken forward. The provision of more material to the defence would need to be matched by commensurate and adequate remuneration.

Indeed, a truly fundamental change in practice and process is needed, given that far more material is digital than was the case in the past, and given the size and intricacies of many prosecutions. Disclosure is a particular problem with larger and more complex cases, which are deemed to require robust case management,[60] and prosecution-led disclosure from the very earliest stage.[61] The CPS Disclosure Manual notes that factors posing difficulties for the prosecutor may include the length of the investigation, the number of defendants, the number of witnesses, applying differential disclosure, dealing with material from joint or linked investigations, historical material, and accessing or obtaining third party material, particularly from foreign jurisdictions.[62] Moreover, particular issues arise in relation to the increasing number of child abuse and sexual offence trials, especially given the sensitivity and sometimes age of the relevant material.[63]

In *R v R and Others*, a case concerning an allegation of 'very substantial' fraud, electronic materials seized in the course of investigation contained a total of seven

---

[53] *Judicial Protocol*, n 45. This replaces the previous judicial document *Disclosure: a Protocol for the Control and Management of Unused Material in the Crown Court* and the section on 'Disclosure' in the *Lord Chief Justice's Protocol on the Control and Management of Heavy Fraud and Other Complex Criminal Cases* (2005).

[54] Ibid, para 16.

[55] *Magistrates' Court Disclosure Review* (2014), https://www.judiciary.gov.uk/wp-content/uploads/2014/05/Magistrates'-Court-Disclosure-Review.pdf. Disclosure in the magistrates' courts was beyond the remit of Gross LJ's, *Review of Disclosure in Criminal Proceedings*, n 49, para 167.

[56] Ibid, para 211. [57] Ibid, para 203. [58] Ibid, para 203. [59] Ibid, para 232.

[60] *Judicial Protocol*, n 45, 38. [61] *Attorney General's Guidelines, n 36*, para 50.

[62] *CPS Disclosure Manual*, n 36, 81.

[63] *Judicial Protocol*, n 45, 45. Also see CPS, *2013 Protocol and Good Practice Model: Disclosure of Information in Cases of Alleged Child Abuse and Linked Criminal and Care Directions Hearings* (2013); S. Leahy, 'Too Much Information? Regulating Disclosure of Complainants' Personal Records in Sexual Offence Trials' [2016] *Crim LR* 229.

terabytes of data.[64] Owing in no small part to this vast quantity, the case proceeded for five years without the prosecution completing primary disclosure. Consequently, the trial judge stayed all counts on a draft indictment as an abuse of process, ruling that the passage of time meant that it was not possible for the defendants to have a fair trial. This was overturned by the Court of Appeal which drew a number of conclusions:

- The prosecution is and must be in the driving seat at the stage of initial disclosure . . .
- The prosecution must then encourage dialogue and prompt engagement with the defence . . .
- The law is prescriptive of the result, not the method . . .
- The process of disclosure should be subject to robust case management by the judge, utilising the full range of case management powers . . .
- Flexibility is critical.[65]

Among other matters, the court endorsed the practice of 'dip sampling' material and the use of search tools by the prosecution to satisfy the disclosure obligation in a practicable and effective manner where the quantity of material to be reviewed would be unmanageable otherwise (though it noted that disclosure of the methodology of such sampling or searching would be important).[66]

Such an approach is adopted by the Serious Fraud Office, for instance, which is turning to technology for answers. In the investigation into corruption and bribery by Rolls-Royce plc, artificial intelligence was used to sift, index, and summarize documents.[67] While that may provide a longer-term solution, at present the software is not readily available, not least because of cost.

i. Sanctions for disclosure failings by the prosecution

A prosecutor's failure to observe time limits in terms of disclosure does not on its own constitute grounds for staying the proceedings for abuse of process, unless it involves such delay by the prosecutor that the accused is denied a fair trial.[68] Evidence may be excluded under s 78 of the Police and Criminal Evidence Act 1984 (PACE) also.

The Court of Appeal has been somewhat uneven in respect of prosecution failings, upholding certain trial judge decisions which de facto bring about the end of trials, while being more pragmatic and sympathetic to the prosecution in many other instances. The gravity of the charged offences and the motivations of the defence in pursuing material are relevant. For instance, in *Barkshire* the Court of Appeal stated that the statutory test for disclosure extends to anything available to the prosecution which might undermine confidence in the accuracy of evidence called by the prosecution, or which might provide a measure of support for the defence at trial.[69] The prosecution

---

[64] *R v R and Others* [2015] EWCA Crim 1941. This is roughly equivalent to more than 5 billion typed pages.
[65] See [32] onwards.   [66] [25].
[67] 'SFO expected to promote Ravn's crime-solving AI robot', *Financial Times*, 12 February 2017.
[68] CPIA, s 10; see *R v O and others* [2011] EWCA Crim 2854.
[69] [2011] EWCA Crim 1885.

case might be undermined as a result of a particular defence which the accused may or may not run. Prosecution failure to make proper disclosure of material relating to the role and activities of an undercover officer, as well as other material supportive of the defence case, where the materials were pertinent to a potential submission of abuse of process by way of entrapment and had the capacity to support the defence of necessity and justification, rendered the trial unfair and the convictions unsafe.

Boardman involved the collapse of a prosecution after the exclusion of communication data that had not been disclosed in a timely fashion.[70] B had been charged with several offences of harassment through text messages and phone calls contrary to the Protection from Harassment Act 1997, allegedly using a phone other than his own. He had requested disclosure by the prosecution of communications data from the sending device as well as his own phone. Though the prosecution listed the data as exhibits in the case, he had not received them eight days before the listed trial date. B applied to adjourn the trial on the basis that his expert needed three weeks to produce his report; adjournment would mean a delay of several months. The judge was not prepared to adjourn and instead ruled that it would be unfair to allow the prosecution to use the telephone evidence in its entirety at such a late stage, and so excluded all of the data under s 78 of PACE. That ruling effectively brought the prosecution to an end. The Court of Appeal dismissed the prosecution's appeal, holding that it was beyond argument that Boardman would have suffered prejudice, given the length of time the complaint had been pending. Though the trial judge recognized the pressure under which the CPS was working, such pressure was shared by defence lawyers and the court and, moreover, that could not be an answer if effective case management was to mean anything. In addition, the court was careful to limit the effect of its decision: 'overzealous pursuit of inconsequential material', in an effort to end the prosecution, would be an abuse of the court process.

Not long after *Boardman*, the Court of Appeal opened its judgment in *R v Salt* by noting that this involved its consideration 'for the second time within the last two months serious failures by the prosecution in relation to the provision of material which led a judge to bring the case to an end'.[71] Two brothers were charged with rape, false imprisonment, and sexual assault; there had been 'grave' failures in relation to disclosure. On the first day of the trial, a police officer attended with three boxes of material which neither counsel nor the CPS had seen. A revised schedule of unused material in the possession of the police was then prepared, containing over 25 further items, and disclosure continued throughout the prosecution case; by day seven of the trial the schedule of unused material contained a further 53 items. The judge viewed the failures to be so 'fundamental and far reaching as to make this a truly exceptional and unique case', and so, notwithstanding the seriousness of the charges, marked the court's 'wholesale condemnation of the prosecution by allowing a stay and refusing the prosecution the right to pursue the case'.[72]

---

[70] [2015] EWCA Crim 175.   [71] [2015] EWCA Crim 662, [1].   [72] [27].

The Court of Appeal noted that proceedings could be stayed for abuse of process not only where a fair trial was impossible but also where it would be contrary to the public interest in the integrity of the criminal justice system that a trial should take place.[73] Where a court was considering whether to stay criminal proceedings as an abuse of process on the basis of the prosecution's failure to make proper disclosure of evidence or unused material, the factors to be taken into account included the gravity of the charges, the denial of justice to the complainants, the necessity for proper attention to be paid to disclosure, the nature and materiality of the failures, the waste of court resources, and the effect on the jury and the availability of other sanctions. Though the undisclosed documents were of limited materiality, the conduct of the CPS and the police was deemed to be reprehensible. That said, the sanctions which a court could impose on them to secure adherence to basic principles of justice lacked proportionality,[74] especially in relation to such 'grave crimes'. Despite all this, the court concluded that a fair trial was possible, noting that a lack of proper compliance with the CPR by those initially representing the defendant had played its part in what had happened. The impact of the CPR on the duties of the defence are illustrated profoundly here: if the defence has not brought to the court's attention what is contended to be a failure by the prosecution in sufficient time for it to be remedied before the trial, this may be critical.[75] In other words, the defence bears an obligation to identify and raise failure by the prosecution in a timely fashion. The court held that it was not in the interests of justice to stay the proceedings on the basis that their continuation would undermine public confidence in the administration of justice.[76] Notably, the court said it would ask the Criminal Procedure Rule Committee to consider whether any further sanctions on those charged with the prosecution of a case could be imposed through new Rules or whether any other steps or sanctions should be taken to secure compliance with the CPR.[77] Moreover, the court 'trust[ed] that the judgments . . . in *Boardman* and in this case will receive the closest study by all Chief Crown Prosecutors and all Chief Constables. There should be no recurrence of failures of this kind by either the CPS or any police force.'[78] Notwithstanding the gravity of the charges, this is a remarkably anodyne response to egregious prosecutorial behaviour, and no disincentive to such practices in future.

Similarly, failure to disclose did not render a conviction unsafe in *Garland*, following a referral by the Criminal Cases Review Commission to the Court of Appeal on the ground that there was material non-disclosure of information available to the police and the Crown.[79] The court noted with approval the statement of Lord Rodger in *McInnes v HM Advocate*,[80] where the equivalent Scottish disclosure regime was challenged under Art 6 of the European Convention on Human Rights (ECHR):

> The significance of any infringement of an accused's Art 6(1) Convention rights will depend on the circumstances. As has been said on many occasions, not every infringement of a particular right will mean that the accused's trial as a whole has been unfair. Obviously,

---

[73] [37]. [74] [72]. [75] [66]. [76] [72]. [77] [71]. [78] [73].
[79] [2016] EWCA Crim 1743. See Ch 12. [80] [2010] UKSC 7, [30].

for example, failure to disclose a police statement of a Crown witness who is not called to give evidence will usually have no affect on the fairness of the trial . . . [T]he law deals in real, not in merely fanciful, possibilities. So . . . an appellate court will only hold that a trial has been unfair and quash the jury's verdict as a miscarriage of justice if there is a real possibility that, if the statements had been disclosed, a jury may reasonably have come to a different verdict.

As noted in *Salt*, the sanctions which a court can impose on the police and prosecution to secure adherence to basic principles of justice in terms of disclosure could be viewed as disproportionate:[81] there is little between a stay or exclusion of evidence that might lead to the collapse of a trial, on the one hand, and essentially condoning prosecution failings, on the other. Indeed, in 2012 a review was carried out by Lord Justice Gross and Lord Justice Treacy, focusing specifically on sanctions for disclosure failure.[82] Though this review considered failures by both the prosecution and the defence, and the sanctions against both parties, it noted that the concerns expressed to them about failures by the prosecution 'outweighed in large measure' the concerns about defence failures, and that as disclosure is a dynamic process, defence failures may sometimes be caused by prosecution delays.[83] Regardless, and perhaps surprisingly, this review did not recommend the creation of any additional sanctions, though recommended that ss 6B and 6D (requiring an updated defence statement and the notification of names of experts instructed by accused) be brought into force.[84] This has not yet occurred. Continuing to focus on the defence, both in terms of perceived weakness and duties to mitigate prosecution failings, is dubious, given the source of the issues in this context. The review did make some ancillary recommendations, relating to the placement of warnings about the consequences of disclosure failures. Taylor describes this review as a missed opportunity, and criticizes its maintenance of 'the timidity which has characterised the approach towards sanctioning inadequate disclosure on the part of investigating officers'.[85] Action from the CPR Committee, as requested in *Salt*, is yet to occur.

ii. Public interest immunity

So far, we have considered the disclosure of non-sensitive material. There are further complexities in the disclosure regime where sensitive material is involved. If the police investigation involved an informer, or touched on a matter of national security, for example, the prosecution might well be reluctant to disclose this information to the defence. In this situation, the prosecution can make a claim of 'public interest immunity' (PII). This area of the law has caused some issues. The basic principle is that PII claims need to be judged by the courts; the prosecution should not decide that

---

[81] *Salt*, n 71, [72].

[82] Lord Justice Gross and Lord Justice Treacy, *Further review of disclosure in criminal proceedings: sanctions for disclosure failure* (2012), https://www.judiciary.gov.uk/wp-content/uploads/JCO/Documents/Reports/disclosure_criminal_courts.pdf.

[83] Ibid, 14.   [84] See section 9.2(B).

[85] C. Taylor, 'The disclosure sanctions review: another missed opportunity?' [2013] *E&P* 272, 283.

relevant material is sensitive and therefore not to be disclosed; non-disclosure needs the approval of the trial judge. Beyond this, the courts recognize three different types of PII claim:[86]

- Type One: the prosecutor must give to the defence notice of application and indicate at least the category of the material held. The defence must have the opportunity to make representations and there is an *inter partes* hearing conducted in open court.

- Type Two: the prosecutor must give to the defence notice of application but the nature of material is not revealed because to do so would have the effect of disclosing that which the prosecutor contends should not in the public interest be disclosed. The defence has the opportunity to address the court on the procedure to be adopted but the application is made to the court in the absence of the defendant or representative.

- Type Three: the prosecutor makes an application to the court without notice to the defence because to do so would have the effect of disclosing that which the prosecutor contends should not in the public interest be disclosed—a 'highly exceptional' class.

The English courts, as well as the European Court of Human Rights (ECtHR), stress the importance of informing the judge whenever material is not being disclosed for PII reasons. The judge can then look out for the defence's interests during the trial. At the start of the trial, for example, it might seem that PII material is not relevant to the defence case; but the case might develop at trial in such a way that the material does become relevant and the decision to withhold it needs to be reassessed. There is less consensus on other issues. Type 2 PII hearings raise particular problems, for here the defence is not able directly to present argument on the key issue: the importance of the sensitive material to its case. In *Jasper v UK*,[87] the defence argued that in this situation the judge should appoint a 'special counsel', who could represent the defence during the PII hearing, being privy to the nature of the sensitive material but not reporting back to the defence on its exact nature.[88] A majority of the Court thought the English courts did not need to go this far to comply with Art 6, but a substantial minority dissented on this point. In *Edwards and Lewis v UK*,[89] the Court seems to have come close to reversing its decision in *Jasper*. Both defendants made entrapment claims at their respective trials. Here the ECtHR thought it especially important that the defence should have some say about certain information that was not disclosed on PII grounds. This was because it was thought unfair to have the judge decide an issue—the validity of

---

[86] Once it becomes clear that a PII application will be required, the prosecutor should make a written application to the court in accordance with r 15.3.

[87] (2000) 30 EHRR 1.

[88] For a discussion of special counsel, and the difficulties they face, see J. Ip, 'The Rise and Spread of the Special Advocate' [2008] *PL* 717.

[89] (2005) 40 EHRR 24. See also *Botmeh v UK* (2008) 46 EHRR 31.

the entrapment claim—while in possession of information relevant to that claim about which the defence was not able to present adversarial argument. The solution, it was thought, was to appoint special counsel. This shows rather less trust in the impartiality of the judiciary than did the decision in *Jasper*.

Unsurprisingly, the decision in *Edwards and Lewis* threw the English courts into some turmoil. A few trial judges appointed special counsel, and the issue quickly came before the House of Lords. Its decision in *R v H and C*[90] is in some ways unhelpful. Rather than giving clear guidance on when special counsel should be appointed, it suggests that the issue should rarely arise because prosecutors can simply apply the test of disclosure found in the CPIA: if sensitive material assists the defence case or undermines the prosecution case, then it should (probably) be disclosed. If the prosecution cannot accept disclosure, it should terminate the prosecution. Where sensitive material does not meet the test in the CPIA, then it need not be disclosed. In neither case should the judge normally be troubled with the decision. While this may sound very sensible, it does not really confront the difficulty that prosecutors seem to encounter in practice. That they often do bring PII issues to the judge's attention suggests that they do not find the basic CPIA test a simple one; rightly or wrongly, they do not trust their own judgement and would rather involve the judge. Keeping the judge out of the picture may make things simpler from the point of view of the appearance of justice and the concerns expressed by the ECtHR, but it may not be the fairest way of dealing with the issues. Beyond this, the House of Lords was prepared to say little more than that the appointment of special counsel should be exceptional. Its reticence may have been due, in part, to the knowledge that the government had requested a referral of the decision in *Edwards and Lewis* to the Grand Chamber of the ECtHR. This request, however, was later withdrawn. In practice, the courts may find more useful guidance in the judgment of the Court of Appeal, which held that special counsel should be appointed whenever sensitive material is relevant to a 'preliminary determinative ruling', such as an application to stay proceedings, or where it is prejudicial to a defendant so that the judge does not feel able to make a decision involving the material without adversarial argument.[91] Later cases confirm that judges should never make rulings on the basis of material of which, because it is subject to PII, the defence are unaware and thus cannot contribute argument.[92] The ECtHR has held that submitting all documents which might reasonably be expected to assist the defence and for which PII was claimed to the disclosure judge, informing the defence of this fact, and ensuring an *inter partes* hearing where detailed submissions could be made on the facts of the case and on the nature of the defence case, were sufficient safeguards to ensure a fair trial.[93] Failure to appoint special counsel or to provide a daily transcript to the disclosure judge to be examined for any material that might have assisted the applicant's case were unnecessary to cater for the 'purely speculative possibility' that a line of defence might emerge.[94] Moreover, the

---

[90] [2004] 2 WLR 335.   [91] [2004] 1 Cr App R 17.
[92] *Ali and Hussain v Revenue and Customs Prosecutions Office* [2008] EWCA Crim 1466.
[93] *McKeown v UK* (2012) 54 EHRR 7, [52].   [94] [53].

Court of Appeal has rejected the contention that judges are unable to put relevant material out of their minds when considering a point of law; this 'compartmentalisation of the judicial mind' avoids the need for special counsel.[95]

There is another matter relating to PII on which judicial guidance has been disappointing. So far we have said nothing about the test the judge should apply when ruling on a PII claim. The basic question here is whether the judge should withhold relevant evidence from the defence in order to protect sensitive information. The ECtHR has suggested that this approach may be acceptable: 'The entitlement to disclosure of relevant evidence is not an absolute right. In any criminal proceedings there may be competing interests, such as national security or the need to protect witnesses at risk of reprisals or keep secret police methods of investigation of crime, which must be weighed against the rights of the accused.'[96] This view is a familiar one; it supposes that the defendant's rights are subject to being traded off against other values. The importance of those other values should not be slighted. An informer whose identity is revealed may be put in danger, and if they are to be protected this may involve very significant disruption to their life. Ordered to disclose the identity of such a person, the prosecution may feel it has no choice but to abandon the proceedings. Yet, it is hardly palatable to withhold relevant evidence from the defence. There is obviously a difficult dilemma here, but given that non-prosecution—rather than the endangerment of the informer—is an option, one should be very wary of using the sort of balancing language that the ECtHR appears to espouse. Another point to bear in mind is that the prosecution may be able to avoid the dilemma described here by not bringing a prosecution which depends crucially on an informer in the first place. If a balancing test is to be used, then it is important to take a wide view of the issues (Could the situation have been avoided? Why not abandon the prosecution?) rather than one which simply weighs the importance of sensitivity against the defendant's rights.

Where PII is concerned, the English courts have tended to distance themselves from the sort of balancing language used by the ECtHR. Yet they have managed to leave considerable ambiguity as to the nature of the test to be applied. In *Keane*, it was suggested that material should be disclosed if it 'may prove the defendant's innocence or avoid a miscarriage of justice'.[97] Of course, the basic rule is that the defendant does not have to prove innocence. It is difficult to know whether this is just a careless choice of words, or whether the test is intended to set a reasonably high threshold. In favour of the latter interpretation, one might suppose that, had the court intended a simple test of relevance to be applied, it would have said so. Things are not clarified by the House of Lords in *H and C*. While the general core of the judgment is that relevant evidence should be disclosed to the defence, there are dicta which suggest that it is acceptable to withhold information so long as it will not be of significant help.[98]

---

[95] *R v May* [2005] EWCA Crim 97, [20]–[21].   [96] *Edwards and Lewis v UK*, n 89, 53.
[97] [1994] 1 WLR 746, 751–2.   [98] See n 90, [18], [37].

There may be good reason for some caution in setting the test for disclosure of PII material. If the test is too wide—including, for example, material which '*may* be relevant' to the defence case—then the judge at a preliminary hearing may feel the need to disclose evidence which turns out not to be relevant to the defence case as it is developed at trial. But the current test for disclosure in the CPIA—'material which might reasonably be considered capable of undermining the case for the prosecution or of assisting the case for the accused'—is sufficiently robust to avoid this problem. Given the difficulty of justifying a balancing test where the defendant's ability to defend himself is concerned, there is a good argument for applying this test at the PII stage. Any material which meets this test should be disclosed. As for the vexed question of special counsel, the Court of Appeal's guidance in *H and C* appears to ensure that special counsel will be appointed in cases where they are most needed, that is, where the judge has a difficult decision to make and will benefit from adversarial argument. The contention in later cases, however, that judges can simply put sensitive material out of their mind when deciding certain issues, is dubious, and should be treated with caution.[99]

iii. Practice and incentives

As numerous studies over decades have shown, there are serious and enduring problems with the operation of the disclosure scheme in practice.[100] One major issue is that decisions about disclosure are made by prosecutors, who are reliant on information provided to them by the police. But the schedules prepared by the police are poor: they often contain insufficient detail to enable prosecutors to make informed decisions about what should be disclosed (about half of cases), and sometimes fail to mention significant information altogether.[101] Ideally, the CPS should scrutinize the schedules carefully, and ask for more information from the police where detail is lacking: in 2008, this happened in less than half of cases where descriptions were inadequate.[102] A more recent joint inspection in 2017 reviewed random volume Crown Court cases, as well as cases identified by the CPS as failing because of disclosure issues.[103] The inspection found obvious disclosure issues prior to charge in 55.5 per cent of all the reviewed cases and, of these, the prosecution dealt with the issues fully in 24.7 per cent, partially in 37.0 per cent, and not at all in 38.3 per cent.[104] In terms of adherence to the Better Case Management timetable for disclosure in contested Crown Court cases, the prosecution did not discharge its duties in a timely manner in 54.4 per cent of the random selection of cases.[105] Throughout, police scheduling was routinely poor, while release

---

[99] See A. Wistrich, C. Guthrie, and J. Rachlinski, 'Can Judges Ignore Inadmissible Information? The Difficulty of Deliberately Disregarding' (2005) 153 *U Pa LR* 1251.

[100] HMCPSI, *The Inspectorate's Report on the Thematic Review of the Disclosure of Unused Material* (2000); J. Plotnikoff and R. Woolfson, *'A Fair Balance'? Evaluation of the Operation of Disclosure Law* (2001).

[101] HMCPSI, *Disclosure: A Thematic Review of the Duties of Disclosure of Unused Material Undertaken by the CPS* (2008), 32–4.

[102] Ibid, 33.   [103] HMCPSI and HMIC, *Making It Fair*, n 17.   [104] Ibid, para 3.3.

[105] Ibid. See Judiciary of England and Wales, *The Better Case Management (BCM) Handbook* (2018), https://www.judiciary.gov.uk/wp-content/uploads/2018/02/bcm-guide-for-practitioners-05032018.pdf.

by the police to the prosecutor of material that may undermine the prosecution case or assist the defence case was rare. In addition, prosecutors failed to challenge poor quality schedules and in turn provided little or no input to the police. To compound matters, the auditing process fell far below acceptable standards. This was seen to lead to chaotic scenes outside the court, with last-minute and often unauthorized disclosure between counsel, unnecessary adjournments, and discontinued cases, and ultimately reflecting badly on the criminal justice system in the eyes of victims and witnesses.[106] All that said, none of the failings was found to be attributable to existing law, procedure, or guidance: rather training, supervision, quality assurance mechanisms, and IT were to blame.[107] The review made a number of recommendations based on this, in addition to proposing consolidation of the numerous Guidances.[108]

It is not surprising to find such problems persisting in the disclosure regime, given that the police have little incentive to make the schedules transparent. There is a tension between the rules and practice, as shaped by the police sense of mission. Police must 'pursue all reasonable lines of enquiry whether these point towards or away from the suspect', retain all relevant material, and notify the CPS of it.[109] Moreover, the police 'cannot decline to make inquiries' in order to avoid having to disclose information that may either undermine the prosecution case or assist the defence.[110] While HMCPSI in 2008 found no evidence of deliberate non-disclosure by the police,[111] Quirk's interview-based study found that police officers admitted that they were reluctant to help the defence through disclosure.[112] One officer noted the possibility of listing potentially disclosable material on the sensitive schedule, so that defendants would not have access to it and be in a position to request disclosure, and the HMCPSI noted its concerns about this. In its view, only 20 per cent of cases judged by the police to involve sensitive material were properly categorized as such; and inadequate descriptions of material on the sensitive schedules were again rarely questioned by prosecutors. The Inspectorate therefore felt unable to provide an 'assurance as to the appropriateness of CPS handling of material categorised as sensitive', noting that 'there is a significant risk that miscarriages of justice may occur'.[113] While some of the problems with the disclosure regime are caused by lack of training and resources—compiling the schedules, reviewing them, and chasing up inadequate descriptions is time-consuming—it is likely that, as Quirk notes, adversarial attitudes and the wish not to help defendants escape conviction (especially when it can be assumed that the majority will plead guilty) plays a role also.

Despite the positive dimensions of the CPIA regime, such as the provision of schedules to the defence which help it to monitor what has not been disclosed, prosecution

---

[106] HMCPSI and HMIC, *Making It Fair*, n 17, para 1.3.   [107] Ibid, para 10.1.   [108] Ibid, para 10.4.

[109] Ministry of Justice, *Criminal Procedure and Investigations Act 1996 (section 23(1)) Code of Practice* (2015), paras 3.5 and 7.2.

[110] *R v Joof and Others* [2012] EWCA Crim 1475, [17].

[111] HMCPSI, *Disclosure*, n 101, 63.

[112] H. Quirk, 'The Significance of Culture in Criminal Procedure Reform: Why the Revised Disclosure Scheme Cannot Work' (2006) 10 *E & P* 42, 48–50.

[113] HMCPSI, *Disclosure*, n 101, 51.

disclosure remains problematic. To some extent, the system will always be reliant on the police, and inevitably the police are reluctant to disclose unused material that may be helpful to defendants. There are no obvious remedies other than further resources and training, which will mitigate if not resolve these shortcomings.[114] Some commentators suggest that the answer lies in adopting the currently forbidden 'keys to the warehouse' approach whereby the defence are given access to all material obtained during the investigation (subject to limited public interest grounds for non-disclosure).[115] It is likely that this could compound rather than ease issues, given the resource and time implications of sifting through significant amounts of material within the current scheme of legal aid. Smith contemplates a further, more radical solution involving the placement of 'Judicial Disclosure Officers' in each police force, who would receive all evidence and determine which material should be disclosed.[116] Issues of resource would obtain here also, of course.

(B) DEFENCE DISCLOSURE

Different principles apply to defence disclosure. Before 1996, there was no general obligation on the defence to disclose details of its case before trial, with some limited exceptions for alibis, expert evidence, and serious fraud trials. The CPIA changed this, imposing an obligation on the defence, in trials on indictment, to disclose details of its case following initial disclosure by the prosecution. Defence disclosure was expanded by the CJA 2003.[117] There is no statutory requirement of defence disclosure in summary trials, though disclosure will sometimes be beneficial to the defence because, by alerting the prosecution to the issues to be raised, it may trigger further prosecution disclosure.

In the Crown Court the defence should provide a defence statement, setting out the details of its case, including any defences and points of law to be raised, and the matters on which it takes issue with the prosecution, as well as the reasons why.[118] The defence must also disclose the names and addresses of the witnesses it intends to call and details of any expert witnesses it has consulted.[119] Understandably, these provisions are controversial,[120] and have been characterized as progressing from their original purpose to assist in the identification of relevant material for further prosecution disclosure to a case management form.[121] The *Code of Practice for Arranging*

---

[114] E.g. Lord Justice Gross, *Review of Disclosure in Criminal Proceedings*, n 49, para 133.

[115] See A. Jordanoska, 'Case Management in Complex Fraud Trials: Actors and Strategies in Achieving Procedural Efficiency' (2017) *Int J L in Context* 336.

[116] Smith, n 19, 730.

[117] See Redmayne, n 30. The provisions were further modified by the Criminal Justice and Immigration Act 2008, s 60.

[118] CPIA, s 6A.

[119] CJA 2003, ss 34–35, which came into force on 1 May 2010 (Criminal Justice Act 2003 (Commencement No 24 and Transitional Provisions) Order 2010 (SI 2010/1183).

[120] See Redmayne, n 30.

[121] A. Edwards 'Case Management Forms' [2011] *Crim LR* 547, 549.

and Conducting Interviews Notified by the Accused provides guidance to police officers wishing to conduct interviews with proposed witnesses whose details are disclosed to the prosecution by the accused.[122] The Code requires the police to notify the defendant's solicitors when they propose to interview a defence witness and the defendant's solicitor is entitled to be present during the interview with the witness's consent, although is not permitted to intervene in questioning.

Defence disclosure has certain parallels with the changes to the right to silence introduced by the Criminal Justice and Public Order Act 1994 (see Chapter 5). Both are enforced by adverse inferences. If a defendant fails to issue a defence statement, or if his defence at trial departs from what was disclosed, an adverse inference may be drawn against him.[123] The Judicial Protocol notes that the prosecution may comment on any failure in defence disclosure (except where the failure relates to a point of law) without leave of the court, but counsel should use a measure of judgement as to whether it is wise to embark on cross-examination about such failure.[124] If the accused is cross-examined about discrepancies between his evidence and the defence statement, or if adverse comment is made, the judge must give appropriate guidance to the jury.

It must be said, however, that adverse inferences from non-disclosure are even less straightforward than those from silence. The defendant's failure to disclose a defence before trial is suspicious only because the law places an obligation on him to do so, and in that situation the inference that the defence is fabricated surely is weak. Indeed, where the defendant fails to disclose a point of law on which he relies, it is difficult to see how any adverse inference could be drawn at all. Further, if disclosure is inadequate, it will often be difficult to judge whether this is the defendant's fault or that of his legal team. These problems no doubt partly explain why the defence disclosure provisions in the CPIA have had such little impact. In contrast to the mass of case law on the inferences from silence provisions, there are few reported cases on the conditions in which an inference from faulty disclosure can be drawn.[125]

The Court of Appeal in *R v Daha Essa* concluded that s 11(5) is 'perfectly compatible' with the ECHR, for the same reasons that s 34 is.[126] It stressed the judicial control of the use of s 11(5): the judge can stop cross-examination if it is unfair, and direct the jury to disregard it if such cross-examination has been embarked upon. Moreover, elucidating the defence does not compromise the right to pre-trial silence, nor does it infringe his entitlement against self-incrimination.[127] Comparable provisions in the St Lucia Criminal Code compelling submission of a defence statement in a positive defence case were held not to breach the constitutional right to pre-trial silence.[128]

---

[122] *Code of Practice for Interviews of Witnesses Notified by Accused order 2010*, http://www.opsi.gov.uk/acts/acts1996/related/ukpgacop_19960025_en.pdf.

[123] s 11.   [124] *Judicial Protocol*, n 45, 21.

[125] The principal decision is *Tibbs* [2000] 2 Cr App R 309. See also *Wheeler* [2001] 1 Cr App R 10; *R (Sullivan) v Crown Court at Maidstone* [2002] 1 WLR 2747.

[126] [2009] EWCA Crim 43, [23]. See Ch 5.

[127] *R v Rochford* [2010] EWCA Crim 1928.

[128] *Sexius v The Attorney-General of St Lucia* [2017] UKPC 26.

Some defence statements are insufficiently detailed to meet the requirements of the Act, though it appears that the situation has improved in terms of practice in this respect. In 2006, the Court of Appeal's Disclosure Protocol called for a 'complete change in the culture' relating to defence disclosure,[129] and in 2008 HMCPSI judged that less than half of defence statements met the criteria in the CPIA.[130] That said, the 2017 joint review found that 73.3 per cent of defence statements were of sufficient quality for the prosecution to work with, though in many cases the defence statement was often served late and sometimes very close to the trial itself.[131] This may well be exacerbated by the pressures of time and resource experienced by defence practitioners.

i. The defendant's obligations

Defence disclosure raises issues of principle. Some commentators consider that it goes against the grain of an adversarial system to require defendants to perform duties which may be helpful to the prosecution. These issues are best considered in the context of wider changes in criminal procedure, which require defendants to cooperate with the courts. A useful starting point is the Court of Appeal's decision in *R v Gleeson*.[132] Here, the defence realized it had a technical defence to the charge made in the indictment. It waited until the end of the prosecution case, and then made a submission of no case to answer on the basis that the common law conspiracy charged by the prosecution was impossible (i.e. it claimed that the defendant had conspired to do something which was not actually an offence). The judge agreed that this was a sound defence, but permitted the prosecution to redraft the indictment so that the charge was statutory conspiracy (to which impossibility is not a defence). The defence appealed on the basis that the judge should not have permitted this course of action. In dismissing the appeal, the Court of Appeal commented on the duties of the defence:

> A prosecution [should] not be frustrated by errors of the prosecutor, unless such errors have irremediably rendered a fair trial for the defendant impossible. For defence advocates to seek to take advantage of such errors by deliberately delaying identification of an issue of fact or law in the case until the last possible moment is, in our view, no longer acceptable, given the legislative and procedural changes to our criminal justice process in recent years.[133]

The CJA amendments make defence obligations somewhat clearer than they were at the time of *Gleeson*. The CPIA now specifies that, in the Crown Court, the defence should disclose any points of law to be relied on, though the sanction specified for failure is the drawing of adverse inferences rather than, as in *Gleeson*, the loss of a watertight defence.

---

[129] Court of Appeal, *Protocol for the Control and Management of Unused Material in the Crown Court* (2006), paras 32–46.

[130] HMCPSI, *Disclosure*, n 101, 48, judged that less than half of defence statements met the criteria in the CPIA.

[131] HMCPSI and HMIC, *Making It Fair*, n 17, para 6.4. Cf R. Denyer, 'The Defence Statement' [2009] *Crim LR* 340, noting that he was 'still waiting' to see effective defence statements.

[132] [2004] *Crim LR* 579.   [133] Ibid, [35].

Shortly after *Gleeson* was decided, the CPR were introduced, and have been amended a number of times. As noted in Chapter 1, these rules set out the duties of the parties and the courts in relation to the conduct of criminal proceedings. The CPR are significant in that they indicate that the defence's concern should not just be to win its own case, but to ensure that the case is dealt with justly, where justice includes the conviction of the guilty. While *Gleeson* suggests that a new vision of criminal adjudication was emerging prior to the introduction of the rules, the CPR marked a 'fundamental change' in criminal procedure.[134] The comments of the Divisional Court in *Malcolm v DPP* are of note:

> Miss Calder's submissions, which emphasised the obligation of the prosecution to prove its case in its entirety before closing its case, and certainly before end of the final speech for the defence, had an anachronistic, and obsolete, ring. Criminal trials are no longer to be treated as a game, in which each move is final and any omission by the prosecution leads to its failure. It is the duty of the defence to make its defence and the issues it raises clear to the prosecution and to the court at an early stage. That duty is implicit in r.3.3 of the Criminal Procedure Rules 2005, which requires the parties actively to assist the exercise by the court of its case management powers, the exercise of which requires early identification of the real issues. Even in a relatively straightforward trial such as the present, in the magistrates' court (where there is not yet any requirement of a defence statement or a pre-trial review), it is the duty of the defence to make the real issues clear at the latest before the prosecution closes its case.[135]

As we have seen, in the Crown Court the defence is under a statutory obligation to disclose its defence to the prosecution before trial. Although there is no such statutory obligation in the magistrates' court, an implication of rr 3.2 and 3.3 is that the defence may be asked to reveal details of its case prior to trial. Thus, in *Robinson v Abergavenny Magistrates' Court*[136] when the defence raised an unanticipated issue at a late stage, the prosecution was granted an adjournment to give it time to respond to the new point. The Divisional Court rejected an application for judicial review of the decision to grant an adjournment, finding that *Gleeson* applied to the magistrates' court as much as to the Crown Court. The defence lawyer was said to have lost sight of his obligations under the CPR, and to be out of touch with the 'modern approach' to litigation.[137] In *R (on the application of DPP) v Chorley Magistrates' Court*, it was suggested that the defendant should have been asked to identify the issues to be raised, and the witnesses needed, at a pre-trial hearing. That he had not done so meant that he should gain no advantage from taking the prosecution by surprise.[138]

In *Kelly v Warley Magistrates' Court*, the District Judge asked the defence to produce a list of its witnesses prior to trial, to enable the prosecution to check their criminal records.[139] As we have seen, the CJA 2003 amended the disclosure provisions of

---

[134] *Lawson v Stafford Magistrates' Court* [2007] EWHC 2490 (Admin), [30].

[135] [2007] EWHC 363 (Admin), [31]. For a very useful review of case law in this area, see P. Fields, 'Clarke and McDaid: A Technical Triumph' [2008] *Crim LR* 612.

[136] [2007] EWHC 2005 (Admin).   [137] Ibid, [27].   [138] [2006] EWHC 1795 (Admin), [26].

[139] [2007] EWHC 1836 (Admin).

the CPIA, adding a requirement that the defence provide a list of its witnesses to the prosecution. In *Kelly*, it was argued that it would be odd if the CPR could introduce a requirement which the government has so far decided not to implement, but this contention did not find favour, Laws LJ doubting 'whether this inchoate legislation can of itself bear the inference that the CPR provide no power to do what the deputy district judge did'.[140] It was nevertheless held that the District Judge had gone too far. Details of defence witnesses were subject to litigation privilege, and the court was concerned that unless the sanctions for failure to comply with a direction to reveal witness details were moderate and proportionate, the judge's direction would amount to an attempt to interfere with privilege rather than simply to regulate proceedings.[141] This would be the case, for example, if the judge had threatened to prohibit the defence from calling a witness whose details had not been provided to the prosecution before trial.

Section 6A is now in force, and the CPR have been amended to take account of *Kelly*. Under r 3.11(c), parties can be asked to provide details of the witnesses they wish to call, and r 3.5(6) now provides a wide power to order any appropriate sanction. As Laws LJ explained, risks attach to early identification of defence witnesses: witnesses could be discouraged from cooperating; there is the risk that false points could be taken, the truth could be distorted, and witnesses manipulated.[142]

A fundamental question is whether this provision overrides litigation privilege,[143] namely which relates to communications made at the stage when litigation is pending or contemplated. Compliance with s 6A and legal professional privilege were considered in *Rochford* where the court held that a failure to amend a defence statement in accordance with a direction made by the judge would not be a contempt of court.[144] In considering whether there was a failure to comply with s 6A, the court stated that if the defendant was going to say at trial that he had been somewhere else at the material time, whether by giving evidence to that effect, calling such evidence from somebody else, or simply by raising it in argument, then not including such material constituted a failure to comply with s 6A. That said, if he was going to make no positive case at all, and 'was simply going to sit tight and ensure that the Crown proved its case', then there would have been no failure to comply with s 6A.[145] The court answered in the affirmative the question of whether legal professional privilege and the defendant's privilege against self-incrimination survive s 6A, on the basis that what he is required to disclose is what is going to happen at the trial, not 'his confidential discussions with his advocate, although of course they may bear on what is going to happen at the trial. Nor is he obliged to incriminate himself if he does not want to.'[146]

Rochford was cited in *Malcolm*, where the defence statement failed 'utterly' to meet the s 6A requirements and was seriously defective.[147] Nonetheless, M's appeal was

---

[140] Ibid, [14].   [141] Ibid, [32]–[35].

[142] *Kelly*, [22] per Laws LJ. See also J. McEwan, 'The Changing Face of Criminal Litigation in England and Wales: Editor's Introduction' (2010) 14(2) *E&P* 89.

[143] See Law Society, *Criminal Procedure Rules: Impact on Solicitors' Duties to the Client* (2008).

[144] [2010] EWCA Crim 1928.   [145] [16].   [146] [21].   [147] [2011] EWCA Crim 2069.

allowed on the facts, as the recorder's repeated criticism of these inadequacies together with the directions he gave to the Crown about witnesses who were to be called would have created in the mind of the informed observer the perception that there was a real possibility that he had become biased against M.

A radical application of the CPR was evident in *R v Musone*, where they were used to justify the exclusion of defence evidence of 'substantial probative value'.[148] Musone had attempted to ambush a co-defendant, by introducing evidence of the co-defendant's bad character at a late stage; this was in breach of a provision requiring early notice of an intention to introduce bad character evidence. It seems that Musone could not have been prevented from doing this had the CPR not been in force. But in order to give the co-defendant a fair trial, the overriding objective was held to allow the judge to exclude the evidence. Similarly, in *R v Ensor* the defence 'failed totally to comply with either the spirit or the letter of the CPR' by failing to inform the prosecution or the court of a defence expert's report on which they intended to rely.[149] The court stated that 'the defence was in grave breach of the Criminal Procedure Rules' and that this was a 'deliberate tactical ploy' and 'nothing less than an attempt to ambush the prosecution'.[150]

Some might argue that the defence should not have to be helpful to the prosecution and that disclosure obligations, as well as some of the developments under the CPR, therefore are problematic. Increased participatory requirements on the defence contribute to a shift away from an adversarial system.[151] Even so, an uncompromising position that the defendant should not be required to disclose has little to be said for it.[152] Exceptions to the old rule that the defence does not have to disclose its case have long been recognized—an alibi notice provision was introduced as early as 1967, and appears to have been uncontroversial. And, as a matter of theory, it is not evident that the defence has a right to win a case by taking the prosecution by surprise. As the CPR's overriding objective recognizes, trials are at least in part a search for the truth, and ambush has no part to play in this. However, in Chapter 4 we noted that the privilege against self-incrimination is a widely recognized principle of criminal procedure, and the privilege was characterized in terms of a defendant's immunity from being placed under a duty to cooperate. Do disclosure obligations and the like infringe this principle? We suggest that they do not do so yet, though more recent developments in fact require defendants to cooperate to some extent. Whereas once we could argue that case law and the CPR merely decided that defendants should not be able to gain an advantage, such as an acquittal on technical grounds, through doing so, now the requirement to prepare a defence statement, and disclose the names and addresses of the witnesses it intends to call and details of any expert witnesses it has consulted, require a new

---

[148] [2007] EWCA Crim 1237.   [149] *R v Ensor* [2009] EWCA Crim 2519.
[150] [32].
[151] A. Owusu-Bempah, 'Defence participation through pre-trial disclosure: issues and implications' (2013) 17 *E&P* 183, 200. Also McEwan, n 142.
[152] See R. Mosteller, 'Discovery Against the Defense: Tilting the Adversarial Balance' (1986) 74 *California L Rev* 1567.

and unfamiliar degree of cooperation. This constitutes a steady erosion of adversarial norms. On the other hand, the statutory disclosure regime is enforced through adverse inferences, which like inferences from silence, can be said not to infringe the privilege. While the courts in cases such as *Malcolm* have been reasonably creative in dealing with procedure—for example, allowing the prosecution to recall a witness to address a late defence point after the justices had retired to decide the case—courts have not used the CPR to undermine aspects of procedure which might be said to embody substantive values. Thus, in *Shaw v DPP* the prosecution, realizing that it had made a mistake, changed the charge on which the defendant was to be tried at a late stage of proceedings. *Gleeson* was distinguished; the change, which suddenly put the defendant in jeopardy of imprisonment, was held to be inappropriate.[153] While *Musone* did involve the use of the CPR to exclude significant defence evidence, the Court of Appeal did note that this outcome should be rare,[154] and stressed that the exclusion was in pursuit of a fair trial for both defendants.

9.3 ABUSE OF PROCESS: AN OVERVIEW

In the remainder of this chapter we focus on the doctrine of abuse of process and its use to control criminal proceedings. We begin with a brief overview of abuse of process before considering its application to two particular areas: delay and entrapment.[155]

The courts, both civil and criminal, have an inherent power to regulate their own process. This extends to being able to stop a case from proceeding in order to prevent the judicial process from being abused; in more technical terms, the case is 'stayed' as an abuse of process. A stay is not equivalent to an acquittal, and it is possible that the authorities could attempt to prosecute the defendant again for the same offence. However, any such prosecution would almost certainly be stayed as an abuse of process itself. Of course, there are competing principles and interests at play here. As Sir Brian Leveson P noted in *Crawley*:

> there is a strong public interest in the prosecution of crime and in ensuring that those charged with serious criminal offences are tried. Ordering a stay of proceedings, which in criminal law is effectively a permanent remedy, is thus a remedy of last resort.[156]

There are two broad categories of case in which proceedings may be stayed:[157]

> namely (i) where it will be impossible to give the accused a fair trial, and (ii) where it offends the court's sense of justice and propriety to be asked to try the accused in the particular circumstances of the case. In the first category of case, if the court concludes that an

---

[153] [2007] EWHC 207 (Admin).
[154] *Musone*, n 148, [60]; also *R v Phillips* [2011] EWCA Crim 2935.
[155] See generally A. Choo, *Abuse of Process and Judicial Stays of Criminal Proceedings* (2nd edn, 2008); J. Rogers, 'The Boundaries of Abuse of Process in Criminal Trials' [2008] *CLP* 289.
[156] [2014] EWCA Crim 1028, [18].
[157] Choo, n 155, 18; *R v Beckford* [1996] 1 Cr App R 94.

accused cannot receive a fair trial, it will stay the proceedings without more. No question of the balancing of competing interests arises. In the second category of case, the court is concerned to protect the integrity of the criminal justice system.[158]

The first category of cases is where the defendant cannot receive a fair trial; an example would be where adverse media publicity has undermined the ability of the trial to proceed in an unbiased manner.[159] The second is where, although the defendant can still receive a fair trial in that he does not face an undue risk of false conviction, it would nevertheless be unfair to try him. A good flavour of the thinking behind this second type of abuse of process is provided by Lord Griffiths in one of the leading authorities, *R v Horseferry Road Magistrates' Court, ex p Bennett*.[160] Here, the defendant had been brought to Britain to stand trial, not through formal extradition procedures but by being arrested and handcuffed to the seat of an aeroplane bound for London:

> In the present case there is no suggestion that the appellant cannot have a fair trial, nor could it have been suggested that it would have been unfair to try him if he had been returned to this country through extradition procedures. If the court is to have the power to interfere with the prosecution in the present circumstances it must be because the judiciary accept a responsibility for the maintenance of the rule of law that embraces a willingness to oversee executive action and to refuse to countenance behaviour that threatens either basic human rights or the rule of law. . . . The courts, of course, have no power to apply direct discipline to the police or the prosecuting authorities, but they can refuse to allow them to take advantage of abuse of power by regarding their behaviour as an abuse of process and thus preventing a prosecution.[161]

A striking example of the application of the doctrine is *R v Grant*,[162] where the police installed a listening device in the exercise yard of the police station where Grant was held. In this way, they were able to overhear privileged conversations between the defendant and his solicitor; however, they apparently learned nothing of relevance to the case against Grant. Despite this, the Court of Appeal held that the trial should have been stayed as an abuse of process:

> we are in no doubt but that in general unlawful acts of the kind done in this case, amounting to a deliberate violation of a suspected person's right to legal professional privilege, are so great an affront to the integrity of the justice system, and therefore the rule of law, that the associated prosecution is rendered abusive and ought not to be countenanced by the court.[163]

The court continued by noting that the police's action 'seriously undermines the rule of law'.[164]

---

[158] *Maxwell* [2010] UKSC 48, [13].
[159] E.g. *R v McCann* (1991) 92 Cr App R 239.
[160] [1994] 1 AC 42.   [161] Ibid, 150.   [162] [2005] EWCA Crim 1089.
[163] Ibid, [54].   [164] Ibid, [57].

Grant was considered in *Warren v Attorney General of Jersey*, where the Privy Council took a rather more generous and conciliatory approach to egregious prosecutorial misconduct. The appellants appealed against a refusal by the Court of Appeal of Jersey to grant a stay of proceedings on the grounds of abuse of process, after the police acted unlawfully and misled the authorities of Jersey and three foreign states.[165] Indeed, without the product of the unlawfulness there would not have been a trial. Despite grave prosecutorial misconduct, a number of factors, taken cumulatively, were deemed to weigh heavily against a stay: the gravity of the offence; the fact that the 'ringleader' was a professional drug dealer who had recently been released from prison for a similar offence; the mitigation by the unwise advice of Crown Advocate of the gravity of the police misconduct; that there had been no attempt to mislead the court; and the real urgency for the police to keep on top of a fast-moving situation. The Board found it impossible to characterize the decision to refuse a stay, on the basis of a difficult balancing exercise, as perverse, or one which no reasonable judge could have reached.[166] Amongst this rather questionable 'balancing', quite how the inappropriate advice from a prosecutor mitigated rather than aggravated the situation regarding state abuse is hard to grasp.

Moreover, the Board in *Warren* considered that the decision in *Grant* was wrong.[167] Though agreeing that the deliberate invasion by the police of a suspect's right to legal professional privilege is a serious affront to the integrity of the justice system which may lead to a stay of proceedings, the Board stated that the particular circumstances of each case must be considered and carefully weighed in the balance. In these circumstances, the trial judge was entitled to refuse a stay and the Court of Appeal should not have held that his decision was wrong. In *Grant*, the stay seemed to be to express disapproval of the police misconduct and to discipline the police, which is not the function of the courts.[168]

As Lord Brown observed:

> In short, the essential principle for which in turn *Maxwell*, and now [*Warren*] . . . should be seen to stand, is that the court seised of the question whether proceedings should be stayed as an abuse of process, (or the analogous question whether a retrial should be ordered), has a very broad discretion indeed.[169]

O'Connor castigates the worrying lack of rigour throughout *Warren*, bemoaning the lack of coherent principle, and suggesting that it has lowered the standard of vigilance against abuses.[170] It is a markedly pragmatic decision, which elevates the pursuit of criminality over any concerns about state overreach.

---

[165] [2011] UKPC 10.   [166] [45]–[51].   [167] [36].   [168] [37].   [169] [80].
[170] P. O'Connor, '"Abuse of Process" after *Warren* and *Mitchell*' [2012] *Crim LR* 672, 677. See also P. Hungerford-Welch, 'Abuse of Process: Does It Really Protect the Suspect's Rights?' [2017] *Crim LR* 3.

9.4 DELAY

Generally, cases should be brought to trial as quickly as possible. There are several reasons why delay should be avoided. First, as we have observed on several occasions, the pre-trial stage involves considerable stress and uncertainty for defendants, as well as for victims. The case should be resolved as soon as possible so that all involved can get on with their lives. Where defendants are concerned, matters are even more serious where bail has been denied. Every day between remand and trial is an extra day in custody; while time served on remand can be taken into account at sentencing if the defendant is found guilty, no compensation is offered in the event of an acquittal. Secondly, human memory declines over time. The longer the period between the alleged crime and the trial, the less likely witnesses are to remember events clearly. Delay therefore makes the trial a less accurate means of adjudicating guilt and innocence. A third possible reason for avoiding delay has been highlighted in government initiatives to bring defendants to trial as quickly as possible—sometimes within days of the alleged crime. It is thought that a speedy response to offending reinforces the connection between the crime and its punishment, bringing home to offenders the consequences of their offending behaviour. Thus, there have been a series of efficiency-based initiatives from *Simple, Speedy, Summary Justice*;[171] *Swift and Sure Justice*;[172] through to Better Case Management (BCM), and TSJ.[173]

The rationale for 'active' case management to avoid delay in respect of criminal cases was reiterated and underlined by Lord Justice Judge in *Jisl*:

> Resources are limited. The funding for courts and judges, for prosecuting and the vast majority of defence lawyers is dependent on public money, for which there are many competing demands. Time itself is a resource. Every day unnecessarily used, while the trial meanders sluggishly to its eventual conclusion, represents another day's stressful waiting for the remaining witnesses and the jurors in that particular trial; and, no less important, continuing and increasing tension and worry for another defendant or defendants, some of whom are remanded in custody, and the witnesses in trials which are waiting their turn to be listed. It follows that the sensible use of time requires judicial management and control.[174]

Of course, it is possible for justice to be too quick, and earlier initiatives in expediting cases to trial raised concerns that the defence had been given insufficient time to prepare for court.[175]

Such concerns endure, though it seems delays are getting worse against a backdrop of continuing financial pressure. The timeliness of service of the Initial Details of the

---

[171] See Home Office, *Delivering Simple, Speedy, Summary Justice* (2006).

[172] Ministry of Justice, *Swift and Sure Justice: The Government's Plans for Reform of the Criminal Justice System* (2012).

[173] HMCPSI, *Business as Usual?*, n 28.   [174] *Jisl* [2004] EWCA Crim 696, [114].

[175] See D. Brown, *Reducing Delays in the Magistrates' Courts*, Home Office Research Findings No 131 (2000); J. Robins, 'The Speed of Fight', *Law Society Gazette*, 3 August 2000, 24.

Prosecution Case remains weak, with only 60.1 per cent of papers served by the CPS in accordance with TSJ timescales.[176] A delay at this juncture has significant knock-on effects. Moreover, backlogs in the Crown Court increased by 34 per cent between March 2013 and September 2015, and waiting time for a Crown Court hearing increased by 35 per cent (from 99 days to 134).[177] Some of this delay is ascribed to the abolition of committal hearings in 2013: in the year to September 2012, cases spent an average of 31 days in magistrates' courts, and a further 100 days waiting to be heard in Crown Court, whereas in the year ending September 2015, cases spent just five days in the magistrates' court on average, but then waited a further 134 days for a Crown Court hearing.[178] The situation in the magistrates' court is a little more positive: although the length of time spent preparing for magistrates' court cases increased from 119 to 133 days (10 per cent) between 2011 and 2015, the amount of time spent in court, including waiting for a court date, reduced from 23 to 22 days. This may be due to more time preparing cases, meaning that more cases are being resolved on the first hearing (71 per cent in 2014/15 compared with 62 per cent in 2010/11) and on average cases are taking slightly fewer hearings to be resolved (1.8 hearings per case in the year ending September 2011 to 1.6 in the year ending September 2015).[179]

Since then the average waiting times for all trials have started to fall: from 15.1 weeks to 14.1 weeks for guilty plea trials between 2016 and 2017, whilst not guilty plea trials decreased from 32.3 weeks to 29.9 weeks.[180] The more complex cases in the Crown Court, which may require ticketed judges who specialize in certain cases, inevitably take longer: the two offence groups with the longest waiting times in 2017 were fraud offences (26.9 weeks) and sexual offences (26.3 weeks).[181] The average number of days from first listing at the magistrates' court to completion in the Crown Court decreased by 19 days from 194 days in 2016 to 175 days in 2017.[182] There was a small increase in first listing at the magistrates' court to completion at the magistrates' court, from six days in 2016 to seven days in 2017.[183]

In the rest of this section, we concentrate on how the courts respond to cases in which there has been considerable delay in bringing a case to trial. There are three main contexts in which pre-trial delay becomes an issue. The first is where a number of years have elapsed between the alleged crime and its prosecution; this may happen, for example, in historical abuse cases where the victim does not feel able to report the crime until adulthood or much later in life. Secondly, where a defendant is remanded in custody time limits are imposed to ensure that the case does not take too long to come to trial. The courts often have to deal with situations where the prosecution argues that there are good reasons for extending the time limits. Finally, the courts also

---

[176] HMCPSI, *Business as Usual?*, n 28, 1.22.

[177] Comptroller and Auditor General, *Efficiency in the criminal justice system*, Session 2015–16, HC 852 (2016), paras 1.5–1.10.

[178] Para 1.10.   [179] Para 1.11.

[180] Ministry of Justice, *Criminal Justice Statistics quarterly, England and Wales, 2017* (2018), 13.

[181] Ibid, 14.   [182] Ibid, 18.   [183] Ibid.

concern themselves with delay between charge and trial, whether or not the defendant is detained. If the prosecution does not bring the case to trial within a reasonable time, the court may stop the prosecution as an abuse of process. Each of these contexts will be dealt with in turn.

(A) DELAY AND 'HISTORIC' OFFENCES

As far as historic offences are concerned, there is a very different approach between summary and indictable offences. For summary offences, proceedings must be started within six months of the alleged offence having taken place.[184] Apart from such cases, in English criminal law there is no statute of limitations.[185] There is thus no bar to bringing a case to court 20, 30, 50, or even more years after the alleged crime was committed. This is of particular significance in relation to sexual abuse cases,[186] which are reported more readily and pursued more robustly than before.

A decision to prosecute an offence which occurred many years ago should not be taken lightly. Quite apart from the difficulty of gathering reliable evidence, it may be argued that it is not right to hold someone to account for something that they did many years ago, given that their personality and circumstances may have changed completely during the intervening years. This is perhaps most pertinent where an adult is prosecuted for a crime committed during their youth. There was some recognition of this in the Code for Crown Prosecutors, which, among the public interest factors against prosecution, once referred to a situation where 'there has been a long delay between the offence taking place and the date of the trial',[187] though this was not included in the 2013 or 2018 Codes.

The primary concern of the courts in delay cases of this type is whether the defendant can have a fair trial, in the sense of defending himself adequately against the charges brought by the prosecution. There are two principal devices available to the courts to deal with this. The first is a warning to the jury about the difficulties caused by delay. The Crown Court Compendium indicates that the jury should be directed: to consider the length of and the reasons for the delay in making the complaint and ask whether or not the delay makes the victim's evidence in court more difficult to believe; to not assume that a late complaint is bound to be false, any more than an immediate complaint definitely would be truthful; and that victims of sexual offences can react in different ways, and some may not speak out until some time has passed.[188]

---

[184] Magistrates' Courts Act 1980, s 127; r 7.2.5.

[185] Though a few offences do have time limits attached to them, e.g. under the Trade Descriptions Act 1968, s 19, prosecutions for indictable offences under the Act must be commenced within three years of the offence, or one year of its discovery, whichever is the earlier.

[186] See CPS, *Abuse of Process Legal Guidance*, https://www.cps.gov.uk/legal-guidance/abuse-process.

[187] *Code for Crown Prosecutors* (2010), para 6.5.

[188] Judicial College, *Crown Court Compendium Part I* (2017), 10–14.

In some cases, the courts will go further than this, and may stay the prosecution on the grounds that it is an abuse of process. An application to stay for abuse of process on the grounds of delay must be determined in accordance with *Attorney-General's Reference (No 1 of 1990)*:[189] it cannot succeed unless, exceptionally, a fair trial is no longer possible owing to prejudice to the defendant caused by the delay which cannot be addressed fairly in the normal trial process. The presence or absence of explanation or justification for the delay is relevant only insofar as it bears on that question.[190]

The relevant principles are summarized in *R v S*:

(i)   Even where delay is unjustifiable, a permanent stay should be the exception rather than the rule;

(ii) Where there is no fault on the part of the complainant or the prosecution, it will be very rare for a stay to be granted;

(iii) No stay should be granted in the absence of serious prejudice to the defence so that no fair trial can be held;

(iv) When assessing possible serious prejudice, the judge should bear in mind his or her power to regulate the admissibility of evidence and that the trial process itself should ensure that all relevant factual issues arising from delay will be placed before the jury for their consideration in accordance with appropriate direction from the judge;

(v)   If, having considered all these factors, a judge's assessment is that a fair trial will be possible, a stay should not be granted.[191]

In *R v TBF*, the Court of Appeal quashed convictions for sexual offences as an abuse of process after delays of between 30 and 40 years, where there was no good reason for the long delay.[192] Although the complainants' mother had confronted the appellant 27 years previously, she had not reported him to the police. The Court of Appeal reviewed the case law, stating that *Galbraith*, *Attorney-General's Reference (No 1 of 1990)*, *R v S*, and the present decision contain all the necessary discussion about the applicable principles.[193] Any application of these is to be regarded as a fact-specific decision rather than an elaboration of or amendment to the governing principles. The Court of Appeal derived the following five propositions in relation to prosecutions brought after a long delay:

i)   the court should stay proceedings on some or all counts of the indictment for abuse of process if, and only if, it is satisfied on balance of probabilities that by reason of delay a fair trial is not possible on those counts;

---

[189] *Attorney-General's Reference (No 1 of 1990)* [1992] QB 630.
[190] *CPS v F* [2011] EWCA Crim 1844, [38]–[40]. See A. Choo, 'Abuse of Process and Delayed Prosecutions' in P. Radcliffe, G. Gudjonsson, A. Heaton-Armstrong, and D. Wolchover (eds), *Witness Testimony in Sexual Cases: Evidential, Investigative and Scientific Perspectives* (2016).
[191] [2006] EWCA Crim 756, [21]. *S* also notes that, contrary to what was said in some of the earlier cases, the defendant does not bear a burden of proof to show that a fair trial would not be possible.
[192] [2011] EWCA Crim 726.   [193] [47].

ii)   it is now recognised that usually the proper time for the defence to make such an
      application and for the judge to rule upon it is at trial, after all the evidence has
      been called;

iii) in assessing what prejudice has been caused to the defendant on any particu-
      lar count by reason of delay, the court should consider what evidence directly
      relevant to the defence case has been lost through the passage of time. Vague
      speculation that lost documents or deceased witnesses might have assisted the de-
      fendant is not helpful. The court should also consider what evidence has survived
      the passage of time. The court should then examine critically how important the
      missing evidence is in the context of the case as a whole;

iv)   having identified the prejudice caused to the defence by reason of the delay, it
      is then necessary to consider to what extent the judge can compensate for that
      prejudice by emphasising guidance given in standard directions or formulat-
      ing special directions to the jury. Where important independent evidence has
      been lost over time, it may not be known which party that evidence would have
      supported. There may be cases in which no direction to the jury can dispel the
      resultant prejudice which one or other of the parties must suffer, but this depends
      on the facts of the case;

v)   if the complainant's delay in coming forward is unjustified, that is relevant to the
      question whether it is fair to try the defendant so long after the events in issue.
      In determining whether the complainant's delay is unjustified, it must be firmly
      borne in mind that victims of sexual abuse are often unwilling to reveal or talk
      about their experiences for some time and for good reason.[194]

An 'extreme' delay was considered in *R v D*, where D appealed against his conviction
for a number of sexual offences against three nieces and the sexual abuse and rape of
his daughter between 39 and 63 years earlier.[195] D argued that the delay had resulted
in missing evidence, due to witnesses having died or becoming infirm, and documents
being destroyed or lost. The Court of Appeal held that the resulting missing evidence
was not so cogent as to amount to a finding of serious prejudice in its absence. Moreover, the trial judge had given the jury appropriate directions regarding the effect of the
delay—D's convictions were safe.[196]

(B) CUSTODY TIME LIMITS

Article 5 of the ECHR protects the right to liberty. Pre-trial detention is permissible
but a defendant so detained is 'entitled to trial within a reasonable time or to release
pending trial'. The ECtHR has held that where the defendant is detained, the prosecution must act with 'special diligence' in bringing the case to trial.[197]

Where indictable offences are concerned, English law has various provisions which
help to ensure that defendants remanded in custody are brought to trial within a

---

[194] [37].   [195] [2013] EWCA Crim 1592.   [196] [24].
[197] *Stögmüller v Austria* (1979) 1 EHRR 155, [5].

reasonable timeframe. A defendant can be remanded in custody for 28 days only; after that period, a new decision must be taken. More importantly, the Prosecution of Offences Act 1985 and regulations issued under it contain provisions on custody time limits. Under these, for example, a defendant charged with an offence triable only on indictment is entitled to trial within 182 days of his case being transferred to the Crown Court.[198] If a time limit expires, a defendant is entitled to be released on bail, but the prosecution may apply for extension of the time limit before expiration. An extension should not be granted unless the court is satisfied that there is good and sufficient cause (the section lists the illness or absence of a judge or important witness as good causes, among others), and that the prosecution has acted 'with all due diligence and expedition'.[199] The court must focus strictly on these two statutory questions, and it is neither desirable nor possible to define what amounts to 'good and sufficient' cause.[200]

CPS compliance to custody time limit (CTL) standards varies across locations and there are numerous 'failures' in their effective monitoring.[201] That said, on the whole, the courts take custody time limits seriously and are reluctant to extend them.[202] Indeed, the High Court stressed that any application to extend a custody time limit must be treated in a 'very serious manner'.[203] While the prosecution is to be judged by 'realistic, not impossible, standards and . . . should not in any event be refused an extension unless its lack of due diligence and expedition has in fact delayed the trial date',[204] the courts will not look favourably, when considering whether there has been due expedition, on 'pretexts such as chronic staff shortages, . . . overwork, sickness, absenteeism or matters of that kind'.[205] Factors such as the complexity of the case and the cooperativeness of the accused are relevant, however. Delay caused by actors external to the prosecution may justify extension of a custody time limit: for example, delays caused by foreign prosecutors[206] or by the late provision of phone logs by a mobile phone company.[207] Such factors are no fault of the prosecuting authorities; some cases will always take longer to come to trial than others, and so long as the prosecution has done all it can, an extension of the time limit seems appropriate.

The contemporary issue of financial constraints and the impact of budget cuts were considered in the otherwise 'routine' case of *R (McAuley) v Coventry Crown Court*.[208] McAuley applied for judicial review of the Crown Court's decision to extend the CTL,

---

[198] Prosecution of Offences (Custody Time Limits) Regulations 1987 (SI 1987/299), reg 5.
[199] Prosecution of Offences Act 1985, s 22(3).
[200] *Campbell-Brown v Central Criminal Court* [2015] EWHC 202 (Admin), [65]–[66].
[201] HMCPSI, *Custody time limits: A report relating to the handling of custody time limits by the Crown Prosecution Service* (2010); HMCPSI, *Custody time limits: Follow-up review of the handling of custody time limits by the Crown Prosecution Service* (2013).
[202] See, generally, A. Samuels, 'Custody Time Limits' [1997] *Crim LR* 260.
[203] *R (Raeside) v CPS* [2012] EWHC 1064 (Admin), [33].
[204] *R (O) v Harrow Crown Court* [2006] UKHL 42, [57].
[205] *R v Manchester Crown Court, ex p McDonald* [1990] 1 WLR 841, 847.
[206] As in ibid.
[207] *R (Thomas) v Central Criminal Court* [2006] EWHC 2138 (Admin).
[208] [2012] EWHC 680 (Admin).

claiming that it had been a systemic failure in HM Courts and Tribunal Service (HMCTS) to provide sufficient funds to enable defendants in custody to be tried within the maximum period allowed by law. HMCTS conceded that the CTL should not have been extended, and the High Court therefore quashed the decision.

The High Court described the CTL as a:

> vital feature of our system of justice which distinguishes it from many other countries. It puts a premium on careful management of all resources and the efficient conduct of business by the court administration under the direction of the judiciary. Not only does it provide sure means of compliance with a principle of the common law as old as Magna Carta that justice delayed is justice denied, but it has the collateral benefit that money is not squandered by the unnecessary detention of persons in prison awaiting trial at significant cost to the taxpayer.[209]

The High Court noted that in the present financial circumstances, pressure on court resources available to try such cases will be tight, but that the Secretary of State when seeking funds for the Ministry of Justice did not make any amendment to the time limit set out in the Regulations or ask Parliament to approve an amendment, and so in routine cases, such as the present, it would not be necessary to extend a CTL unless there were exceptional or unusual circumstances.[210] This puts a subtle gloss on the statutory terminology.

McAuley was cited and considered the same year in *R (Raeside) v CPS* where the High Court emphasized that 'If a case is fixed outside the CTL and there is no express consent to this, it is for the court itself to take the initiative in seeing that an immediate application by the Crown is made and heard as soon as is practicable.'[211]

In rare circumstances, a court may refuse both to extend a CTL and to release the person detained. This was the outcome in *R (O) v Harrow Crown Court*[212] where, under s 25 of the Criminal Justice and Public Order Act 1994, D, who had a previous conviction for rape, could not be granted bail on a charge of rape unless there were exceptional circumstances. The House of Lords held that in this situation there was no breach of Art 5(3), because the lack of due diligence, which prevented an extension of the custody time limit, did not necessarily equate with the lack of 'special diligence' which triggers Art 5(3).

This decision was upheld in *O'Dowd v UK*, where the ECtHR stated that it did not consider that 'due diligence' under s 22(3) could be equated to 'special diligence' as required by Art 5(3).[213] Unlike the domestic courts, the ECtHR examines the proceedings as a whole and assesses any particular periods of inactivity or delay by the authorities within the context of the overall period of pre-trial detention, with particular regard to official recognition of the time already spent in detention and the need to take additional steps to bring about a more speedy trial.[214] The ECtHR was satisfied

---

[209] [25].   [210] [30].   [211] *R (Raeside) v CPS*, n 203, [31].   [212] See n 204.
[213] (2012) 54 EHRR 8, [73].   [214] [73].

that the authorities displayed special diligence in progressing the applicant's case and that any delay attributable to them did not exceed what was reasonable, noting the substantial contribution by O'Dowd to the overall length of his pre-trial detention through his conduct of his defence and his choices regarding his legal representation.[215] In conclusion, the Court found no violation of Art 5(3).[216]

What if a CTL is about to expire, and the prosecutor replaces the original charge against the defendant with a new one? The literal effect of the rules is that a new time limit will start to run with the introduction of the new charge; the obvious problem here is that this may allow the prosecutor to manipulate the rules. In very limited circumstances, this might be an abuse of process. This situation was considered in *R v Leeds Crown Court, ex p Wardle*.[217] The defendant had originally been charged with murder for causing death during a burglary. When the CTL was about to expire, the prosecution substituted the murder charge for one of manslaughter. On appeal to the Crown Court, the judge considered that, had the charge not been changed, an extension of the CTL would not have been granted: the prosecution had not acted with due expedition. Nevertheless, the effect of the new charge was to institute a new time limit, so the defendant lost his automatic right to release on bail. The defendant was, of course, free to make a new application for bail, but this was turned down because he had a previous history of offending on bail and of not surrendering. The case eventually reached the House of Lords. All of the judges expressed some concern about the way the rules allow a new charge to institute a new time limit, but a majority held that the law could not be interpreted in such a way as to allow the defendant's release in this situation. Nor could there be said to have been an abuse of process. Wardle applied to the ECtHR, claiming that his Art 5 rights had been breached, but his application was ruled inadmissible. The Court considered that there had been adequate judicial supervision of the decision to keep him in custody, and that the prosecution had acted with sufficient expedition.[218]

Wardle leaves the law in an unsatisfactory state, and, though cited in argument, was not referred to by the ECtHR in the judgment in *O'Dowd*. *Wardle* involved some dubious performance on the part of the police and prosecutors and, from the facts, it is difficult to see why a charge of murder was ever considered appropriate. The victim, who had a weak heart, seems to have died from a combination of shock and minor injuries, facts which do not suggest any intention to kill or cause serious harm. One would have expected the charge to have been reduced at a much earlier stage. There is also the Crown Court judge's finding that the prosecution had not acted with much urgency in disclosing witness statements and in obtaining video evidence. The just result here would seem to involve blocking the start of a new time limit, and a minority in the House of Lords (Lord Nicholls and Lord Scott) did think that the rules could be read so as to achieve this. Another way of protecting the defendant would be to stay the

---

[215] [76].   [216] [77].   [217] [2002] 1 AC 754.
[218] *Wardle v UK* (2003) 4 EHRLR 459.

proceedings for abuse of process. There was general agreement in the House of Lords that this device might be used in extreme cases: where a new charge was substituted solely to introduce a new time limit. But that was not felt to be the case here, because the charge had also been altered for good reasons, in that the evidence did not support the murder charge. Staying the trial for abuse of process would certainly be a drastic step in *Wardle*, for it would more or less ensure that Wardle could not be tried for a serious crime, so it is no surprise that all the judges were cautious about this remedy. Given that a stay was not thought appropriate in *Wardle*, it seems unlikely that there will be many cases where it will be justified; it will not be often that a prosecutor introduces a new charge *solely* to extend a time limit.

(C) DELAY BETWEEN CHARGE AND TRIAL

There is a common law right to be tried without unreasonable delay or, to put the matter differently, the courts have an inherent jurisdiction to prevent an abuse of their process where there has been unreasonable delay in bringing a case to trial.[219] This general right applies whether or not the defendant is in custody, and so can be distinguished from the issue of custody time limits discussed in the previous section. However, the English courts have insisted that the remedy of staying the prosecution for abuse of process should be invoked sparingly, and only where there has been clear fault on the part of the prosecution or where the delay has seriously prejudiced the defendant.[220] This approach prompts the question of the appropriate remedy for the general run of cases in which delay occurs and whether, in those circumstances, what we have is a right without a remedy. This difficult issue has been brought into sharp relief by the Human Rights Act and by several decisions of the ECtHR. Before returning to the question of remedies for breach, we consider the general approach of the Convention, and how the English courts have interpreted and applied it.

The ECHR provides various guarantees of timely decision making in criminal justice (e.g. Art 5(3), arrestee should be 'brought promptly before a judge'; Art 5(4), person detained 'entitled to take proceedings by which the lawfulness of his detention shall be decided speedily by a court'), but the most relevant for present purposes is the guarantee in Art 6(1)—applicable equally to civil and criminal cases—of a 'fair and public hearing *within a reasonable time* by an independent and impartial tribunal'. It was established by the Court at an early stage that the rationale for this right is that individuals should not be allowed to remain 'too long in a state of uncertainty about their fate',[221] although subsequently the Court has emphasized more broadly 'the

---

[219] See e.g. the Privy Council in *Bell v DPP of Jamaica* [1985] AC 937, and the High Court of Australia in *Jago v District Court of New South Wales* (1989) 87 ALR 577.

[220] For magistrates' courts, see *R v Brentford JJ, ex p Wong* [1981] QB 445; for the Crown Court, see *Attorney-General's Reference (No 1 of 1990)* [1992] QB 630.

[221] *Stögmüller v Austria* (1979) 1 EHRR 155, 5.

importance of rendering justice without delays which might jeopardise its effectiveness and credibility'.[222] We may identify four key questions about the extent and effect of this right—when time begins to run, to what decisions the right applies, what amounts to a breach, and what remedies should be given.

i. When does time begin to run?

For the purposes of both Arts 5 and 6, it was established by the ECtHR in *Deweer v Belgium*[223] that time begins to run from the point of charge, but that the term 'charge' has an autonomous meaning in this context which approximates to whether 'the situation of the [suspect] has been substantially affected'. The *Deweer* approach was applied by the Court in *Heaney and McGuinness v Ireland*,[224] holding that the applicants had been 'charged' for this purpose when served with a notice requiring them to account for their movements, prior to being formally charged with an offence.

However, in *Attorney-General's Reference (No 2 of 2001)*[225] Lord Bingham, with whom all their Lordships concurred on this point, held that time will usually begin to run from the point at which a person is charged (in the English sense) or summoned, adding mysteriously that this is not an inflexible rule. He referred to the ECtHR decision in *Howarth v UK*,[226] where the Court held that time began to run from the point at which the applicant had been interviewed by the Serious Fraud Squad, some four and a half months before he was charged. Without engaging with that decision or the other ECHR jurisprudence, Lord Bingham commented that 'arrest will not ordinarily mark the beginning of that period. An official indication that a person will be reported with a view to prosecution may, depending on the circumstances, do so'.[227]

There are two obvious difficulties with the House of Lords' position. First, Lord Bingham appeared to depart from the ECtHR approach without giving reasons for doing so—he is entitled to do this, but when s 2 of the Human Rights Act 1998 states that a British court 'must take into account' ECtHR jurisprudence, one would expect a discussion of the relevant decisions and good reasons to be offered for taking a different approach. Secondly, Lord Bingham's speech leaves it unclear under what circumstances an English court may properly hold that time begins to run before the point of charge. This is manifestly unsatisfactory: should courts be guided by the ECtHR decisions (such as *Deweer*, *Howarth*, and *Heaney and McGuinness*), or is Lord Bingham signalling an approach that is more flexible from the prosecutor's point of view but different from the Convention jurisprudence?

ii. To which stages of the criminal process does the guarantee apply?

The ECHR jurisprudence indicates that the 'reasonable time' guarantee applies from the time of arrest through to the final stage of appeals. Thus in *Howarth v UK*,[228] a

---

[222] *H v France* (1990) 12 EHRR 74.   [223] (1980) 2 EHRR 30.   [224] (2000) 33 EHRR 264.
[225] [2003] UKHL 68.   [226] (2001) 31 EHRR 861.   [227] [2003] UKHL 68, [28].
[228] (2001) 31 EHRR 861.

two-year delay in dealing with an appeal was held to breach Art 6(1); in *Mellors v UK*,[229] a three-year delay between trial and appeal in Scotland was held unreasonable; and in *Reid v UK*,[230] the Court held that:

> The delays which appear in this case cannot be justified either by the complexity of the case or the exigencies of internal procedure. While one year per instance may be a rule of thumb in Art. 6(1) cases, Art. 5(4) concerning issues of liberty requires particular expedition.

This contrast is not so much between the 'reasonable time' guarantees in the two Articles, as between whether the appellant was in custody or not—the Court has rightly insisted that custody cases call for greater expedition.

In *R (on the application of Lloyd) v Bow Street Magistrates' Court*,[231] the Divisional Court held that the guarantee covers the execution of a sentence or ancillary order made on conviction. Thus, Dyson LJ found no difficulty in applying Art 6(1) to the enforcement of a confiscation order made on conviction for conspiracy to handle stolen goods: 'such proceedings are part and parcel of the confiscation proceedings, which in turn are part and parcel of the original criminal proceedings'. In *Crowther v UK*, the ECtHR found, in relation to the requirement to pay a confiscation order, that a period of over four years of almost 'total inactivity' on the part of Customs had resulted in a breach of Art 6(1).[232] Thus, the question of unreasonable delay may be raised at any point between the initial charge (howsoever interpreted) and the final appeal or final act of enforcing orders of the court.

iii. What amounts to a breach?

It is well established that the length of a delay must be considered in relation to the complexity of the case and the conduct of the public authorities (prosecution, court) and of the defendant.[233] As the ECtHR put it in *Mellors v UK*:

> the reasonableness of the length of proceedings must be assessed in the light of the circumstances of the case and having regard to . . . the complexity of the case, the conduct of the applicant and of the relevant authorities, and the importance of what is at stake for the applicant.[234]

In that case, the delay of three years and two weeks in dealing with the appeal was held unreasonable: the case was not unduly complex, and although the defence contributed in a small way to the delays, the major problem was one of listing the appeal. Similarly, in *Ahmed v Birmingham Magistrates' Court and the CPS*,[235] a Divisional Court held that a delay of some three years in enforcing a summons for dangerous driving and bringing the case to court breached Art 6(1). This was too long 'for the trial of a very simple, uncomplicated case of dangerous driving'. The causes lay in the court's failure

---

[229] App No 57836/00, Judgment of 17 July 2003.
[230] (2003) 37 EHRR 211.   [231] [2004] *Crim LR* 136.
[232] *Crowther v UK*, App No 53741/00, 1 February 2005.   [233] *Konig v Germany* (1978) 2 EHRR 170.
[234] See n 229, [28].   [235] [2003] EWHC 72 (Admin).

to notice that it was sending letters to the wrong address, and in certain periods of unexplained inactivity, and there was no evidence that the defendant was trying to avoid or escape trial.

In *R (on the application of Lloyd) v Bow Street Magistrates' Court*, it had taken some five years for proceedings to be brought against the applicant to enforce the confiscation order in respect of the unpaid portion. Among other delays were two years during which the receiver appointed by the court did nothing, and a further year's delay before the final summons could be heard at Bow Street. Dyson LJ stated:

> Convicted criminals who are the subject of confiscation orders do not attract sympathy, and are not entitled to favoured treatment. But there is nothing surprising about the requirement that, if the prosecuting authorities/magistrates court seek to enforce a confiscation order, they should do so within a reasonable time. It is potentially very unfair on a defendant that he should be liable to be committed to prison for non-payment of sums due under a confiscation order many years after the time for payment has expired, and long after he has been released from custody and resumed work and family life.[236]

This is important in the way that it brings the discussion back to the reasons for respecting the right to be tried without unreasonable delay—the effects on people's lives and decision making about their future.

In *Beggs v UK*, the relevant proceedings in Scotland lasted more than ten years, and were complicated and vast.[237] While some elements of the delays were not caused by the authorities, or were justified, there were periods of inactivity by the judicial authorities.[238] Accordingly, there had been a violation of Art 6(1). The ECtHR highlighted the difficult decisions to be made by the domestic courts where aspects of Art 6 appear to be in conflict: 'In particular, the right to a trial within a reasonable time must be balanced against the need to afford to the defence sufficient time to prepare its case and must not unduly restrict the right of the defence to equality of arms. Thus in assessing whether the length of proceedings was reasonable, particularly in a case where an applicant relies upon the court's responsibility to take steps to advance the proceedings, this Court must have regard to the reasons for the delay and the extent to which delay resulted from an effort to secure other key rights guaranteed by art.6.'[239]

In *Piper v UK*, P complained that the length of proceedings brought against him for drug trafficking, lasting more than 11 years, breached the 'reasonable time' requirement under Art 6(1).[240] This was through no fault of his own, but rather by reason of the working of the British system of administration of justice. Such a delay merited a finding that there had been a breach of Art 6(1), though given the limited prejudice caused by the delay and the fact that only a relatively small proportion of the overall length of the proceedings was attributable to it, it was not 'necessary' in terms of Art 41 to afford the complainant any financial compensation. The ECtHR applied *Beggs* in

---

[236] [2003] EWHC 2294 (Admin), [25].   [237] (2013) 56 EHRR 26, [235].   [238] [261]–[273].
[239] [240].   [240] (2015) 61 EHRR 38.

assessing whether the length of proceedings was reasonable, having regard to the reasons for the delay and the extent to which delay resulted from an effort to secure other key rights guaranteed by Art 6.[241]

iv. What is the appropriate remedy for breach?

The House of Lords accepted in *Porter v Magill*[242] that the right to trial within a reasonable time is a free-standing right safeguarded by Art 6(1): it is no answer to a breach of this right that other rights guaranteed by Art 6, such as the right to a fair trial before an independent and impartial tribunal, have been respected. The more difficult question concerns remedies. The Strasbourg Court has acknowledged that breach of the right does not necessarily render the whole proceedings a nullity,[243] but because it operates after exhaustion of local remedies that Court has never had to consider the proper approach to a case which has been delayed so that the trial has not yet taken place. It has, however, held that each Contracting State must have in place a remedy or range of remedies for breach of the right which are effective in law and in practice.[244] What remedies English law offers was the principal question before the nine members of the House of Lords in *Attorney-General's Reference (No 2 of 2001)*.[245] The House of Lords held by a majority of 7:2 that it will rarely be appropriate to stay the proceedings if they have not yet begun, because there is a strong public interest in having charges tried. A court should therefore consider lesser remedies such as compensation or mitigation of sentence. Thus, Lord Bingham held that:

> The appropriate remedy will depend on the nature of the breach and all the circumstances, including particularly the stage of the proceedings at which the breach is established. If the breach is established before the hearing, the appropriate remedy may be a public acknowledgement of the breach, action to expedite the hearing to the greatest extent practicable and perhaps, if the defendant is in custody, his release on bail. It will not be appropriate to stay or dismiss the proceedings unless (a) there can no longer be a fair hearing or (b) it would otherwise be unfair to try the defendant. The public interest in the final determination of criminal charges requires that such a charge should not be stayed or dismissed if any lesser remedy will be just and proportionate in all the circumstances. The prosecutor and the court do not act incompatibly with the defendant's Convention right in continuing to prosecute or entertain proceedings after a breach is established in a case where neither of conditions (a) or (b) is met, since the breach consists in the delay which has accrued and not in the prospective hearing.

Two judges delivered strong dissents to the majority decision, Lord Hope arguing that the majority approach 'empties the reasonable time guarantee almost entirely of content'.[246] However, in a later Privy Council decision, which provided an opportunity to review more ECHR case law, the dissenting judges reconciled themselves to the majority view.[247]

---

[241] [50].   [242] [2002] 2 AC 357.   [243] *Bunkate v Netherlands* (1993) 19 EHRR 477.
[244] *Kudla v Poland*, App No 30210/96, Judgment of 26 October 2000, [158].
[245] [2003] UKHL 68.   [246] Ibid, [46].   [247] *Spiers v Ruddy* [2007] UKPC D2.

It is clear from the decision in *Attorney General's Reference* that (b) is intended to be a narrow category. It includes 'cases of bad faith, unlawfulness and executive manipulation', but may also go a little further than this. Lord Bingham accepted that there may be cases 'where the delay is of such an order, or where a prosecutor's breach of professional duty is such . . . as to make it unfair that the proceedings against a defendant should continue'. *Darmalingum v The State*[248] was provided as an example of extreme delay; that the delay in the case was 15 years from charge to the close of proceedings suggests that this will be a narrow category. There remains, then, the question whether 'lesser remedies' than a stay are really sufficient in cases where there has been delay that is neither that extreme nor involves a breach of professional duty by the prosecutor. If the rationale of the right to a timely trial is that a defendant should not face excessive uncertainty over his future, then there is a good argument that courts should be prepared to stay proceedings in more than just the narrow category indicated by (b).[249]

9.5 ENTRAPMENT

Many of the pre-trial issues we have considered in this chapter are connected to the fairness of the trial: by regulating disclosure, and considering issues of delay, the pre-trial process offers an opportunity to ensure that the coming trial is as fair as possible. In extreme cases, as in those involving unreasonable delay, a stay for abuse of process can be used to prevent the trial from taking place at all. Our final topic in this chapter considers the use of pre-trial remedies as a response to entrapment. Here, the courts will sometimes prevent a trial from taking place because the police have gone beyond their law enforcement role by 'creating' the crime with which the offender is charged.

Although the majority of recorded offences are reported to the police by members of the public, there are a minority of cases in which the police decide to adopt proactive methods. Typically, these are crimes without direct victims, such as drug-related crimes or those involving a form of conspiracy or other organization. Intelligence-led policing may take different forms,[250] and our concern here is with approaches that rely on the deployment of undercover officers or participant informers. We saw in Chapter 4 that the use of surveillance may impinge on the target person's right to respect for private life, and that this is why the ECtHR has insisted on certain safeguards, which the Regulation of Investigatory Powers Act 2000 attempted to translate into English

---

[248] [2000] 1 WLR 2303.

[249] See further J. Jackson and J. Johnstone, 'The Reasonable Time Requirement: An Independent and Meaningful Right?' [2005] *Crim LR* 3.

[250] For discussion, see M. Maguire, 'Policing by Risks and Targets: Some Dimensions and Implications of Intelligence-Led Policing' (2000) 9 *Policing and Society* 315, and R. Billingsley, T. Nemitz, and P. Bean (eds), *Informers: Policing, Policy, Practice* (2001); S. McKay, *Covert Policing: Law and Practice* (2nd edn, 2015).

law.[251] Proactive methods of law enforcement such as undercover policing and the use of participant informers raise similar questions about the right to respect for private life and the prevention of arbitrary interference by state officials, but they also raise a deeper question about the right to a fair trial under Art 6. If the state, through the police or a police-instigated informant, engages in an operation to test whether a person will commit a crime in a given situation, there is a point at which this becomes state-created crime; and for the state to create a crime and then to prosecute a person for it would be a gross abuse of power. As we will see, the contention is that in this situation it would not be fair to try the defendant at all. This is how the point of principle was put in the leading English decision:

> It is simply not acceptable that the state through its agents should lure its citizens into committing acts forbidden by the law and then seek to prosecute them for doing so. That would be entrapment. That would be a misuse of state power, and an abuse of the process of the courts. The unattractive consequences, frightening and sinister in extreme cases, which state conduct of this kind could have are obvious. The role of the courts is to stand between the state and its citizens and make sure this does not happen.[252]

This does not rule out all forms of proactive policing, as we will see. But it purports to set a limit to the exercise of police power and to create a realm of protection for citizens. It does so both because citizens should not be tempted by state officials in this way; if they are, the trial should be stayed in order to protect the defendant from unjust conviction. As the ECtHR put it in the leading decision of *Teixeira de Castro v Portugal*:

> The Court concludes that the two officers' action went beyond those of undercover agents because they instigated the offence and there is nothing to suggest that without their intervention it would have been committed. That intervention and its use in the impugned criminal proceedings meant that, right from the outset, the applicant was definitively deprived of a fair trial.[253]

Thus, the leading decisions in both Strasbourg and London hold that the appropriate remedy for entrapment is that the proceedings should not take place at all—in England, this indicates a stay of the proceedings for abuse of process.

What form of activity by law enforcement agents amounts to entrapment and justifies this remedy? The House of Lords in *Looseley*[254] concluded that it would be acceptable for the police to target an individual if three conditions are fulfilled. First, they must have reasonable grounds to suspect that person of involvement in the offence or, more broadly, reasonable grounds for suspecting people who frequent a certain place

---

[251] For comments on the extent to which this has been achieved, see Ch 5.

[252] Per Lord Nicholls in *Attorney-General's Reference (No 3 of 2000); Looseley* [2001] UKHL 53. For analysis of the decision, see A. Ashworth, 'Re-Drawing the Boundaries of Entrapment' [2002] *Crim LR* 161.

[253] (1999) 28 EHRR 101, 39. See also *Furcht v Germany* (2015) 61 EHRR 25 where undercover officers had not confined themselves to investigating criminal activity in an essentially passive manner, but exerted such an influence on the subject as to incite the commission of an offence that would otherwise not have been committed.

[254] [2001] UKHL 53.

of being thus involved. Secondly, the officers or informants should be duly authorized to carry out the operation in accordance with the Codes of Practice issued under the Regulation of Investigatory Powers Act 2000: this is a procedural requirement, and is intended to enhance supervision and to remove arbitrariness. For example, the Code of Practice makes it clear that proactive methods should not be used unless less intrusive methods of investigation are likely to be unsuccessful. And, thirdly, if the first two conditions are fulfilled, the officer or participating informant must do no more than provide the suspect with an unexceptional opportunity to commit the offence. Formerly this was sometimes phrased in terms of passive rather than active involvement, but in practice the officer or informant will often have to do some acts in order to provide the opportunity. The key factor is that the officer or informant should act normally, as a potential customer would do in a given situation, and not hold out any extra temptation.

The application and interpretation of the first element of *Looseley* has been problematic. The notion of reasonable suspicion plays an important role in Art 5(1), in justifying restrictions of liberty such as arrest, and has been emphasized by Strasbourg in its various decisions on entrapment.[255] But the difficulty with *Looseley* is the extension of reasonable suspicion to places as well as people.[256] Since entrapment is not the only way of dealing with areas where it is known that offending is taking place but not who the offenders are—it might, for example, be possible to set up a surveillance operation in order to determine which individuals might reasonably be suspected of involvement in offences—it may be argued that this extension of the condition is not Convention-compliant. In fact, the Court of Appeal decision in *Moon* went some way towards accepting this criticism.[257] The police targeted a bus station where they believed drug-dealing was taking place, and after some initial reluctance the defendant supplied heroin to an undercover officer. On appeal, the prosecution accepted that there was no reasonable suspicion that the defendant was anything other than an addict, and on this basis the Court of Appeal held that proceedings should have been stayed.

Moon was distinguished in *R v Jones*,[258] a case concerning an undercover officer's test purchases from a shop of cannabis-growing paraphernalia, together with advice on growing cannabis, under the pretence that this was for the growing of tomatoes. An application to stay for abuse of process was refused by the judge and an appeal was dismissed.

In *R v Moore*,[259] the police set up an undercover operation to target drug and firearm crime in a particular area of London. Undercover officers established themselves as criminals offering cheap goods for sale as a cover story. During the operation, officers

---

[255] *Vanyan v Russia*, App No 53203/99 (2005); *Ramanauskas v Lithuania*, App No 74420/01 (2008); *Milinenev v Lithuania*, App No 74355/01 (2008).

[256] See D. Ormerod and A. Roberts, 'The Trouble with *Teixeira*: Developing a Principled Approach to Entrapment' (2002) 6 *E&P* 38, 51–2.

[257] [2004] EWCA Crim 2872.   [258] [2010] EWCA Crim 925, [15].   [259] [2013] EWCA Crim 85.

were introduced to Ms Moore by her step-father who was said to be a local criminal. One officer (J) told Moore that he had cheap goods for sale, which she purchased from him twice. J then asked her if anyone round there had any cocaine; she replied that she could get it in large quantities and of good quality. She sourced it through her father and supplied cocaine to J. At trial for supply of controlled drugs, Moore made an application to stay the proceedings for abuse of process on the ground of entrapment. The Court of Appeal held that there had been no entrapment as Moore had been provided with an opportunity, which she seized immediately and resolutely, to volunteer herself as a participant in substantial offending.[260]

This case was seen to '[lie] intriguingly between the circumstances of previously decided cases':[261] while Moore was akin to the defendants in *Attorney General's Reference (No 3 of 2000)* and *Moon* in that she had not been involved in the supply of any drugs previously, unlike them she was not an addict lured into a single supply after some persuasion by the undercover officer. The court saw the instant case as similar to *Moon* and not to the *Attorney General's Reference (No 3 of 2000)*.[262] Although the court must concentrate on the nature of the police conduct rather than on the defendant's predisposition, it saw one as the other side of the other: in ascertaining whether the police overstepped some line so as to make their conduct unacceptable. Ultimately the solution lies in the sense of proportion and fairness.[263] Moore 'needed no persuasion whatsoever, but on the contrary seemed to take to the multiple supply of reasonably large quantities of cocaine like a duck to water'.[264]

Rix LJ cited with approval an article by David Ormerod in which he identified five relevant factors in applications to stay based on alleged entrapment:

> (i) reasonable suspicion of criminal activity as a legitimate trigger for the police operation; (ii) authorisation and supervision of the operation as a legitimate control mechanism; (iii) necessity and proportionality of the means employed to police particular types of offence; (iv) the concepts of the 'unexceptional opportunity' and causation; and (v) authentication of the evidence.[265]

Addressing these in turn, first, the court found that there was plainly a reasonable suspicion of drug-dealing (and other criminality) in the area which justified the taking of covert policing operations. The fact that M was not personally suspected in this context, nor a named target, was something to be taken into account but having grounds for suspicion of a particular person is not always essential. Secondly, there was both authorization and supervision, even if this was not 'immaculate'. Thirdly, as for necessity and proportionality, in the context of certain crimes, such as drug-dealing, covert operations are a necessary element in detection, and it was justifiable and proportionate for the police to use the supply of drugs by persons who voluntarily joined in drug-dealing without being lured to do so as stepping stones in the investigation of the existing criminal conspiracies to supply drugs which the operation was tasked

---

[260] [76]. [261] [65]. [262] [76]. [263] [66]. [264] [66].
[265] [52], citing D. Ormerod, 'Recent Developments in Entrapment' [2006] *Covert Policing Rev* 65.

to detect. Fourthly, on the subject of the 'unexceptional opportunity', the undercover officers acted in the ordinary way of drug purchasers rather than using some exceptional manoeuvre to lure Ms Moore into offending. 'The fact that there is a necessary subterfuge does not mean that the boundary has been crossed into unjustifiable entrapment.' Fifthly, the conversations were recorded so there was no question as to what was said.[266]

Roberts is critical of this decision,[267] on the basis that it is akin to 'random virtue testing'. The police behaviour was predicated on a general suspicion that offences were being committed in a relatively large geographical area, which must be differentiated from a suspicion relating to a specific location, such as a park or a particular building. As noted in *Moore*, Ormerod suggests that the interpretation of reasonable suspicion should not extend to 'being used to target all residents of a high crime area'.[268] We suggest that this is not the case. Though the target area for the police operation was wide, Moore readily and willingly supplied drugs, after little prompting. And while we might have serious concerns about police decisions to focus on particular areas and contexts, which may incorporate class or racial biases, deploying entrapment as a remedy is not appropriate.

The scope of the doctrine of abuse of process has been examined in relation to the actions of vigilante paedophile chasers that pose as children online.[269] In very limited instances it may apply to ordinary citizens' behaviour also. While the underlying purpose of the doctrine is not present in relation to the actions of private citizens, sufficiently gross misconduct by a private citizen may in theory found a stay of proceedings as an abuse of process, if the state seeks to rely on the product of that misconduct.[270]

While it is now clear that the courts will stay some prosecutions where there has been state instigation of crime, the theoretical basis for objecting to entrapment is less clear. Indeed, Squires has questioned whether there is any coherent basis for doing so.[271] After all, if a defendant such as Moon had been persuaded to supply heroin to a member of the public, and the police had stumbled upon the transaction, she would have had no defence in law and no claim to have proceedings stayed.[272] Part of Squires's argument, influenced by Seidman,[273] is that the distinction drawn between cases of impermissible entrapment and legitimate police investigations serves to protect the privileged from having their virtue tested (especially as most of us would actually succumb to temptation if a sufficiently attractive offer were made), while allowing the police to

---

[266] [68]–[75].

[267] A. Roberts, 'Case Comment *R. v Moore (Mia)*: Abuse of Process—Entrapment—Defendants Supplying Drugs to Undercover Police Officers' [2014] *Crim LR* 364, 367.

[268] *Moore* [54], citing Ormerod, 73.   [269] *R v TL* [2018] EWCA Crim 1821.

[270] *Council for the Regulation of Health Care Professionals v General Medical Council and Saluja* [2006] EWHC 2784 (Admin).

[271] D. Squires, 'The Problem with Entrapment' (2006) 26 *OJLS* 351.

[272] See K. Hofmeyr, 'The Problem of Private Entrapment' [2006] *Crim LR* 319.

[273] L. Seidman, 'The Supreme Court, Entrapment and Our Criminal Justice Dilemma' [1981] *Supreme Court Rev* 111.

target those who already inhabit an environment where they encounter temptation to commit crime. Thus, in *DPP v Willliams and O'Hare*,[274] the police parked a van in a street with its back doors unlocked, and cartons of cigarettes visible inside. On being confronted with this temptation, the defendants proceeded to take the cigarettes. The Divisional Court held that this was not entrapment, and in *Looseley* the House of Lords agreed that the prosecution was appropriate largely, it seems, because an area of high vehicle crime had been targeted. The 'fact that the defendants may not have previously been suspected or even thought of offending was their hard luck'.[275] Presumably, if the van had been left in a low-crime area, the courts would have found that there was impermissible entrapment.

While Squires's argument is intriguing, it is not entirely convincing. Insofar as his thesis claims to describe the practice of the courts, the decision in *Williams* is the strongest point in its favour. But many commentators doubt that *Williams* was correctly decided,[276] and the later decision in *Moon*, which emphasizes reasonable suspicion of an individual rather than of an area, undermines it. *Williams* was not considered in *Moore*. We suggest, then, that a coherent doctrine of entrapment can be based on the idea that the police can only legitimately target those who they reasonably suspect to be currently involved in criminal activity: *currently* is significant, because otherwise the police would be able to target anyone with previous convictions. At a more normative level, the argument would be that it is not legitimate for the state to seek to use criminal sanctions against those who are not committing crime; its role should be largely reactive. However, there are difficulties with this defence of the entrapment doctrine, which we will address briefly.

Feinberg has defended the sort of position outlined above—that the state should not seek to lure non-criminals into crime—on the grounds that we should face no more than the 'natural odds' of being tempted to commit crime.[277] Some of us may be faced with temptation to commit crime in our normal lives; if we give in, we will be rightly prosecuted. The problem here is that the natural odds, under which some people face fewer temptations to commit crime than others, are not really natural. As Seidman points out,[278] they are the products of political choices and reflect social inequality. This can be conceded, but so long as entrapment is used to target only those who are suspected of ongoing involvement in crime, the entrapment doctrine is no more a tool for preserving social inequality than is the rest of the criminal law. It is true that entrapment could be used in the pursuit of a rather strange programme of equality, whereby the privileged could be faced with temptations to commit crime just as the underprivileged are, but surely the more sensible social programme would be to ameliorate the criminogenic environments that the underprivileged face.

---

[274] (1994) 98 Cr App R 206.   [275] See n 254, [65].   [276] See Choo, n 155, 149–50.

[277] J. Feinberg, 'Criminal Entrapment' in *Problems at the Roots of Law: Essays in Legal and Political Theory* (2003).

[278] L. Seidman, Entrapment and the "Free Market" for Crime, in P. H. Robinson et al (eds), *Criminal Law Conversations* (2009), 493.

A second difficulty the entrapment doctrine faces is how to respond to 'test pur-chase' cases. In *Amin*, plain-clothes police officers flagged down a taxi in an area not covered by its licence.[279] The driver was prosecuted for picking them up, and this was held not to be an abuse of process.[280] Similar tactics are sometimes used to check whether shops are sticking to the terms of their licences.[281] There was no reasonable suspicion of the taxi driver in *Amin*, and while requiring suspicion might be appropri-ate in cases involving shopkeepers, it would be far more difficult in the *Amin* scenario. If it is felt important that the police should be able to test licensees without reasonable suspicion,[282] it might be possible to argue that those who take part in a regulated ac-tivity, such as driving a taxi or selling alcohol, are legitimate targets of virtue-testing. A similar argument was used in respect of the privilege against self-incrimination in Chapter 4, though it should be noted that the argument is potentially unruly.

Finally, if reasonable suspicion plays a key role in setting the bounds of the entrap-ment doctrine, there is a difficult question about the extent to which reasonable suspi-cion may be supplied, or bolstered, after the defendant has been targeted. In *Moon*, the Court of Appeal remarked that a search of the defendant's apartment had uncovered evidence of personal use of drugs rather than of dealing. If the search had found drugs in quantities that indicated dealing, could this have been used to support the argument that Moon was a legitimate target of the police operation? In *Looseley*, the police initially targeted Looseley because they had been given his telephone number in a pub from where they suspected heroin was being dealt. They phoned the number and Looseley agreed to supply them with drugs, which he in fact did on three occasions. It might be argued that while the initial tip-off was insufficient to provide reasonable suspicion that Looseley was currently engaged in drug-dealing, the ease with which he procured drugs provided further evidence that he was a dealer. In *Williams*, it is possible, as acknowl-edged in *Looseley*, that the defendants had not even 'thought of' offending before being confronted with the easy opportunity of the unsecured cigarettes, and this gives strong grounds for arguing that they should not have been prosecuted. But might things have been different had the defendants smashed the window of a car in order to steal a wallet left on the front seat? This behaviour seems to display a rather higher level of commit-ment to offending, and might be taken to be evidence that the defendants were among those responsible for vehicle crime in the area. And in *Moore*, while she had not been involved in criminality before, or at least had not experienced police intervention, she took to it readily and willingly. There are difficult questions here. One argument would be that because the entrapment doctrine is intended to regulate police conduct, a deci-sion to target a particular person cannot be justified after the fact. On the other hand, if the concern is about whether in fact the target was lured into committing a crime that he was not already committing, a wider inquiry may be appropriate.

---

[279] *Nottingham City Council v Amin* [2000] 1 Cr App R 426.
[280] See also *East Riding of Yorkshire Council v Dearlove* [2012] EWHC 278 (Admin).
[281] *DPP v Marshall* [1988] 3 All ER 683.
[282] See also *Stratford on Avon District Council v Dyde* [2009] EWHC 3011 (Admin).

9.6 CONCLUSION

This chapter has examined the procedural mechanisms that seek to ensure that the criminal trial runs efficiently and fairly, and to maintain the integrity of the process as a whole. While these measures embody particular normative positions in prioritizing one aim over another, say, they cannot avoid being affected by pragmatic matters like rapidly advancing technology as well as budget cuts. This is particularly pronounced in relation to disclosure. Moreover, shifting norms in relation to belief in victims' accounts, for instance, have altered prosecution policy and practice in relation to delayed trials, though the courts continue to monitor the reasons for this. All of this is underpinned by the pervasive drive for efficiency in the criminal justice system.

It is regrettable that the Court of Appeal has not taken a more robust approach in respect of disclosure failings. While the choice between a stay and letting the trial continue might seem pronounced and invidious, the current approach constitutes a de facto approbation of questionable prosecution practices. The jurisprudence on entrapment is more mindful of the overreach of state powers, though does not resolve inconsistent police practices that may reflect socio-economic and racial biases.

FURTHER READING

CHOO, A., *Abuse of Process and Judicial Stays of Criminal Proceedings*, 2nd edn, Oxford: Oxford University Press, 2008, 71–96 (on delay).

LEAHY, S., 'Too Much Information? Regulating Disclosure of Complainants' Personal Records in Sexual Offence Trials' [2016] *Crim LR* 229.

QUIRK, H., 'The Significance of Culture in Criminal Procedure Reform: Why the Revised Disclosure Scheme Cannot Work' (2006) 10 *E&P* 42.

SQUIRES, D., 'The Problem with Entrapment' (2006) 26 *OJLS* 351.

QUESTIONS FOR DISCUSSION

1. Does the prosecution disclose too little evidence and the defence too much?

2. Should the courts be less reluctant to stay proceedings for abuse of process in cases involving delay?

3. What, if anything, is wrong with entrapment?

10

PLEA

A key decision for prosecuted individuals is how to plead. With the exception of special pleas such as *autrefois convict* and *autrefois acquit* in cases where the defendant pleads that he or she has been tried previously and cannot lawfully be retried for the offence,[1] and the rare plea of not guilty by reason of insanity, defendants have a choice of two pleas: guilty or not guilty. In some cases, the decision may depend on the offence(s) charged, so that a plea of guilty may be offered to a lesser offence than that charged or to only one or two offences where more offences are charged. In this connection, as we will see, the discussion of prosecutorial decision making in Chapter 7 is particularly relevant. In some cases, the decision on plea may depend on the mode of trial; that is, the level of court in which the charge is likely to be heard. Summary offences are triable only in magistrates' courts, and indictable only offences are tried in the Crown Court, but there is a large middle category of offences triable either way. In these cases, defendants have a right to elect Crown Court trial: the Crown Court has a higher acquittal rate than the magistrates' courts, but there is a longer delay before the trial and, where a conviction results, sentences in the Crown Court tend to be higher than in the magistrates' courts. The incentives therefore are mixed for defendants, whereas prosecutors tend to wish to have as many either way offences as possible dealt with in the magistrates' courts. The system for determining mode of trial is now designed to ensure that as many cases as possible, in the triable either way category, are dealt with by magistrates. Thus, the 'plea before venue' system in place since the Criminal Procedure and Investigations Act 1996 ensures that those who indicate an intention to plead guilty to an either way offence are dealt with in the magistrates' courts (subject to the possibility of committal to the Crown Court for sentence).

If the defendant pleads not guilty, the case goes to trial. If the defendant pleads guilty, there is no trial. Instead, the defence may submit a 'basis of plea', and the prosecution will always give a statement of facts in court; if there is disagreement about the facts on which sentence should be passed, the judge may have to hold a *Newton* hearing to resolve the matter.[2] The European Convention on Human Rights (ECHR) declares that

---

[1] See the discussion of double jeopardy, Ch 12.7.

[2] See the leading case of *Newton* (1982) 4 Cr App R (S) 388, and discussion by A. Ashworth, *Sentencing and Criminal Justice* (5th edn, 2010), ch 11. *Underwood* [2005] 1 Cr App R (S) 90, [6]–[10] provides guidance regarding the *Newton* hearing procedure.

'everyone is entitled to a fair and public hearing', that 'everyone charged with a criminal offence shall be presumed innocent until proven guilty according to law', and that everyone shall have the right 'to examine or have examined witnesses against him'.[3] A defendant who pleads guilty gives up these rights and does not put the prosecution to proof; as we describe later, the English criminal justice system contains an array of incentives designed to produce this outcome. In some countries, those rights have been thought so fundamental that they cannot be waived, with the unavailability of the guilty plea being regarded as a guarantee of defendants' rights.[4] That said, while jurisdictions like France, the Netherlands, Germany, and Italy traditionally did not provide for guilty pleas, this state of affairs is changing.[5] Though reduction in sentences seems to run counter to the trend for increasing severity against terrorism, organized crime, and other serious types of offending, pressures on resources are leading governments to find ways of reducing the number of trials taking place.

In England and Wales, guilty pleas were relatively unusual in the eighteenth century and did not become common until the nineteenth century, when defence lawyers were allowed to play a fuller part.[6] Now the, vast majority of charges result in a guilty plea. The Criminal Procedure Rules (CPR) outline the procedure on a plea of guilty: if the defendant pleads guilty and the court is satisfied that the plea represents a clear acknowledgement of guilt, the court may convict the defendant without receiving evidence.[7] There may be some examination of the plea by a judge at a plea and trial preparation hearing, but not necessarily before passing sentence on a guilty plea. In essence, the guilty plea constitutes a waiver by the defendant of the right to a trial and to put the prosecution to proof. Moreover, since 2015 there has been an online 'make a plea' service, for people charged with traffic offences. 'Users' of the 'service' complete an online form. There have been more than 46,000 plea submissions since 2015.[8]

It is possible, in limited circumstances, to withdraw or appeal a guilty plea. A defendant may apply to withdraw a guilty plea, but must do so as soon as practicable after becoming aware of the reasons for doing so, and before sentence.[9] In terms of appeal, the Court of Appeal has always been reluctant to grant leave to appeal against conviction to a defendant who pleaded guilty in the Crown Court,[10] and would do so only if he did not appreciate the nature of the charge or did not intend to admit he was guilty

[3] See Ch 2.

[4] M. Damaška, 'Evidentiary Barriers to Conviction and Two Models of Criminal Procedure: a Comparative Study' (1973) 121 *U Pa LR* 506.

[5] See Judge F. Tulkens, 'Negotiated Justice' in M. Delmas-Marty and J. R. Spencer (eds), *European Criminal Procedures* (2002); N. Jorg, S. Field, and C. Brants, 'Are Inquisitorial and Adversarial Systems Converging?' in C. Harding et al (eds), *Criminal Justice in Europe* (1995), esp 47–51; L. Leigh and L. Zedner, *A Report on the Administration of Criminal Justice in the Pre-Trial Phase in France and Germany* (1992), 43; H. Jung, 'Plea-Bargaining and its Repercussions on the Theory of Criminal Procedure' (1997) 5 *Eur J Crime, Crim L and Crim Justice* 112; and S. Maffei, 'Negotiations on Evidence and Negotiations on Sentence: Adversarial Experiments in Italian Criminal Procedure' (2004) 2 *J Int Crim J* 1050, 1060.

[6] M. Feeley, 'Legal Complexity and the Transformation of the Criminal Process: The Origins of Plea Bargaining' (1997) 31 *Israel LR* 183; cf the analysis of the socio-political context of early plea-bargaining in the United States in M. Vogel, *Coercion to Compromise* (2007).

[7] r 24.7.   [8] https://www.gov.uk/make-a-plea.   [9] r 24.10.   [10] *Forde* [1923] 2 KB 400, 403.

of it, or if upon the admitted facts he could not in law have been convicted of the offence charged. As stated in *Asiedu*:

> ordinarily, once [the defendant] has admitted such facts by an unambiguous and deliberately intended plea of guilty, there cannot then be an appeal against his conviction, for the simple reason that there is nothing unsafe about a conviction based on the defendant's own voluntary confession in open court.[11]

Section 144 of the Criminal Justice Act 2003 provides a strong incentive to plead guilty:[12]

(1) In determining what sentence to pass on an offender who has pleaded guilty to an offence before that or another court a court must take into account:

   (a) the stage in the proceedings for the offence at which the offender indicated his intention to plead guilty; and

   (b) the circumstances in which this indication was given.

The legislation does not state the amount of the discount, but sentencing guidelines now deal authoritatively with the details.[13] In brief, the discount ranges from one-third for a guilty plea at the first stage of the proceedings, downwards on a sliding scale to one-tenth for a change of plea at the door of the court, and down to zero if the guilty plea is entered during the course of the trial. The guideline makes it clear that if the offence is already close to the custody threshold, a guilty plea may have the effect of reducing the sentence to a non-custodial one.

This chapter begins with an outline of plea and trial preparation hearings before looking at pleas of guilty and not guilty. It then considers some of the principal reasons for changes of plea, looking at charge bargains (where the defendant agrees to plead guilty in exchange for the prosecution reducing the level of the charge or the number of charges), fact bargains (where the defendant agrees to plead guilty only on the basis that the prosecution will put forward a particular version of the facts), and plea negotiation (where the change of plea is motivated by considerations of sentence). The characteristics of the English system are then evaluated in the light of defendants' rights and the supposed advantages to the public.

10.1 PLEA AND TRIAL PREPARATION HEARINGS

In the early 1980s, some magistrates' courts began to hold pre-trial reviews of contested cases, with a view to facilitating an exchange of information between prosecution and defence, identifying issues so as to save time and perhaps bring about pleas

---

[11] *Asiedu* [2015] EWCA Crim 714, [19].

[12] The section was originally enacted as s 48 of the Criminal Justice and Public Order Act 1994. The changes in its terms are not significant for present purposes.

[13] Sentencing Council, *Reduction in sentence for a guilty plea: Definitive guideline* (2017) replacing Sentencing Guidelines Council, *Reduction in Sentence for a Guilty Plea: Revised Guideline* (2007).

of guilty. Research suggested that they had modest advantages in cost–benefit terms: Brownlee, Mulcahy, and Walker found that they had little overall effect on the speed of case disposal, and resulted in relatively few changes of plea to guilty, but they still argued that there were overall cost-savings because the reviews were relatively inexpensive.[14]

Now one of the aims of Transforming Summary Justice (TSJ), the joint criminal justice system initiative, is to obtain more guilty pleas earlier in the process. The explicit rationale for this is to save money, as well as lessening the impact on victims and witnesses and 'assisting' the defendant in credit given for an early guilty plea.[15] TSJ involves the listing of cases as those where a guilty plea is anticipated (GAP cases) and those where a not guilty plea is anticipated (NGAP cases). The former are heard in dedicated magistrates' courts 14 days after charge and ideally are dealt with at the first hearing, whereas NGAP cases are listed in dedicated case management courts 28 days after charge, with the aim of review and preparation happening before the first hearing. TSJ is not having the desired effect: a comparison of the 12 months to June 2016 with the 12 months to December 2016 reveals that the proportion of guilty pleas at first hearing has worsened slightly from 70.1 per cent to 69.3 per cent.[16]

Turning to the Crown Court, in 2001 the Auld Review identified four different types of pre-trial hearing, and was critical of this multiplicity of arrangements and also of their rigidity and bureaucracy. Auld's recommendation was for a more flexible single system: the result was the plea and case management hearing (PCMH).[17] This had many of the functions of the former plea and directions hearing, in terms of taking the defendant's plea, assessing the readiness of prosecution and defence, and so forth. But there was an additional emphasis on active case management by the judge. As the Court of Appeal emphasized in *R v Penner*, the CPR require all issues to be identified and, if necessary, examined at the PCMH.[18] And, of course, the PCMH gave an opportunity to a defendant whose plea was not guilty to ask the judge for an advance indication of sentence, were the plea to change to guilty.

There was a perception that holding a PCMH in cases where not guilty pleas were expected was either unnecessary or too early in the process, resulting in multiple additional hearings and variations in practice.[19] So, as part of Better Case Management (BCM), the PCMH was replaced by a new first hearing in the Crown Court, called the Plea and Trial Preparation Hearing (PTPH). This builds on TSJ in magistrates' courts and is linked to the Early Guilty Plea Scheme, introduced in Crown Courts in 2012. The aim is to identify cases where a defendant is likely to plead guilty and to expedite them through an early guilty plea hearing.

---

[14] I. Brownlee, A. Mulcahy, and C. P. Walker, 'Pre-Trial Reviews, Court Efficiency and Justice: a Study in Leeds and Bradford Magistrates' Courts' (1994) 33 *Howard JCJ* 109; for earlier discussion, see J. Baldwin, *Pre-Trial Justice* (1986).

[15] HM Crown Prosecution Service Inspectorate (HMCPSI), *Business as Usual? Transforming Summary Justice Follow-up Report* (2017), 3.25.

[16] Ibid.   [17] See CPR (2009), rr 3.5 and 3.11.   [18] *R v Penner* [2010] EWCA Crim 1155.

[19] Ministry of Justice, *Plea and Trial Preparation Hearings: Introduction and Guidance* (revised 2015).

A PTPH generally takes place within 28 days of sending from the magistrates' court. In straightforward cases, the PTPH involves consideration of the full prosecution case and enables clear notification of witness requirements. There is an expectation that a plea will be taken at the PTPH and directions given to carry the matter through to an effective trial, so that in straightforward cases no further oral hearing should be required.[20] In more complex cases, a Further Case Management Hearing (FCMH) may be needed. Data for the four months up to April 2016 indicated an average of 2.5 PTPHs per case,[21] and while the CPS set a target of 37.5 per cent of guilty pleas taking place at the first hearing in the 12 months to June 2016 only three CPS Areas performed better than this.[22] Other figures show that prior to the introduction of BCM in 2016 the average number of hearings for guilty plea trials had increased from 3.9 to 4.1 between 2014 and 2015, but this was followed by a decrease from 4.1 to 3.7 hearings between 2015 and 2017.[23] So, there is some progress in terms of expediting guilty plea and lowering the number of trials, but this is slow.

There is evidence of regional variation in practice. Darbyshire's research found that in some courts with long-established judicial pre-trial case management regimes, the CPR and Early Guilty Plea Scheme were seen as a nuisance because of their generous time limits, compared with local deadlines.[24] She found significant differences in basic organization, such as listing and timing of PCMHs and pre-trial hearings, the naming of pre-trial hearings, and the cases in which they were used. Notably, northern courts generally had higher pre-trial guilty plea rates.

PTPHs need not take place in person. The Criminal Practice Direction provides that courts should conduct hearings by live link or telephone where it is lawful and in the interests of justice to do so.[25] It is the duty of the court to make use of technology actively to manage a case, including an obligation to give directions for the use of live links and telephone facilities in pre-trial hearings, including PCMHs.[26] While this may seem cost-efficient and in keeping with technological developments, empirical evidence is not positive. A Ministry of Justice evaluation of a virtual court pilot in Kent and London, where video link was introduced for defendants detained by police, showed them to be more expensive than traditional courts, with defendants less likely to take up legal advice and more likely to receive a prison sentence.[27] Moreover, qualitative research from Transform Justice suggests that video hearings reduce defendants' understanding of, and respect for, the process.[28] This is particularly pronounced for

---

[20] Ibid, 2.8.   [21] HMCPSI, *Better Case Management: A Snapshot* (2016), para 1.11.

[22] Ibid, 3.19.

[23] Ministry of Justice, *Criminal court statistics quarterly, England and Wales, January to March 2018 (annual 2017)* (2018), 16.

[24] P. Darbyshire, 'Judicial Case Management in Ten Crown Courts' [2014] *Crim LR* 30, 48.

[25] 3N.1; also CPR, r 3.5(1), (2)(d).   [26] CPR, r 3.2.

[27] M. Terry, S. Johnson, and P. Thompson, *Virtual Court pilot: Outcome evaluation*, Ministry of Justice Research Series 21/10 (2010).

[28] Transform Justice, *Defendants on video—conveyor belt justice or a revolution in access* (2017), http://www.transformjustice.org.uk/wp-content/uploads/2017/10/Disconnected-Thumbnail-2.pdf.

children and young people.[29] All of this underlines how caution is needed in the digital roll-out that HM Courts and Tribunals Service is heralding uncritically.

10.2 PLEADING GUILTY: RATES AND REASONS

In the magistrates' courts, the rate of guilty pleas is well over 90 per cent. Most of these are relatively minor matters, three-quarters being summary offences that almost always end in a fine. A contested trial in a magistrates' court is therefore fairly rare: in 2013, defendants pleaded not guilty in 9 per cent of the non-motoring cases and 6 per cent of the motoring cases.[30]

Between 2001 and 2009, the guilty plea rate in the Crown Court increased by 14 per cent to 71 per cent, and has declined a little since then to 67 per cent in 2016 and 2017.[31] Again, there is regional variation—the rate in London is 55 per cent, whereas in the North West it is 73 per cent.[32] The overall decline is attributed in part to an increase in sexual offence trials, which have low guilty plea rates. In 2017, the highest guilty plea rate was for drug offences at 80 per cent, and the lowest for sexual offences at 35 per cent. Violence against the person had the second lowest guilty plea rate at 60 per cent.[33] This is due to difficulties in ensuring that witnesses testify in such cases, and perceptions that contesting the charges is worthwhile due to the lack of corroborative evidence in sexual offence cases. Since 2010, the proportion of guilty pleas that were entered 'prior to trial' fell from 68 per cent to 55 per cent in 2017.[34] In 2017, the CPS reported that 77 per cent of guilty pleas in the magistrates' court were at the first hearing, and 41 per cent guilty pleas in Crown Court at the first hearing.[35]

Why do so many defendants plead guilty and forgo their right to be tried? In the early 1970s, Bottoms and McClean interviewed over 200 defendants who pleaded guilty either at a magistrates' court or at the Crown Court: about two-thirds stated that they did so because they were guilty.[36] A similar finding emerged from the later survey by Hedderman and Moxon, although 65 per cent of their respondents also said that the prospect of a lighter sentence was a reason for their decision.[37] Research carried out for the Sentencing Council found that the main factor determining whether or not offenders pleaded guilty was the likelihood of being found guilty at trial. The weight of evidence and legal advice were central in this assessment and crucial in determining when a guilty plea was entered.[38]

---

[29] Standing Committee for Youth Justice, *'They just don't understand what's happened or why': A report on child defendants and video links* (2018).

[30] Magistrates Association, *Single Justice Procedure, position statement*, 14 April 2015.

[31] *Criminal court statistics quarterly*, 11.   [32] Ibid, Table AC9.   [33] Ibid, 12.

[34] Ibid, 12.   [35] CPS, *Key Performance Measures* (2018), https://www.cps.gov.uk/key-measures.

[36] A. E. Bottoms and J. D. McClean, *Defendants in the Criminal Process* (1976), 115.

[37] C. Hedderman and D. Moxon, *Magistrates' Court or Crown Court? Mode of Trial Decisions and Sentencing* (1992), 24.

[38] W. Dawes, P. Harvey, B. McIntosh, F. Nunney, and A. Phillips, *Attitudes to Guilty Plea Sentence Reductions* (2011), [5.1].

What about those who change their plea? This leads to 'cracked trials': a case is listed as a not guilty plea with court time set aside for a contested trial but it 'cracks' after the defendant changes to a guilty or lesser plea, or the prosecution drops the case, after it has been listed. This may occur on the day of the hearing, others a day or two before. Cracked trials cause unnecessary inconvenience and anxiety to victims and other witnesses who are brought to court on what turns out to be a fruitless journey. They also produce inefficiencies in the criminal justice system, since they cause listing difficulties and consequently may result in a wastage of scarce resources, namely court time, judicial time, and public money.[39] The estimated annual cost to the CPS of cases that do not go on to trial, for example due to late guilty pleas, is £21.5 million.[40]

In 2008, 41 per cent of cases listed for trial 'cracked' at the last minute—mostly (62 per cent) because the defendant entered a late plea of guilty, but also because the defendant pleaded guilty to a lesser charge (19 per cent) or the prosecution dropped the case (17 per cent).[41] The introduction of PCMHs had not at that stage brought any significant reduction in cracked trials.[42] Thus, the encouragement of earlier guilty pleas continued to form a major part of the official strategy for increasing 'efficiency' in the criminal process.[43]

Despite various initiatives, the number of 'cracked' trials in magistrates' courts has remained consistent in recent years, with a rate of 30 per cent in 2015[44] and 38 per cent in 2017.[45] The proportion of trials that cracked due to 'acceptable guilty plea(s) entered late' and 'acceptable guilty plea to alternative new charge' has decreased, however, by 5 percentage points and 3 percentage points respectively since 2010.[46]

In the Crown Court, there has been some improvement:[47] in the year to September 2011 30 per cent of cases cracked and 26 per cent were vacated, whereas in 2015 24 per cent cracked and 33 per cent were vacated. Since 2010, the proportion of Crown Court trials that were 'effective' has increased gradually to 51 per cent in 2017, with a corresponding decrease in cracked trials to 34 per cent in 2017.[48] In 2017, criminal damage and arson had the highest proportion of cracked trials at 47 per cent.[49] Late guilty pleas are the main reason for cracked trials; since 2010, the proportion of Crown Court trials cracked for this reason increased by 5 percentage points to 67 per cent in 2017.[50] The percentage of cracked trials due to 'defendant pleads guilty to alternative charge' decreased by 2 percentage points from 2010 to 15 per cent in 2017.[51] Since 2010, the proportion of guilty pleas that were entered 'prior to trial' has fallen, from 68 per cent to 55 per cent in 2017.[52] The proportion where a guilty plea was entered 'at other hearings' also increased, by 5 percentage points to 9 per cent. The proportion of guilty pleas

---

[39] Leveson, *Review of Efficiency in Criminal Proceedings* (2015), 7.1.2.
[40] National Audit Office (NAO), *Efficiency in the Criminal Justice System*, Session 2015–16, HC 852 (2016), 4.
[41] *Judicial Statistics 2008*, Table 6.11.   [42] See section 10.6(E).   [43] Leveson, n 39, 5.5.
[44] NAO, n 40, 1.16.   [45] *Criminal court statistics quarterly*, 4.
[46] NAO, n 40, 1.16. Notably, the proportion that cracked because the prosecution decided not to proceed against the defendant has increased since 2010 by 10 percentage points to 45 per cent in 2017.
[47] Ibid, 1.15.   [48] *Criminal court statistics quarterly*, 9.   [49] Ibid, 10.   [50] Ibid, 9.
[51] Ibid, 12.   [52] Ibid, 11.

entered during trial or at an unknown stage have remained fairly constant throughout the time series, at around 1 per cent and 3 per cent, respectively. In 2014–15, 21 per cent of trials in the magistrates' courts 'cracked' because the defendant pleaded guilty on the day of the trial, and 28 per cent for Crown Court trials.[53]

10.3 PLEADING NOT GUILTY

Why do some defendants persist in their pleas of not guilty, whilst others change their pleas? Once again, the most obvious answer is that they maintain that they are not guilty. It seems that around 60 per cent of defences involve a denial of the basic facts:[54] around one in six of these are alibi defences, and perhaps one-quarter are claims of mistaken identification.[55] The other 40 per cent of defences accept the basic facts but contest guilt on the basis of justification or lack of culpability. Some three-quarters of these seem to amount to a denial of *mens rea*, and almost all the remaining one-quarter claim self-defence.

Just as some people who are innocent eventually plead guilty, some who are guilty plead not guilty. They may do so for a variety of personal reasons, ranging from over-confidence, to shame at the offence, and an unwillingness to admit it publicly in any circumstances (e.g. with sexual offences). Some guilty defendants may be alive to the possibility of acquittal if prosecution witnesses fail to attend court to give evidence. Just as it is recognized that some defendants who change their pleas to guilty on the day of the trial do so because they see that the prosecution witnesses are at the court, so there may be others who, seeing that the prosecution witnesses have not arrived, persist in their plea of not guilty, with the result that the case collapses. While no study has identified the numbers involved, it seems entirely plausible that some defendants benefit from such windfalls. The Home Office mentioned the view that 'delayed guilty pleas are a tactic employed in the hope that witnesses will lose patience and decide not to testify.'[56] The usual official response to this is to reinforce the incentives to plead guilty and to enter that plea early in the process. The difficulty is how to distinguish between the not-guilty pleaders who are guilty and the not-guilty pleaders who are not guilty, a key issue to which we return later. Moreover, account must also be taken of a third group—those who have an arguable point, such as whether a taking was dishonest or whether force was used reasonably in self-defence, and who wish to have that decided by a court.

10.4 CHARGE BARGAINS

The term 'charge bargaining' is used here to encompass two distinct kinds of case. The first is where a defendant faces two or more charges and signifies an intention to plead not guilty to them. It is then possible for the prosecution to drop one or

---

[53] NAO, n 40, 25.   [54] *Judicial Statistics 2008*, 121.   [55] Ibid, 75 and 92.
[56] Home Office, *Justice for All* (2002), 4.41.

more of the others, in return for a plea of guilty to one charge. Either the prosecution or the defence may suggest this way of resolving the matter. Many of these are
cases where several distinct offences are alleged, but some will be cases in which the
prosecution has charged a person with both theft and handling stolen goods, say,
in the expectation that there would be a conviction of only one offence. The second
kind of case is where the defendant faces a serious charge and signifies an intention
to plead not guilty to it. It may be possible for the prosecution to drop the serious
charge in exchange for a plea of guilty to a less serious charge. Much depends on the
relevant substantive criminal law. At some points, the law seems to be ready-made
for this kind of charge bargain: for example, a defendant might intend to plead
not guilty to grievous bodily harm with intent, contrary to s 18 of the Offences
Against the Person Act 1861, but might be willing to plead guilty to the lesser offence of recklessly inflicting grievous bodily harm contrary to s 20 of the same Act.
The same applies if the original charge is under s 20, and the defendant is willing
to plead to the lesser offence under s 47, assault occasioning actual bodily harm.
Elaine Genders has demonstrated the way in which many s 18 charges come to be
downgraded, partly because of the problems of proving intent unless the injury was
particularly serious.[57] In her sample, only 19 per cent of those charged under s 18
were eventually convicted under that section. Similarly, Ralph Henham found that
some 62 per cent of those charged under s 18 pleaded guilty to a lesser offence.[58]
In Chapter 7.4(B), we noted evidence of some downgrading of charges of racially
aggravated offences.

Apart from the specific types of offence just considered, in what proportion of cases
do charge bargains take place? Most of the research focuses on the Crown Court, but
charge bargains are by no means uncommon in magistrates' courts. Thus, both Baldwin[59] and Mulcahy[60] found plenty of evidence of charges being reduced in number or
in seriousness, followed by a change of plea to guilty. Such practices may be the result
of a pre-trial review, whereby the defence lawyer discovers the likely strength of the
prosecution case; or they may emerge by the usual processes of interaction between
prosecution and defence lawyers, either around the court or even by telephone contact.
Mulcahy's interviews with a small number of defence and prosecution lawyers working
in magistrates' courts led to the conclusion that trial avoidance is often thought desirable on both sides.[61] In addition, the lawyers in Newman's ethnographic research saw
bargaining as part of their practice, with guilty pleas as the standard outcome for their
clients and so put pressure on them to plead guilty.[62] If these are fair representations

---

[57] E. Genders, 'Reform of the Offences Against the Person Act: Lessons from the Law in Action' [1999] *Crim LR* 689, 691–3; see also A. Cretney and G. Davis, *Punishing Violence* (1995), 137–8.

[58] R. Henham, 'Further Evidence on the Significance of Plea in the Crown Court' (2002) 41 *Howard JCJ* 151, 153.

[59] J. Baldwin, *Pre-Trial Justice* (1986).

[60] A. Mulcahy, 'The Justification of "Justice": Legal Practitioners' Accounts of Negotiated Case Settlements in Magistrates' Courts' (1994) 34 *BJ Crim* 411.

[61] Ibid.   [62] D. Newman, *Legal Aid Lawyers and the Quest for Justice* (2013), 110–14.

of the general working culture,[63] to which there may of course be exceptions, then it is likely that there will be considerable pressure on some defendants in magistrates' courts to plead guilty.

Similar findings emerged from the study of Health and Safety inspectors by Hawkins: although he found that there were some cases in which inspectors would not bargain, he discovered ample evidence of cases of 'pre-trial manoeuvring over number and type of charges'.[64] His conclusion, however, was that from the inspectors' point of view it was not simply a matter of speed and saving resources: 'while many of the bargains reveal a strong desire to expedite the matter, they also reveal a desire to achieve a commensurate penalty'.[65]

Turning to the Crown Court, as many as 77 of the 112 defendants in McCabe and Purves's sample who changed their plea at a late stage pleaded guilty to only part of the original indictment,[66] whereas in Baldwin and McConville's sample it was only 11 out of 121 late guilty pleaders[67] and in Bottoms and McClean's sample only three out of 68.[68] Most of the research on cracked trials does not provide details of the nature of any negotiation that took place, but some 51 per cent of those in Hedderman and Moxon's sample who changed their plea stated that they did so in the expectation that some charges would be dropped or reduced, resulting in a lighter sentence.[69] It may therefore be assumed that one or other form of charge bargain is a fairly frequent phenomenon.

What are the advantages and disadvantages of this for the prosecution? The chief benefit is that it is assured of at least one conviction, and does not have to risk the hazards of trial, more particularly in the Crown Court where in 2017 56 per cent of contested cases ended in an acquittal.[70] In view of the possibility that witnesses may fail to turn up or may alter their story, or that the jury will be swayed by some non-legal factor, it is tempting for the prosecution to settle for the certainty of a conviction, albeit of a less serious offence (or fewer offences than charged). The Code for Crown Prosecutors (2013) states in para 9.2 that:

> Prosecutors should only accept the defendant's plea if they think that the court is able to pass a sentence that matches the seriousness of the offending, particularly where there are aggravating features. Prosecutors must never accept a guilty plea just because it is convenient.

This brief guidance reveals some of the conflicts besetting a prosecutor when taking a decision about accepting a lesser plea. The final words enjoin prosecutors not to give priority to 'convenience', but presumably this means their own personal convenience in getting a file off their desk. If we revert to the fuller description provided by the 1992

---

[63] See also M. McConville et al, *Standing Accused* (1994), 194–8, and M. Travers, *The Reality of Law* (1997), ch 5 on defence solicitors.

[64] K. Hawkins, *Law as Last Resort* (2003), 105.   [65] Ibid, 108.

[66] S. McCabe and R. Purves, *By-Passing the Jury* (1972).

[67] J. Baldwin and M. McConville, *Negotiated Justice* (1977), ch 2.

[68] Bottoms and McClean, n 36, 126–7.   [69] Hedderman and Moxon, n 37, 24.

[70] *Criminal court statistics quarterly 2018*, Table AC6. This represents a slight fall from 59 per cent in 2015–16, and from 64 per cent in 2010.

version of the Code, we find a more frank acknowledgement of the conflicting forces at work:

> Administrative convenience in the form of a rapid guilty plea should not take precedence over the interests of justice, but where the court is able to deal adequately with an offender on the basis of a plea which represents a criminal involvement not inconsistent with the alleged facts, the resource advantages both to the Service and to the courts generally will be an important consideration.[71]

This seems to suggest that it is proper to accept a plea of guilty to a lesser offence if the maximum sentence for that offence is not too low compared with the seriousness of what the defendant did. Thus, for example, if in the Crown Court a defendant enters a plea of not guilty to a s 18 charge of causing grievous bodily harm with intent (which carries a maximum sentence of life imprisonment) and the defendant then offers to plead guilty to the lesser s 20 offence of inflicting grievous bodily harm (which carries a maximum sentence of five years' imprisonment), the prosecutor should reflect on whether the five-year maximum is appropriate for what was done. However, this guidance is rather naïve when viewed in the light of sentencing law. As Lord Bingham CJ stated, it is 'inconsistent with principle that a defendant should be sentenced for offences neither admitted nor proven by verdict'.[72] In the context of offences under ss 18 and 20, the maximum sentence of five years for s 20 offences must be reserved for the worst conceivable cases, and it would only be in cases of greater harm and greater culpability that a sentence as far up the range as four years would be proper.[73] In practice, therefore, a prosecutor who accepts a plea to s 20 on an indictment charging s 18 would have to be satisfied that a sentence of two or three years would be adequate on the facts.

What are the advantages and disadvantages of charge bargaining from the defendant's point of view? These depend on whether the defendant has committed an offence and, if so, what offence(s). It is easy to say that if the defendant has really committed the higher offence, a plea of guilty to a lesser offence brings a benefit to the defendant in terms of a lower sentence. What is more debatable is the kind of case in which the defendant may be said to have been overcharged in order to put pressure on him or her to plead guilty to the lesser charge. In Chapter 7 we recorded evidence that this does occur, despite injunctions to the contrary in the Code for Crown Prosecutors. To the extent that it does happen, it means that some charge bargains hold no true advantage for the defence and only for the prosecution. By appearing to reduce the charge(s), the prosecutor obtains a plea of guilty to the offence that should really have been charged in the first place.

Much worse is the position of the defendant who maintains innocence of all charges. As we saw at the beginning of this chapter, English sentencing law holds out a massive institutional temptation to plead guilty, stemming from three sources—pleading guilty to a lesser charge should result in a lower sentence for the lesser offence, plus

---

[71] Code for Crown Prosecutors (2nd edn, 1992), para 11.
[72] *Canavan and Kidd* [1998] 1 Cr App R (S) 243, 247.
[73] Sentencing Council, *Assault Definitive Guideline* (2011), 8.

a further discount for pleading guilty, and if the defendant indicates an intention to plead guilty when brought before the magistrates on an either way charge the early plea may result in the magistrates passing sentence or at least committing the case to the Crown Court for sentence with a full discount. These institutional incentives may be known to the defendant, but they may be all the more powerful when conveyed by a lawyer who might be regarded as an expert. Thus, if counsel's advice is that pleading guilty to a lesser charge is likely to result in a non-custodial sentence whereas conviction after a trial might result in custodial sentence, a defendant may well succumb to the pressure to forgo a perfectly reasonable defence. The dependence of the defendant on his or her legal representatives is considerable, and this brings issues of professional ethics to the fore.[74] Moreover, the apparently growing phenomenon of unrepresented defendants is significant here: not only does their less detailed understanding of the discount scheme act as a barrier towards achieving early guilty pleas,[75] a lack of legal advice may induce guilty pleas. This is compounded by the fact that, since 2012, many defendants who do not qualify for legal aid may be liable for their legal costs, even if found not guilty.[76] These practical legal changes purport to reduce the expenditure on unmerited contested trials, but serve to incentivize guilty pleas, as the most pragmatic response for individuals seeking to avoid the risk of significant financial hardship.

10.5 FACT BARGAINS

In some cases, the defendant changes his plea to guilty following negotiation with the prosecution about how the facts of the case should be stated. This informal process might begin with the defendant submitting a written basis of plea, or might involve the preparation of an agreed basis of plea by prosecution and defence. An agreement to minimize a particular aggravating feature, for example, or not to mention the part played by another (e.g. a friend or partner) may be sufficient to persuade the defendant to plead guilty. Again, the principal advantage for the prosecution is that it secures a conviction in the case, even though the 'public interest' may be said to suffer a loss because the sentence is based on facts less serious than what actually occurred. The judge is not bound to accept an agreed basis of plea. The defendant, on the other hand, stands to benefit from the favourable statement of the facts and the discount for pleading guilty, which will lower the sentence further—although it can only be counted

[74] See Ch 3, and L. Bridges, 'Ethics of Representation on Guilty Pleas' (2006) 9 *Legal Ethics* 80.
[75] House of Commons Justice Committee, *Criminal Legal Aid*, Twelfth Report of Session 2017–19, HC 1069 (2018), [83]. That said, the proportion of defendants dealt with in the Crown Court who were known to have had legal representation at their first hearing decreased by 2 percentage points between 2010 and 2016, but has since increased by 2 percentage points to 95 per cent in 2017, the same level as 2010: *Criminal court statistics quarterly*, 17.
[76] Legal Aid, Sentencing and Punishment of Offenders Act 2012, Sch 7, amending the Prosecution of Offences Act 1985.

as a benefit if he or she is actually guilty of a more serious version of the offence than that put to the court.

In *Beswick*,[77] there was evidence that the offender had bitten the victim's ear and crushed his nose with his knee during an altercation. The indictment was for wounding with intent, contrary to s 18 of the Offences Against the Person Act 1861. Just before the trial, the prosecution agreed not only to accept a plea of guilty to s 20 wounding but also to accept that plea on the basis that he merely 'bit at' the victim's ear, without mention of the facial injury. The prosecution statement of facts conformed to that agreement, but the judge refused to sentence on that basis and insisted on a *Newton* hearing at which witnesses were heard in order to determine the true facts.[78] The Court of Appeal approved the course taken by the judge, and stated that:

> The prosecution should not lend itself to any agreement whereby a case is presented to the sentencing judge to be dealt with so far as that basis is concerned on an unreal and untrue set of facts concerning the offence to which a plea of guilty is to be tendered.

The CPR make it clear that the judge has the power to decide whether or not to accept the basis of plea and, if not, to hold a *Newton* hearing.[79]

In cases where the defendant wishes to put forward a plea of guilty on a version of facts that the prosecution is unable to accept, the Code for Crown Prosecutors states that 'the court should be invited to hear evidence to determine what happened, and then sentence on that basis'.[80] The judge should be asked to hold a *Newton* hearing, and if the evidential findings at that hearing go against the defendant, 'some or even the whole of any discount to which he might otherwise have been entitled by reason of his plea of guilty' may be forfeited.[81]

10.6 PLEA BARGAINS

One of the main reasons for our dealing first with charge bargains and fact bargains is that it leaves for separate consideration those cases in which the defendant begins by signifying a plea of not guilty to the charge and subsequently alters the plea to guilty. These are cases where there is no question of reducing the number or level of the charges, and no bargain about the factual basis on which the case will be put forward. The bargain, in effect, is with the law: it is only a bargain because the law holds out the incentive of a reduced sentence to those who plead guilty, starting from a one-third reduction for a guilty plea entered at the first stage of the proceedings. The essence is that the defendant trades a chance of acquittal for a lower sentence than would have been received in the event of conviction after a trial. Institutional incentives to plead guilty are evident in the sentence discount itself, advance indication of sentence, the

---

[77] [1996] 1 Cr App R (S) 343.   [78] On *Newton* hearings, see n 2.   [79] r 24.11.
[80] Para 9.4; the guidance is qualified by the clause 'where this may significantly affect sentence'.
[81] *Elicin and Moore* [2009] 1 Cr App R (S) 561.

'plea before venue' system, diversion schemes, and plea discussions in serious fraud cases. Separately, and cumulatively, they have a considerable impact on the defendant. Most of the discussion here relates to the Crown Court, but the 'guilty plea discount' applies equally in magistrates' courts.

(A) THE SENTENCE DISCOUNT

At the beginning of this chapter the wording of s 144 of the Criminal Justice Act 2003, on reduction of sentence for pleading guilty, was set out. Its broad and unqualified wording is the subject of a Sentencing Council guideline: the discount applies to all courts (including magistrates' courts) and to all forms of sentence (including fines and community sentences). The apparent public benefits which underlie the practice of reducing sentence for pleas of guilty are said to apply just as much to overwhelming cases as to less strong ones.[82] Courts must state that they have reduced sentence under s 144. The early evidence was that compliance with that requirement was variable,[83] but it is increasingly recognized as good sentencing practice to state how much of a reduction in sentence has been given for the guilty plea.[84] Insofar as this practice is followed, it amounts to an authoritative form of communication to offenders and their lawyers, which is likely to heighten the influence of the discount.

There is both statutory authority for, and broad empirical confirmation of, a significant discount for pleading guilty. Insofar as the discount is known to defendants or is brought to their attention by lawyers, it is likely to exert a considerable pressure towards pleading guilty. That, of course, is the purpose of the relevant law. It was formerly thought that the sentence discount did not apply in magistrates' courts, but the law is now clear[85] and the *Magistrates' Court Sentencing Guidelines* remind benches that a timely plea should result in a sentence reduction.[86]

(B) ADVANCE INDICATION OF SENTENCE

The screw was turned further by the procedures for advance indication of sentence recommended in the Auld Report. The Court of Appeal in *Goodyear*[87] overruled the previous authority (*Turner*)[88] and gave what it termed 'guidelines' on the circumstances in which a judge might give an 'advance indication of sentence' to a defendant who is pleading not guilty but wishes to know the likely sentence on a guilty plea. The guidelines are

---

[82] *R v Caley* [2012] EWCA Crim 2821, [24].

[83] R. Henham, 'Bargain Justice or Justice Denied? Sentence Discounts and the Criminal Process' (1999) 63 *MLR* 515; cf also his discussion of a small project in magistrates' courts, R. Henham, 'Reconciling Process and Policy: Sentence Discounts in the Magistrates' Courts' [2000] *Crim LR* 436. For criticisms of the methodology and conclusions of these projects, see A. Sanders, R. Young, and M. Burton, *Criminal Justice* (4th edn, 2010), 446.

[84] See the Sentencing Council, *Reduction in sentence for a guilty plea*, n 13, 5. This was also the view of the High Court of Australia in *Cameron v R* (2002) 209 CLR 339.

[85] Sentencing Council, *Reduction in sentence for a guilty plea*, n 13, 4.

[86] Sentencing Council, *Magistrates' Court Sentencing Guideline* (2017), 16.

[87] [2006] 1 Cr App R (S) 23.

[88] [1970] 2 QB 321, extensively discussed in the 3rd edition at pp 280–2.

detailed, but essentially a defendant may ask the judge (usually at a PCMH) whether the judge could give an indication of the maximum sentence that would be given based on the prosecution case papers, were the plea to be one of guilty, but before taking account of mitigation; the judge may decline to give such an indication; but if an indication is given, this binds the judge and any subsequent judge dealing with the case.[89] The Auld Report thought such a procedure both desirable and acceptable, asking 'What possible additional pressure, unacceptable or otherwise, can there be in the judge, whom [the defendant] has requested to tell him where he stands, indicating more precisely the alternatives?'[90] The court in *Goodyear* likewise concluded that if the defendant seeks the judge's view, 'we do not see why a judicial response to a request for information from the defendant should automatically be deemed to constitute improper pressure on him'. The difference, of course, lies between defence counsel's prediction and the authoritativeness of the judicial indication: the element of roulette has gone, but the judge's indication may impose enormous pressure on the defendant, particularly where the indicated sentence on a change of plea to guilty does not involve immediate imprisonment. The *Goodyear* procedure, in combination with the guideline on reduction of sentence for a guilty plea, imposes considerable pressure on the guilty and innocent alike.

Importantly, this judicial indication must be invited, so as to maintain the freedom of the defendant to choose and determine his plea. In *Nightingale*,[91] the Judge Advocate gave an uninvited sentence indication at a court martial, after which the defendant pleaded guilty. The Court of Appeal stressed that while the provision of realistic advice would inform choice as to plea, the uninvited indication given by the judge, and its impact on the defendant after considering the advice given to him by his legal advisers on the basis of their professional understanding of that statement, created inappropriate additional pressures and narrowed improperly his freedom of choice.[92]

(C) PLEA BEFORE VENUE

There is widespread recognition of the principle that the earlier an intention to plead guilty is made known, the larger the sentence reduction should be. This follows from the rationale for the sentence discount, stated by the Sentencing Council:

> Although a guilty person is entitled not to admit the offence and to put the prosecution to proof of its case, an acceptance of guilt:
>
> a) normally reduces the impact of the crime upon victims;
>
> b) saves victims and witnesses from having to testify; and
>
> c) is in the public interest in that it saves public time and money on investigations and trials.[93]

---

[89] CPD VII C. See further *Asiedu* [2009] 1 Cr App R (S) 420. In *R v Omole* [2011] EWCA Crim 1428, the Court of Appeal held that where the defence requests an indication of the bracket of the Definitive Guidelines into which the case falls a judge should treat it as a request for an indication of the maximum sentence.

[90] R. E. Auld, *Review of the Criminal Courts of England and Wales; Report* (2001), 434–44.

[91] *R v Nightingale* [2013] EWCA Crim 405, [12].   [92] [16] and [17].

[93] Sentencing Council, *Reduction in sentence for a guilty plea*, n 13, 4.

Putting this principle into practice means that the courts should reserve the maximum discount for those who indicate a plea of guilty at the earliest possible stage. Under the 'plea before venue' procedure, all defendants who are charged with triable either way offences are brought before magistrates and asked whether they intend to plead guilty.[94] If they decline to intimate an intention to plead guilty, they may elect to be tried in the Crown Court or, if not, the magistrates will have the decision whether to commit them to the Crown Court for trial or to deal with the case themselves. However, the real incentive is for those who intimate an intention to plead guilty. The magistrates have the power to sentence them, if they decide that the case falls within their sentencing powers,[95] and this might mean a smaller and swifter sentence for the offender. However, that outcome is not certain since the magistrates also have the power to commit the case to the Crown Court for sentence.

It appears that the purpose of the procedure—to avoid late changes of plea and to have more cases dealt with cheaply in the magistrates' courts—has been met in part. However, 'plea before venue' places great pressure on defendants to plead guilty very early, perhaps before they have had disclosure from the prosecution and therefore properly grounded legal advice. In order to secure the maximum sentence reduction of one-third, a defendant has to plead guilty at 'the first stage of proceedings', which is described as 'normally . . . the first hearing at which a plea or indication of plea is sought and recorded by the court'.[96]

Whether a discount of more than one-third for pleading guilty is ever justifiable is a question to be discussed in the concluding part of this chapter.

(D) NEGOTIATED DIVERSION

The focus of this discussion of plea bargains has been upon defendants whose decision to plead guilty is influenced by the sentence reduction. However, another form of bargain is where the possibility of a criminal charge acts as an incentive to participate in some scheme of diversion. An example of this, mentioned in Chapter 6, is the system of conditional cautions, under which the CPS and the police may agree conditionally not to prosecute a person if he agrees to certain conditions for a caution. Those conditions can impose some obligations, such as participation in a programme of work or treatment, and the threat of prosecution is suspended conditionally on compliance with the agreed terms. Thus, the defendant may avoid a criminal conviction by agreeing to the terms for a conditional caution. As we noted,[97] one of the conditions for such

[94] Magistrates' Courts Act 1980, ss 17A–17C.
[95] It was held in *R v Warley Justices, ex p DPP* [1998] 2 Cr App R 307 that the magistrates' courts limit of six months' imprisonment for one offence could be used for cases that might justify a sentence of nine months at the Crown Court, if taking account of the discount meant that six months was the appropriate sentence.
[96] Sentencing Council, *Reduction in sentence for a guilty plea*, n 13, 5.
[97] See Ch 6.2(C); simple police cautions offer the same possibilities for bargains.

a caution must be a free admission of guilt, but earlier research suggests that innocent persons can be tempted to agree to a caution rather than face the threat of something more serious. This type of bargain therefore holds the same advantages and disadvantages as plea bargaining more generally.

(E) PLEA DISCUSSIONS IN SERIOUS FRAUD CASES

In 2009, the Attorney General introduced a new procedure for plea discussions in cases of serious or complex fraud,[98] which now is incorporated into the Criminal Practice Directions.[99] One purpose of this procedure is to encourage defendants in such cases to reach an agreement that avoids the need for a lengthy, costly, and potentially risky trial. It therefore follows that there may be concessions on both sides, which may make sense pragmatically for the prosecution, but may also enable powerful corporate actors to negotiate justice and thereby moderate the impact of the criminal law on them. The idea is that where the defendant intends to plead guilty, the defence and prosecution will work on an agreed basis of plea, combined with sentencing submissions, which would then be submitted to the judge (ideally seven days before the hearing date). The basis of plea should be accompanied by material provided by the prosecution to the defence, and any documents in support of mitigating factors relied upon by the defence. The sentencing submissions should identify the relevant range in the sentencing guidelines, and should also deal with ancillary orders. As with any case involving a basis of plea, the judge remains in control and has the power to reject either the basis of plea or the sentencing submission or both, adopting the appropriate procedural response (such as a *Newton* hearing). The defendant may wish to ask for an advance indication of sentence before engaging in this procedure, and so the comments made in section 10.6(B) may apply here too. The English scheme was drawn up with a view to avoiding some of the excesses encountered in the United States,[100] but its practical impact has been limited, not least because it requires a full admission from the defendant.

In *R v Innospec Ltd*, Thomas J expressed criticism of the actions of the Serious Fraud Office in entering into a plea agreement with Innospec Ltd, a multinational company that manufactured fuel additives and had been involved in the payment of millions of pounds of bribes in Indonesia.[101] In his sentencing remarks, he observed:

> the SFO cannot enter into agreement under the laws of England and Wales with an offender as to the penalty in respect of the offence charged . . . although the sentencing submission proceeded to put forward a specific proposal as opposed to the range as set out

---

[98] *Attorney General's guidelines for prosecutors on plea discussions and presenting a plea agreement to the court in serious fraud cases* (2012), https://www.gov.uk/guidance/plea-discussions-in-cases-of-serious-or-complex-fraud--8.

[99] CPD VII B. For broader discussion, see R. Julian, 'Judicial Perspectives in Serious Fraud Cases' [2008] *Crim LR* 764, esp at 776–8.

[100] E.g. those revealed in *McKinnon v United States* [2008] UKHL 59; see N. Vamos, 'Please Don't Call it Plea-Bargaining' [2009] *Crim LR* 617.

[101] [2010] *Crim LR* 665.

in the authorities, that must have been because the provisions of the consolidated criminal practice direction had not been fully appreciated.... It is in the public interest, particularly in relation to the crime of corruption, that although, in accordance with the Practice Direction, there may be discussion and agreement as to the basis of plea, the court must rigorously scrutinise in open court in the interests of transparency and good governance the basis of that plea and to see whether it reflects the public interest.[102]

A similar note was struck in *R v Dougall*:

In this jurisdiction a plea agreement or bargain between the prosecution and the defence in which they agree what the sentence should be, or present what is in effect an agreed package for the court's acquiescence is contrary to principle. That applies to cases of this kind, as it does to others.[103]

Moreover, the Court of Appeal stressed that the issue of guidelines regarding fraud and corruption prosecutions does not imply that they are more respectable than other forms of crime, or that those who commit fraud or corruption should not be ordered to serve prison sentences. Both *Innospec* and *Dougall* indicate the dangers inherent in plea discussions in respect of corporate criminality.

Linked to plea discussions are deferred prosecution agreements (DPAs) for corporate defendants.[104] As emphasized in *Serious Fraud Office v Rolls-Royce plc*, any penalty under a DPA must be comparable to a fine imposed upon a conviction after a guilty plea, and so the court should take into account any potential reduction for a guilty plea in accordance with s 144 and the Sentencing Council Guideline.[105]

(F) PLEA BARGAINS: THE BALANCE OF ADVANTAGES

What is the balance of advantages of plea bargains for the Crown? They contribute to the smooth running of the system by bringing speed and a reduction of the cost and resources needed to deal with the cases. They ensure a conviction, and avoid the hazards of trial. In the present system, these advantages come at the price of a sentence reduction: it could be claimed that offenders who benefit from the sentence discount are receiving a lower sentence than they deserve (on the basis of harm and culpability), purely for reasons of speed and cost. Those who believe that sentencing should be based on preventive grounds, such as deterrence or incapacitation, would also regard the discount as detracting from its primary purpose. It would be difficult to calculate whether these losses to the system are justified by the advantages, because that would also involve a calculation of how many defendants would persist in a not guilty plea if there were no sentence discount for pleading guilty.

What is the balance of advantages for victims? In general, guilty pleas spare victims the anxiety and possible trauma of having to give evidence in court, and the unpleasantness of hearing all the details of the crime analysed and repeated at length

---

[102] [26]–[27].   [103] *R v Dougall* [2010] EWCA Crim 1048.   [104] See Ch 6.
[105] [2017] Lloyd's Rep FC 249, [119].

in public. For those victims who do give evidence (a minority, because of the large numbers of guilty pleas), the process is often stressful.[106] However, research for the Sentencing Advisory Panel found that some rape victims disagreed with the discount given for pleading guilty and said they would have been prepared to give evidence, if they had been given the choice, in order to ensure that substantial mitigation was not based on this factor.[107] More recent research for the Sentencing Council found that whilst not all surveyed victims supported a reduced sentence for pleading guilty, the majority recognized the benefits to victims and witnesses, especially if the plea was entered at an early stage. Indeed, those who had been a victim or who had witnessed a crime were more likely to be supportive of sentence reductions than the broader general public.[108] In these cases, it is particularly important that the victim or victim's family should be notified of such a significant step, but this does not always happen.[109]

What is the balance of advantages for defendants? The primary benefit is the discount for pleading guilty, which in general promises a substantial reduction in the length of a custodial sentence and may in some cases result in the passing of a non-custodial rather than a custodial sentence. Such sentence reduction may be magnified by the defence lawyer's speech in mitigation: in general, it is much easier to construct a convincing mitigation for someone who has pleaded guilty than for someone who has contested guilt.

These, however, are only advantages for the factually guilty defendant. From the point of view of other defendants, these may be regarded as disincentives to a justifiable challenge to the prosecution case. There are undoubtedly some innocent defendants who feel pressure to plead guilty, because they believe there is a risk that they may not obtain an acquittal and it might appear best to 'cut their losses' in the hope of receiving a non-custodial sentence. Estimates of the number of innocent defendants who take this course vary: Zander and Henderson's figures suggested that up to 11 per cent of guilty pleaders claim innocence,[110] and earlier research suggested that an even higher percentage of guilty pleaders were 'possibly innocent' of one or more charges.[111]

Not enough is known about the mental processes of people placed in this position, but the research on false confessions should be sufficient to dispel any initial reluctance to believe that people could indeed plead guilty when they are innocent.[112] Research has shown that mandatory minimum sentences as well as gender impact on

---

[106] E.g. J. Morgan and L. Zedner, *Child Victims* (1992), 141–3; J. Shapland, J. Willmore, and P. Duff, *Victims in the Criminal Justice System* (1985), 63–7.

[107] Sentencing Advisory Panel, *Advice to the Court of Appeal on Rape* (2002), 41. The Panel drew attention to the possibility of making a Victim Personal Statement to this effect.

[108] W. Dawes, P. Harvey, B. McIntosh, F. Nunney, and A. Phillips, *Attitudes to Guilty Plea Sentence Reductions* (2011).

[109] See the *Victims & Witnesses: Code of Practice for Victims of Crime* (2015).

[110] M. Zander and P. Henderson, *Crown Court Study* (1993), 138–42.

[111] See the summary by P. Darbyshire, 'The Mischief of Plea Bargaining and Sentencing Rewards' [2000] *Crim LR* 895, 903.

[112] See Royal Commission on Criminal Justice (1993), para 4.32, on false confessions of guilt.

the likelihood of false guilty pleas.[113] Moreover, the concept of innocence also needs careful attention: a defendant may have a perfectly arguable defence and should, one might contend, have a right to put the prosecution to disproof of the defence. Yet such a defendant may be advised that running the defence is not worth the risk and the consequent loss of discount, especially if this may make the difference between a custodial and a non-custodial sentence. The sentencing discount positively discourages defendants from putting the prosecution to proof of guilt, not least because it can be as much as a one-third reduction or even the avoidance of a custodial sentence. Indeed, a significant proportion of those who apply to the Criminal Cases Review Commission (CCRC) for a review of their conviction pleaded guilty: a sample of applications from January 2014, January 2015, and January 2016 indicated an average of 26.7 per cent did so.[114] Since 2010, the CCRC has referred 128 cases to the Court of Appeal, 49 of which were guilty plea cases (38 per cent).[115]

The defence lawyer's ethical duty is not to place any pressure on the defendant but to give a frank appraisal of the prospects and of the advantages and disadvantages of continuing with a plea of not guilty. Peter Tague has argued, on the basis of discussions with London barristers, that there are three good reasons for maintaining a not guilty plea—the high chance of acquittal, the relative smallness of the sentence discount (which some would dispute), and the possibility of an appeal in the event of conviction.[116] Tague further argues that the fee structure does not create perverse incentives for barristers to prefer guilty pleas to trials, and that barristers who repeatedly advised lay clients to plead guilty when they and their solicitors preferred to plead not guilty would find themselves being briefed less frequently.[117] However, it remains true that the framework of criminal justice described in sections 10.6(A) to 10.6(F) above, based on a substantial sentencing discount, contains strong incentives for those who are innocent to plead guilty, and that it is the lawyer's duty to explain that.[118]

10.7 POLICIES AND PRINCIPLES

There is much that is unsatisfactory in the rules and practices described in this chapter. Charge bargains are an unavoidable aspect of any system that includes graduated criminal offences (more serious, less serious) and that allows multiple charging. Graduated

---

[113] D. Zimmerman and S. Hunter, 'Factors affecting false guilty pleas in a mock plea bargaining scenario' (2018) 23 *Legal and Criminological Psychology* 53–67; L. Dervan and V. Edkins, 'The Innocent Defendant's Dilemma: An Innovative Empirical Study of Plea Bargaining's Innocence Problem' (2013) 103 *J Crim L and Criminol* 1.

[114] *Response of the Criminal Cases Review Commission (the CCRC) to the Sentencing Council's Reduction in Sentence for a Guilty Plea Guideline*, Consultation (2016), http://www.ccrc.gov.uk/app/uploads/2016/06/CCRC-Sentencing-Council-consultation-April-2016.pdf, [5].

[115] Ibid, [8].

[116] P. Tague, 'Tactical Reasons for Recommending Trials rather than Guilty Pleas in the Crown Court' [2006] *Crim LR* 23.

[117] P. Tague, 'Barristers' Selfish Incentives in Counselling Defendants over Choice of Plea' [2007] *Crim LR* 3.

[118] For a forthright critique, see M. McConville, 'Plea Bargaining: Ethics and Politics' in S. Doran and J. Jackson (eds), *The Judicial Role in Criminal Proceedings* (2000), 81–5, and Bridges, n 74 above.

offences are right in principle,[119] and it is often justifiable to charge more than a single offence. But the result is to place pressure on defendants to plead guilty to something, as a kind of compromise. Fact bargains also seem to have an element of inevitability: defendants may only be prepared to plead guilty on a particular version of the facts, and the prosecution may be persuaded that this is right or acceptable. Plea bargains in the Crown Court operated for many years in a kind of half-light, with the *Turner* rules being flouted so frequently by barristers and trial judges that the Court of Appeal had to use strong language on several occasions in condemning the culture of disobedience.[120] At that time counsel had to predict the sentence that the judge was likely to give, particularly if the judge had declined to see counsel privately. Now the system has brought these matters more into the open, notably with advance indication of sentence and with plea discussions in serious fraud cases. This may make matters clearer to the defendant and the defence lawyer when a defendant is considering a change of plea to guilty; but the amount of pressure is very great, particularly where there is a difference between a custodial and non-custodial outcome. This is compounded by the cuts to legal aid and the phenomenon of unrepresented defendants. From the public point of view, all of this may result in two kinds of unwanted consequences—the conviction (by guilty plea) of some people who are innocent, and the manipulation of criminal justice by some people who are guilty and who 'play the system', for example by waiting until the day of trial in order to see whether key witnesses attend before signifying their plea.

The movement in recent years has therefore between towards greater incentives and greater openness about what is on offer to defendants who are currently pleading not guilty. In 2002, the government stated its objective of getting more defendants to plead guilty and to do so earlier, by means of a 'clearer tariff of sentence discount, backed up by arrangements whereby defendants could seek advance indication of the sentence they would get if they pleaded guilty'.[121] The benefit to witnesses and victims was acknowledged, but savings of court time and public money also loomed large: 'if more defendants pleaded guilty early in the process, the courts and other agencies within the CJS would be able to concentrate on the remaining contested cases'.[122] Many of the measures originated in the report of the Auld Review, which recommended a clear set of graduated sentence discounts and a new system of advance indication of sentence, initiated by the defendant.[123] In reaching his conclusions, Auld LJ took account of a number of concerns raised in the second edition of this book, relating to the difficulty of reconciling the various incentives to plead guilty with the framework of rights to which the UK is a signatory. The Royal Commission on Criminal Justice of 1993 spectacularly failed to make any reference to these rights. The Auld Review did so, but concluded that they do not stand in the way of the recommendations made. Sir Brian Leveson's review in 2015 stated that the rationale behind the Early Guilty Plea

---

[119] Cf A. Ashworth, *Principles of Criminal Law* (6th edn, 2009), ch 3, esp 75–80.
[120] E.g. in *Pitman* [1991] 1 All ER 468 and in *Attorney General's Reference (No 44 of 2000) (Peverett)* [2001] 1 Cr App R 416.
[121] Home Office, *Justice for All* (2002), para 4.42.   [122] Ibid, para 4.41.
[123] Auld Review, n 90, 443–4.

Scheme was to create a national process 'eliciting guilty pleas in an efficient manner by producing the most effective opportunities for those who are guilty to plead at the earliest stage'.[124] Framing this as being about 'opportunities' for the (presumably factually) guilty is notable, and overlooks any negative impact on defendants more widely. Similarly, policy documents on and HMCPSI reviews of initiatives like TSJ make no mention of rights.

The argument here is that the sentence discount for pleading guilty runs contrary to the spirit of at least four of the rights recognized under the ECHR, and possibly counter to their letter too, as well as to the EU Directive on the right to information. This argument starts by considering the rights of a defendant charged with a criminal offence, rather than starting with the objective of making the criminal justice system operate as smoothly and as cost-effectively as possible. The rights to be considered are the presumption of innocence, the privilege against self-incrimination, the right not to be discriminated against in the exercise of Art 6 rights, the right to a fair and public hearing, and the right to information.

(A) THE PRESUMPTION OF INNOCENCE

Article 6(2) of the ECHR declares that 'everyone charged with a criminal offence shall be presumed innocent until proved guilty according to law'. One implication of this seems to be that a defendant has a right to put the prosecution to proof. No one should be recorded as guilty of an offence until the prosecution has proved that guilt, and 'any doubt should benefit the accused'.[125] The question is whether this right can be waived and, if so, under what conditions. The first part of the question may be answered by reference to a 1972 decision of the European Commission on Human Rights, which held that the possibility of pleading guilty does not infringe Art 6(2) so long as there are adequate safeguards against abuse, and that the judge is satisfied that the accused understands the effect of his plea.[126] The second part of the question is more difficult to answer, and the authorities indicate that the presence of a substantial incentive to give up the right to be tried—one-third or more off the sentence for the offence(s)—needs to be reviewed in Strasbourg.

In an early case, *X v UK*,[127] the trial judge had observed when passing sentence that a guilty plea would have constituted a mitigating circumstance. The applicants argued in Strasbourg that this amounted to the imposition of a heavier sentence on the grounds that they had contested the charge, and accordingly that the sentence was in breach of Art 6. In rejecting the application as manifestly ill-founded, the Commission observed:

> It is clear from the statements by the trial judge that he did not increase the applicants' sentence on the ground that they had affirmed their innocence throughout the trial, but

[124] Leveson, n 39, 167.   [125] *Barbera, Messegue and Jabardo v Spain* (1989) 11 EHRR 360, [33].
[126] *X v UK* (1972) 40 CD 64, 67, discussed by B. Emmerson, A. Ashworth, and A. Macdonald, *Human Rights and Criminal Justice* (3rd edn, 2012), 20–74.
[127] (1975) 3 DR 10, 16.

rather refrained from reducing what he deemed to be the proper sentence, having regard to the gravity of the offences concerned.

This is consistent with the theory behind the guilty plea discount in English law,[128] even though it remains true that exercising one's right to be tried has a cost in the sense that the sentence passed in the event of conviction will be higher (possibly 50 per cent higher)[129] than the sentence on a guilty plea. Does the compatibility of a discount for pleading guilty depend on the extent of the inducement involved? In *Deweer v Belgium*,[130] the Court found a violation of Art 6 where the applicant had been offered the choice between paying a relatively modest fine by way of 'compromise' or facing lengthy criminal proceedings. If he had chosen to contest the charge, his butcher's shop would have remained closed by administrative order, thus depriving him of income. The Court held that a procedure under which an accused can waive the right to a hearing on payment of a penalty is not necessarily inconsistent with Art 6, but that such a settlement must be free from 'constraint'. In the present case, there was such disproportionality between the moderate fine and the substantial collateral consequences of contesting the proceedings that the settlement was tainted by constraint and therefore in breach of Art 6. In English cases, the discount on a custodial sentence can be up to one-third,[131] and it is clear that a plea of guilty may make the difference between a custodial sentence and a community sentence.[132] Is a decision to plead guilty made in those circumstances sufficiently free from 'constraint', in the sense applied in *Deweer v Belgium*?

The magnitude of the English discount may suggest that it is not. It is one thing to offer a small inducement to plead guilty, in order to reinforce the proposition that those who are guilty should plead guilty and not try to 'play the system'. It is quite another thing if the extent of the inducement is so great as to 'drown out' that proposition and induce those who are not guilty to change their plea. Auld LJ, in his report, recognized the risk that some innocent defendants might be induced to plead guilty and commented that no system can guarantee that this will not happen. But his primary concern seemed to be that a sentencing system should not be tailored to encourage a defendant who knows he is guilty to 'try his luck', and this is why the sentence discount—and, on his view, a substantial one—is necessary.[133] In our view, this approach ignores the force of the presumption of innocence and sacrifices it too readily to expediency.

The 1993 Royal Commission sought to deal with the problem of innocent defendants thus:

Provided that the defendant is in fact guilty and has received competent legal advice about his or her position, there can be no serious objection to a system of inducements designed

---

[128] See e.g. *Harper* [1968] 1 QB 108.

[129] If the sentence after conviction is three years, and the sentence after an early guilty plea is two years (applying the one-third discount), then the former is 50 per cent higher than the latter.

[130] (1980) 2 EHRR 439.   [131] Sentencing Council, *Reduction in sentence for a guilty plea*, n 13.

[132] Ibid; see also *Howells* [1999] 1 Cr App R (S) 335, per Lord Bingham CJ at 337.

[133] Auld Review, n 90, 439–40.

to encourage him or her so to plead. Such a system is, however, sometimes held to encourage defendants who are not guilty of the offence charged to plead guilty to it nevertheless... This risk cannot be wholly avoided and, although there can be no certainty as to the precise numbers... it would be naive to suppose that innocent persons never plead guilty because of the prospect of the sentence discount.[134]

The only relevant point made subsequently is that 'against the risk that defendants may be tempted to plead guilty must be weighed the benefits to the system and to defendants of encouraging those who are in fact guilty to plead guilty. We believe that the system of sentence discounts should remain.'[135] This kind of 'balancing' argument, which appears to assign no particular weight to the presumption of innocence or any other recognized right, is quite unacceptable. It also overlooks that not all defendants will receive legal advice about their plea.[136] Certainly it would be wrong for the advocates of rights to argue that it behoves us to take *every possible* step to ensure that innocent persons are never convicted. That would result in an immense investment of resources into criminal trials that might cripple the economy. But to dismiss that extreme position is not enough. As Dworkin argues, there is a strong case for maintaining that at all stages of the criminal process our procedures should put the proper value on the fundamental harm of wrongful conviction.[137] What the proper value is may be a matter for debate, but the argument here is that to hold out a substantial sentence discount as a standing incentive for defendants to waive their right to trial goes too far. It fails to give any special weight to the presumption of innocence, whereas its position as a fundamental right ought surely to require this.

(B) THE PRIVILEGE AGAINST SELF-INCRIMINATION

Although not declared expressly in the ECHR, it is now established that the privilege against self-incrimination and the related right of silence are implied rights that form part of the right to a fair trial in Art 6.[138] Leading Strasbourg decisions describe the privilege as a 'generally recognized international standard' which lies 'at the heart of the notion of fair procedure under Article 6', and the same applies to the right of silence.[139] Both have been held to 'presuppose that the prosecution in a criminal case seek to prove their case against the accused without resort to evidence obtained through methods of coercion or oppression in defiance of the will of the accused. In

[134] Royal Commission on Criminal Justice, *Report*, para 7.42. [135] Ibid, para 7.45.
[136] In responding to the Sentencing Council's draft Guideline on reductions in sentence for guilty pleas, the House of Commons Justice Committee recommended that the exception permitting the reduction to apply to later pleas should be expressly extended to any situation where the defendant wishes to obtain legal advice before deciding whether to plead guilty and has been unable to do so. House of Commons Justice Committee, *Reduction in sentence for a guilty plea guideline*, First Report of Session 2016–17, HC 168 (2016), 32. This was not included in the final Guideline.
[137] R. M. Dworkin, 'Principle, Policy, Procedure' in C. Tapper (ed), *Crime, Proof and Punishment* (1981), 212.
[138] See Ch 2.
[139] E.g. *Murray v UK* (1996) 22 EHRR 29 and *Saunders v UK* (1997) 23 EHRR 313, both drawing on Art 14 of the International Covenant on Civil and Political Rights.

this sense the right is closely linked to the presumption of innocence contained in Article 6(2) of the Convention'.[140]

As we discuss elsewhere, the concept of coercion has been quite widely drawn by the Court.[141] The question here is whether the sentence discount for pleading guilty amounts to coercion in an analogous sense.

Two points may be made briefly. The first is that a substantial discount, of one-third or more, may well amount to an inducement of the same magnitude as the financial penalties considered in cases such as *JB v Switzerland*[142] to infringe the privilege against self-incrimination. The second point is that there is a considerable literature on false confessions, as the Royal Commission on Criminal Justice recognized.[143] Difficult as it may be to imagine, some people who are innocent may be induced to plead guilty by the prospect of a non-custodial sentence and no further fuss. Just as the law holds that a confession should not be admitted if it was obtained in consequence of anything said or done which was likely, in the circumstances existing at the time, to render it unreliable, so one might argue that *pari passu* a plea of guilty should not be upheld if it was obtained in consequence of what might be described as a substantial inducement. Indeed, the argument would be that the legal system should not provide such an inducement, whereas English law, through its sentencing discount, clearly does.

(C) THE RIGHT NOT TO BE DISCRIMINATED AGAINST IN THE EXERCISE OF ARTICLE 6 RIGHTS

Article 14 of the ECHR declares that the rights in the Convention 'shall be secured without discrimination on any ground such as sex, race, colour'. Would this principle be breached, either in the letter or in the spirit, if it were found that the operation of the criminal justice system routinely discouraged members of a particular ethnic minority from disputing their guilt?

Persons from a Black, Asian, or Minority ethnic (BAME) background tend to plead not guilty at a higher rate than white individuals.[144] In 2016, white defendants had the highest guilty plea rate for indictable offences at the Crown Court (71 per cent), whereas for all other ethnic groups the rate ranged between 56 and 64 per cent.[145] Black and Asian men are more than one and a half times more likely to enter a 'not guilty' plea than white men; Black, Asian, Mixed ethnic, and Chinese/Other ethnic women were all more likely than white women to enter not guilty pleas at Crown Court, with Asian women more than one and a half times more likely to do so.[146] The

---

[140] *Saunders*, ibid, [68].   [141] See Ch 4.7.   [142] [2001] *Crim LR* 748.

[143] Royal Commission on Criminal Justice, *Report*, para 4.32.

[144] D. Lammy, *An independent review into the treatment of, and outcomes for, Black, Asian and Minority Ethnic individuals in the Criminal Justice System* (2017), ch 3; C. Thomas, 'Ethnicity and the Fairness of Jury Trials in England and Wales 2006–2014' [2017] *Crim LR* 860, 867.

[145] Ministry of Justice, *Statistics on Race and the Criminal Justice System 2016* (2017), 9.

[146] Lammy, n 144, 26. Also Ministry of Justice, *Black, Asian and Minority Ethnic disproportionality in the Criminal Justice System in England and Wales* (2016), 19.

plea decision can have a profound impact. As Lammy notes, 'Admitting guilt can result in community punishment rather than custody, or see custodial sentences reduced by up to a third. Plea decisions are an important factor in the disproportionate make-up of the prison system.'[147] Roger Hood found that not only do black defendants tend to plead not guilty more frequently than white defendants but that, when convicted, they tend to receive longer sentences largely because they have forfeited the discount for pleading guilty.[148] Comparably, a more recent Ministry of Justice study found that pleading not guilty was associated with large increases in the odds of imprisonment.[149] Ethnicity was associated with being sentenced to prison, and plea partially explained this association.

In 2003, the John Report found that 'defendants from African Caribbean and Asian ethnic groups are more likely to be acquitted than white defendants',[150] while 2016 figures showed that Crown Court conviction rates for BAME groups were either proportionate or lower than the White ethnic group,[151] which may be regarded as vindicating many not guilty pleas. As noted in that Ministry of Justice report, how defendants arrive at a plea can be influenced by the legal advice they receive, the type of legal representation they have, if any, the level of trust they place in any sentencing discounts they may receive for early guilty pleas, their assessment of their chances with a jury, as well as whether they actually committed the offence with which they were charged.[152] All such dimensions have considerable racial and socio-implications and potential biases.

This state of affairs can be regarded as a form of indirect discrimination: a general principle (the sentence discount) has a disproportionate impact on members of ethnic minorities simply because they exercise a right (the right to be tried and to be presumed innocent until convicted). The Royal Commission seemed to recognize this, but merely expressed its support for 'the recommendation made by Hood that the policy of offering sentence discounts should be kept under review'.[153] In fact, Hood argued that 'it is time [i.e. now] to consider all the implications of a policy which favours so strongly those who plead guilty'.[154] The Auld Review recognized that 'it is important to discover why one group of defendants, distinguished only by their ethnicity, should behave differently from others when faced with the same choices',[155] and called for research to determine why this is so and whether the discount for pleading guilty was relevant to this. However, it appears that Auld was sceptical of these arguments, and took the general position that if members of ethnic minorities sought to exercise their right to be tried, they should take the consequence of a more severe sentence if found guilty.

---

[147] Lammy, n 144, 25 (footnote omitted).   [148] R. Hood, *Race and Sentencing* (1992), 125.

[149] K. Hopkins, N. Uhrig, and M. Colahan, *Associations Between Ethnic Background and Being Sentenced to Prison in the Crown Court in England and Wales in 2015* (2016), 7.

[150] Gus John Partnership, *Race for Justice* (2003), para 37. For a summary of the early research, see M. Fitzgerald, *Ethnic Minorities and the Criminal Justice System* (1993), 26.

[151] Ministry of Justice, *Black, Asian and Minority Ethnic disproportionality in the Criminal Justice System in England and Wales* (2016), 19.

[152] Ibid, 28.   [153] Royal Commission on Criminal Justice, *Report*, para 7.58.

[154] Hood, n 148, 182.   [155] Auld Review, n 90, 441.

This overlooks the powerful argument about indirect discrimination, an argument that strongly favours the abolition (or substantial diminution) of the guilty plea discount.[156]

(D) THE RIGHT TO A 'FAIR AND PUBLIC' HEARING

Article 6(1) of the ECHR declares that 'everyone is entitled to a fair and public hearing', and goes on to describe the limited situations in which 'the press and public may be excluded from all or part of the trial'. One characteristic of cases in which there is a guilty plea is that there is no real public hearing. An added characteristic of cases in which there is a plea bargain is that the crucial negotiation takes place in the absence not only of the public but also of the accused person. There is good reason to believe that a case determined in this way would not satisfy Art 6(1). Of course, it may be replied that there is always some form of public hearing, at which the defendant pleads guilty, prosecution and defence speeches are made, and the judge decides on sentence. But if it can be established that the defendant's fate was determined by words spoken in private, of which only some were relayed to the defendant by counsel, this might cause some reconsideration of the ECtHR approach.[157]

(E) THE RIGHT TO INFORMATION

The EU Directive on the right to information, as examined in Chapter 5, provides under Art 6 a right to information about the accusation and Art 7 a right of access to the materials of the case. Any guilty plea should be based on the evidence held by the prosecution and on legal advice, though we have seen that pre-trial disclosure by the CPS is often inadequate in practice. This is compounded by the tight timeframes. The prosecutor must serve initial details of the prosecution case on the defendant if requested, and must do so as soon as practicable; and no later than the beginning of the day of the first hearing.[158] Thus, the point at which a defendant is eligible for the guilty plea maximum sentence discount, namely the first stage of proceedings, might be the same point at which the initial details of the prosecution case may be shared. This does not seem to comply with the right to information.

10.8 CONCLUSION

From the point of view of principle, there are powerful arguments in favour of reassessing the sentence discount for those who plead guilty. It is certainly against the spirit of four fundamental rights and freedoms recognized in the ECHR—the presumption of innocence, the privilege against self-incrimination, the right to equal treatment in the exercise of rights, and the right to a fair and public hearing—and is

---

[156] In M. Tonry, *Punishment and Politics* (2004), 75 and 87, it is argued that this reasoning should lead to the abolition of the guilty plea discount.

[157] See the case of *X v UK*, n 126, and accompanying text.   [158] CPR, r 8.2(2).

probably against the letter of two of them. The right to information is compromised also. The sentence discount sustains a number of perverse incentives that are liable to distort both the pursuit of truth and the protection of rights, in the context of charge, fact, and plea bargains.

One major difficulty is the size of the sentence discount: it can be as much as one-third (although less for a late change of plea), and can certainly make the difference between immediate custody and a non-custodial sentence. These are formidable incentives, applicable both to those who are guilty and to those who are innocent. It has been argued here that discounts of this kind are so great that they place unfair pressure on those who maintain their innocence and wish to put the prosecution to proof—a strong temptation to 'cut one's losses' and plead guilty in exchange for a lesser sentence, particularly if it is non-custodial. A fairer system (assuming that the discount is to be retained) would be to offer a small incentive of no more than a 10 per cent reduction, aimed at preserving the freedom of choice of someone who maintains innocence and at ensuring that the exercise of the right to be presumed innocent until proved guilty does not have a significant cost.[159]

There have been significant steps towards increasing the openness of plea negotiations, with a greater involvement of judges, through advance indication of sentence and plea discussions in serious fraud cases. Sentencing guidelines—now covering most offences—should increase the predictability of sentencing. But there remains the question whether increased transparency and increased judicial involvement do not amount to increased pressure on the guilty and the innocent alike. The Royal Commission of 1993 concluded that a system in which the judge gave such a sentence indication would amount to placing undue pressure on defendants, largely because the involvement of a judge made the pressure greater than simply the prediction of counsel. But Auld LJ disagreed:

> That comparison is precisely what a defendant considering admitting his guilt wants to know. He knows and will, in any event, be advised by his lawyer that a plea of guilty can attract a lesser sentence and broadly what the possible outcomes are, depending on his plea. So what possible additional pressure, unacceptable or otherwise, can there be in the judge, whom he has requested to tell him where he stands, indicating more precisely the alternatives?[160]

Such a system of sentence indication may succeed in reducing the element of uncertainty, but it surely imposes additional pressure through the involvement of the authoritative figure of the judge. Given the magnitude of the possible difference between the two sentences, the real question is whether the pressure is so great as to impinge on the defendant's freedom of choice in the exercise of fundamental rights. If such an inducement were made to someone before he or she confessed a crime to the

---

[159] Of course, any reduction in the amount of the discount would have to form part of a general reappraisal of sentence levels and approaches to sentencing. We are certainly not arguing for any overall increase in the severity of sentences: other adjustments would have to be made.

[160] Auld Review, n 90, ch 10, para 112.

police, the prevailing principle is that the confession should be ruled inadmissible.[161] False confessions do occur. Our submission is that the same considerations should apply in the context of changes of plea from not guilty to guilty.

Could the greater involvement of the judge be turned into an advantage for defendants, as a means of protecting the defendant's rights rather than imposing undue pressure? The overriding assumption is that it is necessary, for purposes of efficiency and cost-effectiveness, to increase the proportion of guilty pleas and of early guilty pleas, and any proposal about greater involvement of judges in assessing case papers and in ascertaining that innocent defendants were not being pressured into pleading guilty would undoubtedly be dismissed as too costly. But even if this is true—and until it has been thoroughly investigated, it would be unwise to make the assumption—then the question is plainly one of expense rather than respect for rights, which regrettably is the current pervading sentiment in the criminal justice context. In this chapter, we have noted the strong structural incentives to plead guilty and to enter that plea at the first stage of the proceedings, and we have argued that these incentives undermine safeguards for the innocent. Stephen Schulfhofer has advanced the same view in powerful terms:

> Contractual exchange, under appropriate conditions, can leave both parties better off. But the converse is also true. When the conditions necessary for welfare-enhancing transactions are not met, contractual exchange can leave both parties worse off. In criminal justice, pervasive structural impediments to efficient, welfare-enhancing transactions have produced just this situation. With trials in open court and deserved sentences imposed by a neutral factfinder, we protect the due process right to an adversarial trial, minimize the risk of unjust conviction of the innocent, and at the same time further the public interest in effective law enforcement and adequate punishment of the guilty. But plea negotiation simultaneously undercuts all of these interests. The affected parties are represented by agents who have inadequate incentives for proper performance; prospects for effective monitoring are limited or non-existent; and the dynamics of negotiation can create irresistible pressure for defendants falsely to condemn themselves. As a result, plea agreements defeat the public interest in effective law enforcement at the same time that they deny defendants the benefits of a vigorous defence and inflict undeserved punishment on innocents who could win acquittal at trial.[162]

These words were written in an American context, and the somewhat optimistic description of trials seems rather overdone. Indeed, this point is taken up by Robert Scott and William Stuntz who ask whether it is really desirable to push more innocent people to trial, on the basis that some of them will be convicted and will then receive harsher sentences than they would have done if they had pleaded guilty:

> This result stands every known theory of distributional justice on its head. We would think it common ground that losses, equally unjust losses, are better spread than concentrated, all else being equal. Schulhofer, like most critics of plea bargaining, seems to

---

[161] It would be inconsistent to create an exception for the sentence discount: see the discussion in Ch 4.
[162] S. J. Schulhofer, 'Plea-Bargaining as Disaster' (1992) 101 *Yale LJ* 1979, 2008–9.

prefer a few innocent defendants serving long prison terms to a larger number serving a few years apiece.[163]

Their view is certainly contestable: if all known theories of distributional justice point in the direction of more convictions of the innocent, then that is a good reason for not subscribing to them. From the rights perspective, the right of innocent persons not to be convicted ought to be recognized as a strong right with a high value, not something to be traded off simply for supposed efficiency gains. Scott and Stuntz would insist that, in a world where there are going to be convictions of innocent people, we must face the choice to which they refer, and not avoid it. Their approach, in the leading article on which Schulhofer was commenting, is to eschew both extremes—to argue both against the existing system of plea negotiation and against the abolition of all plea negotiations—and to press the case for reconfiguring the bargaining process in order to make it fairer. They start from the position that modern criminal justice systems are so demanding of resources that in most countries there is an 'inability to test innocence claims at acceptable cost'.[164] Some reforms in this country, in the form of advance indication of sentence and plea discussions in serious fraud cases, appear to have moved towards the greater information for defendants on the choice to be made, and clearer sentencing guidance to enhance predictability, that Scott and Stuntz recommend. This is offset by the increased pressure on defence practitioners, and by the lack of legal advice before plea for all defendants. However, as argued earlier, the size of the discount available in England and Wales is too great, the pressure it exerts on defendants is too much, the effect on innocent defendants (especially those from certain racial minorities) is unacceptable, and the system as a whole fails to place a sufficiently high value on preventing wrongful convictions.[165] Moreover, the ability to negotiate benefits powerful and corporate defendants for the most part. Successive governments have failed to give priority to avoiding undue pressure on the innocent in their search for ways of achieving the efficiencies they desire.

FURTHER READING

McConville, M. and Marsh, L., 'Factory Farming and State-Induced Pleas' in J. Hunter, P. Roberts, S. N. M. Young, and D. Dixon (eds), *The Integrity of Criminal Process: From Theory into Practice*, London: Bloomsbury, 2016.

McEwan, J., 'Truth, Efficiency, and Cooperation in Modern Criminal Justice' (2013) 203 *CLP* 66.

Tonry, M., *Punishment and Politics*, Cullompton: Willan, 2004, ch 4.

[163] R. E. Scott and W. J. Stuntz, 'A Reply: Imperfect Bargains, Imperfect Trials and Innocent Defendants' (1992) 101 *Yale LJ* 2011, 2013.
[164] R. E. Scott and W. J. Stuntz, 'Plea Bargaining as Contract' (1992) 101 *Yale LJ* 1909, 1951.
[165] Cf the argument of Dworkin, n 137 and accompanying text.

QUESTIONS FOR DISCUSSION

1. Are charge bargains inevitable?

2. Is the procedure for advance indication of sentence a worthwhile innovation?

3. Are the rights-based arguments against the sentence discount for pleading guilty convincing at the level of principle? Even if they are, would there be insuperable problems in devising a practical system that took them into account?

11

THE TRIAL

The trial is the focal point of criminal procedure. Case preparation in the earlier stages of the process is carried out in the light of the possibility that the case may go to court. The rules governing trials therefore shape decisions made by police and prosecutors. While it is true that the majority of defendants plead guilty, and that the system encourages trial avoidance in this manner, the trial remains important because defendants' decisions on whether or not to plead guilty are often informed by what they believe to be the probability of conviction. Furthermore, where defendants do not plead guilty, a decision has to be made on whether or not they actually are guilty. The mechanism for making this crucial decision deserves close consideration.

Many aspects of the trial can only be understood through detailed analysis of the rules of evidence and fact-finding processes, which is beyond the scope of the present work. Rather, we consider courtroom processes, the role of the jury, and some of the protective measures for witnesses, all of which are closely connected to issues of procedural fairness, in the light of contemporary technological developments and efficiency initiatives. Before proceeding to this, we briefly consider theoretical perspectives on the trial.

Clearly, a primary function of the trial, as of the criminal process as a whole, is accurate decision making. The trial is an attempt to sort the innocent from the guilty and to determine the level of wrongdoing of the guilty, though it is constrained by the high standard of proof (beyond reasonable doubt) which protects the innocent from wrongful conviction. For some writers, there is little more to the trial than this; although other values might in theory play a role in the trial, they are not sufficiently compelling to outweigh the strong interest in accurate fact-finding.[1] As a description of actual trial practices, this view has little to be said for it (which hints that it is deficient as a theory, too). Anglo-American jurisdictions (as well as the regime under the European Convention on Human Rights (ECHR)) recognize the importance of a fair trial, where fairness comprises more than accuracy. In England and Wales, the abuse of process jurisdiction, discussed in Chapter 9, is a good example of this. Thus, there is widespread agreement that the criminal trial is not a purely instrumental process. Saying just what it is in addition to an instrumental process, however, is more difficult and here there is less agreement.

---

[1] See L. Laudan, *Truth, Error and Criminal Law: An Essay in Legal Epistemology* (2006).

The simplest way to incorporate values other than accuracy in a theory of the trial is to depict the trial as a side-constrained instrumental process, where things such as the need to respect the defendant's rights restrain the pursuit of truth. In contrast, a more complex theory would argue that values other than accurate fact-finding are an intrinsic part of the trial, and thus should not be seen as constraints on accuracy but as an integral part of the trial's aims. One way of grounding this vision of the trial is provided by Duff and his co-authors who have argued that the trial should be seen as a communicative process in which the defendant is called to answer for alleged wrong-doing, and to account for that wrongdoing should it be proved.[2] Because, for Duff et al, the trial is a process or moral engagement with the accused, accuracy is no longer a primary aim, but is intertwined with moral values. This is an ambitious theory, and there may be questions about the extent to which the criminal trial should be modelled as a process of moral dialogue when it involves the application of state power to an individual.[3] A slightly different, and influential, way of acknowledging the integral position of values other than accuracy to the criminal trial is to stress the need for criminal verdicts to be legitimate.[4] At one level, it is hard to disagree with this—who would argue that trial verdicts should be illegitimate? But unpacking the notion of legitimacy is not straightforward; advocates of legitimacy have tended to explain legitimacy in terms of public confidence or trust, but public attitudes are sufficiently fickle that they offer no guarantee that the trial would respect the defendant's rights or result in more than a largely instrumental trial process. Legitimacy therefore probably needs some objective grounding, but explaining just why certain actions of the state should affect the legitimacy of the trial remains difficult.

The difference between these theories should not be overstated. Indeed, the distinction between side-constrained instrumentalism and intrinsic theories may be one with no practical difference.[5] Most theorists who reject pure-instrumentalism share a broadly similar vision of the trial—though we will point up possible disagreements about certain cases later in the chapter. As we explained in Chapter 2, our own vision of the trial, and of the wider criminal process to which it is central, emphasizes respect for dignity and rights. We located important rights as internal values in the criminal process, so, for what it is worth, these values are properly seen as intrinsic to the trial rather than as side constraints. While we are cautious about the language of legitimacy, this account could be translated into such terms by suggesting that respect for rights is a primary objective constraint on legitimacy.[6] However, while this makes it clear that respect for rights is an important part of the account of the trial, it says little about what makes trials distinctive as processes which involve rights and what particular rights

---

[2] R. A. Duff et al (eds), *The Trial on Trial, Vol 3: Towards a Normative Theory of the Criminal Trial* (2007).

[3] See M. Redmayne, 'Theorizing the Criminal Trial' (2009) 12 *New Crim LR* 287.

[4] A view taken in I. Dennis, *The Law of Evidence* (6th edn, 2017) and P. Roberts and A. Zuckerman, *Criminal Evidence* (2nd edn, 2010).

[5] See Redmayne, n 3.

[6] This seems to be Choo's position: A. Choo, *Abuse of Process and Judicial Stays of Criminal Proceedings* (2nd edn, 2008), 190.

and values a trial might engage. This is a complex topic, and we will do no more at this point than note that one important aspect of the trial is its association with the rule of law.[7] As Waldron explains, when someone is accused of breaking the law:

> they should have an opportunity to request a hearing, make an argument, and confront the evidence before them prior to the application of any sanction associated with the norm. The Rule of Law is violated when the institutions that are supposed to embody these procedural safeguards are undermined. In this way the Rule of Law has become associated with political ideals such as the separation of powers and the independence of the judiciary.[8]

Criminal trials might also engage the rule of law in another way. Trials are constrained by the demand that 'citizens be protected from oppression and their dignity respected';[9] more ambitiously, they provide an opportunity to examine the actions of the state in prosecuting crime—calling the state to account, as it has been put. This helps to explain why close scrutiny of the legality of police actions in investigating crime may become an important part of a criminal trial.

11.1 MODES OF TRIAL

(A) MAGISTRATES' COURT AND CROWN COURT

There are two different levels of court in England and Wales with substantial differences in the trials that take place in them. The least serious cases are tried in the magistrates' courts and the more serious ones in the Crown Court; in practice, the vast majority of cases—at least 95 per cent—are dealt with in the magistrates' court. The principal distinction between the two courts is that cases in the Crown Court are tried by a professional judge sitting with a jury, and cases in the magistrates' court are tried by lay magistrates, or by a professional District Judge sitting alone. Lay magistrates are unpaid and hear cases on a part-time basis; they typically sit in benches of three and are advised on legal points by a clerk. There is considerable debate about the relative merits of the two types of trial, and it is important to understand something about these issues before considering the way in which cases are allocated between the different courts.

First, it is not unusual to have two levels of court; most jurisdictions have more elaborate procedures for trying the more serious cases. Given limited resources, this is entirely appropriate. Accurate adjudication is more important in serious than non-serious cases, because the cost of error (of either mistaken conviction or mistaken acquittal) is greater. This does not, of course, mean that trials in the lower tier of court should be cursory, or that defendants tried there should face an undue risk of mistaken conviction. One of the concerns about the magistrates' court is that defendants

---

[7] See Duff et al, n 2, 94–6.
[8] J. Waldron, 'The Concept and the Rule of Law' (2008) 43 *Georgia L Rev* 1, 8.   [9] Duff et al, n 2, 95.

do in fact face an unacceptable risk of false conviction. It is often remarked that the conviction rate is higher in the magistrates' court than in the Crown Court. According to Crown Prosecution Service (CPS) statistics, 62 per cent of defendants in contested trials in the magistrates' courts are convicted, compared with 54 per cent in the Crown Court.

Between 78–82 per cent of persons proceeded against in the magistrates' courts are convicted (see Table 11.1). Of contested trials in the Crown Court, 18–20 per cent end in acquittal.[10] Since 2007, 78–80 per cent of individuals who were tried in the Crown Court for indictable offences were found guilty (see Table 11.2). The proportion is even larger for individuals who pleaded not guilty to summary offences in the Crown Court, with 95–97 per cent convicted each year (see Table 11.3).

It is not obvious how to interpret these differences. In the inevitable absence of knowledge of the proportion of innocent and guilty defendants in each court, it is impossible to say whether one court is more accurate, or even lenient, than the other. It should also be noted that the cases dealt with in each court have different characteristics. Those tried in the Crown Court are more complex, and many summary offences have no *mens rea* element; it may therefore be that cases heard in the magistrates' courts are simply easier to prove.[11]

Moving beyond acquittal and conviction rates, there has been a general perception among defendants and lawyers that trials in the Crown Court are fairer than magistrates' trials.[12] There are several reasons why Crown Court trial may be fairer. Juries typically come fresh to a case; they are not 'case hardened' in the way magistrates may be. Trial by judge and jury is also an effective way of keeping certain information—such as the fact that the defendant has previous convictions—away from the fact-finder.[13] Juries tend to be more representative of the general population than magistrates, and in some circumstances this may make them superior fact-finders, for they will have a wider range of life experiences.[14] Indeed, these reasons seem connected to the reason for having trials in the first place, which is, primarily, to make accurate decisions. There are, of course, other reasons why jury trial is thought to be fair, but there is likely to be

---

[10] Criminal Justice System Statistics publication, *Crown Court: Pivot Table Analytical Tool for England and Wales, Time Period: 12 months ending December 2007 to 12 months ending December 2017.*

[11] See P. Darbyshire, 'For the New Lord Chancellor—Some Causes for Concern About Magistrates' [1997] *Crim LR* 861, 869–72. We do know that at Crown Court the conviction rate is considerably higher for summary offences than for indictable offences (97 per cent vs 78 per cent), which lends some support to this argument, but as these figures include guilty pleas they are not quite on point. Criminal Justice System Statistics publication, *Crown Court: Pivot Table Analytical Tool for England and Wales 2007–2017.*

[12] See C. Hedderman and D. Moxon, *Magistrates' Court or Crown Court? Mode of Trial Decisions and Sentencing* (1992), 20, where 62 per cent of defendants and 70 per cent of solicitors are said to support the statement 'magistrates are on the side of the police'. See also Darbyshire, above n 11, 869.

[13] On the problems of achieving this in the magistrates' court, see M. Wasik, 'Magistrates' Knowledge of Previous Convictions' [1996] *Crim LR* 851; P. Darbyshire, 'Previous Misconduct and the Magistrates' Courts—Some Tales from the Real World' [1997] *Crim LR* 105.

[14] See M. Redmayne, 'Theorizing Jury Reform' in R. A. Duff et al (eds), *The Trial on Trial, Vol 2: Judgment and Calling to Account* (2006).

Table 11.1 Magistrates' Court proceedings

	2007	2008	2009	2010	2011	2012	2013	2014	2015	2016	2017
Proceeded against in MC	1,732,506	1,640,023	1,694,410	1,653,190	1,580,024	1,484,602	1,441,308	1,467,844	1,492,160	1,456,177	1,392,139
Convicted	1,351,070	1,292,539	1,331,212	1,283,333	1,232,640	1,160,753	1,111,742	1,147,599	1,177,919	1,176,117	1,146,720

Table 11.2 Crown Court proceedings for indictable offences

	2007	2008	2009	2010	2011	2012	2013	2014	2015	2016	2017
Tried in the Crown Court for indictable offences	78580	83887	91875	100263	96127	84469	79572	82755	84466	76402	67987
Found guilty	61472	67226	73420	79461	76999	67701	64764	67034	67914	60943	54486

Table 11.3 Crown Court proceedings for summary offences

	2007	2008	2009	2010	2011	2012	2013	2014	2015	2016	2017
Tried in the Crown Court for summary offences	3,462	3,553	3,963	4,862	4,119	3,239	3,003	3,188	3,412	3,350	2,932
Found guilty	3,362	3,453	3,805	4,681	3,941	3,109	2,901	3,041	3,285	3,211	2,839

more debate about the merits of such reasons. For example, juries are able to exercise 'jury equity' by reaching a verdict in defiance of the law.[15] Jury equity, or jury nullification as it is know in the United States, is controversial, because it seems to undermine the rule of law.[16] However, one of the values associated with the rule of law in the view of writers such as Waldron and MacCormick,[17] is that legal decisions are contestable and open to argument; in this way, jury equity may be less threatening to legal values than is sometimes supposed. As a deliberate decision to disapply the law, jury equity is likely to be rare; however, jury decision making is probably characterized by discretion and moral judgement to a greater degree than judicial decision making,[18] and this is to some extent encouraged by the criminal law, which often uses open-textured standards such as reasonableness to define criminal liability. Jury trial is often praised for helping to ensure that the defendant is tried by his peers, but this probably adds little to the points just made.

It should be noted that jury trial has merits beyond those associated with the interests of defendants. The jury is, in various ways, a democratic institution. Jury trial gives citizens some input into the application of the criminal law.[19] The institution of the jury helps to ensure that the criminal law is expressed in terms comprehensible to ordinary people, and it also serves an educational and social function.[20] Bringing lay people into the courtroom means that the pursuit of criminal justice is not a closed shop, dominated by lawyers and other professionals. It makes trials genuinely public and helps to prevent the state abusing its power. However, not all of these merits are the exclusive preserve of the jury; the use of lay magistrates also helps to keep the law simple and serves a civic function.

As well as these general points about the respective institutional virtues of magistrates and jury trial, there is research on magistrates' trials which supports the criticism that this is a cursory form of justice. Some time ago, McBarnet commented on the 'ideology of triviality'[21] which she found prevailing in the magistrates' courts: the presumption that the cases dealt with there were not important and that full due process protections were not appropriate. McConville et al were also critical of the quality of justice in magistrates' courts, commenting that defendants in the lower courts, rather than benefiting from a presumption of innocence, typically face an

---

[15] A case often used to illustrate this is the acquittal of Clive Ponting, who was charged with leaking information in breach of the Official Secrets Act for reasons which many would have regarded as reflecting the public interest. Although he had no defence in law, he was acquitted by the jury. See G. Drewry, 'The *Ponting* Case—Leaking in the Public Interest' [1985] *PL* 203.

[16] For a variety of perspectives on jury equity, or 'nullification', see J. Kleinig and J. Levine (eds), *Jury Ethics: Juror Conduct and Jury Dynamics* (2006).

[17] See Waldron, n 8; N. MacCormick, 'Rhetoric and the Rule of Law' in D. Dyzenhaus (ed), *Recrafting the Rule of Law* (1999).

[18] See N. Finkel, 'Jurors' Duties, Obligations and Rights: The Ethical/Moral Roots of Discretion' in Kleinig and Levine, n 16.

[19] See ibid.

[20] See R. Matthews, L. Hancock, and D. Briggs, *Jurors' Perceptions, Understanding, Confidence and Satisfaction in the Jury System: A Study in Six Courts* (2004), 64–6.

[21] D. McBarnet, *Conviction: Law, the State and the Construction of Justice* (1983), 144.

uphill struggle in persuading the court that the prosecution case is not made out.[22] In Morgan and Russell's study, only 30 per cent of regular court users professed to having 'a great deal' or 'a lot' of confidence in lay magistrates, as compared to nearly 90 per cent with this level of confidence in professional magistrates.[23] At the same time, only 8 per cent said they had 'no' or 'very little' confidence in the lay magistracy. A more recent study carried out for the Ministry of Justice stressed the changes that have been made in the magistrates' courts, including initiatives that prioritize speedy, summary justice, as well as improved training.[24] This study, which involved interviews and discussion groups with judges, court staff, and professional and lay court users, found that magistrates were seen as more representative of the national working population in terms of gender and ethnicity than District Judges.[25] Respondents saw magistrates as fair, due to their lay status, as well as the balance provided by having three people on the bench. In contrast, a noted strength of District Judges was the speed with which they deal with cases.

The differences between the two types of trial make the allocation of cases between them an important issue. From the point of view of the government, case allocation is particularly critical because it has significant resource implications. A typical trial in the magistrates' courts costs around ten times less than a Crown Court trial,[26] and Crown Court trials cost an average of £1,900 per day for staff and judicial and juror costs, compared with £1,150 in a magistrates' court.[27] It was estimated that £36.1 million is the minimum additional cost of cases that could be heard in either court going to the Crown Court rather than the magistrates' court in 2014–15.[28] Moreover, there are concerns about the number of Crown Court trials that begin on time, and their growing length: in 2014–15 just 33 per cent of trials in the Crown Court were deemed to be 'effective', in going ahead as planned on the day they were due to start,[29] while their increasing length meant an additional cost of £44 million for the year ending September 2015 over 2010–11.[30] The situation has improved somewhat: 51 per cent of Crown Court trials were effective in 2017, with a corresponding decrease in cracked and ineffective trials.[31] Since 2010, the proportion of magistrates' court trials that were effective increased by 4 percentage points to 47 per cent. There is considerable regional difference in these contexts.[32] Measures that will keep more cases at the lower level are seen to have the potential to make considerable savings, though as we have seen there is an ideological drive for swifter summary justice too.

[22] M. McConville et al, *Standing Accused: The Organization and Practices of Criminal Defence Lawyers in Britain* (1994), ch 9.

[23] R. Morgan and N. Russell, *The Judiciary in the Magistrates' Courts* (Home Office and Lord Chancellor's Department, 2000), 60.

[24] Ipsos MORI for the Ministry of Justice, *The strengths and skills of the Judiciary in the Magistrates' Courts* (2011), 1.

[25] Ibid, ch 3.

[26] Home Office, *Digest 4: Information on the Criminal Justice System in England and Wales* (1999), 69.

[27] National Audit Office (NAO), *Efficiency in the criminal justice system* (2016), 10.   [28] Ibid, 4.

[29] Ibid.   [30] Ibid.

[31] *Criminal court statistics quarterly, England and Wales, January to March 2018 (annual 2017)* (2018), 9.

[32] NAO, n 27, 3.4.

The primary tool for case allocation is the classification of offences into three types: summary, either way, and offences triable only on indictment. The first and last categories are straightforward. Summary offences, the least serious criminal offences, can only be tried in the magistrates' court. Offences triable only on indictment, a category comprising the most serious offences, can only be tried in the Crown Court. Things are more complicated with either way (also referred to as 'indictable') offences. This large category comprises some common offences such as theft and assault occasioning actual bodily harm. Here, a decision must be taken as to where the case will be tried. The decision is for the magistrates, and is taken at a mode of trial hearing. They must follow the *Sentencing Council's guideline on Allocation (mode of trial)* when deciding whether to send defendants charged with 'either way' offences for trial in the Crown Court, or to try the case themselves.[33] This provides that, in general, either way offences should be tried summarily unless: the likely sentence would clearly be in excess of the magistrate court's powers after taking into account personal mitigation and any potential reduction for a guilty plea; or for reasons of unusual legal, procedural, or factual complexity, the case should be tried in the Crown Court, such as where a very substantial fine is the likely sentence. In cases with no factual or legal complications, the magistrates' court may retain jurisdiction, notwithstanding that the likely sentence might exceed its powers.[34]

Magistrates have quite limited sentencing powers, so the more serious either way offences are best dealt with in the Crown Court, where they can be sentenced appropriately. Whereas there was once a £5,000 cap on fines, this was removed by s 85 of the Legal Aid, Sentencing and Punishment of Offenders Act 2012. Moreover, though magistrates can impose no more than six months' imprisonment, s 154 of the Criminal Justice Act (CJA) 2003 would extend this to 12 months: it has not yet been brought into force, but there have been a number of recent calls for such extension.[35] As noted earlier, even disregarding sentencing powers, the more elaborate fact-finding procedures of a Crown Court trial should be used in the most serious cases. If the magistrates decide to send the case to the Crown Court, the case will be dealt with there. If, however, the decision is to retain the case in the summary jurisdiction, that is not an end to the matter. The defendant may override this decision by choosing to be tried in the Crown Court.[36] A complicating factor is that if the magistrates try the case themselves and find the defendant guilty, they may commit the case to the Crown Court for sentencing if, on reflection, they conclude that their sentencing powers are not sufficient. In practice, the vast majority (about 90 per cent) of either way offences sent to the Crown Court are sent because magistrates decline jurisdiction.[37] The prosecution's arguments on appropriate venue are usually the dominant factor in mode of trial hearings.[38]

---

[33] CPR, Part 9; and CPD II 9A.1.   [34] *Sentencing Council Guideline on Allocation (mode of trial)* (2015).
[35] Magistrates Association, *Investigation of cases sent by magistrates to Crown Court for sentence* (2015), 2.5; *The Times*, 'Double sentencing powers for magistrates, urges lord chief justice', 19 September 2017.
[36] Magistrates' Courts Act 1980, s 20.
[37] *CPS Annual Report 2008–2009*, Annex B. More recent figures are not available.
[38] See S. Cammiss, 'Deciding Upon Mode of Trial' (2007) 46 *Howard JCJ* 372.

Over the years, various steps have been taken to ensure that as many cases as possible are tried summarily. Some either way offences have been reclassified as summary: for example, common assault, driving whilst disqualified, and criminal damage up to a value of £5,000. The *Sentencing Council Guideline on Allocation* creates a presumption in favour of summary trial.[39] Moreover, the 'plea before venue' arrangement allows defendants to indicate whether or not they intend to plead guilty before the magistrates make the mode of trial decision.[40] The idea here is that if the defendant indicates that he intends to plead guilty, the magistrates will be more prepared to deal with the case themselves.

Exemplifying the drive for efficiency, the Criminal Justice and Courts Act 2015 introduced 'trial by a single justice on the papers', otherwise known as the Single Justice Procedure (SJP).[41] The SJP permits proceedings to be initiated by any 'relevant prosecutor', including the police, by means of an SJP Notice which is served on the accused.[42] This applies to cases involving adults charged with summary only non-imprisonable offences, such as speeding, vehicle excise duty, and fare evasion, which comprise about 850,000 cases per annum. In 2016, the SJP was extended to other prosecutors such as TV Licensing, the Environment Agency, train operating companies, and local authorities.[43] SJP cases are dealt with on the papers by a single magistrate sitting with a legal adviser, without the attendance of either prosecutor or defendant. The case is not heard in a traditional courtroom, and the defendant responds to the charge either online or in writing. Between April 2015 and April 2017, 667,168 cases were dealt with using SJP, of which 599,921 were disposed of.[44]

While there are undoubted efficiency benefits to the SJP, which applies currently to a limited range of crimes that might be regarded as minor or 'regulatory', it impacts on the principle of open justice, and may disincentivize not guilty pleas.[45] Such matters were raised by the House of Commons Justice Committee which noted concerns about potential extension of the SJP.[46] The Committee welcomed Lord Justice Fulford's intention to issue a protocol setting out guidance for magistrates on when they should sit in open court, and recommended that these concerns be taken into account in the preparation of that protocol.[47] This is yet to be issued.

Despite some setbacks, the pursuit of efficiency through the roll-out of automated justice seems ineluctable. The Ministry of Justice suggested that a subset of cases currently dealt with by means of SJP could be dealt with through an online process where the defendant chooses to plead guilty and is informed of the prospective penalty before confirming acceptance: this would result in an instant conviction and a fine being

---

[39] See n 34, 1.   [40] See Ch 10.   [41] s 46.   [42] CPR, r 24.9(2).

[43] The Criminal Justice Act 2003 (New Method of Instituting Proceedings) (Specification of Relevant Prosecutors) Order 2016 (SI 2016/430).

[44] https://insidehmcts.blog.gov.uk/2017/06/16/revolutionising-summary-justice-an-update-on-the-single-justice-procedure/.

[45] See Ch 10.

[46] House of Commons Justice Committee, *The role of the magistracy*, Sixth Report of Session 2016–17, HC 165 (2016), [26].

[47] Ibid.

imposed without the involvement of a magistrate.[48] This typifies the trend away from lay justice and oversight, to an administrative and mechanical mode of criminal justice. Such a development has implications for the trial process as well as for individual rights. As Jane Donoghue rightly highlights, the implications of a criminal conviction are not well recognized by the public, and the creation of online systems for summary offences provides few safeguards.[49] Moreover, the Prisons and Courts Bill 2017 sought to create an online magistrates' court, with listings and case results also online; it would incorporate viewing booths in an effort to preserve some degree of open justice.[50] The Bill fell with the government and has not been replaced, though the sentiment remains, as is evident from this Ministry of Justice consultation statement:

> The starting point for our approach is that only what has to be done at a physical venue—most trials and sentencing—will be done there. The remainder will be dealt with outside the courtroom using modern technology.[51]

It is regrettable that the growth and deployment of court technologies has not been accompanied by sufficient scrutiny of their impact upon defendant and witness participation, case outcomes, or the broader normative or social consequences.[52] Moreover, it seems that efficiency concerns and budget cuts have led the CPS to delegate most magistrates' court advocacy to less qualified Associate Prosecutors.[53] This lends weight to Marsh's contention that 'magistrates' courts reflect a rapid "assembly-line" approach to the disposals of cases'.[54]

As noted, a defendant can elect trial by jury in the Crown Court for either way cases.[55] There have long been suggestions that this right should be abolished;[56] while attempted by the Labour government, the two relevant Mode of Trial Bills did not receive parliamentary support.[57] The proposed legislation would have allowed defendants to argue their preference for jury trial before the magistrates and, in making their decision, magistrates were to take into account the possible effect of a conviction on a defendant's livelihood and reputation. Though this was a problematic construction with questionable class-based implications and other biases, the issue remains: the Leveson Review heard many, though not unanimous, calls for change, on the basis that a court not a defendant should decide how he is to be tried.[58]

---

[48] Ministry of Justice, *Impact Assessment: Online convictions/statutory fixed fine* (2016), https://consult. justice.gov.uk/digital-communications/transforming-our-courts-and-tribunals/supporting_documents/Impactassessment.PDF, 1.

[49] J. Donoghue, 'Reforming the Role of Magistrates: Implications for Summary Justice in England and Wales' (2014) 80 *MLR* 995, 1016–18.

[50] https://www.lawgazette.co.uk/law/courts-bill-viewing-booths-to-preserve-open-justice/5059937.article.

[51] Ministry of Justice, *Fit for the future: transforming the Court and Tribunal Estate* (2018), 1.15.

[52] Donoghue, n 49, 1024.

[53] L. Soubise, 'Prosecuting in the Magistrates' Courts in a Time of Austerity' [2017] *Crim LR* 847.

[54] L. Marsh, 'Leveson's Narrow Pursuit of Justice: Efficiency and Outcomes in the Criminal Process' (2016) 45 *Common L World Rev* 51, 60.

[55] Magistrates' Courts Act 1980, s 20.   [56] Royal Commission on Criminal Justice, *Report* (1993), 87.

[57] A good account of the mode of trial saga is Windlesham, *Responses to Crime, Vol 4: Dispensing Justice* (2001), ch 7.

[58] The Rt Hon. Sir Brian Leveson President of the Queen's Bench Division, *Review of Efficiency in Criminal Proceedings* (2015), [336].

Indeed, there remains a reasonable argument for removing the right to elect jury trial in either way cases. Relatively few jurisdictions allow defendants a comparable choice,[59] and there is nothing like a right to choose trial venue in the ECHR. The argument that the decision is one for the courts, to be taken primarily on grounds of case seriousness, is a strong one. While there is something to the argument that certain types of case are especially suited to jury trial, regardless of their seriousness (an example is theft, which can involve the broad evaluative issue of dishonesty, defined in the case law in terms of the standards of ordinary and reasonable people[60]), there is a danger that in practice this argument will become the one that certain people (e.g. those without previous convictions) have a greater claim to jury trial than others, a contention that should be resisted. To say this, is not to say that there is a strong case for removing the right to elect. Pressure for reform has been driven by the desire for efficiency, and as we have stressed, there are reasons to regard efficiency-based arguments with caution. To the extent that jury trial is valuable—and earlier we have very briefly sketched some reasons for thinking that it is—any proposal to reduce the number of jury trials should be viewed sceptically. It should be noted, however, that jurors themselves consider that many of the cases they hear are too trivial to justify the disruption to their lives involved in hearing them.[61] That view counts for something and suggests the need to reflect carefully on where and how we draw the line between summary and Crown Court jurisdictions, free of the rhetorical bombast about the right to jury trial that has dominated much of the debate.[62]

(B) TRIAL BY JUDGE AND JURY AND TRIAL BY JUDGE ALONE

Though Crown Court trial has traditionally been trial by judge and jury, there have been attempts to allow certain cases in the Crown Court to be tried by a judge sitting alone. The CJA 2003 allows for trial without jury in cases where there is evidence of jury-tampering.[63] In addition, the Act contained provisions on trial by judge alone in cases of serious fraud,[64] but this was repealed by s 113 of the Protection of Freedoms Act 2012.[65] The original version of the Criminal Justice Bill also included provisions on jury waiver, allowing defendants to opt for trial by judge alone rather than jury trial,[66] but this clause was controversial and was dropped during the legislative process.

In the previous section we reviewed some of the arguments in favour of jury trial, and drew comparisons between jury trial and magistrates' trial. A slightly different

---

[59] An exception is New Zealand: N. Cameron, S. Potter, and W. Young, 'The New Zealand Jury' (1999) 62 *Law & Contemporary Probs* 103.

[60] *Ivey (Appellant) v Genting Casinos (UK) Ltd* [2017] UKSC 67.   [61] See Matthews et al, n 20, 63.

[62] See e.g. B. Houlder, 'The Importance of Preserving the Jury System and the Right of Election for Trial' [1997] *Crim LR* 875.

[63] CJA 2003, ss 44–46.   [64] Ibid, s 43.

[65] Sir Brian Leveson noted that if fraud trials are to continue to be conducted with juries, appropriate funding is needed. *Review of Efficiency in Criminal Proceedings*, n 58, [358].

[66] Clause 36 of the original Bill, available at: www.publications.parliament.uk/pa/cm200203/cm-bills/008/2003008.htm.

question is now relevant: what are the key differences between trial by judge and trial by jury? While we saw that magistrates have a higher conviction rate than jurors, it is not clear that in the Crown Court judges would convict more defendants than juries would, and the limited number of cases mean any differences are not statistically significant.

In Northern Ireland, trial by judge alone has existed since 1973, in the 'Diplock' courts.[67] There, jury acquittal rates have generally been slightly higher than that of Diplock judges.[68] However, jury acquittal rates in Northern Ireland may have been higher than elsewhere,[69] and the Diplock acquittal rates are close, on average, to those of juries in England and Wales. In the United States, judicial acquittal rates are generally higher than those of juries:[70] though when judges are asked how they would have decided jury cases which they have presided over, they tend to report that they would have convicted in slightly more cases than the actual juries did.[71] At a more qualitative level, Jackson and Doran's study of Diplock courts found that the trials in them had a different atmosphere to jury trials; in jury trials more emotive arguments might be used. These authors also noted the difficulty of involving the judge both in managing the trial and in bearing responsibility for the verdict, in that this might at least appear to compromise judicial independence.[72]

As noted previously, of the three exceptions to jury trial originally included in the Criminal Justice Bill, the only one to have become law is the exception for cases where there is a risk of interference with the jury. In *R v Twomey*, the Court of Appeal considered the operation of this provision.[73] Twomey's trial was underway when the judge received information that members of the jury had been approached with a view to putting pressure on them. The judge discharged the jury, but refused to continue the trial sitting by himself (an option under s 46 of the CJA 2003) because he had seen inadmissible and prejudicial material. He also refused to rule that a new trial should take place without a jury on the grounds that it would be possible to put in place measures to protect the jury. The Court of Appeal disagreed with both decisions. In a judgment which put considerable emphasis on resource issues, it held that a judge in the position of the judge in *Twomey* should ordinarily continue the trial sitting alone.[74] It found that the proposed protective measures could not effectively guard against threats to the jurors' families, and that even if they could: 'it would be unreasonable to impose that package with its drain on financial resources and police manpower on the police, and, no less important, it would be totally unfair to impose the additional burdens

[67] Northern Ireland (Emergency Provisions) Act 1973.

[68] See J. Jackson and S. Doran, *Judge Without Jury* (1995), 35.

[69] See J. Jackson, K. Quinn, and T. O'Malley, 'The Jury System in Contemporary Ireland' (1999) 62 *Law & Contemporary Probs* 202, 227.

[70] A. Leipold, 'Why are Federal Judges so Acquittal Prone?' (2005) 83 *Washington ULQ* 151.

[71] D. Givelber and A. Farrell, 'Judges and Juries: The Defense Case and Differences in Acquittal Rates' (2008) 33 *Law & Social Inquiry* 31.

[72] See n 68. See further J. Jackson, S. Doran, and M Seigel, 'Rethinking Adversariness in Non-Jury Criminal Trials' (1995) 23 *Am J Crim L* 1.

[73] *R v Twomey* [2009] 2 Cr App R 25.   [74] Ibid, [20].

consequent on the deployment of this package on individual jurors'.[75] It also noted that protective measures might prejudice the jury against the defendant.

The significance of the right to jury trial was emphasized subsequently in *J, S, M v R*, which concerned a successful appeal against an order to conduct the trial of the defendants by a judge alone.[76] The estimated length of the trial was two weeks, which was deemed 'an important consideration in the context of both the burdens on the jury of any necessary protection, and its impact on the public, both in terms of cost, and of the inevitably significant drain on police resources'.[77] While the Court of Appeal agreed that there was and continued to be a real and present danger of jury tampering,[78] it disagreed with the trial judge that the necessary protective measures would either impose an unacceptable burden on the jurors by intruding for a prolonged period on their ordinary lives, or that the jury would be inhibited from giving the case proper attention and returning a true verdict.[79] The Court of Appeal stressed that ordering the trial of a serious criminal offence without a jury remains and must remain the decision of last resort. The court described 'extreme cases, where the necessary protective measures constitute an unreasonable intrusion into the lives of the jurors' as those involving a constant police presence in or near their homes, or police protection at all times. This sets the bar rather high in terms of the level of protection and intervention that will be canvassed to ensure a jury trial. Indeed, in *KS v R* a 'fairly limited level of jury protection' was deemed to sufficient to outweigh the potential threat.[80]

That said, the Court of Appeal will approve judge-only trials where the statutory conditions are fulfilled, and it is fair and in the interests of justice to continue the trial without the jury. Such was the situation in *R v McManaman*, where the jury was discharged and a trial for rape continued without the jury after a third party, who was in the gallery, sent a Facebook friend request to one of the jurors.[81] The Court of Appeal endorsed the trial judge proceeding on the basis that the statutory conditions were fulfilled. The court observed that it did not have to be shown that a defendant had instigated jury tampering; this is not what the legislation requires, and fundamentally the concern is to protect the integrity of a jury.[82]

While we have suggested that jury trial incorporates certain important values, it should not be insisted on at any cost. There is a good case to be made for allowing a non-jury trial in cases where jurors would otherwise be put at risk; jurors have rights as well as defendants (e.g. under Arts 5 and 8 of the ECHR). Given that much of the evidence in *Twomey* was secret, it is impossible to judge whether the case for non-jury trial was made out on the facts. What is problematic, though, is the Court of Appeal's insistence that in this situation a part-heard trial should normally be continued by the presiding judge. If jurors are likely to be prejudiced by being subject to protective measures, then surely there is a substantial risk that the judge, who in the course of the hearing to discharge the jury will have heard detailed evidence about

[75] Ibid, [33].   [76] [2010] EWCA Crim 1755.   [77] [2].   [78] [4].   [79] [7].
[80] *KS v R* [2010] EWCA Crim 1756. See L. Campbell, 'The Prosecution of Organised Crime: Removing the Jury' (2014) 18 *E&P* 83–100.
[81] [2016] EWCA Crim 3, [30].   [82] [22].

attempts to intimidate jurors, will also be prejudiced.[83] If, as was the case in *Twomey*, the evidence of intimidation is partly withheld from the defence, the situation is in tension with the decision in *Edwards and Lewis v UK*, where lack of adversarial argument on matters of 'determinative importance'[84] was found to be problematic: in the *Twomey* scenario, the judge will be privy to unchallenged information that may colour the determinative decision whether to convict. If there is concern about the wasted resources involved in stopping the trial part way through, one solution would be to have the application to discharge the jury heard by a judge other than the one conducting the trial.

When it comes to serious fraud cases, arguments for departing from the norm of jury trial have been more controversial. The principal argument for reform in this area is that certain trials involve issues so complex that they are not well suited to lay fact-finding. Connected to this is the argument that fraud trials could be made to run more speedily were there no need to explain complex issues to the jury and that long trials place undue demands on jurors; jurors in the Jubilee Line corruption case sat for nearly two years, and while they report having been pleased to be involved in the trial, the lengthy proceedings placed a heavy cost on their lives, especially in terms of employment.[85] The argument that juries cannot understand fraud cases has little empirical support.[86] It seems that in practice a jury of 12 will include individuals who are capable of understanding the issues involved and of explaining them, where need be, to other jurors.[87] Further, the complexity of a trial is not fixed: measures can be taken to educate jurors about business practices and to explain things to them simply and clearly, and cases might be split into separate trials of distinct issues.

The Criminal Justice Bill 2003 originally contained a provision on 'jury waiver', which would have allowed defendants in the Crown Court to opt for trial by judge alone. The choice of juryless trial could have been refused in exceptional cases only. This provision was removed at a late stage in the legislative process.[88] Letting defendants waive jury trial is, at first sight, an appealing idea,[89] but it is in fact potentially very radical. It would have allowed defendants effectively to bring the institution of trial by jury to an end: all it would take would be for every defendant to decline jury trial. Of course, it is extremely unlikely that this would happen: jury trial is often thought to be in the interests of defendants, and it is probable that sufficient numbers of defendants share

---

[83] See A. Wistrich, C. Guthrie, and J. Rachlinski, 'Can Judges Ignore Inadmissible Information? The Difficulty of Deliberately Disregarding' (2005) 153 *U Pa L Rev* 1251.

[84] (2005) 40 EHRR 24, [57].

[85] See S. Lloyd-Bostock, *Report on Interviews with Jurors in the Jubilee Line Case* (2006).

[86] See e.g. T. Honess, M. Levi, and E. Chapman, 'Juror Competence in Processing Complex Information: Implications from a Simulation of the Maxwell Trial' [1998] *Crim LR* 763; R. Lempert, 'Civil Juries and Complex Cases: Taking Stock After Twelve Years' in R. Litan (ed), *Verdict: Assessing the Civil Jury System* (1993); N. Vidmar, 'The Performance of the American Civil Jury: An Empirical Perspective' (1998) 40 *Arizona L Rev* 849.

[87] This seems to have been the situation in the Jubilee Line case: see Lloyd-Bostock, n 85.

[88] See 'Blunkett Furious as Lords Throw out Reform of Jury Trial', *The Guardian*, 20 November 2003.

[89] See S. Doran and J. Jackson, 'The Case for Jury Waiver' [1997] *Crim LR* 155.

this view that trial by judge alone would have remained exceptional.[90] All the same, the theoretical possibility of de facto jury abolition should prompt us to look carefully at the jury waiver proposal.

The superficially appealing logic behind jury waiver is that to the extent that jury trial is justified as being in the interests of defendants, there can be no objection to allowing defendants to forego it in favour of some other appropriate trial arrangement. There is no denying that defendants have legitimate interests in the means by which they are tried: interests in impartial and accurate fact-finding arrangements which adequately weight the presumption of innocence. But these things are also in the interests of the courts and of society as a whole. It is more difficult to find legitimate interests defendants might have in a particular form of trial which are not shared in this manner. Perhaps there are some cases where defendants have a legitimate concern about jury trial: if, for example, the case is one likely to arouse strong emotions[91] or if the defence case will raise complex issues which the jury may have difficulty understanding[92] (though, as noted earlier, we should be wary of accepting that certain issues are too complex for jury trial), it may be appropriate to allow trial by judge alone. But a problem with the provision in the Criminal Justice Bill was that, with very limited exceptions, it simply left the decision to the defendant, with no acknowledgement that decisions about mode of trial affect the community's interests in the trial system as well. In some jurisdictions which allow waiver of jury trial, the prosecution is allowed to make representations on the issue,[93] and this seems more appropriate. Such a possibility was contemplated by Sir Brian Leveson, who suggested that the judge should decide on a case-by-case basis whether to accede to the defendant's request for trial without jury, after hearing representations from both sides, rather than imposing a general statutory limit on offences to which the option could apply. Further, the judge should be entitled to override the defendant's wish for trial by judge alone if the public interest required a jury.[94] These are sensible proposals.

It is worth mentioning the effect that the contemporary ubiquity of technology and social media has on the jury. As well as enabling some jury tampering, the advent of the internet and social media has served as a temptation for some jurors to research the ongoing case,[95] though as the Court of Appeal noted '[t]he overwhelming majority of jury trials proceed without jury irregularities'.[96] In terms of the use of the internet, if the jury has considered material adverse to the defendant which he has had no opportunity to address, and if this extraneous material affects the fairness of the trial,

[90] An opinion poll in England found that a quarter of respondents would opt for trial by judge rather than by jury: J. Roberts and M. Hough, *Public Opinion and the Jury: An International Literature Review* (2009), 32. See also M. Zander and P. Henderson, *Crown Court Study* (1993), 172: 30 per cent of defendants said they would not choose jury trial.

[91] See N. Vidmar, 'Generic Prejudice and the Presumption of Guilt in Sex Abuse Trials' (1997) 21 *Law & Human Behavior* 5.

[92] An example might be *R v Adams* [1996] 2 Cr App R 467.   [93] See Jackson and Doran, n 68.

[94] Leveson, *Review of Efficiency in Criminal Proceedings*, n 58, [345].

[95] C. Thomas, *Are juries fair?*, Ministry of Justice Research Series 1/10 (2010), 49–50.

[96] *R v Thompson and others* [2010] EWCA Crim 1623.

the conviction is likely to be unsafe.[97] Specific guidance about the use of the internet must now be given to jurors[98] and failure to adhere to these instructions is contempt.[99] Moreover, following the recommendations of the Law Commission,[100] the Criminal Justice and Courts Act 2015 created several indictable offences of juror misconduct. The Act makes it an offence for jurors to 'research the case during the trial period', to share research with another member of the jury during the trial period, and to engage in 'conduct from which it may reasonably be concluded that the [juror] intends to try the issue otherwise than on the basis of the evidence presented in the proceedings on the issue'.[101] In addition, a judge may order jurors to surrender any electronic communications devices for a period.[102]

(C) RACE AND MODE OF TRIAL

So far we have not considered the implications of the defendant's race or ethnic origin in the debates about mode of trial. Defendants from Black, Asian, and Minority ethnic groups (BAME) may feel that a tribunal with members from their, or another, racial minority will afford them a fairer trial, or to put it another way, that a lack of diversity may lead to bias, unconscious or otherwise. As Lammy noted, '[a] fundamental source of mistrust in the CJS among BAME communities is the lack of diversity among those who wield power within it. Nowhere is this more apparent than in our courts, where there is a gulf between the backgrounds of defendants and judges'.[103] To what extent should mode of trial decisions take these issues into account?

Something should first be said about how representative, in terms of race, the different forms of tribunal are. The magistracy as a whole seems to be reasonably representative of the country's population: in 2018, 12 per cent of magistrates declared themselves to be Black, Asian, or from a Minority ethnic background.[104] Notably, BAME representation was greater among judges aged under 60: this is significant as 55 per cent of magistrates are aged over 60.[105] There are regional differences of BAME representation, ranging from 28 per cent of magistrates in London, 25 per cent in Birmingham and Solihull, down to 2 per cent in Cumbria, Devon, and Cornwall, and 5 per cent overall in Wales.[106] The situation is less positive in terms of diversity for professional magistrates (District Judges): only 7 per cent are not White.[107] In the Crown Court and beyond, the numbers are lower

---

[97] *R v Karakaya* [2005] 2 Cr App R 5; *Thompson*, [11].   [98] *Thompson*, n 96, [12].

[99] *R v Fraill* [2011] EWCA Crim 1570; *Attorney General v Dallas* [2012] EWHC 156 (Admin).

[100] Law Commission, *Contempt of Court (1): Juror Misconduct and Internet Publications*, Law Com No 340 (2013).

[101] Criminal Justice and Courts Act 2015, ss 71–73, creating new ss 20A–20C of the Juries Act 1974. See K. Crosby, 'Juror Punishment, Juror Guidance and the Criminal Justice and Courts Act 2015' (2015) *Crim LR* 578–93.

[102] Juries Act 1974, s 15A as inserted by the 2015 Act.

[103] The Lammy Review, *An independent review into the treatment of, and outcomes for, Black, Asian and Minority Ethnic individuals in the Criminal Justice System* (2017), 37 (footnotes omitted).

[104] Ministry of Justice, *Judicial Diversity Statistics 2018* (2018), 13.   [105] Ibid, 6.

[106] Ibid, Table 3.   [107] Ibid, Table 1.1.

still: 4 per cent of Circuit Judges declared themselves as BAME and 7 per cent of Court of Appeal judges.[108] This may be relevant as BAME rates of being committed to the Crown Court for trial are disproportionate when compared to figures for white defendants.[109] While there have been improvements, due in part to the efforts of the Judicial Diversity Committee, these are precarious gains: the House of Commons Justice Committee expressed concern that current difficulties in recruitment to the Criminal Bar, due to legal aid cuts and working conditions, could have a negative impact on future recruitment to, and diversity within, the judiciary, in particular the criminal courts.[110]

Just as with magistrates, the fact that the jury is a multi-member body makes it more likely to be diverse. A detailed study by Thomas, confirming earlier research,[111] found that jury pools were a good representation of the ethnic make-up of the communities from which they were drawn.[112] However, because juries are in principle selected randomly, there is no guarantee that a black or Asian defendant will be tried by a jury including a juror from a minority ethnic group. The Crown Court Study in 1993 found that nationally 65 per cent of juries were all white, while in 2007 it was stated that most juries in most Crown Courts in England and Wales are likely to be all white, due to the demographics of the catchment areas.[113]

There is some empirical evidence on race and jury decision making. In a four-year project, drawing on data from four Crown Courts (Blackfriars, Reading, Manchester Minshull Street, and Southwark), Thomas found evidence that individual jurors decided a staged case differently depending on their ethnicity—an effect she termed 'same race leniency' (though it might equally be termed 'other race harshness'). Specifically, 'BME defendants were less likely to be found guilty than White defendants, while the White defendant was much more likely to be found guilty by BME jurors than White jurors'.[114] But any such bias could not be detected in decisions of the jury as a whole. Further, and in line with earlier research from the United States,[115] Thomas found that where a racial issue was made salient in the case presented to the jury, differential treatment could not be detected in individual juror votes.[116]

Thomas's subsequent research published in 2010 and 2017 affirmed that jury verdicts constitute one stage in the criminal justice system where BAME groups do *not* face persistent disproportionality.[117] Thomas's 2010 study covered 18 months, 500,000 charges, and 16,000 jury verdicts by deliberation, while the later study was more

---

[108] Ibid, 5.

[109] Ministry of Justice, *Black, Asian and Minority Ethnic disproportionality in the Criminal Justice System in England and Wales* (2016), 28.

[110] House of Commons Justice Committee, *Criminal Legal Aid*, Twelfth Report of Session 2017–19, HC 1069 (2018), 87.

[111] M. Zander and P. Henderson, *Crown Court Study* (1993), 241; Matthews et al, n 20, 19–20.

[112] C. Thomas, *Diversity and Fairness in the Jury System* (2007).   [113] Ibid.   [114] Ibid, 164.

[115] S. Sommers and P. Ellsworth, 'How Much Do We Really Know About Race and Juries? A Review of Social Science Theory and Research' (2003) 78 *Chicago-Kent L Rev* 997.

[116] See Thomas, n 112, 166–7.

[117] Ibid, i; C. Thomas, 'Ethnicity and Fairness of Jury Trials in England and Wales 2006–2014' [2017] *Crim LR* 860.

extensive, covering eight years, over three million charges, and almost 400,000 jury verdicts. Both studies found that though BAME defendants in England and Wales are over-represented amongst those facing a jury verdict (as they are charged disproportionately with offences tried in the Crown Court and plead not guilty to these charges consistently more often than white defendants), they are not convicted disproportionately by juries. For offences that make up over three-quarters of all jury verdicts, jury conviction rates were either similar for white and BAME defendants or white defendants were convicted substantially more often than BAME defendants. The analysis found an overall jury conviction rate of 66 per cent for BAME defendants and 64 per cent for white defendants.[118] These small differences in jury conviction rate by defendant ethnicity are a strong indication that factors other than ethnicity are likely to be more relevant to jury verdicts.[119] All that said, while it appears that juries deliver equitable results, regardless of the ethnic make-up of the jury, or of the defendant in question, concerns about the appearance of fairness with all-white juries remain.[120]

Racial issues are not only relevant to jury composition. The magistrates' court and Crown Court benches should as far as possible reflect the social characteristics of society as a whole, if only because everyone should have an equal opportunity of sitting on the bench, and to ensure a diversity of world views and experiences in judicial decision making. However, when we come to look at the choice between magistrates' court and Crown Court, and between trial by jury and trial by judge alone, race raises more complex issues. In some cases, minority ethnic defendants may have concerns about possible jury bias. There are reported cases where jurors are said to have made racially discriminatory remarks, and, because of the basic rule that jury deliberations should remain secret, the courts have found it difficult to deal with this situation.[121] If a defendant fears that the jury which tries him may be biased, then this is just the sort of situation where there is a case for jury waiver: the defendant may well prefer trial by a judge, where the verdict will be supported by reasons.

When it comes to the choice between magistrates' court and Crown Court, concerns about racial discrimination provide some support for the right to elect Crown Court trial. There is enduring evidence that black defendants are more likely to elect Crown Court trial than are white defendants.[122] As noted in the Lammy Review, many BAME defendants neither trust the advice that they are given, nor believe they will receive a fair hearing from magistrates, which leads to them pleading not guilty and then electing for a jury trial at the Crown Court, rather than be tried in a magistrate's court, despite the higher sentencing powers available at the former.[123] This should make us cautious about removing the right to elect jury trial, because it may indirectly discriminate against

[118] Ibid, 873, fig 3.   [119] Ibid, 873.   [120] Thomas, *Are juries fair?*, n 95, 24.

[121] *R v Quereshi* [2002] 1 WLR 518; *R v Connor, R v Mirza* [2004] UKHL 2. See generally R. Pattenden and G. Daly, 'Racial Bias and the English Criminal Trial Jury' (2005) 64 *CLJ* 678.

[122] See M. Fitzgerald, *Ethnic Minorities and the Criminal Justice System* (1993), 21, 45. S. Cammiss and C. Stride, 'Modelling Mode of Trial' (2008) 48 *BJ Crim* 482, found some evidence that minority ethnic defendants were more likely to be sent to the Crown Court by the magistrates.

[123] Lammy, n 103, 27.

black defendants. At its strongest, the argument is this: black suspects are charged by the police at lower standards of evidence than are white suspects,[124] though the situation seems fairer as regards CPS charging practices.[125] As they enter the system, then, the cases against black defendants tend to be weaker, and to be charged at a higher level than is merited (see Chapters 7 and 10). In terms of magistrates' decisions, Lammy bemoaned the fact that systematic scrutiny is hindered by the absence of reliable data, such as whether defendants plead 'guilty' or 'not guilty'.[126] Nonetheless, Lammy identified some worrying disparities for BAME women that require further analysis and investigation: of those tried at magistrates' court, Black, Asian, Mixed ethnic and Chinese/Other women were all more likely to be convicted than White women.[127]

BAME defendants may, therefore, choose Crown Court trial for the better chance of acquittal offered there, and also because the CPS is more likely to reduce charges in order to secure a guilty plea once the case has gone to Crown Court. Removing the right to elect would thus deny BAME defendants a means of protecting themselves against discriminatory police charging practices. There is empirical research to support this view of the merits of the right to elect,[128] but there is also evidence which cautions against oversimplifying the situation. Hood et al found that some black defendants were worried about jury bias; they also found that, overall, slightly more black defendants complained about unfair treatment in the Crown Court than in the magistrates' court.[129]

The possibility of indirect discrimination is a reason against removing the right to elect jury trial, at least until more is known about why BAME defendants might favour this mode of trial. It also points to the importance of ensuring that proceedings in the magistrates' courts are as fair as possible. In the Hood et al study, around one-third of minority ethnic defendants, when asked what could be done to improve things, pointed to the need for more minority ethnic District Judges and magistrates; magistrates themselves took the same view.[130] The authors suggest organizing magistrates' rotas so that, 'in those areas where a substantial proportion of defendants are from minority ethnic backgrounds, at least one magistrate from such a background will be sitting on the Bench'.[131] Random selection has never been the principle in the magistrates' court, therefore this proposal deserves serious consideration.

(D) PROFESSIONAL AND LAY MAGISTRATES

A final issue about the way in which cases are allocated between different decision makers concerns the balance between lay and professional magistrates ('District Judges'). There are significant differences between professional and lay magistrates:

---

[124] See C. Phillips and D. Brown, *Entry into the Criminal Justice System: A Survey of Police Arrests and Their Outcomes* (1998), 183–6.

[125] Lammy, n 103, 17.   [126] Ibid.   [127] Ibid, 32, Table 2.

[128] See L. Bridges, 'Taking Liberties', *Legal Action*, 6 July 2000, 6.

[129] R. Hood, S. Shute, and F. Seemungal, *Ethnic Minorities in the Criminal Courts: Perceptions of Fairness and Equality of Treatment* (2003), 31–5. The position was reversed for Asian defendants.

[130] Ibid, 117, 131.   [131] Ibid, 135.

District Judges work more quickly, are less likely to grant adjournments, and sentence more harshly.[132] They are also less representative of the general population in terms of race, gender, and age. In economic terms, professional magistrates are more expensive, though this is hard to quantify or ascertain accurately.[133] Whereas District Judges are salaried, the fact that they work alone, more quickly, and rarely require advice from a clerk limits the difference in efficiency or economic terms, in terms of court work; to the extent that District Judges use custody more frequently than lay magistrates, they perhaps will impose greater costs on the criminal justice system.[134]

Despite the differences between the two types of magistrate, there was once little formal policy on how cases should be allocated between them. Following the Ministry of Justice study on *The strengths and skills of the Judiciary in the Magistrates' Courts* in 2011, a working group was established, including senior members of the judiciary, the Magistrates Association, and HM Courts and Tribunal Service (HMCTS), which agreed a *Protocol on Judicial Deployment in the Magistrates' Courts* in 2012. Serious cases such as terrorism, extradition, or serious sex cases in the Youth Court should always be allocated to District Judges, as well as lengthy or complex or interlinked cases, and a share of more routine court business, including case management and pre-trial reviews.[135] District Judges and magistrates should occasionally sit in mixed benches, with a particular view 'both to improving the case management skills of magistrates and to improving the culture of collegiality'.[136] Despite this initiative, a survey commissioned by the Magistrates Association in 2016 found that that over 20 per cent of its members considered the allocation of work to be inappropriate either most or some of the time and, of these, over 80 per cent were concerned about factually complex cases being retained by District Judges.[137] The House of Commons Justice Committee recommended amendment of the protocol to support judicial deployment in the magistrates' court, and recommended consideration be given to allowing magistrates to sit without legal advisers when sitting with a District Judge.[138] This has yet to occur.

11.2 CROWN COURT TRIAL: THE ROLES OF THE JUDGE AND JURY

Crown Court trial involves a division of responsibility between judge and jury. Generally speaking, questions of law are for the judge whereas questions of fact are for the jury. But this division is not rigid: the judge will often make factual evaluations when deciding whether or not evidence is admissible.[139] Judges also play a role in guarding

---

[132] Ibid, 48–54. Ipsos, n 24.   [133] Hood et al, n 129.
[134] Ibid, viii. Ipsos, n 24.   [135] *Protocol on Judicial Deployment in the Magistrates' Courts*, [5].
[136] Ibid.   [137] House of Commons Justice Committee, *The role of the magistracy*, n 46, [16].
[138] Ibid, [20].
[139] See generally R. Pattenden, 'Pre-Verdict Judicial Fact-Finding in Judicial Trials with Juries' (2009) 29 *OJLS* 1; R. Pattenden, 'The Proof Rules of Pre-Verdict Judicial Fact-Finding in Criminal Trials by Jury' (2009) 125 *LQR* 79.

against false conviction by ensuring that a weak case does not go to the jury. We came across this in Chapter 7 where, in discussing the role of the CPS, it was noted that a substantial proportion of acquittals are on the basis of an order or direction from the judge to the jury, rather than because the jury has acquitted of its own accord. Judges also have some influence in cases that do go to the jury. At the end of the trial the judge sums up on the facts, and can emphasize aspects of the evidence which he or she deems to be important. Convictions are occasionally quashed because a judge has gone too far and given a one-sided summing-up.[140] Many cases nowadays will involve the judge giving some direction to the jury on fact-finding: perhaps a warning about suspect evidence, or a direction on how to draw an inference from a particular factual scenario. The *Crown Court Compendium on Jury and Trial Management and Summing Up* attests to the importance of the judge's role in guiding the jury.[141] Moreover, the European Court of Human Rights (ECtHR) regards such directions as an important component of the right to a fair trial: given that the jury does not give reasons for its decision, carefully stated judicial warnings are the best guarantee that the jury has taken important factors into account.[142]

The principles underlying the division of roles between judge and jury are well illustrated by the debates surrounding the test the judge should apply in deciding whether there is a case to go to the jury. The leading case is *Galbraith*, which clarified conflicts in the case law. Under *Galbraith*, the judge should direct a verdict of acquittal if evidence to prove any element of the prosecution case is lacking. That much is relatively simple; things are more difficult 'where there is some evidence but it is of a tenuous character'. Here, the court identified two principles:

> (a) Where the judge comes to the conclusion that the prosecution case, taken at its highest, is such that a jury properly directed could not properly convict upon it, it is his duty, upon a submission being made, to stop the case. (b) Where however the prosecution evidence is such that its strength or weakness depends on the view to be taken of a witness's reliability, or other matters which are generally speaking within the province of the jury and where on one possible view of the facts there is evidence upon which a jury could properly come to the conclusion that the defendant is guilty, then the judge should allow the matter to be tried by the jury.[143]

A crucial issue is what is meant by the prosecution case 'taken at its highest'. The rest of the quotation implies that the judge should assume that the witness is 'reliable', and apply the test on that basis. Of course, the defendant may suggest that the witness is lying or mistaken, but that is a matter for the jury. The usual criticism of this approach is that it affords insufficient protection to defendants. The judge may have serious misgivings about the reliability of a key witness, but unless the witness's

---

[140] *R v Wood* [1996] 1 Cr App R 207; *R v Bryant* [2005] EWCA Crim 2079.

[141] Judicial College, *The Crown Court Compendium, Part I: Jury and Trial Management and Summing Up* (2017).

[142] See *Condron v UK* (2001) 31 EHRR 1.

[143] [1981] 1 WLR 1039, 1042. See also *R v P* [2008] 2 Cr App R 6.

evidence is self-contradictory,[144] the case should still be left to the jury. It is often pointed out that it seems odd that the trial judge should apply this test, while the Court of Appeal when reviewing the safety of a conviction applies a much broader test of whether the conviction is 'unsafe'. While the Court of Appeal shows great deference to the jury when applying this test, the 'unsafe' test does allow it to quash a conviction because of doubts about a witness.[145] The defence of *Galbraith* involves arguing that it is important to reserve some questions for the jury, and to avoid so far as possible the judge encroaching on the jury's domain. This policy, whereby issues of witness credibility are reserved for the jury, in fact underlies considerable parts of the law of evidence.[146]

The thin nature of the distinction involved here can be seen by examining the facts of *Hill*.[147] In this case, the defendant had been observed selling a 'small dark substance' to customers. Tried for supplying cannabis, Hill argued that the observations of the police officers were insufficient to make out a case for him to answer. The Court of Appeal agreed, and quashed his conviction. Without suggesting that there is anything wrong with this decision, it is not easy to articulate why the prosecution case, taken at its highest, did not warrant a conviction while, on slightly different facts, it would have done. If, for example, Hill's customer had testified that he had purchased from Hill a substance that was cannabis, the case would almost certainly have been strong enough to go to the jury.[148] No matter what doubts the judge had about the witness, he could not, within the confines of the *Galbraith* rule, have stopped the case. To answer that questions of credibility are for the jury is not immediately convincing: why, one might ask, should the nature of the substance which police officers saw Hill selling not be an issue for the jury? If there is a difference between the scenarios, it lies not in credibility but in the degree of risk to which the defendant is exposed in leaving the case to the jury.

The *Galbraith* rule appears even harder to support when one notes that there are a number of exceptions to it.[149] There are some credibility issues which judges do decide, and where a decision against the prosecution may bring the case to a halt. We have already come across examples: s 76 of the Police and Criminal Evidence Act 1984 (PACE) can result in the exclusion of a confession where the prosecution cannot convince the judge of its reliability (see Chapter 5), and the *Turnbull*[150] rule can result in a case depending substantially on poor quality eyewitness evidence being withdrawn from the jury (see Chapter 4). The Court of Appeal has also held that unconvincing confessions from a mentally handicapped defendant should be withdrawn from the jury, even where the case does not raise a s 76 issue.[151] The CJA 2003 requires judges to direct an acquittal where the prosecution case is based on a statement made out of

---

[144] *Slippey* [1988] *Crim LR* 767.

[145] A good example is *R v B* [2003] EWCA Crim 319, discussed in Ch 9.

[146] See e.g. *R v Turner* [1975] QB 834; *R v H* [1995] 2 AC 596.   [147] (1993) 96 Cr App R 456.

[148] The courts are prepared to recognize lay expertise in drug identification: *R v Chatwood* [1980] 1 WLR 874.

[149] See I. Dennis, *The Law of Evidence* (6th edn, 2017), 4-007.   [150] [1977] QB 224.

[151] *Mackenzie* (1993) 96 Cr App R 98.

court which is thought to be unconvincing.[152] In practice, too, *Galbraith* is sometimes ignored: cases depending on the testimony of child witnesses are sometimes stopped when a judge has doubts about the witness's evidence.[153] It is possible to reinterpret *Galbraith* so as to reconcile these seeming exceptions with it: the situations just described, it might be argued, relate to doubts about the reliability of testimony, rather than about the sincerity of the witness (in the sense of whether the witness is deliberately lying). Although *Galbraith* itself seemed to raise both types of issue, it might be argued that the issue which really needs to be reserved to the jury is that of whether or not the witness is lying. There may be a policy reason for this distinction, though not, perhaps, a terribly convincing one in the criminal setting: judges are doubtless reluctant to say that they think a witness may be lying. It is rather more diplomatic to leave this sort of decision to the secrecy of the jury room.

Galbraith involves an important issue: it determines just when a defendant will be put at risk of criminal conviction. It is difficult to find convincing reasons for the current rule, and the case law, as we have seen, recognizes a number of exceptions to it. The Criminal Cases Review Commission, a body with considerable experience of the possible causes of false conviction, has noted that 'Judges sometimes allow cases go to the jury for decision where the prosecution evidence can hardly be said to support a conviction beyond reasonable doubt.... Trial judges should be more vigorous in ruling that there is no case to answer.'[154] It would be better, both in terms of consistency and of protecting defendants, to allow a judge to stop a case whenever it is thought that a conviction would be unsafe.[155]

All that said, *Galbraith* was endorsed and applied in *CPS v F*, where its authority was described as 'undiminished'.[156] The Court of Appeal emphasized that its principles were neither modified nor extended for the purposes of addressing trials of historic unreported sexual crimes. In cases where the state of prosecution evidence is so unsatisfactory, contradictory, or so transparently unreliable that no jury, properly directed, could convict, the judge must direct the jury that there is no case to answer and to return a 'not guilty' verdict. In making this direction, the judge must bear in mind the constitutional primacy of the jury, and not usurp its function.[157]

Galbraith concerns the question of when the judge should direct the jury to acquit. But what about the converse situation, where the prosecution case is strong and the defence has no answer to it? Here we see an example of the asymmetry of criminal procedure.[158] As the House of Lords confirmed in *Wang*,[159] a judge is never permitted to direct a jury to convict. If the defendant has no good defence in law, the judge can make this very plain to the jury, but the jury must never be told that it has to

---

[152] CJA 2003, s 125.

[153] See G. Davis et al, *An Assessment of the Admissibility and Sufficiency of Evidence in Child Abuse Prosecutions* (1999), 47–8.

[154] Memorandum to Home Affairs Committee, 2005–6, HC 1703, para 3.1.

[155] This was the recommendation of the Royal Commission on Criminal Justice, n 56, 59.

[156] [2011] EWCA Crim 1844, [36].   [157] Ibid.   [158] For further discussion, see Ch 13.

[159] [2005] UKHL 9.

convict. The justification for this is jury equity. Controversially, the principle is that a jury should always have the power to acquit a defendant in defiance of the law.

In terms of directions of law to the jury, traditionally these were given for the first time in the summing-up, which may not necessarily be the best way to help the jurors.[160] Recognizing that this involved jurors being directed to evaluate the evidence at a stage when the evidence had concluded, some members of the judiciary began to give directions earlier in the trial.[161] This approach, encouraged by Sir Brian Leveson, has been adopted formally in the Criminal Procedure Rules (CPR): the judge must give the jury directions about the law at any time that will help them to evaluate the evidence, and also when summing up the evidence for them, to such extent as is directly relevant and necessary.[162] The Better Case Management (BCM) Handbook notes that a single national process with standard directions should assist both prosecution and defence.[163] Whether implemented in practice is another matter.

11.3 CONFRONTATION AND THE PROTECTION OF WITNESSES

In this section, we examine one area of the law which is closely tied to processual norms: the law relating to hearsay and the confrontation and protection of witnesses. Article 6(3) of the ECHR gives a defendant the right to 'examine or have examined witnesses against him'. It is convenient to refer to this as the right of confrontation, though as Ian Dennis notes, this is less a single unified right but rather a bundle of rights.[164] In recent years, courts have been faced with difficult questions about the extent to which law and practice conflict with the right(s) to confrontation. Key questions concern the extent to which out-of-court statements can be presented at trial in lieu of the presence of the witness who made them, and in what circumstances witnesses can be allowed to give evidence with 'special measures' or even anonymously.

(A) OUT-OF-COURT STATEMENTS

As regards out-of-court statements, the primary rule has long been that such 'hearsay' statements are inadmissible. The person who made the statement should attend trial, where they can be cross-examined. However, exceptions to the rule against hearsay have been expanded over time.[165] If a witness has made a statement prior to trial—typically, but not necessarily, to the police—that statement may now be presented in court

---

[160] *Crown Court Compendium, Part 1* (2017), 1–4.   [161] Leveson, n 58, [283].   [162] CPR, r 25.14.

[163] Judiciary of England and Wales, *The Better Case Management (BCM) Handbook* (2018), 4.

[164] I. Dennis, 'The Right to Confront Witnesses: Meanings, Myths and Human Rights' [2010] *Crim LR* 255. He suggests that it includes the right to public trial; to face-to-face confrontation; to cross-examination; and to know the identity of the accuser.

[165] See generally J. Spencer, *Hearsay Evidence in Criminal Proceedings* (2nd edn, 2014).

in certain circumstances. Under s 116 of the CJA 2003 the circumstances are that the witness is unavailable to attend the trial because she: is dead; is physically or mentally unfit to attend; is outside the UK and attendance is not practical; cannot be found, despite attempts having been made; or will not give evidence through fear. Where fear is the reason for non-attendance, s 116 requires that an interests of justice test be satisfied before the out-of-court statement is admitted, which includes considering the 'risk that its admission or exclusion will result in unfairness to any party to the proceedings (and in particular to how difficult it will be to challenge the statement if the relevant person does not give oral evidence)'. But the interests of justice are relevant to the other grounds of unavailability as well, because of the applicability of s 78 of PACE.[166]

If a witness statement is admitted against the defendant under s 116, will this be incompatible with the confrontation right in Art 6(3)? There is a large ECHR case law on the interpretation of this right, and while the case law is not entirely consistent, it is clear that the answer to this question will depend on various issues, prominent among them the extent to which the defendant was able to challenge the statement, and whether the statement is the 'sole or decisive' evidence against the defendant. The following passage is indicative of the ECtHR's approach:

> evidence must normally be produced at a public hearing, in the presence of the accused, with a view to adversarial argument. There are exceptions to this principle, but they must not infringe the rights of the defence. As a general rule, paragraphs 1 and 3 (d) of Article 6 require that the defendant be given an adequate and proper opportunity to challenge and question a witness against him, either when he makes his statement or at a later stage … where a conviction is based solely or to a decisive degree on depositions that have been made by a person whom the accused has had no opportunity to examine or to have examined, whether during the investigation or at the trial, the rights of the defence are restricted to an extent that is incompatible with the guarantees provided by Article 6.[167]

As is examined below, this strict rule has been moderated somewhat.[168]

The English courts have tended to be sceptical of the requirements laid down in the Strasbourg cases,[169] leading to a successful challenge in *Al-Khawaja and Tahery v UK*,[170] and a subsequent series of domestic and ECHR cases examining the English approach and the 'sole or decisive' rule. In *Al-Khawaja*, the complainant had died after making a statement to the police; in *Tahery*, the witness declined to give evidence through fear (though the defendant, Tahery, does not seem to have done anything to cause the fear; the witness was scared of the reaction from other members of the Iranian community). In both cases, the witness statements were admitted at trial. The ECtHR found that the statements were a decisive basis for the applicants' convictions. The government largely conceded this, but relied on the argument that the applicants had still been able to challenge the statements, and that this should be considered to

---

[166] CJA, s 126(2)(a).   [167] *Luca v Italy* (2003) 36 EHRR 46, [39]–[40].
[168] *Al-Khawaja and Tahery v UK* (2012) 54 EHRR 23.
[169] See *R v M(KJ)* (2003) 2 Cr App R 322; *R v Sellick and Sellick* [2005] EWCA Crim 651.
[170] (2009) 49 EHRR 1.

counterbalance the absence of the witnesses. Among the means of challenge were that in *Al-Khawaja* the defence could have pointed out inconsistencies in the applicant's statements, and in *Tahery* it could have called other witnesses who might have cast doubt on the statement. It is unclear to what extent the Court accepted that such means of challenge might counterbalance the inability to examine the witness. While 'the Court doubt[ed] whether any counterbalancing factors would be sufficient to justify the introduction in evidence of an untested statement which was the sole or decisive basis for the conviction of an applicant',[171] this is not an absolute statement, and the Court does seem to have taken the government's counterbalancing argument seriously by examining it on its merits. On the facts, however, it was not convinced by the argument. As regards *Tahery*, this may be right; it seems that all of the potential witnesses to the crime were reluctant to give information, which only left Tahery's own testimony, something unlikely to carry much weight. The conclusion is more debatable in *Al-Khawaja*: the Court noted that the inconsistencies in the complainant's accounts were minor, and that her allegation corresponded with that of another complainant, with whom collusion could be ruled out. But surely the issue is the *potential* for challenge provided by these other items of evidence, not the fact that they happen not to support the defence case; otherwise the prosecution is put in a worse position to the extent that the impugned evidence is reliable.

The Court of Appeal responded to this ruling by arguing that, for a number of reasons, it was wrong. In *Horncastle*, it read the ECtHR as having laid down an absolute rule that where the evidence of an absent witness is the sole or decisive basis for conviction, counterbalancing factors, such as the ability to challenge the statement through other evidence, cannot make up for the absence of confrontation.[172] As we suggested in the previous paragraph, the judgment in *Al-Khawaja* may not support such a reading. Be that as it may, the Court of Appeal argued that such an absolutist position is not supported by previous ECtHR decisions, nor is it cogent as a matter of principle. For the Court of Appeal, the question is 'whether the evidence can be assessed and tested so that it is safe to rely upon it'; the absolutist position presumes 'that all hearsay evidence which is critical to a case will be potentially unreliable in the absence of testing in open court [and that] the fact-finder cannot be trusted to assess the weight of such evidence'. 'The importance of the evidence within the case is an entirely separate issue from its reliability'.[173] The court went on to give various examples of hearsay evidence which it thinks would be reliable enough to determine a case standing alone.

The Court of Appeal's decision was endorsed by the Supreme Court in *R v Horncastle*.[174] Lord Phillips, giving judgment for the court, found that, notwithstanding the requirement on domestic courts to take account of the Strasbourg jurisprudence in applying clearly established principles, on rare occasions it might decline to do so where concerned that the Strasbourg judgment did not sufficiently appreciate or accommodate some aspect of English law. This was such a case.[175] Lord Phillips stressed

[171] Ibid, [37].   [172] [2009] EWCA Crim 964, [41].   [173] Ibid, [58], [60], [64].
[174] [2009] UKSC 14.   [175] [11].

that the sole or decisive rule had been introduced in *Doorson v Netherlands* without full consideration of whether there was justification for imposing the rule as an over-riding principle applicable equally to continental and common law jurisdictions.[176] He drew attention to the 'paradox' produced by the sole or decisive test: 'It permits the court to have regard to evidence if the support that it gives to the prosecution case is peripheral, but not where it is decisive. The more cogent the evidence the less it can be relied upon.'[177]

Al-Khawaja and Tahery v UK was then heard by the Grand Chamber of the ECtHR,[178] which tempered its previous approach. The Grand Chamber concluded that admitting a statement by a witness who did not attend the trial and whose evidence was the sole or decisive basis for a conviction would not necessarily breach Art 6(1) and Art 6(3)(d), as long as there were sufficient counterbalancing factors, including strong procedural safeguards, to offset the prejudice to the defendant of not being able to cross-examine the absent witness. Where a conviction is based solely or decisively on the evidence of absent witnesses, the court must subject the proceedings to the 'most searching scrutiny'.[179] The Grand Chamber advocated a narrow interpretation of 'decisive', namely evidence of such significance or importance as is likely to be deter-minative of the outcome of the case.[180] Moreover, despite its dicta in *Luca*, the sole or decisive rule should not be applied in an inflexible manner.[181] The ECtHR concluded that, notwithstanding the difficulties caused to Al-Khawaja by admitting the statement and the dangers of doing so, there were sufficient counterbalancing factors to conclude that admitting the witness statement did not breach Art 6.[182] In contrast, the decisive nature of the witness statement against Tahery, without strong corroborative evidence, meant the jury were unable to conduct a fair and proper assessment of its reliability. There were not sufficient counterbalancing factors to compensate for the difficulties to the defence, and thus there was a violation of Art 6(1) read in conjunction with Art 6(3)(d).[183]

The judgment is a curious mix: the ECtHR purports not to yield to the arguments of the UK, which are addressed and sought to be rebutted in turn, while ultimately moderating the interpretation of its own jurisprudence. Moreover, it is less than clear as to what truly distinguished the different findings for Al-Khawaja and Tahery—the judgment's focus on corroboration may well be problematic. As Redmayne suggests, some of the more puzzling aspects of the Grand Chamber's decision may result from the process of compromise, in recognizing the lack of justification for a strict sole or decisive rule, and watering down a hard-line reiteration of the rule to avoid antagoniz-ing the UK.[184] While this decision cannot be characterized as a complete capitulation by the ECtHR, given the upholding of Tahery's complaint, it does represent a prag-matic admission of the jurisdictional specificity of protections for the defendant, and a tempering of the more rigid rule exhorted previously. Overall, the Grand Chamber's

---

[176] [107].   [177] [91].   [178] (2012) 54 EHRR 23.
[179] [147].   [180] [131].   [181] [146].   [182] [158].   [183] [165].
[184] M. Redmayne, 'Hearsay and Human Rights: *Al-Khawaja* in the Grand Chamber' (2012) 75 *MLR* 865.

decision has defused some tension between the ECtHR and the English courts over hearsay law.[185]

The first subsequent Court of Appeal judgment following this decision was *R v Ibrahim*,[186] where Ibrahim had been convicted of rape based on the untested hearsay evidence of the complainant who had died before the trial. In finding that this evidence should not have been admitted, and that so doing had infringed Ibrahim's rights under Art 6, the Court of Appeal examined the relationship between *Horncastle* and *Al-Khawaja and Tahery*:

> 88. It seems to us that there is a difference in approach between the Supreme Court's decision in *Horncastle* and the Grand Chamber's decision in *Al-Khawaja*. First and foremost, the Supreme Court declined to apply 'the sole or decisive' test, at least to the two cases before it. The Grand Chamber confirmed that this test remained part of the Strasbourg jurisprudence, although it accepted that the consequence of concluding that a particular piece of untested hearsay evidence was 'sole or decisive' did not automatically mean that the particular trial where that evidence was admitted was unfair.
>
> 89. This difference may be more one of form than substance, however. Thus, the Court of Appeal talked of a conviction being based 'solely or to a decisive degree on hearsay evidence admitted under the [2003 Act]' and the Supreme Court talked of the hearsay evidence being 'critical evidence'. That may not be very different from the Grand Chamber's concept of 'sole or decisive'. Next, the Court of Appeal and the Supreme Court both emphasise that when the untested hearsay evidence is 'critical', the question of whether the trial is fair will depend on three principal factors. First, the English courts accept that there has to be good reason to admit the untested hearsay evidence. To decide this under English law there must be compliance with the statutory code. The Grand Chamber necessarily puts this requirement on a more general basis, but it emphasised the need for 'justification'. Secondly, and we think most importantly, all three courts stipulate that there must be an enquiry as to whether that evidence can be shown to be reliable. Thirdly, all three courts are concerned with the extent to which there are 'counterbalancing measures' and if so whether they have been properly applied in deciding whether to admit the 'critical' untested hearsay evidence or to allow the case to proceed. In the case of England and Wales those 'counterbalancing measures' must include all the statutory safeguards in the 'code', as well as a proper application of common law safeguards, such as proper directions in the summing up. The Grand Chamber emphasised the same thing at paragraph 144 and particularly in its 'general conclusion on the sole or decisive rule' at paragraph 147 . . .

In *R v Riat*, the Court of Appeal emphasized that:

> For the purposes of a Crown Court in England and Wales dealing day to day with cases of this kind, five propositions are central:
>
> i) the law is, and must be accepted to be, as stated in UK statute, viz the Criminal Justice Act 2003 ('CJA 03');
>
> ii) if there be any difference, on close analysis, between the judgment of the Supreme Court in Horncastle and that of the ECtHR in Al-Khawaja & Tahery, the obligation

---

[185] Ibid, 873.   [186] [2012] EWCA Crim 837, CJA 2003.

of a domestic court is to follow the former: see *R(RJM) v SSWP* [2009] 1 AC 311 at [64] and *Ibrahim* at [87];

iii) there are indeed differences in the way in which principle is stated, but these may well be more of form than of substance; in particular, the importance of the hearsay evidence to the case is undoubtedly a vital consideration when deciding upon its admissibility and treatment, but there is no over-arching rule, either in the ECtHR or in English law, that a piece of hearsay evidence which is 'sole or decisive' is for that reason automatically inadmissible;

iv) therefore, both because of point (ii) and because of point (iii), the Crown Court judge need not ordinarily concern himself any further with close analysis of the relationship between the two strands of jurisprudence and need generally look no further than the statute and *Horncastle*; we endeavour to set out below the principal questions which must be addressed;

v) however, neither under the statute, nor under *Horncastle*, can hearsay simply be treated as if it were first hand evidence and automatically admissible.[187]

The ECtHR has applied its reformulated interpretation of the confrontation doctrine in an application arising from *Horncastle,* holding that there was no breach of Art 6.[188] It reiterated that where sole or decisive absent witness evidence has been admitted, the key question is whether counterbalancing measures, which permit a fair and proper assessment of reliability, were present. It rejected the applicants' argument that any decisive evidence must be reliable, or at the very least shown not to be unreliable to any significant extent, before it can be fairly admitted.[189] The ECtHR concluded that the Supreme Court's decision not to apply the 'sole or decisive rule' in the applicants' case, as it was understood following the judgment of the Chamber in *Al-Khawaja and Tahery*, does not lead to a violation of Art 6.[190]

It is obvious that in *Horncastle* the Court of Appeal and the Supreme Court interpreted the concern over confrontation as one that is focused purely on reliability. But this is not the only way to understand confrontation. The Sixth Amendment to the US Constitution guarantees the defendant's right 'to be confronted with the witnesses against him'.[191] The confrontation right was invigorated by the US Supreme Court which, in *Crawford v Washington*,[192] held that evidence that was admissible under reliability-based exceptions to the hearsay rule might still be inadmissible on grounds of violation of the confrontation right. At one point, it observed that 'Dispensing with confrontation because testimony is obviously reliable is akin to dispensing with jury trial because a defendant is obviously guilty.'[193] One interpretation of this is that confrontation is a 'dignitarian' right; that is, it reflects respect for human dignity rather than the need to protect defendants from

---

[187] [2012] EWCA Crim 1509, [2] followed in *R v Shabir* [2012] EWCA Crim 2564.
[188] *Horncastle v UK* [2014] ECHR 1394.   [189] [138].   [190] [139].
[191] For analysis, and comparison with the ECHR approach, see R. Friedman, 'The Confrontation Right Across the Systemic Divide' in J. Jackson, M. Langer, and P. Tillers (eds), *Crime, Procedure and Evidence in a Comparative and International Context* (2008).
[192] 541 US 36 (2004).   [193] Ibid, 62.

false conviction.[194] As it was put, if rather mysteriously, in *Coy v Iowa*: 'there is something deep in human nature that regards face-to-face confrontation between accused and accuser as essential to a fair trial in a criminal prosecution.'[195] In the United States, confrontation is interpreted as a strong right. It will result in the exclusion of evidence even if that evidence is not the 'sole or decisive' element of the state's case, and there is no question of counterbalancing through rebuttal evidence. However, the right only applies to 'testimonial' evidence: broadly speaking, evidence given in contemplation that it might be used in a criminal prosecution. Thus, in *Davis v Washington* statements made during an emergency call to the police, when the caller's mind would have been preoccupied with getting help, were admissible in the absence of the witness.[196] Further, the confrontation right can be forfeited by the defendant if, for example, he kills or frightens the witness with the intention of preventing her from testifying.[197] The ECtHR has hinted that it would recognize some sort of forfeiture doctrine.[198]

From the current jurisprudence it is not clear whether the ECtHR views the European confrontation right as being, in whole or in part, dignitarian. The concerns expressed in *Al-Khawaja* are mainly focused on the ability of the defence to demonstrate the unreliability of the evidence. We do not know how the ECtHR would respond to a case where the disputed testimony is 'obviously reliable'—whether it would still insist on confrontation. But it is true that the dignitarian case for confrontation is not an easy one to make; the cases where there is intuitively the strongest case for confrontation—'testimonial' cases, in the US terminology—are usually ones where there are also reliability concerns, and it may be this that drives the feeling that confrontation is such an important right. If we rule out a dignitarian basis for confrontation, then the Court of Appeal's argument of principle in *Horncastle* appears plausible. However, although it gives various examples of hearsay evidence which is both reliable and decisive, the examples are problematic: they tend either not to involve 'testimonial' statements, and thus not to make the strongest case for confrontation,[199] or to be under-described. Examples of testimonial hearsay evidence that could convict a defendant standing alone are probably very rare. The more significant part of the Court of Appeal's argument is that counterbalancing factors can justify the admission of decisive hearsay by providing some equivalent of cross-examination. And here, there is a good argument for admissibility on the facts of *Al-Khawaja*. There, the victim's death does not raise suspicions about the motive for the witness not wanting to face the defendant in court (as might be present in a case of a witness who refuses to attend court, as in *Tahery*), and

---

[194] See M. Redmayne, 'Confronting Confrontation' in P. Roberts and J. Hunter (eds), *Criminal Evidence and Human Rights* (2012), ch 12.

[195] 487 US 1012, 1017 (1988).   [196] 547 US 813 (2006).

[197] *Giles v California*, 554 US 353 (2008).   [198] See *Al-Khawaja*, n 170, [37].

[199] There is some suggestion in the Strasbourg case law that something like the 'testimonial' requirement may operate before the confrontation right is triggered: see *X v UK* (1992) 15 EHRR CD 113, finding an application 'manifestly ill-founded' where the complaint was against the use of anonymous witnesses whose evidence did not 'implicate' the defendant, but provided evidence of the background to events.

was not foreseeable, so the prosecution could not have been expected to arrange some sort of confrontation prior to trial.[200] Further, the evidence in the case allowed some checking for consistency, providing an—albeit very approximate—substitute for cross-examination, and some reassurance that the evidence was not moulded by the police[201] (the victim had initially complained spontaneously to a neighbour).

(B) ANONYMOUS WITNESSES

The cases discussed so far involve the defence being unable to question a prosecution witness. The ECHR case law also deals with the situation where the defence can question a witness, but is compromised by not knowing his or her identity. Anonymity may seriously limit the ability to cross-examine: often the defence will not be able to explore potential reasons for giving false testimony. Genuine confrontation—the ability to examine the witness—may be lost. In numerous cases, the English courts allowed witnesses to testify anonymously, shielding their identity by allowing them to give evidence from behind a screen, but in a welcome change from the usual minimalist response to Convention rights, in *R v Davis* the House of Lords held that in the absence of legislative authority this practice was not permissible;[202] indeed, the House of Lords admonished the Court of Appeal for giving too little weight to rights and resorting too readily to a process of balancing.[203] Davis had been 'gravely impeded'[204] in his cross-examination of witnesses: his defence was that the witnesses who identified him were part of a conspiracy led by an ex-girlfriend, but in court he could not even be sure which of the witnesses she was and so could not question her effectively.

The use of anonymous witnesses is permissible under the ECHR, but certain conditions must be met. Significantly, the case law recognizes that there is a need to balance the rights of defendants and witnesses in this area:

> It is true that Article 6 does not explicitly require the interests of witnesses in general, and those of victims called upon to testify in particular, to be taken into consideration. However, their life, liberty or security of person may be at stake, as may interests coming generally within the ambit of Article 8 of the Convention. Such interests of witnesses and victims are in principle protected by other, substantive provisions of the Convention, which imply that Contracting States should organise their criminal proceedings in such a way that those interests are not unjustifiably imperilled. Against this background, principles of fair trial also require that in appropriate cases the interests of the defence are balanced against those of witnesses or victims called upon to testify.[205]

In *Doorson* itself, the Court found that there had been no breach of Art 6. There were counterbalancing factors in place, in that the defence was able to point to factors

---

[200] Contrast the facts of *R v Cole, R v Keet* [2008] 1 Cr App R 5, where the slow onset of dementia might have afforded this opportunity.

[201] A concern in some of the confrontation literature: W. O'Brien, 'The Right of Confrontation: US and European Perspectives' (2005) 121 *LQR* 481.

[202] [2008] UKHL 38.   [203] Ibid, [16], [34].   [204] Ibid, [32].

[205] *Doorson v The Netherlands* (1996) 22 EHRR 330, [70].

undermining the credibility of the anonymous witnesses, and their evidence was not the 'sole or decisive' basis for conviction. As with absent witnesses, the 'sole or decisive' criterion is significant: 'it should be recalled that, even when "counterbalancing" procedures are found to compensate sufficiently the handicaps under which the defence labours, a conviction should not be based either solely or to a decisive extent on anonymous statements'.[206] Of course, this has been tempered somewhat by the subsequent interpretations in *Al-Khawaja* and *Horncastle*.

The government quickly responded to *Davis* by passing emergency legislation. The Criminal Evidence (Witness Anonymity) Act 2008 permitted witnesses to give evidence anonymously, subject to various conditions, and was replaced subsequently, with little change, by provisions in the Coroners and Justice Act 2009. The legislation lays down three conditions for anonymity:[207] anonymity must be (a) necessary to protect a person or prevent serious damage to property or 'real harm' to the public interest; (b) consistent with a fair trial for the defendant; and (c) in the interests of justice because the witness's testimony is important and she would not testify otherwise. The Act goes on to specify various considerations to be taken into account when assessing whether points (a)–(c) are satisfied.[208] These include the defendant's right to know the identity of a witness; the extent to which the witness's credibility will be an issue; whether the witness's evidence can be tested under anonymity; and whether the witness's evidence might be the sole or decisive evidence implicating the defendant. Anonymity orders have been made in a significant number of trials. According to the CPS, 129 applications for witness anonymity were granted between the legislation coming into force in July 2008 and December of that year (this would have involved a smaller number of trials, as many trials would involve multiple anonymous witnesses).[209]

The original legislation was given detailed consideration by the Court of Appeal in *R v Mayers*.[210] The court made a number of significant points, for example noting the crucial importance of prosecution investigation and disclosure in order to give the defence as full a basis as possible for cross-examination. It considered alternative measures to protect witnesses, but noted that protections such as witness relocation constitute a 'tumultuous' interference with a witness's life, as well as with that of their family.[211] It found that the witness's fear need not be caused by the defendant. In one of the cases in this conjoined appeal it put considerable weight on the fact that the victim had been attacked in public, in full view of onlookers, and found that this would give a sound basis for the witnesses to be afraid of the consequences of testifying without anonymity.[212] In two of the four cases, the Court of Appeal concluded that the defendants had received a fair trial. But in one the conviction was quashed because there were doubts about the credibility of the witness, and the available evidence did not allow a proper opportunity for her evidence to be tested. In another it held that there

---

[206] Ibid, [76].   [207] s 88.   [208] s 89.

[209] Human Rights Joint Committee, *Eighth Report 2008–9 (Legislative Scrutiny: Coroners and Justice Bill)*, para 1.119.

[210] [2009] 1 Cr App R 30.   [211] Ibid, [9].   [212] See also *R v Powar* [2009] EWCA Crim 594.

is no provision for anonymous hearsay; that is, for an anonymous witness statement to be presented in court.

Most significantly, perhaps, *Mayers* confirms what is implicit in the legislation: that whether the evidence of an anonymous witness is the sole or decisive evidence is only a factor to be considered when making an anonymity order. If anonymous evidence is the mainstay of the prosecution case, that will not prevent an order being made nor render the trial unfair.[213] Moreover, when considering whether anonymous evidence is sole or decisive, it appears that each witness is to be considered individually: if there is more than one anonymous witness then anonymous evidence is not sole or decisive.[214]

In *Chisholm*, the Court of Appeal rejected the complaint that the judge did not give in open court the reasons for the witness anonymity orders; indeed, setting out the reasons would have defeated the purpose of the orders.[215] Moreover, an unnecessary witness anonymity order is not necessarily problematic as long as it does not have any adverse effect on the fairness of the trial or the safety of the conviction.[216] In *Donovan*, the decision to grant anonymity meant that the jury was prevented from hearing admissible and substantive material which was relevant to the question whether either or both witnesses may have been lying or may have had any motivation for lying.[217] The trial was held to be unfair as material of potential value to the defence, providing grounds for believing that both witnesses may have had a motive for incriminating the defendant, was available but the trial judge did not allude to it.

In *Ellis v UK*, the ECtHR emphasized that when a witness gave evidence anonymously certain counterbalancing factors could guard against an unfair trial.[218] The Court observed that the problems posed by absent witnesses (as in Al-*Khawaja and Tahery*) and anonymous witnesses (as in the present case) were not different in principle. However, the precise limitations on the defence's ability to challenge a witness in these two types of cases differ: unlike absent witnesses, anonymous witnesses are confronted in person by defence counsel, who may pursue any inconsistencies in their account, and their demeanour under questioning can be observed. Though the evidence of one of the anonymous witness was not the 'sole evidence', the ECtHR accepted, like the trial judge, that there was a possibility that it might have been decisive in respect of some of the applicants.[219] The ECtHR was satisfied that the jury could conduct a fair and proper assessment of the reliability of the witness's evidence, in the light of 'the trial judge's impeccable approach to the question of anonymity, the admission of evidence and the direction of the jury, as well as the extensive disclosure which had occurred in the case which permitted extensive and effective cross-examination of [the witness]'.[220] The ECtHR emphasized that there was a clear public interest in ensuring that ongoing, gang-related violence and revenge killings were prosecuted, and that allowing witnesses to give evidence anonymously was an important tool in enabling such prosecutions.[221] In contrast, and understandably, in *Balta and Demir v Turkey* the ECtHR held, unanimously, that there had been a violation

---

[213] See n 210, [23].   [214] Ibid, [25], [75].   [215] [2010] EWCA Crim 258, [24].
[216] *Willett* [2011] EWCA Crim, [45].   [217] [2012] EWCA Crim 2749, [18].
[218] [2012] ECHR 813.   [219] [81].   [220] [82]–[88].   [221] [80].

of Art 6(1) taken in conjunction with Art 6(3)(d).[222] The applicants had been convicted
of membership of an illegal organization, on the basis of statements by an anonymous
witness whom the applicants were unable to question at any stage of the proceedings.
The procedural safeguards that existed in Turkey had not been implemented so as to
counterbalance the handicap to the defence arising from the lack of direct confrontation.

(C) SPECIAL MEASURES FOR VULNERABLE AND INTIMIDATED WITNESSES

A cognate but distinct scheme of 'special measures' to facilitate the giving of evidence by
vulnerable and intimidated witnesses was introduced by the Youth Justice and Criminal
Evidence Act 1999 (YJCEA). Vulnerable witnesses are all child witnesses (those aged
under 18) and any witness whose quality of evidence is likely to be diminished because
they: are suffering from a mental disorder; have a significant impairment of intelligence
and social functioning; or have a physical disability or are suffering from a physical disorder.[223] Complainants in sexual offence cases are defined as falling into this category
automatically unless they wish to opt out,[224] as are witnesses to certain offences involving
guns and knives.[225] Intimidated witnesses are those suffering from fear or distress in relation to testifying in the case.[226] Special measures are available to prosecution and defence
witnesses but not to the defendant,[227] and are subject to the discretion of the court.

Special measures may include screens to shield the witness from the defendant;[228] a live
link enabling the witness to give evidence during the trial from outside the court;[229] evidence given in private;[230] removal of wigs and gowns by judges and barristers;[231] a video-
recorded interview to be admitted by the court as the witness's evidence-in-chief;[232] or
examination of the witness through an intermediary.[233] Section 101 of the Coroners and
Justice Act 2009 inserted a new s 22A into the YJCEA making special provision for adult
complainants in sexual offence trials in the Crown Court. The section provides, on application by a party to the proceedings, for the automatic admissibility of a video-recorded
statement as evidence in chief under s 27 of the YJCEA, unless this would not be in the
interests of justice or would not maximize the quality of the complainant's evidence.

Special measures have been held to be compliant with Art 6.[234] As noted by Baroness
Hale, under the 1999 Act:

> All the evidence is produced at the trial in the presence of the accused, some of it in pre-
> recorded form and some of it by contemporaneous television transmission. The accused

---

[222] *Balta and Demir v Turkey*, App No 48628/12.   [223] YJCEA, s 16.   [224] s 17(4).
[225] Sch 1A, as inserted by the Coroners and Justice Act 2009.   [226] YJCEA, s 17.
[227] Ibid, s 16(1); see *Speaking Up for Justice: Report of the Interdepartmental Working Group on the Treatment of Vulnerable or Intimidated Witnesses in the Criminal Justice System* (1998); M. Burton, R. Evans, and A. Sand-ers, 'Protecting Children in Criminal Proceedings: Parity for Child Witnesses and Child Defendants' (2006) 18(3) *Child and Family Law Quarterly* 397; P. Cooper and D. Wurtzel, 'A Day Late and a Dollar Short: In Search of an Intermediary Scheme for Vulnerable Defendants in England and Wales' [2013] *Crim LR* 4.
[228] YJCEA s 23.   [229] s 24.   [230] s 25.   [231] s 26.   [232] s 27.   [233] s 29.
[234] *R (D) v Camberwell Green Youth Court* [2005] UKHL 4, citing *Kostovski v Netherlands* (1989) 12 EHRR 434, 447–8, inter alia.

can see and hear it all. The accused has every opportunity to challenge and question the witnesses against him at the trial itself. The only thing missing is a face to face confrontation, but the appellants accept that the Convention does not guarantee a right to face to face confrontation.[235]

A ground rules hearing, involving the prosecutor, the magistrates/judge, and the trial advocates, and the intermediary (where engaged), will be held to discuss and establish how to enable a witness who is vulnerable or who has a communication need can give their best evidence.[236] The court must take 'every reasonable step' to facilitate the participation of any person, including the defendant.[237] The Criminal Practice Directions provide useful guidance on how judges should deal with children and vulnerable witnesses.[238] In *Lubemba*, Hallett LJ, the Vice President of the Court of Appeal (Criminal Division), referred in detail to available toolkits and the text of the Direction, which guide the questioning of vulnerable witnesses.[239] She outlined the appropriate role and actions of the trial judge, as well as emphasizing the importance of the ground rules hearing.[240]

There is a curious and unsustainable perception underpinning the 1999 Act that defendants are not vulnerable, at least not in such a way as to require equivalent protections to other such witnesses.[241] The extent to which this exclusion is compliant with Art 6 is questionable.[242] And as Fairclough reminds us, vulnerability among defendants and offenders is pervasive.[243] Following the ECtHR ruling in *SC v UK* that an 11-year-old defendant with limited intellectual ability, learning difficulties, and a poor attention span could not participate in the trial process effectively,[244] a limited live-link provision was extended to defendants,[245] and it remains the only special measure available to defendants statutorily.[246] It appears that knowledge of this provision's existence is poor and so is little used,[247] despite it being a measure that, if used carefully, could have significant implications for the trial participation and Art 6 rights of the defendant.

---

[235] *R (D) v Camberwell Green Youth Court*, [49] per Baroness Hale. See L. Ellison, 'Case Comment—Youth Court: Whether Legislative Provision Requiring Special Measures Direction to be Given in Relation to Child Witnesses in Need of Special Protection in Manner Compatible with Convention Requirement for a Fair Trial' [2005] *Crim LR* 497.

[236] P. Cooper, P. Backen, and R. Marchant, 'Getting to Grips with Ground Rules Hearings: A Checklist for Judges, Advocates and Intermediaries to Promote the Fair Treatment of Vulnerable People in Court' [2015] *Crim LR* 420.

[237] CPR, r 3.9(3)(b).

[238] 3E.1–6. See in particular CPR, Part 3, CPD 1 General matters 3D: *Vulnerable People in the Courts* and CPD 1 General matters 3E: *Ground Rules Hearings to Plan the Questioning of a Vulnerable Witness or Defendant*. See also the Judicial College's *Young Witness Bench Checklist 2012*.

[239] *Lubemba* [2014] EWCA Crim 2064.   [240] Ibid, [43].

[241] Cf Vulnerable Witnesses (Scotland) Act 2004.

[242] D. Birch, 'A Better Deal for Vulnerable Witnesses?' [2000] *Crim LR* 223, 242.

[243] S. Fairclough, 'Speaking Up for Injustice: Reconsidering the Provision of Special Measures Through the Lens of Equality' [2018] *Crim LR* 4–19.

[244] [2005] 40 EHRR 10.   [245] YJCEA, s 33A.

[246] See S. Fairclough '"It doesn't happen . . . and I've never thought it was necessary for it to happen": Barriers to vulnerable defendants giving evidence by live link in Crown Court trials' (2017) 21(3) *E&P* 209; also J. McEwan, 'Vulnerable Defendants and the Fairness of Trials' [2013] *Crim LR* 100–13.

[247] Fairclough, ibid, 215–16.

The Coroners and Justice Act 2009 inserted a statutory power to appoint an intermediary for a defendant giving evidence by means of s 33BA of the YJCEA but this has
not yet been brought in force. The power of a judge is therefore still governed by the
inherent power of the court at common law to appoint an intermediary if needed.[248]
Indeed, this had occurred in *Rashid*, where the trial judge had permitted R to have an
intermediary during his evidence. In his appeal against conviction on the ground that
he needed an intermediary during the whole trial, the Court of Appeal stated that 'in
all but the rarest case, the advocates [are], as an ordinary part of their duties as competent advocates, able to do what was needed so that the applicant was fully able to
participate in every aspect of the trial (when no intermediary was present) until the
applicant gave evidence'.[249] As noted by the High Court in *R v Secretary of State for
Justice*, '[t]he most pressing need for the help of an intermediary self-evidently bites at
the point of maximum strain, that is when an accused should he do so elects to give an
account of himself by entering the witness box and submitting to cross-examination'.[250]
The court noted the 'jeopardy in which he is and which crystallises at that point', and
that the 'intelligent observer would be puzzled' by why a witness for the Crown could
be supported by an intermediary but the defendant against whom he gave evidence
denied one under the same scheme.[251]

The Court of Appeal made a number of observations on how young or vulnerable defendants should be treated in court in *R v Grant-Murray and Henry; R v Mc-
Gill, Hewitt and Hewitt*,[252] a case involving five unsuccessful applications appealing
their convictions for joint enterprise murder. The court confirmed, 'if confirmation is
needed, that the principles in *Lubemba* apply to child defendants as witnesses in the
same way as they apply to any other vulnerable witness'.[253] It also emphasized the importance of training,[254] and said it would be difficult to conceive of an advocate being
competent to act in a case involving young witnesses or defendants without specific
training.[255] Moreover, in its *Report on Unfitness to Plead* the Law Commission recommended mandatory screening of defendants under the age of 14 for participation difficulties.[256] All of this seems most sensible.

11.4 CONCLUSION

Despite its statistical rarity, which is becoming even more pronounced in relation to
corporate offenders, the criminal trial remains the animating and culminating feature
of the criminal process. It is a costly and risky enterprise, however, and so we have
seen that measures that seek to minimize reliance on a contested trial, such as guilty
pleas and prosecution agreements, are incentivized more and more. For those trials

---

[248] *R (C) v Sevenoaks Youth Court* [2009] EWHC 3088 (Admin).   [249] [2017] EWCA Crim 2.
[250] [2014] EWHC 1944 (Admin), [36].   [251] Ibid, [47].   [252] [2017] EWCA Crim 1228.
[253] Ibid, [226].   [254] Ibid, [226]; (and see *Rashid*, n 249 [80]).   [255] Ibid, [226].
[256] Law Commission, *Report on unfitness to plead: Vol 1*, Law Com No 364 (2016), 7.130.

that are pursued, numerous efforts are being made to ensure that more of them are effective, in taking place on the planned date, and in running swiftly, predictably, and efficiently. While these initiatives are understandable and laudable, the preoccupation with quantification and economy savings to the detriment of other values is unfortunate and overlooks the potential impacts on defendants and witnesses, unintended or otherwise.

When a contested trial does take place, it looks rather different than was the case just a decade ago. Significant changes have been wrought: in the magistrates' courts fewer and fewer cases are opposed, trials are shorter, and some powers to try cases have been transferred online. The apparent efficiency savings that derive from this mean that the preference is for ever more 'summary' justice. The chosen mode of trial is not just a matter of principle but of pragmatism—the cheaper and quicker the process, the better it is perceived to be in the current political climate.

Despite some efforts to remedy biases and unfairness, issues of diversity, and the lack thereof, persist in the criminal trial. There are significant racial and socio-economic implications of trial in magistrates' court and Crown Court, and whether that trial is by judge and jury or by judge alone. Plea decisions influence the mode of trial. While individual choices here are understandable and sensible on a number of levels, they reflect and can embed racial unfairness from earlier stages in the process. A more optimistic note may be sounded in respect of jury trials and ethnicity, though the incorporation of myths and cultural biases is a problematic dimension of lay decision making.

The negative experience of witnesses throughout the trial has prompted a reconsideration of available protective devices. Traditional trial structures and processes have been altered in seeking to protect witnesses and mitigate secondary victimization, especially of already vulnerable and/or intimidated parties. But the exclusionary rhetoric and practice, in overlooking the implications and protections for vulnerable defendants, continues. And it is in relation to confrontation and the protection of witnesses that the interplay between domestic and European courts has been most pronounced in respect of confrontation.

Beyond these significant doctrinal concerns, technology and digital advances have effected considerable changes to the trial process. There are important positive dimensions to this. While broadcasting and photography have been banned in the courts since 1925,[257] the workings of the courts are more open than ever in some respects, due to the live tweeting of certain trials. This mitigates the diminished number of legal correspondents in the print media, which has limited quality coverage of criminal trials in newspapers. Moreover, some use of live links can be helpful and sensible. That said, the extent to which technological developments in respect of the trial compound the disillusionment and detachment of defendants is not considered in policy initiatives. Speedy trials and remote links may be appealing politically, but they have significant implications for the rights and perceptions of the defendant. Linked to the push for

---

[257] CJA 1925, s 41.

digital trials are virtual hearings out of hours.[258] There has been a drive to have longer opening hours for courts, and this is being piloted, to much concern from the Bar.[259] How this impacts on diversity, both in a gender and ethnic sense, has not been examined adequately. Altered modes, forms, and timings of trials will impact on the different parties and cohorts in distinct ways. Such reforms further maintain the illusion that criminal justice cuts do not have real consequences, for defendants, innocent or otherwise, and for the working lives of practitioners.

FURTHER READING

DUFF, R. A., FARMER, L., MARSHALL, S., AND TADROS, V. (eds), *The Trial on Trial. Vol 3: Towards a Normative Theory of the Criminal Trial*, Oxford: Hart, 2007.

McEWAN, J., 'Vulnerable Defendants and the Fairness of Trials' [2013] *Crim LR* 100.

REDMAYNE, M., 'Theorizing the Criminal Trial' (2009) 12 *New Crim LR* 287.

REDMAYNE, M., 'Confronting Confrontation' in P. Roberts and J. Hunter (eds), *Criminal Evidence and Human Rights*, London: Bloomsbury, 2012, ch 12.

QUESTIONS FOR DISCUSSION

1. How should we decide which cases should be tried by jury? If it is accepted that jury trial is appropriate in some cases, should there be exceptions to the principle that jurors are selected at random?

2. What is the rule in *Galbraith*? Is it appropriate?

3. Should defendants have an absolute right to confront the witnesses against them? If not, what exceptions should there be?

---

[258] D. Kirk, 'Reflections of a Former Prosecutor' (2014) 78 *J Crim L* 99. https://www.lawgazette.co.uk/practice/judge-spearheading-late-night-courts-confronts-the-critics/5062314.article.

[259] See https://insidehmcts.blog.gov.uk/2017/10/24/next-steps-in-testing-our-proposals-for-court-hours-pilots; https://www.thetimes.co.uk/article/leading-barristers-threaten-boycott-of-night-court-plan-jxbvlsf3r. HMCTS, Flexible Operating Hours Pilots Prospectus, October 2017.

12

APPEALS, REVIEWS, AND RETRIALS

The appeals process serves many purposes. From the legal system's point of view, perhaps the most important purpose is the development and clarification of the law. A common law system could hardly exist unless appeals offered a means of reviewing the law. In performing this role, appeals allow the higher courts to exert some control over the lower courts. These are important functions of appeals and add much to an understanding of the forces shaping the appeals system. Of course, from the point of view of litigants, appeals offer a chance to challenge a result they are unhappy with. Such challenges have provided the criminal justice system with some of its most memorable images: the photographs of victims of long-running miscarriages of justice, such as the 'Guildford Four' and the 'Birmingham Six', celebrating their freedom on the steps of the Court of Appeal have a dramatic resonance. However, like much media coverage of the criminal justice system, such images, if taken to be representative of what the appeals system is all about, are apt to mislead. For one thing, it is not only the Court of Appeal that hears criminal appeals. Further, while the criminal appeals system does play an important role in securing the acquittal of those who dispute the facts on which they were found guilty, the majority of appeals do not revolve around questions of fact. Most appeals involve legal issues. The legal issues vary: in a large number of appeals the question is solely about whether the sentence given by the court was correct.[1] Other appeals involve questions about the criminal law: whether, for example, the court applied the correct definition of some legal concept such as 'intention' or the correct definition when the law has changed subsequently.[2] We will not consider such appeals in this chapter. The focus will be on the atypical, but important, appeals on questions of fact. We will also look at some appeals on questions of law, but only where the legal questions involve the defendant's procedural rights. These 'due process appeals' have given rise to difficult questions about when the courts should quash the convictions of the factually guilty. These appeals might be said to perform a third function of the appeals system. As we saw in the previous chapter, the criminal courts

---

[1] In 2016/17, the Court of Appeal heard 1,183 sentence appeals and 215 conviction appeals: *In the Court of Appeal (Criminal Division) 16/17* (2018), Annexes C and D. Both figures have been declining for some years.

[2] *R v Chapman* [2013] EWCA Crim 1370.

offer an opportunity to review, and on occasion to condemn, executive action, and this scrutiny is at its most prominent in appeal courts. And beyond this, the work of the Criminal Cases Review Commission, and the payment of compensation in limited instances, go some way towards mitigating the harm caused by miscarriages of justice through unjust convictions.

Before moving on to consider these issues, it is helpful to offer a brief overall sketch of the criminal appeals system. As well as the distinctions just mentioned, there is also a difference in the way prosecution and defence appeals are treated: in general, prosecution appeals are more restricted than defence appeals, though some reforms have diminished this distinction. Bearing this in mind, both prosecution and defence have rights of appeal from decisions of the magistrates' courts. The defence can appeal on questions of fact; here, appeal is to the Crown Court, which hears the appeal as a specially constituted panel of two judges sitting with a magistrate. This type of criminal appeal is unique in that it involves a rehearing of the case: the witnesses will be heard again, and their evidence assessed afresh. In most other appeals, the court will hear argument from the parties, but it is rare for an appeal court to hear evidence from witnesses. Both prosecution and defence are also able to appeal from the magistrates' court on questions of law. Here, appeal is by way of 'case stated' to the Administrative Court, a division of the High Court. The magistrates are asked to supply a statement of the facts of the case as they have found them, as well as their legal conclusions; this will provide the basis on which the court hears the appeal. Both parties are also able to challenge the magistrate's decision on legal grounds by way of judicial review;[3] these appeals are again heard by the Administrative Court. From the Administrative Court, further appeal is possible to the Supreme Court: leave will only be granted for points of law of general public importance.[4] The Administrative Court also hears appeals from the Crown Court when it sits as a court of appeal for appeals from the magistrates' court; these appeals may be by way of case stated or by judicial review.[5]

From the Crown Court as a court of first instance, a defendant is able to appeal against a finding of guilt on grounds of either fact or law. Appeal is to the Court of Appeal, from where either party may appeal to the Supreme Court in limited circumstances. The prosecution has fewer appeal rights. Since 1987, it has been able to appeal certain pre-trial rulings to the Court of Appeal; this jurisdiction was originally confined to serious fraud cases but was enlarged in 1996 to include all lengthy or complex cases.[6] The Criminal Justice Act (CJA) 2003 now allows prosecution appeals on rulings

---

[3] The judicial review procedure would occasionally allow a decision of fact to be challenged, where the magistrates can be shown to have drawn an unreasonable conclusion.

[4] This was challenged unsuccessfully on Art 6 and other grounds in *R v Dunn* [2010] EWCA Crim 1823; see C. Knight, 'Second Criminal Appeals and the Requirement of Certification' [2011] *LQR* 188.

[5] The Law Commission suggested that all appeals from the Crown Court should be to the Court of Appeal: *The High Court's Jurisdiction in Relation to Criminal Proceedings: A Consultation Paper* (2007), though revised this proposal in the subsequent report in 2010: Law Com No 324, [1.28].

[6] Under the CJA 1987, s 9 and Criminal Procedure and Investigations Act 1996, ss 35–36. Section 309 of the CJA 2003 added 'seriousness' to the criteria for appeal from preparatory hearings under the Criminal Procedure and Investigations Act 1996.

made by the judge during the trial; if the prosecution is not successful in the Court of Appeal the effect will often be the acquittal of the defendant. These prosecution appeals involve points of law. Until relatively recently, the situation was that the prosecution was not able to appeal against an acquittal in the Crown Court.[7] One exception to this rule was introduced in 1996, when the prosecution was given the power to challenge an acquittal that was tainted by, for example, threats of violence to jurors or witnesses.[8] In 2003, the CJA took things further, allowing appeals against acquittals in serious cases where significant new evidence of guilt emerges after the trial. With both these exceptions to the 'double jeopardy' principle there is a fairly complex process designed to ensure that an acquittal is not too easily challenged.

12.1 RESTRICTIONS ON APPEAL RIGHTS

The foregoing sketch is one-dimensional in that it illustrates the different avenues of appeal but says nothing about the conditions for appeal. A very important aspect of the appeal process is the way in which appeals are restricted and discouraged. All appeals from the Crown Court sitting as a court of first instance involve some sort of leave, either from the trial judge or from the Court of Appeal itself. This important filtering exercise will be discussed further later in the chapter. Where the prosecution is concerned, we have already seen that appeal rights are on the whole less generous. Although the CJA 2003 extended prosecution appeal rights by allowing interlocutory appeals from legal rulings by a Crown Court judge, prosecutors may well be discouraged from exercising this right by the possibility that, if they lose the appeal, the defendant will be acquitted.[9] Where defendants are concerned, there are also disincentives. For example, in the magistrates' court the appeal avenue to the Divisional Court by way of case stated or as an application for judicial review will generally only allow parties to appeal questions of law. A defendant who contends that the magistrates have made a factual mistake can appeal to the Crown Court. Although this right of appeal initially looks to be generous—the defendant does not need leave to appeal—there is a disincentive in that the Crown Court can increase his sentence. According to Pattenden, the power to increase sentence 'is not used very often'; however, 'this fact is probably not well known'.[10] The power may well dissuade defendants from exercising their right of appeal; indeed, some commentators suspect that it exists partly for this

---

[7] The Attorney General is able to obtain a ruling on a point of law arising in a case in which the defendant was acquitted, but this is not a true appeal as the defendant's acquittal is unaffected. The power is found in the CJA 1972, s 36.

[8] Criminal Procedure and Investigations Act 1996, s 54.

[9] Though in this respect contrast ss 58 and 62 of the CJA 2003. These provisions are discussed in more detail later.

[10] R. Pattenden, *English Criminal Appeals 1844–1994* (1996), 219. Cf *R v St Albans Crown Court, ex p Cinnamond* [1981] 2 WLR 681, where a period of driving disqualification was increased from three to 18 months.

purpose.[11] Another restriction on appeal to the Crown Court is that the right can only be exercised by those who have pleaded not guilty.[12] As we saw in Chapter 10, the vast majority of convictions at summary trial are achieved by way of guilty plea. This might not be troubling were it not for the fact that the guilty plea is not always a reliable indicator of guilt. The Crown Court has gone some way towards mitigating this rule by allowing a case where a guilty plea can be shown to be 'equivocal', or to have been made under duress, to be remitted to the magistrates for reconsideration.[13]

Turning to consider appeal to the Court of Appeal from trial in the Crown Court, we find a similar disincentive. Although the Court of Appeal does not have the power to increase sentence on a defence appeal, it can achieve something very similar. It may take several months for a defendant's appeal to be heard by the Court of Appeal. Many defendants will have spent this time in custody, and normally the time served in custody up to the failure of an appeal will be counted as part of their sentence. The Court of Appeal, however, has the power to rule that time served will not be subtracted from the sentence, as a 'loss of time' order.[14] Effectively, then, the time served is treated as an additional punishment for defendants who are thought to be wasting the court's time. While it seems that this power is used rarely, the Court of Appeal has made clear that it will use it against applications that are considered to be without merit. In *R v Fortean*, the court ordered 42 days' loss of time, considerably longer than what seemed in practice to have been the limit of 28 days. It commented:

> This court is coping, with considerable effort, with over 6,000 applications each year for leave to appeal. It is anxious to deal promptly with those which raise properly arguable grounds of appeal, whether in the end they are successful or not. It is an important feature of this jurisdiction, unlike some others, that the trial process is concluded with sentence. An appeal is not built into the trial process but must be justified on properly arguable grounds. This also means that the sentence is operative pending appeal. That reinforces the need to attend promptly to those who have appeals of arguable substance. The court's ability to do that is significantly hampered by meritless applications such as the present.... We make it clear that this power may be exercised in *any* meritless application which should never have been pursued after due warning. That counsel or solicitors have associated themselves with such a renewal will be relevant, but it will not necessarily avoid such an order if there was no justification for continuing the case.[15]

In *R v Gray*, the Court of Appeal revisited the question of when it is appropriate to make a loss of time order.[16] Citing *Fortean*, the court noted the 'pattern of unjustified renewals of applications for leave to appeal against conviction' which 'take up a wholly disproportionate amount of staff and judicial resources . . . [and] waste significant sums of public money . . .'[17] Importantly, advice of counsel to apply for leave to appeal

---

[11] Ibid; J. Sprack, *A Practical Approach to Criminal Procedure* (15th edn, 2016), 458.
[12] Magistrates' Courts Act 1980, s 108.   [13] *R v Dodd* (1982) 74 Cr App R 50.
[14] Criminal Appeal Act 1968, s 29.
[15] [2009] EWCA Crim 437, [10], [17]. See also *R v Hart* [2006] EWCA Crim 3239.
[16] [2014] EWCA Crim 2372.   [17] Ibid, [2].

does not protect applicants in precluding the making of such an order.[18] Subsequently, in *R v Jeffers* the court considered the making of a loss of time order but decided against it, instead extracting an undertaking from counsel that the decision in *Gray* be promulgated widely.[19]

As noted in previous chapters, there is a perception that more and more defendants in criminal courts are unrepresented.[20] This is particularly pronounced in relation to appeals: applications for leave to appeal lodged by applicants acting in person has continued to increase to 9.8 per cent in 2017.[21] This imposes demands in terms of case management; such applicants are often of limited means and in custody.[22] The impact of self-representation and an effort to mitigate this through the use of third party advice was considered in *R v Conaghan*, a ruling on four renewed applications for leave to appeal against conviction which were listed together because each defendant had been helped in presenting his application by a third party who was not legally qualified.[23] Hallett LJ observed that: 'It has become increasingly common in the Court of Appeal Criminal Division for the court to receive applications by unqualified third parties to represent an applicant and address the court, usually at renewed applications for leave hearings where public funding is exhausted.' Hallett LJ criticized the presentation of totally unmeritorious applications by '[t]hird parties with a personal interest in the proceedings, or with a cause they wish to advance, or simply with the best of intentions', which raise the applicant's hopes, take up a very considerable amount of the court's time and resources, and put an applicant at risk of a loss of time order.

The loss of time rule and the power to increase sentence in the Crown Court have problematic implications. Rather like the sentence discount for a guilty plea, their effect is to discourage defendants from pursuing their legal rights, even if this is in accordance with the advice of legal counsel. As with the sentence discount, the justification for this is that such powers are necessary in order to prevent the courts from being overwhelmed by unmeritorious cases. In both areas, this claim is difficult to assess: with the sentence discount there is some evidence to suggest that the number of newly contested cases would not be that great.[24] With the loss of time rule, it appears that when the court's intention to use the power was announced in a Practice Direction,[25] the number of appeals was halved.[26] What cannot be known, of course, is how many meritorious appeals are deterred. While in *Fortean* and *Gray* the Court

---

[18] Ibid, [7], citing *Hart*, [43]; renewing an application on the advice of counsel will not necessarily prevent a loss of time order.

[19] [2015] EWCA Crim 1435, [24] et seq.

[20] See Transform Justice, *Justice Denied? The experience of unrepresented defendants in the criminal courts* (2016).

[21] *In the Court of Appeal (Criminal Division) 16/17* (2018), 4. Approximate percentages for previous years are: 2016: 9.21 per cent, 2015: 6.6 per cent, 2014: 5 per cent, 2013: 3.4 per cent, and 2012: 2.53 per cent.

[22] *In the Court of Appeal (Criminal Division) 15/16* (2017), 20.

[23] *R v Conaghan and Others* [2017] EWCA Crim 597.

[24] M. Tonry, *Punishment and Politics* (2004), 87.   [25] [1970] 1 All ER 119.

[26] See *Monnell and Morris v UK* (1988) 10 EHRR 205, 30.

of Appeal justified tougher use of the loss of time rule on the grounds that it is over-whelmed, the number of applications to it by defendants has been decreasing in the last two decades. Further, in the Court of Appeal the arguments are complicated by the system of leave to appeal. Leave offers a means of filtering out the weakest cases before they result in a full court hearing, and this might be thought to be a more rational way of dealing with the possible flood of appeals than the threat of extra punishment. Of course, even the initial filtering process requires judicial resources, which are stretched, but it is doubtful that the current system makes the best use of judicial resources.[27]

The loss of time rule has been challenged before the European Court of Human Rights (ECtHR).[28] The Court held that the rule did not infringe Art 6 (fair trial) nor, more surprisingly, Art 5(1) (right to liberty and security of person). The exception in Art 5(1)(a), which allows 'lawful detention of a person after conviction by a compe-tent court', was held to apply to the loss of time rule. This, it must be said, is puzzling. The ECtHR acknowledged that this exception does not permit just any lawful deten-tion after conviction: there must be some rational connection between the convic-tion and the detention. Given that the time added to the sentence through the loss of time rule is not part of the punishment for the offence for which the defendant was convicted, it is not easy to see what this connection could be. The Court's explanation was that:

> Whilst the loss of time ordered by the Court of Appeal is not treated under domestic law as part of the applicants' sentences as such, it does form part of the period of detention which results from the overall sentencing procedure that follows conviction. As a matter of English law, a sentence of imprisonment passed by a Crown Court is to be served subject to any order which the Court of Appeal may, in the event of an unsuccessful application for leave to appeal, make as to loss of time.[29]

The difficulty here is that this reasoning could be used to justify any further deten-tion ordered after conviction: if, after an unsuccessful appeal, it was the practice of the Court of Appeal to toss a coin as a means of deciding whether or not to double the appellant's sentence, this too could be said to be one of the conditions understood to be imposed by a Crown Court sentence. Subsequent decisions of the ECtHR have taken a rather tougher line to the use of detention as a means of controlling appeals processes, and the decision in *Monnell* might now be subject to rethinking.[30]

As has been pointed out, the requirement for leave to appeal is in principle a more rational way of dealing with the problem of a flood of appeals. The system works as follows. A convicted defendant needs to obtain leave before his appeal will be heard by the Court of Appeal. This can be obtained from the judge who tried him but, as the

---

[27] See J. Spencer, 'Does our Present Criminal Appeals System Make Sense?' [2006] *Crim LR* 677.
[28] *Monnell and Morris v UK*, n 26.   [29] Ibid, 46.
[30] B. Emmerson, A. Ashworth, and A. Macdonald, *Human Rights and Criminal Justice* (3rd edn, 2012), 900–1.

Table 12.1 Convictions and applications for leave to appeal

Year	Number of defendants convicted after a not guilty plea in trial cases in the Crown Court	Number of applications for leave to appeal against conviction received by the Court of Appeal	Number of applications for leave to appeal against conviction considered and granted by single judge in the Court of Appeal	Percentage of applications for leave to appeal against conviction granted by single judge in the Court of Appeal
2010	11,957	1,488	242	16.3
2011	12,275	1,535	221	14.4
2012	12,490	1,697	252	14.8
2013	11,518	1,554	168	10.8
2014	11,121	1,419	153	10.8
2015	12,106	1,517	196	13.1
2016	11,655	1,368	67	4.9
2017	11,238	1,264	79	6.3

Source: *Royal Courts of Justice Annual Tables—2017*, Table 3.7, and *Criminal court statistics quarterly*, Table AC8.

appeal will often involve some criticism of the judge, it is more common for appellants to apply to the Court of Appeal for leave to appeal. When an application is made, it will first be considered by a single judge. If the application is unsuccessful at this stage, it can be renewed; the renewed application is considered by the 'full court': a panel of two or three judges sitting in open court. If leave to appeal is granted, the appeal proceeds to a full hearing by the Court of Appeal.

In 2017, about 11 per cent of all those convicted in the Crown Court sought leave to appeal against their convictions. The proportion of applications for leave granted by the single judge is declining (see Table 12.1).

Of the large majority that is refused, around one-third make a renewed application to the full court. On this renewed attempt to get leave, between one-fifth and one-third were successful. All of these proportions have been declining in the past decade (see Table 12.2).

It is not obvious what to make of these figures: there is no telling what is a reasonable overall success rate, though the decline in the percentage granted by a single judge and of the success of appeals is noteworthy. What is also significant is that many who have their applications turned down by the single judge persist and have a reasonable chance of success on the renewed application to the full court. This suggests that the initial stage, where the application is considered by a single judge, is somewhat haphazard. Other evidence supports this. JUSTICE, a body with considerable experience of miscarriage of justice cases, suggested that the process 'is regarded as particularly

Table 12.2 Applications for leave to appeal

	Number of applications renewed	Number of applications to renew granted by Full Court	Number of appeals allowed	Percentage of appeals allowed from total applications for leave to appeal received by the Court of Appeal
2010	370	148	187	12.6
2011	425	167	196	12.8
2012	495	110	151	8.9
2013	437	94	110	7.1
2014	442	136	147	10.4
2015	556	70	125	8.2
2016	321	73	90	6.6
2017	358	62	64	5.1

Source: Royal Courts of Justice Annual Tables—2017, Tables 3.7 and 3.8.

susceptible to inconsistency'.[31] In his review of the criminal courts, Lord Justice Auld drew attention to some of the problems with the system: the single judge is required to consider applications for leave 'out of normal court sitting hours and in addition to preparatory work for each day's sitting.... The norm is that they are done in the evenings, sometimes over the weekend and during vacation periods.'[32] It seems that the system is not properly resourced, and it is therefore not surprising that inconsistent decisions are made at the initial stage. The marked decrease in applications granted by a single judge in the Court of Appeal in 2016 and 2017 is also cause for concern.

Returning to appeals from the magistrates' court to the Crown Court, it is worth looking at the available figures to see how they compare with those for the Court of Appeal. In 2017, the Crown Court heard 13,251 appeals against conviction from 10,187 appellants: this represents less than 1 per cent of all those found guilty in the magistrates' courts. In 42 per cent, the appeal was allowed.[33] It is obvious that the rate of appeal is very low, and it is likely that some innocent defendants do not pursue an appeal.[34] This may in part be due to the fear of an increased sentence and perhaps also to poor legal advice, but it may also be due to defendants simply not perceiving it worthwhile to appeal against a conviction, especially if the punishment has been slight. Beyond these figures, and the inferences that can be drawn from them, little is known

---

[31] *Remedying Miscarriages of Justice* (1994), 8.

[32] Auld LJ, *Review of the Criminal Courts of England and Wales: Report* (2001), 639.

[33] Ministry of Justice, *Criminal court statistics quarterly, England and Wales, January to March 2018 (annual 2017)* (2018), Table C8.

[34] See K. Malleson and S. Roberts, 'Streamlining and Clarifying the Appellate Process' [2002] *Crim LR* 272, 274.

about the appellate process in the Crown Court. This remains an under-researched area of the criminal process.

12.2 CHALLENGING JURY VERDICTS

Our focus now turns to the Court of Appeal, where it will remain for much of the rest of the chapter. When the Royal Commission on Criminal Justice reported in 1993, considerable critical attention was focused on the Court of Appeal. The court was seen to have played a key role in the long-running miscarriage of justice cases that were finally rectified in the late 1980s and early 1990s. The Birmingham Six and Guildford Four had both had appeals dismissed by the court soon after their convictions; the Birmingham Six had also had a second appeal turned down in 1986. There was a widespread perception that the Court of Appeal had been unduly sceptical of claims of miscarriage of justice during the 1980s, and that some defendants had had their appeals dismissed unjustly.[35] Connected to this complaint that the court has been oversceptical is a criticism that it has tended to show too much deference to jury verdicts, in other words, that the court is reluctant to interfere with a jury's decision to convict a defendant. There is a good deal of truth in the claim that the court shows considerable deference to the jury.[36] But, as Pattenden observes, the Court of Appeal is also reluctant to overturn findings of fact by a trial judge (as when a judge makes a preliminary finding of fact when making an admissibility decision).[37] Indeed, the Court of Appeal even shows considerable deference to its own previous decisions when a defendant appeals his conviction for a second time.[38] There seems to be a general reluctance to challenge the factual (as opposed to legal) decisions of criminal courts, whereas civil appeal courts play a more interventionist role. There are various possible reasons for the reluctance on the criminal side; some of these apply more to jury decisions than to the decisions of judges. First, the Court of Appeal is at a disadvantage in relation to the trial court. The trial court will have seen and heard the witnesses in the case, whereas the Court of Appeal will only have access to the transcript of the original trial. While the court may hear some live evidence, its role is restricted to that of reviewing the case, rather than rehearing it. Further, the jury does not give reasons for its decisions, thus the Court of Appeal lacks access to the precise reasons why the jury became convinced of the defendant's guilt. Secondly, the jury plays a crucial role in the criminal justice system, deciding whether or not defendants are guilty in the most serious contested cases. The criminal justice system puts considerable trust in the jury to make these

---

[35] On the appeal of the Birmingham Six, see C. Mullin, *Error of Judgement* (1990), chs 41–4. More generally, see J. Rozenberg, 'Miscarriages of Justice' in E. Stockdale and S. Casale (eds), *Criminal Justice under Stress* (1992); A. Zuckerman, 'Miscarriage of Justice and Judicial Responsibility' [1991] *Crim LR* 492.

[36] This is made plain in *Pendleton* [2001] UKHL 66.

[37] R. Pattenden, 'The Standard of Review for Mistake of Fact in the Court of Appeal, Criminal Division' [2009] *Crim LR* 15.

[38] See *R v Stock* [2008] EWCA Crim 1862.

decisions, as it does in judges to conduct trials properly. If the Court of Appeal interfered with trial verdicts too readily, it would put itself in the uncomfortable position of
questioning the ability of trial courts to reach correct verdicts: it might be thought to
be undermining the very system which it oversees. A third reason why the court may
be reluctant to interfere with decisions of trial courts, and its own previous decisions,
is finality: there is some value in seeing the verdict as an authoritative ruling on a disputed issue; this allows interested parties to get on with their lives with a clear view of
their legal position. If verdicts are too readily overturned, then this sense of finality will
be eroded. Finally, as we have already seen, the Court of Appeal is very conscious of the
finite resources in the criminal justice system. If verdicts were overturned too readily,
there might be more appeals.

It is not surprising, then, that the Royal Commission on Criminal Justice commented that:

> In its approach to the consideration of appeals against conviction, the Court of Appeal
> seems to us to have been too heavily influenced by the role of the jury in Crown Court
> trials. Ever since 1907, commentators have detected a reluctance on the part of the Court
> of Appeal to consider whether a jury has reached a wrong decision. This impression is un-
> derlined by research conducted on our behalf. This shows that most appeals are allowed on
> the basis of errors at the trial, usually in the judge's summing up. We are all of the opinion
> that the Court of Appeal should be readier to overturn jury verdicts than it has shown itself
> to be in the past.[39]

In the aftermath of the Royal Commission's report, there were a number of changes to
the appeals system. The Criminal Cases Review Commission (CCRC) was established
to take over the role of the Home Office in investigating miscarriages of justice and
referring cases back to the Court of Appeal where defendants have exhausted their
normal appeal rights. There were also modifications to the Criminal Appeal Act 1968,
which governs the powers of the Court of Appeal. The Act now provides that the Court
of Appeal 'shall allow an appeal against conviction if they think the conviction is unsafe' and shall 'dismiss such an appeal in any other case'.[40] The Act also made changes
to the court's power to hear 'fresh' evidence. As noted earlier, the Court of Appeal is
basically a court of review: it does not rehear cases. But sometimes new evidence will
emerge after the conclusion of a trial, throwing doubt on the original verdict. Here,
the question arises whether the Court of Appeal should hear such 'fresh' evidence.
There is some concern that a defendant will simply fail to call important evidence at
his initial trial, knowing that, should he be convicted, he will be able to challenge the
verdict on appeal by revealing the evidence then, or that a convicted defendant could
attempt to circumvent the restriction on calling fresh evidence by trial by deploying
one defence against a jury, and if this fails dismiss the original counsel and then bring

---

[39] Royal Commission on Criminal Justice, *Report* (1993), 162.
[40] Criminal Appeal Act 1968, s 2(1). The amendments were introduced by the Criminal Appeal Act 1995.

in new counsel to put an alternative defence in front of the Court of Appeal or retrial.[41] For this reason, the reception of fresh evidence is not automatic; the court will be very reluctant to admit it if it could have been adduced at the original trial. The Royal Commission criticized the Court of Appeal for being too reluctant to admit fresh evidence, and the Criminal Appeal Act now provides that the court should hear fresh evidence where this is 'necessary or expedient in the interests of justice', having regard to a number of factors such as 'whether the evidence appears to the court to be capable of belief' and 'whether there is a reasonable explanation for failure to adduce the evidence' at the original trial.[42]

The legal framework described in the previous paragraph obviously leaves considerable discretion to the Court of Appeal. Before examining how the court approaches conviction appeals, one more aspect of its powers needs to be mentioned. If the court decides that a conviction is unsafe, that does not necessarily mean that the appellant will go free. Since 1964, the court has had the power to order a retrial.[43] Thus, if there remain doubts about the appellant's guilt, he can be retried by a new jury. Most appeals to the Court of Appeal where it has to decide whether the interests of justice require a retrial concern questions including whether the alleged offence is sufficiently serious to justify a retrial; whether, if re-convicted, the appellant would be likely to serve a significant period or further period in custody; the appellant's age and health; and the wishes of the victim of the alleged offence.[44] Retrial will not always be appropriate: there may have been such a lapse of time since the original trial that it is no longer practical. In some cases, there will have been such media attention around the case that there will be doubts about the fairness of a new trial.[45]

Retrials are used with some frequency, being ordered in between one-quarter and two-fifths of the appeals allowed since 2010 (see Table 12.3).[46]

The jurisdiction to permit a second retrial must be exercised with extreme caution,[47] and a second retrial should be confined to the very small number of cases in which the crime was of extreme gravity and the evidence against the defendant very powerful.[48] While this two-part test would usually suffice in identifying where the interests of justice lay, a wider consideration stretching beyond those factors might sometimes be required.[49] Where the case did not involve murder, particularly strong justification would be needed to satisfy the test of extreme gravity.[50]

---

[41] *R v Smith* [2013] EWCA Crim 2388, [90].

[42] Criminal Appeal Act 1968, s 23. As observed in *Erskine* [2009] EWCA Crim 1425 (at [39]) 'the discretion to receive fresh evidence is a wide one focusing on the interests of justice'. See A. Roberts, 'Evidence: *R. v Avorgah (Moise)* Commentary' [2016] *Crim LR* 491.

[43] The history of this reform is described in R. Nobles and D. Schiff, *Understanding Miscarriages of Justice* (2000), 62–4. See J. Chalmers and F. Leverick, 'When Should a Retrial be Permitted After a Conviction is Quashed on Appeal?' (2001) 74 *MLR* 721–49.

[44] *R v Maxwell* [2010] UKSC 48, [20].   [45] On the approach to this, see *Stone* [2001] *Crim LR* 465.

[46] *Judicial and Court Statistics 2008*, Table 1.7.

[47] *R v Bell* [2010] EWCA Crim 3.   [48] [46].

[49] *R v Burton* [2015] EWCA Crim 1307, [22].   [50] [31].

Table 12.3 Successful appeals against conviction in which retrial ordered

	Number of appeals against conviction allowed	Number of retrials ordered	Percentage of successful appeals against conviction in which retrials is ordered
2010	187	56	29.9
2011	196	52	26.5
2012	151	39	25.8
2013	110	40	36.4
2014	147	40	27.2
2015	125	60	48
2016	90	42	46.7
2017	64	26	40.6

Source: *Royal Courts of Justice Annual Tables—2017*, Table 3.8.

R v Maxwell remains the only appeal to Supreme Court (or indeed to the House of Lords) from a decision to order a retrial.[51] It is an unsatisfactory decision. M's original convictions for murder and robbery had been quashed on the ground of prosecutorial misconduct, following an unchallenged finding by the CCRC that the police had deceived the trial court by concealing, and lying about, the provision of improper payments and benefits to a key informer in exchange for his evidence. The behaviour of the police was egregious, ongoing, and endemic. The Court of Appeal quashed M's convictions, finding that had the trial judge known about the police misconduct, he might either have stayed the prosecution as an abuse of process or excluded the informer's evidence. However, it also found that M had made post-conviction admissions which constituted clear and compelling evidence of his guilt, and so ordered a retrial.

A divided Supreme Court dismissed M's appeal against the Court of Appeal's decision. The appeal was dismissed by Lords Dyson, Rodger, and Mance. The question of whether a retrial was required in the interests of justice was an exercise of judgement in which a number of relevant factors had to be weighed in the balance:

> a decision under section 7 of the 1968 Act as to whether the interests of justice require a retrial calls for an exercise of judgment which should only be upset on appeal if it was plainly wrong in the sense that it is one which no reasonable court could have made or if the court took into account immaterial factors or failed to take into account material factors.[52]

Lord Dyson reiterated that it is not the function of the criminal courts to refuse a retrial on the grounds of misconduct so as to mark disapproval and to discipline the police.[53] He followed the finding of the Court of Appeal that while the evidence without

---

[51] [2010] UKSC 48.   [52] [19] per Lord Rodger.   [53] [24].

which there would be no order for a retrial consisted of admissions which the appellant would not have made but for the original misconduct which led to his conviction
and failed appeal, it was not determinative of whether a retrial was required.[54] The
Court of Appeal had carried out a difficult balancing exercise, weighing up 'appalling
misconduct by the police', which, had it been known at the time of the trial, would
not have resulted in the conviction, and a particularly shocking and serious alleged
offence, and new and compelling evidence untainted by the prosecutorial misconduct.
Lord Dyson concluded that the Court of Appeal was 'right to respect the strength of
the public interest in seeing that that those against whom there is prima facie admissible evidence that they are guilty of crimes, especially very serious crimes, are tried.
This public interest is all the greater where, as in the present case, there is compelling
evidence of guilt.'[55]

In a robust dissent, Lord Brown stated that to describe police misconduct on this
scale merely as shocking and disgraceful downplayed the gravity of its impact upon
the integrity of the prosecution process. He found it hard to imagine a worse case of
sustained dishonesty designed to secure a conviction at all costs.[56] Moreover, but for
the prosecutorial misconduct which initially ensured M's conviction and then ensured
the failure of his appeal, he would never have made the admissions upon which it was
sought to prosecute him afresh.[57] This led Lord Brown to conclude that it would be
inappropriate to retry on fresh evidence, given the 'but for' character of this case and
the enormity of the unpunished police misconduct.[58] Lord Collins stressed in dissent
that though the power not to order a retrial should not be used as a form of discipline,
the 'interests of justice' are not limited to the individual case. The police misconduct
must be seen in the wider context of the preservation of the rule of law, and of public
confidence in the criminal justice system.[59]

As we have seen, in 1993 the Royal Commission urged the Court of Appeal to overturn jury verdicts more readily. One way of trying to assess whether there has been any
change in the court's attitude since then is to look at the statistics. In the early 1990s,
about one-third of applications were granted leave to appeal. Once in front of the full
court, about 43 per cent of appeals were allowed. By 2010, slightly fewer were granted
leave (23 per cent) and there was a similar success rate once in front of the court.
Since then, the proportion granted leave has decreased still further and fluctuates in
the teens, with a low of 11 per cent in 2017, of which around one-third are successful.
All of this suggests that the court is becoming more reluctant to overturn jury verdicts,
rather than more inclined to do so (see Table 12.4).

When it comes to the introduction of fresh evidence, it again seems that the Court of
Appeal's working practices have changed little. Roberts has replicated the Royal Commission research, by examining 300 appeals heard by the court in 2002, and again in

---

[54] [26].   [55] [34].   [56] [83] per Lord Brown.   [57] [102].   [58] [105].
[59] [115] per Lord Collins.

Table 12.4 Results of appeals heard by Full Court

Year	Number of appeals against conviction allowed by Full Court	Number of appeals against conviction heard by Full Court dismissed
2010	187	309
2011	196	307
2012	151	241
2013	110	236
2014	147	228
2015	125	180
2016	90	162
2017	64	126

Source: *Royal Courts of Justice Annual Tables—2017*, Table 3.8.

the first six months of 2016.[60] She found that fresh evidence was a ground of appeal in more cases than it had been in 1990: 23 grounds of appeal from 300 cases in 1990 involved fresh evidence, compared with 37 in 2002, and 42 in 2016. Given that all of these cases had passed the leave stage, it suggests that the court is, in some sense, being more receptive to fresh evidence (this issue is very hard to be precise about, because the court sometimes hears fresh evidence '*de bene esse*', that is, without specifying whether it passes the test in s 23, but may then declare the fresh evidence unconvincing). While the increasing number of appeals based on fresh evidence is potentially evidence of a more liberal approach to the leave filter, Roberts notes that the majority of fresh evidence appeals in the 2016 sample were renewed applications to appeal having initially being rejected by the single judge and therefore were still seeking leave to appeal.[61] The evidence was admitted by the court in eight of the 42 cases (19 per cent) in 2016 which is significantly lower than 61 per cent in 1990. This suggests that the court is much more restrictive than it was in 1990. Moreover, 20 of the appeals in 2016 were non-counsel applications and in many of those the applicant had drafted his or her own grounds of appeal.

Roberts found that fresh evidence was a slightly less successful ground of appeal in 2002 than in 1990 (a 27 per cent success rate as compared to 35 per cent in 1990). Of the eight appeals where fresh evidence was admitted in 2016, just one was allowed and seven were dismissed. In two cases, a retrial was ordered. In 2016, the number of appeals which succeeded on the basis of fresh evidence was very small, at 2 per cent of the total fresh evidence cases and 0.3 per cent of all 300 cases.[62]

[60] S. Roberts, 'The Royal Commission on Criminal Justice and Factual Innocence' (2004) 1 *JUSTICE Journal* 86, 91; S. Roberts 'Fresh Evidence and Factual Innocence in the Criminal Division of the Court of Appeal' (2017) 81 *J Crim L* 303.
[61] Ibid, 319.　　[62] Ibid, 320.

It is obvious that an argument from fresh evidence is a relatively rare ground of appeal, making up only around 7 per cent of grounds in 2010.[63] As the Royal Commission noted, appeals are far more likely to be successful where it is argued that a (legal) error was made at trial. It is especially difficult for a defendant to mount a successful appeal when he can point to no error at trial and has no fresh evidence. Such appeals are often referred to as 'lurking doubt' appeals.[64] The appellant is basically arguing that the jury made a mistake on the evidence as was presented to it at trial, and here one would expect the court to be most sensitive about its role in relation to that of the jury. Roberts found this ground of appeal referred to in seven of the 300 appeals from 2002, and in only one of these was it successful.[65] Following the decision in *R v Pope*, it seems even less unlikely that this ground will be deployed.[66] The court held that only in the 'most exceptional circumstances' would a conviction be quashed on this ground alone, and 'even more exceptional' if the attention of the court is confined to a re-examination of the material before the jury.[67] Unsurprisingly, there is no mention of lurking doubt in Roberts's 2016 study.

In a fresh evidence appeal, an appellant is on firmer ground. His argument is not that the jury simply got it wrong, but that there is evidence, never heard by the jury, which makes the conviction unsafe. This raises the question of how the Court of Appeal should react to the fresh evidence, as was considered by the House of Lords in *Pendleton*.[68] The question is sometimes said to involve a choice between a 'jury impact' test, which considers whether the fresh evidence might have had an impact on the trial jury, and a test whereby the Court of Appeal concentrates on its own re-action to the evidence. The previous authority, *Stafford*, had rejected the jury impact test; rather the court should come to it its own view of the significance and credibility of the evidence.[69] It is not always easy to see the difference between these two approaches. The sort of difference the particular test might make is alluded to in *Stafford*, where it was noted that the appellant had 'urged that the court should recognise that reasonable men can come to different conclusions on contested issues of fact and that, although the court came to the conclusion that the fresh evidence raised no reasonable doubt as to the guilt of the accused, they should nonetheless quash the conviction if they thought that a jury might reasonably take a different view.'[70] That there is an issue worth arguing about here is also hinted at by the Royal Commission, which contended that *Stafford* was open to criticism 'insofar as it concerns a decision by the court to hear and evaluate itself the fresh evidence and despite it to reject the appeal. In our view, once the court has decided to receive evidence that is relevant and capable of belief, and which could have altered the outcome of the case, it should quash the conviction and order a retrial unless that is not practicable or desirable.'[71]

---

[63] More recent data are not available. In response to an FOI request in August 2018, the Ministry of Justice stated that it does not hold such information.

[64] See L. Leigh, 'Lurking Doubt and the Safety of Convictions' [2006] *Crim LR* 809.

[65] See n 60.   [66] [2012] EWCA Crim 2241.

[67] [14].   [68] [2001] UKHL 66.   [69] *Stafford v DPP* [1973] 3 All ER 763, 765.

[70] Ibid, 765.   [71] See n 39, 175.

Presumably evidence can be capable of belief even if the court itself does not believe it. Under the Royal Commission's approach, it seems that the court would avoid taking a view on the credibility of a witness called to present fresh evidence (rather along the lines of *Galbraith*[72]). Where, however, a retrial is impracticable, the Commission thought that the only approach was to follow *Stafford*, and to allow the court to decide the issue for itself.

The simplest thing to say about *Pendleton* is that it rejects the criticisms of the Royal Commission and follows *Stafford*. The outcome is that the court should come to its own view of the safety of the conviction, and therefore the question of the practicality of a retrial does not arise until it is decided whether or not the conviction should be quashed. The appellant had argued that this approach undermined the role of the jury: only the jury impact test truly recognized the centrality of the jury in trial on indictment. The response of the House of Lords was that this got things the wrong way round: the real way to respect the jury was to be rather more reluctant to overturn its verdict. According to Lord Hobhouse, 'it is the appellant's argument which is unprincipled since it is he who is seeking to escape from the verdict of a jury merely upon the possibility... that the jury might have returned a different verdict'.[73] Lord Hobhouse distanced himself from the jury impact test.[74] Lord Bingham's judgment, however, with which the other judges expressed agreement, was more equivocal. While endorsing *Stafford*, Lord Bingham suggested that the jury impact test might have some use:

> First, it reminds the Court of Appeal that it is not and should never become the primary decision-maker. Secondly, it reminds the Court of Appeal that it has an imperfect and incomplete understanding of the full processes which led the jury to convict. The Court of Appeal can make its assessment of the fresh evidence it has heard, but save in a clear case it is at a disadvantage in seeking to relate that evidence to the rest of the evidence which the jury heard. For these reasons it will usually be wise for the Court of Appeal, in a case of any difficulty, to test their own provisional view by asking whether the evidence, if given at the trial, might reasonably have affected the decision of the trial jury to convict. If it might, the conviction must be thought to be unsafe.[75]

Evidently *Pendleton* left some uncertainty over the question of what approach should be taken to fresh evidence cases. It is therefore unsurprising to find varying approaches in the later Court of Appeal case law. One of the first cases to consider *Pendleton* was *Hakala*,[76] which associated itself with the more restrictive approach of Lord Hobhouse rather than the jury impact dicta of Lord Bingham. *Pendleton* was interpreted as simply confirming the decision in *Stafford*. But in other cases it has been said that after *Pendleton* the test is whether the jury would inevitably have convicted.[77] That view echoes the jury impact line, but lies in stark contrast to Auld LJ's statement in *Maloney* that: 'The issue is not whether the Court considers, in the light of the proposed fresh

---

[72] [1989] 1 WLR 1039; see discussion in Ch 11.
[73] See n 68, [36].   [74] Ibid, [32].   [75] Ibid, [19].   [76] [2002] EWCA Crim 730.
[77] See *Gray* [2003] EWCA 1001 at 13; *Ward* [2003] EWCA Crim 3191 at 9.

evidence, that a jury might conceivably have reached a different decision if it had heard it. So,...the Court should beware against adopting, consciously or unconsciously, a train of thought that unless they can be certain the jury would have convicted had they heard the proffered fresh evidence, the conviction must be unsafe.'[78]

Pendleton was considered by the Privy Council in *Dial v Trinidad*. The majority judgment (with which, significantly, Lord Bingham agreed), stressed that *Pendleton* had decided that the Court of Appeal should take its own view of cases involving fresh evidence:

> Where fresh evidence is adduced on a criminal appeal it is for the Court of Appeal, assuming always that it accepts it, to evaluate its importance in the context of the remainder of the evidence in the case. If the court concludes that the fresh evidence raises no reasonable doubt as to the guilt of the accused it will dismiss the appeal. The primary question is for the court itself and is not what effect the fresh evidence would have had on the mind of the jury. That said, if the court regards the case as a difficult one, it may find it helpful to test its view 'by asking whether the evidence, if given at the trial, might reasonably have affected the decision of the trial jury to convict'.[79]

Despite the decision in *Dial* (which the Lord Chief Justice drew to the attention of the CCRC[80]), one can still find references in the case law to the proper test being the possible impact of the fresh evidence on the jury.[81]

There seems to be a move away from this, exemplified in *R v Burridge* where the court concluded with 'no doubt' that both in *Stafford* and *Pendleton* the House of Lords 'rejected the proposition that the jury impact test was determinative, explaining that it was only a mechanism in a difficult case for the Court of Appeal to "test its view" as to the safety of a conviction'.[82] Indeed, it underlined that Lord Bingham was part of the majority judgment articulated by Lord Brown in *Dial*. In *Ahmed*, the court rejected the submission that a conviction would be rendered unsafe by the existence of material which the jury did not have and which might have affected its decision, stating that 'in most cases of arguably relevant fresh evidence it will be impossible to be 100 per cent sure that it might not possibly have had some impact on the jury's deliberations, since *ex hypoethesi* the jury has not seen the fresh material. The question which matters is whether the fresh material causes this court to doubt the safety of the verdict of guilty.'[83]

In *R v Noye*, the court stated that its approach should now be regarded as settled, recounting the line of authority.[84] Subsequently, in *O'Donnell v R* the court described whether or not the material submitted might have affected the jury's verdict, as 'not

---

[78] [2003] EWCA Crim 1373 at 45.

[79] *Dial and Another v State of Trinidad and Tobago* [2005] UKPC 4, [31], quoting *Pendleton*.

[80] See L. Elks, *Righting Miscarriages of Justice? Ten Years of the Criminal Cases Review Commission* (2008), 68–9.

[81] E.g. *R v Carter* [2009] EWCA Crim 1739; *R v F* [2008] EWCA Crim 2014; *R v Kennedy* [2007] EWCA Crim 3132.

[82] [2010] EWCA Crim 2847, [101].   [83] [2010] EWCA Crim 2899, [24].

[84] *Noye* [2011] EWCA Crim 650, [25].

the acid test on appeal but only an advisable cross-check', citing *Pendleton*.[85] This 'well trodden line of authority' was applied in the content of fresh evidence based on scientific advances in *George v R*, a case that hinged on circumstantial evidence.[86] The court concluded that 'in the light of the new material, we are not prepared to conclude that these verdicts remain safe: the fresh evidence might reasonably have affected the decision of the trial jury'.[87]

The relevant test(s) to be applied relation in relation to an appeal based on fresh evidence due to the non-disclosure of evidence was considered in *R v Garland*.[88] As the Supreme Court stated in *McInnes v HM Advocate* in relation to the consequence of any failure to disclose: 'The test that should be applied is whether, taking all the circumstances of the trial into account, there is a real possibility that the jury would have arrived at a different verdict.'[89] Though *Pendleton*, *Burridge*, and *Ahmed* were cases of fresh evidence and not of non-disclosure, this was not material when determining the test to be applied, as in both instances the evidence in question was not before the jury.[90] The court in *Garland* neatly resolved any issues in the case law, stating that 'We do not consider that there is any inconsistency between these two lines of authority. Any apparent differences are, in our view, a matter of emphasis.'[91]

One might wonder how much is at stake here. Commentators presume that the jury impact approach is more liberal, and more likely to result in a successful appeal, but the difference between the approaches can seem very thin: as it was put in *Pendleton*: 'If the Court has no reasonable doubt about the verdict, it follows that the Court does not think that the jury could have one; and, conversely, if the Court says that a jury might in the light of the new evidence have a reasonable doubt, that means that the Court has a reasonable doubt.'[92] There are, however, cases where *Pendleton* has been used to justify a decision which might not otherwise have been made. An appeal in *Mills and Poole* had been heard by the Court of Appeal in 1996 and dismissed. In 2002, the CCRC referred the case back to the court, giving as one of its reasons for doing so the decision in *Pendleton*. In considering the new appeal, which was allowed, *Pendleton* appears to have made the court particularly cautious about making its own judgements as to the credibility of witnesses.[93] In *R v CCRC, ex p Farnell*,[94] an application for judicial review of a decision by the CCRC not to refer a case to the Court of Appeal was successful; *Pendleton* was again used to justify the decision. The case in question involved a claim of provocation. The Commission had expressed the view that the Court of Appeal was unlikely to find the defendant's actions excusable, but the High Court called attention to passages in *Pendleton* where the Court of Appeal was warned not to trespass on the

---

[85] [2012] EWCA Crim 2393, [35]. Pendleton's 'risk assessment' was applied recently in *R v Pabon* [2018] EWCA Crim 420, [72].

[86] *George v R* [2014] EWCA Crim 2507.   [87] [52].   [88] *R v Garland* [2016] EWCA Crim 1743.

[89] *McInnes v HM Advocate* [2010] UKSC 7, [19]–[20] cited in *R v Kelly* [2015] EWCA Crim 500, [42]. See Ch 9.

[90] *Garland* [2016] EWCA Crim 1743, [50].   [91] [52].   [92] See n 68, [15].

[93] See *R v Mills and another (No 2)* [2004] 1 Cr App R 7 at 79, 83.

[94] [2003] EWHC 835 (Admin).

jury's territory. It seems the Commission should have asked whether the Court of Appeal might find that *a jury* could consider Farnell's actions excusable.

This review of the Court of Appeal's case law in the aftermath of *Pendleton* might suggest that all is chaos. There is something to that view. Certainly the Court of Appeal have found it difficult to explain how they approach fresh evidence. Beneath the conflicting dicta, however, there is probably a reasonable degree of consistency. Much depends on the overall strength of the case against a defendant. If the court has some doubt about the safety of the conviction, then, as in *Mills and Poole*, *Pendleton* may be used as a justification for allowing the appeal. Where there is less doubt, the court may feel no need to consider the jury's view of things. It may also feel able to decide for itself a reasonably self-contained issue, such as whether new expert evidence is convincing. But some appeals raise wider issues: in *Pendleton*, the defendant's defence had never been put before the jury, and in *Mills and Poole* there were questions about several aspects of the prosecution case. Here, the court is likely to be aware of its role as a court of review: it cannot easily make judgements about witnesses it has never seen, or about how new lines of defence affect the case as a whole. Reference to the jury's perspective is a means of explaining this difficulty. 'It all depends on the facts' is often an unsatisfactory way of summarizing a complex area of case law, but there is considerable truth in it here.

This leaves a question at a more conceptual level. The debate about *Stafford* and *Pendleton* is partly a theoretical one. Lord Devlin was highly critical of the decision in *Stafford* because he believed it undermined the role of the jury.[95] We saw earlier that the Royal Commission on Criminal Justice, too, thought the *Stafford* approach wrong. But, unless the wide use of retrials is advocated—and they will often be impractical or, worse, put an innocent defendant in jeopardy—it is hard to see how the Court of Appeal deciding the case on its own view of the merits undermines the jury. The original jury cannot be asked for its opinion, so a decision has to be made somehow. The argument might be that, because we do not know why the jury convicted, we should presume that the fresh evidence might have made a difference. That seems to be an argument that the defendant should be given the benefit of any doubt. But the law only requires that defendants be given the benefit of reasonable doubt, and whether there is a reasonable doubt is precisely the question the Court of Appeal, under *Stafford* and *Dial*, should be asking itself. There is no reason of principle for adopting the jury impact test; indeed, to adopt it on grounds of respect for the jury would seem to rule out allowing appeals on the basis of lurking doubt when there is no new evidence, and we would not advocate that. But where the jury impact test may be useful is in guarding against the sort of approach the Court of Appeal took to notorious cases such as the Birmingham Six appeals, where it would do its best to explain away any flaw revealed in the prosecution evidence.[96] In *Dial*, Lord Steyn ended his dissenting judgment with

---

[95] Devlin, *The Judge* (1979), 148–76.

[96] See R. Nobles and D. Schiff, *Understanding Miscarriages of Justice* (2000), ch 5.

a rhetorical flourish, criticizing the judge who had upheld the defendants' convictions: 'It is always important for a judge to bear in mind what Learned Hand J in his famous address during the Second World War, in Central Park, New York City, called the spirit of liberty. He said that the spirit of liberty is the spirit which is not too sure that it is right. The need for such an approach is immeasurably increased where the issue at stake is killing a man by the cruel and barbaric punishment of the death penalty. This spirit is not evident in the judgment of de la Bastide CJ. Instead his judgment is expressed in certainties and absolutes with some questionable and speculative assumptions in favour of the State.'[97]

When judging the performance of the Court of Appeal whether the court is taking an unduly sceptical attitude to fresh evidence seems the better question to ask than whether it should adopt a jury impact or some other test. Whether the court is being too sceptical is very difficult to judge. The court might be criticized for building considerable flexibility into its approach to appeals, but it is not so easy to say whether this leads it to uphold convictions that it should not. However, in at least one relatively recent appeal there were signs of the court taking the sort of attitude criticized by Lord Steyn. *Stock* involved a long-running allegation of miscarriage of justice.[98] Stock had been convicted of robbery in 1970. His case was considered by the Court of Appeal for the fourth time in 2008, this being the second time that it had been referred to the Court of Appeal by the CCRC. The Court of Appeal put considerable weight on its earlier judgments, and on occasion indulged in some rather speculative interpretations of the evidence.[99] The fact that evidence relied on by the appellant involved events being recollected that took place a long time before was held against him.[100] Elks, a former member of the CCRC, suggests that the decision in *Stock* echoes the sort of attitude to miscarriages of justice evident in cases such as the Birmingham Six.[101] It would be too hasty to conclude that the Court of Appeal has slipped back to the dark days of the 1980s, but given its track record, its judgments in appeals against conviction require constant and critical scrutiny. Tony Stock died in 2012, still maintaining his innocence.

12.3 DUE PROCESS APPEALS

In the previous section we concentrated on cases where the appellant's argument is basically that he is innocent, and that the jury came to a mistaken factual conclusion. In this section we discuss another type of appeal, where the defendant's principal contention is that there has been a failure of due process at trial and that, because of this, his conviction should be quashed whether or not he is guilty. Appeals of this type are dealt

---

[97] See n 79, [64].

[98] [2008] EWCA Crim 1862. See also *R v Pinfold* [2009] EWCA Crim 2339, though there the Court of Appeal's decision is perhaps less open to criticism.

[99] Ibid, [55]–[56].　　　[100] Ibid, [46].　　　[101] L. Elks, *R v Stock* (2008) 9 *Arch News* 3.

with under the same statutory framework as the 'fact' appeals considered previously: in other words, the Court of Appeal should quash the conviction if it is 'unsafe'. This is a slightly strange test to apply to due process appeals. Before 1995, the test was in terms of whether the conviction was 'unsafe *or unsatisfactory*'. The revised wording followed a recommendation of the Royal Commission and was intended to simplify the language of the statute. It was not intended to change the practice of the Court of Appeal which had previously been prepared to allow due process appeals.[102] In the event, however, the new test led to some uncertainty about the Court of Appeal's powers. The tensions in the case law reflect not just differing views on the statutory language, but also deeper matters of principle.

The issues are well illustrated by the facts and decision in *Chalkley and Jeffries*.[103] The defendants were charged with conspiracy to rob. The principal evidence against them was a tape recording of their conversations, which had been obtained by placing a bugging device in Chalkley's home after he had been arrested on a pretext. The trial judge refused to exclude this evidence, and this led the defendants to plead guilty. On appeal it was held that, even if the trial judge's ruling as to the admissibility of the evidence had been wrong, the convictions were not unsafe. One of the issues here concerns the effect of a guilty plea on an appeal against conviction. It was held that, unless it could be shown that a mistaken decision by the judge left the accused with no alternative in law but to plead guilty, a guilty plea would normally preclude a successful appeal.[104] (The caveat—'normally'—is aimed at cases where a plea was made by mistake or without intention to admit the truth of the charge.) A further issue concerned the interpretation of the Criminal Appeal Act following the 1995 amendments. Auld LJ's conclusion was that: 'The Court has no power under the substituted section 2(1) to allow an appeal if it does not think the conviction unsafe but is dissatisfied in some way with what went on at the trial.'[105] Thus, what we are here referring to as 'due process appeals' should, on Auld's view, no longer be allowed.

Chalkley, then, gives a simple answer to the question we are considering. However, other cases take a different view of the Court of Appeal's powers under the amended Criminal Appeal Act, and the consensus now seems to be that *Chalkley* was wrongly decided.[106] For example, in *Mullen* the Court of Appeal held that the defendant's trial had involved an abuse of process and that, whether or not he was guilty, his conviction should be quashed.[107] Similarly, in *Davis, Johnson and Rowe* it was recognized that: 'A conviction may be unsafe even where there is no doubt about guilt but the trial process has been "vitiated by serious unfairness…".'[108] There are many other dicta to like effect.

---

[102] J. Smith, 'The Criminal Appeal Act 1995: Appeals Against Conviction' [1995] *Crim LR* 920; D. Schiff and R. Nobles, 'Criminal Appeal Act 1995: The Semantics of Jurisdiction' (1996) 59 *MLR* 573.

[103] [1998] 2 Cr App R 79.

[104] Ibid, 94. On the approach to guilty pleas, see further *R v Kelly and Connolly* [2003] EWCA Crim 2957.

[105] Ibid, 98.

[106] *Hakala*, n 76, [5], stated that *Chalkley* is not to be followed on this point.

[107] (1999) 2 Cr App R 143.

[108] [2001] 1 Cr App R 115, 132, quoting *Smith* (1999) 2 Cr App R 238.

But *Chalkley* is significant in that it highlights the tensions in this area, between respect for due process and the need for accurate verdicts.

It is accepted, then, that the Court of Appeal should allow due process appeals and that the Criminal Appeal Act permits it to do so. However, what is not clear is just when it should quash a conviction on due process grounds. What can be said with a good deal of certainty is that if the original trial was vitiated by an abuse of process, then an appeal will be successful. However, 'abuse of process' is a relatively narrow category. It covers cases where a defendant has been entrapped, where he has been prejudiced by undue delay between charge and trial, cases of disguised extradition (as in *Mullen*), situations where the prosecution has reneged on an agreement, and various other things. As we saw in Chapter 9 with the example of delay, the Court of Appeal is anxious to restrict the use of stays for abuse of process as far as possible, and they will only be available in cases where the prosecutor's conduct falls seriously below acceptable standards, as in the situations just described. This prompts the question: where a trial has been unfair in some way that does not amount to an abuse of process, should the defendant's conviction nevertheless be quashed? While statements such as the one made in *Davis*, quoted above, suggest that the answer to this question is 'yes', the case law has not yet made it clear just when unfairness short of abuse of process results in 'unsafety', nor is there agreement among commentators as to how this question should be answered.[109]

Of course, a critical, complicating factor here is Art 6 of the European Convention on Human Rights (ECHR), the precise content of which is determined largely by the judges in Strasbourg rather than by the English judiciary. This means that the Court of Appeal is no longer able to define trial fairness in such a way that its own conception of unfairness coincides with just those cases where it is prepared to quash a conviction irrespective of guilt. The Court of Appeal has, as it were, lost control of the definition of fairness. And, to complicate things further, the ECHR demands that a remedy be provided to anyone whose rights—including fair trial rights—are infringed.[110] An obvious remedy would be the quashing of a conviction. If this approach were taken, the concept of unsafety in the Criminal Appeal Act would be identical to the ECHR concept of fairness: whenever a trial was unfair under Art 6, the Court of Appeal would quash a defendant's conviction. At first sight, this is an attractive approach, with which the courts have flirted: in *Togher*, it was said that 'if a defendant has been denied a fair trial, it will be almost inevitable that the conviction will be regarded as unsafe',[111] and in *R v A* it was said that the 'guarantee of a fair trial under Article 6 is absolute: a conviction obtained in breach of it cannot stand'.[112] But it is now clear that these observations are not good law. Even where an appellant has had a judgment in his favour from the ECtHR, establishing a breach of Art 6, the Court of Appeal will not necessarily find a conviction unsafe.[113] As noted, the Convention requires a remedy be given for a

---

[109] See I. Dennis, 'Fair Trials and Safe Convictions' (2003) 56 *CLP* 211; N. Taylor and D. Ormerod, 'Mind the Gap: Safety, Fairness and Moral Legitimacy' [2004] *Crim LR* 266.
[110] ECHR, Art 13.   [111] *R v Togher and others* [2001] 3 All ER 463, 33.   [112] [2002] 1 AC 45, 25.
[113] *R v Lewis* [2005] EWCA Crim 859; *Dowsett v CCRC* [2007] EWHC 1923 (Admin).

breach of Art 6, but that need not be the quashing of a conviction: it can be an award of damages, a reduction in sentence, or merely an acknowledgement that a right has been breached.[114] However, it may be that such remedies will not always be a sufficient response to a breach of Art 6, or some other procedural right. Taylor and Ormerod suggest that using these remedies to respond to an Art 6 breach 'fails to elevate human rights to their proper status in the overall context in which decisions are to be made'.[115] On this view, the court should be prepared to quash some convictions gained in breach of Art 6 even if the defendant is plainly guilty. This brings us back to the question asked earlier: in which cases should this occur?

In due process appeals there is a tension between the role of the courts as fact-finders, and their role in upholding the moral integrity of the criminal process. In developing a framework for considering when unfair convictions should be quashed and when upheld, we are not attracted by solutions which put significant weight on concepts such as legitimacy and moral integrity, unless more is said about exactly what these terms mean. Instead, our approach is a protective, or remedial, one. Defendants should not be disadvantaged by breach of their rights. Where a conviction is gained via a breach of Art 6, therefore, that conviction should be held to be unsafe and quashed. Key here is a causal question. The court will have to ask whether, if Art 6 had not been breached, the defendant would have been convicted. As before, this will sometimes prove difficult to answer. There will doubtless be a temptation to find, in cases where defendants have obviously committed serious crimes, that the Art 6 breach did not cause the conviction. In some cases, a retrial will be possible and that offers a way out of some of the more difficult dilemmas the court may face.

We doubt whether adoption of the remedial approach to breaches of Art 6 would greatly change the practice of the Court of Appeal. The most significant change would be in cases, such as *Chalkley* and *Togher*, where the defendant has pleaded guilty. The guilty plea in *Chalkley* was obviously caused by the judge's decision to admit the challenged evidence. Were this decision to be found in breach of Art 6, or to infringe the domestic conception of fairness under s 78, then on our account the conviction should be quashed. This would result in the factually guilty walking free, but if our commitment to fair trials is to mean anything, that is surely an appropriate outcome: it is what would have happened had the defendants' rights been respected in the first place. In *Togher*, the decision is not so straightforward: there would be a difficult decision as to whether the undisclosed material, which went to the credibility of prosecution witnesses, might have caused the jury to acquit. If it might have, the conviction would, on our account, be unsafe. In *Togher*, unlike in *Chalkley*, a retrial would probably be a viable option.

If the remedial approach is an appropriate way of marking the gravity of Art 6 breaches, it is not so obvious that it provides a solution to all due process appeals. In *Clarke and McDaid*, the House of Lords decided that the defendants' convictions

---

[114] Dennis, n 109; Emmerson, Ashworth, and Macdonald, n 30, 21, 27.   [115] See n 109, 279.

should be quashed because of a technical error: the bill of indictment had not been signed by an officer of the court.[116] This decision raises slightly different issues to the ones we have been discussing so far. As a matter of statutory interpretation, it was held that the signature was an essential step for there to be a valid trial. The error did not disadvantage the defendants in any material sense; the trial would have proceeded to conviction in exactly the same way had the indictment been signed. It might therefore seem odd that the convictions were quashed. However, there is probably a class of procedural errors that should be seen as invalidating a conviction regardless of whether they disadvantage a defendant, as when a court simply has no jurisdiction: if a summary offence is tried in error by the Crown Court, for example.[117] Seen in this light, *Clarke* might not be such a problematic decision. A further difficulty for our account is a case involving far more serious malpractice. In *Mullen*, the defendant had been illegally deported from Zimbabwe in order to avoid proper extradition procedures.[118] It may be that he suffered no real disadvantage through this, in that he could have been deported through legal means, albeit in a more protracted process. In cases like *Mullen*, involving serious abuse of power by the executive, the conviction should still be quashed. Legitimacy must play some role in decisions to exclude evidence and to stay proceedings for abuse of process, and here it provides one explanation for why Mullen's conviction should have been quashed.

For those who think that the courts should never acquit those who have committed serious crimes (Mullen was convicted of conspiracy to cause explosions), *Mullen* is a controversial decision. This was certainly the government's view, and in 2006 it published a 'consultation' paper (on which views were only canvassed on *how*, not whether, to change the law), proposing to prevent the Court of Appeal from quashing convictions in cases where defendants are plainly guilty.[119] The proposals were widely condemned by the legal establishment,[120] and a modified provision was included in the Criminal Justice and Immigration Bill. This would have specified that a conviction is not unsafe where there is no reasonable doubt about guilt, with a proviso that an appeal could be allowed if it would 'seriously undermine the proper administration of justice to allow the conviction to stand'. This probably did little more than state the position the Court of Appeal had already come to (though it might have prevented the decision in *Clarke and McDaid*), but was still controversial. The government dropped the provision in order to ensure passage of the rest of the Bill through Parliament.

---

[116] [2008] UKHL 8.
[117] See J. Spencer, 'Quashing Convictions for Procedural Irregularities' [2007] *Crim LR* 835.
[118] [1999] 2 Cr App R 143.   [119] Home Office, *Quashing Convictions* (2006).
[120] See Elks, n 80, 47–9.

12.4 POST-APPEAL REVIEW OF CONVICTIONS: THE CRIMINAL CASES REVIEW COMMISSION

Many defendants will find that their appeal is unsuccessful. Others will not appeal; after a certain time (28 days where appeals against conviction in the Crown Court are concerned), their right to appeal will lapse. In these situations, normal appeal rights have been exhausted. However, that is not quite an end to the matter. It is possible to have a conviction referred back to the Crown Court or Court of Appeal.[121] This may occur where, for example, new evidence emerges to throw doubt on the conviction. The system used to be that a decision on whether or not to refer a case back to the Court of Appeal was made by the Home Secretary, on advice from civil servants in the Home Office.[122] In the wake of the Royal Commission on Criminal Justice, a new body was set up to take over this role. The CCRC started work in 1997.

The CCRC investigates claims of miscarriage of justice and refers cases back to the appropriate appeal court. Although the Commission's powers involve both magistrates' court and Crown Court cases,[123] and challenges to sentence as well as verdicts, here we concentrate on the most common situation, where an application is made to have a conviction referred back to the Court of Appeal. The usual procedure is that an application will be made to the CCRC.[124] The Commission will consider whether the application is eligible: it may only exceptionally make a reference if the applicant did not appeal at the time of his original conviction, and many applications are rejected because the applicant did not.[125] If eligible, the application will be investigated. In some cases, this can be done fairly rapidly but others will involve considerable work. The Commission has the power to initiate police investigations,[126] and to obtain information.[127] At the end of the process, a decision is made whether or not to refer a case to the Court of Appeal. If a preliminary decision is made not to make a referral, the applicant or his lawyer will usually be informed of the proposed reasons for non-referral and be invited to comment. The Criminal Appeal Act 1995 sets out the criteria for making a referral, which should not be made unless 'the Commission consider that there is a real possibility that the conviction . . . would not be upheld'. The grounds on which the conviction would not be upheld must involve 'an argument, or evidence, not raised in the proceedings which led to it or any appeal or application for leave to appeal against it',

---

[121] There also remains the possibility of a pardon. See Pattenden, n 10, 378–84.

[122] Ibid, ch 10.

[123] Referrals of convictions in the magistrates' courts are rare. See K. Kerrigan, 'Miscarriages of Justice in the Magistrates Court: The Forgotten Power of the CCRC' [2006] *Crim LR* 143.

[124] For useful description of the CCRC's working methods, see D. Kyle, 'Correcting Miscarriages of Justice: The Role of the Criminal Cases Review Commission' (2004) 52 *Drake L Rev* 657.

[125] Criminal Appeal Act 1995, s 13. Almost half of all the applications the CCRC receives relate to cases that are either ineligible or are 'no appeal' cases where there are no exceptional circumstances: *CCRC Annual Report 2017/18* (2018), 13.

[126] Criminal Appeal Act 1995, s 19.

[127] Ibid, ss 18 and 18A, as amended by the Criminal Cases Review Commission (Information) Act 2016.

unless there are exceptional circumstances.[128] While historically 68 per cent of people applying to the CCRC have done so without the help of a lawyer, this has increased to 80 per cent.[129] This is noteworthy as legally represented applicants have a significantly increased chance of a better outcome—8 per cent of represented applicants had their cases referred compared with 2.1 per cent of unrepresented applicants.[130]

The CCRC notes that its cases coalesce around certain themes, which impact on referral numbers considerably; one issue often leads to multiple cases being referred.[131] Over the years, these themes have included: sex offences involving a changed understanding of the significance of medical findings; shaken baby and sudden-infant-death cases; HMRC controlled deliveries of drugs cases; cases linked to the disbanded West Midlands Police Serious Crime Squad, and youth confession cases from Northern Ireland. The CCRC observed that in 2018 there was no clear or dominant theme.

As well as these themes, Kyle gives a useful flavour of the sort of case the CCRC investigates:

> From the Commission's perspective, cases that result in referral tend to fall into two broad categories. The first is cases in which relevant new evidence appears, occasionally if rarely being wholly exculpatory, but more often being of a nature that, had it been heard by the jury, might reasonably have caused them to come to a different verdict. This includes cases, quite often encountered, in which new psychiatric evidence supports the argument that an applicant should have been convicted of manslaughter by reason of diminished responsibility or provocation, rather than murder. The second category, more closely aligned to the types of issues raised by applicants themselves, involves some flaw in the investigation, prosecution, or trial process not brought about by malice but rather, in plain terms, because someone has not done his or her job properly—and this may well be something to which the defence lawyers have contributed.[132]

At the centre of the Commission's task is a predictive exercise: it should not make a referral just because it thinks there has been a miscarriage of justice, but only if it believes that the Court of Appeal may quash the conviction. Thus, its decision must be informed by the Court of Appeal's working practices. The Criminal Appeal Act underlines this by requiring a new argument or evidence, but even without this provision something new would generally be needed, because that is what the Court of Appeal itself demands. The referral criteria have been discussed by the Divisional Court, in a case involving judicial review of a CCRC decision.[133] Significantly, the judgment was given by Lord Bingham, who was then Lord Chief Justice. The 'real possibility test' he explained, 'plainly denotes a contingency which in the Commission's judgment is more than an outside chance or bare possibility but which may be less than a probability or likelihood or racing certainty'.[134] In cases concerning fresh evidence, 'the Commission

---

[128] Criminal Appeal Act 1995, s 13.   [129] *CCRC Annual Report 2017/18* (2018), 11.
[130] J. Hodgson and J. Horne, *The Extent and Impact of Legal Representation on Applications to the Criminal Cases Review Commission (CCRC)* (2009).
[131] *CCRC Annual Report 2017/18*, 18–19.   [132] See n 124, 672.
[133] *R v CCRC, ex p Pearson* [2000] 1 Cr App R 141.   [134] Ibid, 149.

must ask itself a double question: do we consider that…there is a real possibility that the Court of Appeal will receive the fresh evidence? If so, do we consider that there is a real possibility that the Court of Appeal will not uphold the conviction?'[135] A little more guidance is available to the Commission in the form of statements made by the court itself in referral cases. The court has on occasion been critical of the Commission for referring to it cases which it regards as a waste of its time.[136] Less bluntly, the court has been prepared to give the Commission a lesson on the law, commenting in *Sharp*, a case that apparently came 'nowhere near' the criteria for the admissibility of fresh evidence, that 'had the Commission had its attention drawn to the authorities that we have set out in this judgment, which it does not appear to have had before it, it would have taken a very different view of Mr Sharp's application'.[137]

The CCRC acts as a safety net outside the courts, which means in theory that the principle of finality has less drastic consequences,[138] and it represents 'an integral part of the protection available in this jurisdiction against the risk and consequences of wrongful conviction'.[139] As the Court of Appeal stated in *R (Charles) v CCRC*:

i)   The CCRC exercises an important residual jurisdiction in the interests of justice.

ii) The decision whether or not a case satisfies the threshold conditions and is to be referred to the CACD [Court of Appeal Criminal Division] is for the CCRC and not the Court; it is not for the Court to usurp the CCRC's function.

iii) The judgment required of the CCRC is unusual, carrying with it the predictive exercise as to the view the CACD might take.

iv) The threshold conditions serve as an important filter, not least in preventing the CACD from inundation with threadbare cases; they also assist in striking the right balance between the interests of justice on the one hand and those of finality on the other.

v)   Even if the threshold conditions are satisfied, the CCRC retains a discretion not to refer a case to the CACD.

vi) Though the decisions of the CCRC, whether or not to refer cases to the CACD, clearly are subject to judicial review . . . (1) the CCRC should not be vexed with inappropriate applications impacting on scarce resources; the Court's scrutiny at the permission stage is thus of importance; (2) on a judicial review, CCRC *reasons* should not be subjected to a 'rigorous audit' to establish that they were not open to legal criticism.[140]

As will be obvious from the material already covered in this chapter, the Commission's predictive task is not an easy one. There is a fair degree of unpredictability in the Court of Appeal's approach to appeals, especially as regards the test to be applied in fresh evidence cases. Despite this, the Commission is reasonably good at predicting

[135] Ibid, 150. [136] *R v Ellis* [2003] EWCA Crim 3930; *R v Gerald* [1999] *Crim LR* 315.
[137] [2003] EWCA Crim 3870 at 33. See also the criticism of the Commission at 26.
[138] *R v Smith* [2013] EWCA Crim 2388, [92]. [139] [2017] EWHC 1219 (Admin), [2].
[140] Ibid, [47].

what the court will do: about 67 per cent of its referrals are successful.[141] As with many of the statistics in this chapter, there is no good way of judging whether this is too high, too low, or about right.[142] Indeed, in 2015 the House of Commons Justice Committee recommended that the CCRC should be less cautious in its application of the test, though suggested that any change to the test itself would have to be in the light of a change to the Court of Appeal's grounds for allowing appeals.[143] One can be reasonably sure, however, that were the success rate to fall far below 50 per cent, the Court of Appeal, mindful of being 'burdened with a mass of hopeless appeals',[144] would use its criticisms of referrals to prompt a more careful approach from the Commission. Some think that the success rate indicates that the Commission is too conservative; unsurprisingly, the Commissioners themselves deny the criticism that the CCRC is a 'handmaid' of the Court of Appeal, adopting an uncritical approach to miscarriages of justice.[145] The decision to refer *Stock* to the Court of Appeal for a second time, a referral that involved criticism of the court's interpretation of the evidence in the previous referral, is some testament to the CCRC's independence. As for the Commission's case load, this is not insignificant: since 1997 it has considered in the region of 23,000 applications, and referred around one in every 35 for appeal at an average rate of 33 cases a year (around 3 per cent).[146] It refers more cases to the Court of Appeal than the Home Office did.[147]

Carolyn Hoyle and Mai Sato have carried out a major, independent empirical assessment of how the CCRC operates, examining 146 cases from applications received since 2000, from six categories of cases relating to: historical institutional abuse, contemporary sexual offences, forensic and expert evidence, police investigations, court-directed investigations, and asylum.[148] They looked at the applications for each case, the case records, and the statement of reasons, as well as spending four years visiting the CCRC and interviewing current and former members of staff. While their findings were broadly very positive, they found some evidence of inconsistency in how the CCRC works, as well as issues of speed of response.[149] They identified variability in the

---

[141] *CCRC Annual Report 2017/18*, 11.

[142] The Commission view it as about right, but others think it too high: see Home Affairs Committee, *The Work of the Criminal Cases Review Commission, Oral and Written Evidence Tuesday 27 January 2004*, Q 27, 74; R. Nobles and D. Schiff, 'The Criminal Cases Review Commission: Reporting Success?' (2001) 64 *MLR* 280.

[143] House of Commons Justice Committee, *Criminal Cases Review Commission*, Twelfth Report of Session 2014–15, HC 850 (2015), [16] and [20]; also see S. Heaton, *A critical evaluation of the utility of using innocence as a criterion in the post conviction process*, Doctoral thesis, University of East Anglia (2013).

[144] *Ex p Pearson*, n 133, 149.

[145] See Kyle, n 124; Elks, n 80, 345–7. An interesting perspective from a former member of the Scottish CCRC is P. Duff, 'Straddling Two Worlds: Reflections of a Retired Criminal Cases Review Commissioner' (2009) 72 *MLR* 693. On criticism of the CCRC and the test for referral to the Court of Appeal, see H. Quirk, 'Identifying Miscarriages of Justice: Why Innocence in the UK is Not the Answer' (2007) 70 *MLR* 759.

[146] *CCRC Annual Report 2017/18*, 11.

[147] Nobles and Schiff, n 142, 282–3.

[148] C. Hoyle and M. Sato, *Reasons to Doubt: Wrongful Convictions and the Criminal Cases Review Commission* (2019).

[149] Ibid, ch 4.

CCRC's work, such as regarding its inclination to conduct empirical investigations in given cases.[150] Of course, some variability is inevitable in the exercise of discretion, but the CCRC is now seeking to guard against this by being more consultative internally in its decision-making processes.[151]

Moreover, they note that CCRC staff were not surprised by Roberts's findings[152] that the Court of Appeal is becoming more reluctant to quash convictions based on fresh evidence. Carolyn Hoyle and Mai Sato question what the CCRC does about this: 'Does it fall in line, and select and construct its referrals accordingly, or does it push back and try to shift the Court's behaviour?'[153]

Ultimately, their empirical work establishes and clarifies how the Court of Appeal's evolving jurisprudence affects the CCRC decision-making field and frames. The CCRC's Casework Guidance Notes are shaped by the Court of Appeal's prior response to CCRC referrals and to direct appeals, and this ties the CCRC into a close and deferential relationship with the court.[154] They conclude that the relationship could be more challenging and occasionally combative without comprising its symbiotic nature. Another practical and feasible suggestion they make is the long-term digital data storage of all Crown Court trials, which would expedite some CCRC reviews.[155]

The CCRC appears to have a reputation for careful investigation and to do its job well.[156] While some have hoped that the Commission would come to play a vocal role in criminal justice debates, using its expertise to propose general lessons about the causes of miscarriages of justice, it has not found this easy.[157] That said, the CCRC has been one of the most positive additions to the criminal justice landscape in recent decades, though its ability to correct miscarriages of justice is limited by the Court of Appeal's interpretation of its own powers. Its role is also limited by its budget. Since creation it seems to have been underfunded,[158] and the Chief Executive in the 2017/18 report stressed that 'Things have not been easy in recent years; money has been tighter even with standstill budgets and workloads higher than we would have liked.'[159] Administrative reforms have meant that it has still been able to reduce its case backlog and thus waiting times for review,[160] but it is crucial that it continues to receive adequate support from government. In 2015, the House of Commons Justice Committee considered the adequacy of the CCRC's resources, powers, and working practices, leading it to recommend that the CCRC be granted additional funding in order to reduce the backlog in applications, alongside a discretion to refuse to investigate certain categories of cases so that it can better focus its resources on more serious and deserving cases.[161]

---

[150] Ibid, ch 12, and 319.   [151] Ibid, ch 6.   [152] See n 60.
[153] Hoyle and Sato, n 148, 331.   [154] Ibid, 33.   [155] Ibid, 321.
[156] See A. James, N. Taylor, and C. Walker, 'The Criminal Cases Review Commission: Economy, Effectiveness and Justice' [2000] *Crim LR* 140.
[157] See House of Commons Justice Committee, [53].   [158] James et al, n 156, 145.
[159] *CCRC Annual Report 2017/18*, 10.   [160] Ibid, 16.
[161] House of Commons Justice Committee, [35].

12.5 MISCARRIAGES OF JUSTICE

The criminal process aims to offset and prevent, to the greatest extent possible, miscarriages of justice. While this term has a distinct legal meaning, and often is used as a synonym for wrongful conviction, it can encompass also wrongful arrest or other state intervention, and failure to pursue prosecutions, for instance. Indeed, Clive Walker regards a miscarriage of justice as the state's violation of an individual's rights (whether suspect, defendant, convict, victim, or witness), and stressed that miscarriages of justice can be institutionalized within, and ensue from, the misapplication of laws.[162] Many social harms are created through miscarriages of justice, to the wrongfully convicted, to the victim of the crime, to the criminal justice system, and public confidence in it.[163]

Throughout the book we have highlighted miscarriages of justice in the form of disproportionality, biases, and abuses in state investigation and prosecution of crime, as well as issues relating to the treatment of the victims of crime. Our particular focus in this section is on the narrower understanding of miscarriages of justice, whereby an individual is wrongfully convicted, and on the extent to which the state seeks to remedy or respond to the harm caused. Such wrongful convictions often result from errors or issues in police investigation,[164] though other causes might be mistakes in forensic science, expert testimony, or issues with the defence argument.

The British state's response to miscarriages of justice remains inadequate and unacceptable. Section 133 of the CJA 1988 provides for the payment of compensation for miscarriages of justice, on application to the Secretary of State. As enacted, s 133 stated that when a person has been convicted of a criminal offence and when subsequently his conviction has been reversed or he has been pardoned on the ground that a new or newly discovered fact shows beyond reasonable doubt that there has been a miscarriage of justice, compensation shall be paid to him or, if he is dead, to his personal representatives, unless the non-disclosure of the unknown fact was attributable to him. The 1988 Act does not define miscarriage of justice. In *R (Adams) v Secretary of State for Justice*, the Supreme Court used four categories of miscarriages of justice as a framework for discussion, in seeking to determine when an applicant could be compensated in accordance with s 133:

(1) Where the fresh evidence shows clearly that the defendant is innocent of the crime of which he has been convicted.

(2) Where the fresh evidence is such that, had it been available at the time of the trial, no reasonable jury could properly have convicted the defendant.

[162] C. Walker, 'Miscarriages of Justice in Principle and Practice' in C. Walker and K. Starmer, *Miscarriages of Justice: A Review of Justice in Error* (1999), 33–7.
[163] M. Naughton, *Rethinking Miscarriages of Justice: Beyond the Tip of the Iceberg* (2007).
[164] B. Forst, 'Wrongful Convictions in a World of Miscarriages of Justice' in C. Huff and M. Killias (eds), *Wrongful Convictions and Miscarriages of Justice: Causes and Remedies in North American and European Criminal Justice Systems* (2013), ch 2.

(3)   Where the fresh evidence renders the conviction unsafe in that, had it been available at the time of the trial, a reasonable jury might or might not have convicted
the defendant.

(4)   Where something has gone seriously wrong in the investigation of the offence or
the conduct of the trial, resulting in the conviction of someone who should not
have been convicted.[165]

The Supreme Court was divided as to the correct construction of s 133, and ultimately
a bare majority of five Justices held that the provision does not require a claimant to
prove beyond reasonable doubt that he was innocent of the particular offence, rather
he must prove that a new or newly discovered fact so undermines the case against
him that no conviction could be based upon it. All nine Justices held that categories 1
and 2 fell within the meaning of the phrase 'miscarriage of justice', and that s 133 was
compatible with Art 6(2).[166]

So as to 'restore the definition of a miscarriage of justice to the pre-*Adams* position',[167] the Anti-social Behaviour, Crime and Policing Act 2014 inserted s 133(1ZA)
restricting compensation to cases in which a new or newly discovered fact shows beyond reasonable doubt that the person did not commit the offence, in other words,
category 1 cases. This amended provision was challenged unsuccessfully in *R (Hallam)
v Secretary of State for Justice* and *R (Nealon) v Secretary of State for Justice* on the basis
that it was incompatible with the presumption of innocence in Art 6(2).[168] Hallam had
been convicted of murder aged 17; the Court of Appeal later quashed his conviction,
after his having spent more than seven years in custody. Nealon had served 17 years for
attempted rape, before a successful appeal after referral by the CCRC. Despite this, their
applications for compensation were rejected by the Secretary of State. They sought judicial review of that decision, arguing that s 133(1ZA) was unlawful as it was contrary to
the presumption of innocence as protected by Art 6(2). The Divisional Court dismissed
their claims on the basis that Art 6(2) does not apply to compensation decisions under
s 133, notwithstanding the authority of the ECtHR,[169] and that even if Art 6(2) were to
apply, there was no incompatibility.[170] On appeal, the Court of Appeal considered that
it was bound by *Adams* to hold that Art 6(2) was not applicable to s 133.[171]

Leave to appeal was granted to Hallam and Nealon, and a hearing before the UK Supreme Court was held in May 2018. By a majority of 5:2, the Supreme Court dismissed
their appeals.[172] The majority of the court found that while Art 6(2) had been engaged,

---

[165] [2011] UKSC 18, [9] per Lord Phillips, following Dyson LJ in the Court of Appeal [2009] EWCA Civ
1291.
[166] H. Quirk and M. Requa, 'The Supreme Court on Compensation for Miscarriages of Justice: Is it Better
that Ten Innocents are Denied Compensation than One Guilty Person Receives It?' (2012) 75 MLR 387–400.
[167] Public Bill Committee, 11 July 2013, col 463 (Damian Green MP).
[168] [2016] EWCA Civ 355.
[169] *R (Adams) v Secretary of State for Justice* [2011] UKSC 18, [2012] 1 AC 48.
[170] [2015] EWHC 1565 (Admin).   [171] [2016] EWCA Civ 355.
[172] *R (Hallam) v Secretary of State for Justice* and *R (Nealon) v Secretary of State for Justice* [2019] UKSC 2.

it did not follow that the ECtHR would find a violation,[173] as its jurisprudence was deemed not to be 'coherent or settled' on whether Art 6(2) applied in respect of claims not involving any criminal charge.[174] And even if Art 6(2) did have such a wider application, Lord Mance was not persuaded that s 133(1ZA) was incompatible with Art 6(2).[175] Though she declined to do so, Lady Hale added that her view of the appropriateness of making a declaration of incompatibility had nothing to do with her view of the merits of the amendment to s 133.[176]

Lord Reed, in a powerful and persuasive dissenting judgment with which Lord Kerr agreed, expressed difficulty in accepting that and how the Supreme Court could diverge from a construction of the Convention which it knows to be out of step with the approach of the ECtHR.[177] Lord Reed described as 'unrealistic' the distinction between a requirement that innocence be established, and a requirement that innocence be established by a new or newly discovered fact and nothing else.[178] Indeed, someone making an application under s 133 must be someone whose conviction has been quashed because of the impact of a new or newly discovered fact, and in most such cases there will be no other reason for the quashing of the conviction. Lord Reed concluded that the implication of the Secretary of State's decision that the new or newly discovered fact does not establish the person's innocence is likely to be that, although that fact has led to the quashing of the conviction, innocence has not been established. 'The decision therefore casts doubt on the innocence of the person in question and undermines the acquittal.'[179]

This decision of the Supreme Court affirms the human-rights compliance of a regrettable policy and legislative development, which limits profoundly the compensating of those who suffer miscarriages of justice. While such individuals may deploy the civil law to pursue the police and state agents for wrong conviction, the narrowing of the parameters to include category 1 cases only is deeply problematic.

12.6 PROSECUTION APPEALS

We saw earlier that the structure of the appeals process reveals a marked asymmetry between prosecution and defence appeal rights. Prosecutors have fewer opportunities to appeal than defendants. Where prosecutors do have appeal rights, as in the magistrates' court, these tend to be restricted so as to allow appeals on points of law, rather than challenges to fact-finding. The CJA 2003 enables the prosecution to challenge decisions as to points of law made by judges in the Crown Court. Most significantly, the

---

[173] See Lord Mance, [61]; Lady Hale, [81]–[82].
[174] Lord Mance, [73]. See L. Campbell, 'Criminal Labels, the European Convention on Human Rights and the Presumption of Innocence' (2013) 76 *MLR* 681.
[175] [74].   [176] [82].
[177] [175], e.g. in *Allen v UK* (2013) 63 EHRR 10.
[178] [184].   [179] [184].

same Act allows the reopening of jury acquittals when they are challenged on factual grounds. The creation of this exception to the double jeopardy principle has been controversial. Even with these developments, however, the picture remains asymmetrical. In order to understand the law in this area, then, we need to begin by thinking about the reasons for this asymmetry.[180] Because double jeopardy raises particular issues of principle, we discuss it separately in the next section.

We want the courts to make good decisions: to find facts accurately, to interpret the law properly, and to apply it to the facts in an appropriate manner. In general, appeals offer a means of enhancing these values: the trial court's conclusions can be checked and reassessed. Where questions of law are concerned, the process also allows appeal courts to develop and clarify the law, for the benefit of all trial courts. There are reasons for restraining and filtering appeals: appeal courts cannot work effectively if overloaded, trial courts need to retain some independence, and there is value in coming to a final decision reasonably quickly. While nothing in this picture yet explains why we should want appeal rights to be asymmetrical, the last point mentioned—that there are reasons for restraining appeals—does point us towards an explanation. Because mistaken convictions are much more serious than mistaken acquittals, the need to rectify a mistaken conviction carries far more weight in overcoming the reasons for restraining appeals. Nevertheless, this insight does not provide a very clear picture of how an appeals process might be structured: it explains why we might find asymmetry in an appeals system, but does not *require* asymmetry. If, for example, we decided that the restraint reasons were not very compelling, we might want to give prosecutors and defendants equal appeal rights. This position would be perfectly compatible with an acknowledgement that there are better reasons to permit defence appeals than prosecution appeals. There is, however, one further reason for asymmetry, which applies particularly to jury trial. Jury equity, or jury nullification, is the practice whereby a jury acquits a guilty defendant for reasons of principle. Jury equity is seen by some as being an important value in a jury trial. Allowing appeals against jury acquittals might allow prosecutors to undermine jury equity.[181] This argument will not persuade everyone;[182] as we saw in Chapter 11, jury equity is controversial. There might also be some way of distinguishing nullification cases from others, and allowing appeals in the latter but not the former. Another argument that often emerges in the debates around appeals is that prosecution appeals should be avoided because they subject defendants to stress and uncertainty. While this point should not be overlooked, again it does not give us a very clear picture of how we should structure appeal rights. As a matter of practice, it is not taken to rule out all prosecution appeals. Even when a defendant appears to have secured a victory, as in having his acquittal quashed in the Court of Appeal, he may still face a retrial or further appeal to the Supreme Court.

---

[180] Cf L. Laudan, *Truth, Error and Criminal Law: An Essay in Legal Epistemology* (2006), ch 8.

[181] See P. Westen and R. Drubel, 'Towards a General Theory of Double Jeopardy' [1978] *Supreme Court Rev* 81.

[182] See J. Spencer, n 27, 687–8.

Further, defence appeals too may impose stress and uncertainty on victims, or even on an 'alternative suspect' who may fear that, once the conviction is overturned, he will be prosecuted for the crime.[183]

It is not surprising, then, to find that the asymmetry in appeal rights is unstable, and that new avenues of prosecution appeal have been created. The foregoing discussion suggests that the best way to assess these changes is to examine them individually. The discussion here will focus on the issues in broad outline rather than the technical detail. The CJA 2003 for the first time gave prosecutors rights of appeal during trial on indictment. Previous appeal rights were restricted to preparatory hearings in serious and lengthy cases. Under s 58, the appeal can relate to any ruling made up to the start of the summing-up, including a submission of no case to answer. The prosecution must tell the Crown Court judge of any decision to appeal 'immediately',[184] and the Act has a practical way of restricting such appeals to rulings which severely affect the prosecution case. If the Court of Appeal confirms the judge's ruling, the outcome will be the acquittal of the defendant; the prosecution must also agree to the defendant's acquittal if it abandons the appeal or if leave is refused. As this implies, prosecution appeals, like defence appeals, require leave, either from the trial judge or the Court of Appeal. The Court of Appeal cannot allow the appeal just because it disagrees with the judge's exercise of a discretion: the decision must be wrong in law or unreasonable.[185] A practical problem with allowing 'interlocutory' appeals—appeals during the course of a trial—is that proceedings will be suspended, creating delay and prolonging the defendant's stress. Provisions allow for the more urgent appeals to be expedited,[186] but in practice a jury, once empanelled, cannot be kept waiting for very long. The usual result of a successful prosecution appeal, then, will be that the Court of Appeal will order a retrial, but it may only do so if this is in the interests of justice.

A more wide-ranging power of appeal is to be found in s 62 of the Act, although this section is not yet in force and no implementation date has been set. Section 62 applies to certain serious offences, such as rape, murder, robbery, and arson.[187] It allows the prosecution to challenge any evidential ruling, and here an unsuccessful appeal does not result in acquittal. It would be unsatisfactory if the trial could be put on hold over just any ruling with which the prosecution disagrees—a decision not to allow an inference from silence, for example—and the Act has a solution of sorts to this problem. The evidentiary ruling must 'significantly weaken' the prosecution case.

Section 58 has proved reasonably popular in terms of its use (see Table 12.5).

---

[183] As in the case of the murder of Wendy Sewell, for which Stephen Downing had his conviction quashed in 2001: see 'Guilty Secret of Town with Blood on its Hands', *The Observer*, 11 February 2001; 'Bakewell Killer Hunt Reopens After 25 Years', *The Observer*, 14 April 2002. Cf 'Cleared of Murder—But Still the Sole Suspect', *The Guardian*, 28 February 2003.

[184] CPR, r 38.2; see *R v Quillan* [2015] EWCA Crim 538.

[185] CJA 2003, s 67.

[186] Ibid, s 64.

[187] Sch 4, Part 1 contains a list of around 30 serious offences.

Table 12.5 Appeals under s 58 of the Criminal Justice Act 2003

Year	Number of appeals under s 58
2010	24
2011	28
2012	44
2013	37
2014	37
2015	38
2016	43
2017	28

Source: Ministry of Justice, Freedom of Information Act (FOIA) request ref: 180731022, 13 August 2018.

The case law emphasizes that the only condition for an appeal under s 58 is whether the prosecution is prepared to agree to the defendant's acquittal should it be unsuccessful:[188] the ruling it challenges need not be one that significantly undermines its case, although this will usually be so in practice if the prosecution is prepared to give the acquittal undertaking.

Further, the fact that s 62 refers to 'evidentiary' rulings does not mean that the prosecution cannot challenge a decision to exclude evidence under s 58.[189] Now that the width of s 58 has been recognized,[190] it may be that there is little point in implementing s 62.

In principle, there is little to object to in these powers: such prosecution appeal rights serve the ends of justice by allowing the scrutiny of the decisions of trial judges. It may also be of use in avoiding the situation where the law develops in a lopsided manner. If only defendants can appeal legal rulings, an anti-defendant bias in the application of the law may be prevented, but an untoward pro-defendant bias, even if unlikely, may remain hidden. There have been some concerns about these powers, however. The Law Commission, when reviewing this area of the law, was initially cautious about creating prosecution rights of appeal, and would not have allowed appeal against a successful submission of no case to answer.[191] It expressed the concern that

---

[188] *R v R* [2007] EWCA Crim 370.

[189] *R v Y* [2008] EWCA Crim 10. Case management decisions can also be challenged: *R v C* [2007] EWCA Crim 2352.

[190] See D. Ormerod; A. Waterman, and R. Fortson, 'Prosecution Appeals—Too Much of a Good Thing?' [2010] *Crim LR* 169 where they suggest that while this might be an 'unintentionally wide avenue of appeal', there is little danger of it exacerbating the Court of Appeal's already large workload.

[191] Law Commission, *Prosecution Appeals Against Judges' Rulings*, Consultation Paper No 158 (2000). This stance was modified in Law Commission, *Double Jeopardy and Prosecution Appeals*, Law Com No 267 (2001), in which it was proposed that appeals be allowed on the first, but not the second, limb of *Galbraith* (i.e. on a decision whether there is no evidence to support part of the prosecution's case, but not on whether such evidence as there is, taken at its highest, is sufficient to convict).

the defence might be discouraged from making such a submission by the fear that, if successfully appealed, there would be a new trial and thus a loss of any tactical advantage gained during the original trial. This emphasis on tactical factors did not impress commentators.[192] The Commission also expressed some concern over equality of arms, noting that given that the defence has no interlocutory appeal rights, it might seem odd to provide the prosecution with them. One response to this is that prosecution interlocutory appeals are the equivalent of defence appeals after the jury verdict, which prosecutors do not possess; however, it may be questioned whether it is right to make defendants wait until they have been convicted before they can challenge a ruling which is obviously wrong.[193]

The principal objection to the appeals in the CJA 2003 may well be practical. Dealing at the moment largely with defence appeals post-trial, we have seen that the Criminal Division of the Court of Appeal continues to be stretched in terms of resources, and that this may affect the quality of decision making at the leave stage, and encourage loss of time orders. Prosecution appeals put further pressure on the court. Linked to this is the question of delay. Compared to its European counterparts, English criminal procedure has generally resolved criminal matters speedily. This is due partly, no doubt, to the 'concentrated' nature of criminal proceedings in this jurisdiction, with the key stage being the trial.[194] Interlocutory appeals are a threat to this tradition. The net result may well be defendants spending longer on remand,[195] and in a state of uncertainty about the outcome of the proceedings against them.

Reform of criminal procedure rarely stands still for long. Now that we have prosecution appeals during the trial, attention may well turn to prosecution appeals post-verdict, which might involve a challenge to the judge's directions to the jury on the substantive law. Indeed, if interlocutory appeals under ss 58 and 62 of the CJA 2003 come to disrupt trials by regularly throwing them into hiatus, it may well be argued that the appropriate place for those appeals is at the end of the trial. The Law Commission saw no case for post-verdict prosecution appeals,[196] but Lord Justice Auld did raise the question of the power to appeal 'perverse' jury verdicts (this turned out to be one of the most controversial proposals in his report).[197] Some jurisdictions— Canada is an example[198]—allow the prosecution to appeal points of law after a jury acquittal. Although such appeals raise difficult issues, they should not be ruled out of contemplation.

---

[192] See R. Pattenden, 'Prosecution Appeals Against Judges' Rulings' [2000] *Crim LR* 971; I. Dennis, 'Prosecution Appeals and Retrial for Serious Offences' [2004] *Crim LR* 619.

[193] See Spencer, n 27. It would, however, be difficult to find a way of limiting defence appeals: there is no obvious equivalent of the prosecution's acquittal undertaking.

[194] M. Damaška, *Evidence Law Adrift* (1997), ch 3.

[195] See Ch 8.

[196] Law Commission, n 191.

[197] Auld, n 32, 636–7.

[198] See K. Roach, 'Canada' in C. Bradley (ed), *Criminal Procedure: A Worldwide Study* (1999), 77.

12.7 DOUBLE JEOPARDY AND RETRIALS

The traditional double jeopardy principle meant that jury acquittals were final, as were acquittals by the magistrates once the appeals process was over. In addition, the principle protects defendants from retrial for an offence for which they have already been convicted. The law here involves some technical issues, because it needs to establish when a new charge is the 'same' as one for which the defendant has already stood trial.[199] In simple terms, if the new trial involves substantially the same facts as a prior one, the defendant will not be retried, either because he has a 'plea in bar' of trial or because the trial should be stayed as an abuse of process. We will not discuss these technical points; as before, we concentrate on the arguments of principle.

In 1996 an exception to the double jeopardy principle was introduced, allowing an acquittal to be quashed and a new trial to take place in cases where the acquittal is found to be 'tainted' by the commission of an 'administration of justice offence involving interference with or intimidation of a juror or witness'.[200] This power has never been used. The CJA 2003 went much further, creating a 'fresh evidence' exception to the double jeopardy principle.[201] Where new evidence emerges throwing doubt on an acquittal, an application can be made to the Court of Appeal to quash the acquittal and order a new trial. The court should only do so if there is 'new and compelling' evidence.[202]

'New' is defined in terms of whether it was adduced in the proceedings resulting in the acquittal, and 'compelling' in terms of whether the evidence is substantial, reliable, and 'in the context of the outstanding issues [i.e. the issues in dispute at the trial], it appears highly probative of the case against the acquitted person'.[203] If this test is satisfied, the acquittal will not necessarily be quashed: first, an interests of justice test must be considered. The considerations here include whether a fair trial is possible (it may not be, owing to, for example, media coverage or delay) and 'whether it is likely that the new evidence would have been adduced in the earlier proceedings against the acquitted person but for a failure by an officer or by a prosecutor to act with due diligence or expedition'.[204] A very significant point about the power to quash acquittals is that it is retrospective: it applies to acquittals secured before the new power is implemented as well as those secured after implementation. The power is also restricted to a number of serious offences, including murder, manslaughter, and serious sexual and drug offences.[205] Ireland, Scotland, New Zealand, and various Australian jurisdictions have followed England's lead and introduced new evidence exceptions to the double jeopardy rule.

---

[199] See *Connelly* [1964] AC 1254; *Beedie* [1998] QB 356 and, generally, A. Choo, *Abuse of Process and Judicial Stays of Criminal Proceedings* (2008), 21–56.
[200] Criminal Procedure and Investigations Act 1996, s 54.
[201] CJA 2003, Part 10.   [202] Ibid, s 78.   [203] Ibid, s 78(3)(c).   [204] Ibid, s 79(2)(c).
[205] Sch 5, Part 1 contains a list of 29 'qualifying offences'.

The application of this test is not limited to direct evidence,[206] and evidence which was available but was not used in the original trial may still be 'new' under s 78(2). For example, in *R v B* the Crown applied under s 76 for B's acquittal to be quashed and a retrial ordered. At B's original trial in 1999 the judge had excluded DNA evidence on the basis that the Police and Criminal Evidence Act 1984 had not been complied with, following which the Crown offered no evidence and B was acquitted. This exclusion then was held to be wrong.[207] The Court of Appeal viewed this evidence as plainly compelling, and held it to be new under the terms of s 78(2).

The second matter is the meaning of compelling. In two cases involving a co-defendant who, on being convicted, offered to give evidence against his acquitted co-accused, the court thought that the co-defendant's mixed motives (he might gain favourable treatment by helping the authorities) meant that the new evidence could not be classified as 'compelling'. In one of these cases, *R v G*, it suggested the new evidence would have to meet a very high standard: it should be 'evidence which cannot realistically be disputed'.[208] The court has also suggested that a test based on whether an acquittal in the light of the new evidence would be 'perverse' is appropriate,[209] but that is probably putting it too high. In *Andrews*, the case in which the 'perverse' standard was mentioned, a more accurate description of the evidence was that it was 'strong supporting evidence... the evidence that the respondent was guilty of the rape... is now significantly more powerful than it was. In our judgment if it had been available at the first trial, or if it now were to be deployed at a second trial, the high probability is that the respondent would have been or will be convicted'.[210] This was held to be sufficient to justify quashing the acquittal. In *R v Celaire*, a high probability of conviction also seems to have been the standard applied.[211] In *R v Whittle*, a subsequent confession to murder by a previously acquitted man was deemed to be the outpouring of a drunken, agitated person rather than reliable, substantial, and highly probative evidence.[212] His confession required 'hesitant circumspection' and was not sufficient to constitute new and compelling evidence to justify a retrial.[213] In *R v Dobson*, a case involving the killers of Stephen Lawrence, the court held that compelling 'does not mean that the evidence must be irresistible, or that absolute proof of guilt is required. In other words, the court should not and is certainly not required to usurp the function of the jury, or, if a new trial is ordered, to indicate to the jury what the verdict should be'.[214]

Re-investigation of a case may reveal new and compelling evidence, such as in *R v Weston* where blood from the deceased was found on the respondent's boots through reinvestigation. The court concluded that the interests of justice were served by quashing the acquittal and ordering a retrial.[215] As stressed in *R v MH*, however, in relation

[206] *R v A* [2008] EWCA Crim 2908.   [207] *R v B* [2012] EWCA Crim 414.
[208] *R v G* [2009] EWCA Crim 1207, [5]. See also *R v B* [2009] EWCA Crim 1036; *R v Miell* [2008] 1 WLR 627.
[209] *R v Andrews* [2008] EWCA Crim 2908, [28].   [210] Ibid, 38.   [211] [2009] EWCA Crim 633.
[212] *R v Whittle* [2010] EWCA Crim 2934.   [213] [24].
[214] *R v Dobson* [2011] EWCA Crim 1255, [20].   [215] [2010] EWCA Crim 1576.

to new evidence pertaining to an examination (not previously undertaken) of the victim's clothing:

> inaction, indifference or sloppiness are, of course, highly material and there can be no suggestion that the legislation permits an investigation to be undertaken in a half-hearted manner on the basis that if it fails, more can then be done and permission will be given to set aside the general rule preventing double jeopardy to allow a new trial. On the other hand, that is not to say that human error by a police officer or a scientist is necessarily determinative against an application.[216]

It would obviously be wrong for the police or the CPS to impose a limit on the extent of an investigation on the basis that if a prosecution fails, a subsequent investigation can lead to an application under s 78 of the 2003 Act and a further prosecution.[217] The ultimate test is whether a retrial is necessary to preserve the integrity of the criminal justice system.[218]

Commenting before enactment, the Joint Committee on Human Rights regarded the double jeopardy provision as probably conflicting with the UK's international human rights obligations.[219] The International Covenant on Civil and Political Rights (ICCPR) does not permit 'retrial' after an acquittal, though in exceptional circumstances, 'reopening' of a trial is acceptable. The distinction is that reopening would involve new evidence, not evidence that was available to the prosecutor at the original trial. The position under the ECHR is less clear: Art 4 of Protocol 7, which the UK has not yet signed, permits a retrial on evidence of 'new or newly discovered' facts. It is not clear whether this would allow the use of evidence known to be available at the time of the first trial. While the Court of Appeal may refuse to quash a conviction under the interests of justice test if the new and compelling evidence was originally available, as the Joint Committee argued, it does not appear acceptable to rely on discretion to protect human rights.

There are, of course, deeper issues at stake here than whether or not the law is compatible with international human rights doctrine. This reform was controversial;[220] we need to ask whether any change to double jeopardy can be justified. Put another way: what is the value of the double jeopardy principle? Most people would share the intuition that it is wrong for the state to have unlimited power to question acquittals. If a defendant is acquitted, the state should not be permitted to have another go, to see whether on the next occasion a conviction can be achieved. What is not so obvious, however, is exactly why this is regarded as wrong, nor whether there should be exceptions to the general principle. The intuition presumably has something to do with the importance of having limits on state power, but this idea needs a good deal of

---

[216] *R v MH* [2015] EWCA Crim 585, [48].   [217] [57].   [218] *R v K* [2013] EWCA Crim 1820, [76].

[219] Joint Committee on Human Rights, *Criminal Justice Bill: Further Report*, Eleventh Report of 2002–3, 27–38.

[220] See in particular P. Roberts, 'Double Jeopardy Law Reform: A Criminal Justice Commentary' (2002) 65 *MLR* 393.

unpacking. The state is powerful in all sorts of ways. To pick one comparison which is particularly germane to the present discussion, there is no limitation on the number of times a person can be tried for different crimes. If a person is acquitted of burglary, there is nothing to stop the state from immediately charging him with burglary again, so long as the charge relates to a different burglary. In this way, a person's life could be made a constant misery by serial prosecution. It is true that where the new charge is for exactly the same crime, the prosecution will find it easier to bring the case: having established a case to answer once, it could easily put the defendant in genuine jeopardy of conviction again. But, especially when one bears in mind the possibility that the state can manufacture evidence, this distinction is not sufficiently absolute to rob the comparison of its force. In thinking about double jeopardy, then, it is worth asking why we object to that rather than to serial jeopardy.

Some of the reasons given for the double jeopardy principle are not especially convincing.[221] It is true that, in general, repeated prosecution increases the risk of false conviction.[222] However, this applies to serial jeopardy as much as to double jeopardy. What is more, the risk can be controlled by devices such as the requirement for 'compelling' new evidence. It is also suggested that the new trial will cause distress to the accused,[223] but we are prepared to accept such distress when ordering retrials after successful appeals and, again, serial jeopardy surely causes equal distress. Finality is perhaps a more promising value to draw on in order to support the double jeopardy principle.[224] There is value to the parties, and to society as a whole, in accepting that a contested issue has been resolved. We are prepared to put aside concerns about finality when there is evidence that an innocent person has been convicted, but this can be seen to reflect the fact that, as explained earlier, the conviction of the innocent is a much more serious wrong than acquittal of the guilty. While there is much to be said for this explanation, it would not rule out the creation of exceptions to the double jeopardy principle. Finality might sometimes be thought worth sacrificing in order to secure the conviction of the guilty.

Ian Dennis has made much of this last point.[225] He cautiously supported the exception to the double jeopardy principle, and justifies it by appeal to the value of legitimacy, which he takes to be the controlling value of, if not the whole of the criminal process, at least the trial. On his account, when new evidence emerges to throw doubt on an acquittal, the verdict risks losing its legitimacy. Verdict legitimacy can be restored, however, by a new trial. The strength of Dennis's account is that it recognizes that the criminal process does not exist just to protect the interests of defendants. However, the key role that legitimacy plays here is at least questionable. As we have observed before, legitimacy is a rather vague value. An opponent of double jeopardy

---

[221] For further discussion, see P. Roberts, 'Justice for All? Two Bad Arguments (and Several Good Suggestions) for Resisting Double Jeopardy Reform' (2002) 6 E&P 197.

[222] Law Commission, *Double Jeopardy*, Consultation Paper No 156 (1999), 37.

[223] Ibid, 37–8.   [224] Ibid, 35–8.

[225] I. Dennis, 'Rethinking Double Jeopardy: Justice and Finality in Criminal Process' [2000] *Crim LR* 933; Dennis, n 192.

reform could as easily argue that the value of finality is such that it is never appropriate to reopen an acquittal (while eschewing the language of legitimacy, this, in effect, was Paul Roberts's argument against the reform).[226]

We think an argument for the double jeopardy principle can be put in slightly different terms than the ones explored so far. When the state invokes the machinery of criminal process against a defendant, it puts him at risk of conviction; in some cases, of false conviction. In order to have the moral authority to do this, the state should consider its trial procedures to be generally reliable; to the extent that it thinks they are not, it lacks the moral authority to use them to put people in jeopardy of conviction.[227] This suggests that the state is bound by the verdicts of its trial procedures; it is, we might say, estopped from calling them into question. To demand that a defendant face the jeopardy of conviction a second time is for the state to admit that its trial procedure is unreliable, and this undermines its authority to demand that the defendant stand trial again. This does not, of course, prevent defendants from calling a verdict into question: there is no inconsistency when this occurs.

We suggest that this account has some value in explaining the contours of the double jeopardy principle. The brief discussion of the ICCPR framework earlier, implies that there is particular antipathy towards retrying an acquitted defendant by using evidence that was in the possession of the prosecution at the original trial. In this situation, the estoppel principle should bite with full force. Where new evidence emerges after the trial—by chance, as it were—there is an argument that things are different. The failure in the trial procedure might be said to be outside the state's responsibility. There is reason to be cautious about this argument: one can always imagine future technological breakthroughs that will give us new evidence, and in that sense trials will never be as reliable as they could be. Nevertheless, courts have to operate within the realm of present-day possibility; the state should not be able to distance itself from trial verdicts by saying that things may be different in the future. In the same way, when new evidence does emerge to throw doubt on an acquittal, it might be argued that the state should not be able to revisit the acquittal.

We saw earlier that the initial exception to the double jeopardy principle in England and Wales was the 'tainted acquittal' procedure introduced by the Criminal Procedure and Investigations Act. On the account sketched here, this is none too objectionable. Where the trial process has been undermined in some way, especially by the defendant, it could be said that the state has less reason to be committed to the verdict. It is worth noting that the New Zealand Law Commission, which examined the double jeopardy rule around the time that the Law Commission for England and Wales was doing so, concluded that only an exception along the lines of the tainted acquittal procedure was acceptable.[228] Its proposals were in some ways narrower than

[226] See n 221.
[227] For something like this argument, see R. Nozick, *Anarchy, State and Utopia* (1974), 102–8.
[228] New Zealand Law Commission, *Acquittal Following Perversion of the Course of Justice*, Report 70 (2001).

the English provisions: the exception would only apply where the accused himself had tainted the acquittal. But in other respects they were wider: perjury at the original trial would be included among the administration of justice offences that can trigger reopening of the verdict. In terms of theoretical coherence, there is a lot to be said for reform along these lines. In the event, however, the New Zealand legislature adopted a reform which went further, creating a new evidence exception much like that in England and Wales.[229]

This reform to the law has resulted in a media campaign to reopen an acquittal.[230] Moreover, it appears that most applications to quash acquittals are granted. Of the 21 applications to quash an acquittal since enactment of the CJA 2003, 14 resulted in the quashing of the acquittal and an order for a retrial.[231] One of the few refusals to quash an individual's acquittal for murder in the light of new DNA evidence was in *R v Reilly*, on the basis that R was detained in a high-security psychiatric hospital and only had weeks left to live due to terminal cancer, and so a retrial would not be in the interests of justice.[232]

12.8 CONCLUSION

Like other facets of the criminal process, the work of the appeal courts has been affected by budget cuts. Its heavy workload impacts on the length of time appeals take to progress, and it is questionable whether the practices of single judges and the full court are immune from pressures of time and resource that are evident across the public sector. Some cuts are self-perpetuating and self-reproducing—limiting legal aid increases the likelihood of self-representation and thus delays are worsened through efforts to enable worthwhile participation by the parties. Such fiscal pressures affect the work of the CCRC also. And, of course, there are ideological reasons for the limiting of resources for both the appeal courts and the system of compensation.

Despite these negative trends, on a positive note the work of the Court of Appeal is much more open than was once the case. While broadcasting and photography have been banned in the courts of England and Wales since 1925,[233] the Crime and Courts Act 2013 reversed the wider prohibition, and cameras have been allowed into the appeal courts since October 2013.[234] This development is understandable and sustainable, as the court does not hear evidence or involve jurors. This has been significant for public awareness of the appeal process.

---

[229] Crimes Amendment Act (No 2) 2008, s 6.

[230] See 'Should Wendell Wilberforce Baker be Tried Again for Rape?', *The Times*, 28 July 2009, reporting on a documentary, *Double Jeopardy*, broadcast on BBC1, 30 July 2009. Baker was tried and convicted in 2013.

[231] Ministry of Justice, FOI Request ref: 180813015, 7 September 2018. These 14 included cases such as *R v K* [2013] EWCA Crim 1820 (where the new evidence was from six other women in the same area as the original alleged attack) and *R v H* [2014] EWCA Crim 1816 (the new evidence was from the original complainant and two other women).

[232] *R v Reilly* [2017] EWCA Crim 1333.   [233] CJA 1925, s 41.   [234] ss 31 and 32.

Further potential for positive reform could lie in a revaluation of the Court of Appeal's grounds for allowing appeals. We endorse the view that close consideration should be given to allowing the Court of Appeal to quash a conviction where it has a serious doubt about the verdict, even without fresh evidence or fresh legal argument.[235] Of course, this has implications for the work of the CCRC.

FURTHER READING

DENNIS, I., 'Prosecution Appeals and Retrial for Serious Offences' [2004] *Crim LR* 619.

QUIRK, H., 'Identifying Miscarriages of Justice: Why Innocence in the UK is Not the Answer' (2007) 70 *MLR* 759.

SPENCER, J., 'Does our Present Criminal Appeals System Make Sense?' [2006] *Crim LR* 677.

QUESTIONS FOR DISCUSSION

1. What criteria should courts use to decide whether to quash a conviction?

2. With exceptions to double jeopardy and the ability to appeal pre-trial rulings, do prosecutors now have too many appeal rights?

---

[235] House of Commons Justice Committee, *Criminal Cases Review Commission*, Twelfth Report of Session 2014–15, HC 850 (2015), [28].

13

CIRCUMVENTING THE TRIAL THROUGH PREVENTIVE ORDERS

The focus of the preceding chapters has been on the process by which criminal cases are dealt with. In Chapters 6 and 7 we noted the possibility of diverting criminal cases from the formal criminal process, by means of an array of out-of-court disposals. Subsequent chapters have examined key stages in the process of cases that are prosecuted as criminal offences, including pre-trial remand, plea-bargaining, trial, and appeal. However, one notable feature of the English legal system has been the development and subsequent reining in of civil preventive orders—orders that may be made by a civil court, orders that contain prohibitions created by the court as a response to conduct by the defendant, and orders the breach of which amounts to a criminal offence. It will therefore be seen that the civil preventive order involves a kind of hybrid or two-step process (first, the making of the order according to civil procedure and, secondly, criminal proceedings in the event of breach), with several implications for the criminal process and for the rights of defendants.

13.1 THE CORE OF CRIMINAL PROCEDURE

In Chapter 2 we noted that the European Convention on Human Rights (ECHR) declares that before a person can be convicted of a criminal offence, that person is entitled to a fair trial with a range of procedural safeguards. It is significant that these rights are additional to those declared for civil trials. Thus, according to Art 6(1) of the ECHR, defendants in civil and criminal trials are entitled to 'a fair and public hearing within a reasonable time by an independent and impartial tribunal'. But, according to Arts 6(2) and 6(3), defendants in criminal trials have additional rights including the presumption of innocence, the right to legal assistance, and the right to confront witnesses; and, as we have seen, the European Court of Human Rights (ECtHR) has expanded that list of additional rights by recognizing certain rights (e.g. equality of arms and the privilege against self-incrimination) as 'implied' into Art 6. The purpose of these additional safeguards is to provide fundamental guarantees against arbitrary state conduct and potential misuse of its authority, an authority that is considerable when the public censure of conviction and state punishment are at stake.[1] As Duff, Farmer, Marshall, and Tadros have argued, the criminal trial is a process of considerable social importance, required to determine whether the accused should be held accountable and criminally liable for certain conduct, and in order to achieve this the state must establish the legitimacy of its own claim to hold the defendant to account, by observing 'norms that require defendants to be treated as citizens of a liberal polity, not as mere subjects of power'.[2]

One feature of recent legislative activity has been the expansion of the criminal law through the creation of thousands of offences.[3] Whatever view one takes of that development, each of those offences is subject to criminal procedure, in some form or other. Thus, in principle, if the government wishes a new crime to be created, it must accept that the additional safeguards of criminal procedure will apply to it.

13.2 THE MEANING OF 'CRIMINAL' IN EUROPEAN HUMAN RIGHTS LAW

Because of the importance attached to additional safeguards in criminal cases, the ECtHR has developed two 'anti-subversion' doctrines to restrict the ability of governments to re-label new measures as civil, administrative, or regulatory in order to place them outside the criminal law. What the ECtHR has done is to give an 'autonomous meaning' to certain terms in the Convention: this means that only the Court's definition of those terms is authoritative, and that the classification of a measure in domestic law as 'civil' or 'disciplinary' is not determinative. Thus, the Court has insisted that the term 'criminal charge' in Art 6 is interpreted autonomously, so that a measure (howsoever labelled in domestic law) may be regarded as criminal if it involves a fault requirement and/or if it provides for the imposition of punishment.[4] There is an extensive ECHR case law on this, which has resulted in legal measures from several countries being held to be 'criminal' in substance, despite their domestic designation.[5] It has also insisted that the term 'penalty' in Art 7 has an autonomous meaning, so that even if a measure is preventive in purpose, it may nevertheless be considered to be punitive in

---

[1] See A. Ashworth and L. Zedner, 'Preventive Orders: A Problem of Under-Criminalization?' in R. A. Duff et al (eds), *The Boundaries of the Criminal Law* (2010).

[2] A. Duff, L. Farmer, S. Marshall, and V. Tadros (eds), *The Trial on Trial, Vol 3: Towards a Normative Theory of the Criminal Trial* (2007), 288.

[3] See J. Chalmers, '"Frenzied law making": overcriminalization by numbers' (2014) 67 *Current Legal Problems* 483; J. Chalmers, F. Leverick, and A. Shaw, 'Is Formal Criminalisation Really on the Rise? Evidence from the 1950s' [2015] *Crim LR* 177.

[4] The leading cases are *Engel v Netherlands* (1979) 1 EHRR 647 and *Benham v UK* (1996) 22 EHRR 293.

[5] E.g. *Garyfallou AEBE v Greece* (1999) 28 EHRR 344 (regulatory penalties), and *Ravnsborg v Sweden* (1994) 18 EHRR 38 (contempt of court); see generally B. Emmerson, A. Ashworth, and A. Macdonald, *Human Rights and Criminal Justice* (3rd edn, 2012), ch 3.

effect and therefore to be a 'penalty' to which the non-retroactivity principle applies.[6] These judicial doctrines have the effect of constraining governmental attempts to circumvent the additional safeguards in criminal cases, by insisting that if a measure is in substance a criminal charge or a penalty, designating it as some other kind of legal form cannot be permitted. If it is held to be a 'criminal charge' or 'penalty', the relevant safeguards must apply.

13.3 CIVIL PREVENTIVE ORDERS AND THE EVOLUTION OF THE ASBO

Since introduction in 1998, the Anti-Social Behaviour Order (ASBO) became a notorious feature of English law.[7] Its origins lay in various Labour Party documents of the mid-1990s, which made it clear that nuisance behaviour by neighbours was significantly detrimental to the quality of life of many people, not least those living in public or low-cost housing.[8] It was also believed that the criminal process was not effective in dealing with such behaviour, partly because a criminal offence focuses on a particular event without capturing the full effects of a course of conduct, and partly because the victims of such conduct were often unwilling to give evidence in court against people with whom they had to mix every day. It was against this background that the notion of a civil preventive order was developed, a legal form that would allow evidence to be given according to civil procedure, if necessary by public officials who had witnessed or been told of the objectionable conduct, and which would then enable a court to make an order containing various prohibitions, the breach of which would be criminal.

According to s 1 of the 1998 Act, a court could make an ASBO where it found that: the defendant acted in an anti-social manner, that is, 'in a manner that caused or was likely to cause harassment, alarm or distress'; and that the order was necessary to protect persons from further such behaviour. The court could then make an order 'which prohibits the defendant from doing anything described in the order' for a minimum of two years. Breach of the terms of the order without reasonable excuse was a criminal offence with a maximum penalty of five years' imprisonment. Most cases were brought to a magistrates' court by the local authority or the police. In the early years, there was little enthusiasm for applying for ASBOs in most areas of the country, so that between January 1999 and the end of 2002 only about 1,000 ASBOs were made. In 2002, it became possible for a criminal court to make an ASBO as a supplement to a

---

[6] The leading cases are *Welch v UK* (1995) 20 EHRR 247 and *Ibbotson v UK* (1999) 27 EHRR CD 332; for further analysis, see Emmerson, Ashworth, and Macdonald, ibid, 873ff.

[7] Crime and Disorder Act 1998, s 1.

[8] For detailed discussion, see E. Burney, *Making People Behave: Anti-Social Behaviour, Politics and Policy* (2nd edn, 2009); P. Squires and D. E. Stephen, *Rougher Justice: Anti-Social Behaviour and Young People* (2005); for shorter discussions, see A. Ashworth, 'Social Control and Anti-Social Behaviour: The Subversion of Human Rights?' (2004) 120 *LQR* 263 and S. Macdonald, 'A Suicidal Woman, Roaming Pigs and a Noisy Trampolinist: Refining the ASBO's Definition of Anti-Social Behaviour' (2006) 69 *MLR* 183.

sentence imposed on a convicted offender,[9] and subsequently such ASBOs accounted for the majority of orders made.[10] Overall, 3,440 were made in 2004, 4,090 in 2005, and 2,822 in 2006. Of the 20,231 ASBOs issued between 1 June 2000 to 31 December 2010, 56.5 per cent (11,432) were breached at least once, with 8,492 (42.0 per cent) of these breached more than once.[11] Just under 68 per cent of young people breached their ASBOs at least once by the end of 2010, compared to 50.4 per cent of adults. Of the ASBOs breached at least once, 52.5 per cent were given an immediate custodial sentence, with an average custodial sentence length of 5.2 months.[12] Some sentences were much greater: 20 months' imprisonment for breach of an ASBO prohibiting begging was appropriate where the offender had previous convictions for breach of the same order.[13]

As noted in the previous edition of this book, ASBOs attracted strong and persistent criticism from many quarters, due to the broad scope of the powers given to the authorities and the paucity of safeguards for defendants. Section 1 of the 1998 Act delegated a wide rule-making discretion to the courts, insofar as a court acting under civil procedure, essentially, was able to make criminal laws for that defendant. The decision to make an ASBO or other preventive order was therefore 'a form of criminalization: an *ex ante* prohibition, not an *ex post facto* verdict', and the power thus conferred on the civil court was of enormous width and potency.[14] In addition, the application of ASBOs was problematic: just under half of those receiving ASBOs were young people, despite the government's claim that the measure was not aimed at the young, and some orders were imposed on mentally disturbed and other vulnerable persons who needed support rather than intervention through the criminal justice system. Moreover, there was little engagement with the causes of problematic behaviour. Furthermore, the maximum penalty for the offence of breaching a prohibition in an ASBO was five years and could be regarded as disproportionate, not least as it was higher than the maximum penalty for many offences (e.g. assault, affray, assaulting a police officer). In view of the high maximum penalty and the other objections set out, it was arguable that the ASBO was not compatible with European human rights law, being in substance a penalty or criminal charge, despite being labelled a civil preventive order. Though never considered by the ECtHR, the House of Lords rejected the argument that the ASBO was in substance a criminal charge. The House held that the two stages or steps in the ASBO were distinct, and each of them complied with the necessary procedural safeguards.[15] The first step, when the court determines whether to make an ASBO and what prohibitions to insert into it, was entirely civil. At this stage there was 'no question' of a

---

[9] The power was introduced by s 64 of the Police Reform Act 2002.   [10] Burney, n 8, 171.

[11] Ministry of Justice, *Statistical Notice: Anti-Social Behaviour Order (ASBO) Statistics England and Wales 2010* (13 October 2011), 2.

[12] Ibid, at 4.   [13] *R v Fagan* [2010] EWCA Crim 2449.

[14] See the argument of A. P. Simester and A. von Hirsch, 'Regulating Offensive Conduct through Two-Step Prohibitions' in A. von Hirsch and A. P. Simester (eds), *Incivilities: Regulating Offensive Behaviour* (2006).

[15] *Clingham v Royal Borough of Kensington and Chelsea; R (on behalf of McCann) v Crown Court at Manchester* [2003] 1 AC 787.

conviction being registered: the order is simply preventive. The second step occurs only if the order is breached, which is a criminal offence; criminal procedure applies in its entirety to the breach proceedings. The only concession made by the House of Lords was to hold that the standard of proof in the initial civil proceedings should be high, equivalent to the standard in criminal proceedings (beyond reasonable doubt), in view of the possible consequences of breach of the order.

Following a consultation on the Coalition government plans 'to streamline the tool-kit used to tackle anti-social behaviour',[16] a White Paper *Putting victims first: more effective responses to anti-social behaviour* was published in 2012.[17] This led to the passing of the Anti-social Behaviour, Crime and Policing Act 2014, which replaced ASBOs with injunctions, Criminal Behaviour Orders (CBOs), and a range of other community measures.

Under s 1 of the 2014 Act, the High Court, the county court, or the Youth Court may grant an injunction against a person aged 10 or over if the court is satisfied, on the balance of probabilities, that he or she has engaged or threatens to engage in anti-social behaviour, and that the court considers it just and convenient (rather than necessary as was the cases with ABSOs) to grant the injunction to prevent him or her from so doing. In contrast to ASBOs, such an injunction granted before the person has reached the age of 18 must be for no more than 12 months. An injunction may include prohibitions and/or positive requirements (e.g. attendance at alcohol/drug rehabilitation programmes, the removal of rubbish, etc) and these must avoid, as far as practicable, interference with work or school times. An injunction that includes a requirement must specify the individual or an organization who is responsible for supervising compliance.[18] This seeks to remedy one of the key concerns about ASBOs, that they did not address the underlying causes of problematic behaviour.

As was the case with ASBOs, various persons may apply for an injunction under s 1, including a police chief officer, a local authority, a housing provider, Transport for London, and the Environment Agency.[19] Now, before applying for an injunction such a person must consult the local youth offending team about the application if the respondent is aged under 18; and inform any other body or individual the applicant thinks appropriate of the application.[20] An application for an injunction may be made without notice being given to the respondent.[21]

One definition of anti-social behaviour, given in s 2(1)(a), is comparable to that in the 1998 Act: conduct that has caused, or is likely to cause, harassment, alarm, or distress to any person. Beyond this, there is a more expansive definition in s 2(1)(b) which applies only where the injunction is applied for by a housing provider, a local authority, or a chief officer of police: conduct capable of causing nuisance or annoyance to a person in relation to that person's occupation of residential premises. Nuisance or annoyance is a lower threshold. A third definition is provided in s 2(1)(c), that is, conduct capable of causing housing-related nuisance or annoyance to any person,

---

[16] https://www.gov.uk/government/consultations/more-effective-responses-to-anti-social-behaviour.
[17] Cm 8367 (2012).   [18] s 3.   [19] s 5.   [20] s 14.   [21] s 6.

where 'housing-related' means directly or indirectly relating to the housing management functions of a housing provider, or a local authority.

In contrast to the situation with ASBOs, breach of the injunction is not a crime, but rather constitutes contempt of court, punishable by an unlimited fine or imprisonment for up to two years by the county court. In the case of a young person under the age of 18, breach of the civil injunction will result in a supervision order, or a detention order if, in view of the severity or extent of the breach, no other power available to the Youth Court is appropriate.[22] For both adults and young people, proving breach of an injunction must be beyond reasonable doubt.

The Anti-social Behaviour, Crime and Policing Act 2014 also introduced the Criminal Behaviour Order (CBO), which may be imposed after conviction in addition to the sentence handed down, or the conditional discharge order.[23] The court may make a CBO if satisfied, beyond reasonable doubt, that the offender has engaged in behaviour that caused or was likely to cause harassment, alarm, or distress to any person; and the court considers that making the order will help to prevent the offender from engaging in such behaviour. There is no obligation on the court to include in the CBO a positive requirement addressing the underlying cause of the offending; it is simply enabled to do so.[24] For a young person, a CBO must be a fixed period between one and three years, and for an adult the minimum duration is two years.

The more restrained scheme under the 2014 Act is not immune from the liberal critique of ASBOs and other civil preventive orders elaborated on earlier. Concerns remain about the conflation of criminal and other less harmful behaviour, and the inconsistency in application of the provisions. Moreover, the prospect of supervision of young people and in more egregious cases detention, indicates the interventionist nature of measures that seek to counter anti-social behaviour without addressing the social or structural causes that may be at play.

Historically, the ASBO grew out of dissatisfaction with the criminal law (and, partly, with the protections that it accords to accused persons). As for whether the ASBO and subsequent orders derive support from any normative theory, Peter Ramsay argues that traditional liberal critiques, such as the one presented above, fail to take account of the argument that as citizens we have the duty to assure others that we will respect their interests. Thus, the autonomy of the individual is a fundamental element of the good life, but each person's autonomy is 'intrinsically vulnerable to the spontaneous self-interested preferences of others', which supplies a reason why 'behaviour which fails to reassure [should be] controlled by a preventative order'.[25] He argues that reasoning of this kind underlies the promotion of the ASBO and other civil preventive orders. He does not conclude that this theory of vulnerable autonomy is a convincing rationale, but argues that it has some legitimacy in the context of prevailing political ideologies.[26]

---

[22] Sch 2, para 1.   [23] s 22.   [24] *DPP v Bulmer* [2015] EWHC 2323 (Admin).
[25] P. Ramsay, 'The Theory of Vulnerable Autonomy and the Legitimacy of Civil Preventative Orders' in B. McSherry, A. Norrie, and S. Bronitt (eds), *Regulating Deviance* (2009), 131.
[26] Ibid, 138–9.

13.4 THE RANGE OF CIVIL PREVENTIVE ORDERS

The hybrid legal form provided by the ASBO was emulated in a range of measures, such as the risk of sexual harm order[27] and the serious crime prevention order.[28] Other civil preventive measures were introduced that could be imposed after conviction only, such as the violent offender order,[29] the travel restriction order,[30] and the sexual offences prevention order.[31] Akin to the changes in respect of the ASBO, the risk of sexual harm order was repealed by the 2014 Act and replaced by the sexual risk order (SRO).[32] Now a chief officer of police or the Director General of the National Crime Agency may apply to the magistrates' court for an SRO which will be granted if the court is satisfied 'that the defendant has, whether before or after the commencement of this Part, done an act of a sexual nature' as a result of which it is necessary to make such an order for the purpose of protecting the public or any particular members of the public from harm from the defendant, or protecting children or vulnerable adults generally, or any particular children or vulnerable adults, from harm from the defendant outside the UK.[33] An SRO prohibits the person from doing anything described in the order for a minimum of two years.[34]

A serious crime prevention order can be made by the High Court without conviction, if satisfied that a person has been involved in serious crime, including 'conducting himself in a way that was likely to facilitate the commission by him or another of a serious offence',[35] and where the court has reasonable grounds to believe that the order would protect the public by preventing, restricting, or disrupting the person's involvement in serious crime.[36] The order may contain prohibitions, restrictions, or requirements that are appropriate for the above purposes, such as prohibitions on certain property or financial dealings, on travel, or on the use of certain premises. The legislation includes certain procedural protections but the sanction for breach is a prison sentence of up to five years, and there are further powers on breach such as forfeiture of assets.

Akin to the CBO, the violent offender order applies to a restricted group of people—those who have been convicted of a specified offence (essentially, an offence contrary to s 20 of the Offences Against the Person Act 1861 or worse, for which a sentence of at least 12 months' imprisonment was imposed). The court may make a VOO if a chief constable persuades it that the person has 'acted in such a way as to give reasonable cause to believe that it is necessary' for the order to be made, for the purpose of protecting the public from serious harm. The order may run from two to five years, and may include prohibitions, restrictions, or conditions on matters such as not going to

---

[27] Sexual Offences Act 2003, s 123. See further S. Shute, 'New Civil Preventative Orders: Sexual Offences Prevention Orders; Foreign Travel Orders; Risk of Sexual Harm Orders' [2004] *Crim LR* 417.

[28] Serious Crime Act 2007, s 1.   [29] Criminal Justice and Immigration Act 2008, s 98.

[30] Criminal Justice and Police Act 2001, s 33.   [31] Sexual Offences Act (SOA) 2003, s 104.

[32] s 113 and Sch 5. See H. Davies, *Civil Prevention Orders Sexual Offences Act 2003 ACPO Commissioned Review of the Existing Statutory Scheme and Recommendations for Reform* (2013).

[33] SOA 2003, s 122A.   [34] s 7.   [35] Serious Crime Act, s 2(1)(c).   [36] s 1.

certain places or not having contact with certain people. Closely related to these civil preventive orders were control orders under the Prevention of Terrorism Act 2005. After the events of 9/11, the British legislature passed the Anti-Terrorism, Crime and Security Act 2001, which contained a number of provisions that the government justified as necessary to protect the country against terrorism. One of the measures was the indefinite detention without trial of suspected international terrorists. This was implemented but its compatibility with the ECHR was challenged successfully in the courts. In *A and others v Secretary of State for the Home Department*,[37] the House of Lords declared these powers of detention without trial to be incompatible with Convention rights. Clearly, the powers breached the right to liberty declared by Art 5, but the government relied on its derogation from Art 5 as a justification. This justification was scrutinized by their Lordships, who held inter alia that the derogation could not be supported under Art 15 since it was restricted to suspected *international* terrorists.

As a result of this ruling, the government abandoned the power of indefinite detention without trial and invented the control order.[38] This was presented as another attempt to deal with the problem of persons who could not be deported because the potential receiving country was one that might use torture against the person, and whom it was thought inadvisable to prosecute in the UK because that might lead to the secret processes of the security services becoming known. In essence, the executive (the Home Secretary) could impose a control order so as to restrict the actions of certain persons. Broadly speaking,[39] the order confined its subject to a particular dwelling for a certain number of hours each day, and controlled the subject's interactions with people, and his use of the telephone and internet. As with other civil preventive orders, the consequence of a breach was conviction with a maximum sentence of five years' imprisonment. Control orders were also challenged in the courts, on the ground that in substance they amounted to a deprivation of liberty contrary to Art 5, whereas the government's view was that this was merely a restriction on liberty, which therefore did not engage Art 5. This challenge brought into focus a third form of anti-subversion doctrine, the autonomous meaning given by the Strasbourg Court to the term 'deprivation of liberty'. As that Court had declared in *Guzzardi v Italy*,[40] it is for the Court to determine whether in substance a particular restriction amounts to a deprivation of liberty. In *JJ v Secretary of State for the Home Department* (2007),[41] the House of Lords had to consider whether the particular restrictions imposed by a certain control order (including confinement to a particular apartment for 18 hours per day, no use of telephone or internet, no pre-arranged meetings with others during the hours of liberty except with approval, and so on) were such as to amount, in substance, to a deprivation of liberty contrary to Art 5. By a majority, the House of Lords held that it did amount to a deprivation of liberty, but the House made it clear that some reduction in the

---

[37] [2004] UKHL 56; see now *A v UK* (2009) 49 EHRR 625.

[38] See generally L. Zedner, Preventive Justice or Pre-Punishment? The Case of Control Orders' (2007) 59 *CLP* 174.

[39] See ibid for discussion of the precise details of derogating and non-derogating control orders.

[40] (1981) 3 EHRR 333.   [41] [2007] UKHL 45.

constraints would bring the control order back into the realm of a mere restriction on liberty, which would be outside Art 5.

This preventive regime was moderated somewhat by the Terrorism Prevention and Investigation Measures Act 2011, which abolished control orders[42] and provided for the creation of Terrorism Prevention and Investigation Measures (TPIMs).[43] Ostensibly, TPIMs are narrower in reach and involve more judicial oversight and mechanisms for review when compared to their predecessor. That said, they remain problematic because they are imposed on unconvicted persons, they still involve intrusive restrictions, and because not all of the material relied upon is disclosed to the subject of the order but rather to a special advocate instructed on his behalf.[44]

The Home Secretary may impose a TPIM on an individual if the conditions in s 3 are satisfied, namely that he is satisfied, on the balance of probabilities,[45] that the individual is, or has been, involved in terrorism-related activity; that some or all of this is new terrorism-related activity; that the TPIM is necessary for purposes connected with protecting members of the public from a risk of terrorism, and with preventing or restricting the individual's involvement in terrorism-related activity. In addition, the High Court must give the Home Secretary permission to impose a TPIM under s 6, or he must reasonably consider that the urgency of the case requires the imposition of a TPIM without such permission.[46] Review of the Home Secretary's decision will thus occur retrospectively. Another safeguard is sought to be provided by means of the requirement that the Home Secretary must consult the relevant police chief officer about whether there is evidence available that could realistically be used for the purposes of prosecuting the individual for an offence relating to terrorism before applying for/imposing a TPIM.[47]

Schedule 1 outlines the types of measures that may be imposed in a TPIM, including restrictions on overnight residence, travel, property, and association. In contrast to control orders, there is a two-year limit on imposition of measures without new terrorism-related activity. A TPIM is in force for one year and may be extended on one occasion as long as the Home Secretary is satisfied, on the balance of probabilities, that the individual is, or has been, involved in terrorism-related activity, and that the TPIM remains necessary on the grounds in s 3. Moreover, s 11 provides for review by the Home Secretary of ongoing necessity during the period that a TPIM notice is in force.

David Anderson, then Independent Reviewer of terrorism legislation, stated in his first report into TPIMs that 'Nobody could feel entirely comfortable about [the TPIM regime], or wish it to survive for any longer than necessary. I nonetheless conclude

---

[42] s 1.   [43] s 2.

[44] The Counter-Terrorism and Security Act 2015 raised the threshold from reasonable belief.

[45] This was defined in s 4, and amended by the Counter-Terrorism and Security Act 2015, narrowing the definition of terrorism-related activity in the Act by removing conduct which gives 'support or assistance' to individuals who are known or believed by the individuals concerned to be involved in the 'encouragement or facilitation of acts of terrorism'. This followed recommendation 3 of David Anderson QC; *Terrorism Prevention and Investigation Measures in 2013 Second Report of the Independent Reviewer on the Operation of the Terrorism Prevention and Investigation Measures Act 2011* (2014).

[46] s 3(5).   [47] s 10.

that it provides a broadly acceptable response to some intractable problems.[48] And the regime does survive: the Terrorism Prevention and Investigation Act 2011 (Continuation) Order 2016 extended the Secretary of State's TPIM powers under the Act, which were due to expire on 14 December 2016, for a further five years until 13 December 2021. While TPIMs' preventive effect is hard to ascertain and quantify, intelligence on TPIM subjects is not leading to prosecution (save in respect of TPIM breaches, where the conviction rate is low).[49] As of 31 August 2017, there were six TPIM notices in force, five in respect of British citizens. All six subjects were relocated.[50]

13.5 CONCLUSION

Throughout the book we have drawn attention to the considerable expansion of the criminal law, stemming from the tendency of the government to create a new criminal offence whenever a social problem achieves a high profile in the media. Profligate criminalization this may be, but at least the creation of a crime brings with it the additional procedural safeguards for which Arts 6(2) and 6(3) provide, so that a person cannot be convicted of that crime unless certain protections are accorded during the criminal process. In Chapters 6 and 7 we noted the rapid growth of out-of-court penalties: the power to impose (or, some would say, offer) such penalties lies with either the Crown Prosecution Service or with the police or other law enforcement agency, but respect for the additional safeguards available for criminal charges is retained by the opportunity that the person has to refuse the out-of-court penalty and to insist on the matter being heard in court. Article 6 is satisfied, the Strasbourg Court has held,[51] so long as the ticketed person can insist on having a court hearing—even though, as we noted, there may be powerful pressures to accept the out-of-court penalty.

Although there are grounds for questioning the form that out-of-court disposals take in English law, and the degree of power they place in the hands of enforcement officers, we noted in Chapter 6 that there may be good reasons of proportionality (as well as efficiency and economy) to deal with some minor cases without bringing them to court. Similarly, it can be said that there may be good reasons for dealing with some types of social problem through regulatory, civil, or other non-criminal channels, rather than resorting to the criminal law—indeed, this is implicit in the criticism of criminalization over the last decades. Thus, in this chapter we have charted the rise and fall of a form of hybrid or two-step civil preventive order to deal with certain types of social problem. Trying to use non-criminal methods

---

[48] D. Anderson QC, *Terrorism Prevention and Investigation Measures in 2012: First Report of the Independent Reviewer on the Operation of the Terrorism Prevention and Investigation Measures Act 2011* (2013), 11.55.

[49] Anderson, *Second Report*, n 45, 5.1–5.8 and 6.3(c).

[50] Max Hill QC, Independent Reviewer of Terrorism Legislation, *The Terrorism Acts in 2016: Report of the Independent Reviewer Of Terrorism Legislation on the Operation of the Terrorism Acts 2000 and 2006* (2018), 3.9.

[51] *Ozturk v Germany* (1984) 6 EHRR 409.

of dealing with social problems may attract considerable support, not least as it may suggest an attempt to tackle the causes of the problem, rather than simply to punish its manifestations after the event. However, what we have observed, in the evolution of the ASBO and other civil preventive orders that endure the demise of ASBOs, is the imposition of one or more prohibitions on an individual with a view to preventing nuisance or harm, reinforced by the use of sentences of imprisonment for breach. Thus, the development of the civil preventive order cannot really be supported by those who argue in favour of greater use of the civil law instead of the criminal law, since some civil preventive orders retain a sting in the tail, with imprisonment for breach. It has been argued here that this high maximum penalty colours the whole approach of the civil preventive order, aligning it much more with the criminal law and certainly calling for greater safeguards at the (civil) stage of drafting and imposing the prohibitions.

Granted that the civil preventive order currently stands outside criminal procedure in English law, what are the limits of the technique? It has been argued elsewhere that the civil preventive order seems to fall into 'a jurisprudential black hole',[52] in which there is no presumption of innocence, no ban on retrospectivity, and no prospect of the additional safeguards that are available in criminal cases. Whether there are any operative restraining principles for the civil preventive orders that survive the decline of the ASBOs is difficult to divine. The English courts insisted on standards of certainty and specificity (avoiding over-breadth) in the framing of ASBO prohibitions,[53] and the ECHR jurisprudence offers some support for three restraining principles—the principle of necessity, that it must be established that the restrictions are necessary to prevent the harm; the principle of subsidiary, that less intrusive measures must have been considered and adjudged to be insufficient; and the principle of proportionality, that the measures taken must not be out of proportion to the danger apprehended, taking account of any relevant rights of the individual (such as the right to respect for private life under Art 8 of the Convention).[54] These restraining principles have influenced the demise of the ASBO, and could structure the decisions of the courts on imposing particular prohibitions in particular cases.

FURTHER READING

ASHWORTH, A. and ZEDNER, L., 'Preventive Orders: A Problem of Under-Criminalization?' in R. A. Duff et al (eds), *The Boundaries of the Criminal Law*, Oxford: Oxford University Press, 2010.

---

[52] A. Ashworth, 'Criminal Law, Human Rights and Preventative Justice' in B. McSherry, A. Norrie, and S. Bronitt (eds), *Regulating Deviance* (2009), 100.

[53] The leading decisions are *Boness, Bebbington and others* [2006] 1 Cr App R (S) 690, *H Stevens and Lovegrove* [2006] 2 Cr App R (S) 463, and *W and F* [2006] 2 Cr App R (S) 724.

[54] Two relevant decisions supporting these principles are *Witold Litwa v Poland* (2001) 33 EHRR 1267 and *Enhorn v Sweden* (2005) 41 EHRR 643.

RAMSAY, P., 'The Theory of Vulnerable Autonomy and the Legitimacy of Civil Preventative Orders' in B. McSherry, A. Norrie, and S. Bronitt (eds), *Regulating Deviance*, Oxford: Hart, 2009.

QUESTIONS FOR DISCUSSION

1. Are there good social reasons for the government to make greater use of civil or hybrid orders, for the purpose of social control?

2. How strong are the objections to the favoured model of the civil preventive order in English law?

14

CRIMINAL PROCESS VALUES

Chapters 4 to 12 of the book have discussed key stages of decision making in the criminal process, making reference to issues of policy and principle in the relevant law and practices. It is time now to reflect more generally upon the values that appear to dominate the English criminal process, the values that ought to dominate it, and how change might be brought about, in the context of austerity and diminishing resource allocation, for both economic and ideological reasons. We start by offering some general observations about the criminal process.

Early in Chapter 1, a distinction was drawn between three types of decision at the pre-trial stage: processual decisions, which are concerned with the progress of the case from arrest through to court, or as far as the case goes; dispositive decisions, which divert a case from the process of prosecution and trial and which may dispose of the case through some kind of undertaking or penalty; and the temporizing decision, remand, which determines whether or not the defendant should be at liberty between first court appearance and trial. While there is often a tendency to regard these decisions as discrete rational determinations, it will have become apparent that they cannot be assessed properly without having regard to the system or process of which they form part. Thus, for example, each decision is shaped by the flow of information to the decision maker and by the way in which 'facts' and opinions are selected, constructed, and communicated—all of which may be influenced as much by power relations between the parties as by the law. Additionally, each decision maker may be not only subject to rules or guidelines, as the case may be, but also influenced by an occupational culture and by the expectations of others both within and outside the system. It is therefore important not to neglect the serial view of decisions, noting that decisions by the public and by ordinary police officers or by the personnel of regulatory agencies may have considerable implications for later determinations; that decisions on charge may have implications for mode of trial; that decisions on mode of trial may have implications for remand and for plea; and so forth. Moreover, events which occur early in the process—a mistaken identification, a false confession—can have profound implications later on. The fragility of various types of evidence should caution us to view claims about the 'facts' of cases, or about innocence and guilt, with a degree of scepticism.

Little has been said, in the foregoing chapters, about the differences between accusatorial and inquisitorial systems of criminal justice. The conventional view of the English criminal process is as accusatorial, eschewing the idea of an impartial inquiry into the case by a neutral official in favour of the notion that a fair result emerges from an adversarial process in which the prosecution constructs a case for convicting the defendant and the defendant attempts to undermine or discredit that case. One reason for not dwelling on this contrast is the complexity and nuances of the adversarial/inquisitorial distinction, both in theory and in practice.[1] Another reason may be found in what may be termed the 'theory of convergence', which suggests that the trend in Europe has been away from a clear dichotomy of approaches and towards a more unified framework.[2] Such convergence is said to have been assisted by the European Convention on Human Rights (ECHR). However, the dynamics here are not straightforward. Jackson has suggested that the model promoted under the Convention is distinctive rather than an amalgam of features associated with accusatorial and inquisitorial systems, and that it is unlikely that a single model of proof will emerge under the Convention because differences between jurisdictions mean that ECHR requirements will be implemented in different ways in different jurisdictions.[3] Independently of the Convention, one can point to aspects of particular legal systems which appear to be influenced by elements of a foreign procedural tradition, such as the role now played by the Criminal Procedure Rules (CPR) in England and Wales, and the introduction of forms of plea-bargaining in France and Germany.[4] But it is still problematic to talk of convergence, in part because jurisdictional legal traditions and cultures play a powerful role in the way that these developments evolve,[5] and indeed there is some sense of systems transcending or advancing beyond such models.[6] Perhaps the better lesson to draw from these developments is that it is questionable in the first place to measure actual legal systems against an ideal type of the accusatorial or inquisitorial system.[7] Does the significance of the CPR make the English criminal process less accusatorial?[8] If party control of proceedings is the essence of the accusatorial system, then it must be recognized that there is no pure accusatorial system, because ethical duties to the court and exclusionary rules have always limited the ability of the parties to conduct proceedings how they want, though this is being limited further by the overriding objective and corresponding duties to cooperate. Further, a claim that the English system

---

[1] The best-known work is by M. Damaška, *The Faces of Justice and State Authority* (1976), and 'Evidentiary Barriers to Conviction and Two Models of Criminal Procedure: A Comparative Study' (1973) 121 *U Pa LR* 506.
[2] For further discussion, see N. Jorg, S. Field, and C. Brants, 'Are Inquisitorial and Adversarial Systems Converging?' in C. Harding et al (eds), *Criminal Justice in Europe* (1995); J. Spencer, 'Adversarial vs inquisitorial systems: is there still such a difference?' (2016) 20 *Int J Human Rights* 601–16.
[3] J. Jackson, 'The Effects of Human Rights on Criminal Evidentiary Processes: Convergence, Divergence or Realignment?' (2005) 68 *MLR* 737, 740.
[4] See especially Chs 10 and 11.
[5] J. Ogg, 'Adversary and Adversity: Converging adversarial and inquisitorial systems of justice—a case study of the Italian criminal trial reforms' (2013) 37 *Int J Comp and Applied Crim Justice* 31.
[6] A. Freiberg, 'Post-adversarial and post-inquisitorial justice: Transcending traditional penological paradigms' (2011) 8 *Eur J Criminol* 82.
[7] See further the essays in Part 1 of J. Jackson, M. Langer, and P. Tillers (eds), *Crime, Procedure and Evidence in an International and Comparative Context* (2008).
[8] J. McEwan 'From Adversarialism to Managerialism: Criminal Justice in Transition' (2011) 31 *Legal Studies* 519–46.

is becoming less accusatorial often conveys a value judgement: that important defence rights are being eroded, for example. But this requires careful assessment in the individual case, not comparison with some non-existent ideal type. Much the same could be said when it comes to deployment of Packer's models.

14.1 THE AVOIDANCE OF CRIMINAL TRIALS

In the course of this book it has become evident that whereas the rhetoric of English criminal procedure tends to place emphasis on trial by jury according to the laws of evidence, the practice is otherwise. Most cases are heard in magistrates' courts not in the Crown Court with a jury, and the vast majority of cases proceed on a plea of guilty, which means that no trial of guilt ever takes place. In no sense is this a 'natural' or 'unavoidable' phenomenon: the system is structured so as to produce it. There are incentives towards the avoidance of trials, incentives that do not exist in some other legal systems. The most notable of these is the sentence discount for a plea of guilty, up to one-third off the sentence that would otherwise be given for the offence. There are also disincentives to appealing against court decisions, introduced for similar reasons. For some time, there have been increasing fiscal pressures towards having fewer cases dealt with in the Crown Court and more in the magistrates' courts, manifested in such changes as the reclassification of certain offences as 'summary only' in 1988, and the introduction of the 'plea before venue' system in 1997. This drive for efficiency was given added impetus by the government's austerity programme, and there is little evidence that this will abate at any time. However, in addition to these structural factors there are also cultural influences pulling in the same direction. Defence lawyers and prosecutors act cooperatively at some stages, particularly in plea negotiations.[9] This is underlined further by the requirement to agree matters under the CPR. What ought to be different ethical orientations may thus become submerged beneath the working practices and occupational cultures of the local groups of professionals.

It is not only for cases that are pursued to conviction that the system tends strongly towards trial-avoidance. The trend towards diversion is designed to take cases out of the formal criminal process and to dispose of them separately, again for both ideological and pragmatic reasons. The continued vitality of diversion, despite a generally repressive penal climate, seems to stem from the confluence of some very different arguments—that the painful consequences of being prosecuted may themselves be too severe a response to some forms of wrongdoing; that there is scant evidence that formal court processes are more effective in preventing reoffending; that encounters with the court system may create stigma and disadvantage that makes future law-abidance more difficult; that diversion is far less expensive and time-consuming than court proceedings; and that it is an effective way of closing the 'justice gap' by clearing up more offences. Although it is likely that considerations of cost and clear-up rates weigh most

---

[9] See Ch 3.

heavily with policymakers, the result may also be to advance the other arguments in favour of diversion.

It would be wrong, however, to overlook the disadvantages. On a general plane, a widely used discretion not to prosecute may be regarded as undermining the principle of legality and the idea of the rule of law. For example, the Sexual Offences Act 2003 created several offences that criminalized perfectly normal acts between teenagers:[10] the government's response was that no prosecutions would be brought for such conduct, and the Crown Prosecution Service (CPS) drew up guidelines to that end.[11] The official view is that these broad offences are needed to catch the minority of sexual predators, but the counter-argument is that if guidelines for prosecutors can be drawn up, then the law itself should be drafted so as to decriminalize unproblematic and non-predatory acts. The law should not give such discretion to prosecutors to determine the effective ambit of a widely cast law, and citizens should not have to trust prosecutors not to criminalize them inappropriately.[12] On a more specific plane, existing methods of diversion are often inseparable from incentives for the suspect or defendant to accept them. Rather like the discount for pleading guilty, the incentive to accept a Penalty Notice for Disorder (PND) or caution may prove a powerful practical inducement to terminate one's involvement with the criminal justice system quickly and without the anxiety of a court appearance. However, the European Court of Human Rights (ECtHR) has insisted, and English law generally provides, that anyone who does not wish to accept diversion can decline and invite the prosecution to bring the case before a court.[13] This is crucial, given that cautions, PNDs, reprimands, and final warnings are recorded nationally and may be cited in court or revealed through the vetting required for many positions of employment.[14] Proper safeguards, such as access to legal advice, should be made available and there should be a principle that any sentence the court passes on a subsequent finding of guilt should not be significantly more onerous than the penalty voluntarily rejected by the defendant. Moreover, while some methods of diversion incorporating restorative justice principles may enhance the rights of victims, diversion in cases of serious sexual harm may downplay and diminish the offences' gravity.

These remarks are at a general level, and the practical operation of the system may vary to some extent according to the type of crime alleged. In the previous chapters, we have noted the special difficulties arising in certain types of case: for example, the problems of investigating and prosecuting offences of intimate partner violence and serious sexual assaults have led to changes in law and in practice that may be said to create special sub-systems for such cases.[15] There is certainly a sub-system for cases of serious fraud, following the establishment and ongoing work of the Serious Fraud Office, the introduction of plea negotiation, and the availability of Deferred Prosecution

---

[10] J. Spencer, 'The Sexual Offences Act 2003: Child and Family Offences' [2004] *Crim LR* 347.

[11] See https://www.cps.gov.uk.   [12] See V. Tadros, 'Crimes and Security' (2008) 71 *MLR* 940.

[13] *Ozturk v Germany* (1984) 6 EHRR 409.

[14] See J. Purshouse, Non-Conviction Disclosure as Part of an Enhanced Criminal Record Certificate: Assessing the Legal Framework from a Fundamental Human Rights Perspective [2018] *Public Law* 668.

[15] See particularly Ch 7.

Agreements (DPAs) for corporate offenders.[16] While in principle it is right to contemplate separate procedural approaches to circumvent practical difficulties arising in certain types of case, there is a danger that the social concerns (sometimes expressed in terms of victims' interests or rights) motivating these changes may lead to a neglect of fundamental rights for suspects and defendants, and that once special measures are justified in one area they will become 'normalized' and spread to other areas of the criminal process.[17] Politicians are particularly fond of claiming that a new method of combating a particular type of crime is vital, and that the best approach is to curtail the rights of suspects and defendants, which they then purport to justify as being in the greater public interest or for public protection.[18] This form of assertion is most frequently encountered in the context of the 'war against terrorism', and more recently this style of reasoning has been deployed in the context of organized crime.[19]

Implicit in those arguments is the principle that there are general norms of the criminal process which apply to all offences, and therefore that any difference of legal framework for particular types of case calls for justification. In Chapters 6 and 7, we argued that the English criminal process lacks an overall strategy for pre-trial justice. Different agencies continue to operate in different ways: the police and the CPS may converge in their operations, but the regulatory agencies continue to follow their distinct paths and priorities. These variations, not to mention the discretionary powers that go with them, leave open the possibility of inconsistencies in approach that may discriminate on improper grounds such as class, social position, race, and gender. What is absent from pre-trial justice is a common starting point for all types of case: there is no conception that people who commit offences of similar seriousness should receive similar responses (unless there are strong grounds for doing otherwise), and no real attempt to provide guidance on the relative gravity of the various types of offence. The regulatory agencies have policies that are markedly different from those of the police, not to mention between each other: this means that offences of a similar degree of seriousness may receive different responses according to the context (in a public place, on company premises, in a shop, in a customs shed at a channel port, and so forth). The responses differ at the point of enforcement and investigation, and also in the forms of diversion used. Like sentencing, diversion decisions are dispositive. Unlike sentencing, there are no open hearings and there are no general principles applicable across the diverse contexts of tax, customs, health and safety, pollution, and so on.

Both processual and dispositive decisions, as we have seen, tend towards the avoidance of trials. One feature of pre-trial processes that has become evident from the foregoing chapters is the tendency of some decisions to be taken in anticipation of the decisions of other agencies. There are, in fact, several influences flowing in different

---

[16] See Chs 6.2 and 10.5.

[17] See O. Gross, '"Control Systems" and the Migration of Anomalies' in S. Choudhry (ed), *The Migration of Constitutional Ideas* (2007); L. Campbell, 'Organized Crime and National Security: A Dubious Connection?' (2014) 17 *New Crim L Rev* 220.

[18] See the discussion of such arguments in Chs 1 and 2.

[19] L. Campbell, *Organised Crime and the Law: A Comparative Analysis* (2013).

directions. Almost all the 'input' received by the CPS has come from the police, who have therefore exerted considerable practical influence through their construction of case files. We have noted how some of the working practices of the CPS (in relation to bail and mode of trial decisions, for example) may be shaped by local magistrates or justices' clerks or the local judiciary. Equally, some defence solicitors will tailor their approach on bail and other matters to the particular prosecutor, justices' clerk, or bench of magistrates. Magistrates may sometimes defer to the police or to the CPS rather than applying their judgement independently on remands or mode of trial. It is not always easy to be sure of the existence of undue influence in these relationships: it is sometimes theoretically possible that two different parties are applying the same test and reaching the same conclusion, but the research cited on prosecutions (Chapter 7), on remands (Chapter 8), and on mode of trial (Chapter 11) is strongly suggestive of other, less ethical approaches. This can only be compounded by the increased financial pressures on the system and individuals working within it.

Two people who have less central roles than may be thought appropriate are the defendant and the victim. We have seen that under existing practice in both the Crown Court and magistrates' courts, the defendant is excluded from plea negotiations and has to depend on the mediated words of legal representatives.[20] Direct information for the defendant at this often crucial stage is relatively rare, which places much emphasis on the quality of legal representation. There is clear evidence that this is inconsistent, and that it is not always motivated by a desire to secure the defendant's rights but is sometimes diluted by a desire to curry favour with the police, or to obtain the maximum fee for the minimum work, or not to 'pull the stops out' for a client deemed unworthy.[21] In the face of strong structural and cultural pulls towards trial avoidance and negotiated outcomes, an independent and ethical approach from a well-resourced defence lawyer is vital to protect the suspect-defendant.

Victims, too, may be marginalized as the criminal process moves forward. Efforts to improve the flow of information to victims have not been wholly successful, despite more structured entitlements, including the right to review scheme. Decisions on prosecution and non-prosecution, bail, and acceptance of pleas are not always communicated to the victim. However, as argued above, while the case for greater support and information for victims is a strong one, the arguments for victim involvement in decision making are not.

14.2 THE PRINCIPLED APPROACH

The scourge of many debates about criminal justice policy is the concept of 'balance'. As it is often expressed, the 'balancing' of conflicting interests is presented as if there is no particular weighting of or priority among the interests. They are all

[20] J. Baldwin, *Pre-Trial Justice* (1986); A. Mulcahy, 'The Justifications of "Justice"' (1994) 34 *BJ Crim* 411.
[21] M. McConville et al, *Standing Accused* (1994), 273 and 281; D. Newman, *Legal Aid Lawyers and the Quest for Justice* (2013).

matters to be taken into consideration, and somehow a 'balance' emerges. Some-times the process is given an apparent respectability by quoting probabilities that a certain consequence will ensue—for example, the low risk of innocent people being convicted. The existence of a low risk on one side of the equation may be presented as if it tips the scales in that direction. However, as argued in Chapter 2, this would be to short-circuit the course of reasoning and to ignore the strength of some of the authoritatively recognized rights. It is time, now, to restate the argument in the light of the material in the intervening chapters.

The principled approach to criminal justice—unlike Packer's two models—is explicitly normative. The purpose of the criminal process is to bring about accurate determinations through fair procedures. The approach therefore emphasizes various rights and principles that ought to be safeguarded: some rights, such as the right not to be wrongly convicted, may be defended on a philosophical basis, but the rights declared by the ECHR are recognized and were brought into English law by the Human Rights Act 1998. The European Convention is largely about fair procedures, and its rights are designed to eliminate arbitrariness and to promote fairness rather than to achieve particular outcomes. The effect of the 1998 Act may therefore be described as the constitutionalization of the criminal process, insofar as the Act recognizes the fundamental status of Convention rights in English law through, for example, the courts' duty to take decisions compatibly with the Convention (s 6) and to interpret statutes 'so far as possible' compatibly with Convention rights (s 3). Thus, the Act has had significant effects on the shape of the English criminal process, in matters such as disclosure and public interest immunity, adverse inferences from silence, pre-trial remands, surveillance, entrapment, and so on. However, it was argued in Chapter 2 that the British courts and some politicians have paid insufficient attention to the differing strengths of the Convention rights, and have made the mistake of treating rights under Art 6 as if they were qualified in the same way as those in Arts 8–11. Rectification of this mistake, which has led to the importation of broad 'balancing' notions into fair trial guarantees by way of a modified concept of proportionality, should lead to a further strengthening of the human rights approach.

None of this is to suggest that the Convention should be regarded as a solution to the ills of the criminal process, and indeed to do so would be questionable given the waxing and waning desire of the Conservative Party that the UK withdraw from the ECHR. Both in Chapter 2 and subsequently, attention has been drawn to some short-comings of the Convention. Its coverage of rights is incomplete and patchy: if one were drawing up a new document, there would be several obvious candidates for inclusion that pertain to the criminal process—for example, victims' rights, protection for witnesses, special rights for young people and for women (whether as defendants, victims or witnesses), fault requirements for convictions, and so on. That said, the Convention is treated by the ECtHR as a living instrument, enabling the Court to develop certain implied rights—such as the privilege against self-incrimination and the principle of equality of arms—and apply other rights in a creative fashion. There have also been protocols that have added rights to the Convention on matters such as double jeopardy, capital punishment, and the right to personal property.

14.3 DISCRIMINATION AND NON-DISCRIMINATION

The principle of equality before the law, or non-discrimination, ought to be respected as a fundamental element in the administration of justice. In its present form, the Convention does not declare it to be so: Art 14 declares a right not to be discriminated against in the exercise of other Convention rights, but only the declaration and ratification of a new Protocol on Non-Discrimination will achieve the wider recognition of the principle. It would then be necessary to use the principle as the basis for positive obligations that would recognize the case for special treatment of certain groups. We have noted in previous chapters that special procedures to protect vulnerable and mentally disordered people are vital, both for their dignity as well as the reliability and integrity of the criminal process.[22] The same should apply to members of minority ethnic groups, in respect of whom we have noted evidence that people from certain backgrounds are disadvantaged in decisions to prosecute or caution and in the process of plea negotiation.[23] Increases in the number of people from ethnic minorities in the legal profession and criminal justice agencies are necessary, but they are unlikely to solve the above problems. Moreover, there is some discrimination on grounds of gender in the criminal process: while some sentencing of women and girls may seem lenient, remand decisions call this into question.[24]

A case for positive discrimination has long been recognized in relation to young suspects and defendants. The special procedures introduced for child defendants and child witnesses under the Youth Justice and Criminal Evidence Act 1999 stood in contrast to the consistently tough rhetoric used in relation to young defendants. That said, significant questions remain about the extent and adequacy of these provisions, and the degree to which they protect and enable the participation of young defendants throughout the criminal process. Beyond the trial, the Anti-Social Behaviour Orders, with their stripped-down procedural protections, were a major concern (see Chapter 13), so their replacement is to be welcomed.

A further source of discrimination, discussed at several points in the foregoing chapters, may be found in factors connected with social class or wealth. It is evident from Chapters 6 and 7 that any systematic examination of the prosecution policies of the police compared with those of the regulatory agencies would reveal a diversity of approaches, amounting in general to a less formal, less public, and less severe response to lawbreaking by employers, taxpayers, and others in established professions. It is hardly surprising that statistics about the social background of offenders show a predominance of those from the lower socio-economic groups when the enforcement process is skewed against those groups and in favour of those from the higher occupational categories. However, changing this would present a structural problem of immense proportions for the English criminal justice system. Those who adopt a desert or retributive approach might argue that the first task should be to decide on the relative seriousness of all these

---

[22] See Ch 6 on diversion.   [23] See Chs 7 and 10.

[24] Prison Reform Trust, *Transforming Lives reducing women's imprisonment* (2014); House of Commons Justice Committee, *Women offenders: after the Corston Report*, Second Report of Session 2013–14, HC 92 (2013).

offences, whether 'white collar', 'normal', 'financial', 'commercial', 'domestic', or however they may be labelled. The second task might then be to ensure that the criminal law may only be invoked at a certain level of seriousness, whatever the context of the offence, and not below that level. This would represent an attempt to achieve equality before the law, in the hope of preventing the use of the criminal process for relatively minor offences by impecunious or poorly connected defendants when at the same time ensuring that corporate or wealthy defendants do not benefit from a less vigorous approach where their offences are serious. That change of emphasis would not be easy to achieve, however, for many reasons—the need for a significant shift of resources to allow equivalent enforcement of regulatory offences, the need to reconsider the ways in which certain regulatory offences are drafted, and the possibility that wealthy or corporate 'deviants' might deploy their considerable resources to devise means of 'creative compliance' with the law.[25]

An alternative approach in relation to wealthy or corporate offenders is to adopt a form of restorative justice, abandoning the search for equivalent measures of punishment and instead requiring corporations who offend to make due reparation to those harmed by their offending behaviour.[26] Indeed, one could regard DPAs as such. This approach is premised not only on a rejection of the retributive paradigm for punishment but also on the difficulty and expense involved in holding companies responsible according to traditional criminal procedures and doctrines.[27] Braithwaite and Fisse argue that companies should be served with a notice that presumes liability and requires them to state what remedial measures they propose to take, in respect of both any individual victims and the wider community. In their scheme, this would release resources otherwise devoted to prosecuting corporate crime and enable law enforcement agencies to devote more resources to dealing fairly with other forms of crime.[28] Thus, companies would be taken out of the criminal process and their offences dealt with by different procedures, not so much on principle but rather as a means of controlling scarce resources. This overlooks the important stigmatizing function of the criminal law, and the extent to which companies could absorb the cost of remedying harm through civil means within their budgets. An alternative might be to keep companies within the criminal process and to raise the threshold for dealing with individual offenders, putting fewer inadequate and minor offenders in prison.

Important as it is to acknowledge and address unfair discrimination in the criminal law, in the enforcement process, and in criminal procedure it remains supremely difficult to do so within an unequal society, with discriminatory institutions and practices. The criminal process should not be regarded as something

---

[25] See D. McBarnet and C. Whelan, 'The Elusive Spirit of the Law: Formalism and the Struggle for Legal Control' (1991) 54 *MLR* 848.

[26] B. Fisse and J. Braithwaite, *Corporations, Crime and Accountability* (1993).

[27] L. Campbell, 'Corporate Liability and the Criminalisation of Failure' (2018) 12 *Law and Financial Markets Rev* 57.

[28] For which the authors also have proposals based on restorative justice, reinforced by strong sanctions: J. Braithwaite and P. Pettit, *Not Just Deserts: A Republican Theory of Criminal Justice* (1990), discussed critically in A. von Hirsch and A. Ashworth (eds), *Principled Sentencing* (3rd edn, 2009), ch 5.

separate from wider social issues and capable of separate treatment. Discrimination on grounds of race, gender, age, and other criteria will be hard to remove from the criminal process for so long as its manifestations are present in everyday social life. This is not to deny the importance of efforts to remove discrimination from the criminal process, but it is to argue that there are structural factors that make it likely that some discriminatory effects might be found even if law enforcers were scrupulously fair in their own actions.

14.4 PROMOTING THE PRINCIPLES

How should the principled approach outlined in Chapter 2 and in this chapter be put into practice? Many lawyers would tend to look to a network of rules or to a system of legal regulation as the means of advancing the desired principles. It has often been remarked that many stages in the criminal process are characterized by wide swaths of little-regulated discretion, from which it is assumed that the path of reform involves restrictions on or the complete removal of discretion. However, this would be naïve. It would be to assume that the existence of rules eliminates the practices that discretion allows. There are plenty of examples of rules being circumvented or neutralized, for instance by the police (Chapters 3–5), by prosecutors (Chapter 7), and by counsel and judges (Chapter 10). Thus, the mere enactment of rules in primary legislation should not be regarded as sufficient, or even as more effective than discretion complemented by guidelines. Working practices need to be changed, and this is where questions of ethics and of training come to the fore.

We noted in Chapter 1 that the origins of many recent miscarriages of justice lie in the early parts of the criminal justice system, particularly police investigation, the collection and assessment of forensic evidence, and disclosure. One of the most welcome developments was the creation of the Criminal Cases Review Commission, discussed in Chapter 12. The Commission is, however, currently a remedial rather than a preventive mechanism,[29] and it remains necessary to focus attention on the working practices of the police and other law enforcement agencies, and also the CPS and defence lawyers, at the early stages in the process. Significant advances have been made in the treatment of certain fragile forms of evidence in the criminal process—notably confessions and eyewitness evidence—but further improvements should be made to eyewitness identification procedures, and thought needs to be given to new issues such as voice identification. Appropriate legal advice should be available in these early stages, and this means ensuring that the system of payment for defence solicitors is sufficient and rewards early advice and case preparation appropriately. Moreover, it is not just the prosecution of some

---

[29] The Commission has frequently stated that it will use its experience of miscarriage of justice cases to make recommendations for improving the criminal process. It has found it difficult to do so but some of its general observations are reported in Ch 13.

weak cases that is a cause for concern, or unwarranted arrests followed by detention. The attrition rate, in particular for sexual offences, is also in need of constant
scrutiny and may embody miscarriages of justice of a different kind inasmuch as
guilty people are not prosecuted or are acquitted because of the way the system is
organized. Thus, there is a need to review procedures for encouraging witnesses
to give evidence by the increased availability of video links and other mechanisms,
and for witness protection, subject to proper safeguards for the defence. Unfortunately, however, some changes to criminal procedure savour more of reducing the
rights of the defence for symbolic reasons rather than of improving adequately the
position of victims.

   What should happen when a breach of one or more pre-trial procedures is uncovered? Much has been made, by some academics[30] and even by some British
judges[31] of the 'integrity principle'. The argument is that the integrity of the court,
or more widely of the criminal justice system, would be compromised if it were
to act on evidence that had been obtained as a result of a departure from proper
procedure. At one level, the argument is persuasive, and the imagery of 'tainting'
or 'the fruit of the poisoned tree' seems apposite. Yet in other respects, the integrity
principle leaves certain questions unanswered. Should every departure from procedure, no matter how small or inconsequential, be regarded as calling into question the integrity of a court or the whole system? If not, by what criteria can we tell
whether integrity is compromised? Questions of this kind raise a doubt whether
the integrity principle can be a satisfactory operating standard for the courts: attractive as it is in clear and gross cases, it needs considerable refinement if it is to
be suitable for the general run of situations.[32] More relevant to the objective of
promoting a principled approach to criminal justice is the protective principle: that
a court should not act on evidence if that would deprive the defendant of a protection that should have been assured. In other words, a deviation from procedures
may only be overlooked if the evidence in question was not obtained as a result of
its breach. The defendant should not be disadvantaged by an investigator's non-
observance of the procedures.

   Of course, that leaves the question of just what procedures are proper. Once we
move away from the rules in the Police and Criminal Evidence Act 1984 which
give suspects various rights, there are a host of difficult questions: when, if ever, is
deception, or covert recording, or entrapment, proper? There is simply no avoiding the fact that, in general, an evaluation of the criminal process involves difficult
questions about what values should be respected. Other examples are questions such
as: When might a breach of the privilege against self-incrimination be appropriate?

---

   [30] E.g. I. Dennis, *Criminal Evidence* (2017), ch 2E; J. Hunter, P. Roberts, S. Young, and D. Dixon (eds), *The Integrity of Criminal Process* (2016).
   [31] E.g. Lord Lowry in *R v Horseferry Road Magistrates' Court, ex p Bennett* [1994] 1 AC 42, and Lord Nicholls in *R v Looseley* [2001] UKHL 53. See also the judgments in *A v Home Secretary* [2005] UKHL 71.
   [32] For fuller analysis, see A. Ashworth, 'Exploring the Integrity Principle in Evidence and Procedure' in P. Mirfield and R. Smith (eds), *Essays for Colin Tapper* (2003).

When is it appropriate to keep a suspect's DNA profile or algorithm from a facial image on a database? How wide should arrest powers be? When is jury trial appropriate? Are there exceptions to the right of confrontation? Human rights documents will not always provide clear, or convincing, answers to such questions, and there is room for reasonable disagreement on them. But our argument is that any attempt to answer these questions must involve careful analysis of the values at stake. All too often this does not happen.

The promotion of a principled approach requires not only the provision of appropriate remedies in cases where the principles are not put into practice, but also programmes of training and supervision and guidance for the professionals concerned. No doubt it would be argued that there are professional organizations to take care of such matters, and the role of the Law Society and the Bar Council will be cited. However, the discussion of occupational cultures which began in Chapter 3 and continued in subsequent chapters makes it plain that there is, at the very least, a risk not only that simply changing the rules will fail but also that leaving the task of changing practices to the professional organizations is unlikely to succeed. The risk of failure would be greatest where the particular occupational culture is adverse and strong. It is therefore necessary to attempt to reshape the occupational cultures of some of those working within the criminal process. As a first step, more detailed ethical principles need to be drawn up which spell out the role responsibilities of prosecutors and defence lawyers, and the constraints on their pursuit of these goals. The ethical principles should ideally be supported by examples of situations in which they are intended to bite. This would be a means of challenging occupational cultures in a direct way. In order to do that, of course, it would be necessary to have a reasonably accurate impression of the operation of occupational cultures in practice, and the available research (discussed in previous chapters) provides some evidence of unethical practices (without suggesting that these are prevalent). Thus, it is vital to incorporate into training the reasons for respecting rights, and to reorient professional goals and official performance indicators in a way that reveres and rewards respect for rights over the mere obtaining of convictions. Compounding all of this, the impact of austerity measures and poor funding of both the CPS and legal aid have led to a diminution of the ability of individuals and institutions to prosecute and defend with the care which is warranted in the criminal process.

None of this means that convicting the guilty is unimportant; rather, it emphasizes that this worthy goal should be achieved by fair processes. This is not just a matter of ensuring that Parliament, the courts, and public authorities uphold Convention rights. There is also evidence that people in general regard fair procedures as an essential element in a criminal justice system.[33] Fair processes matter.

---

[33] T. Tyler, *Why People Obey the Law* (1990); J. Jackson, B. Bradford, M. Hough, A. Myhill, P. Quinton, and T. Tyler, 'Why do People Comply with the Law?: Legitimacy and the Influence of Legal Institutions' (2012) 52 *BJ Crim* 105.

14.5 THE CRIMINAL PROCESS OF THE FUTURE

Any detailed reform proposals such as those advanced in this book are likely to have a modest effect if other aspects of the criminal justice system remain little changed and under-resourced, and any changes in the criminal justice system may have a modest effect if social structures and policies remain little changed. Moreover, considerations of cost and public expenditure must be taken into account by anyone who forsakes the cover of academic discussion to venture some policy proposals. Recognizing cost as a constraint does not, however, argue against fundamental change. Indeed, despite the Leveson Review's purported focus on efficiency, the report was not costed. Rather than resorting to the imagery of 'balance' at each stage of the process, the challenge is to ensure or maximize respect for rights while enhancing convictions of the guilty, looking critically at the roles of the professional groups, at their powers, and at their practices. In addition to debating the rights of victims, the approach would be to examine wider social methods of preventing crime that could lead to fewer victims (and fewer offenders), such as the increased availability of pre-school education, improved housing, and other changes in social policy. It is unlikely that changing the criminal process itself will make much difference to crime rates and the safety of citizens: altering the rules of the criminal process is attractive to governments, not least because it is much easier than tackling fundamental issues of social policy, but also because the symbolic effects of appearing 'tough on crime' are expected to have favourable electoral consequences.

The human rights approach to criminal justice advocated in Chapter 2 runs counter to much contemporary policy, although it has its basis in the UK's international obligations (notably the ECHR, and to a lesser extent EU Directives, though Brexit will of course impact on this). However, neither the Convention nor other international instruments—nor, it may be added, any known general theory—provides a comprehensive set of principles for the criminal process. In practice, there will always be some choices to be made, and some trade-offs to be agreed. What is distinctive about the approach advocated here is that it insists on a weighted approach, with justifications given for the different priority given to different rights. It also insists on evidence rather than rhetoric, and on evidence of actual enhancements in prevention or protection rather than evidence of reductions in the risk people believe they face.[34]

---

[34] For argument to the same effect on criminal justice policy and sentencing, see M. Tonry, *Punishment and Politics* (2004).

BIBLIOGRAPHY

ABRAMSON, J. (1994), *We, The Jury: The Jury System and the Ideal of Democracy*, New York: Basic Books.

ALL PARTY PARLIAMENTARY GROUP FOR CHILDREN (2014), *'It's all about trust': Building good relationships between children and the police Report of the inquiry held by the All Party Parliamentary Group for Children 2013–2014*, London: TSO.

ALLDRIDGE, P. (2017), *Criminal Justice and Taxation*, Oxford: Oxford University Press.

ALLEN, R. (2008), 'Theorizing About Self-Incrimination', *Cardozo L Rev*, 30: 751.

ALMOND, P. (2013) *Corporate manslaughter and regulatory reform*, London: Palgrave Macmillan.

ALSCHULER, A. (1983), 'Implementing the Criminal Defendant's Right to Trial', *U Chi LR*, 50: 931.

ALSCHULER, A. (1997), 'Constraint and Confession', *Denver U L Rev*, 74: 957.

AMERICAN BAR ASSOCIATION (1980), *Standards Relating to the Prosecution Function and the Defense Function*, Chicago: American Bar Association.

AMOS, M. (2009), 'Problems with the Human Rights Act 1998 and How to Remedy Them: Is a Bill of Rights the Answer?', *MLR*, 72: 883.

ANDERSON, D. (2013), *Terrorism Prevention and Investigation Measures in 2012: First Report of the Independent Reviewer on the Operation of the Terrorism Prevention and Investigation Measures Act 2011*, London: TSO.

ANDERSON, D. (2014), *Terrorism Prevention And Investigation Measures in 2013 Second Report Of The Independent Reviewer On The Operation Of The Terrorism Prevention And Investigation Measures Act 2011*, London: TSO.

ANGIOLINI, THE RT HON. DAME ELISH DBE QC (2017), *Report of the Independent Review of Deaths and Serious Incidents in Police Custody*, London: TSO.

ARLEN, J., and ALEXANDER, C., eds (2018), *Research Handbook on Corporate Crime and Financial Misdealing*, Cheltenham: Edward Elgar.

ARLEN, J. and ALEXANDER, C. (2018), 'Does Conviction Matter? The Reputational and Collateral Effects of Corporate Crime', in Arlen, and Alexander, eds, qv.

ASHWORTH, A. (2002), *Human Rights, Serious Crime and Criminal Procedure*, London: Sweet & Maxwell.

ASHWORTH, A. (2002), 'Re-Drawing the Boundaries of Entrapment', *Crim LR*, 161.

ASHWORTH, A. (2002), 'Responsibilities, Rights and Restorative Justice', *BJ Crim*, 43: 578.

ASHWORTH, A. (2003), 'Exploring the Integrity Principle in Evidence and Procedure' in Mirfield and Smith, eds, qv.

ASHWORTH, A. (2004), 'Criminal Justice Reform: Principles, Human Rights and Public Protection', *Crim LR*, 516.

ASHWORTH, A. (2004), 'Social Control and "Anti-Social Behaviour": The Subversion of Human Rights?', *LQR*, 120: 263.

ASHWORTH, A. (2007), 'Security, Terrorism and the Value of Human Rights' in Goold and Lazarus, eds, qv.

ASHWORTH, A. (2008), 'Self-Incrimination in European Human Rights Law—A Pregnant Pragmatism?', *Cardozo L Rev*, 30: 751.

ASHWORTH, A. (2009), 'Criminal Law, Human Rights and Preventative Justice' in McSherry, Norrie, and Bronitt, eds, qv.

ASHWORTH, A. (2009), *Principles of Criminal Law*, 6th edn, Oxford: Oxford University Press.

ASHWORTH, A. (2015), *Sentencing and Criminal Justice*, 6th edn, London: Butterworths.

ASHWORTH, A. and FIONDA, J. (1994), 'The New Code for Crown Prosecutors: Prosecution, Accountability and the Public Interest', *Crim LR*, 894.

ASHWORTH, A. and STRANGE, M. (2004), 'Criminal Law and Human Rights', *EHRLR*, 121.

ASHWORTH, A. and WASIK, M., eds (1998), *Fundamentals of Sentencing Theory*, Oxford: Oxford University Press.

ASHWORTH, A. and ZEDNER, L. (2008), 'Defending the Criminal Law: Reflections on the Changing Character of Crime, Procedure and Sanctions', *Crim Law & Phil*, 2: 21.

ASHWORTH, A. and ZEDNER, L. (2010), 'Preventive Orders: a Problem of Under-Criminalization?' in Duff, Farmer, Marshall, and Tadros, eds, qv.

ASHWORTH, A. and ZEDNER, L. (2014), *Preventive Justice*, Oxford: Oxford University Press.

ATTORNEY GENERAL (2013), *Attorney General's Guidelines on Disclosure*, London: TSO.

AUDIT COMMISSION (1996), *Misspent Youth: Young People and Crimes*, London: Audit Commission.

AULD, R. E. (2001), *Review of the Criminal Courts of England and Wales; Report*, London: The Lord Chancellor's Department.

AUSTIN, R. C. (2007), 'The New Powers of Arrest', *Crim LR*, 459.

BAILEY S. and TAYLOR, N. (2009), *Civil Liberties: Cases, Materials and Commentary*, 6th edn, Oxford: Oxford University Press.

BALDWIN, J. (1986), *Pre-Trial Justice*, Oxford: Oxford University Press.

BALDWIN, J. (1992), *The Supervision of Police Investigations in Serious Criminal Cases*, Royal Commission on Criminal Justice Research Study No 4, London: HMSO.

BALDWIN, J. (1993), 'Legal Advice at the Police Station', *Crim LR*, 371.

BALDWIN, J. (1997), 'Understanding Judge Ordered and Directed Acquittals in the Crown Court', *Crim LR*, 536.

BALDWIN, J. and McCONVILLE, M. (1977), *Negotiated Justice*, Oxford: Martin Robertson.

BALDWIN, R. (2004), 'The New Punitive Regulation', *MLR*, 67: 351.

BALDWIN, R. and HAWKINS, K. (1984), 'Discretionary Justice: Davis Reconsidered', *PL*, 570.

BARCLAY, G. C., ed (1999), *Digest 4: Information on the Criminal Justice System in England and Wales*, London: Home Office.

BARCLAY, G. C. and MHLANGA, B. (2000), *Ethnic Differences in Decisions on Young Defendants Dealt With by the Crown Prosecution Service*, Section 95 Findings 1, London: Home Office.

BARKOW, A., and BARKOW, R., eds (2011), *Prosecutors in the Boardroom: Using Criminal law to Regulate Corporate Conduct*, New York: NYU Press.

BILLINGSLEY, R., NEMITZ, T., and BEAN, P., eds (2001), *Informers: Policing, Policy, Practice*, Cullompton: Willan.

BIRCH, D. (1995), 'Corroboration: Goodbye to All That?', *Crim LR*, 524.

BIRCH, D. (1999), 'Suffering in Silence: A Cost–Benefit Analysis of Section 34 of the Criminal Justice and Public Order Act 1994', *Crim LR*, 769.

BIRCH, D. (2000), 'A Better Deal for Vulnerable Witnesses?', *Crim LR*, 223.

BITTNER, E. (1967), 'The Police on Skid Row: A Study in Peacekeeping', *Am Soc Rev*, 32: 699.

BLACKSTOCK, J., CAPE, E., HODGSON, J., OGORODOVA, A., and SPRONKEN, T. (2014), *Inside Police Custody: An Empirical Account of Suspects' Rights in Four Jurisdictions*, Mortsel and Cambridge: Intersentia.

BLAND, N. and MILLER, J. (2000), *Police Stops, Decision-Making and Practice*, Police Research Series, Paper 130.

BLAKE, M. and ASHWORTH, A. (1998), 'Some Ethical Issues in Prosecuting and Defending Criminal Cases', *Crim LR*, 16.

BLAKE, M. and ASHWORTH, A. (2004), 'Ethics and the Criminal Defence Lawyer', *Legal Ethics*, 7: 167.

BLANDON-GITLIN, I., SPERRY, K., and LEO, R. (2010), 'Jurors Believe Interrogation Tactics are not Likely to Elicit False Confessions: Will Expert Witness Testimony Inform them Otherwise?', *Psychology, Crime & Law*, 16.

BLANDÓN-GITLIN, I., SPERRY, K., and LEO, R. (2011), 'Jurors believe interrogation tactics are not likely to elicit false confessions: will expert testimony inform them otherwise?', *Psychology, Crime & Law*, 17: 239.BLOCK, B., CORBETT, C., and PEAY, J. (1993), *Ordered and Directed Acquittals in the Crown Court*, Royal Commission on Criminal Justice Research Study No 15, London: HMSO.

BOGAN, P. (2013), 'Adverse Inference: When Interview and Trial Offence Differ', *Arch Rev*, 4.

BOTTOMS, A. K. and McCLEAN, J. D. (1968), 'The Granting of Bail: Principles and Practice', *MLR*, 31: 40.

BOTTOMS, A. K. and McCLEAN, J. D. (1976), *Defendants in the Criminal Process*, London: Routledge.

BOWLING, B. and MARKS, E. (2017), 'The Rise and Fall of Suspicionless Searches', *King's LJ* 28: 62.

BOWLING, B. and PHILLIPS, C. (2002), *Racism, Crime and Justice*, Harlow: Longman.

BOWLING, B. and PHILLIPS, C. (2007), 'Disproportionate and Discriminatory: Reviewing the Evidence on Police Stop and Search', *MLR*, 70: 936.

BRADFORD, B. (2015), 'Unintended consequences' in R. Delsol and M. Shiner (eds), *Stop and Search: The Anatomy of a Police Power*, London: Palgrave Macmillan.

BRADLEY, C. (1993), 'The Emerging International Consensus as to Criminal Procedural Rules', *Michigan J Int L* 14: 171.

BRADLEY, K. (2009), *The Bradley Report: Lord Bradley's Review of People with Mental Health Problems or Learning Disabilities in the Criminal Justice System*, London: Department of Health.

BRAITHWAITE, J. and PETTIT, P. (1990), *Not Just Deserts: A Republican Theory of Criminal Justice*, Oxford: Oxford University Press.

BRANTS, C. and FIELD, S. (1995), 'Discretion and Accountability in Prosecution' in Fennell, Harding, Jörg, and Swart, eds, qv.

BRIDGES, L. (2000), 'Taking Liberties' *Legal Action*, 6 July.

BRIDGES, L. (2006), 'Ethics of Representation on Guilty Pleas', *Legal Ethics*, 9: 80.

BRIDGES, L. and CAPE E. (2008), *CDS Direct: Flying in the Face of the Evidence*, London: Centre for Crime and Justice Studies, King's College London.

BRIDGES, L. and CHOONGH, S. (1998), *Improving Police Station Legal Advice*, London: Law Society.

BROOKE, D., TAYLOR, C., GUNN, J., and MADEN, A. (2000), 'Substance Misuse as a Marker of Vulnerability Among Male Prisoners on Remand', *BJ Psychiatry*, 177: 248.

BROOKMAN, F. and PIERPOINT, H. (2003), 'Access to Legal Advice for Young Suspects and Remand Prisoners', *Howard JCJ*, 42: 452.

BROWN, D. (2000), *Reducing Delays in the Magistrates' Courts*, Home Office Research Findings No 131, London: Home Office.

BROWN, D. and ELLIS, T. (1994), *Policing Low-Level Disorder*, Home Office Research Study 135, London: Home Office.

BROWNLEE, I. (2004), 'The Statutory Charging Scheme in England and Wales: Towards a Unified Prosecution System?', *Crim LR*, 896.

BROWNLEE, I. (2007), 'Conditional Cautions and Fair Trial Rights: Form versus Substance in the Diversionary Agenda', *Crim LR*, 129.

BROWNLEE, I., MULCAHY, A., and WALKER, C. P. (1994), 'Pre-Trial Reviews, Court Efficiency and Justice: A Study in Leeds and Bradford Magistrates' Courts', *Howard JCJ*, 33: 109.

BUCKE, T. and BROWN, D. (1997), *In Police Custody: police powers and suspects' rights under the revised PACE codes of practice*, Home Office Research Study 174, London: Home Office.

BUCKE, T., STREET, R., and BROWN, D. (2000), *The Right of Silence: the Impact of the Criminal Justice and Public Order Act 1994*, Home Office Research Study 199, London: Home Office.

BURNEY, E. (2009), *Making People Behave: Anti-Social Behaviour, Politics and Policy*, 2nd edn, Cullompton: Willan.

BULL, R., VALENTINE, T., and WILLIAMSON, T., eds (2009), *Handbook of Psychology of Investigative Interviewing: Current Developments and Future Directions*, Chichester: Wiley.

BURNEY, E. and PEARSON, G. (1995), 'Mentally Disordered Offenders: Finding a Focus for Diversion', *Howard JCJ*, 34: 291.

BURNEY, E. and ROSE, G. (2002), *Racist offences—How is the Law Working?*, Home Office Research Study 244, London: Home Office.

BURROWS, P., HENDERSON, P., and MORGAN, P. (1994), *Improving Bail Decisions: the Bail Process Project*, London: Home Office Research and Planning Unit.

BURTON, M. (2001), 'Reviewing Crown Prosecution Service Decisions not to Prosecute', *Crim LR*, 374.

BURTON, M., EVANS, R., and SANDERS, A. (2006), 'Protecting Children in Criminal Proceedings: Parity for Child Witnesses and Child Defendants', *Child and Family Law Quarterly* 18: 397.

BUXTON, R. (2009), 'The Private Prosecutor as Minister of Justice', *Crim LR*, 427.

CAMERON, N., POTTER, S., and YOUNG, W. (1999), 'The New Zealand Jury', *Law & Contemporary Prob*, 62: 103.

CAMMISS, S. (2007), 'Deciding Upon Mode of Trial', *Howard JCJ*, 46: 372.

CAMMISS, S. and STRIDE, C. (2008), 'Modelling Mode of Trial', *BJ Crim*, 48: 482.

CAMPEAU, H. (2015), '"Police Culture" At Work: Making Sense Of Police Oversight' *BJ Crim* 55: 669.

CAMPBELL, L. (2010), 'A Rights-Based Analysis of DNA Retention: "Non-Conviction" Databases and the Liberal State', *Crim LR*, 889.

CAMPBELL, L. (2010), 'DNA Databases and Innocent Persons: Lessons From Scotland?', *The Juridical Review* 285.

CAMPBELL, L. (2013), 'Criminal Labels, the European Convention on Human Rights and the Presumption of Innocence', *MLR*, 76: 681.

CAMPBELL, L. (2013), *Organised Crime and the Law: A Comparative Analysis*, Oxford: Hart.

CAMPBELL, L. (2014), 'Organized Crime and National Security: A Dubious Connection?', *New Crim L Rev* 17: 220.

CAMPBELL, L. (2014), 'The Prosecution of Organised Crime: Removing the Jury', *E&P*, 18: 83.

CAMPBELL, L. (2017), 'Criminal Records and Human Rights', *Crim LR*, 695.

CAMPBELL, L. (2018), 'Corporate Liability and the Criminalisation of Failure', *Law and Financial Markets Rev*, 12: 57.

CAMPBELL, L. and LORD, N., eds (2018), *Corruption in Commercial Enterprise: Law, Theory and Practice,* London: Routledge.

CAMPBELL, L. and PURSHOUSE, J., (2018), 'Privacy, Crime Control and Police use of Automated Facial Recognition Technology', *Crim LR*, 188.

CANE, P. and TUSHNET, M., eds (2003), *The Oxford Handbook of Legal Studies*, Oxford: Oxford University Press.

CAPE, E. (1999), 'Sufficient Evidence to Charge?', *Crim LR*, 874.

CAPE, E. (2003), 'The Revised PACE Codes of Practice: A Further Step Towards Inquisitorialism', *Crim LR*, 355.

CAPE, E. (2004), 'The Rise (and Fall) of a Criminal Defence Profession', *Crim LR*, 408.

CAPE, E. (2006), 'Rebalancing the Criminal Justice Process: Ethical Challenges for Criminal Defence Lawyers', *Legal Ethics*, 9: 56.

CAPE, E. (2007), 'Modernising Police Powers—Again?', *Crim LR*, 934.

CAPE, E. (2010), 'Adversarialism "lite": developments in criminal procedure and evidence under New Labour', *Criminal Justice Matters* 79: 25.

CAPE, E. (2015), 'Transposing the EU Directive on the Right to Information: A Firecracker or a Damp Squib?', *Crim LR*, 48.

CAPE, E. (2017), *Defending Suspects at Police Stations*, 6th edn, London: Legal Action Group.

CAPE, E. (2017), 'Recording Interviews With Body-Worn Cameras: The Latest Pace Codes Consultation', *The Justice Gap*.

CAPE, E. (2017), 'The Police Bail Provisions of the Policing and Crime Act 2017', *Crim LR*, 587.

CAPE, E. and EDWARDS, R. (2010), 'Police Bail Without Charge: The Human Rights Implications', *CLJ*, 69: 529.

CAPE, E. and HODGSON, J. (2014), 'The Right of Access to a Lawyer at Police-Stations: Making the European Union Directive Work in Practice', *New J Eur Crim L*, 5: 450.

CAPE, E. and SMITH, T. (2016), *The practice of pre-trial detention in England and Wales: research report*, Bristol: University of the West of England.

CAPE, E. and YOUNG, R., eds (2008), *Regulating Policing: the Police and Criminal Evidence Act 1984, Past, Present and Future*, Oxford: Hart.

CARLILE, A. (2009), *Report on the Operation in 2008 of the Terrorism Act 2000 and of Part I of the Terrorism Act 2006*, London: Home Office.

CARSON, D. (1989), 'Prosecuting People with Mental Handicaps', *Crim LR*, 87.

CHALMERS, J. (2014), '"Frenzied law making": overcriminalization by numbers', *CLP*, 67: 483.

CHALMERS, J. and LEVERICK, F. (2001), 'When Should a Retrial be Permitted After a Conviction is Quashed on Appeal?', *MLR* 74: 721.

CHALMERS, J., LEVERICK, F., and SHAW, A. (2015), 'Is Formal Criminalisation Really on the Rise? Evidence from the 1950s', *Crim LR*, 177.

CHAN, J. (1996), 'Changing Police Culture', *BJ Crim*, 36: 109.

CHIEF SURVEILLANCE COMMISSIONER (2017), *Chief Surveillance Commissioner Annual Report of the Chief Surveillance Commissioner to the Prime Minister and to the Scottish Ministers for 2016–2017*, HC 299, SG/2017/222.

CHOO, A. (2008), *Abuse of Process and Judicial Stays of Criminal Proceedings*, 2nd edn, Oxford: Oxford University Press.

CHOO, A. (2016), 'Abuse of Process and Delayed Prosecutions' in Radcliffe, Gudjonsson, Heaton-Armstrong, and Wolchover, eds, qv.

CHOONGH, S. (1998), 'Policing the Dross: A Social Disciplinary Model of Policing', *BJ Crim*, 38: 623.

CHOUDHRY, S., ed (2007), *The Migration of Constitutional Ideas*, Cambridge: Cambridge University Press.

CLARE, I., GUDJONSSON, G., and HARARI, M. (1998), 'Understanding of the Current Police Caution (England and Wales)', *J Community & Applied Social Psychology*, 8: 323.

CLARKE, C. and MILNE, R. (2001), *National Evaluation of the PEACE Investigative Interviewing Course*, London: Home Office.

CLARKE, C., MILNE, R., and BULL, R. (2011), 'Interviewing suspects of crime: The impact of PEACE training, supervision, and the presence of a legal advisor', *J Investigative Psychology and Offender Profiling*, 8: 149.

CLARKSON, C., CRETNEY, A., DAVIS, G., and SHEPHERD, J. (1994), 'Assaults: The Relationship between Seriousness, Criminalisation and Punishment', *Crim LR*, 4.

CLEARY, J. (2014), 'Police Interviewing and Interrogation of Juvenile Suspects', *Law & Human Behavior* 38: 271.

CLOUGH, J. and JACKSON, A. (2012), 'The game is up: Proposals on incorporating effective disclosure requirements into criminal investigations', *The Criminal Lawyer*, 3.

COLLEGE OF POLICING (2014), *A Code of Practice for the Principles and Standards of Professional Behaviour for the Policing Profession of England and Wales*, Coventry: College of Policing.

COMMISSION FOR RACIAL EQUALITY (1992), *Juvenile Cautioning: Ethnic Monitoring in Practice*, London: CRE.

COMMISSION JUSTICE PÉNALE ET DROITS DE L'HOMME (1991), *La Mise en Etat des Affaires Pénales*, Paris: la Documentation Francaise.

COMPTROLLER AND AUDITOR GENERAL (2016), *Efficiency in the criminal justice system*, Session 2015–16, HC 852, London: National Audit Office.

COOPER, P. and MATTISON, M. (2017), 'Intermediaries, vulnerable people and the quality of evidence: An international comparison of three versions of the English intermediary model', *Int J Evidence & Proof*, 21: 351.

COOPER, P. and WURTZEL, D. (2013), 'A Day Late and a Dollar Short: In Search of an Intermediary Scheme for Vulnerable Defendants in England and Wales, *Crim LR*, 4.

COOPER, P., BACKEN, P., and MARCHANT, R. (2015), 'Getting to Grips with Ground Rules Hearings: A Checklist for Judges, Advocates and Intermediaries to Promote the Fair Treatment of Vulnerable People in Court', *Crim LR* 420.

CORRE, N. and WOLCHOVER, D. (2004), *Bail in Criminal Proceedings*, 3rd edn, Oxford: Oxford University Press.

COUNCIL OF EUROPE (1987), *The Simplification of Criminal Justice*, Recommendation R(87)18 (1987), Strasbourg: Council of Europe.

COUNCIL OF EUROPE (2000), *Crime and Criminal Justice in Europe*, Strasbourg: Council of Europe.

COURT OF APPEAL (2006), *Protocol for the Control and Management of Unused*

Material in the Crown Court, London: Ministry of Justice.

COYLE, I. and THOMSON, D. (2013), 'Opening up a can of worms: how do decision-makers decide when witnesses are telling the truth?', *Psychiatry, Psychology & Law* 21: 475.

CRAIG, P. (2004), 'Grounds for Judicial Review: Substantive Control over Discretion' in Feldman, ed, qv.

CRANSTON, R. (1979), *Regulating Business*, Oxford: Oxford University Press.

CRETNEY, A. and DAVIS, G. (1995), *Punishing Violence*, London and New York: Routledge.

CRIMINAL CASES REVIEW COMMISSION (2017), *Annual Report and Accounts 2016/17*, Birmingham: Criminal Cases Review Commission.

CRIMINAL CASES REVIEW COMMISSION (2018), *Annual Report 2017/18*, Birmingham: Criminal Cases Review Commission.

CRIMINAL JUSTICE SYSTEM (2007), *Delivering Simple, Speedy, Summary Justice: An Evaluation of the Magistrates' Courts Tests*, London: Criminal Justice System.

CRIMINAL LAW REVISION COMMITTEE (1972), *Eleventh Report: Evidence (General)*, Cmnd 4991, London: HMSO.

CROSBY, K. (2015), 'Juror Punishment, Juror Guidance and the Criminal Justice and Courts Act 2015', *CrimLR*, 578.

CROWN PROSECUTION SERVICE (2009), *The Public Prosecution Service—Setting the Standard*, London: DPP.

CROWN PROSECUTION SERVICE (2009), *Supporting Victims and Witnesses with Mental Health Issues*, https://www.cps.gov.uk.

CROWN PROSECUTION SERVICE (2013), *Charging* (The Director's Guidance), 5th edn, London: CPS.

CROWN PROSECUTION SERVICE (2013), *Code for Crown Prosecutors*, London: CPS.

CROWN PROSECUTION SERVICE (2017), *Violence against Women and Girls: crime report 2016–2017*, London: CPS.

CROWN PROSECUTION SERVICE (2018), *Code for Crown Prosecutors*, London: CPS.

CROWN PROSECUTION SERVICE (2018), *Disclosure Manual*, London: CPS.

CROWN PROSECUTION SERVICE (no date), *Cautioning and Diversion Guidance*, London: CPS.

CROWN PROSECUTION SERVICE (no date), *Policy on Prosecuting Cases of Domestic Violence*, London: CPS.

CROWN PROSECUTION SERVICE (no date), *Restorative Justice Legal Guidance*, London: CPS.

CROWN PROSECUTION SERVICE and METROPOLITAN POLICE SERVICE (2018), *The joint review of the disclosure process in the case of R v Allan*, London: CPS.

DAMAŠKA, M. (1973), 'Evidentiary Barriers to Conviction and Two Models of Criminal Procedure: a Comparative Study', *U Pa LR*, 121: 506.

DAMAŠKA, M. (1976), *The Faces of Justice and State Authority*, New Haven, CT: Yale University Press.

DAMAŠKA, M. (1997), *Evidence Law Adrift*, New Haven, CT: Yale University Press.

DARBYSHIRE, P. (1997), 'For the New Lord Chancellor: Some Causes for Concern about Magistrates', *Crim LR*, 861.

DARBYSHIRE, P. (1997), 'Previous Misconduct and the Magistrates' Courts—Some Tales from the Real World', *Crim LR*, 105.

DARBYSHIRE, P. (2000), 'The Mischief of Plea Bargaining and Sentencing Rewards', *Crim LR*, 895.

DARBYSHIRE, P. (2011), *Sitting in Judgment: The Working Lives of Judges*, Oxford: Hart.

DARBYSHIRE, P. (2014), 'Judicial Case Management in Ten Crown Courts', *Crim LR*, 30.

DAVIES, F. G. (1995), 'CPS Charging Standards: A Cynic's View', *JP*, 159: 203.

DAVIES, F. G. (1997), 'Ten Years of the Crown Prosecution Service: the Verdict', *JP*, 161: 207.

DAVIES G. and VENNARD, J. (2006), 'The Experience of Ethnic Minority Magistrates', *Howard JCJ*, 45: 485.

DAVIES, H. (2013), *Civil Prevention Orders, Sexual Offences Act 2003: ACPO Commissioned Review of the Existing Statutory Scheme and Recommendations for Reform*, London: ACPO.

DAVIS, G., HOYANO, L., KEENAN, C., MAITLAND, L., and MORGAN, R. (1999), *An Assessment of the Admissibility and Sufficiency of Evidence in Child Abuse Prosecutions*, London: Home Office.

DAVIS, J., VALENTINE, T., MEMON, A., and ROBERTS, A. (2015), 'Identification on the Street: A field comparison of police street identifications and video lineups in England' *Pyschology, Crime & Law* 21: 9.

DAW, R. (1994), 'The CPS Code—A Response', *Crim LR*, 904.

DAWES, W., HARVEY, P., MCINTOSH, B., NUNNEY, F., and PHILLIPS, A. (2011), *Attitudes to guilty plea sentence reductions*, London: Sentencing Council.

DE SCHUTTER, O. and RINGELHEIM, J. (2008), 'Ethnic Profiling: A Rising Challenge for European Human Rights Law', *MLR*, 71: 358.

DEFLEM, M. ed (2016) *The Politics of Policing: Between Force and Legitimacy, Sociology Crime, Law and Deviance*, Bingley: Emerald.

DEHAGHANI, R. (2016), 'Custody Officers, Code C and Constructing Vulnerability: Implications for Policy and Practice', *Policing* 11: 74.

DEHAGHANI, R. (2017), 'Automatic Authorisation: An Exploration of the Decision to Detain in Police Custody', *Crim LR*, 187.

DELMAS-MARTY, M., and SPENCER, J. R., eds (2002) *European Criminal Procedures*, Cambridge: Cambridge University Press.

DELSOL, R. (2015), 'Effectiveness' in R. Delsol, *Stop and Search: The Anatomy of a Police Power*, London: Palgrave Macmillan.

DEMPSEY, M. (2009), *Prosecuting Domestic Violence*, Oxford: Oxford University Press.

DENNIS, I. (2000), 'Rethinking Double Jeopardy: Justice and Finality in Criminal Process', *Crim LR*, 933.

DENNIS, I. (2003), 'Fair Trials and Safe Convictions', *CLP*, 56: 211.

DENNIS, I. (2004), 'Prosecution Appeals and Retrial for Serious Offences', *Crim LR*, 619.

DENNIS, I. (2010), 'The Right to Confront Witnesses: Meanings, Myths and Human Rights', *Crim LR*, 255.

DENNIS, I. (2017), *The Law of Evidence*, 6th edn, London: Sweet & Maxwell.

DENYER, R. (2009), 'The Defence Statement', *Crim LR*, 340.

DERSHOWITZ, A. (2006), *Pre-Emption*, New York: W. W. Norton.

DERVAN, L. and EDKINS, V. (2013), 'The Innocent Defendant's Dilemma: An Innovative Empirical Study of Plea Bargaining's Innocence Problem', *J Crim L and Criminol*, 103: 1.

DEVLIN, P. (1976), *Report to the Secretary of State for the Home Department of the Departmental Committee on Evidence of Identification in Criminal Cases*, London: HMSO.

DEVLIN, P. (1979), *The Judge*, Oxford: Oxford University Press.

DHAMI, M. (2002), 'Do Bail Information Schemes Really Affect Bail Decisions?', *Howard JCJ*, 41: 245.

DHAMI, M. (2004), 'Conditional Bail Decision-Making in the Magistrates' Court', *Howard JCJ*, 43: 27.

DHAMI, M. (2005), 'From Discretion to Disagreement: Explaining Disparities in Judges' Pre-Trial Decisions', *Behavioural Sciences and the Law*, 23: 367.

DINGWALL, G. and HARDING, C. (1998), *Diversion in the Criminal Process*, London: Sweet & Maxwell.

DIRECTOR OF PUBLIC PROSECUTIONS (2013) Charging *(The Director's Guidance) 2013*, 5th edn (revised arrangements), https://www.cps.gov.uk/legal-guidance/charging-directors-guidance-2013-fifth-edition-may-2013-revised-arrangements.

DIRECTOR OF PUBLIC PROSECUTIONS (2013) Adult Conditional Cautions *(The Director's Guidance) 2013*, 7th edn, London: CPS.

DISLEY, E., TAYLOR, C., KRUITHOF, K., WINPENNY, E., LIDDLE, M., SUTHERLAND, A., LILFORD, R., WRIGHT, S., MCATEER, L., and FRANCIS, V. (2016), *Evaluation of the Offender Liaison and Diversion Trial Schemes*, Cambridge: Rand.

DIXON, D. (1990), 'Safeguarding the Rights of Suspects in Police Custody', *Policing and Society*, 1: 115.

DIXON, D. (1997), *Law in Policing: Legal Regulation and Police Practices*, Oxford: Oxford University Press.

DIXON, D. (2008), 'Authorise and Regulate: A Comparative Perspective on the Rise and Fall of a Regulatory Strategy' in Cape and Young, eds, qv.

DIXON, D. and TRAVERS, G. (2007), *Interrogating Images: Audio-Visually Recorded Police Questioning of Suspects*, Sydney: Sydney Institute of Criminology.

DOHERTY, C. and EAST, R. (1985), 'Bail Decisions in Magistrates' Courts', *BJ Crim*, 25: 251.

DOLINKO, D. (1986), 'Is there a Rationale for the Privilege Against Self-Incrimination?', *UCLA L Rev*, 33: 1063.

DONOGHUE, J. (2014), 'Reforming the Role of Magistrates: Implications for Summary Justice in England and Wales', *MLR*, 80: 995.

DORAN, S. and GLENN, R. (2000), *Lay Involvement in Adjudication*, Belfast: TSO.

DORAN, S. and JACKSON, J. D. (1997), 'The Case for Jury Waiver', *Crim LR*, 155.

DORAN, S. and JACKSON, J. D., eds (2000), *The Judicial Role in Criminal Proceedings*, Oxford: Hart.

DRESSLER, J. and MICHAELS, A. (2006), *Understanding Criminal Procedure, Vol 1: Investigations*, 4th edn, Newark, NJ: LexisNexis.

DREWRY, G. (1985), 'The Ponting Case—Leaking in the Public Interest', *PL*, 203.

DRIZIN, S. and LEO, R. (2004), 'The Problem of False Confessions in the Post-DNA World', *North Carolina L Rev*, 82: 891.

DROR, I. and FRASER-MACKENZIE, P. (2009), 'Cognitive Biases in Human Perception, Judgment, and Decision Making: Bridging Theory and the Real World' in Rossmo, ed, qv.

DROR, I. and ROSENTHAL, R. (2008), 'Meta-Analytically Quantifying the Reliability and Biasability of Forensic Experts', *J Forensic Sciences*, 53: 900.

DUFF, P. (2009), 'Straddling Two Worlds: Reflections of a Retired Criminal Cases Review Commissioner', *MLR*, 72: 693.

DUFF, P. and HUTTON, N., eds (1999), *Criminal Justice in Scotland*, Aldershot: Ashgate.

DUFF, R. A. (1986), *Trials and Punishments*, Cambridge: Cambridge University Press.

DUFF, R. A. (2005), 'Strict Liability, Legal Presumptions and the Presumption of Innocence' in Simester, ed, qv.

DUFF, R. A., FARMER, L., MARSHALL, S., and TADROS, V., eds (2006), *The Trial on Trial, Vol 2: Judgment and Calling to Account*, Oxford: Hart.

DUFF, R. A., FARMER, L., MARSHALL, S., and
TADROS, V., eds (2007), *The Trial on Trial,
Vol 3: Towards a Normative Theory of the
Criminal Trial*, Oxford: Hart.

DUFF, R. A., FARMER, L., MARSHALL, S., and
TADROS, V., eds (2010), *The Boundaries
of the Criminal Law*, Oxford: Oxford
University Press.

DWORKIN, R. M. (1981), 'Principle, Policy,
Procedure', in Tapper, ed, qv.

DYZENHAUS, D., ed (1999), *Recrafting the
Rule of Law*, Oxford: Hart.

EDWARDS, A. (2011), 'Case Management
Forms', *Crim LR*, 547.

EDWARDS, A. (2012), 'Legal Aid, Sentencing
and Punishment of Offenders Act 2012—
The Financial Procedural and Practical
Implications', *Crim LR*, 584.

ELKS, L. (2008), '*R v Stock*', *Arch News*, 9: 3.

ELKS, L. (2008), *Righting Miscarriages of
Justice? Ten Years of the Criminal Cases
Review Commission*, London:
JUSTICE.

ELLIS, L. and DIAMOND, S. (2003), 'Race,
Diversity, and Jury Composition: Battering
and Bolstering Legitimacy', *Chicago-Kent L
Rev*, 78: 1033.

ELLIS, R. and Biggs, S. (2013), 'Simple
Vautions', *Arch Rev*, 6.

ELLISON, L. (2005), 'Case Comment—Youth
Court: Whether Legislative Provision
Requiring Special Measures Direction to
be Given in Relation to Child Witnesses
in Need of Special Protection in Manner
Compatible with Convention Requirement
for a Fair Trial', *Crim LR*, 497.

ELLISON, L. (2007), 'Promoting Effective
Case-Building in Rape Cases: A
Comparative Perspective', *Crim LR*, 691.

EMMERSON, B., ASHWORTH, A., and
MACDONALD, A. (2012), *Human Rights
and Criminal Justice*, 3rd edn, London:
Sweet & Maxwell.

EPSTEIN, R. (2011), 'Deferred Prosecution
Agreements on Trial: Lessons from the
Law of Unconstitutional Conditions' in
Barkow and Barkow, eds, qv.

EQUALITY AND HUMAN RIGHTS
COMMISSION, (2012), *Briefing paper, Race
disproportionality in stops and searches
under Section 60 of the Criminal Justice
and Public Order Act 1994*, Manchester:
Equality and Human Rights Commission.

EVANS, R. (1993), 'Comparing Young
Adult and Juvenile Cautioning in the
Metropolitan Police District', *Crim LR*,
572.

EVANS, R. (1993), 'Evaluating Young Adult
Diversion Schemes in the Metropolitan
Police District', *Crim LR*, 490.

EVANS, R. (1996), 'Challenging a Police
Caution using Judicial Review', *Crim LR*,
104.

EVANS, R. and ELLIS, R. (1997), *Police
Cautioning in the 1990s*, Home Office
Research Findings No 33, London: Home
Office.

EVANS, R. and WILKINSON, C. (1990),
'Variations in Police Cautioning', *Howard
JCJ*, 29: 155.

FAIRCLOUGH, S. (2017), '"It doesn't happen . . . and I've never thought it was
necessary for it to happen": Barriers to
vulnerable defendants giving evidence by
live link in Crown Court trials', *E&P*
21: 209.

FAIRCLOUGH, S. (2018), 'Speaking Up for
Injustice: Reconsidering the Provision
of Special Measures Through the Lens of
Equality', *Crim LR*, 4.

FEELEY, M. (1979), *The Process is the
Punishment*, New York: Russell Sage
Foundation.

FEELEY, M. (1997), 'Legal Complexity and the
Transformation of the Criminal Process:
The Origins of Plea Bargaining', *Israel LR*,
31: 183.

FEELEY, M. and SIMON, J. (1994), 'Actuarial Justice: The New Emerging Criminal Law' in Nelken, ed, qv.

FEILZER, M. and HOOD, R. (2004), *Differences or Discrimination?*, London: Youth Justice Board.

FEINBERG, J. (2003), 'Criminal Entrapment' in Feinberg, ed, qv.

FEINBERG, J., ed (2003), *Problems at the Roots of Law: Essays in Legal and Political Theory*, Oxford: Oxford University Press.

FELD, B. (2013), *Kids, Cops and Confessions: Inside the Interrogation Room*, New York: NYU Press.

FELDMAN, D. J., ed (2009), *English Public Law*, 2nd edn, Oxford: Oxford University Press.

FENNELL, C. (2003), *The Law of Evidence in Ireland*, 2nd edn, Dublin: LexisNexis.

FENNER, S., GUDJONSSON, G., and CLARE, I. (2002), 'Understanding of the Current Police Caution (England and Wales) Among Suspects in Police Detention', *J Community & Applied Social Psychology*, 12: 83.

FIELD, S. (2008), 'Early Intervention and the "New" Youth Justice: A Study of Initial Decision-making', *Crim LR*, 177.

FIELDS, P. (2008), 'Clarke and McDaid: A Technical Triumph', *Crim LR*, 612.

FINDLEY, K. and SCOTT, M. (2006), 'The Multiple Dimensions of Tunnel Vision in Criminal Cases', *Wisconsin L Rev*, 2: 291.

FINKEL, N. (2006), 'Jurors' Duties, Obligations and Rights: The Ethical/Moral Roots of Discretion' in Kleinig and Levine, eds, qv.

FIONDA, J. (1995), *Public Prosecutors and Discretion: A Comparative Study*, Oxford: Clarendon Press.

FISHER, H. (1977), *Report of an Inquiry by the Hon. Sir Henry Fisher into the circumstances leading to the trial of three persons on charges arising out of the death of Maxwell Confait and the fire at 27 Doggett Road, London SE6*, London: HMSO.

FISSE, B. and BRAITHWAITE, J. (1993), *Corporations, Crime and Accountability*, Sydney: University of Sydney Press.

FITZGERALD, M. (1993), *Ethnic Minorities and the Criminal Justice System*, Royal Commission on Criminal Justice Research Study No 20, London: HMSO.

FITZGERALD, M. (1999), *Final Report into Stop and Search*, London: Metropolitan Police Service.

FLACKS, S. (2017), 'The stop and search of minors: A "vital police tool"?', *Criminol & Crim Justice* 18: 364.

FOOTE, C. (1954), 'Compelling Appearance in Court: the Administration of Bail in Philadelphia', *U Pa LR*, 102: 1031.

FORST, B. (2013), 'Wrongful Convictions in a World of Miscarriages of Justice' in Huff and Killias, eds, qv.

FOSTER, J. (2003), 'Police Cultures' in Newburn, ed, qv.

FOSTER, J., NEWBURN, T., and SOUHAMI, A. (2005), *Assessing the Impact of the Stephen Lawrence Inquiry*, London: Home Office.

FREED, D. J. and WALD, P. (1964), *Bail in the United States*, New York: Vera Institute of Justice.

FREIBERG, A. (2011), 'Post-adversarial and post-inquisitorial justice: Transcending traditional penological paradigms', *Eur J Criminol*, 8: 82.

FRIEDMAN, R. (2008), 'The Confrontation Right Across the Systemic Divide' in Jackson, Langer and Tillers, eds, qv.

FUKURAI, H. and KROOTH, R. (2003), *Race in the Jury Box: Affirmative Action in Jury Selection*, Albany, NY: State University of New York Press.

GARDNER, J. (1998), 'Punishment—in Proportion and in Perspective' in Ashworth and Wasik, eds, qv.

GARLAND, F. and MCEWAN, J. (2012), 'Embracing the overriding objective: difficulties and dilemmas in the new criminal climate', *E&P*, 16: 233.

GAROUPA, N., OGUS, A., and SANDERS, A. (2011), 'The Investigation and Prosecution of Regulatory Offences: Is There an Economic Case for Integration?', *CLJ*, 70: 236.

GARRETT, B. (2011), *Too Big to Jail; How Prosecutors Compromise with Corporations*, Cambridge, MA: Harvard University Press.

GARRETT, B. (2014), *Convicting the Innocent: Where Criminal Prosecutions Go Wrong*, Cambridge, MA: Harvard University Press.

GELSTHORPE, L. and PADFIELD, N., eds (2003), *Exercising Discretion: Decision-Making in the Criminal Justice System and Beyond*, Cullompton: Willan.

GENDERS, E. (1999), 'Reform of the Offences Against the Person Act: Lessons from the Law in Action', *Crim LR*, 689.

GILL, P., JEFFREYS, A., and WERRETT, D. (1985), 'Forensic application of DNA "fingerprints"', *Nature*, 318: 577.

GIVELBER, D. and FARRELL, A. (2008), 'Judges and Juries: The Defense Case and Differences in Acquittal Rates', *Law & Social Inquiry*, 33: 31.

GLIDEWELL, I. (1998), *Review of the Crown Prosecution Service: a Report*, Cm 3960, London: TSO.

GOLDKAMP, J. and GOTTFREDSON, M. R. (1985), *Policy Guidelines for Bail: An Exercise in Court Reform*, Philadelphia, PA: Temple University Press.

GOOLD, B. and LAZARUS, L., eds (2007), *Security and Human Rights*, Oxford: Hart.

GOOLD, B., LAZARUS, L., and SWINEY, G. (2007), *Public Protection, Proportionality and the Search for Balance*, London: Ministry of Justice.

GOTTFREDSON, M. and HIRSCHI, T. (1990), *A General Theory of Crime*, Stanford, NJ: Stanford University Press.

GREENAWALT, K. (1981), 'Silence as a Moral and Constitutional Right', *William & Mary L Rev*, 23: 15.

GRIFFITHS, A. and MILNE, B. (2006), 'Will it All End in Tiers? Police Interviews with Suspects in Britain' in Williamson, ed, qv.

GROSS L. J. (2011), *Review of Disclosure in Criminal Proceedings*, London: Courts and Tribunals Judiciary.

GROSS L. J. and TREACY L. J. (2012), *Further review of disclosure in criminal proceedings: sanctions for disclosure failure*, London: Courts and Tribunals Judiciary.

GROSS, O. (2007), '"Control Systems" and the Migration of Anomalies' in Choudhry, ed, qv.

GUDJONSSON, G. (2003), *The Psychology of Interrogations and Confessions: A Handbook*, Chichester: Wiley.

GUDJONSSON, G. (2007), 'Investigative Interviewing' in Newburn, Williamson, and Wright, eds, qv.

GUS JOHN PARTNERSHIP (2003), *Race for Justice*, London: CPS.

HALLIDAY, S. and SCHMIDT, P., eds (2004), *Human Rights Brought Home: Socio-Economic Perspectives on Human Rights in the National Context*, Oxford: Hart.

HAMER, D. (2009), 'The Expectation of Incorrect Acquittals and the "New and Compelling Evidence" Exception to Double Jeopardy', *Crim LR*, 63.

HARCOURT, B. (2007), *Against Prediction: Profiling, Policing and Punishing in an Actuarial Age*, Chicago, IL: University of Chicago Press.

HARDING, C., FENNELL, P., JÖRG, N., and SWART, B., eds (1995), *Criminal Justice in Europe*, Oxford: Clarendon Press.

HARRIS, D. and JOSEPH, S., eds (1995), *The International Covenant on Civil and Political Rights and United Kingdom Law*, London: Butterworths.

HARRIS, D., O'BOYLE, M., and WARBRICK, C. (2014), *Harris, O'Boyle and Warbrick,*

Law of the European Convention on Human Rights, 3rd edn, Oxford: Oxford University Press.

HAWKINS, K. (1984), *Environment and Enforcement*, Oxford: Oxford University Press.

HAWKINS, K., ed (1992), *The Uses of Discretion*, Oxford: Oxford University Press.

HAWKINS, K. (2003), *Law as Last Resort*, Oxford: Oxford University Press.

HEALTH AND SAFETY EXECUTIVE (2009), *Enforcement Policy Statement*, https://www.hse.gov.uk.

HEATON, S. (2013), 'A critical evaluation of the utility of using innocence as a criterion in the post conviction process', Doctoral thesis, University of East Anglia.

HEATON-ARMSTRONG, A., SHEPHERD, E., and WOLCHOVER, D., eds (1999), *Analysing Witness Testimony*, London: Blackstone Press.

HEATON-ARMSTRONG, A., WOLCHOVER, D., and MAXWELL-SCOTT, A. (2006), 'Obtaining, Recording and Admissibility of Out-of-Court Witness Statements' in Heaton-Armstrong, Shepherd, Gudjonsson, and Wolchover, eds, qv.

HEATON-ARMSTRONG, A., SHEPHERD, E., GUDJONSSON, G., and WOLCHOVER, D., eds (2006), *Witness Testimony: Psychological, Investigative and Evidential Perspectives*, Oxford: Oxford University Press.

HEDDERMAN, C. and HOUGH, M. (1994), *Does the Criminal Justice System Treat Men and Women Differently?*, Home Office Research Findings No 10, London: Home Office.

HEDDERMAN, C. and MOXON, D. (1992), *Magistrates' Court or Crown Court? Mode of Trial Decisions and Sentencing*, Home Office Research Study 125, London: Home Office.

HEINZ, W. (1989), 'The Problems of Imprisonment', in Hood, ed, qv.

HELMHOLZ, R., GRAY, C., LANGBEIN, J., MOGLEN, E., SMITH, H., and ALSCHULER, A. (1997), *The Privilege Against Self Incrimination: Its Origins and Development*, Chicago, IL: University of Chicago Press.

HENHAM, R. (1999), 'Bargain Justice or Justice Denied? Sentence Discounts and the Criminal Process', *MLR*, 63: 515.

HENHAM, R. (2000), 'Reconciling Process and Policy: Sentence Discounts in the Magistrates' Courts', *Crim LR*, 436.

HENHAM, R. (2002), 'Further Evidence on the Significance of Plea in the Crown Court', *Howard JCJ*, 41: 151.

HERRMANN, J. (1974), 'The Rule of Compulsory Prosecution and the Scope of Prosecutorial Discretion in Germany', *U Chi LR*, 41: 468.

HERRMANN, J. (1992), 'Bargaining Justice: a Bargain for German Criminal Justice?', *U Pittsburgh LR*, 53: 755.

HILL, M. (2018), *The Terrorism Acts in 2016: Report of the Independent Reviewer of Terrorism Legislation on the Operation of the Terrorism Acts 2000 and 2006*, London: Independent Reviewer of Terrorism Legislation.

HILSON, C. (1993), 'Discretion to Prosecute and Judicial Review', *Crim LR*, 639.

HM CROWN PROSECUTION SERVICE INSPECTORATE (1998), *Cases Involving Domestic Violence, Thematic Report*, London: HMCPSI.

HM CROWN PROSECUTION SERVICE INSPECTORATE (1999), *Adverse Cases*, London: HMCPSI.

HM CROWN PROSECUTION SERVICE INSPECTORATE (1999), *Central Casework Section*, London: HMCPSI.

HM CROWN PROSECUTION SERVICE INSPECTORATE (2000), *The Inspectorate's Report on the Thematic Review of the Disclosure of Unused Material*, London: HMCPSI.

HM Crown Prosecution Service Inspectorate (2002), *Report of a Joint Inspection into the Investigation and Prosecution of Cases involving Allegations of Rape*, London: HMCPSI.

HM Crown Prosecution Service Inspectorate (2002), *Report on the Thematic Review of Casework Having a Minority Ethnic Dimension*, London: HMCPSI.

HM Crown Prosecution Service Inspectorate (2003), *Streets Ahead: A Joint Inspection of the Street Crime Initiative*, London: HMCPSI.

HM Crown Prosecution Service Inspectorate (2004), *A Follow Up Review of CPS Casework with a Minority Ethnic Dimension*, London: HMCPSI.

HM Crown Prosecution Service Inspectorate (2007), *Discontinuance*, London: HMCPSI.

HM Crown Prosecution Service Inspectorate (2008), *Disclosure: A Thematic Review of the Duties of Disclosure of Unused Material Undertaken by the CPS*, London: HMCPSI.

HM Crown Prosecution Service Inspectorate (2008), *Inspection of CPS Direct*, London: HMCPSI.

HM Crown Prosecution Service Inspectorate (2010), *Custody time limits: A report relating to the handling of custody time limits by the Crown Prosecution Service*, London: HMCPSI.

HM Crown Prosecution Service Inspectorate (2013), *Custody time limits: Follow-up review of the handling of custody time limits by the Crown Prosecution Service*, London: HMCPSI.

HM Crown Prosecution Service Inspectorate (2013), *Review into the Disclosure handling in the case of R v Mouncher and Others*, London: HMCPSI.

HM Crown Prosecution Service Inspectorate (2016), *Communicating with victims*, London: HMCPSI.

HM Crown Prosecution Service Inspectorate (2016), *Thematic Review of the CPS Rape and Serious Sexual Offences Units*, London: HMCPSI.

HM Crown Prosecution Service Inspectorate (2016), *Transforming Summary Justice: An early perspective of the CPS contribution*, London: HMCPSI.

HM Crown Prosecution Service Inspectorate (2017), *Business as Usual? Transforming Summary Justice Follow-up Report*, London: HMCPSI.

HM Crown Prosecution Service Inspectorate (2017), *Case Finalisations: An Inspection into the Timeliness and Accuracy of Recording Case Finalisations onto the Crown Prosecution Service Case Management System*, London: HMCPSI.

HM Crown Prosecution Service Inspectorate and HM Inspectorate of Constabulary (2004), *Violence at Home: A Joint Thematic Inspection of the Investigation and Prosecution of Cases Involving Domestic Violence*, London: HMCPSI and HMIC.

HM Crown Prosecution Service Inspectorate and HM Inspectorate of Constabulary (2008), *Joint Thematic Review of the New Charging Arrangements*, London: HMCPSI and HMIC.

HM Crown Prosecution Service Inspectorate and HM Inspectorate of Constabulary (2014), *Achieving best evidence in child sexual abuse cases—a joint inspection*, London: HMCPSI and HMIC.

HM Crown Prosecution Service Inspectorate and HM Inspectorate of Constabulary (2015), *Joint Inspection of the Provision of Charging Decisions*, London: HMCPSI and HMIC.

HM Crown Prosecution Service Inspectorate and HM Inspectorate of Constabulary (2016), *Delivering Justice in a Digital Age: Joint inspection of digital case preparation and presentation in the criminal justice system*, London: HMCPSI and HMIC.

HM Crown Prosecution Service Inspectorate and HM Inspectorate of Constabulary (2017), *Making It Fair: A Joint Inspection of the Disclosure of Unused Material in Volume Crown Court Cases*, London: HMCPSI and HMIC.

HM Crown Prosecution Service Inspectorate, HM Inspectorate of Constabulary, and HMI Probation (2013), *Living in a different world: Joint review of disability hate crime*, London: HMCPSI, HMIC, and HMI Probation.

HM Government and College of Policing (2014), *Out of Court Disposals Consultation Response*, London: TSO and College of Policing.

HM Inspectorate of Constabulary (2002), *Under the Microscope Refocused: A Revisit to the Thematic Inspection Report on Scientific and Technical Support*, London: HMIC.

HM Inspectorate of Constabulary (2013), *Stop and search powers: Are the police using them effectively and fairly?*, London: HMIC.

HM Inspectorate of Constabulary (2014), *Crime-recording: making the victim count. The final report of an inspection of crime data integrity in police forces in England and Wales*, London: HMIC.

HM Inspectorate of Constabulary (2015), *Increasingly everyone's business: A progress report on the police response to domestic abuse*, London: HMIC.

HM Inspectorate of Constabulary (2015), *Witness for the prosecution:*

Identifying victim and witness vulnerability in criminal case files, London: HMIC.

HM Inspectorate of Constabulary (2016), *State of Policing: The Annual Assessment of Policing in England and Wales 2015*, London: HMIC.

HM Inspectorate of Constabulary and HM Crown Prosecution Service Inspectorate (2011), *Exercising Discretion: The Gateway to Justice A study by Her Majesty's Inspectorate of Constabulary and Her Majesty's Crown Prosecution Service Inspectorate on cautions, penalty notices for disorder and restorative justice*, London: HMIC and HMCPSI.

HM Inspectorate of Constabulary and HM Crown Prosecution Service Inspectorate (2017), *Living in fear—the police and CPS response to harassment and stalking: A joint inspection by HMIC and HMCPSI*, London: HMIC and HMCPSI.

HM Inspectorate of Constabulary and Fire & Rescue Services (2017), *A progress report on the police response to domestic abuse*, London: HMICFRS.

HM Inspectorate of Constabulary and Fire & Rescue Services (2017), *PEEL: Police Legitimacy*, London: HMICFRS.

HM Inspectorate of Prisons (2012), *Thematic Report by HM Inspectorate of Prisons Remand prisoners: A thematic review*, London: HMIP.

HM Inspectorate of Probation (2017), *Probation Hostels' (Approved Premises) Contribution to Public Protection, Rehabilitation and Resettlement*, London: HMIP.

HM Inspectorate of Probation, HM Inspectorate of Prisons, and HM Crown Prosecution Service Inspectorate (2012), *Facing Up To Offending: Use of restorative justice in the criminal justice system*, London: HMIP, HMIP, and HMCPSI.

HODGSON, J. (1994), 'Adding Injury to Injustice: The Suspect at the Police Station', *J Law & Soc*, 21: 85.

HODGSON, J. (2002), 'Human Rights and French Criminal Justice' in Halliday and Schmidt, eds, qv.

HODGSON, J. (2003), 'Codified Criminal Procedure and Human Rights: Some Observations on the French Experience', *Crim LR*, 165.

HODGSON, J. and HORNE, J. (2009), *The Extent and Impact of Legal Representation on Applications to the Criminal Cases Review Commission*, London: CCRC.

HOHL, K. and STANKO, E. (2015), 'Complaints of Rape and the Criminal Justice System: Fresh Evidence on the Attrition Problem in England and Wales', *Eur J Criminol* 12: 324.

HOFMEYR, K. (2006), 'The Problem of Private Entrapment', *Crim LR*, 319.

HOME AFFAIRS COMMITTEE (2002), *The Conduct of Investigations into Past Cases of Abuse in Children's Homes*, 4th Report, HC 836, London: TSO.

HOME AFFAIRS COMMITTEE (2004), *The Work of the Criminal Cases Review Commission*, HC 289-I, London: TSO.

HOME AFFAIRS COMMITTEE (2014), *Leadership and standards in the police*, Third Report of Session 2013–14, HC 67-I, London: TSO.

HOME AFFAIRS COMMITTEE (2015), *Police bail*, Seventeenth Report of Session 2014–15, HC 962, London: TSO.

HOME AFFAIRS COMMITTEE (2016), *College of Policing: three years on*, Fourth Report of Session 2016–17, HC 23, London: TSO.

HOME AFFAIRS SELECT COMMITTEE (2012), *Drugs: Breaking the Cycle—Formal Minutes*, London: TSO.

HOME OFFICE (1997), *No More Excuses: a New Approach to Tackling Youth Crime in England and Wales*, London: Home Office.

HOME OFFICE (1998), *Speaking Up for Justice*, London: Home Office.

HOME OFFICE (1999), *Digest 4: Information on the Criminal Justice System in England and Wales*, London: Home Office.

HOME OFFICE (1999), *Interception of Communications in the United Kingdom*, Cmnd 4368, London: Home Office.

HOME OFFICE (2002), *Justice for All*, Cmnd 5563, London: Home Office.

HOME OFFICE (2003), *Crime in England and Wales 2002/2003*, London: Home Office.

HOME OFFICE (2006), *Delivering Simple, Speedy, Summary Justice*, London: Home Office.

HOME OFFICE (2006), *Quashing Convictions*, London: Home Office.

HOME OFFICE (2006), *Rebalancing the Criminal Justice System in Favour of the Law-Abiding Majority: a consultation paper*, London: Home Office.

HOME OFFICE (2008), *Government Proposals in Response to the Review of the Police and Criminal Evidence Act 1984*, London: Home Office.

HOME OFFICE (2009), *DNA Retention Policy: Re-Arrest Hazard Rate Analysis*, London: Home Office.

HOME OFFICE (2009), *Keeping the Right People on the DNA Database: Science and Public Protection*, London: Home Office.

HOME OFFICE (2009), *Operation of Police Powers Under the Terrorism Act 2000 and Subsequent Legislation*, London: Home Office.

HOME OFFICE (2009), *Regulation of Investigatory Powers Act 2000: Consolidating Orders and Codes of Practice: A Public Consultation Paper*, London: Home Office.

HOME OFFICE (2009), *Written Ministerial Statement: DNA and Fingerprint Retention*, London: Home Office.

HOME OFFICE (2010), *Policing in the 21st Century: Reconnecting Police and the People*, London: Home Office.

HOME OFFICE (2017), *Police powers and procedures*, London: Home Office.

HOME OFFICE (2018), *Crime outcomes in England and Wales: year ending March 2018*, London: Home Office.

HOME OFFICE (2018), *Operation of police powers under the Terrorism Act 2000 and subsequent legislation: Arrests, outcomes, and stop and search, Great Britain, financial year ending March 2018*, Statistical Bulletin 09/18, London: Home Office.

HONESS, T., LEVI, M., and CHAPMAN, E. (1998), 'Juror Competence in Processing Complex Information: Implications from a Simulation of the Maxwell Trial', *Crim LR*, 763.

HOOD, R. G., ed (1989), *Crime and Criminal Policy in Europe: Proceedings of a European Colloquium*, Oxford: Centre for Criminological Research.

HOOD, R. G. (1992), *Race and Sentencing*, Oxford: Oxford University Press.

HOOD, R. G., SHUTE, S., and SEEMUNGAL, F. (2003), *Ethnic Minorities in the Criminal Courts: Perceptions of Fairness and Equality of Treatment*, Lord Chancellor's Department Research Series No 2/03, London: Lord Chancellor's Department.

HOPKINS, K., UHRIG, N., and COLAHAN, M. (2016), *Associations between ethnic background and being sentenced to prison in the Crown Court in England and Wales in 2015*, London: Ministry of Justice.

HORRY, R. MEMON, A., MILNE, R., WRIGHT, D., and DALTON, G. (2013), 'Video Identification of Suspects: A Discussion of Current Practice and Policy in the United Kingdom', *Policing: A Journal of Policy and Practice* 7: 307.

HORRY, T., et al (2014), 'Archival analyses of eyewitness identification test outcomes: what can they tell us about eyewitness memory?' *Law & Human Behavior* 38: 94.

HORWELL, R., (2017), *Mouncher Investigation Report*, London: Home Office.

HOULDER, B. (1997), 'The Importance of Preserving the Jury System and the Right of Election for Trial', *Crim LR*, 875.

HOUSE OF COMMONS COMMITTEE OF PUBLIC ACCOUNTS (2013), *The Criminal Justice System*, Fifty-Ninth Report of Session 2013–14, HC 1115, London: TSO.

HOUSE OF COMMONS CONSTITUTIONAL AFFAIRS COMMITTEE (2004), *Draft Criminal Defence Service Bill*, HC 746-I, London: TSO.

HOUSE OF COMMONS JUSTICE COMMITTEE (2009), *The Crown Prosecution Service: Gatekeeper of the Criminal Justice System*, London: TSO.

HOUSE OF COMMONS JUSTICE COMMITTEE (2013), *Women offenders: after the Corston Report*, Second Report of Session 2013–14, HC 92, London: TSO.

HOUSE OF COMMONS JUSTICE COMMITTEE (2015), *Criminal Cases Review Commission*, Twelfth Report of Session 2014–15, HC 850, London: TSO.

HOUSE OF COMMONS JUSTICE COMMITTEE (2015), *Criminal courts charge*, Second Report of Session 2015–16, HC 586, London: TSO.

HOUSE OF COMMONS JUSTICE COMMITTEE (2016), *Efficiency in the criminal justice system*, First Report of Session 2016–17, HC 72, London: TSO.

HOUSE OF COMMONS JUSTICE COMMITTEE (2016), *Reduction in sentence for a guilty plea guideline*, First Report of Session 2016–17, HC 168, London: TSO.

HOUSE OF COMMONS JUSTICE COMMITTEE (2016), *The role of the magistracy*, Sixth Report of Session 2016–17, HC 165, London: TSO.

HOUSE OF COMMONS JUSTICE COMMITTEE (2018), *Criminal Legal Aid*, Twelfth Report of Session 2017–19, HC 1069, London: TSO.

HOUSE OF COMMONS JUSTICE COMMITTEE (2018), *Disclosure of evidence in criminal cases*, Eleventh Report of Session 2017–19, HC 859, London: TSO.

HOYANO, A., HOYANO, L., DAVIS, G., and GOLDIE, S. (1997), 'A Study of the Impact of the Revised Code for Crown Prosecutors', *Crim LR*, 556.

HOYLE, C. (1998), *Negotiating Domestic Violence*, Oxford: Oxford University Press.

HOYLE, C. and SATO, M. (2019), *Reasons to Doubt: Wrongful Convictions and the Criminal Cases Review Commission*, Oxford: Oxford University Press.

HUCKLESBY, A. (1996), 'Bail or Jail? The Practical Operation of the Bail Act 1976', *JLS*, 23: 213.

HUCKLESBY, A. (1997), 'Court Culture: an Explanation of Variations in the Use of Bail by Magistrates' Courts', *Howard JCJ*, 36: 129.

HUCKLESBY, A. (1997), 'Remand Decision Makers', *Crim LR*, 269.

HUCKLESBY, A. (2004), 'Not Necessarily a Trip to the Police Station: The Introduction of Street Bail', *Crim LR*, 803.

HUCKLESBY, A. (2011), *Bail Support Schemes for Adults*, Bristol: Policy Press.

HUGHES, M., BAIN, S, GILCHRIST, E., and BOYLE, J. (2013), 'Does providing a written version of the police caution improve comprehension in the general population?', *Psychology, Crime & Law* 19: 549.

HUFF, C., and KILLIAS, M., eds (2013), *Wrongful Convictions and Miscarriages of Justice: Causes and Remedies in North American and European Criminal Justice Systems*, Boca Raton, FL: CRC Press.

HUMAN GENETICS COMMISSION (2009), *Nothing to Hide, Nothing to Fear? Balancing Individual Rights and the Public Interest in the Governance and Use of the National DNA Database*, London: Central Office of Information.

HUMPHREYS, C. (1955), 'The Duties and Responsibilities of Prosecuting Counsel', *Crim LR*, 739.

HUNGERFORD-WELCH, P. (2017), 'Abuse of Process: Does it Really Protect the Suspect's Rights?', *Crim LR*, 3.

HUNTER, J., ROBERTS, P., YOUNG, S., and DIXON, D., eds (2016), *The Integrity of Criminal Process: From Theory into Practice*, Oxford: Hart.

HUTTER, B. (1988), *The Reasonable Arm of the Law*, Oxford: Oxford University Press.

HYNES, P. and ELKINS, M. (2013), 'Suggestions for Reform to the Police Cautioning Procedure', *Crim LR*, 966.

ILIADIS, M. and FLYNN, A. (2017), 'Providing a Check on Prosecutorial Decision-Making: An Analysis of the Victims' Right to Review Reform', *BJ Crim*, 58: 550.

INDEPENDENT POLICE COMPLAINTS COMMISSION (2009), *Police Complaints: Statistics for England and Wales 2008/09*, London: Independent Police Complaints Commission.

INDEPENDENT POLICE COMPLAINTS COMMISSION (2013), *Consultation Response to Police and Crime Committee*, London: IPCC.

INDEPENDENT POLICE COMPLAINTS COMMISSION (2015), *Referring complaints, conduct matters and death or serious injury matters to the IPCC—a review of current police force practice*, London: IPCC.

INSTITUTE OF RACE RELATIONS (2015), *Dying for Justice*, London: Institute of Race Relations.

INTERNATIONAL ASSOCIATION OF PROSECUTORS (2006), *Standards for Prosecutors: an Analysis of the United Kingdom National Prosecuting Agencies*, The Hague: International Association of Prosecutors.

IOANNOU, M. and HAMMOND, L. (2015), 'The detection of deception within investigative contexts: Key challenges and core issues', *J Investigative Psychology and Offender Profiling* 12: 107.

IP, J. (2008), 'The Rise and Spread of the Special Advocate', *PL*, 717.

IPSOS MORI for the MINISTRY OF JUSTICE (2011), *The strengths and skills of the Judiciary in the Magistrates' Courts*, Ministry of Justice Research Series 9/11, London: Ministry of Justice.

IRVING, B. (1980), *Police Interrogation: A Study of Current Practice*, London: HMSO.

IRVING, B. and DUNNIGHAN, C. (1993), *Human Factors in the Quality Control of CID Investigations*, Royal Commission on Criminal Justice Research Study No 21, London: HMSO.

JACKSON, J. D. (2003), 'Justice for All: Putting Victims at the Heart of Criminal Justice?', *JLS*, 30: 309.

JACKSON, J. D. (2005), 'The Effects of Human Rights on Criminal Evidentiary Processes: Convergence, Divergence or Realignment?', *MLR*, 68: 737.

JACKSON, J. D. (2006), 'Ethical Implications of the Enhanced Role of the Crown Prosecutor', *Legal Ethics* 9: 35.

JACKSON, J. D. (2009), 'Re-Conceptualizing the Right of Silence as an Effective Fair Trial Standard', *ICLQ*, 58: 835.

JACKSON, J. D. and DORAN, S. (1995), *Judge without Jury*, Oxford: Oxford University Press.

JACKSON, J. D. and JOHNSTONE, J. (2005), 'The Reasonable Time Requirement: An Independent and Meaningful Right?', *Crim LR*, 3.

JACKSON, J. D., LANGER, M., and SEIGEL, M. (1995), 'Rethinking Adversariness in Non-Jury Criminal Trials', *Am J Crim L*, 23: 1.

JACKSON, J. D., LANGER, M., and TILLERS, P., eds (2008), *Crime, Procedure and Evidence in a Comparative and International Context*, Oxford: Hart.

JACKSON, J. D., QUINN, K., and O'MALLEY, T. (1999), 'The Jury System in Contemporary Ireland', *Law & Contemporary Probs*, 62: 202.

JACKSON, J. D., WOLFE, M., and QUINN, K. (2000), *Legislating Against Silence: The Northern Ireland Experience*, Belfast: Northern Ireland Office.

JACKSON, J., BRADFORD, B., HOUGH, M., MYHILL, A., QUINTON, P., and TYLER, T. (2012), 'Why do People Comply with the Law?: Legitimacy and the Influence of Legal Institutions', *BJ Crim*, 52: 105.

JAMES, A., TAYLOR, N., and WALKER, C. (2000), 'The Criminal Cases Review Commission: Economy, Effectiveness and Justice', *Crim LR*, 140.

JEFFERSON, T. and WALKER, M. (1992), 'Ethnic Minorities in the Criminal Justice System', *Crim LR*, 83.

SIR BILL JEFFREY (2014), *Independent criminal advocacy in England and Wales*, London: Ministry of Justice.

JEREMY, D. (2008), 'The Prosecutor's Rock and Hard Place', *Crim LR*, 925.

JOHNSTON, E. (2015), 'The innocent cannot afford to plead guilty: The impact of the criminal court charge', *Crim L and Justice Weekly*, 179: 670.

JOHNSTON, E. and SMITH, T. (2017), 'The digital revolution: Body-worn cameras and street interviews', *Crim L and Justice Weekly* 181: 769.

JOHNSTONE, G. (2011), *Restorative Justice: Ideas, Values, Debates*, 2nd edn, Cullompton: Willan.

JOINT COMMITTEE ON HUMAN RIGHTS (2003), *Criminal Justice Bill: Further Report*, HC 724, London: TSO.

JOINT COMMITTEE ON HUMAN RIGHTS (2009), *Legislative Scrutiny: Coroners and Justice Bill*, HC 362, London: TSO.

JOINT COMMITTEE ON HUMAN RIGHTS (2009), *Legislative Scrutiny: Policing and Crime Bill (gangs injunctions)*, London: TSO.

JONES, P. R. and GOLDKAMP, J. S. (1991), 'Judicial Guidelines for Pre-Trial Release: Research and Policy Developments in the United States', *Howard JCJ*, 30: 140.

JORDANOSKA, A. (2017), 'Case Management in Complex Fraud Trials: Actors and Strategies in Achieving Procedural Efficiency', *Int J L in Context* 336.

JORG, N., FIELD, S., and BRANTS, C. (1995), 'Are Inquisitorial and Adversarial Systems Converging?' in Harding, Fennell, Jörg, and Swart, eds, qv.

JUDICIAL COLLEGE (2017), *The Crown Court Compendium*, Part I: Jury and Trial Management and Summing Up, London: Judicial College.

JUDICIAL STUDIES BOARD (2007), *Anti-Social Behaviour Orders: a Guide for the Judiciary*, 3rd edn, London: Judicial Studies Board.

JUDICIARY OF ENGLAND AND WALES (2013), *Judicial Protocol on the Disclosure of Unused Material in Criminal Cases*, London: Judiciary of England and Wales.

JUDICIARY OF ENGLAND AND WALES (2018), *The Better Case Management (BCM) Handbook*, London: Judiciary of England and Wales.

JULIAN, R. (2008), 'Judicial Perspectives in Serious Fraud Cases', *Crim LR*, 764.

JUNG, H. (1993), 'Criminal Justice: A European Perspective', *Crim LR*, 237.

JUNG, H. (1997), 'Plea-Bargaining and its Repercussions on the Theory of Criminal Procedure', *Eur J Crime, Crim L and Crim Justice*, 5: 112.

JUSTICE (1970), 'The Prosecution Process in England and Wales', *Crim LR*, 668.

JUSTICE (1994), *Remedying Miscarriages of Justice*, London: JUSTICE.

JUSTICE (1998), *Under Surveillance*, London: JUSTICE.

KASSIN, S. M. (2003), 'Behavioral Confirmation in the Interrogation Room: On the Dangers of Presuming Guilt', *Law & Human Behavior*, 27: 187.

KASSIN, S. M. (2014), 'False Confessions: Causes, Consequences, and Implications for Reform', *Policy Insights from the Behavioral and Brain Sciences*, 112.

KASSIN, S. M. and FONG, C. (1999), '"I'm Innocent": Effects of Training on Judgments of Truth and Deception in the Interrogation Room', *Law & Human Behavior*, 23: 499.

KASSIN, S. M. and GUDJONSSON, G. (2004), 'The Psychology of Confessions: A Review of the Literature and Issues', *Psychological Science in the Public Interest*, 5: 33.

KASSIN, S. M. and MCNALL, K. (1991), 'Police Interrogation and Confession: Communicating Promises and Threats by Pragmatic Implication', *Law & Human Behavior*, 5: 233.

KASSIN, S. M., GOLDSTEIN, C. C., and SAVITSKY, K. (2003), 'Behavioral Confirmation in the Interrogation Room: On the Dangers of Presuming Guilt', *Law & Human Behavior* 27: 187.

KASSIN, S. M., DRIZIN, S., GRISSO, T., GUDJONSSON, G, LEO, R., and REDLICH, A. (2010), 'Police-Induced Confessions: Risk Factors and Recommendations', *Law & Human Behavior*, 34: 3.

KAYE, D. and SMITH, M. (2004), 'DNA Databases for Law Enforcement: The Coverage Question and the Case for a Population-Wide Database' in Lazer, ed, qv.

KAYE, T. (1991), 'Unsafe and Unsatisfactory'? *Report of the Independent Inquiry into the Working Practices of the West Midlands*

Serious Crime Squad, London: Civil Liberties Trust.

KELLOUGH, G. and WORTLEY, S. (2002), 'Remand for Plea: Bail Decisions and Plea Bargaining as Commensurate Decisions', *BJ Crim*, 42: 186.

KEMP, V. (2010), *Transforming Legal Aid: Access to Criminal Defence Services*, London: Ministry of Justice.

KEMP, V. (2013), '"No Time for a Solicitor": Implications for Delays on the Take-Up of Legal Advice', *Crim LR*, 184.

KEMP, V. (2014), 'PACE, Performance Targets and Legal Protections', *Crim LR*, 278.

KEMP, V. and BALMER, N. (2008), *Criminal Defence Services: Users' Perspectives (Interim Report)*, London: Legal Services Commission.

KEMP, V., BALMER, N., and PLEASENCE, P. (2012), 'Whose Time is it Anyway? Factors Associated with Duration in Police Custody', *Crim LR*, 736.

KEMP, V., PLEASENCE, P., and BALMER, N. (2011), 'Children, Young People and Requests for Police Station Legal Advice: 25 years on from PACE', *Youth Justice*, 11: 28.

KENDALL, J. (2018), *Regulating Police Detention: Voices from Behind Closed Doors*, Bristol: Policy Press.

KENNEDY, M., TRUMAN, C., KEYES, S., and CAMERON, A. (1997), 'Supported Bail for Mentally Vulnerable Defendants', *Howard JCJ*, 36: 158.

KERRIGAN. K. (2006), 'Miscarriages of Justice in the Magistrates Court: The Forgotten Power of the CCRC', *Crim LR*, 143.

KING, M. (1981), *The Framework of Criminal Justice*, London: Croom Helm.

KING, N. J. (1994), 'The Effects of Race-Conscious Jury Selection on Public Confidence in the Fairness of Jury Proceedings: An Empirical Puzzle', *Am Crim LR*, 31: 1177.

KIRK, D. (2014), 'Reflections of a Former Prosecutor', *J Crim L*, 78: 99.

KLEINIG, J. and LEVINE, J., eds (2006), *Jury Ethics: Juror Conduct and Jury Dynamics*, Boulder, CO: Paradigm.

KNIGHT, C. (2011), 'Second Criminal Appeals and the Requirement of Certification', *LQR*, 188.

KRAINA, C. and CARROLL, L. (2006), *Penalty Notices for Disorder: Review of Practice across Police Forces*, London: Office for Criminal Justice Reform.

KYLE, D. (2004), 'Correcting Miscarriages of Justice: The Role of the Criminal Cases Review Commission', *Drake L Rev*, 52: 657.

KYMLICKA, W. (2002), *Contemporary Political Philosophy: An Introduction*, 2nd edn, Oxford: Oxford University Press.

LAMMY, D. (2017), *The Lammy Review: An Independent Review into the Treatment of, and outcomes for, Black, Asian and Minority Ethnic Individuals in the Criminal Justice System*, London: Ministry of Justice.

LANGER, M. (2004), 'From Legal Transplants to Legal Translations: The Globalization of Plea-Bargaining and the Americanization Thesis in Criminal Procedure', *Harvard Int LJ*, 45: 1.

LASSITER, G., SLAW, R., BRIGGS, M., and SCANLAN, C. (2006), 'The Potential for Bias in Videotaped Confessions', *J Applied Social Psychol*, 22: 1838.

LAUDAN, L. (2006), *Truth, Error and Criminal Law: An Essay in Legal Epistemology*, Cambridge: Cambridge University Press.

LAW COMMISSION (1999), *Double Jeopardy*, Consultation Paper No 156, London: TSO.

LAW COMMISSION (2000), *Prosecution Appeals Against Judges' Rulings*, Consultation Paper No 158, London: TSO.

LAW COMMISSION (2001), *Bail and the Human Rights Act 1998*, Consultation Paper No 157, London: TSO.

LAW COMMISSION (2001), *Double Jeopardy and Prosecution Appeals*, Report No 267, London: TSO.

LAW COMMISSION (2007), *The High Court's Jurisdiction in Relation to Criminal Proceedings: A Consultation Paper*, London: TSO.

LAW COMMISSION (2013), *Contempt of Court (1): Juror Misconduct and Internet Publications*, Law Com No 340, London: TSO.

LAW COMMISSION (2016), *Report on Unfitness to Plead: Vol 1*, Law Com No 364, London: TSO.

LAW SOCIETY (2008), *Criminal Procedure Rules: Impact on Solicitors' Duties to the Client*, London: Law Society.

LAZER, D., ed (2004), *DNA and the Criminal Justice System: The Technology of Justice*, Cambridge, MA: MIT Press.

LEAHY, S. (2016), 'Too Much Information? Regulating Disclosure of Complainants' Personal Records in Sexual Offence Trials', *Crim LR*, 229.

LEGAL SERVICES COMMISSION (2005), *Code for the Criminal Defence Service*, London: Legal Services Commission.

LEGAL SERVICES COMMISSION (2008), *Evaluation of CDS Direct First Phase Expansion*, London: Legal Services Commission.

LEGAL SERVICES COMMISSION (2013), *Annual Report and Accounts 2012–13*, London: Legal Services Commission.

LEIGH, L. (2006), 'Lurking Doubt and the Safety of Convictions', *Crim LR*, 809.

LEIGH, L. (2007), 'Private Prosecutions and Diversionary Justice', *Crim LR*, 289.

LEIGH, L. (2013), 'Cautioning—whatever happened to common sense', *CL & J*, 177: 269.

LEIGH, L. and ZEDNER, L. (1992), *A Report on the Administration of Criminal Justice in the Pre-Trial Phase in France and Germany*, Royal Commission on Criminal Justice Research Study No 1, London: HMSO.

LEIPOLD, A. (2005), 'Why are Federal Judges so Acquittal Prone?', *Washington ULQ*, 83: 151.

LEMPERT, R. (1993), 'Civil Juries and Complex Cases: Taking Stock After Twelve Years' in Litan, ed, qv.

LENG, R. (2000), 'The Exchange of Information and Disclosure' in McConville and Wilson, eds, qv.

LENNON, G., (2016), 'Stop and search powers in UK terrorism investigations: a limited judicial oversight?' *Int J Human Rights*, 20: 634.

LENSING, H. and RAYAR, L. (1992), 'Notes on Criminal Procedure in the Netherlands', *Crim LR*, 623.

LEVESON, THE RT HON. SIR B. (2015), *Review of Efficiency in Criminal Proceedings*, London: Judiciary of England and Wales.

LEVI, M. (1993), *The Investigation, Prosecution and Trial of Serious Fraud*, Royal Commission on Criminal Justice Research Study No 14, London: HMSO.

LIEBLING, A. and KRARUP, H. (1993), *Suicide Attempts and Self-Injury in Male Prisons*, Cambridge: Institute of Criminology.

LIEBLING, A., MARUNA, S., and MCARA, L. eds (2017) *The Oxford Handbook of Criminology*, 6th edn, Oxford: Oxford University Press.

LIPPERT-RASMUSSEN, K. (2006), 'Racial Profiling Versus Community', *J Applied Philosophy*, 23: 191.

LISTER, S. (2013), 'The New Politics of the Police: Police and Crime Commissioners and the "Operational Independence" of the Police', *Policing: A Journal of Policy and Practice*, 7: 239.

LITAN, R., ed (1993), *Verdict: Assessing the Civil Jury System*, Washington, DC: The Brookings Institution.

LLOYD-BOSTOCK, S. (2006), Report on Interviews with Jurors in the Jubilee Line Case, London: HMCPSI.

LOADER, I. (2006), 'Fall of the Platonic Guardians: Liberalism, Criminology and Responses to Crime in England and Wales', *BJ Crim*, 46: 561.

LOFTUS, B. (2008), 'Dominant Culture Interrupted', *BJ Crim*, 48: 756.

LOFTUS, B. (2009), *Police Culture in a Changing World*, Oxford: Oxford University Press.

LOFTUS, B. (2010), 'Police Occupational Culture: Classic Themes, Altered Times', *Policing and Society*, 20.

LOFTUS, B. and GOOLD, B. (2012), 'Covert surveillance and the invisibilities of policing', *Criminol & Crim Justice*, 12: 275.

LORD, N. and KING, C. (2018), 'Negotiating Non-Contention: Civil Recovery and Deferred Prosecution in Response to Transnational Corporate Bribery' in Campbell and Lord, eds, qv.

LUBAN, D. (1993), 'Are Criminal Defenders Different?', *Mich LR*, 91: 1729.

LUDLOW, A. (2017), 'Marketizing Criminal Justice' in Liebling, Maruna, and McAra, eds, qv.

LUNDY, L. KILKELLY, U., BYRNE, B., and KANG, J. (2012), *The UN Convention on the Rights of the Child: a study of legal implementation in 12 countries*, New York: UNICEF.

LUSTGARTEN, L. (2002), 'The Future of Stop and Search', *Crim LR*, 603.

McBARNET, D. (1983), *Conviction: Law, the State and the Construction of Justice*, London: Macmillan.

McBARNET, D. and WHELAN, C. (1991), 'The Elusive Spirit of the Law: Formalism and the Struggle for Legal Control', *MLR*, 54: 848.

McCABE, S. and PURVES, R. (1972), *By-Passing the Jury*, Oxford: University of Oxford Penal Research Unit.

McCANDLESS, R., FEIST, A., ALLAN, J., and MORGAN, N. (2016), *Do initiatives involving substantial increases in stop and search reduce crime? Assessing the impact of Operation BLUNT 2*, London: Home Office.

McCARTNEY, C. (2006), *Forensic Identification and Criminal Justice: Forensic Science, Justice and Risk*, Cullompton: Willan.

McCONVILLE, M. (1992), 'Videotaping Interrogations: Police Behaviour On and Off Camera', *Crim LR*, 532.

McCONVILLE, M. (1993), *Corroboration and Confessions: The Impact of a Rule Requiring that No Conviction Can Be Sustained on the Basis of Confession Evidence Alone*, London: TSO.

McCONVILLE, M. (2000), 'Plea Bargaining: Ethics and Politics' in Doran and Jackson, eds, qv.

McCONVILLE, M. and BALDWIN, J. (1981), *Prosecution, Courts and Conviction*, Oxford: Oxford University Press.

McCONVILLE, M. and MARSH, L. (2015), 'Adversarialism goes West: Case Management in Criminal Courts', *IJEP*, 19: 172.

McCONVILLE, M. and MARSH, L. (2016), 'Factory Farming and State-Induced Pleas' in Hunter, Roberts, Young, and Dixon, eds, qv

McCONVILLE, M. and WILSON, G., eds (2002), *The Handbook of the Criminal Justice Process*, Oxford: Oxford University Press.

McCONVILLE, M., SANDERS, A., and LENG, R. (1991), *The Case for the Prosecution*, London: Routledge.

McCONVILLE, M., HODGSON, J., BRIDGES, L., and PAVLOVIC, A. (1994), *Standing Accused*, Oxford: Oxford University Press.

MacCORMICK, N. (1999), 'Rhetoric and the Rule of Law' in Dyzenhaus, ed, qv.

MACDONALD, S. (2006), 'A Suicidal Woman, Roaming Pigs and a Noisy Trampolinist:

Refining the ASBO's Definition of Anti-Social Behaviour', *MLR*, 69: 183.

MACDONALD, S. (2008), 'Constructing a Framework for Criminal Justice Research: Learning from Packer's Mistakes', *New Crim LR*, 11: 257.

McEWAN, J. (2010), 'The Changing Face of Criminal Litigation in England and Wales: Editor's Introduction', 14(2) *E & P*, 14(2): 89.

McEWAN, J. (2011), 'From Adversarialism to Managerialism: Criminal Justice in Transition', *Legal Studies* 31: 519.

McEWAN, J. (2013), 'Vulnerable Defendants and the Fairness of Trials', *Crim LR*, 100.

McGLYNN, C. (2017), 'Rape Trials and Sexual History Evidence: Reforming the Law on Third Party Evidence', *J Crim L* 81: 367.

McGLYNN, C., WESTMARLAND, N., and GODDEN, N. (2012), '"I Just Wanted Him to Hear Me": Sexual Violence and the Possibilities of Restorative Justice', *J Law and Society* 39: 213.

McGLYNN, C., WESTMARLAND, N., and JOHNSON, K. (2017), 'Under the radar: the widespread use of "Out of Court resolutions" in policing domestic violence and abuse in the United Kingdom', *BJ Crim*, 58: 1.

MACHURA, S. (2002), 'Interaction Between Lay Assessors and Professional Judges in German Mixed Courts', *International Rev Penal Law*, 72: 451.

McKAY, S. (2015), *Covert Policing: Law and Practice*, 2nd edn, Oxford: Oxford University Press.

McKENZIE, I., MORGAN, R., and REINER, R. (1990), 'Helping the Police with their Enquiries: The Necessity Principle and Voluntary Attendance at the Police Station', *Crim LR*, 22.

McMAHON, M. (1990), 'Net-Widening: Vagaries in the Use of a Concept', *BJ Crim*, 30: 121.

MACNAIR, M. (1990), 'The Early Development of the Privilege Against Self-Incrimination', *OJLS*, 10: 66.

MACPHERSON, SIR W. (1999), *The Stephen Lawrence Inquiry: Report of an Inquiry*, Cm 4261, London: TSO.

McSHERRY, A., NORRIE, A., and BRONITT, S., eds (2009), *Regulating Deviance*, Oxford: Hart.

MAFFEI, S. (2006), *The European Right to Confrontation in Criminal Proceedings*, Groningen: Europa Law.

MAGISTRATES ASSOCIATION (2015), *Investigation of cases sent by magistrates to Crown Court for sentence*, London: Magistrates Association.

MAGUIRE, M. (2000), 'Policing by Risks and Targets: Some Dimensions and Implications of Intelligence-Led Policing', *Policing and Society*, 9: 315.

MAGUIRE, M. (2007), 'Crime Data and Statistics' in Maguire, Morgan, and Reiner, eds, qv.

MAGUIRE, M. and JOHN, T. (1996), 'Covert and Deceptive Policing in England and Wales: Issues in Regulation and Practice', *Eur J Crime, Crim Law and Crim Justice* 4: 316.

MAGUIRE, M. and McVIE, S. (2017), 'Crime Data and Criminal Statistics: A Critical Reflection' in Liebling, Maruna, and McAra, eds, qv.

MAGUIRE, M. and NORRIS, C. (1992), *The Conduct and Supervision of Criminal Investigations*, Royal Commission on Criminal Justice Research Study No 5, London: HMSO.

MAGUIRE, M., MORGAN, R., and REINER, R., eds (2007), *The Oxford Handbook of Criminology*, Oxford: Oxford University Press.

MALLESON, K. and ROBERTS, S. (2002), 'Streamlining and Clarifying the Appellate Process', *Crim LR*, 272.

MALLOY, L., SHULMAN, E., and CAUFFMAN, E. (2014), 'Interrogations, confessions, and guilty pleas among serious adolescent offenders', *Law & Human Behavior* 38: 181.

MARSH, L. (2016), 'Leveson's Narrow Pursuit of Justice: Efficiency and Outcomes in the Criminal Process', *Common L World Rev*, 45: 51.

MATTHEWS, R., HANCOCK, L., and BRIGGS, D. (2004), *Jurors' Perceptions, Understanding, Confidence and Satisfaction in the Jury System*, Research Development and Statistics Directorate, Findings 177, London: Home Office.

METROPOLITAN POLICE AUTHORITY (2007), *Counter-Terrorism: The London Debate*, London: Metropolitan Police Authority.

MIDDLETON, D. (2005), 'The Legal and Regulatory Response to Solicitors Involved in Serious Fraud', *BJ Crim*, 45: 810.

MILLER, J., BLAND, N., and QUINTON, P. (2000), *The Impact of Stops and Searches on Crime and the Community*, Police Research Series, Paper 127, London: Home Office.

MINISTRY OF JUSTICE (2008), *Offender Management Caseload Statistics 2007*, London: Ministry of Justice.

MINISTRY OF JUSTICE (2008), *Punishment and Reform: our Approach to Managing Offenders*, London: Ministry of Justice.

MINISTRY OF JUSTICE (2009), *Judicial and Court Statistics 2008*, London: Ministry of Justice.

MINISTRY OF JUSTICE (2009), *Statistics on Race and the Criminal Justice System 2007/8*, London: Ministry of Justice.

MINISTRY OF JUSTICE (2011), *Modernising the Criminal Justice System: The CJS Efficiency Programme*, London: Ministry of Justice.

MINISTRY OF JUSTICE (2011), *Statistical Notice: Anti-Social Behaviour Order (ASBO) Statistics England and Wales 2010*, London: Ministry of Justice.

MINISTRY OF JUSTICE (2012), *Digital Strategy*, London: Ministry of Justice.

MINISTRY OF JUSTICE (2012), *Swift and Sure Justice: The Government's Plans for Reform of the Criminal Justice System*, London: Ministry of Justice.

MINISTRY OF JUSTICE (2013), *Simple Cautions for Adult Offenders*, London: Ministry of Justice.

MINISTRY OF JUSTICE (2013), *Transforming Legal Aid: Delivering a more credible and efficient system*, London: Ministry of Justice.

MINISTRY OF JUSTICE (2013), *Transforming Legal Aid: Next Steps*, London: Ministry of Justice.

MINISTRY OF JUSTICE (2016), *Black, Asian and Minority Ethnic disproportionality in the Criminal Justice System in England and Wales*, London: Ministry of Justice.

MINISTRY OF JUSTICE (2017), *Self harm in prison custody*, London: Ministry of Justice.

MINISTRY OF JUSTICE (2017), *Statistics on Race and the Criminal Justice System 2016*, London: Ministry of Justice.

MINISTRY OF JUSTICE (2018), *Female Offender Strategy*, Cm 9642, London: Ministry of Justice.

MINISTRY OF JUSTICE (2018), *Fit for the future: transforming the Court and Tribunal Estate*, London: Ministry of Justice.

MINISTRY OF JUSTICE (2018), *Offender Management Statistics Bulletin, England and Wales Annual 2017*, London: Ministry of Justice.

MINISTRY OF JUSTICE (2018), *Out of Court Disposals Pilot: Cautions Reoffending Analysis*, London: Ministry of Justice.

MIRFIELD, P. (1997), *Silence, Confessions and Improperly Obtained Evidence*, Oxford: Oxford University Press.

MIRFIELD, P. and SMITH, R., eds (2003), *Essays for Colin Tapper*, London: LexisNexis.

MITSILEGAS, V. (2016), 'The Uneasy Relationship between the UK and European Criminal Law: From Opt-Outs to Brexit?', *Crim LR*, 517.

MOECKLI, D. (2007), 'Stop and Search Under the Terrorism Act 2000', *MLR*, 70: 654.

MORENO, Y. and HUGHES, P. (2008), *Effective Prosecution*, Oxford: Oxford University Press.

MORGAN, J. and ZEDNER, L. (1992), *Child Victims*, Oxford: Oxford University Press.

MORGAN, P. M. (1992), *Offending Whilst on Bail*, Research and Planning Unit Paper 65, London: Home Office.

MORGAN, P.M. and HENDERSON, P. (1998), *Remand Decisions and Offending on Bail*, Home Office Research Study 184, London: Home Office.

MORGAN, R. (1996), 'The Process is the Rule and the Punishment is the Process', *MLR*, 59: 306.

MORGAN, R. (2001), 'International Controls on Sentencing and Punishment' in Tonry and Frase, eds, qv.

MORGAN, R. (2002), 'Magistrates: The Future According to Auld', *JLS*, 29: 308.

MORGAN, R. (2008), *Summary Justice: Fast—But Fair?*, London: Centre for Crime and Justice Studies, King's College.

MORRIS, A. (2002), 'Critiquing the Critics: A Brief Response to Critics of Restorative Justice', *BJ Crim*, 42: 578.

MORRIS, N. and TONRY, M. (1990), *Between Prison and Probation*, New York: Oxford University Press.

MOSTELLER, R. (1986), 'Discovery Against the Defense: Tilting the Adversarial Balance', *California L Rev*, 74: 1567.

MOSTON, S. and STEPHENSON, G. (1993), *The Questioning and Interviewing of Suspects outside the Police Station*, Royal Commission on Criminal Justice Research Study No 22, London: HMSO.

MOTT, J. (1983), 'Police Decisions for Dealing with Juvenile Offenders', *BJ Crim*, 23: 249.

MOXON, D., ed (1985), *Managing Criminal Justice*, London: HMSO.

MOXON, D. and HEDDERMAN, C. (1994), 'Mode of Trial Decisions and Sentencing Differences between Courts', *Howard JCJ*, 33: 97.

MULCAHY, A. (1994), 'The Justifications of "Justice": Legal Practitioners' Accounts of Negotiated Case Settlements in Magistrates' Courts', *BJ Crim*, 34: 411.

MULLIN, C. (1990), *Error of Judgement*, Dublin: Poolbeg Press.

MUNRO, V. and KELLY, L. (2009), 'A Vicious Cycle?: Attrition and Conviction Patterns in Contemporary Rape Cases in England and Wales' in J. Brown and M. Horvath (eds), *Rape: Challenging Contemporary Thinking*, Cullompton: Willan.

MURPHY, P., ECKERSLEY, P., and FERRY, L. (2016), 'Accountability and transparency: Police forces in England and Wales', *Public Policy and Administration* 32: 197.

MURRAY, K. (2018), 'The Modern Making of Stop and Search: The Rise of Preventative Sensibilities in Post-War Britain', *BJ Crim* 58: 588.

MURRAY, R. (2012), 'Police interviewing loophole must be tackled urgently', *Law Society Gazette*, 26 April 2012.

MVA and MILLER, J. (2000), *Profiling Populations Available for Stops and Searches*, Police Research Series, Paper 131, London: Home Office.

NANCE, D. (1994), 'Civility and the Burden of Proof', *Harvard J Law & Public Policy*, 17: 647.

NAREY, M. (1997), *Review of Delay in the Criminal Justice System* ('The Narey Report'), London: Home Office.

NASH, R. and WADE, K. (2009), 'Innocent But Proven Guilty: Using False Video Evidence to Elicit False Confessions and Create False Beliefs', *Applied Cognitive Psychology*, 23: 624.

NATIONAL AUDIT OFFICE (1997), *The Crown Prosecution Service*, London: National Audit Office.

NATIONAL AUDIT OFFICE (2006), *Crown Prosecution Service: Effective Use of Magistrates' Courts Hearings*, London: National Audit Office.

NATIONAL AUDIT OFFICE (2016), *Efficiency in the Criminal Justice System*, Session 2015–16, HC 852, London: National Audit Office.

NATIONAL DNA DATABASE STRATEGY BOARD (2018), *Annual Report 2016/17*, London: TSO.

NATIONAL POLICING IMPROVEMENT AGENCY (2009), *National Investigative Interviewing Strategy*, London: National Policing Improvement Agency.

NPCC and CPS (2018), *The National Disclosure Standards*, London: NPCC and CPS.

NAUGHTON, N. (2007), *Rethinking Miscarriages of Justice: Beyond the Tip of the Iceberg*, London: Palgrave Macmillan.

NELKEN, D., ed (1994), *The Futures of Criminology*, London: Sage.

NEW ZEALAND LAW COMMISSION (2001), *Acquittal Following Perversion of the Course of Justice*, Report No 70, Wellington: New Zealand Law Commission.

NEWBURN, T., ed (2003), *Handbook of Policing*, Cullompton: Willan.

NEWBURN, T., WILLIAMSON, T., and WRIGHT, A., eds (2007), *Handbook of Criminal Investigation*, London: Routledge.

NEWMAN, D. (2013), *Legal Aid Lawyers and the Quest for Justice*, Oxford: Hart.

NEWTH, T. (2008), *HMRC Investigations and Enquiries*, Haywards Heath: Tottel.

NEYROUD, P. (2003), 'Policing and Ethics' in Newburn, eds, qv.

NEYROUD, P. (2006), 'Ethics in Policing: Performance and the Personalization of Accountability in British Policing and Criminal Justice', *Legal Ethics*, 9: 16.

NEYROUD, P. (2018), *Out of Court Disposals Managed by the Police: A Review of the Evidence*, London: NPCC.

NICOLSON, D. and WEBB, J. (1999), *Professional Legal Ethics*, Oxford: Oxford University Press.

NISSMAN, C. M. and HAGEN, E. (1982), *The Prosecution Function*, Washington, DC: Lexington.

NOBLES, R. and SCHIFF, D. (2000), *Understanding Miscarriages of Justice*, Oxford: Oxford University Press.

NOBLES, R. and SCHIFF, D. (2001), 'The Criminal Cases Review Commission: Reporting Success?', *MLR*, 64: 280.

NORTHERN IRELAND LAW COMMISSION (2012), *Report: Bail in Criminal Proceedings*, NILC 14, London: TSO.

NOZICK, R. (1974), *Anarchy, State and Utopia*, New York: Basic Books.

NUFFIELD COUNCIL ON BIOETHICS (2007), *The Forensic Use of Bioinformation: Ethical Issues*, London: Nuffield Council on Bioethics.

O'BRIEN, W. (2005), 'The Right of Confrontation: US and European Perspectives', *LQR*, 121: 481.

O'CONNOR, P. (1992), 'Prosecution Disclosure: Principle, Practice and Justice', *Crim LR*, 464.

O'CONNOR, P. (2012), '"Abuse of Process" after Warren and Mitchell', *Crim LR*, 672.

O'MALLEY, P. (1999), 'Volatile and Contradictory Punishment', *Theoretical Criminology*, 3: 175.

OFFICE FOR CRIMINAL JUSTICE REFORM (2007), *Out-of-court Disposals for Adults: a Guide to Alternatives to Prosecution*, London: Office for Criminal Justice Reform.

OFSHE, R. and LEO, R. (1997), 'The Decision to Confess Falsely: Rational Choice and Irrational Action', *Denver U L Rev*, 74: 979.

OGG, J. (2013), 'Adversary and Adversity: Converging adversarial and inquisitorial systems of justice—a case study of the Italian criminal trial reforms', *Int J Comp and Applied Crim Justice*, 37: 31.

ORMEROD, D. (2001), 'Sounds Familiar?—Voice Identification Evidence', *Crim LR*, 595.

ORMEROD, D. (2006), 'Recent Developments in Entrapment', *Covert Policing Review*, 6.

ORMEROD, D. and ROBERTS, A. (2002), 'The Trouble with *Teixeira*: Developing a Principled Approach to Entrapment', *E&P*, 6: 38.

ORMEROD, D. and ROBERTS, A. (2003), 'The Police Reform Act 2002', *Crim LR*, 141.

ORMEROD, D., WATERMAN, A., and FORTSON, R. (2010), 'Prosecution Appeals—Too Much of a Good Thing?', *Crim LR*, 169.

OSNER, N., QUINN, A., and CROWN, G. (1993), *Criminal Justice Systems in Other Jurisdictions*, The Royal Commission on Criminal Justice, London: HMSO.

OWUSU-BEMPAH, A. (2013), 'Defence participation through pre-trial disclosure: issues and implications' *E&P* 17: 183.

OWUSU-BEMPAH, A. (2014), 'Silence in Suspicious Circumstances', *Crim LR*, 126.

OWUSU-BEMPAH, A. (2017), *Defendant Participation in the Criminal Process*, London: Routledge.

PACKER, H. (1968), *The Limits of the Criminal Sanction*, Stanford, CA: Stanford University Press.

PADFIELD, N. (1993), 'The Right to Bail: A Canadian Perspective', *Crim LR*, 510.

PADFIELD, N. (2018), 'Even More Court Closures', *Crim LR*, 351.

PARKER, H., SUMNER, M., and JARVIS, G. (1989), *Unmasking the Magistrates*, Milton Keynes: Open University Press.

PARRY, G. (2014), 'The Curse of Babel and the Criminal Process', *Crim LR*, 802.

PATTENDEN, R. (1996), *English Criminal Appeals, 1844–1994*, Oxford: Oxford University Press.

PATTENDEN, R. (2000), 'Prosecution Appeals Against Judges' Rulings', *Crim LR*, 971.

PATTENDEN, R. (2009), 'Pre-Verdict Judicial Fact-Finding in Judicial Trials with Juries', *OJLS*, 29: 1.

PATTENDEN, R. (2009), 'The Proof Rules of Pre-Verdict Judicial Fact-Finding in Criminal Trials by Jury', *LQR*, 125: 79.

PATTENDEN, R. (2009), 'The Standard of Review for Mistake of Fact in the Court of Appeal, Criminal Division', *Crim LR*, 15.

PATTENDEN, R. and DALY, G. (2005), 'Racial Bias and the English Criminal Trial Jury', *CLJ*, 64: 678.

PATTENDEN, R. and SKINNS, L. (2000), 'Choice, Privacy, and Publicly Funded Legal Advice at Police Stations', *MLR*, 73.

PEARSE, J. and GUDJONSSON, G. (1996), 'Police Interviewing Techniques at Two South London Police Stations', *Psychology, Crime & Law*, 3: 63.

PEAY, J. (2017), 'Mental Health, Mental Disabilities, and Crime' in Liebling, Maruna, and McAra, eds, qv.

PECK, M. (2006), *The Fraud (Trials Without a Jury) Bill 2006–07*, House of Commons Research Paper 06/57, London: House of Commons Library.

PEERS, S., HERVEY, T., KENNER, J., and
WARD, A (2014), *The EU Charter of
Fundamental Rights: A Commentary*,
London: Bloomsbury.

PHILLIPS, C. and BOWLING, B. (2017),
'Ethnicities, Racism, Crime and Criminal
Justice' in Liebling, Maruna, and McAra,
eds, qv.

PHILLIPS, C. and BROWN, D. (1998), *Entry
into the Criminal Justice System: A survey of
Police Arrests and Their Outcomes*, Home
Office Research Study No 185, London:
Home Office.

PHILLIPS, M., MCAULIFF, B., KOVERA, M.,
and CUTLER, B. (1999), 'Double-blind
Photoarray Administration as a Safeguard
Against Investigator Bias', *J Applied
Psychology*, 84: 940.

PHILPOTTS, G. J. O. and LANCUCKI, L. B.
(1979), *Previous Convictions, Sentence and
Reconvictions*, Home Office Research Study
53, London: HMSO.

PIETH, M., and IVORY, R. eds (2011)
*Corporate Criminal Liability: Emergence,
Convergence and Risk*, New York: Springer.

PIKE, G., BRACE, N., and KYNAN, S.
(2002), *The Visual Identification of
Suspects: Procedures and Practice*, Home
Office Briefing Note 2, London: Home
Office.

PIZZARUSSO, A., ed (1994), *Italian Studies in
Law, Vol. II*, Dordrecht: Martinus Nijhoff.

PLAYER, E. (2007), 'Remanding Women in
Custody: Concerns for Human Rights',
MLR, 70: 402.

PLAYER, E., ROBERTS, J., JACOBSON, J.,
HOUGH, M., and ROBOTTOM, J. (2010),
'Remanded in Custody: Recent Trends in
England and Wales', *Howard JCJ*,
49: 231.

PLEASENCE, P., KEMP, V., and BALMER, N.
(2011), 'The Justice Lottery? Police Station
Advice 25 Years On from PACE', *Crim
LR*, 3.

PLOTNIKOFF, J. and WOOLFSON, R. (2001), 'A
Fair Balance'? Evaluation of the Operation
of Disclosure Law*, London: Home Office.

PLUGGE, E., DOUGLAS, N., and FITZPATRICK,
R. (2006), *The Health of Women in Prison*,
Oxford: Department of Public Health,
University of Oxford.

POLICE COMPLAINTS AUTHORITY (2004),
*Stop and Search Complaints 2000–2001,
Summary Report*, London: Police
Complaints Authority.

PRATT, J. (2007), *Penal Populism*, London:
Routledge.

PRISON REFORM TRUST (2011), *Innocent
Until Proven Guilty: Tackling the Overuse of
Custodial Remand*, London: Prison Reform
Trust.

PRISON REFORM TRUST (2014), *Transforming
Lives reducing women's imprisonment*,
London: Prison Reform Trust.

PURSHOUSE, J. (2018), 'Non-conviction
Disclosure as Part of an Enhanced
Criminal Record Certificate: Assessing
the Legal Framework from a Fundamental
Human Rights Perspective', *Public Law* 668.

PURSHOUSE, J. and CAMPBELL, L. (2019),
'Privacy, Crime Control and Police Use of
Automated Facial Recognition Technology'
Crim LR 188.

QUINTON, A., ed (1967), *Political Philosophy*,
Oxford: Oxford University Press.

QUINTON, P. (2011), 'The formation of
suspicions: police stop and search practices
in England and Wales', *Policing and Society*
21: 357.

QUINTON, P., TIRATELLI, M., and BRADFORD,
B. (2017), *Does More Stop and Search Mean
Less Crime? Analysis of Metropolitan Police
Service Panel Data, 2004–14*, Coventry:
College of Policing.

QUIRK, H. (2006), 'The Significance of
Culture in Criminal Procedure Reform:
Why the Revised Disclosure Scheme
Cannot Work', *E&P*, 10: 42.

QUIRK, H. (2007), 'Identifying Miscarriages of Justice: Why Innocence in the UK is Not the Answer', *MLR*, 70: 759.

QUIRK, H. (2016), *The Rise and Fall of the Right of Silence*, London: Routledge.

QUIRK, H. and REQUA, M. (2012), 'The Supreme Court on Compensation for Miscarriages of Justice: Is it Better that Ten Innocents are Denied Compensation than One Guilty Person Receives It?', *MLR*, 75: 387.

RADCLIFFE, P., GUDJONSSON, G., HEATON-ARMSTRONG, A., and WOLCHOVER, D. (2016), *Witness Testimony in Sexual Cases: Evidential, Investigative and Scientific Perspectives*, Oxford: Oxford University Press.

RAIFERTAIGH, U. (1997), 'Reconciling Bail Law with the Presumption of Innocence', *OJLS*, 17: 1.

RAINE, J. and WILLSON, M. (1996), 'The Imposition of Conditions in Bail Decisions', *Howard JCJ*, 35: 256.

RAINE, J. and WILLSON, M. (1997), 'Police Bail with Conditions', *BJ Crim*, 37: 593.

RAMSAY, P. (2004), 'What is Anti-Social Behaviour?', *Crim LR*, 908.

RAMSAY, P. (2009), 'The Theory of Vulnerable Autonomy and the Legitimacy of Civil Preventative Orders' in McSherry, Norrie, and Bronitt, eds, qv.

REDMAYNE, M. (2004), 'Disclosure and its Discontents', *Crim LR*, 441.

REDMAYNE, M. (2006), 'Theorizing Jury Reform' in Duff, Farmer, Marshall, and Tadros, qv.

REDMAYNE, M. (2007), 'Rethinking the Privilege Against Self-Incrimination', *OJLS*, 27: 209.

REDMAYNE, M. (2008), 'English Warnings', *Cardozo L Rev*, 30: 1047.

REDMAYNE, M. (2009), 'Theorizing the Criminal Trial', *New Crim LR*, 12: 287.

REDMAYNE, M. (2012), 'Confronting Confrontation' in Roberts and Hunter, eds, qv.

REDMAYNE, M. (2012), 'Hearsay and Human Rights: Al-Khawaja in the Grand Chamber', *MLR* 75: 865.

REID, K. (2009), 'Race Issues and Stop and Search: Looking Behind the Statistics', *J Crim L*, 73: 165.

REINER, R. (2007), *Law and Order: An Honest Citizen's Guide to Crime and Control*, Cambridge: Polity Press.

REINER, R. (2010), *The Politics of the Police*, 4th edn, Oxford: Oxford University Press.

REINER, R. (2016), 'Conservatives and the Constabulary in Great Britain: Cross-Dressing Conundrums' in Deflem M., ed, qv.

REINER, R. (2017), 'Is Police Culture Cultural?', *Policing: A Journal of Policy and Practice*, 11: 236.

RENNING, C. (2002), 'Influence of Lay Assessors and Giving Reasons for the Judgement in German Mixed Courts', *Int Rev Penal Law*, 72: 481.

RICHARDSON, G., OGUS, A., and BURROWS, P. (1982), *Policing Pollution*, Oxford: Oxford University Press.

RIDLEY, A., VAN RHEEDE, V., and WILCOCK, R. (2015), 'Interviews, intermediaries and interventions: Mock-jurors', police officers' and barristers' perceptions of a child witness interview', *Investigative Interviewing: Research and Practice*, 7: 21.

RISSE, M. and ZECKHAUSER, R. (2004), 'Racial Profiling', *Philosophy & Public Affairs*, 32: 131.

ROACH, K. (1999), *Due Process and Victims' Rights: the New Law and Politics of Criminal Justice*, Toronto: University of Toronto Press.

ROACH, K. (2003), 'The Criminal Process' in Cane and Tushnet, eds, qv.

ROBERTS, A. (2008), 'Pre-Trial Defence Rights and the Fair Use of Eyewitness Identification Procedures', *MLR*, 71: 331.

ROBERTS, A. (2014), 'Case Comment: *R. v Moore (Mia)*: Abuse of Process—Entrapment—Defendants Supplying Drugs to Undercover Police Officers', *Crim LR*, 364.

ROBERTS, A. (2016), 'Evidence: *R. v Avorgah (Moise)* Commentary', *Crim LR*, 491.

ROBERTS, A., DAVIS, J., VALENTINE, T., and MEMON, N. (2014), 'Should We Be Concerned About Street Identifications?', *Crim LR*, 633

ROBERTS, D. (1993), 'Questioning the Suspect: The Solicitor's Role', *Crim LR*, 368.

ROBERTS, J. and HOUGH, M. (2009), *Public Opinion and the Jury: An International Literature Review*, London: Ministry of Justice.

ROBERTS, J. and MANIKIS, M. (2011), *Victim Personal Statements: A Review of Empirical Research*, London: Ministry of Justice.

ROBERTS, P. (2002), 'Double Jeopardy Law Reform: A Criminal Justice Commentary', *MLR*, 65: 393.

ROBERTS, P. (2002), 'Justice for All? Two Bad Arguments (and Several Good Suggestions) for Resisting Double Jeopardy Reform', *E&P*, 6: 197.

ROBERTS, P., and HUNTER, J. eds (2012), *Criminal Evidence and Human Rights*, London: Bloomsbury

ROBERTS, P. and SAUNDERS, C. (2008), 'Introducing Pre-Trial Witness Interviews—A Flexible New Fixture in the Crown Prosecutor's Toolkit', *Crim LR*, 831.

ROBERTS, P. and ZUCKERMAN, A. (2010), *Criminal Evidence*, 2nd edn, Oxford: Oxford University Press.

ROBERTS, S. (2017), 'Fresh Evidence and Factual Innocence in the Criminal Division of the Court of Appeal', *J Crim L*, 81: 303.

ROBERTSON, G., DELL, S., GROUNDS, A., and JAMES, K. (1992), 'Mentally Disordered Remand Prisoners', Home Office Research Bulletin No 32, London: Home Office.

ROBINS, J. (2000), 'The Speed of Fight', *Law Society Gazette*, 3: 24.

ROBINSON, P. (2001), 'Punishing Dangerousness: Cloaking Preventive Detention as Criminal Justice', *Harvard LR*, 114: 1429.

ROBINSON, P., GARVEY, S., and FERZAN, K., eds (2009), *Criminal Law Conversations*, Oxford: Oxford University Press.

ROCK, P. (1993), *The Social World of an English Crown Court*, Oxford: Clarendon Press.

ROCK, P. (2004), *Constructing Victims' Rights: The Home Office, New Labour and Victims*, Oxford: Clarendon Press.

ROGERS, J. (2006), 'Restructuring the Exercise of Prosecutorial Discretion in England', *OJLS*, 26: 775.

ROGERS, J. (2008), 'The Boundaries of Abuse of Process in Criminal Trials', *CLP*, 289.

ROGERS, J. (2017), 'A Human Rights Perspective on the Evidential Test for Bringing Prosecutions', *Crim LR*, 678.

ROLLOCK, N. (2009), *The Stephen Lawrence Inquiry 10 Years On: A Critical Review of the Literature*, London: The Runnymede Trust.

ROSSMO, K., ed (2008), *Criminal Investigative Failures*, London: CRC.

ROYAL COMMISSION ON CRIMINAL JUSTICE (1993) (chair: Viscount Runciman), *Report*, Cmnd 2263, London: HMSO.

ROYAL COMMISSION ON CRIMINAL PROCEDURE (1981) (chair: Sir Cyril Phillips), *Report*, Cmnd 8092, London: HMSO.

ROZENBERG, J. (1992), 'Miscarriages of Justice' in Stockdale and Casale, eds, qv.

RUTHERFORD, A. (1993), *Criminal Justice and the Pursuit of Decency*, Oxford: Oxford University Press.

SAMUELS, A. (1997), 'Custody Time Limits', *Crim LR*, 260.

SANDERS, A. (1985), 'Class Bias in Prosecutions', *Howard JCJ*, 24: 176.

SANDERS, A. (1988), 'The Limits to Diversion from Prosecution', *BJ Crim*, 28: 513.

SANDERS, A. (2001), *Community Justice: Modernising the Magistracy in England and Wales*, London: IPPR.

SANDERS, A. (2002), 'Core Values, the Magistracy and the Auld Report', *JLS*, 29: 324.

SANDERS, A. (2008), 'Can Coercive Powers be Effectively Controlled or Regulated? The Case for Anchored Pluralism' in Cape and Young, eds, qv.

SANDERS, A. (2016), 'The CPS—30 Years On', *Crim LR*, 82.

SANDERS, A. and BRIDGES, L. (1990), 'Access to Legal Advice and Police Malpractice', *Crim LR*, 494.

SANDERS, A. and YOUNG, R. (2007), 'From Suspect to Trial' in Maguire, Morgan, and Reiner, eds, qv.

SANDERS, A., YOUNG, R., and BURTON, M. (2010), *Criminal Justice*, 4th edn, London: Butterworths.

SANDERS, A., HOYLE, C., MORGAN, R., and CAPE, E. (2001), 'Victim Impact Statements: Can't Work, Won't Work', *Crim LR*, 447.

SAURON, J.-L. (1990), 'Les Vertus de l'Inquisitoire, ou l'Etat au Service des Droits', *Pouvoirs*, 55: 53.

SAVAGE, S. (2013), 'Thinking Independence: Calling the Police to Account through the Independent Investigation of Police Complaints', *BJ Crim*, 53: 94.

SCHIFF, D. and NOBLES, R. (1996), 'Criminal Appeal Act 1995: The Semantics of Jurisdiction', *MLR*, 59: 573.

SCHULHOFER, S. (1984), 'Is Plea Bargaining Inevitable?', *Harv LR*, 97: 1037.

SCHULHOFER, S. (1992), 'Plea Bargaining as Disaster', *Yale LJ*, 101: 1979.

SCHULHOFER, S. and NAGEL, I. (1997), 'Plea Negotiations under the Federal Sentencing Guidelines', *Northwestern ULR*, 91: 1284.

SCOTT, R. E. and STUNTZ, W. J. (1992), 'Plea Bargaining as Contract', *Yale LJ*, 101: 1909.

SCOTT, R. E. and STUNTZ, W. J. (1992), 'A Reply: Imperfect Bargains, Imperfect Trials and Innocent Defendants', *Yale LJ*, 101: 2011.

SCOTTISH LAW COMMISSION (2009), *Discussion Paper on Double Jeopardy*, Edinburgh: Scottish Law Commission.

SCOULAR, J. and O'NEILL, M. (2007), 'Regulating Prostitution: Social Inclusion, Responsibilization and the Politics of Prostitution Reform', *BJ Crim*, 47: 764.

SEALE-CARLISLE, T. M. and MICKES, L. (2016), 'US line-ups outperform UK line-ups', *Royal Society Open Science*, doi:10.1098/rsos.160300.

SEDLEY, S. (2001), 'Wringing Out the Fault: Self-Incrimination in the 21st Century', *NILQ*, 52: 107.

SEIDMANN D. and STEIN, A. (2000), 'The Right to Silence Helps the Innocent', *Harvard L Rev* 114: 430.

SEIDMAN, L. (1981), 'The Supreme Court, Entrapment and Our Criminal Justice Dilemma', *Supreme Court Rev*, 111.

SEIDMAN, L. (2009), 'Entrapment and the "Free Market" for Crime' in Robinson, Garvey, and Ferzan, eds, qv.

SENTENCING COUNCIL (2011), *Assault Definitive Guideline*, London: Sentencing Council.

SENTENCING COUNCIL (2017), *Reduction in Sentence for a Guilty Plea Definitive Guideline*, London: Sentencing Council.

SENTENCING COUNCIL (2018), *Out-of-court-disposals*, London: Sentencing Council.

SHAPLAND, J., DUFF, P., and WILLMORE, J. (1985), *Victims in the Criminal Justice System*, Aldershot: Gower.

SHEPHERD, E. and GRIFFITHS, A. (2013), *Investigative Interviewing: The Conversation Management Approach*, 2nd edn, Oxford: Oxford University Press.

SHEPHERD, E. and MILNE, R. (1999), 'Full and Faithful: Ensuring Quality, Practice and Integrity of Outcome in Witness Interviews' in Heaton-Armstrong, Shepherd, and Wolchover, eds, qv.

SHUTE, S. (2004), 'New Civil Preventative Orders: Sexual Offences Prevention Orders; Foreign Travel Orders; Risk of Sexual Harm Orders', *Crim LR*, 417.

SIMESTER, A. P., ed (2005), *Appraising Strict Liability*, Oxford: Oxford University Press.

SIMESTER, A. P. and VON HIRSCH, A. (2006), 'Regulating Offensive Conduct through Two-Step Prohibitions' in von Hirsch and Simester, eds, qv.

SIMON, W. H. (1993), 'The Ethics of Criminal Defense', *Mich LR*, 91: 1703.

SKINNS, L. (2009), 'I'm a Detainee; Get me Out of Here', *BJ Crim*, 49: 399.

SKINNS, L. (2009), '"Let's Get it Over With": Early Findings on the Factors Affecting Detainees' Access to Custodial Legal Advice', *Policing and Society*, 19: 58.

SKINNS, L. (2011), 'The Right to Legal Advice in the Police Station: Past, Present and Future', *Crim LR*, 19.

SKOLNICK, J. (1966), *Justice without Trial*, New York: Wiley.

SLAPPER, G. (2001), *Organisational Prosecutions*, Aldershot: Ashgate.

SLAPPER, G. and TOMBS, S. (2000), *Corporate Crime*, London: Longman.

SMITH, J. C. (1994), 'The Right to Life and the Right to Kill in Law', *New LJ*, 144: 354.

SMITH, J. C. (1995), 'The Criminal Appeal Act 1995: Appeals against Conviction', *Crim LR*, 920.

SMITH, T. (2018), 'The "Near Miss" of Liam Allan: Critical Problems in Police Disclosure, Investigation Culture and the Resourcing of Criminal Justice', *Crim LR*, 711.

SOMMERS, S. and ELLSWORTH, P. (2003), 'How Much Do We Really Know About Race and Juries? A Review of Social Science Theory and Research', *Chicago-Kent L Rev*, 78: 997.

SOOTHILL, K. (2009), 'Keeping the DNA Link', *NLJ*, 159: 1021.

SOUBISE, L. (2017), 'Prosecuting in the Magistrates' Courts in a Time of Austerity', *Crim LR*, 847.

SPENCER, J. R. (2004), 'The Sexual Offences Act 2003: Child and Family Offences', *Crim LR*, 347.

SPENCER, J. R. (2006), 'Does our Present Criminal Appeals System Make Sense?', *Crim LR*, 677.

SPENCER, J. R. (2007), 'Arrest for Questioning', *CLJ*, 66: 282.

SPENCER, J. R. (2007), 'Quashing Convictions for Procedural Irregularities', *Crim LR*, 835.

SPENCER, J. R. (2014), *Hearsay Evidence in Criminal Proceedings*, 2nd edn, Oxford: Hart.

SPENCER, J. R. (2016), 'Adversarial vs inquisitorial systems: is there still such a difference?', *Int J Human Rights*, 20: 601.

SPIELMANN, D. (2016), 'Companies in the Strasbourg Courtroom', *Cambridge J Int and Comp L*, 5: 404.

SPRACK, J. (2016), *A Practical Approach to Criminal Procedure*, 15th edn, Oxford: Oxford University Press.

SQUIRES, D. (2006), 'The Problem with Entrapment', *OJLS*, 26: 351.

SQUIRES, P. and STEPHEN, D. E. (2005), *Rougher Justice: Anti-Social Behaviour and Young People*, Cullompton: Willan.

STANDING COMMITTEE FOR YOUTH JUSTICE, (2018), *'They just don't understand what's happened or why': A report on child defendants and video links*, London: Standing Committee for Youth Justice.

STARMER, K. (2012), 'Finality in Criminal Justice: When Should the CPS Reopen a Case?' *Crim LR*, 526.

STEWART, H. (2016), 'The Privilege Against Self-Incrimination: Reconsidering Redmayne's Rethinking', *E&P*, 95.

STEPHEN, H. (1926), *The Conduct of an English Criminal Trial*, London: University of London Press.

STOCKDALE, E. and CASALE, S., eds (1992), *Criminal Justice Under Stress*, London: Blackstone Press.

STONE, C. (1988), *Bail Information for the Crown Prosecution Service*, London: Vera Institute of Justice.

STONE, V. and PETTIGREW, N. (2000), *The Views of the Public on Stops and Searches*, Police Research Series Paper 129, London: Home Office.

STRANG, H. (2002), *Repair or Revenge: Victims and Restorative Justice*, Oxford: Oxford University Press.

STRANG, H., SHERMAN, L., MAYO-WILSON, E., WOODS, D., and ARIEL, B. (2013), *Restorative Justice Conferencing (RJC) Using Face-to-Face Meetings of Offenders and Victims: Effects on Offender Recidivism and Victim Satisfaction. A Systematic Review*, London: Restorative Justice Council.

SUKUMAR, D., HODGSON, J., and WADE, K. (2016), 'Behind Closed Doors: Live Observations of Current Police Station Disclosure Practices and Lawyer–Client Consultations', *Crim LR*, 900.

SUKUMAR, D., HODGSON, J., and WADE, K. (2016), 'How the timing of police evidence disclosure impacts custodial legal advice', *E&P*, 200.

TADROS, V. (2008), 'Crimes and Security', *MLR*, 71: 940.

TAGUE, P. (2006), 'Tactical Reasons for Recommending Trials rather than Guilty Pleas in the Crown Court', *Crim LR*, 23.

TAGUE, P. (2007), 'Barristers' Selfish Incentives in Counselling Defendants over Choice of Plea', *Crim LR*, 3.

TAK, P. J. P. (1986), *The Legal Scope of Non-Prosecution in Europe*, Helsinki: HEUNI.

TAPPER, C., ed (1981), *Crime, Proof and Punishment*, London: Butterworths.

TAYLOR, C. (2013), 'The disclosure sanctions review: another missed opportunity?', *E&P*, 272.

TAYLOR, N. and ORMEROD, D. (2004), 'Mind the Gap: Safety, Fairness and Moral Legitimacy', *Crim LR*, 266.

TEMKIN, J. (2000), 'Prosecuting and Defending Rape: Perspectives from the Bar', *J L & Soc*, 27: 219.

TEMKIN, J. (2002), *Rape and the Legal Process*, 2nd edn, Oxford: Oxford University Press.

TERRY, M., JOHNSON, S., and THOMPSON, P. (2010), *Virtual Court pilot: Outcome evaluation*, Ministry of Justice Research Series 21/10, London: Ministry of Justice.

THOMAS, C. (2007), *Diversity and Fairness in the Jury System*, London: Ministry of Justice.

THOMAS, C. (2010), *Are juries fair?*, Ministry of Justice Research Series 1/10, London: Ministry of Justice.

THOMAS, C. (2017), 'Ethnicity and Fairness of Jury Trials in England and Wales 2006–2014', *Crim LR*, 860.

THE RT HON. THE LORD THOMAS OF CWMGIEDD (2018), 'The Criminal Procedure Rules: 10 Years On', *Crim LR*, 395.

TONRY, M. (2004), *Punishment and Politics*, Cullompton: Willan.

TONRY, M. and FRASE, R., eds (2001), *Sentencing and Sanctions in Western Countries*, Oxford: Oxford University Press.

TRANSFORM JUSTICE (2016), *Justice Denied? The experience of unrepresented defendants in the criminal courts*, London: Transform Justice.

TRANSFORM JUSTICE (2017), *Defendants on video—conveyor belt justice or a revolution in access?*, London: Transform Justice.

TRANSFORM JUSTICE (2017), *Less is more- the case for dealing with offences out of court.*

TRANSFORM JUSTICE (2018), *Presumed innocent but behind bars—is remand overused in England and Wales?*, London: Transform Justice.

TULKENS, F. (2002), 'Negotiated Justice' in Delmas-Marty and Spencer, eds, qv.

TYLER, T. (1990), *Why People Obey the Law*, New Haven, CT: Yale University Press.

VALENTINE, T. (2006), 'Forensic Facial Identification' in Heaton-Armstrong, Shepherd, Gudjonsson and Wolchover, eds, qv.

VALENTINE, T. and HEATON, P. (1999), 'An Evaluation of the Fairness of Police Lineups and Video Identifications', *Applied Cognitive Psychology*, 13: 59.

VALENTINE, T., DARLING, S., and MEMON, A. (2006), 'Do Strict Rules and Moving Images Increase the Reliability of Sequential Identification Procedures?', *Applied Cognitive Psychology*, 21: 933.

VALENTINE, T., HUGHES, C., and MUNRO, R. (2009), 'Recent Developments in Eyewitness Identification Procedures in the United Kingdom' in Bull, Valentine, and Williamson, eds, qv.

VALENTINE, T., DAVIS, J., MEMON, A., and ROBERTS, A. (2012), 'Live Showups and Their Influence on a Subsequent Video Line-up', *Applied Cognitive Psychology*, 26: 1.

VAMOS, N. (2009), 'Please Don't Call it Plea-Bargaining', *Crim LR*, 617.

VAN BUEREN, G. (2005), *Commentary on the U.N. Convention on the Rights of the Child*, Leiden: Martinus Nijhoff.

VAN KEMPEN, P. (2011), 'The Recognition of Legal Persons in International Human Rights Instruments: Protection Against and Through Criminal Justice?' in Pieth and Ivory, eds, qv.

VAN ZYL SMIT, D. and ASHWORTH, A. (2004), 'Disproportionate Sentences as Human Rights Violations', *MLR*, 67: 541.

VICTIMS' COMMISSIONER (2015), *A Review of Complaints and Resolution For Victims of Crime*, London: Victims' Commissioners.

VICTIM SUPPORT (1995), *The Rights of Victims of Crime*, London: Victim Support.

VIDMAR, N. (1997), 'Generic Prejudice and the Presumption of Guilt in Sex Abuse Trials', *Law & Human Behavior*, 21: 5.

VIDMAR, N. (1998), 'The Performance of the American Civil Jury: An Empirical Perspective', *Arizona L Rev*, 40: 849.

VOGEL, M. (2007), *Coercion to Compromise*, Oxford: Oxford University Press.

VON HIRSCH, A., and ASHWORTH, A. (2005), *Proportionate Sentencing*, Oxford: Oxford University Press.

VON HIRSCH, A., ASHWORTH, A., and ROBERTS, J., eds (2009), *Principled Sentencing*, London: Hart.

VON HIRSCH, A., and SIMESTER, A. P., eds (2006), *Incivilities: Regulating Offensive Behaviour*, Oxford: Hart.

WADDINGTON, P. A. J. (1999), 'Police (Canteen) Culture: an Appreciation', *BJ Crim*, 39: 286.

WADDINGTON, P. A. J., STENSON, K., and DON, D. (2004), 'In Proportion: Race, and Police Stop and Search', *BJ Crim*, 44: 889.

WALDRON, J. (2003), 'Security and Liberty: the Image of Balance', *J Political Philosophy*, 11: 191.

WALDRON, J. (2008), 'The Concept and the Rule of Law', *Georgia L Rev*, 43: 1.

WALKER, C. (1999), 'Miscarriages of Justice in Principle and Practice' in Walker and Starmer, qv.

WALKER, C. (2004), 'Terrorism and Criminal Justice—Past, Present and Future', *Crim LR*, 311.

WALKER, C. (2007), 'The Treatment of Foreign Terror Suspects', *MLR*, 70: 427.

WALKER, C., and STARMER, K. (1999), *Miscarriages of Justice: A Review of Justice in Error*, Oxford: Oxford University Press.

WALMSLEY, R. (2017), *World pre-trial/ remand imprisonment list*, 3rd edn, *World Prison Brief*.

WALSH, D. and BULL, R. (2015), 'Interviewing suspects: Examining the association between skills, questioning, evidence disclosure, and interview outcomes', *Psychology, Crime & Law*, 21: 661.

WALSH, D., MILNE, B., and BULL, R. (2016), 'One way or another? Criminal investigators' beliefs regarding the disclosure of evidence in interviews with suspects in England and Wales', *J Police and Criminal Psychology*, 31: 127.

WALTERS, M., WIEDLITZKA, S., OWUSU-BEMAPH, A., and GOODALL, K. (2017), *Hate Crime and the Legal Process—Final Report*, Brighton: Universith of Sussex.

WARBURTON, H., MAY, T., and HOUGH, M. (2005), 'Looking the Other Way: The Impact of Reclassifying Cannabis on Police Warnings', *BJ Crim*, 45: 113.

WARD, A. and PEERS S., eds (2004), *The EU Charter of Fundamental Rights*, Oxford: Hart.

WARD, T. and GARDNER, P. (2003), 'The Privilege Against Self Incrimination: In Search of Legal Certainty', *Eur Human Rights L Rev*, 387.

WASIK, M. (1996), 'Magistrates: Knowledge of Previous Convictions', *Crim LR*, 851.

WELLS, G. (2006), 'Eyewitness Identification: Systemic Reforms', *Wisconsin L Rev* 615.

WELLS, G. and OLSON, E. (2003), 'Eyewitness Identification', *Annual Review of Psychology*, 54: 277.

WELLS, G., MEMON, A., and PENROD, S. (2006), 'Eyewitness Evidence: Improving its Probative Value', *Psychological Science in the Public Interest*, 7: 45.

WELSH, L. (2013), 'Are magistrates' courts really a "law free zone"? Participant observation and specialist use of language', *Papers from the British Criminology Conference* 3.

WELSH, L. (2017), 'The effects of changes to legal aid on lawyers' professional identity and behaviour in summary criminal cases: a case study', *J Law and Society*, 44: 559.

WESTEN, P. and DRUBEL, R. (1978), 'Towards a General Theory of Double Jeopardy', *Supreme Court Rev*, 81.

WESTERA, N., KEBBELL, M., and MILNE, R. (2011), 'Interviewing witnesses: Will investigative and evidential requirements ever concord?', *Brit J Forensic Practice*, 13: 103.

WHITE, R. (2006), 'Investigators or Prosecutors or, Desperately Seeking Scotland: Re-Formulation of the "Philips Principle"', *MLR*, 69: 143.

WILLIAMS, C. (2008), 'An Analysis of Discretionary Rejection in Relation to Confessions', *Melbourne U L Rev*, 32: 302.

WILLIAMSON, T., ed (2006), *Investigative Interviewing: Rights, Research, Regulation*, Cullompton: Willan.

WILLIAMSON, T. (2006), 'Towards Greater Professionalism: Minimizing Miscarriages of Justice' in Williamson, ed, qv.

WINDLESHAM, LORD (2001), *Responses to Crime, Volume 4: Dispensing Justice*, Oxford: Oxford University Press.

WISTRICH, A., GUTHRIE C., and RACHLINSKI, J. (2005), 'Can Judges Ignore Inadmissible Information? The Difficulty of Deliberately Disregarding', *U Pa LR*, 153: 1251.

WOLCHOVER, D. (2008), 'Viper Disappointments in the PACE Review', *Arch News*, 10: 4.

WOLCHOVER, D. and HEATON-ARMSTRONG, A. (2004), 'Ending the Farce of Staged Street Identifications', *Arch News*, 3: 5.

WOLCHOVER, D. and HEATON-ARMSTRONG, A. (2006), 'Improving Visual Identification Procedures Under PACE Code D' in Heaton-Armstrong, Shepherd, Gudjonsson, and Wolchover, eds, qv.

WOLCHOVER, D. and HEATON-ARMSTRONG, A. (2014), 'Street Identification', *CJ&L*, 178.

WOOLF, H. and TUMIN, S. (1991), 'Prison Disturbances April 1990: Report of an Inquiry', Cmnd 1456, London: HMSO.

YOUNG, R. (2008), 'Street Policing after PACE: The Drift to Summary Justice' in Cape and Young, eds, qv.

YOUNG, R. and SANDERS, A. (2004), 'The Ethics of Prosecution Lawyers', *Legal Ethics*, 7: 190.

YOUNG, R. and WILCOX, A. (2007) 'The Merits of Legal Aid in the Magistrates' Courts Revisited', *Crim LR*, 109.

ZANDER, M. (2000), 'Why Jack Straw's Jury Reform Has Lost the Plot', *NLJ*, 150: 723.

ZANDER, M. (2012), 'If the PACE Codes are not law, why do they have to be followed?' *Crim Law and Justice Weekly*, 176: 713.

ZANDER, M. (2015), *Zander on PACE: The Police and Criminal Evidence Act 1984*, 7th edn, London: Sweet & Maxwell.

ZANDER, M. and HENDERSON, P. (1993), *Crown Court Study*, Royal Commission on Criminal Justice Research Study No 19, London: HMSO.

ZEDNER, L. (2005), 'Securing Liberty in the Face of Terror', *J Law & Society*, 32: 507.

ZEDNER, L. (2007), 'Preventive Justice or Pre-Punishment? The Case of Control Orders', *CLP*, 59: 174.

ZEDNER, L. (2007), 'Seeking Security by Eroding Rights: The Side-Stepping of Due Process' in Goold and Lazarus, eds, qv.

ZIMMERMAN, D. and HUNTER, S. (2018), 'Factors affecting false guilty pleas in a mock plea bargaining scenario', *Legal and Criminological Psychology*, 23: 53.

ZUCKERMAN, A. (1991), 'Miscarriage of Justice and Judicial Responsibility', *Crim LR*, 492.

INDEX